The Penguin Dictionary of

ECONOMICS

Graham Bannock
R.E. Baxter

Eighth Edition

PENGUIN BOOKS

PENGUIN BOOKS

Published by the Penguin Group
Penguin Books Ltd, 80 Strand, London WC2R 0RL, England
Penguin Group (USA) Inc., 375 Hudson Street, New York, New York 10014, USA
Penguin Group (Canada), 90 Eglinton Avenue East, Suite 700, Toronto, Ontario,
Canada M4P 2Y3 (a division of Pearson Penguin Canada Inc.)
Penguin Ireland, 25 St Stephen's Green, Dublin 2, Ireland (a division of Penguin Books Ltd)
Penguin Group (Australia), 250 Camberwell Road, Camberwell,
Victoria 3124, Australia (a division of Pearson Australia Group Pty Ltd)
Penguin Books India Pvt Ltd, 11 Community Centre, Panchsheel Park, New Delhi – 110 017, India
Penguin Group (NZ), 67 Apollo Drive, Rosedale, Auckland 0632, New Zealand
(a division of Pearson New Zealand Ltd)
Penguin Books (South Africa) (Pty) Ltd, 24 Sturdee Avenue, Rosebank, Johannesburg 2196, South Africa

Penguin Books Ltd, Registered Offices: 80 Strand, London WC2R 0RL, England

www.penguin.com

First published 1972
Second edition 1978
Third edition 1984
Fourth edition 1987
Fifth edition 1992
Sixth edition 1998
Seventh edition 2003
Eighth edition 2011
3

Copyright © Graham Bannock, R.E. Baxter and R. Rees, 1972, 1978, 1984
Copyright © Graham Bannock, R.E. Baxter and Evan Davis, 1987, 1992, 1998, 2003
Copyright © Graham Bannock and R.E. Baxter, 2011
All rights reserved

The moral right of the authors has been asserted

Set in ITC Stone Serif 7.5/9.75 pt
Typeset by Jouve (UK), Milton Keynes
Printed in England by Clays Ltd, St Ives plc

ISBN: 978–0–141–04523–8

www.greenpenguin.co.uk

MIX
Paper from
responsible sources
FSC   FSC® C018179
www.fsc.org

Penguin Books is committed to a sustainable
future for our business, our readers and our
planet. This book is made from paper certified
by the Forest Stewardship Council.

Contents

Foreword to the Fifth Edition

'. . . no dictionary of a living tongue can ever be perfect, since while it is hastening to publication, some words are budding, and some falling away.'

Samuel Johnson, *The Dictionary of English* (1755)

'In the case of economics there are no important propositions that cannot, in fact, be stated in plain language.'

J.K. Galbraith, *Annals of an Abiding Liberal* (1979)

Our labours in regularly improving and updating this book have been rewarded, to date, by total sales, worldwide, in excess of 500,000 copies. For this fifth edition we have continued the process of revision. Some seventy entries have been deleted and many others abbreviated to make space for over 150 new entries taking account of new developments in economic theory and practical affairs.

Both the intended readership and the scope and method of the book are unaltered. The dictionary is planned as a companion to two kinds of users of economics. First, for the general reader who wants to follow economic discussion in the press or elsewhere and for the increasing number of people who need some knowledge of economics in their daily work, in teaching, business, the civil service, representative bodies and the professions. Secondly, it is aimed at students – especially those up to the second-year university courses in the subject – but also others, e.g. those at business schools for whom economics is part of the curriculum.

Our distinctive approach remains unique. This approach consists of a micro-encyclopaedic treatment with extensive cross-referencing, up-to-date institutional material and a level of exposition that attempts to combine a reasonable degree of academic rigour with brevity and practical relevance.

Our subject is large and growing continuously and we have had to be highly selective. Words in common usage are not normally included unless they have a specialized meaning in economics. Economic theory, including international, monetary and welfare economics, has been treated fairly comprehensively. We have also given considerable emphasis to the history of economics in keeping with our view of the subject as a developing one. Individual economists are included only where they have made an important and definable contribution to the body of economic thought as it exists today. We have been particularly sparing in our inclusion of contemporary economists (other than Nobel Prize-winners), so that many distinguished living members of the profession are left out. We have tried to include all the key terms used by econometricians and statisticians that are in general use. Our treatment of financial and business economics, public finance, international trade and development and payments has been more selective still but, institutions apart, we hope that nothing important has been omitted.

We have been helped and encouraged by the response we have received from our readers. We hope that they will continue to point out to us any errors or omissions.

G.B.
R.E.B.
E.D.
May 1991

Foreword to the Eighth Edition

It is now thirty-eight years since *The Penguin Dictionary of Economics* was first published. This Eighth Edition represents the most extensive revision we have carried out. The changes we have made reflect the developing world economy and the continued evolution of our subject. We have added some seventy-five significant new entries, deleted fifty and revised and updated several hundred. We have continued to record the ebb and flow of economic doctrine and have attempted to point out what is controversial. We have also maintained the trend in earlier editions of shifting the balance of material on to a more international basis. In keeping with the origins of the 2007–2009 credit crisis, we have enhanced coverage of financial economics. Those who have been awarded a Nobel Prize since the publication of the last edition have also been included. In other respects the basic plan of the work with its micro-encyclopaedic treatment and extensive cross-referencing system, as described in the Foreword to the Fifth Edition above, remains unchanged.

Evan Davis, our collaborator on four previous editions, did not participate in this one because of other commitments but we gratefully acknowledge his generosity in allowing us to use his entries where appropriate.

We wish to acknowledge the exceptional contribution of our copy editor, Jane Robertson, in expunging errors and improving the text in so many ways. We continue to get ideas and suggestions from our readers which we greatly appreciate. We are also grateful, as always, for the support we have received from Dee Baxter and Françoise Bannock.

G.B.
R.E.B
May 2010

Single and double arrows (➤ ➤➤) in the text indicate, respectively, *see* and *see also*, where a point is either amplified or complemented in another entry.

Words or phrases in entries are placed in *italics* if they are definitions or illustrations of the use of a term which may be cross-referenced from another entry, but for which no separate entry is provided. This usage is in addition to the normal use of italics for the titles of published works and where special emphasis is required.

THE DICTIONARY

'A' shares ➤ share.

above the line ➤ below the line.

absolute cost advantage ➤ barriers to entry.

absorption costing ➤ management accountancy.

abstinence theory of interest ➤ interest, abstinence theory of.

acceleration principle The hypothesis that the level of ➤ investment in an economy varies directly with the rate of change of output. Given technological conditions and the relative prices of ➤ capital and ➤ labour, a certain size of capital stock will be chosen to produce a particular level of output. If this level of output changes, then, other things being equal, the desired size of capital stock will also change. Net investment is, by definition, the amount by which the capital stock changes, so it follows that the amount of investment depends on the size of the change in output. At its simplest, the hypothesis asserts that investment will be *proportional* to the rate of change of output, at all levels of output. However, under more realistic assumptions the relationship may cease to be a simple, proportional, one. There may, for example, be spare capacity over some range of increasing output, so that the capital stock does not have to be increased until full capacity is reached; or the capital intensity (➤ capital-intensive) of production may vary as the level of output varies. In addition, the relation will be influenced by ➤ expectations, time lags, etc. As well as being very important in explaining the determination of investment expenditure in the economy, the acceleration principle also plays an important part in theories of the ➤ business cycle, e.g. the ➤ accelerator–multiplier model, and the theory of ➤ economic growth, e.g. in the ➤ Harrod–Domar model. ➤➤ accelerator coefficient.

accelerator coefficient The factor that determines how much ➤ investment is induced by a change in output (➤ acceleration principle). Its value is influenced by the availability of spare capacity, the productivity of capital, the rate of ➤ interest and the price of labour. ➤ capital–output ratio; productivity.

accelerator–multiplier model A model of economic growth, incorporating the effects of the ➤ acceleration principle and the ➤ multiplier. An increase in government expenditure, for example, raises consumers' incomes which, through the multiplier, leads to an increase in output which in turn, through the accelerator, raises investment. The increase in expenditure in investment itself raises incomes and the process is repeated. The model reveals that the multiplier and the accelerator interrelate in a way that can produce a cyclical pattern to economic growth. ➤➤ Harrod–Domar model; Samuelson, P.A.

accelerator theory of investment ➤ acceleration principle; business cycle.

acceptance The act of accepting, i.e. agreeing to honour a promissory note such as a ➤ bill of exchange. By extension, the document itself.

account 1 A record of financial transactions in the form of ➤ stocks or flows (➤➤ balance of payments; balance sheet; current account; social accounting).

2 An arrangement between a seller and a buyer under which a period of ➤ credit is allowed before payment, e.g. the period in which ➤ stock exchange transactions take place and after the end of which settlement must be made. Up to the end of an account, transactions are made without payment and account dates are thus of vital importance to speculators.

account day The day on which all transactions made during the previous ➤ account at the ➤ stock exchange must be settled (hence, *settlement day*). On the New York and London Stock Exchanges the markets use rolling accounts which are settled a fixed number of days after the transaction.

accounting equation, basic ➤ balance sheet.

accounting standards Rules to be followed in the preparation of company accounts. National standards are issued by such bodies as the Financial Accounting Standards Board (FASB) in the United States and the Accounting Standards Board (ASB) in the UK. The International Accounting Standards Board (IASB), based in London, is working to reach worldwide agreement on its International Financial Reporting Standards (IFRS). So far over 100 countries have 'required or permitted' these standards, including the European Union, but full agreement has yet to be reached with the United States and Japan, though it is hoped to achieve it by 2011.

accruals ➤ accrued expenses.

accrued expenses The cost of services utilized in advance of payment and written into a company's accounts as ➤ liabilities.

acquisition ➤ takeover.

active labour-market policies Measures taken to increase the employment prospects of the unemployed (➤ long-term unemployment) without creating upward pressure on wage levels. Such policies include, for example, job counselling (job broking), training, direct job creation in the public sector, and employment subsidies to firms. They differ from the passive measure of paying out state benefits to the unemployed. The distinguishing characteristic of active labour-market measures is that they do not rely on general macroeconomic growth to generate employment (➤ Keynesian unemployment), nor do they include measures designed to price the unemployed into existing jobs (➤ classical unemployment). Active measures have been most extensively pursued in Sweden where, after 300 days, benefits for the unemployed are replaced by options for work or training. The UK has emulated some of these ideas for 18–24 year olds through a comprehensive *welfare to work* package for those unemployed for over six months. This embodies a 'carrot-and-stick' approach, combining the threat of loss of benefit with the opportunity of a place on a training scheme, community work, or a temporary job subsidy. Similar schemes have been adopted in the USA through, for example, the Personal Responsibility and Work Opportunity Reconciliation Act 1996. Whilst active labour-market policies are widespread, the ➤ International Labour Organization reported in 2004 that there was a considerable variation in the amount of support given to such policies between countries. Countries in Europe may spend about 1.6 per cent of Gross Domestic Product on such measures, compared with the USA and Japan which spend about 0.2 per cent. ➤➤ workfare.

activity analysis ➤ linear programming.

activity-based costing ➤ management accountancy.

activity rate ➤ labour force.

actuary Someone trained in the calculation of ➤ risk and ➤ premiums for ➤ assurance purposes.

adaptive expectations The formulation of beliefs about the future value of variables based on their past value and direction of movement. If economic agents used adaptive expectations to predict inflation next year, they would take this year's rate and adjust it. The adjustment would depend on how wrong they had been last year when predicting inflation this year – if they had underestimated inflation, they would upwardly revise their prediction for next year. Adaptive expectations are perhaps naïve, in that they will, respectively, always under- or overestimate a variable which is consistently rising or falling. The assumption that people hold them is crucial in allowing certain economic policies to have an effect (➤ policy ineffectiveness theorem) and has been criticized as *ad hoc*. ➤➤ expectations; rational expectations.

ADB ➤ Asian Development Bank.

administered prices Strictly, prices that are set by management decision rather than by negotiation between buyer and seller. True ➤ market prices are to be found only in the ➤ stock exchange and other places where prices change constantly. Most retail and industrial prices are set by management, though they will be altered in response to competition. The term administered prices is often used to refer to price-fixing by a ➤ monopoly firm, a ➤ cartel or a government body.

ADR ➤ American Depository Receipt.

***ad valorem* tax** ➤ tax, *ad valorem*.

advanced countries States with the highest levels of ➤ national income per head, e.g. the member countries of the ➤ Organisation for Economic Co-operation and Development. ➤➤ developing countries; least-developed countries; transition, economies in.

advances Loans (➤ bank loan).

adverse selection The problem that, in certain markets, the inability of one trader to assess the quality of the other makes it likely that poor-quality traders will predominate. Noted by ➤ Akerlof in 1970, adverse selection is sometimes referred to as the *lemon problem*. A popular example of the phenomenon is in the secondhand-car market, where *sellers* know whether or not their car is a lemon (i.e. performs badly), but where *buyers* cannot make that judgement without running the car. Given that buyers cannot tell the quality of the car they are buying, all cars of the same model will end up selling at the same price, regardless of whether they are lemons or not. The risk of purchasing a lemon will lower the price buyers are prepared to pay for any car and, because secondhand prices are low, people with non-lemon cars will be little inclined to put them on the market.

There are three ingredients in this problem: (a) a random variation in product quality in the market; (b) ➤ asymmetric information about product quality between traders in the market; and (c) a greater willingness for poor-quality traders to trade at low prices than for high-quality ones to do so. (Lemon car owners will still put their cars on the market when the prices drop; other car owners will not.) There are many important markets where adverse selection is held to be significant, notably insurance and the market for credit. ➤➤ market failure.

advertising Paid announcements to persuade or inform members of the public. Outside the theoretical world of ➤ perfect competition, advertising of goods and services is necessary to ensure that potential buyers are informed and helps to make markets function efficiently. However, advertising can create or increase ➤ barriers to entry into an industry and enhance product differentiation (➤ differentiation, product) and, it has been argued, promote ➤ concentration. Proponents of heavy advertising expenditure argue that it provides a ➤ signalling mechanism whereby high-quality producers publicly demonstrate their commitment to their product – something they would do only if they genuinely believed that it had a long-term future – while others point out that consumers may have little choice in a concentrated industry but to bear the cost of unnecessary advertising which serves only to keep out new entrants. 'Own brand' products in supermarkets (which are not advertised) have not replaced advertised brands, and this could be explained by the power of advertisers to manipulate consumer psychology.

AfDB ➤ African Development Bank.

African Development Bank (AfDB) A regional international bank (➤ banking) founded in 1964 for assisting in the economic growth of the independent African states. In 1972, an affiliated organization, the African Development Fund, was set up with a membership open, unlike that of the bank, to non-African states. It is through this fund that loans are made to African member states at low or nil ➤ rates of interest (➤➤ soft loan). Affiliation to the fund has enabled the bank to broaden its sources of funds for investment. In 1982, the African members of the bank agreed to open its membership to non-African states. In 1998, members agreed to increase the capital of the bank by about $8 billion, to about $30 billion. The bank has fifty-three African member states and twenty-four other member states, with the latter having a share of capital of 40 per cent. ➤➤ Asian Development Bank; Caribbean Development Bank; Colombo Plan; development assistance; Inter-American Development Bank.

African Development Fund ➤ African Development Bank.

agency costs The inefficiencies associated with employing a representative to perform a task for you, rather than carrying it out yourself. In any situation in which people are employed to perform a task, those employees – or agents – may well have their own interests, quite separate from those of the employer (often referred to as the 'principal'). Agency costs refer to the loss of efficiency in the conduct of a task from the fact that agents may let their own interests temper their behaviour. For example, a travel agent may sell a more expensive ticket than necessary to obtain a bigger commission. Agency costs – in practice very common in all sorts of economic relationships – only prevail where the behaviour of the agent is hard to monitor directly. ➤ principal–agent problem.

aggregate concentration ➤ concentration.

aggregate demand The sum of all expenditure within an economy, making up ➤ gross domestic product. The main categories are: (a) consumers' expenditure on goods and services; (b) government spending (➤ public expenditure); (c) ➤ investment in capital goods and stocks (➤ inventories); and (d) ➤ exports of goods and services, less expenditure on ➤ imports of goods and services. Since ➤ Keynes, economists have debated how far the level of aggregate demand affects the total level of output and ➤➤ economic growth. ➤ national income; policy ineffectiveness theorem.

aggregate supply The total of all goods and services produced in an economy. Prior to ➤ Keynes, it was believed that ➤ national income was determined by aggregate supply (➤ Say). Keynes shifted the emphasis on to ➤ aggregate demand, with supply meeting whatever demand existed up to a point. Supply factors have since received more consideration in the determination of total output. ➤➤ supply-side economics.

aggregated rebate ➤ deferred rebate.

aggregation problem ➤ Cambridge School.

aid ➤ development assistance.

AIM Alternative Investment Market ➤➤ unlisted securities market(s).

Akerlof, George A. (b. 1940) Economist from the University of California at Berkeley and joint winner of the Nobel Prize in 2001 for his work on the effect of ➤ asymmetric information and ➤ adverse selection on the functioning of markets. His most famous paper by far, 'The Market for Lemons: quality uncertainty and the market mechanism', *Quarterly Journal of Economics* (1970), was written in his first year as an assistant professor at Berkeley, and describes the impact of adverse selection on the secondhand-car market.

Professor Akerlof was educated at Yale and the Massachusetts Institute of Technology, and, apart from when at Berkeley, spent time at the London School of Economics between 1978 and 1980. He also spent a year at the Indian Statistical Institute in New Delhi in 1968. This convinced him that standard economics was not rich enough to explain all the market behaviour we observe. Akerlof's economics has been characterized by a preoccupation with the conventions of behaviour, institutions or inertias that might impede the frictionless functioning of markets. He contributed to the ➤ efficiency wage hypothesis, with an account of workers whose productivity was low on account of them holding a sense of injustice at their low wages. He was also a proponent of ➤ new Keynesianism, trying to explain why wages and prices might be sticky, as companies would quite rationally use simplistic rules-of-thumb to set prices. In aggregate, these might have a serious effect for the economy as a whole, and indeed, provide an argument for why monetary policy may be more effective at stimulating the economy than ➤ new classical economics has acknowledged.

Allais, Maurice (1911–2010) Educated at the École Polytechnique and the École Nationale Supérieure des Mines in Paris, Allais became director of the Centre d'Analyse Économique at the École Nationale Supérieure in 1944, where he taught notable economists like Malinvaud and ➤ Debreu. He became the first French citizen to win the ➤ Nobel Prize for Economics in 1988. His main work is his book *A la recherche d'une discipline économique* (1943), a report on ➤ general equilibrium and ➤ economic efficiency without any assumption of ➤ convexity. His name is best known for the Allais paradox, an attempt to show the impact of psychological factors on consumer decision-making in conditions of ➤ risk. The paradox is as follows. If you offer people either a certain $500 or a lottery ticket that gives them a 10 per cent chance of winning $2500, an 89 per cent chance of winning $500 and a 1 per cent chance of winning nothing, they often take the certain $500. But if you offer them a choice between two lottery tickets, one which gives them an 11 per cent chance of winning $500 and an 89 per cent chance of winning nothing, or another one that offers them a 10 per cent chance of winning $2500 and a 90 per cent chance of winning nothing, they often take the second one. Interestingly, however, the effective choice being made is the same in both cases, and consistent consumers should pick either the first option both times or the second option both times. ➤ behavioural economics; neuro-economics.

Allais paradox ➤ Allais, M.

allocative efficiency ➤ economic efficiency.

Alternative Investment Market (AIM) ➤ unlisted securities market(s).

American Depository Receipt (ADR) A document issued by a US bank against ➤ shares deposited with it or a bank overseas. The ADR gives title to the underlying shares and is traded as such on ➤ stock exchanges.

amortization Provision for the repayment of ➤ debt by means of accumulating a 'sinking fund' through regular payments which, with accumulated ➤ interest, may be used to settle the debt in instalments over time, or in a lump sum. The term is also used as a synonym for ➤ depreciation.

Andean Pact A ➤ customs union agreed at Cartagena in 1969 between Chile, Peru, Colombia, Bolivia and Ecuador. Venezuela joined the pact in 1973, but Chile terminated her agreement in 1976. Free trade was established between the member states, although it was not until 1994 that a Common External Tariff regime was agreed. In 1996, the Trujillo Act committed the member states to the setting up of an Economic Community (➤ European Union). In 1999, a Framework Agreement was concluded for the establishment of a ➤ Free Trade Area with ➤ Mercosur. ➤➤ Central American Common Market; Latin American Integration Association; Union of South American Nations.

annually managed expenditure (AME) The portion of public spending in the UK that is managed on a year-by-year basis, rather than on a rolling three-year budget. The biggest components are: (a) social security spending; (b) debt interest; (c) local authority self-financed spending; and (d) contributions to the European Union. Annually managed expenditure is sometimes seen as spending that is *demand-led*, i.e. spending over which government has little short-term control, but simply has to cover as the bills come in. It contrasts with departmental spending that can be more easily allocated in advance. ➤ public expenditure.

annual percentage rate (APR) A legally standardized form for presenting the ➤ rate of interest and all the associated costs of a loan in the UK. The idea behind the APR is to prevent lenders quoting low interest rates while, in effect, making the loan expensive by charging arrangement fees and demanding frequent payments. The APR is the ➤ compound interest you would pay if all costs associated with the loan were collected as interest. (➤ competition policy)

annuity 1 A constant annual payment.
   2 A guaranteed series of payments in the future purchased for a lump sum. Annuities are described as 'certain' where payment is specified for a fixed number of years. A 'life' annuity payment continues until the death of the person for whom it was purchased. Annuities may be 'immediate', where payment commences on purchase, or 'deferred', where payment starts at a future specified date. Some annuities, at higher cost, offer protection against the erosion of the real value of income through ➤ inflation, e.g. by a guaranteed increase of 5 per cent each year. Other variations include ➤ indexation and with-profits annuities where income is tied to the profits of a life fund. The price of an annuity is based on the ➤ present value of the stream of income payments it provides, and it varies with ➤ rates of interest and, in the case of life annuities, the age and sex of the person who will draw the annuity.

anti-trust (US) Legislation to control ➤ monopoly and restrictive practices in favour of ➤ competition policy. It applies not only to amalgamations of firms (➤ trust) but also to single companies. In the USA the Sherman Act (1890) made monopoly or the restraint of trade illegal. The Clayton Act (1914) clarified earlier legislation and prohibited specific activities, notably ➤ price discrimination, ➤ exclusive dealing, and ➤ interlocking directorates and shareholdings among competitors. The Celler–Kefauver Act (1950) amended the Clayton Act and closed a loophole which allowed companies to buy competitors' assets as long as they did not acquire their shares. The Robinson–Patman Act (1936) strengthened the provisions in the Clayton Act against price discrimination and made it illegal to sell goods to retailers and wholesalers at different prices unless justified by differences in the cost of supply. Anti-trust policy is overseen by the *Federal Trade Commission*, a federal government agency created in 1914 that cooperates with, but is independent of, the Anti-Trust Division of the Department of Justice. Anti-trust suits led to the break-ups of Standard Oil in 1911 and of AT&T in 1982. Suits against IBM (1969) and Microsoft (1998) did not result in break-ups as intended. The Microsoft case ended in a *consent decree* – a judicial agreement that the company should cease certain practices. United States anti-trust law is intended to be non-discretionary, in contrast to the UK approach that is more pragmatic. Section 4 of the Clayton Act created a private right to recover triple damages inflicted by violation of the Act. Private actions against monopolies have been far more numerous than government actions. ➤➤ Chicago School; competition policy; Glass-Steagall Act 1933; monopoly; shipping conference.

APACS Association of Payment Clearing Services. ➤ clearing house.

APC ➤ average propensity to consume.

appreciation Increase in the value of ➤ assets; the antonym of ➤ depreciation. Appreciation may occur through rising ➤ prices as a result of ➤ inflation, increased scarcity or increases in earning power. ➤➤ currency appreciation.

appropriation account A business account showing how net ➤ profit is distributed between ➤ dividends, reserves, ➤ pension funds, etc.

appropriation accounts ➤ public expenditure.

APR ➤ annual percentage rate.

APS ➤ average propensity to save.

arbitrage The exploitation of differences between the prices of financial ➤ assets or ➤ currency or a ➤ commodity within or between markets by buying where prices are low and selling where they are higher. If wheat is cheaper in Chicago than in London after allowing for transport and dealing costs, it will pay to buy in Chicago and sell in London. If interest rates are higher on a euro deposit in London than in Frankfurt, a higher return will be obtained by switching funds from one centre to the other. It will also pay to switch funds from a euro deposit in Frankfurt to a sterling deposit in London if the interest rate differential is greater than the cost of covering against the risk of a fall in the exchange rate of the pound against the euro (➤ forward exchange market). Unlike ➤ speculation, arbitrage does not normally involve significant risks, since the buying and selling operations are carried out more or less simultaneously and the profit made does not depend upon taking a view on future price changes. By eliminating price differentials, arbitrage contributes to the achievement of ➤ equilibrium. ➤ Price discrimination between markets is difficult or impossible where possibilities for arbitrage exist. ➤ carry trade; efficient markets hypothesis.

arbitration The process in which parties to a dispute allow a third party, who has no other direct involvement, to suggest or impose a solution. Each party will be more inclined to go to arbitration if it thinks both that it has a good chance of winning, and that the cost of resolving the dispute will be lower than by other means. The logic behind arbitration is that disputants find it easier to agree with a third party than to resolve their argument themselves. Arbitration can be (a) binding, in which case each party agrees in advance that it will do whatever the arbiter decides; or (b) non-binding, in which case the parties are free to reject the arbiter's advice. *Pendular arbitration* is that in which the arbiter can only accept the point of view of one side or the other, but is not allowed to advocate a compromise solution. The idea behind this is to encourage the disputants to make reasonable offers to each other before the arbiter makes a decision. ➤➤ bargaining theory of wages; game theory.

arc elasticity ➤ elasticity.

arithmetic progression A sequence of numbers in which the *differences* between all adjacent numbers in the sequence are the same, e.g. 2, 4, 6, 8, 10 . . . ➤➤ geometric progression.

Arrow, Kenneth Joseph (b. 1921) After graduation at Columbia University and a period at the Cowles Commission, Professor Arrow went to Stanford University in 1949, where he became a professor in 1953. In 1968, he accepted a Chair at Harvard University, but returned to Stanford University in 1979. He was awarded the ➤ Nobel Prize for Economics in 1972 (with ➤ Hicks). His publications include *Social Choice and Individual Values* (1951), 'Existence of an Equilibrium for a Competitive Economy' (with ➤ Debreu, *Econometrica* 1954), *Studies in Mathematical Theory of Inventory and Production* (1958), *Public Investment, the Rate of Return, and Optimal Fiscal Policy* (1970), *Essays in the Theory of Risk-Bearing* (1971) and *General Competitive Analysis* (with Frank Hahn, 1971).

Professor Arrow showed that it was logically impossible to devise a constitution for a community that would always ensure that outcomes would be ranked in a way that appeared desirable (➤➤ impossibility theorem). He made important contributions to ➤ general equilibrium analysis that placed the theory on a firmer basis after the work of ➤ Walras. Professor Arrow has also made contributions to the theory of decision-making under uncertainty (➤ risk) and to ➤ growth theory.

Arrow–Debreu general equilibrium model A mathematical model of a market economy that consists of consumers with ➤ demand functions for commodities, and firms with ➤ production functions to produce those commodities. It was a breakthrough in ➤ general equilibrium analysis. The model was developed in the early 1950s, and succeeded in showing that, in principle, it was possible to posit the existence of a logically consistent set of prices across the economy that would ensure demand and supply were in equilibrium in the markets for commodities themselves, and for the inputs for production that were needed to make the commodities. ➤➤ Arrow, K.J.; Debreu, G.; Walras, M.E.L.

articles of association ➤ Memorandum of Association.

ASEAN ➤ Association of South East Asian Nations.

Asian Development Bank (ADB) The Asian Development Bank, based in Manila, was established in 1966, following the recommendations of the United Nations Economic and Social Commission for Asia and the Pacific. It was formed 'to foster economic growth and cooperation in the region of Asia and the Pacific and to contribute to the acceleration of economic development of the ➤ developing countries of the region'. It encourages economic and financial cooperation among the regional members. In 2008, 64 per cent of the total subscribed ➤ capital of US$3.9 billion was contributed by the forty-eight countries within the region, which included 36 per cent of this total from its three developed countries of Japan, Australia and New

Zealand. The remaining nineteen, non-regional, countries contributed US$1.4 billion. The bank's affiliate – the Asian Development Fund – gives ➤ soft loans to the poorest nations in the region. A strategic guidance, looking forward to 2020, was adopted by the Bank in 2008 which had three aspects: Inclusive Growth, Environmental Sustainable Growth and Regional Integration. The Bank's instruments are loans, mostly to governments and the public sector, grants and technical assistance. Some loans are made to the private sector, together with equity investment and technical assistance. In 2008, loans made by the Bank totalled US$10.5 billion. ➤➤ African Development Bank; Caribbean Development Bank; Colombo Plan; development assistance; Inter-American Development Bank.

Asia–Pacific Economic Cooperation (APEC) A forum of, originally, fifteen Pacific Rim countries, formed in 1989 on the initiative of Australia. In 1992, a secretariat was opened in Singapore and in 1994 agreement was reached for the establishment of a ➤ free trade area in stages by 2020. At a meeting in Osaka in 1995, the member countries agreed to reduce import tariffs (➤ tariffs, import) and liberalize services, public procurement contracts and ➤ foreign investment. It was accepted that flexibility should be allowed in the implementation of measures by the developing countries in the group and in relation to particularly sensitive areas, e.g. agriculture. In 2009, there were twenty-one members: Australia, Brunei, Canada, Chile, China, Hong Kong, Indonesia, Japan, Malaysia, Mexico, New Zealand, Papua New Guinea, Peru, the Philippines, Russia, Singapore, South Korea, Taiwan, Thailand, the USA and Vietnam. ➤ Association of South East Asian Nations; North American Free Trade Agreement.

assay To test for the purity of gold or other minerals; to determine the worth of something. ➤ seignorage.

assessable profits The taxable ➤ profit of a business, normally after the deduction of ➤ capital allowances, interest and other business expenses. It differs, however, from accounting profit not only because of different treatment of ➤ depreciation, but because some business expenses (e.g. some forms of entertaining) are not allowable in computing taxable profit.

assets 1 A business accounting term. On the ➤ balance sheet of a company, everything the company owns and which has a money value is classified as an asset, total assets being equal to total liabilities. Assets fall into the following categories, roughly in order of the extent to which realizing their money value would disrupt the company's business: (a) *current assets*: ➤ cash, bank deposits and other items that can readily be turned into cash, e.g. bills receivable, ➤ stock and work in progress, and marketable ➤ securities; (b) *trade investments*: ➤ investment in subsidiary or associated companies; (c) *fixed assets*: ➤ land, buildings, plant and machinery, vehicles and furniture, usually at cost less ➤ depreciation written off; and (d) *intangible assets*: goodwill, patents, etc. The assets of an individual are those possessions or the liabilities of others to him, which have a positive money value.

2 *Financial assets* are titles to cash, e.g. a bank ➤ deposit or income and/or ➤ capital gains. Financial assets may be classified according to their ➤ liquidity, the protection they offer against ➤ inflation (➤ indexation) or changes in ➤ exchange rates and the risk of default. Some financial assets are income-certain, e.g. ➤ gilt-edged securities, while some are not, e.g. ➤ ordinary shares. Some assets are capital-certain, e.g. a fixed-interest security that is redeemable at par (➤ par value; redeemable securities), but ordinary shares are subject to a price risk.

3 *Real assets* are tangible assets such as land, buildings or equipment.

asset specificity The feature of durable or fixed ➤ assets which have no, or limited, alternative uses (e.g. a nuclear power station), and which, once built, therefore generate ➤ sunk costs.

assisted areas Regions that attract government assistance because of their persistent high levels of unemployment relative to the rest of the country. First introduced in the UK in the 1930s. Since the accession of the UK to the ➤ European Union (EU), the assisted areas are defined according to EU guidelines which include having a GDP per capita of less than 75 per cent of the EU average. Under EU rules, state aid must not distort competition within the Union and 'structural' and 'cohesion' funds are available for the assistance in member states. National measures for assisted areas and their boundaries are agreed with the Commission. The latest agreed map of assisted areas is for the period 2007–13. ➤ regional policy.

Association of South East Asian Nations (ASEAN) An association set up in 1967 by five countries in South East Asia: Indonesia, Malaysia, the Philippines, Singapore and Thailand. In 1976, the ASEAN agreed to a list of industrial projects covering petrochemicals, fertilizers, steel, soda ash, newsprint and rubber, on which the group would cooperate in the construction of major plants. The ASEAN also agreed to set up a permanent secretariat. Brunei joined the ASEAN in 1984, Vietnam in 1995, Myanmar and Laos in 1997 and Cambodia in 1999. The member nations of the ASEAN have agreed to the aim of establishing an economic community by 2015. Some tariffs on imports of manufactures have been reduced. Regional ➤ free trade agreements have been concluded with Australia, China, India, Japan, New Zealand and South Korea. ➤ Asia–Pacific Economic Cooperation.

assurance That branch of ➤ insurance under which a company is made to pay a ➤ capital sum on a specified date or on the death of the person assured. The former contract or policy is called *term* or *endowment* assurance, and the latter *whole-of-life*. Both types of policy may be with or without ➤ profits. By paying a higher ➤ premium, the policyholder can receive a share of the profits earned by the life fund. Policies may also be linked in some way to ➤ equities so that the final payment is determined by the stock market prices current at the time (➤ unit trust). Life assurance is an important form of private ➤ savings.

asymmetric information Information concerning a transaction that is unequally shared between the two parties to the transaction. The most famous application of the problems that asymmetric information can create has been ➤ Akerlof's discussion of the secondhand-car market (➤ adverse selection). Other important applications relate to the ➤ principal–agent problem and ➤ moral hazard. ➤➤ information, economics of; mechanism design; screening; signalling.

Atkinson index An index of income ➤ inequality, proposed by A.B. Atkinson in 1970, which takes into account assumptions about social economic welfare and reflects the decreasing ➤ marginal utility of money as incomes rise. The central idea upon which the index is constructed is that of Equally Distributed Equivalent (EDE) income. The EDE is that income which, if distributed equally, would yield the same level of social economic welfare as that yielded by actual incomes. A shift to a more equal income distribution may lead to a fall in total income, although social economic welfare remains the same. There is a trade-off between equality of incomes and total income which a society must balance when deciding between alternative economic policies which involve changes in income distribution.

The index may be summarized as follows:

$$A = 1 - \frac{Y_e}{Y}$$

Y_e = EDE   If A = 0 perfect equality

Y = Actual Income   A → 1 increasing inequality

➤➤ Gini coefficient; income, distribution of; social welfare function.

ATM Automatic teller machines (➤ credit card).

auction A type of transaction in which the buyer of an item and the price paid for it are chosen after a number of different potential buyers has each made some declaration of their willingness to pay for the item. Auctions can be held in a variety of forms: (a) the *English auction*, in which the bidders sequentially offer higher prices, with the last remaining bidder paying his/her last offered price; (b) the *Dutch auction*, in which a list of sequentially lower prices are offered by the seller, until a potential buyer accepts one of these prices and then pays that price for the product; (c) the *sealed-bid auction*, in which each bidder is given one chance to make an offer, in ignorance of the offers of other bidders, and in which the highest offer is accepted; and (d) the *second-price* (or ➤ Vickrey) *auction*, which is exactly like a sealed-bid auction, except that the highest bidder has to pay only the price offered by the second-highest bidder. Economists have used ➤ game theory to study how auctions should be conducted, and what strategy should be adopted in each case by the bidders.

Austrian school A tradition of economic thought originating in the work of Carl ➤➤ Menger (1840–1921), who was Professor of Economics at Vienna until 1903. Menger's principal achievement was the construction of a marginal utility theory of value (➤ value, theories of). He was succeeded in the Chair by von ➤➤ Wieser (1851–1926) who developed his work, and in addition, clearly formulated the important concept of ➤ opportunity cost. ➤➤ Böhm-Bawerk (1851–1914), who followed, made his main contributions in the fields of ➤ capital and interest-rate theory (➤ rate of interest). The perspective of the Austrian School differs sharply from that of mainstream economics. The members of the school do not, for example, accept the usefulness of the concept of general market ➤ equilibrium. They argue that in reality markets are characterized by constant change and creative discovery through entrepreneurship (➤ entrepreneur). As a consequence of this, planned economies tend to break down since the necessary information for planning can never be available and mathematical models of the economy can be misleading. The Austrian tradition was followed in the work of von ➤➤ Mises and von ➤➤ Hayek, and, later, in work by ➤➤ Hicks, J.R.; ➤➤ Jevons, W.S.; Longfield, S.M.

authorized capital The amount of share ➤ capital fixed in the ➤ Memorandum of Association and the articles of association of a company as required by the Companies Acts (➤ company law). Also known as *nominal capital* or *registered capital*.

auto-correlation A ➤ correlation, not between two different variables, but between successive values of one variable. It is used most frequently to refer to a potential problem in ➤ least-squares regression, when the residual of the regression is auto-correlated, i.e. appears to have a systematic pattern, and therefore deviates from the assumption of randomness usually made. Auto-correlation, or serial correlation, requires other analytical methods to be adopted.

automatic stabilizers ➤ built-in stabilizers.

autonomous investment Investment expenditure which is not induced by changes in output (➤ acceleration principle). Examples of such investment are: (a) government expenditure on infrastructure; and (b) firms' expenditure on new plant to exploit an invention.

average A single number calculated to summarize and represent the values of items in a set (➤➤ frequency distribution). The most common such measure is the *arithmetic mean*. This is calculated by adding together the values of the items in the set and dividing the total by the number of items. For example, suppose that the wages of five employees were $400, $420, $480, $500 and $550 per week respectively. The arithmetic mean is ($400 + $420 + $480 + $500 + $550) divided by 5 = $470. There is an implied assumption in the arithmetic mean that the values from which the mean is calculated are more or less of the same order of magnitude. For example, if another employee were included who earned $970 per week, the arithmetic mean would show an average wage of the six employees to be $553 per week, which would be misleading as all but one earned less than this. ➤➤ standard deviation.

The *median* avoids this problem of extremes by taking that value for which there is an equal number of items with values below it as above it. For example, in the above example of five employees, the median is $480, as there are two employees with wages above and two with wages below this. If we include the sixth employee, the median is the arithmetic mean of the two middle values (as there is an even number of items), i.e. ($480 + $500) divided by 2 = $490. The median, therefore, is less affected by extreme values and will be less than the arithmetic mean where the items include an extreme high value and will be higher than the arithmetic mean where there is an extreme low value.

The third important measure of average is the *mode*. This is simply the 'most popular' value in a set of numbers. For example, suppose, out of a total of fifty employees, five earned $400, ten earned $420, twenty-five earned $480, five earned $500 and five earned $550 per week, respectively. The mode would be $480 per week, because more employees earned that wage than any other of the wages specified. It is to be noted that, unlike the other two measures, the mode is totally uninfluenced by other items in the set.

A fourth measure of average is the *geometric mean*. This is calculated by multiplying the items in the set and taking the nth root, where n is the number of items in the set. For instance, the geometric mean of 3 and 12 is the square root of ($3 \times 12 = 36$) = 6. In general, the formula can be written as log (geometric mean) = $\log x_1 + \log x_2 + \log x_3 \ldots + \log x_n$ *divided* by n. In the above example of five employees' wages, the geometric mean works out at $467, compared with the arithmetic mean of $470. If the additional employee earning $970 is added, the arithmetic mean rises to $553, an increase of 18 per cent, but the geometric mean rises only to $527, an increase of 13 per cent. This is a general characteristic of the geometric mean. It tends to constrict the effects of large-value items and enhance the effect of low-value items. ➤ consumer price index. ➤➤ weighted average.

average cost Total production costs per unit of output. It is calculated by adding total ➤ fixed costs to total ➤ variable costs and dividing by the number of units produced. The effect of indivisibilities (➤ economies of scale) is that average costs fall as output expands, spreading the fixed cost over more units. After a time, however, average variable costs may increase as, for example, workers are paid overtime to operate machinery nearer to its full capacity and more has to be spent on maintenance. This is said to give short-run average-cost curves a characteristic U-shape. In the ➤ long run, all costs are variable because more fixed ➤ assets can be acquired or surplus capacity scrapped. The shape and slope of the long-run average-cost curve, when all costs are variable, will be determined by the extent of long-run economies of scale (if any).

average-cost pricing The pricing of goods or services so as just to cover the ➤ average cost of production. The firm engaging in this will neither make a profit nor loss. ➤➤ marginal-cost pricing.

average propensity to consume The proportion of income, whether of individuals, households or countries, spent on goods and services, other than for ➤ investment. ➤➤ consumption function; marginal propensity to consume; savings ratio.

average propensity to save The proportion of income, whether of individuals, households or countries, which is not spent on consumption. ➤ average propensity to consume; ➤➤ savings ratio.

average revenue Total sales value divided by the number of units sold and equal, therefore, to average ➤ price.

Averch–Johnson effect The tendency of companies, the ➤ rate of return of which is regulated, to engage in excessive accumulation of capital in order to expand the volume of their profits. If companies are told that they are not allowed to earn more than a 15 per cent return on capital, there is a strong incentive for them to over-invest in order to earn that 15 per cent on as large a capital base as possible, even if it would be more efficient for them to have less capital and higher ➤ variable costs. The 'A. J. Thesis' was put forward in 1962 in an article in the *American Economic Review* entitled 'Behaviour of the Firm Under Regulatory Restraint' by Harvey Averch and Leland Johnson. ➤ rate-of-return regulation; ➤➤ price regulation; regulation; yardstick competition.

avoidable costs ➤ prime costs.

B

backwardation **1** In a ➤ commodity market, the amount by which the spot ➤ price (including the cost of stocking over time) exceeds the forward price. ➤➤ forward exchange market; spot market.

2 On the ➤ stock exchange, a sum of ➤ money paid by a ➤ bear to a ➤ bull for the right to delay delivery of ➤ securities sold forward at a fixed price. A bear will have sold securities to a bull for delivery on a certain date in the expectation that, by that date, the market price will have fallen. If it does not in fact fall, he may consider it worth while to pay a backwardation so as to defer delivery of the shares until the next account period.

3 A temporary situation in which one ➤ market maker has a lower offer price than another's bid price.

BACS Bankers' Automated Clearing Service (➤ clearing house).

bad banks ➤ Troubled Asset Relief Program.

'bad money drives out good' The idea that an injection of a low-quality coinage into a monetary system will dissuade holders of high-quality coins from parting with cash. Before paper ➤ money (➤ banknote) became universally accepted as a means for settling ➤ debts, precious metals were the most common forms of money. Gold and silver coins were struck bearing a ➤ face value equivalent to the value of their metal content. Debasement of the coinage occurred when the face value was kept above the value of the metal content of the coinage. The holders of the correctly valued coinage became unwilling to exchange for the debased coinage because they would obtain less metal in exchange than if they bought direct. The result was that the 'good', undebased, coinage did not circulate. The process is referred to as ➤ Gresham's law, and is an early application of the idea of ➤ adverse selection.

balanced budget A situation in which the government's planned expenditure equals its expected income. In public finance it refers to a situation where current income from ➤ taxation and other receipts of central government are sufficient to meet payments for goods and services, ➤ transfer payments and debt interest. Government budgets are often in deficit (do not balance) on both ➤ current account and ➤ capital account and these deficits are financed by net borrowing and changes in the ➤ money supply (➤ public-sector borrowing requirement). As a result of high levels of public expenditure to counter the 2007–2009 credit crisis, budget deficits rose to unprecedented levels for peace-time. As a percentage of ➤ nominal gross domestic product, projected government financial balances (imbalances) for 2009 were –11.2 for the USA, –7.4 for Japan and –12.6 for the UK, the highest in the ➤ OECD. The importance of the budget balance and how it is financed is that it may affect levels of demand and prices in the economy and the willingness of investors to buy sovereign bonds (➤ sovereign risk) (➤ fiscal policy; Keynes; structural budget deficit). ➤➤ public sector.

balanced budget multiplier The effect upon the ➤ national income of equal changes in government expenditure and revenues. If government expenditure is increased by $1000 million and income-tax rates are increased to raise an additional $1000 million in revenue, ➤ aggregate demand may not, as might be expected, remain the same, since a proportion of personal ➤ disposable income would have been saved. Whereas all the increase in government expenditure results in increased demand, some of the reduction in personal incomes leads to a fall in savings rather than expenditure. If the ➤ savings ratio were 10 per cent, then the additional demand would be $100 million, which would have a ➤ multiplier effect upon the national income.

balanced growth The state of an economy in which there is a constant relationship between the components of aggregate ➤ national income. Consumption expenditure, ➤ investment and employment grow at the same rate as national income. The model is applied to the study of equilibrium conditions in ➤ growth theory. ➤➤ steady-state growth.

balance of payments A tabulation of the credit and debit transactions of a country with foreign countries and international institutions during a specific period. The data are collated on the principle of ➤ double-entry bookkeeping, although, by convention, the figures are published in a single column with positive (credit) and negative (debit) signs. The entries in the account should, therefore, add up to zero but because of measurement problems they fail to do so in practice and recourse has to be made to a ➤ balancing item. Transactions are divided into two broad groups: (a) ➤ current account, and (b) capital account. The *current account* is made up of trade in goods (also called merchandise or visible trade), and in services plus the profits and interest earned from overseas ➤ assets, net of those paid abroad. It is the current account that is generally referred to in discussion of the state of the balance of payments. The *capital account* is made up of such items as the inward and outward flow of money for ➤ investment and international grants and loans.

The main groups making up a country's international accounts are compared in the table below for China, India, the USA and the UK.

The overall deficits or surpluses in the balance of payments are brought into balance by movements in the ➤ gold and foreign exchange reserves or liabilities to non-residents. The balance of payments reflects many factors but specifically: (a) the state of ➤ aggregate demand at home and the state of demand abroad; and (b) the ➤ exchange rate and the relative costs of domestic production. Governments can only influence the balance by changing demand, or by changing the exchange rate.

A current account surplus can be seen as an accumulation of foreign assets, and is thus equivalent to a form of national saving. It is certainly true that the balance of payments of different countries has tended to reflect savings levels. A deficit in the balance of payments is not necessarily a bad thing, any more than a surplus

Balance of payments

2007   **BnUS$**

	China	India	USA	UK
Imports of goods	956	219	2017	625
Exports of goods	1218	146	1162	440
Goods trade balance	+262	−73	−855	−185
Imports of services	130	49	378	212
Exports of services	122	86	497	295
Services trade balance	−8	+37	+119	+83
Current account (% GDP)	+11.3	−1.0	−5.3	−3.8

Foreign direct investment

2006

	China	India	USA	UK
Inwards	691	88	2394	1280
Outwards	112	35	3177	1522
Net outwards	−579	−53	+784	+243

Source: OECD Statistical Abstracts, 2009.

need be a good thing. It is a form of borrowing which could be used to enhance domestic investment to the benefit of future growth. On the other hand, if a deficit is caused by an unsustainable period of excess demand, perhaps occasioned by an excessive ➤ budget deficit, it will persist until the home market has reached ➤ equilibrium brought about by, say, a reduction in the offsetting surplus on capital account or a significant drop in the exchange rate.

Although, in principle, there are many measures that can be taken in a direct attempt to correct a disequilibrium in a country's balance of payments, many, such as import ➤ tariffs, import ➤ quotas, ➤ import deposits and ➤ export incentives are now constrained by the rules of the ➤ World Trade Organization or the ➤ European Union, and are generally reckoned to be ineffective in the long term. More generally, however, the rapid development of ➤➤ globalization has enabled an expansion in the surpluses on the balance of payments of developing countries such as China, which has resulted in financial flows into the advanced countries such as the USA, which exacerbates problems of fiscal and monetary management. ➤ competitiveness; J-curve.

balance of trade The difference between a nation's imports of goods and services and its exports of them. It is the most important element of the ➤ balance of payments.

balance sheet A statement of the ➤ wealth of a business, other organization or individual on a given date, usually the last day of the ➤ financial year; not to be confused with the profit and loss account (➤ double-entry bookkeeping), which records changes in the company's wealth over one year. A balance sheet is in two parts: (a) on the left-hand side or at the top, ➤ assets, and (b) on the right-hand side or at the bottom, ➤ liabilities. The assets of the company – ➤ debtors, cash, investments and property – are set out against the claims or liabilities of the persons or organizations owning them – the ➤ creditors, lenders and shareholders – so that the two parts of the balance sheet are equal. This is the principle of double-entry bookkeeping. The fact that the assets and liabilities are equal does not mean that the ➤ equity shareholders owe as much as they own; they are included among the claimants.

According to the *basic accounting equation*, assets = liabilities + equity; therefore, assets – liabilities = equity. Equity, shareholders' interest or net worth (which are all the same thing) calculated from the balance sheet in this way may not reflect its true market value, since assets are normally written into the balance sheet at historical cost (➤ book value) without any adjustment for ➤ appreciation (➤ inflation accounting).

Until the 1981 Companies Act the law did not, in the UK, lay out requirements for financial reporting of companies in detail or to any particular format, so that the layout and content of balance sheets varied considerably. The Companies Acts now require accounts to be set out in conformity with the European Economic Community (EEC) (➤ European Union) Fourth Directive (➤ company law). Notes to the accounts provide breakdowns of some of the elements of the balance sheet (e.g. tangible assets), as well as other information required by statute, e.g. details of directors' and employees' remuneration.

balancing allowance ➤ capital allowances.

balancing item Data for the ➤ balance of payments accounts are collated on the principle of ➤ double-entry bookkeeping. For example, the value of a shipment of the export from the UK of a motor vehicle to the USA will be recorded as a credit item. The payment for the motor vehicle by the US importer by, for example, depositing a sum to the account of the UK exporter in a bank in New York will be recorded as a debit item to the same amount. In principle, for every credit item, there is a corresponding debit item and for every debit item a corresponding credit item, although, by convention, the figures are published in a single column with positive (credit) and negative (debit) signs. The entries in the account should, therefore, add up to zero. In practice, this is difficult to achieve for a number of reasons, e.g. the difficulty of collecting accurate information, a difference in the timing between the two sides of the balance, or a change in exchange rates. Because of such measurement problems, recourse has to be made to the ➤ balancing item which simply adjusts the difference between the sums of the credit and the sums of the debit entries in the balance of payments accounts so that they add up to zero.

Balassa–Samuelson Effect The productivity of that part of a growing economy open to international trade will increase faster than other sectors as it is subject to the prevailing competitive market conditions of international markets. This raises relative wages in the tradable sector, which have to be matched by the non-tradable sector, leading to a higher rate of inflation, coupled with an appreciation in the ➤ real exchange rate. A fixed exchange rate would lead to a higher inflation rate (➤ European Economic and Monetary Union). The effect is named from seminal papers published in 1964 by Bela Balassa (1928–91), 'Purchasing-power parity doctrine. A reappraisal' and by P.A. ➤ Samuelson, 'Theoretical notes on trade problems'.

bank, commercial ➤ commercial banks.

bank, joint-stock ➤ commercial banks.

bank, overseas ➤ overseas banks.

bank, secondary ➤ secondary bank.

bank advances ➤ bank loan.

bank bill ➤ bill of exchange.

bank clearings ➤ clearing house.

bank credit ➤ credit.

Leabharlann
Chontae Ceatharlach
00236851

bank deposits The amount of money standing to the ➤ credit of a customer of a bank. Bank deposits are ➤ assets of its customers and ➤ liabilities of the bank. Deposits may arise from the payments of ➤ cash or a ➤ cheque to a bank for credit to a customer, or by transfer into an account from another account, including a ➤ loan from a bank to its customer. Bank deposits are simply IOUs written in the books of the bank. They do not necessarily reflect actual holdings of cash by the bank. Since bank deposits are used in the settlement of debts, they are ➤ money in the economic sense, so that by creating deposits, banks create money (➤ banking). A deposit may be on ➤ current account or ➤ deposit account. These two types of account are known as ➤ demand deposits and ➤ time deposits in the USA. Bankers' deposits are deposits by a ➤ commercial bank at the ➤ central bank.

banker's draft A ➤ cheque drawn by a bank as opposed to a bank's customer. Banker's drafts are drawn at the request of a customer, and that customer's account is debited when it is drawn. They are regarded as ➤ cash, since they cannot be returned unpaid and are used when a creditor is not willing to accept a personal cheque in payment.

Bank for International Settlements (BIS) An institution, with head offices in Basle, set up on the basis of a proposal by the Young Committee in 1930. The original purpose was to enable the various national ➤ central banks to coordinate through their own central bank the receipts and payments arising mainly from German war reparations. It was hoped, however, that it would develop beyond this, but many of the functions that it might have performed were taken over by the ➤ International Monetary Fund (IMF) after the Second World War. It has, however, in recent years played a more active part in attempting to mitigate the effects of international financial ➤ speculation, acts as a trustee for international government loans and plays an important role in cooperation over banking regulation. Although the major functions of a central bank for central banks are performed by the IMF, the meetings of the central board have been an important means of central bank cooperation. From the 1970s the Basle Committee on Banking Supervision of the BIS has developed international standards for ➤ capital adequacy. The BIS carries out research in financial and monetary economics and compiles statistics. In June 2007 and again a year later the BIS warned that excessive exposure to collateralized credit made the global economy vulnerable to recession. The BIS is owned and controlled by its fifty-five member financial institutions (➤ central banks or monetary authorities), including the ➤ European Central Bank, which have the right to vote and attend the annual general meetings of the organization.

banking   The business of accepting ➤ deposits and lending ➤ money. Banking defined in this way, however, is carried out by some other ➤ financial intermediaries that perform the functions of safeguarding deposits and making ➤ loans. ➤ Building societies and ➤ finance houses, for example, are not normally referred to as banks and are not regarded as being part of the banking system in the narrow, traditional sense. The deposits of some types of bank (e.g. the UK National Savings Bank) cannot be used in the settlement of debts until they are withdrawn, but a deposit in a commercial bank can be used to settle debts by the use of ➤ cheques or ➤ credit transfer. When the manager of a branch of one of the clearing banks opens an overdraft account for a customer, the loan creates a deposit, i.e. a book debt has been incurred to the customer in return for a promise to repay it. Whether or not the overdraft is secured by ➤ collateral security (e.g. an ➤ insurance policy, or some other ➤ asset), when the customer draws upon the loan the bank has added to the total ➤ money supply. In ➤ balance-sheet terms, the deposit is a claim on the bank (i.e. a ➤ liability) while the customer's promise to repay it (or the collateral security) is an asset to the bank. In the absence of government controls on lending, the limitation on the bank's ability to create deposits is its obligation, if it is to remain in business, to pay out ➤ current account deposits in cash on demand. Since customers meet most of their needs for money by using credit cards and writing cheques on their deposits, the cash holdings the banks need form only a small fraction of their total deposits. (The settlement of debts between the clearing banks is made by electronic transfer (➤ clearing house).) This ratio between their deposit liabilities and their cash holdings is called the ➤ cash ratio (sometimes called the primary ratio). Banks also hold other ➤ liquid assets (➤ bills of exchange, ➤ Treasury bills, loans at call and other loans to the money market, ➤ liquidity ratio (secondary ratio)). The object of the banker is, of course, to keep reserves as near as possible to the minimum, since there is only a relatively low return in the money market and no return at all on holdings of cash. The banking system is based on confidence in the system's ability to meet its obligations. In the short run, no bank is able to meet all its obligations in cash and, if demands upon it exhausted its cash reserves, the bank would be obliged to close its doors.

The prevention of bank failure and the protection of bank customers against fraud and loss is one objective of the control and regulation of the banking system which is the responsibility, in the UK, of the Financial Services Authority. That regulation now relies on prudential ratios (➤ capital adequacy) to minimize failure and instability in the banking system. There is also increasing emphasis on assessing the adequacy of the bank's own risk management systems as an instrument of bank supervision (➤ capital adequacy).

The Bank of England remains responsible, in the UK, for ensuring the financial system generally is secure (guarding against ➤ systemic risk). Since the money supply is a basic tool of economic policy, the government also wishes to exert control over the creation of credit by the banking system through its finance ministry. In the UK, this function is also performed by the Bank of England (➤ central bank). Direct controls on bank lending in the interests of controlling the ➤ money supply were removed in 1971 in an attempt to introduce more competition into the banking system. There are now no longer any significant reserve ratios as such. The Bank of England now relies on interest rates to influence inflation (➤ Monetary Policy Committee).

Recent decades have seen substantial growth and change in the banking system. The main features have been an increase in the importance of ➤ overseas banks operating in the UK and other non-clearing banks, the increasing use of new parallel markets as sources of funds for the banks and a decline in the number of merchant banks (➤ investment banks). At the same time, traditional distinctions between the various types of bank are breaking down as most ➤ financial intermediaries diversify their activities. Building societies and investment banks are offering high-interest cheque accounts, non-banks such as multiple retailers are entering the banking market, and some building societies have incorporated as banks (➤ incorporation). The clearing banks have become major providers of ➤ mortgage lending for house purchase and provide non-banking financial services such as insurance broking, ➤ equity purchases, traveller's cheques and, of course, ➤ credit cards. ➤ banknote (for the origin of banking).

Although the main features of banking in different countries may be similar there are important differences. In particular, the US and German banking systems are more fragmented than most, although everywhere a few very large banks account for a large proportion of banking assets and this ➤ concentration is tending to increase. From 1933 until 1999 the ➤ Glass-Steagall Act prevented US commercial banks from acting as investment banks. Banks are everywhere prone to failure since increasing lending can be profitable but banking liabilities tend to be much more ➤ liquid than their assets so that when confidence is impaired, damaging bank 'runs' may occur. About one fifth of US banks failed in 1931–2 and some failed in Europe also. More recently there was a secondary banking crisis in Britain in the early 1970s, a Savings and Loan Associations (➤ savings bank) crisis in the US in the 1980s, a wave of bank failures in Scandinavia in the early 1990s, an Asian Banking crisis in 1997 and of course widespread bank failures in 2007–8.

To increase confidence in banking systems most governments have guaranteed consumer bank deposits against loss, within limits. Moreover, because of the importance of banks to the functioning of economies, governments have generally bailed out larger banks as 'too big to fail' when they got into difficulty (➤ moral hazard). The increasing use of ➤ securitization and ➤ derivatives, along with ➤ globalization, have meant that problems in the financial sector are now rapidly transmitted between countries.

These issues came to the fore again in dramatic fashion in the 2007–2009 credit crisis which followed the puncturing of a ➤ sub-prime credit boom. In this crisis governments around the world were forced to support banking systems by capital injections or outright ownership, the acquisition of ➤ toxic assets and other means. These costly measures, along with more general measures to promote economic activity on Keynesian lines (➤ Keynesian economics; ➤ quantitative easing) seem to have mitigated the crisis. Various longer term measures have been implemented or proposed, including a bank levy to provide insurance against future bank failures, tighter regulation of banks, including enhanced ➤ capital adequacy requirements and even restriction on the range of bank activities and bank size.

banking, retail ➤ commercial banks.

banking, wholesale ➤ wholesale banking.

banking and currency schools The representatives of the two sides of opinion in a controversy which centred on Sir Robert Peel's Bank Charter Act 1844. This Act effectively limited the creation of ➤ banknotes to the ➤ Bank of England and regulated their issue. The *banking school* argued that, given that banknotes were convertible into gold, there was no need to regulate the note issue because the fact of convertibility would constrain any serious overissue. Moreover, it was pointless to try to regulate the issue of banknotes because the demand for currency would be met by an expansion of ➤ bank deposits, which would have the same effect as an expansion of the note issue. The *currency school*, on the other hand, argued that the check offered by convertibility would not operate in time to prevent serious commercial disruption. Banknotes should be regarded as though they were the gold specie they in fact represented, and consequently the quantity at issue should fluctuate in sympathy with the ➤ balance of payments. ➤➤ banking; fiduciary issue; gold standard; money supply.

bank loan A sum borrowed from a bank, normally for a fixed period of two to three years or more for a specific purpose, usually by a commercial concern. The term is also used to include overdrafts and ➤ personal loans. In this broader sense, bank loans are more commonly known as *bank advances*, while total *bank lending* includes commercial paper (promissory notes) and ➤ acceptances. In the UK, 60–70 per cent of loans outstanding by banks and ➤ building societies to residents by value is for business purposes, even though the ➤ commercial banks make ➤ mortgage loans for house purchase on a large scale.

Bank loans are normally secured (➤ collateral security), repaid in regular instalments and with interest charged at rates which vary with the bank's ➤ base rate. UK banks have been compared unfavourably with those in other countries in the extent to which they provide long-term loans to industry. It is true that until about thirty years ago the bulk of bank advances was in the form of overdrafts that are repayable on demand. This was partly because the banks in the UK have not in general been able to attract long-term deposits, and it is regarded as bad banking practice 'to borrow short and lend long'. However, commercial customers of the banks in the UK have also preferred overdraft finance, which is cheaper and more flexible than other types of borrowing, provided the banks were willing to renew overdraft facilities and allow, as they have done, much overdraft borrowing to become 'hard core'. In recent years, the UK banks have greatly increased contractual medium-term lending (➤ term loan), and this type of advance now accounts for well over half the bank advances to non-personal customers. Most medium-term lending is for periods of five to seven years, and lending for longer periods than this is still less common in the UK than in some European countries. ➤ business finance.

banknote A note issued by a bank undertaking to pay the bearer the ➤ face value of the note on demand. Banknotes in England had their origin in the receipts issued by London goldsmiths in the seventeenth century for gold deposited with them for safe-keeping. The practice of ➤ banking had its origin in the activities of these goldsmiths, who began lending money and whose deposit receipts came to be used as money. Later, the goldsmiths issued banknotes, and so did the banks that developed later still. Today, only the ➤ Bank of England and the Scottish and Irish banks in the UK are allowed to issue banknotes and only Bank of England notes are ➤ legal tender in England and Wales. Since 1931, when banknotes became inconvertible to gold, the promise on a banknote to 'pay the bearer on demand' has simply been an undertaking that the note is legal tender. Thus, the Currency and Bank Notes Act 1954, which regulates the issue of banknotes in the UK, refers to the ➤ fiduciary issue. Only four denominations of notes are now issued to the general public, the largest being the £50 note. (The 10s note was replaced by the 50p coin in 1969 and a £1 coin was introduced in 1983, entirely replacing the £1 note in 1986.) ➤ banking and currency schools. In the US the US Treasury is responsible for currency issues, not the central bank (➤ Federal Reserve System).

US dollar bills since 1969 have been printed in denominations of $1, 5, 10, 20 and 50 only. US paper money, as in the UK, is a fiduciary issue.

Bank of China (PBC) The People's Bank of China was founded in 1948 and initially consolidated the state-owned ➤ commercial banks. Subsequently the commercial banks were spun off and from 1995 the PBC began to function as a ➤ central bank. Bank supervision is not carried out today by the PBC but by the China Banking Regulatory Commission. China's gold and foreign exchange reserves at the end of 2009 valued in US dollars were 2.4 trillion, by far the largest in the world. These reserves are held by the State Administration of Foreign Exchange (SAFE) which is an affiliate of the PBC. The People's Bank formulates and implements ➤ monetary policy under the guidance of the State Council. It sets reserve requirements for the commercial banks and has been able to control the money supply because of the fixed exchange rate against the US dollar. From 1995 small adjustments to the ➤ exchange rate have been made possible based on a basket of currencies, so it is now more properly described as a 'managed float' (➤ managed currency).

Bank of England The ➤ central bank of the UK. Founded in 1694 by a group of private bankers, chiefly to raise money for the Crown, it was chartered first to operate as a commercial *joint-stock bank* (➤ commercial banks). In succeeding centuries its royal charter favoured the circulation of its notes, and it became a leading banker to other banks. The Bank Charter Act 1844 recognized it as the central note-issuing authority and the ➤ lender of last resort. By 1870, it was recognized as responsible for the general level of interest rates, which it regulated through the ➤ bank rate, and thus for the general state of ➤ credit in the country. By the early twentieth century the bank was recognized as the central organ for the execution of national financial and monetary policy, under the overall direction of the government. In 1946, the bank was nationalized, thus completing its identification with the state.

The Bank of England (which covers the whole of the United Kingdom) acts as a banker for the commercial banks, transactions between which (outside the ➤ clearing-house system) are settled between accounts held at the bank. The commercial banks maintain reserves at the central bank, but (apart from the relatively small *Cash Ratio Deposit* (*CRD*) which are non-interest bearing) the commercial banks themselves determine how large these reserves should be: there are no mandatory reserve requirements as in some other countries. The bank aims to achieve monetary stability through changes in rates of interest, taking into account the annual inflation target set by government. At the end of 2009 that target was 2 per cent measured by the ➤ Consumer Price Index.

The Bank of England Act 1998 conferred sole responsibility on the bank for determining UK interest rates, a function until then exercised by the Treasury. The ➤ Monetary Policy Committee at the bank sets the policy rate (*bank rate*) which is reviewed at monthly meetings. The bank influences interest rates by ➤ bank rate, which is the rate it pays on the voluntary reserves of the commercial banks and ➤ building societies held by it, and also by ➤ open market operations. Since 1997 the bank influences interest rates primarily by transactions in ➤ repos, whereas previously this was done via the ➤ discount houses. Since 1997, the bank has had statutory responsibility for the effectiveness and stability of the financial system as a whole (➤ systemic risk), while the Financial Services Authority now supervises the individual banks and building societies for prudential risk (➤ capital adequacy). This division of responsibility between the bank and the FSA may change because it was subjected to heavy criticism during the 2007–2009 credit crisis (➤ banking).

The bank no longer manages the government debt issue (➤ national debt) but engages in ➤ gilt repos as part of its daily market operations (➤ gilt stripping). *Eligible securities* for use by the bank's counterparties (➤ counterparty risk) as ➤ collateral security for lending include ➤ gilt-edged securities, sterling ➤ Treasury bills, eligible bank bills (➤ bills of exchange) and euro-denominated securities (➤ European Economic and Monetary Union) issued by the European Economic Area (➤ European Free Trade Association), central governments and major international institutions where eligible for use in ➤ European Central Bank operations. The bank is now organized into four operational areas: (a) monetary analysis and statistics; (b) markets; (c) financial stability; and (d) banking services. Financial stability is defined as reducing threats to the financial system as a whole and acting as ➤ lender of last resort. ➤➤ banking; quantitative easing.

Bank of France The Banque de France, the ➤ central bank of France, was established in 1800 and is the oldest in the world after the Bank of Sweden and the ➤ Bank of England. In 1998 the bank's legislation was amended to ensure conformity with the ➤ Maastricht Treaty. Since 1 January 1999 the Bank of France has been an integral part of the European system of central banks (➤➤ European Central Bank) without any independent power to determine monetary policy.

Bank of Japan (BOJ) Japan's ➤ central bank (Nippon Ginko) was founded in 1882, acts as ➤ lender of last resort, manages ➤ monetary policy and issues ➤ currency, the yen, which floats independently (➤ exchange rate). It does not regulate the banking system, which since 1998 has been the role of the Financial Supervisory Agency. The autonomy of the BOJ was enhanced in the 1998 Bank of Japan Act and the bank takes the final decision on monetary policy.

bank overdraft ➤ overdraft.

bank rate The ➤ rate of interest at which the ➤ central bank lends to the banking system. In the UK the operational rate of the ➤ Bank of England has been referred to as bank rate for most of its history, although other terms have been used at different times: ➤ repo rate and minimum lending rate. The ➤ commercial banks and building societies quote their own interest rates for customers as percentage points over bank rate or base rate. For the US equivalent ➤ Federal Reserve System.

bankruptcy A declaration by a court of law that an individual or company is insolvent, i.e. cannot meet ➤ debts on the due dates (➤ insolvency). A bankruptcy petition may be filed either by the debtor or by his creditors requesting a receiving order. An inquiry into the debtor's affairs is then conducted by a registered insolvency practitioner, who retains temporary control of the debtor's financial affairs. If he thinks fit, the practitioner may call a meeting of the debtor's creditors and, if they wish it, declare the debtor bankrupt. The debtor's assets are then realized and distributed among his creditors. In the case of a company, it goes into ➤ liquidation. Until he is discharged (i.e. has paid off his debts and been declared a discharged bankrupt in law) a bankrupt may not incur ➤ credit without making it known that he is an undischarged bankrupt, nor may he serve as a director in a limited company without permission from the court.

The UK Enterprise Act 2002 amended the Insolvency Act 1986, to provide companies with protection from creditors and enable them to be reorganized before their assets are distributed. The objectives of this procedure are similar to those of Chapter 11 of the Bankruptcy Reform Act 1978 in the US. General Motors, the largest motor company in the world, filed for Chapter 11 bankruptcy in June 2009 and emerged a month later as a company owned by the US Treasury.

bargaining The interaction between participants to a transaction by which they decide on an allocation of the surplus they create by entering the transaction. If a car is worth $10,000 to a potential buyer and $9000 to the owner, there is a potential welfare gain of $1000 to be made by a sale. The buyer would be willing to buy it at $9999, and the seller would sell it at $9001. Somehow, a price has to be fixed between these two *reservation prices*. In this case, once they have decided to enter the transaction, the negotiation between them can be likened to a ➤ zero-sum game, or to a problem of ➤ bilateral monopoly. Economists have used ➤ game theory to look at the best bargaining strategies, and the potential outcomes of more complicated bargaining situations, e.g. one in which the surplus to be divided shrinks the longer the parties negotiate. ➤ arbitration.

bargaining theory of wages A theory of wage determination based on negotiations between employers and unions. The theory has been set within a number of different assumptions, e.g. as a ➤ game theory problem in which both sides wish to divide the firm's profits but also to maximize them: an exercise in ➤ cost–benefit analysis where each is aware of the costs of a strike and the risks of participating in one. These theories are complementary to those based on ➤ supply and ➤ demand analysis (➤ price theory) in the sense that the bargaining is seen to be carried out within the framework of the conditions existing at the time in the ➤ labour market (➤ wage-fund theory). ➤➤ arbitration; bargaining.

barriers to entry Economic or technical factors that prevent, or make it difficult, for firms to enter a market and compete with existing suppliers. An established firm may enjoy an *absolute cost advantage* which might arise from the possession of patent rights to certain production processes or a long-term contract for the supply of energy or the ownership of sources of raw materials. In the same way, existence of ➤ economies of scale might mean that a new entrant would have to invest large sums and produce on a large scale in order to compete on price. If the market were small in relation to the ➤ optimum scale of production, new entrants might calculate that the risk of entry would be unacceptably high because any new supplier would reduce the output of all suppliers below the optimum, so that either the new or an existing supplier would fail.

Product differentiation (➤ differentiation, product) can also raise the cost of entry by necessitating heavy expenditure on advertising and the support of dealer outlets to overcome significant buyer preferences. ➤ Collusion on pricing and restrictive practices, such as ➤ full-line forcing and ➤ exclusive dealing, may exclude newcomers, as may legislation, e.g. a requirement for licensing. Potential exporters may suffer long delays waiting product approval under food safety regulations. Barriers to entry may allow established firms to charge prices above the level that would obtain in the absence of these barriers. ➤➤ competition policy; contestability; monopoly; protection; sunk costs; World Trade Organization.

barriers to exit Restrictions on the ability of a company to withdraw from an activity, or to redeploy its resources to an alternative activity. Such restrictions may be imposed by government and designed to protect communities by discouraging the closure of plant by the imposition of high social charges on exit. In this case, they may also act as deterrents to new entry into a sector (which becomes more risky if exit is expensive), and as an impediment to economic transformation. However, the economics of ➤ industrial organization has used ➤ game theory as a device for analysing business behaviour, and this can demonstrate the paradoxical logic that companies may want to restrict *their own* ability to withdraw from an industry. Such a strategy might be rational, as a means of persuading a potential competitor not to enter the industry, on the grounds that the incumbent is committed to remaining.

Barro, Robert J. (b. 1944) ➤ Ricardian equivalence.

barter Acquiring goods or services by means of exchange for other goods or services, rather than for ➤ money. A form of barter has grown into a serious business activity. Corporations specializing in barter deals offer to buy surplus products in exchange for credits that the company disposing of the goods can use to buy other goods and services (e.g. TV advertising time) specified by the barter corporation. These corporations have sufficient financial weight to be able to obtain large discounts for the goods and services they offer for trade. ➤ counter trade.

base period The reference date from which an ➤ index number of a ➤ time series is calculated. For example, the price index of commodities produced in the UK has a base period of 1995. The base year may be changed to reflect any changes over time in the composition of items making up the index. ➤➤ Laspeyres index; weighted average.

base rate The ➤ rate of interest which forms the basis for the charges for ➤ bank loans and overdrafts or deposit rates of the ➤ commercial banks. Since 1971, the

UK banks have fixed their base rates independently of one another, though obviously they cannot differ very much for long periods. Prior to 1971, the banks agreed on their deposit and overdraft rates, but this ➤ cartel arrangement has been abandoned. Very large first-class risk companies may borrow at 1 per cent above base rate or even less, but small firms and individuals will have to pay several percentage points more than this. Base rates will be generally close to short-term ➤ money market rates but change less frequently, so when, as sometimes happens, rates on the ➤ interbank market rise much above base rate, large companies have taken advantage of the interest-rate differential, borrowing on overdraft and lending in that market (➤➤ Bank of England).

Basle II ➤ capital adequacy.

Basle Agreements ➤ capital adequacy.

battle of the sexes A situation – popularly characterized in the economics of ➤ game theory – in which people or institutions have a strong interest in coordinating their behaviour, but disagree over quite how to behave. An example would be in the setting of an industry standard for, say, a pipe fitting. Everybody may agree that it is overwhelmingly important that some standard fitting is agreed, but each firm may take its own view as to what that standard should be. The characterization of such situations as a 'battle of the sexes' derives from a simple analogy used in game theory to caricature them: a husband and wife want to spend the evening together, but what should they do? His first choice is to go to the ballet with her; while she wants to go and watch some boxing with him. Assuming these are the only possible activities, the ranking of different ways of spending the evening in order of preference are:

> Go to ballet with her
> Go to boxing with her
> Go to ballet alone
> Go to boxing alone

Her preferences are to:

> Go to boxing with him
> Go to ballet with him
> Go to boxing alone
> Go to ballet alone

It should, of course, be possible to agree on an evening together, but the crucial feature of these situations is the possibility that a struggle by husband and wife to get their first-best option may result in them each getting the third-best option. For example, if he insists on going to the ballet, and she insists on going to the boxing, they may end up going their own way, even though both would prefer to be together. It is generally recognized that if the situation is commonly repeated, it is easier to reach agreement than if it occurs once only (➤ repeated games). ➤ prisoner's dilemma.

Bauer, Peter T. (1915–2002) ➤ economic development.

Baumol effect The idea that services become relatively more expensive as economies develop, and that manufactured goods become relatively less expensive. It was outlined in 1967 by Baumol who argued that increases in ➤ productivity led to lower prices and productivity improved through investment in new technology, and there was more scope for such investment in capital- rather than labour-intensive industries. As manufacturing industries tend to be more capital-intensive than services, they would enjoy relatively falling prices.

It is true that in less developed countries the prices of manufactured goods tend to be very high compared to the prices of services, whereas in rich countries services tend to be very expensive. But the Baumol effect should not be overstated: many non-manufacturing sectors (such as telecommunications) have enjoyed spectacular increases in productivity based on new technology. Moreover, it is argued that it is hard to measure productivity in service industries, where outputs are often hard to define precisely. (It is difficult to tell just how the productivity of e.g. a lawyer or teacher should be defined.)

The Baumol effect is partly used to explain the growth of government spending, as government primarily provides services rather than goods to the public. ➤➤ public expenditure.

Bayes' theorem A formula in ➤ probability theory for calculating the chance that an unknown prior event occurred, given that a known subsequent event occurred, based on the work of Thomas Bayes (1702–61). We might use Bayes' theorem, for example, to gauge whether a doctor prescribed the right drugs to a patient, by seeing whether the patient recovered from a sickness or not. When we see whether the patient recovers, we can make an assessment that the right drugs were given, but not a perfect one: after all, the patient might get better without the right medicine, and may not get better even with the right medicine. But clearly, if the patient gets better, that makes it more likely the right drugs were given. Bayes' law puts a precise probability on that event. More specifically, suppose that before the event we believe that there is a fifty–fifty chance the doctor gives the right prescription. Suppose, too, that one in ten patients who are wrongly prescribed recovers, and one in two patients who are correctly prescribed recovers. Then, the observation that a patient did recover makes it five times more likely that they were rightly prescribed than wrongly prescribed.

More generally, the theorem says that the probability of a prior event E having occurred, given that a subsequent event S occurred, is equal to the prior probability of E times the probability of S occurring given E occurred, all divided by the probability of S occurring one way or the other. In the above example, this is:

Probability that the *wrong* medicine
was prescribed given that
the patient got better $= \dfrac{0.5 \times 0.1}{0.05 + 0.25} = 16.6$ per cent

Probability that the *right* medicine
was prescribed given that
the patient got better $= \dfrac{0.5 \times 0.5}{0.05 + 0.25} = 83.3$ per cent

The theorem has led to considerable controversy among statisticians, who argue about the validity of ascribing a probability to a past event.

bear A ➤ stock exchange speculator who sells ➤ stocks or ➤ shares that he/she may or may not possess because a fall in prices is expected and, therefore, can be bought (back) later at a ➤ profit; the antonym of ➤ bull. A bear who sells ➤ securities that he/she does not possess is described as having 'sold short'. If possessing the securities solds, he/she is described as a 'covered' or 'protected' bear. A 'bear market' is one in which prices are falling.

bearer bonds ➤ Bonds, the legal ownership of which is vested in the holder, no ➤ transfer deed being required since there is no central register of ownership. An endorsed ➤ cheque, or a cheque made payable to a bearer, or a ➤ banknote, are similar in nature to bearer ➤ securities. Bearer bonds normally have dated interest ➤ coupons attached to them that can be presented to the issuer of the security for payment.

bearer securities ➤ bearer bonds.

Becker, Gary Stanley (b. 1930) An idiosyncratic and controversial economist and winner of the ➤ Nobel Prize for Economics in 1992. Becker was educated at Princeton University and lectured at Chicago University until 1957; he went then to Columbia University where he stayed until 1970, when he returned to Chicago. He has been Professor of Economics and Society at Chicago University since 1983. Becker has been more prominent than any other member of the profession in using economic reasoning in the analysis of social behaviour. His publications include: *The Economics of Discrimination* (1957), *An Economic Analysis of Fertility* (1960), 'A Theory of the Allocation of Time' (*Economic Journal*, 1965), 'Crime and Punishment: An Economic Approach' (*Journal of Political Economy*, 1968), *A Treatise on the Family* (1981) and, with his wife Guity Nashat Becker, *The Economics of Life* (1996). His style has been to explain all sorts of normal human behaviour in the language of economics and rational choice. Nowhere is this more obvious than in his analysis of the family. He discusses the allocation of work within the household, and the impact of changing household technology on, for example, female participation in the labour market, and on the level of divorce. He is also responsible for path-breaking work in formulating and formalizing the microeconomic foundations of our understanding of investments in training and ➤ education in the creation of human capital. ➤➤ sow's ear effect.

'beggar-my-neighbour' policy The enactment of an economic policy for the benefit of a country's economy which has an adverse effect on the economies of other countries. Such policies may be aimed directly at restricting imports, such as applying high import tariffs (➤ tariffs, imports) or ➤ quotas which curtail the ➤ exports of trading partners or a ➤ devaluation of the currency to expand the country's own exports. (➤ protection)

behavioural assumption The pattern of human motivation built into any economic theory. For example, the theory of the firm (➤ firm, theory of the) assumes that entrepreneurs are profit-maximizers; the cobweb theory (➤ cobweb model) assumes that market suppliers are motivated by price in the period preceding that in which they sell their supply. ➤➤ model.

behavioural economics The branch of economics that is concerned with understanding human decision-making more realistically than simply as a rational process. It draws heavily upon psychology as a discipline, and at its crudest can be seen as a means of cataloguing ways in which people appear systematically to make what seem like mistakes in their judgements in traditional economic terms. An early example of this type of study is the ➤ Allais paradox. Many examples can be drawn from people's decisions under uncertainty. People put a disproportionate weight on vivid but unlikely outcomes, e.g. winning the lottery, compared to pedestrian but likely outcomes, e.g. not winning the lottery. Another important observation is that people are loss-averse, in that they hate losing money more than they enjoy gaining it, and they are more loss-averse than traditional economics of ➤ diminishing marginal utility would predict. It is also observed that there is a bias to the status quo in much of our decision-making. Thus, for example, employees automatically enrolled in a pension are far more likely to stay in the pension than those who are not automatically enrolled, even if employees are able to override the automatic choices made for them.

While some postwar economists, notably Simon (➤ Simon, Herbert), did look at decision-making as a special subject in its own right (➤➤ bounded rationality), behavioural economics took off with the contributions of Tversky and ➤ Kahneman. They produced a model of behaviour that viewed most human decisions as being made not as maximizing some absolute goal, but as a two-stage procedure in which people first set some reference value of the goal and then, secondly, strive to perform relative to the reference. The status quo might be a reference point. This might explain why people appear less keen to sell a share that is falling in price, even if they would not go out of their way to buy the same share if they didn't already own it. Behavioural economics is a branch of the subject with numerous applications. J.M. ➤ Keynes emphasized the importance of 'animal spirits' rather than calculated decision-taking in investment decisions, and this aspect of economics is just as applicable to ➤ macroeconomics as to ➤ microeconomics. ➤ business cycles; endogenous preferences.

behavioural theory of the firm An approach to the study of firms that analyses how decisions are reached within them, rather than, as is more traditional, assuming that their behaviours conform to the pursuit of some single goal. It was primarily developed by Cyert, March and ➤ Simon. The main tenets of the behavioural theory are: (a) that firms attempt ➤ satisficing, rather than adopting, maximizing behaviour; and (b) that the firm is a set of individuals and groups, each of which has its own aspirations. These groups, sometimes in coalitions, continuously bargain over the decisions the firm makes, leading to the pursuit of many complex goals. The theory has not displaced the traditional approach, for a number of reasons – most notably that it fails to generate any specific predictions about what firms would actually do in any particular circumstances. Its primary influence has been in reminding economists of the facts that, in practice, maximizing profits may be expensive for a firm (acquiring full and unbiased information from all departments is no easy task) and institutional factors may impede the single-minded pursuit of any one goal. ➤➤ firm, theory of the; X-efficiency.

bell curve ➤ normal distribution.

below the line Items in an account that are underneath the line at which a total is made. If *above the line*, an item is included in the total. In reported results for quoted companies (➤ quotation), *extraordinary items* that arise from transactions that are outside the ordinary activities of a business (e.g. the sale of an office building) may be taken below the line for the purposes of calculating ➤ earnings per share, whereas *exceptional items* that do derive from the ordinary activities may be taken above the line for that purpose.

benefit–cost analysis ➤ cost–benefit analysis.

Bentham, Jeremy (1748–1832) The leading philosopher of ➤ utilitarianism. Self-interest was deemed the sole stimulus to human endeavour, and the pursuit of happiness an individual's prime concern. The purpose of government should be to maximize the sum of the happiness of the greatest number of individuals. ➤ Human Development Index.

Bernoulli, Daniel (1700–1782) ➤ Bernoulli's hypothesis.

Bernoulli's hypothesis A proposition by Daniel Bernoulli (1700–1782) that a decision as to whether or not to accept a ➤ risk depended not just on money but also on ➤ utility. For example, a bet would appear to be worth accepting if, at the toss of a coin, you won $10 for every head and lost only $5 for every tail. Given the coin is unbiased, there is an equal chance of a head or a tail turning up. However, if $5 was all you had in the world, the bet would not seem so attractive. The $5 would have a high utility attached to it and Bernoulli suggested that this is what counted in such decisions. ➤➤ marginal utility of money; risk aversion.

Bertrand competition A model of price competition between firms in which each charges the price that would be charged under ➤ perfect competition (➤ marginal-cost pricing). The model arrives at a result by assuming that each firm sets its prices on the (incorrect) expectation that other firms will not move their prices in response. This inevitably leads to a downward spiral in prices until marginal cost is arrived at. As a model, it contrasts with that of ➤ Cournot, who found that price and output in a duopoly situation would be somewhere between the extremes of ➤ monopoly and perfect competition. The Bertrand result can be seen as a ➤ Nash equilibrium outcome. ➤➤ oligopoly.

beta 1 In finance theory, the degree to which the returns on a particular financial asset track those of the rest of the market. A beta of 1 indicates that an asset, on average, moves with the rest of the market. A higher beta indicates that it moves in the same direction as the market but with more extremity. A negative beta indicates that the return on an asset grows when returns elsewhere in the market are falling, and vice versa. Assets with a low beta are held to be attractive, as they perform well when the market generally is doing badly. Under the ➤ capital asset pricing model, it is believed that they are highly priced for this reason.

2 The Greek letter β, commonly used in econometrics to represent the relationship between the ➤ dependent variable and the independent variable. If ➤ regression analysis produces an estimate of a high beta, relative to the scale of the units involved, it means the relationship is strong. ➤➤ null hypothesis.

Beveridge, William Henry (Lord Beveridge) (1879–1963) Director of the London School of Economics from 1919 to 1937, Lord Beveridge's work in economics arose from a continual interest throughout his life in the problem of ➤ unemployment. His major contribution to the subject was published in *Unemployment* (1931).

He was a major influence in the setting-up of labour exchanges, and his 1942 report, *Social Insurance and Allied Services* that became known as the Beveridge Report, led to the extension of welfare services. His definition of full employment, which he gave in *Full Employment in a Free Society* (1944) as being reached at a level of 3 per cent unemployed, became a reference point for subsequent government policy. ➤ Sismondi, J.C.L.S. de.

Bhagwati, Jagdish N. (b. 1934) ➤ immiseration.

Big Bang Term used to encapsulate the changes occurring on the London ➤ stock exchange before and after 27 October 1986 when the strict segregation between jobbers (➤ market maker) and ➤ brokers and fixed commissions on securities, purchases and sales were abolished. In July 1983, the government agreed to exempt the stock exchange from the provisions of the Restrictive Trade Practices Acts 1956 and 1976 in return for lifting a number of restrictions on competition, including fixed commissions. In 1982, the Stock Exchange Council had raised the limit on any one outside shareholder in a stock exchange member firm from 10 to 29.9 per cent and, on 1 March 1986, this limitation on outside shareholdings was removed completely. Average commission rates fell by about 40 per cent to 0.26 per cent immediately following the Big Bang, but many bargains (transactions) are now carried out at net prices, i.e. the market maker quotes a price direct to the purchaser (who may be a large ➤ institutional investor) that includes his profit margin. Commission rates for small transactions have risen with the introduction of higher minimum charges. Many banks and other financial institutions, both domestic and foreign, have acquired interests in, or control of, stock exchange companies since March 1986, while increased competition has led to mergers, a few failures and the withdrawal of some firms from certain activities, e.g. dealing in ➤ gilt-edged securities. Other changes associated with the Big Bang have been the closure of the trading floor in March 1987, a major extension in off-the-floor electronic dealing and a major expansion in dealings in international ➤ equities.

bilateral agencies Organizations of one country, as distinct from ➤ multilateral agencies. The term is used mainly to refer to national aid (➤ development assistance) agencies as, for example, USAID in the USA and the Department for International Development in the UK.

bilateralism The agreement between two countries to extend to each other specific privileges in their ➤ international trade that are not extended to others. These privileges may, for example, take the form of generous import ➤ quotas or favourable import duties (➤ tariffs, import). In so far as such agreements tend to proliferate, and in that they impose artificial restraints on the free movement of goods between countries, in the long run they could have an unfavourable effect on international trade compared with ➤ multilateralism, under which there is no discrimination by origin or destination. Bilateralism became widespread in the 1930s as countries tried to protect themselves from the fall in international trade during the Great Depression. However, the ➤ General Agreement on Tariffs and Trade (GATT) was established in 1947 on multilateral principles. The GATT and its successor organization, the ➤ World Trade Organization, have since pursued a policy designed to eliminate bilateralism and other restrictions on international trade.

The success of this policy has been constrained somewhat by the setting up of ➤ customs unions and ➤ free trade areas (➤ counter trade).

bilateral monopoly A market in which a single seller (a ➤ monopoly) is confronted with a single buyer (a ➤ monopsony). Under these circumstances, the theoretical determination of output and price will be uncertain and will be affected by the interdependence of the two parties. ➤➤ bargaining.

bill A document giving evidence of indebtedness of one party to another. A bill may simply be a written order for goods which can be used as security for a loan to the supplier from a bank, or it may be a security such as a ➤ Treasury bill or ➤ bill of exchange.

bill broker A firm or individual dealing in ➤ Treasury bills and ➤ bills of exchange on the London ➤ money market. Traditionally, a bill broker was a ➤ discount house. ➤➤ broker.

bill of exchange An IOU used in ➤ international trade by which the drawer undertakes unconditionally to pay to the drawee a sum of ➤ money at a given date, usually three months ahead. In principle, a bill of exchange is similar to a postdated ➤ cheque and, like a cheque, it can be endorsed for payment to the bearer or any named person other than the drawee. A bill of exchange has to be 'accepted' (endorsed) by the drawee before it becomes negotiable. This function is normally performed by an accepting house, but bills may also be accepted by a bank (it is then known as a *bank bill*) or by a trader (*trade bill*). Once accepted, the drawee does not have to wait for the bill to mature before getting his money; he can sell it on the ➤ money market for a small discount (➤ discount house). Bills of exchange, also referred to as *commercial bills*, were first developed in inland trade by merchants who wished to resell goods before making payment for them. They later became of great importance in international trade, but their use declined with the development of other means of ➤ credit.

bill of sale A document that gives evidence of transfer of ownership, but not of possession, of goods. It is not often used nowadays, but was once a common method of raising a ➤ loan on the security of personal possessions, the borrower retaining possession of goods until the ➤ debt is repaid. ➤➤ mortgage.

BIMBO ➤ management buy-out.

birth rate The *crude birth rate* is the average number of live births occurring in a year for every 1000 of ➤ population. The United Nations, in its *World Population Prospects Database, 2008*, estimated that there was a worldwide decline in crude birth rates between 1970/75 and 2005/2010, with those of the ➤ advanced countries falling from 16.1 to 11.2 and those of the ➤ developing countries falling from 36.1 to 22.3. Other statistical measurements computed for the study of population trends include: (a) the *general fertility rate*, which measures the average number of live births per 1000 for all women between the ages of 15 and 54; (b) *the rate specific* for age of mother in which the number of live births per 1000 is given for different age groups of mother; and (c) *total period fertility rate* which is the average number of children who would be born to a woman if she gave birth at *the rate specific* through her childbearing years. Theoretically, the replacement fertility rate is 2.0 but allowing for early mortality and the larger number of male births than female births, it is higher than this. The world average is 2.33 with a rate of 3.0 in poorer countries. There has been a general decline in fertility rates throughout the world with the increase in real incomes. ➤➤ death rate; population.

BIS ➤ Bank for International Settlements.

black economy ➤ informal economy.

black market The trading in illicit or illegally acquired goods. Not to be confused with black economy (➤ informal economy).

Black–Scholes formula A formula used to establish a fair price for ➤ options in financial markets. The formula, which is used to solve what had previously been considered a difficult problem, was published in 1973. It was based on looking at the price of a basket of financial assets which carried the same risk and return as an option. ➤ Merton, R.; Scholes, M.

Böhm-Bawerk, Eugen von (1851–1914) A member of the ➤ Austrian School who took over the Chair of Economics at Vienna from von ➤ Wieser. His analyses of the rate of ➤ interest and ➤ capital have had an important influence on the development of these aspects of economic theory. His major publications include *Capital and Interest* (1884) and *The Positive Theory of Capital* (1889). The nature of the rate of interest could be found, he argued, in the three propositions: (a) that people expect to be better off in the future; (b) that people put a lower valuation on future goods than on present goods ('jam today is better than jam tomorrow' – the two 'psychological' factors (a) and (b) making people willing to pay to borrow against their future income to spend on consumer goods now (➤➤ time preference)); and (c) the proposition that goods in existence today are technically superior to those coming into existence at some future date because today's goods could be capable of producing more goods during the interval (➤➤ Fisher, I.; interest, productivity theories of). Capital is associated with roundabout methods of production. In order to reap a harvest you could send workers into the fields to pluck the ears of corn. A more efficient method is to spend capital on making scythes and then use these to cut the corn. An even more efficient method is to spend even more capital manufacturing reaping machinery and use this to harvest your corn. Progress is achieved through the use of ➤ labour in more roundabout methods of production. There is, therefore, a widening of the gap between initial ➤ input and final output (➤➤ input–output analysis). Capital supplies the necessary subsistence to labour during the 'waiting time' before new consumer goods are produced (➤➤ wage-fund theory). This waiting time is extended to yield increased ➤ productivity until, in equilibrium, productivity is equated with the ➤ rate of interest. This theory was later developed into a theory of the ➤ business cycle by members of the Austrian School (➤➤ Hayek, F.A. von; Hicks, J.R.; Mises, L. von; Wicksell, K.).

bond 1 A form of fixed-interest ➤ security issued by central or local governments, companies, banks or other institutions. Bonds are usually a form of long-term security but do not always carry fixed interest, may be irredeemable, and may be secured or unsecured. Economists frequently make use of the term in theoretical analysis, e.g. of choices between holding cash and other financial assets, in which a bond is a proxy for a whole range of securities. *Eurobonds* have been defined by Morgan Guaranty, the investment bankers, as a 'bond underwritten by an international syndicate and sold in countries other than the country of the currency in which the issue is denominated'. There is no specific ➤ stock exchange for these bonds (➤➤ bearer bonds; eurocurrency). The term has also been given to types of non-fixed-interest security, e.g. property bonds, that provide the holder with a yield on funds invested in property, or 'managed bonds', in which the funds are placed in a variety of investments. Nowadays, and almost always in the USA, the term includes ➤ debentures. ➤➤ deep discounted bond.

2 A term used to describe goods in a warehouse on which customs duty (➤ tariffs, import) has not yet been paid.

bonus issue, or scrip issue, capitalization issue (US stock dividend, stock split)
Virtually synonymous terms describing ➤ shares given without charge to existing shareholders in proportion to the shares already owned. A *scrip issue* does not add to the ➤ capital employed by the firm, but is made where the capital employed has been increased by withholding profits, and is, therefore, out of line with the ➤ issued capital. Consequently, it is a purely bookkeeping transaction. ➤ Dividends, for example, will, after a scrip issue, be divided among a larger number of shares, so that the dividend per share will fall in proportion to the number of bonus shares issued. ➤➤ new-issue market; rights issue.

book value The value of ➤ assets in the ➤ balance sheet of a firm. This is often the purchase price, and may be less than the market value. ➤➤ inflation accounting.

bounded rationality The idea that economic agents may not have the cognitive power to make decisions about their optimum behaviour very precisely. Thus they may intend to be rational, but in practice make choices on the basis of rules of thumb. In particular, it may be that agents don't act to maximize some goal, but merely to reach a satisfactory outcome in it. The phrase was coined by ➤ Simon, who applied the concept to the study of organizational behaviour. ➤➤ satisficing; transactions costs.

branch banking A ➤ banking system, most highly developed in the UK, in which the small number of ➤ commercial banks have a large number of branches (some 10,000 in Britain). Many other ➤ advanced countries have a much larger number of banks with fewer branches. A banking system in which each bank is a separate enterprise without affiliations with other banks or branches is called *unit banking*. In the USA, it was believed that branch banking led to ➤ concentration of the banking system and lack of competition. Now, prohibitions on branch banking have been relaxed and, although branch banking is growing, the majority of commercial banks are still purely local, with five or fewer branches.

Bretton Woods An international conference held at Bretton Woods, New Hampshire, USA, in July 1944 to discuss alternative proposals relating to postwar international payments problems put forward by the US, Canadian and UK governments. The agreement resulting from this conference led to the establishment of the ➤ International Monetary Fund and the ➤ International Bank for Reconstruction and Development. ➤➤ Keynes plan; Smithsonian Agreement.

broker An intermediary between a buyer and a seller in a highly organized market, e.g. a ➤ stockbroker or commodity broker or a market operator working on his own account, e.g. a pawnbroker (➤ bill broker). On the ➤ stock exchange, a broker is the intermediary between a ➤ market maker and the public.

brokerage Commission or fee charged by a ➤ broker. It is characteristic of the broking profession that it operates only in highly organized markets where margins are relatively small.

Buchanan, James McGill (b. 1919) Professor Buchanan studied at the University of Tennessee prior to obtaining his Ph.D. at the University of Chicago in 1948. He became Professor of Economics at the University of Virginia in 1956 and was appointed, in 1969, Director of the Center for Study of Public Choice, and is currently Professor at George Mason University, Virginia. Professor Buchanan was awarded the ➤ Nobel Prize in Economics in 1986. His published work includes: *The Calculus of Consent: Logical Foundations of Constitutional Democracy* (1962), *Public Finance in Democratic Process: Fiscal Institutions and Individual Choice* (1966), *The Demand and Supply of Public Goods* (1968), *Cost and Choice: An Inquiry in Economic Theory* (1969), *Theory of Public Choice: Political Applications of Economics* (1972), *The Limits of Liberty: Between Anarchy and Leviathan* (1975), *Freedom in Constitutional Contracts: Perspectives of a Political Economist* (1977), *Democracy in Deficit: The Political Legacy of Lord Keynes* (1977) and *The Power to Tax: Analytical Foundations of a Fiscal Constitution* (1980).

Professor Buchanan established, and inspired study in, ➤ public-choice theory. As 'economic man' acted in his own self-interest, so government officials behaved, also. Government actions, therefore, will be pursued according to the self-interest of public officials rather than necessarily for the public good. For example, unpopular but inevitably necessary corrective action may be delayed by governments to force others into the responsibility, and political costs, of taking action. Given that this is the case, the rules of the game by which the politicians serve the public are important in determining how far public desires are served. Professor Buchanan thus takes seriously the issue of constitutions and the constraints they apply on the state. An example might be whether countries should have ➤ hypothecation or whether a ➤ balanced budget provides a welcome discipline on the political process in determining the level of government spending. ➤➤ public-choice theory.

budget An estimate of ➤ income and expenditure for a future period as opposed to an account which records financial transactions. Budgets are an essential element in the planning and control of the financial affairs of a nation or business, and are made necessary essentially because income and expenditure do not occur simultaneously. In modern large-scale business, the annual budget, which is normally broken down into monthly and weekly periods, is a complex document that may take several months to prepare. The starting point will be an estimate of sales and income for the period, balanced by budgets for purchasing, administration, production, distribution and research costs. There will also be detailed budgets of ➤ cash flow and ➤ capital expenditure. These are often also made for periods of further than one year ahead, so that borrowing requirements and capacity requirements can be assessed (➤ capital budgeting). A *flexible budget* is one based on different assumed levels of plant activity.

The UK's national budget sets out estimates of central government expenditure and revenue for the financial year, and is normally presented by the Chancellor of the ➤ Exchequer to Parliament late in the previous financial year. The Labour government, which came to power in 1997, decided to pre-release a Green Paper outlining the background to the budget, and certain options. The budget is formally concerned with ➤ Consolidated Fund revenue and not with ➤ National Insurance or local government finance, although, in practice, all spending and revenue decisions are discussed. In his statement, the Chancellor reviews economic conditions and government expenditure for the past year, makes forecasts for the coming year and announces proposed changes in ➤ taxation. These changes normally become effective immediately, but are subject to parliamentary debate and approval in the Finance Bill and Act. With the increasing importance of government expenditure in the economy, the annual budget is an important instrument in government economic policy. Fiscal changes may have more to do with decisions to modify the budget surplus or deficit in the interest of demand management (➤ balanced budget) than with planned expenditure which, in any case, is essentially discussed and presented earlier in the year. ➤ supply services; ➤➤ public expenditure.

budgetary control A system of control which checks actual ➤ income and expenditure against a ➤ budget so that progress towards set objectives may be measured and remedial action taken if necessary. Budget-control statements comparing actual and estimated expenditure are issued weekly or monthly. These statements will be issued in considerable detail to department heads, and in less detail to higher management. Budget-control statements must, if any necessary remedial action is to be taken in time, be issued as soon as possible after the close of the period to which they relate, and for this reason need not be of the same accuracy as accounting statements and may be based on estimated data. The development of computerized accounting procedures has greatly facilitated budgetary control. ➤➤ resource accounting and budgeting.

budget deficit ➤ balanced budget; crowding-out; public sector borrowing requirement; ➤➤ Keynesian economics; Ricardian equivalence.

budget line ➤ indifference curve analysis.

building society An institution that accepts ➤ deposits, upon which it pays ➤ interest and makes ➤ loans for house purchase secured by ➤ mortgages. Traditionally the societies were all owned by their members (➤ mutual company) comprising their customers.

There were over 500 building societies in the UK in the 1960s but by 2008 the number had fallen to fifty-five, as a result of mergers and incorporation as banks (➤ banking). Building societies are unique to the UK, though elsewhere similar functions are performed by ➤ savings banks. Originally highly localized in their operations, the building societies began increasingly to operate on a national scale. The Building Societies Act 1986 introduced major changes and allowed the societies to widen their services from their traditional property-mortgage business, to include loans to individuals for other purposes, money transmission and foreign-exchange services, personal financial planning services (acquisition and disposal of shares, insurance, pension schemes), estate agency, valuation and conveyancing services. The Act also provided for a regulatory agency, the Building Societies Commission, but since the year 2000 the societies have been regulated by the Financial Services Authority. ➤ financial intermediaries.

built-in stabilizers Institutional features of the economy that, without explicit government intervention, automatically act to dampen down fluctuations in employment and ➤ national income. Examples of these are: (a) aggregate unemployment benefits and welfare payments, which automatically increase when unemployment increases and fall when unemployment falls, so that this part of government expenditure adjusts automatically in the desired direction to offset in part changes in other components of ➤ aggregate demand; and (b) government taxation, which falls in total as national income falls and rises as national income rises, both because the burden of ➤ income taxes changes and because, with changes in ➤ consumption expenditures, sales tax revenues change. Since an increase in taxation tends to restrain expenditure and a fall in taxation to stimulate it, taxation 'automatically' counteracts inflationary and deflationary pressures in the economy (➤ deflation; inflation). These built-in stabilizers rarely have sufficient force to render positive corrective policies unnecessary. ➤➤ cyclically adjusted budget deficit; fiscal drag.

bull A ➤ stock exchange speculator who purchases ➤ stocks and ➤ shares in the belief that prices will rise and that he will be able to sell them again later at a profit (➤ speculation); the opposite of a ➤ bear. The market is said to be *bullish* when it is generally anticipated that prices will rise.

bullion Gold, silver or other precious metal in bulk, i.e. in the form of ingots or bars rather than in coin. Gold bullion is used in international monetary transactions between ➤ central banks and forms partial backing for many ➤ currencies (➤ gold standard). A *bullion market* is a gold market.

Bundesbank The ➤ central bank of Germany, based in Frankfurt. It was formally established in 1957, although its origins can be traced to 1875. Its constitution demands that it maintains the internal and external value of the currency. To help it resist short-term political pressures, the bank is shielded from governmental interference in the conduct of monetary policy, although the powerful Bundesbank president is effectively appointed by the government. During the life of the European Monetary System, the Bundesbank was dominant in establishing monetary policy for the entire European Union, with other member states gradually converging on Germany's low ➤ inflation rate. The Bundesbank is now one of the seventeen central banks participating in ➤ European Central Bank; European Economic and Monetary Union.

business angels ➤ risk capital.

business cycle Economic activity never runs along a straight line but traces a fluctuating wave with varying amplitude and duration. The economic variables exhibiting these cycles may be macroeconomic, such as the ➤ Gross Domestic Product, industrial production, agricultural output, consumer or wholesale price levels and international trade. Often associated with the approach of a cycle to its peak is the growth of ➤ speculation. This may be centred on an almost infinite variety of economic activities, commodities, industries, real estate or financial instruments of many kinds.

Financial stampedes have been a recurring feature of economic activity for centuries from the 'Tulipmania' speculation in Dutch bulbs in the early seventeenth century to the recent rise in real-estate prices inflated by financial instruments that concealed their underlying risks and led to the recession of 2008–2009. However, these irrational – at least in their final stages – speculative excesses (➤ behavioural economics), although often feeding off a particular phase of a business cycle, are not necessarily an integral part of its structure.

Cycles of varying duration began to be explored from the nineteenth century. Clement Juglar (➤ Juglar Cycle), employing for the first time the mathematical analysis of time series, detected cycles of about nine or ten years. Cycles of much longer duration were found by Nikolai Kondratiev (➤ Kondratiev Cycle) in a study of prices and interest rates from the eighteenth century through to the 1920s. This work was evaluated by ➤ Schumpeter who discussed the possibility of long waves of about fifty years. Simon ➤ Kuznets and others have identified cycles of from fourteen to twenty-two years' duration and Joseph Kitchin (1861–1932) shorter cycles of about three to five years. The hierarchy of business cycles also includes those centred around particular industries or commodities. The textbook example is that of the ➤ 'cobweb model' which illustrates how cyclical swings occur in any market in which there is a lag between demand and the supply response. It is typical of agriculture in which there is a long time interval between the planting of seed and the harvesting of crops. Jan ➤ Tinbergen published in 1931 a mathematical model following similar principles to show how cyclical fluctuations in shipbuilding occur because of the time lapse between changes in freight rates and the launch of additional shipping tonnage.

The business cycle appears to be an inherent characteristic of the free-market capitalist system (➤ capitalism). Karl ➤ Marx believed that recessions simply reflected the 'fundamental contradiction of capitalism'. Schumpeter believed that cycles were inherent in the capitalist system and essential for continuing long-run growth. Cycles were generated by the 'creative destruction' of 'swarms of innovations' which led to an increase in the money supply in support of new investment, which was followed by falling prices with the consequential increase in competition leading to recession. For ➤ Hayek, in the upturn there was a fall in real wages because prices rose faster than money wages and this induced firms to switch to more labour-intensive production. Eventually, this caused a drop in total investment.

The converse happened in the recession. The trigger for change may, therefore, be inherent in the recession phase. ➤ Samuelson, ➤ Hicks, Goodwin, ➤ Phillips and Kalecki in the 1940s and 1950s developed theories that combined the ➤ multiplier with the ➤ accelerator theory of investment (➤ accelerator–multiplier model) which demonstrated how their interrelation can cause an oscillating path for National Income. ➤ Friedman, in his analysis of US monetary history, noted the correlation between money supply and economic activity and suggested that the business cycle was a monetary phenomenon. Several theories of the cycle embrace the notion of ➤ rational expectations, or the idea that expectations are more forward looking. ➤ New Keynesianism suggests that fluctuations in ➤ aggregate demand account for the cycle. ➤ New classical economics explains it in terms of *unanticipated* fluctuations in demand. More recently, attention has been paid to the effects of shocks to the economy from technology and taste changes. These 'real' phenomena can, it is suggested, account for many economic fluctuations (➤ real business cycle theory). It has been a matter of economic policy of governments to dampen the amplitude of the cycle so that the trend path of output is followed without much fluctuation. (➤ Frisch, R.A.K.; Jevons, W.S.; policy ineffectiveness theorem; stabilization policy; stop–go).

business finance The provision of ➤ money for commercial use. The ➤ capital requirements of business may be divided into short and medium term, or long term. Short-term capital consists of the current ➤ liabilities of a business plus medium-term capital. The main sources of short- and medium-term capital (for a company) can be further subdivided into internal, and external, as follows:

Internal: ➤ retained earnings, including ➤ accrued expenses and tax reserves. ➤➤ cash flow; corporation tax; self-financing.

External: Temporary ➤ loans from sister companies, directors and others; ➤ bills of exchange; ➤ factoring; trade creditors and expense creditors, and short-term ➤ trade investments.

Short-term capital should, in theory, only be used for investment in relatively liquid assets (➤➤ liquid) so that it is readily available to discharge the liability if necessary. Thus, these sources of short-term capital may be used for finished goods in stock and work in progress, trade debtors, prepaid expenses, cash in hand and at the bank.

Correspondingly, the main sources of long-term liabilities or capital can be subdivided in the same way as follows:

Internal: Reserves, retained earnings and ➤ depreciation provisions.

External: Share capital, i.e. ➤ ordinary shares, ➤ preference shares, long-term loans including ➤ mortgages, ➤ leaseback arrangements and ➤ debentures.

Long-term capital may be used for long-term investment in fixed assets (e.g. land, buildings, plant, equipment and machinery, etc.), in goodwill, patents and trademarks and long-term trade investments.

There are important differences in the sources of capital open to large and small firms. The latter do not have access to the ➤ stock exchange and rely more heavily upon family and friends for equity capital, as well as upon the ➤ commercial banks. The main institutional sources of business finance are the commercial banks, ➤ investment banks, ➤ finance houses, factoring companies and the institutions concerned with new issues (➤ new-issue market). ➤ Insurance companies and ➤ pension funds hold a large proportion of all quoted securities (➤ quotation). A number of other institutions specialize in providing ➤ term loans and ➤ risk capital, especially for innovation and smaller businesses.

business saving That part of the net revenue of a firm that is not paid out as interest, ➤ dividends or ➤ taxation, but rather is kept in the business as reserves and ➤ depreciation allowances or to finance new ➤ investment. Sometimes called *retentions*. ➤➤ self-financing.

business taxation ➤ corporation tax.

buyer's market A ➤ market in which prices are falling, owing, for example, to an excess of ➤ supply of the goods or services traded compared with ➤ demand. ➤➤ price system.

by-product The output from a process designed for the production of some other product. It is a necessary outcome of the production process and cannot be avoided. Its ➤ opportunity cost is zero. ➤ economies of scope.

C

cabotage The transportation of goods or passengers wholly within one country by vehicles, ships or aircraft which are foreign-owned. Many countries prohibit or place restrictions on such operations. For instance, under the Jones Act (the Merchant Marine Act) 1920, US ships are given preference in the carriage of US domestic cargo, and the Merchant Marine Act 1936 enables the US government to impose penalties on foreign vessels that have been built cheaply by means of subsidy if they operate in US domestic trade. Similar restrictions apply to passenger traffic. Restrictions imposed on cabotage road transport throughout the ➤ European Union were eased for operations owned by enterprises of member states in 1998 and for shipping cabotage in 1999 and 2004. ➤ free trade.

calculus of variations A branch of mathematics that is concerned with tracing the optimal path of variables over time. It is to ➤ dynamics what the ➤ Lagrange multiplier is to static analysis. An example of the use of the calculus of variations would be to work out the path of economic growth in terms of the ➤ capital stock and ➤ investment (➤ optimal-growth theory).

call An unpaid portion of the price of a ➤ share. This may appear when an applicant for a new share issue pays only part of the price of the share on application and the remainder on allotment, or when the issued shares of a company are not fully paid up (➤ paid-up capital).

call option A contract giving a right to buy ➤ shares from the dealer making the contract at the price ruling at the time within a specified future period, usually three months. Call ➤ options carry a ➤ commission to the dealer on the price of the shares traded. The opposite of *put option* (➤➤ derivatives).

Cambridge School A system of economic thought influenced by economists at the University of Cambridge, England. ➤ Marshall (1842–1924) held the Chair of Political Economy until 1908, as did ➤ Pigou (1877–1959) until 1944, and during this period the School was characterized by the theory of late ➤ classical economics. After the end of the Second World War, the School attempted to refute what became known as ➤ neo-classical economics and developed ideas based on those of ➤ Keynes (1883–1946), although linked also with the early classical period. The leading figures in the postwar debate were ➤ Robinson (1903–83) and Nicholas Kaldor (1908–86). The Cambridge School emphasized a ➤ macroeconomic approach compared with the ➤ microeconomic approach of the neo-classical school. The Cambridge School denied that there was a direct functional relationship between the rate of ➤ profit and the capital intensity of an economy. They have demonstrated the possibility of ➤ capital reswitching (➤ Wicksell effect, price) and have criticized the neo-classical school for leaping to conclusions about the aggregates derived from microanalysis. For example, they argue that the aggregate ➤ production function of the ➤ Cobb–Douglas type is not compatible in practice with the microfunctions from which it is derived. The neo-classical theory of ➤ distribution which relates relative factor prices (➤ factors of production) to relative ➤ marginal revenue productivities is deficient in throwing light on aggregate-factor distributed shares of product (➤ Euler, L.). Per contra, they themselves are criticized for neglecting ➤ microeconomic theory.

Cantillon, Richard (1680–1734) An Irish international banker who wrote *Essai sur la nature du commerce en général*, which was not published until 1755 but had circulated from about 1730. This work was one of the first synoptic descriptions and analyses of the economic process. His views on the importance of agriculture, based on its receipt of pure ➤ rent, and his analysis of the circulation of wealth, foreshadowed the ➤ Physiocrats and the ➤ *Tableau économique*, respectively.

capacity utilization rate The output of a plant, firm or a whole economy divided by its output at full capacity. ➤➤ excess capacity; output gap.

capital 1 Assets that are capable of generating income and that have themselves been produced. Capital is one of the four ➤ factors of production, and consists of the machines, plant and buildings that make production possible, but excludes raw materials, ➤ land and ➤ labour. All capital is itself, however, the product of labour and raw materials, and can be seen as holding the stored value of them. If a Stone Age man spent one day producing a tool (a capital good) he gained no utility from doing so at the time. He did, however, save labour by using the tool thereafter. By building the tool he had, in effect, put some labour away for use at a later date. The essence of capital, therefore, is that it represents deferred consumption.
2 In more general usage, any asset or stock of assets – financial or physical – capable of generating income. ➤➤ wealth.

capital, authorized ➤ authorized capital.

capital, cost of 1 The ➤ rate of interest paid on the ➤ capital employed in a business. Since capital will usually be drawn from a variety of sources, it will be an average cost derived from weighting the cost of each source, including ➤ equity capital, by its proportion of the total. A high cost of capital is considered detrimental to ➤ investment though the state of business confidence may be more important.
2 The cost of raising additional capital, i.e. the marginal cost. The marginal cost of capital on a discounted ➤ cash flow basis may be used as the minimum level of return in assessing investment projects. ➤ capital asset pricing model; Modigliani–Miller theorem.

capital, issued ➤ issued capital.

capital, marginal efficiency of ➤ internal rate of return.

capital, marginal productivity of ➤ internal rate of return.

capital, nominal ➤ authorized capital.

capital, registered ➤ authorized capital.

capital, sources of ➤ business finance.

capital, working ➤ working capital.

capital account ➤ balance of payments.

capital adequacy A measure of the value of capital owned by the shareholders of a financial institution relative to the amount the institution has lent out. Various regulatory bodies set minimum ➤ capital requirements for financial institutions such as ➤ unit trusts and banks (➤ banking). These requirements take the form of *reserve asset ratios*, a minimum proportion of liquid assets. For banks, these requirements were mainly used to control monetary aggregates (➤ money supply) but now increasingly they are aimed at preventing failure and instability in the financial system (*prudential regulation*).

In the USA, the member banks in the ➤ Federal Reserve System are subject to a legal *reserve requirement* that they are required to maintain at their Federal Reserve Bank. The reserves are related to the size and type of ➤ deposits. By raising or lowering reserve requirements the Federal Reserve can tighten or loosen bank credit but this is more usually done by ➤ open market operations. The ➤ Bank of China by contrast relies heavily on changes in reserve requirements to influence bank credit. In the UK, the ➤ Bank of England does not any longer impose significant reserve requirements on banks but the Financial Services Authority does, under national capital adequacy standards.

The increasing globalization of the world financial system has encouraged international agreement on capital adequacy standards. In 1998 the Basle Agreements (Basle I) provided for common prudential ratios (capital adequacy ratios) and definitions of *risk-adjusted assets*. Banks operating in signatory countries had to have minimum ➤ capital equal to 8 per cent of risk-adjusted assets. Different kinds of capital are given weights (➤ weighted average) deemed to reflect their degree of risk. For example, no adjustments are necessary (have a zero weight) for Triple A rated sovereign bonds issued by ➤ advanced countries (➤ rating agencies). Tier 1, or *core capital,* includes shareholder ➤ equity and perpetual ➤ preference shares. Tier 2, or supplementary capital, includes subordinated-term debt and unrealized holding gains, for example.

The capital adequacy requirements were revised in the Basle II Agreements, first published in 2004 and have been implemented in most advanced countries, though only by larger banks in the USA. The 2007–2009 credit crisis has led to the consideration of further revisions (Basle III) which include standards for ➤ liquidity as well as capital and aimed for implementation by 2012. It may be noted that the Basle Agreements did not prevent the 2007–2009 credit crisis in which some banks failed or had to be supported by governments. Some banks lost the bulk of their capital requirements and this led to some contagion affecting apparently sound banks. (➤➤ CoCo bond)

capital allowances Reductions in tax (➤ taxation) liability that are related to a firm's ➤ capital expenditure. In most countries, expenditure on new capital assets is encouraged by various kinds of allowances, and annual ➤ depreciation is recognized as an expense of the business in calculating tax liability. The taxation authorities' methods of depreciating an ➤ asset are not necessarily the same as those used by the company in the published ➤ accounts. Where a company may claim depreciation for tax purposes at will (e.g. to write off the whole of the cost of an asset against tax in a single year, or to spread it over twenty years as it chooses) this is known as *free depreciation* or *depreciation at choice*.

capital asset pricing model A model of the market for different financial assets that suggests that asset prices will adjust to ensure that the return an asset makes precisely compensates investors for the risk of that asset when held with a perfectly diversified *portfolio*. The model has dominated economists' understanding of the financial sector. Under simplifying assumptions, the following propositions hold: (a) everybody will hold a portfolio of assets which is as diversified as possible (➤➤ diversification); (b) this means the particular risks of each individual asset will be unimportant because the ups and downs of assets' performances will tend to cancel out (➤➤ portfolio theory); (c) there will, nevertheless, be some remaining market risk – the risk of factors that affect all the assets together; (d) this risk depends on how closely the assets' performances coincide; (e) the risk any particular asset adds to a portfolio will thus depend only on how closely its performance tracks that of the rest of the portfolio; (f) the price of assets that closely track other assets will be low because they are unattractive – when other assets do well, they do well and vice versa (➤ beta); and (g) the price of assets that hardly move at all with the market will be high, because they pay out good returns when they are needed most.

The capital asset pricing model is a development of this chain of reasoning. It can be used to calculate an expected return on any particular asset, as a function of the rate of return on riskless assets, plus a risk premium based on the degree to which the asset tracks the market. It thus provides one basis for assessing a cost of capital (➤ capital, cost of) for a company. ➤ efficient markets hypothesis; Markowitz, H.; Sharpe, W.

capital budgeting The adoption of financial plans for managing and monitoring expenditure on non-recurrent expenditure. Capital is generally hard to plan for within ➤ cash flow accounts as, in any one period, the relationship between cost incurred and value derived is very small. ➤➤ resource accounting and budgeting.

capital charges Charges in the ➤ accounts of a company or individual for interest paid on ➤ capital, ➤ depreciation or repayment of ➤ loans.

capital consumption ➤ capital stock.

capital deepening ➤ capital widening.

capital employed The ➤ capital in use in a business. There is no universally agreed definition of the term. It is sometimes taken to mean ➤ net assets (i.e. fixed plus current assets minus current ➤ liabilities), but more usually ➤ bank loans and ➤ overdrafts are included and other adjustments made for purposes of calculating the return on *net capital employed* (➤ rate of return), e.g. the exclusion of intangible assets and the revaluation of ➤ trade investments at market prices. ➤➤ investment appraisal.

capital expenditure The purchase of fixed ➤ assets (e.g. plant and equipment), expenditure on ➤ trade investments or acquisitions of other businesses and expenditure on current assets (e.g. stocks); to be distinguished from ➤ capital formation.

capital formation ➤ net investment in fixed ➤ assets, i.e. additions to the stock of real ➤ capital. *Gross fixed capital formation* includes ➤ depreciation; *net capital formation* excludes it.

capital gains A realized increase in the value of a capital ➤ asset as when a share is sold for more than the price at which it was purchased. Most countries tax capital gains for individuals and for companies, except where they are within the normal course of business as in the case of ➤ stockbrokers, where they are taxed on the overall profits arising from their operations. The tax treatment of capital gains varies between countries, for example some vary the rate of tax according to the length of the holding.

In the UK, individuals now pay Capital Gains Tax (CGT) at a flat rate of 18 per cent (2009–10) but there is an annual exemption for the first £10,100 and tax losses can be carried forward. There are reliefs for individuals disposing of business assets where the rate charged is effectively 10 per cent. Proceeds from the sale of principal private residences are exempt from CGT. Companies pay ➤ corporation tax on capital gains. In the UK, ➤ indexation of certain gains was allowed but this has recently been abandoned in the interests of simplification.

In the US individuals pay income tax on short-term gains (under one year) and a flat rate of 15 per cent on 'long-term' gains of over one year. This regime was introduced in 2003 but is expected to change shortly. Corporations pay corporate income tax on capital gains. The taxation of capital gains is controversial because it may discourage risk-taking and since part of the gain may be the result of ➤ inflation.

The discrimination against short-term gains is intended to discourage ➤ speculation.

capital gearing ➤ gearing.

capital goods ➤ capital.

capital-intensive The production of a commodity in which a higher proportion of ➤ capital is used in the mix of inputs compared with other factor inputs, such as labour. ➤➤ factors of production.

capitalism A social and economic system in which individuals are free to own the means of production and maximize ➤ profits, and in which resource allocation is determined by the ➤ price system. There are no countries which are comprehensively capitalist as everywhere the state owns some of the means of production and the operation of the price system is muted by ➤ regulation and market imperfections (➤ market failure). ➤ Marx argued that capitalism would be overthrown because it inevitably led to the exploitation of labour. In fact, although subject to ➤ depression, capitalism has delivered enormous increases in living standards over the past 200 years. ➤ economic development. (➤➤ socialism)

capitalization **1** The amount and structure of the ➤ capital of a company.

2 The conversion of accumulated ➤ profits and reserves into ➤ issued capital.

3 *Market capitalization* is the market value of a company's issued ➤ share capital, i.e. the quoted price of its shares multiplied by the number of shares outstanding.

capitalization issue ➤ bonus issue.

capitalized ratios Ratios which describe the ➤ capital structure of a company, by indicating the proportion of each type of ➤ security issued.

capitalized value The ➤ capital sum at current ➤ rates of interest required to yield the current earnings of an ➤ asset. For example, if the earnings of an asset were $5 per annum and the appropriate rate of interest were 5 per cent, its capitalized value would be $100, as an asset worth $100 yields an annual return of $5. The general formula for capitalizing the value of an asset is to divide the annual income by the annual rate of interest (all multiplied by 100). ➤➤ annuity.

capital loss A reduction in the ➤ money value of an ➤ asset; opposite of ➤ capital gain.

capital market The ➤ market for long-term loanable funds as distinct from the ➤ money market, which deals in short-term funds. There is no clear-cut distinction between the two markets although, in principle, capital-market ➤ loans are used by industry and commerce mainly for fixed ➤ investment. The capital market is an increasingly international one and in any country is not one institution but all those institutions that match the ➤ supply and ➤ demand for long-term capital and claims on capital, e.g. the ➤ stock exchange, banks and ➤ insurance companies. The capital market, of course, is not concerned solely with the issue of new claims on capital (the *primary* or ➤ new-issue market), but also with dealings in existing claims (the ➤ secondary market). The marketability of ➤ securities is an important element in the efficient working of the capital market, since investors would be much more reluctant to make loans to industry if their claims could not be disposed of easily. All advanced countries have highly developed capital markets, but in ➤ developing countries the absence of a capital market is often as much of an obstacle to the growth of investment as a shortage of savings, and governments and industrialists in these countries are obliged to raise capital in the international capital market, i.e. that composed of the national capital markets in the advanced countries. ➤➤ business finance; public finance.

capital movements ➤ foreign investment.

capital–output ratio The ratio derived by dividing the level of output into the stock of ➤ capital required to produce it. The incremental capital–output ratio is a change in output divided into a change in capital stock, i.e. ➤ investment. The relationship between incremental capital (investment) and output is described by the ➤ acceleration principle and the incremental capital–output ratio is the ➤ accelerator coefficient. The interdependence of capital and output plays an important role in ➤ growth theory, in which various assumptions about the ratio are explored. For example: (a) the ratio may be assumed to be a fixed constant as the economy grows or, as in Marxian economics (➤ Marx, K.) it may be assumed to increase, implying that the rate of profit earned on investment falls (➤ profit, falling rate of); (b) labour and capital may be substitutable depending on wages and the rate of interest; and (c) capital-embodied technical progress may occur, meaning that new investment is more efficient than old, so that the ratio falls as old capital is replaced (➤ technology). ➤➤ capital theory.

capital reserves ➤ company reserves.

capital reswitching A phenomenon that played an important part in the controversy over ➤ capital theory between a group of economists led by ➤ Robinson at Cambridge, England, and a group at Cambridge, Massachusetts, USA, led by ➤ Samuelson and ➤ Solow. Specifically, it can be shown that the proposition that ➤ investment increases as the required ➤ rate of return (➤ internal rate of return) falls may not be valid. We could imagine that, as the required rate of return falls, firms would switch from fewer to more ➤ capital-intensive methods of production, thus increasing the rate of investment. However, it is possible to show that under quite plausible circumstances the rate of return could reach a level at which firms would switch back (i.e. reswitch) from more to less capital-intensive production methods, thus causing investment to fall as the required rate of return falls. This possibility then undermines the ➤ neo-classical economics on which the Cambridge, Massachusetts, argument was based (➤ Wicksell effect, price).

capital stock The total amount of physical ➤ capital in the economy or, less commonly, in a firm or industry. In theory, the most important valuation of the stock is the ➤ present value of the ➤ income stream it will generate in the future, and changes in the capital stock should provide a guide to changes in the productive potential of the economy. Since the different parts of the capital stock, roads, machinery and buildings cannot be added together, in practice they have to be valued to produce an estimate of the capital stock at the prices of a given year. *Capital consumption* is the replacement value of capital used up in the process of production, an identical concept to the ➤ depreciation provisions in company accounts, though not necessarily measured in the same way.

capital structure The sources of long-term ➤ capital of a company. A company's capital structure is determined by the numbers and types of ➤ shares it issues and its reliance on fixed-interest debt (➤ gearing). A company's choice between different sources of finance will be determined by their cost, the type of business it is, its past and expected future earnings, ➤ taxation and other considerations. ➤➤ business finance; capital, cost of.

capital theory That part of economic theory concerned with analysis of the consequences of the fact that production generally involves inputs that have themselves been produced. The existence of these 'produced means of production', or ➤ capital, has profound implications for the nature of the economic system. A central element is the role of time and inter-temporal planning. The production of capital requires the sacrifice of current consumption in exchange for future, possibly uncertain, consumption, and the mechanisms by which this process is organized influence the growth and stability of the economy in important ways. The existence of capital is also central to the analysis of the ➤ income distribution. Two major and controversial questions have been: what determines the income derived by the owners of capital relative to that of the suppliers of labour, and can their share be justified in terms of their contribution to the production of output? An understanding of the nature and implications of capital is fundamental to an understanding of our economic system and, indeed, as one leading contributor to the subject has remarked, the problem in attempting to define capital theory is to do it in such a way 'as to embrace something less than the whole of economics' (Bliss, in *Capital Theory and the Distribution of Income*, 1975). ➤➤ Böhm-Bawerk, E. von.

capital transfer tax ➤ inheritance tax.

capital widening Increasing the quantity of capital without altering the proportions of the other ➤ factors of production. This will occur where the ➤ capital stock and employment are both increasing. Where the capital stock is increased and the numbers employed remain constant or fall, then production has become more capital-intensive and *capital deepening* has occurred.

captives ➤ risk capital.

carbon tax ➤ polluter-pays principle.

Caribbean Basin Initiative (CBI) The Caribbean Basin Economic Recovery Act, passed by the US Congress in 1983, granted preferential and tariff-free access to the US market for a range of goods exported from a number of countries in the Caribbean and Central America. These privileges excluded some commodity groups, e.g. textiles and clothing, sugar and oil. The agreement was originally scheduled to end in 1995, but Congress passed an Act in 1990 that made the provisions of the 1983 Act permanent. In 2000, the US–Caribbean Basin Trade Partnership Act extended the provisions to give some of the member countries tariff-free access on a wider range of goods. In 2010, there were nineteen member countries, of which eight countries benefited from the 2000 agreement. ➤➤ Caribbean Community and Common Market.

Caribbean Community and Common Market (CARICOM) Formed in 1973, the Caribbean Community has fourteen member states: Belize, Guyana and Surinam on the Central American mainland and Antigua, Barbados, Dominica, Grenada, Jamaica, Montserrat, St Kitts/Nevis/Anguilla, St Lucia, St Vincent and the Grenadines and Trinidad/Tobago in the Caribbean. The Bahamas is also a member of the Community, although not of the Common Market. The Community has a secretariat in Georgetown, Guyana. The British Virgin Islands, the Turks and Caicos Islands and Anguilla are associate members. Haiti became a provisional member in 1992. A Common External Tariff has been set up and restrictions on foreign exchange and the free movement of skilled workers have been eased. The aim is the eventual establishment of a common market with monetary union. ➤➤ Caribbean Basin Initiative, ➤ Caribbean Development Bank; Central American Common Market; customs union; Regional Trade Agreements.

Caribbean Development Bank (CDB) A regional development bank, established in 1970, that channels ➤ soft loans and grants for the financing of agricultural and industrial projects in the Caribbean. It has twenty regional members and five others (Canada, China, Germany, Italy and the UK). ➤ development finance institutions.

CARICOM ➤ Caribbean Community and Common Market.

carry-over Postponement of settlement of an ➤ account on the ➤ stock exchange until the following period, involving payment of a ➤ rate of interest on the account. Also called contango (➤ backwardation).

carry trade A currency carry trade exploits the difference between the cost of borrowing in one currency compared with the yield from an investment in another.

A trader borrows finance at a low interest rate in the funding currency and buys a high-yielding asset in the target currency. Profitability depends on stability between the rates of exchange of the two currencies. Growth in this activity leads to the strengthening of the exchange rate of the target currency and a weakening in that of the funding currency, which is a second source of profit as the trader repays his loan in the depreciated currency. However, any change in expectations or currency market volatility can lead to a rapid withdrawal of carry trade funds and a consequential collapse in the target currency exchange rate and a rapid rise in the funding currency exchange rate. (➤ exchange rate)

Cartagena Agreement ➤ Andean Pact.

cartel An association of producers to regulate ➤ prices by restricting output and competition. Cartels are illegal in the USA but have been promoted by governments to achieve 'rationalization', as in Germany in the 1930s. They tend to be unstable because a single member can profit by undercutting the others, while price-fixing stimulates the development of substitutes. The most prominent example of an international cartel is the ➤ Organization of Petroleum Exporting Countries. ➤➤ oligopoly; prisoner's dilemma.

cascade tax ➤ turnover tax.

cash 1 Coins and ➤ banknotes.
   2 ➤ Legal tender in the settlement of ➤ debt.

cash flow The flow of ➤ money payments to or from a firm. Expenditure is sometimes referred to as a 'negative' cash flow. The *gross cash flow* of a business is the gross ➤ profit (after payment of a fixed ➤ rate of interest) plus ➤ depreciation provisions in any trading period, i.e. that sum of money which is available for ➤ investment, ➤ dividends or payment of taxes. The *net cash flow* is retained ➤ earnings and depreciation provisions before or after tax (➤ taxation). Net cash flows of a particular project are usually defined as those arising after taxes have been paid, expenditure on repairs and maintenance carried out, any necessary adjustments made to ➤ working capital, and account taken of any residual value of ➤ assets at the end of the life of a project or other miscellaneous income accruing to the project or business. This term is important in ➤ investment appraisal. 'Cash-flow statement' is often used synonymously with 'statement of ➤ sources and uses of funds'. ➤➤ budget.

cash-flow accounting ➤ inflation accounting.

cash ratio 1 The ratio of a bank's ➤ cash holdings to its total deposits ➤ liabilities (➤➤ banking; liquidity ratio).
   2 For an individual firm, the proportion of its current liabilities that are accounted for by cash in hand, including ➤ bank deposits, and sometimes payments due from customers.

cash ratio deposit ➤ Bank of England.

Cassel, Gustav (1866–1945) ➤ purchasing-power parity theory.

CBI ➤ Caribbean Basin Initiative.

CCA Current-cost accounting (➤ inflation accounting).

CD ➤ certificate of deposit.

CDB ➤ Caribbean Development Bank.

Celler-Kefauver Act ➤ anti-trust (US).

census A statistical survey covering every member of a ➤ population; population, census of; ➤➤ sample.

Central American Common Market (CACM) A common market of four Central American states – Guatemala, El Salvador, Honduras and Nicaragua – agreed at Managua, Nicaragua, in the General Treaty of Central American Economic Integration signed in December 1960. This treaty came into operation in June 1961, and a headquarters was established in San Salvador. Costa Rica joined in 1963 and Panama in 1991. ➤ Free trade between the member countries was expected to be established by June 1966. An agreement on the Equalization of Import Duties and Charges was made in September 1959, and subsequent agreements have established a Common External Tariff ➤ tariffs, import. In 1961, the Central American Bank for Economic Integration was formed to finance industrial projects, housing and hotels in the region. In 1964, the five ➤ central banks agreed to establish, in the long term, a common ➤ currency. The Common Market suffered a setback by the imposition of import duties on a number of commodities by Costa Rica in 1971 and Nicaragua in 1978. However, at a meeting in 1990, the members reaffirmed their determination to establish the Market as agreed at Managua and to reduce the Common External Tariff to a maximum of 20 per cent. In 2005, the Dominican Republic–Central American Free Trade Agreement was approved for a free trade area between CACM, the USA and the Dominican Republic which became effective in 2008. ➤ Andean Pact; customs union; Inter-American Development Bank; Latin American Integration Association; Mercosur.

central bank A bankers' bank and ➤ lender of last resort (➤ Bank of England). All developed and most ➤ developing countries have a central bank that is responsible for exercising control of the ➤ credit system, sometimes under instruction from government and, increasingly often, under its own authority. Central banks typically execute policy through their lead role in setting short-term interest rates (➤ rate of interest) which they control by establishing the rate at which loans of last resort will be made and by ➤ open market operations. Some central banks also use other devices to control ➤ money supply (e.g. such as special deposits) though this is now out of fashion (➤ capital adequacy). With an increasing consensus that ➤ monetary policy plays an important part in determining ➤ aggregate demand, the stability of the ➤ business cycle and the rate of ➤ inflation, central banks have found themselves in a central role in economic management. The success of those that operated at arm's length from political authority – notably in the USA and, before ➤ European Economic and Monetary Union, Germany (➤ Bundesbank) – has led other nations to follow in granting independence. The premisses are that the temptation to engage in ➤ overheating will be diminished if monetary authorities do not have to face an election every few years, and that ➤ credibility of policy will be greater if a bank is in charge.

Some independent central banks have more power than others. In the UK, New Zealand and Canada, the central bank essentially decides on the level of interest

rates, but does so to aim at an ➤ inflation target set by the government. The constitution of the ➤ European Central Bank requires the bank to set its own target. Apart
from their function of making broad economic judgements, central banks (e.g. the
Bank of England, the ➤ Bank of France, and the Bank of Canada) control the note
issue (➤ banknote), act as the government's bank, accept ➤ deposits from, and
make ➤ loans to, the ➤ commercial banks and the ➤ money market, and conduct
transfers of ➤ money and ➤ bullion with central banks in other countries. In many
countries the central bank supervises and regulates the commercial banks and
other financial intermediaries but there has been a trend to separate this function
from prudential regulation (➤ capital adequacy; systemic risk) concerned with the
stability of the financial system as a whole (➤ financial services regulation). ➤ Bank
for International Settlements; Bank of China; Bank of France; Bank of Japan; Federal Reserve System; quantitative easing.

central government ➤ public sector.

central government borrowing requirement ➤ public sector borrowing requirement.

certificate of deposit (CD) A negotiable claim issued by a bank in return for a
term ➤ deposit. Certificates of deposit are ➤ securities that are purchased for less
than their face value, which is the bank's promise to repay the deposit and thus
offer a ➤ yield to maturity. Certificates of deposit, which are traded in the ➤ money
market, were first issued in New York in the 1960s and thus denominated in dollars.
Sterling CDs followed in 1968.

certificate of incorporation A document issued by the Registrar of Companies
certifying the legal existence of a company after certain legal requirements for
registration have been met. ➤➤ company law.

certificate of origin A certificate that specifies the country of origin of an export
or import. A certificate of origin would be required by a customs authority for such
purposes as determining whether an import should benefit from a preferential tariff
(➤ tariffs import) which may have been agreed with specific countries (e.g. those in
a ➤ free trade area or ➤ customs union) or whether, for example, a product is liable
to an anti- ➤ dumping tax. Somewhat different rules may be applied depending on
the purpose for which the country of origin is required to be specified. The ➤ European Union, for instance, generally determines origin by the location at which the
last major manufacturing activity took place but applies a somewhat less stringent
definition to some imports from ➤ developing countries benefiting from the
➤ generalized system of preferences. ➤ World Customs Organization.

CGT Capital gains tax (➤ capital gains).

Chamberlin, Edward Hastings (1899–1967) After a period at the University of
Michigan, Professor Chamberlin joined Harvard University as a tutor in 1922 and
became a Professor of Economics there in 1937. His publications include *Theory of
Monopolistic Competition* (1933), *Towards a More General Theory of Value* (1957) and
The Economic Analysis of Labor Union Power (1958). In *Theory of Monopolistic Competition* he proposed a new emphasis for economic theory which broke away from the
old concepts of pure or ➤ perfect competition or pure ➤ monopoly. These two

cases he saw as special limiting ones. In between was 'monopolistic competition', which was the condition under which most industries, in fact, operated. Each firm pursued a policy of product differentiation by special packaging or advertising so that it created a 'penumbra' of monopoly around its product. He also analysed the problem of selling costs, e.g. advertising. ➤➤ monopolistic (imperfect) competition; Robinson, J.V.

chaos theory A branch of mathematics that is concerned with the time path of ➤ dependent variables in systems of non-linear equations. The odd feature of these systems is that, even though the observed variable is not random in that it is governed by a perfectly simple equation, it behaves in a way that looks very chaotic and unpredictable. This is because, in these systems, very small changes in initial conditions lead to large changes in the outcomes that result. It makes accurate long-term forecasting of the variable impossible. The weather is taken as an archetypal chaotic system, and economists have questioned whether certain variables (e.g. stock market prices) might not best be understood in the same way.

CHAPS Clearing House Automated Payments System (➤ clearing house).

Chapter 11 bankruptcy ➤ bankruptcy.

charge account (US) ➤ credit account.

chartist A stock market analyst who predicts share price movements solely from a study of graphs on which individual ➤ share prices, price indices and sometimes trading volumes are plotted. This technique is called *technical analysis*. Unlike *fundamental analysis* – which requires the study of financial accounts of companies – technical analysis is based upon the belief that all the necessary information is in the share price. In contrast to both chartists and fundamentalists, the adherents of the ➤ efficient markets hypothesis believe that stock market prices adjust rapidly and fully to all information as soon as it becomes available, and that neither existing nor past price levels are of any help in predicting the future.

cheque An order written by the drawer to a ➤ commercial bank to pay on demand a specified sum to a bearer, a named person or corporation. Although still quite important, the use of cheques (in the UK, for example, it peaked in 1990) is gradually giving way to other forms of ➤ credit transfer, ➤ credit cards and electronic payments systems. The banks plan to phase out the use of cheques in the UK in 2018.

Chicago School The free market and monetarist (➤ monetarism) economic thinking that has been associated with the Economics Department at Chicago University, and with ➤ Friedman in particular. The Chicago School is most closely associated with the complementary ideas that: (a) in ➤ microeconomics, markets allocate resources most efficiently, and government intervention should be very limited; and (b) in ➤ macroeconomics, with the monetarist thesis that, as monetary growth causes inflation, discretionary policies to manage ➤ aggregate demand should be avoided, and that government should stick to rules aiming at a steady, low rate of growth of money supply. Common to both beliefs is the idea that the unregulated actions of private individuals are usually socially benign. For that reason, the School has tended to argue for a 'light touch' in ➤ competition policy, and has suggested that most problems of ➤ monopoly are created by government regulation, rather than solved by it. The School has also suggested that ➤ vertical restraints are typically harmless. ➤➤ *laissez-faire*.

CHIPS Clearing House Interbanks Payments System (➤ clearing house).

Chi-squared test A test whether, in a ➤ sample, the number of results occurring in each class interval taken as a whole is acceptably close to what is expected. For example, if a dice is unbiased it is to be expected that when the dice is thrown each number 1 to 6 has an equal chance of occurring. Suppose, taking a sample of 300 throws, we get the following result:

SCORE	1	2	3	4	5	6	TOTAL
Observed frequency	41	62	49	53	37	58	300
Expected frequency	50	50	50	50	50	50	300

$$\chi^2 = \int_1^s \left(v_r - n_r\right)^2 / v_r$$

Where n_r (r = 1,2,3 . . . s)
   v_r (r = 1,2,3 . . . s)
In the above example r = 1 to 6
               n the observed frequency for each number 1 to 6 in each class 's'
               v the expected frequency.
And therefore $\chi^2 = 9.36$
For each number of degrees of freedom, which in the example is 5, there is a χ^2 distribution giving values for a range of probabilities. In the example, the value of 9.36 indicated that there is a ten per cent probability that the dice is unbiased.

c.i.f. Cost, insurance and freight, or charged in full. The seller of the goods must pay the costs of carriage to the port of destination (at which point the buyer takes over the title for the goods) specified in the contract of sale and must insure the goods against loss or damage during transit. ➤ f.o.b.

classical economics The dominant body of economic thinking in the period from ➤ Smith's *Wealth of Nations*, which was published in 1776, to ➤ Mill's *Principles of Political Economy* (1848). It was dominated by the work of ➤ Ricardo. The French ➤ Physiocrats had laid stress on the position of agriculture in the economy, claiming that this sector was the source of all economic wealth.

Smith rejected this view and drew attention to the development of manufacturing and the importance of labour ➤ productivity. Ultimately, ➤ labour was the true measure of ➤ value. Ricardo took up this idea and propounded a theory of relative prices based on costs of production in which labour costs played the dominant role, although he accepted that ➤ capital costs were an additional element. Capital was important, not only by improving labour productivity, but also by enabling labour to be sustained over the period of waiting before work bore fruit in consumable output. This was the idea of the wages fund (➤ wage-fund theory). Wages were dependent on two forces: (a) the demand for labour, derived from the availability of capital, or savings, to finance the wage bill; and (b) the supply of labour, which was fixed in the short run, but in the long run was dependent on the standard of living. The latter was related to the level of subsistence. This was not regarded as merely the basic necessities required to keep the workers alive and to reproduce themselves. It was determined by custom, and accepted to be increasing as real living standards improved.

➤ Malthus, in his theory of population, pointed to the need for restraint because of the presumption that there was a natural tendency for the growth of population to outstrip agricultural output. Ricardo analysed the implications of the productivity of land at the margin of cultivation. The Physiocrats and Smith had attributed agricultural ➤ rent to the natural fertility of the soil, but Ricardo refuted this. Rent existed because of the poor fertility of the final increment of land taken under cultivation. Because of competition, ➤ profits and labour costs must be the same everywhere and, therefore, a surplus must accrue to all land that was more fertile than that on the margin. This surplus was rent. The presumption of competition was the foundation of classical thought. The classical economists believed that, although individuals were each motivated by self-interest and personal ambition, free competition ensured that the community as a whole benefited. As Smith put it, 'It is not from the benevolence of the butcher that we expect our dinner, but from [his] regard to [his] own interest.' As a consequence, they concluded that government interference should be kept to a minimum. The classical economists gave little attention to macroeconomic problems (➤ macroeconomics), such as the ➤ business cycle. Most of the classicists accepted ➤ Say's 'law of markets', the gist of which purported to maintain the impossibility of any severe economic recession (➤ depression) arising from an overall deficiency in ➤ aggregate demand. (Malthus disputed this. He argued that increased savings would not only lower consumption but would also increase output, through increased investment. However, his view was not accepted.)

The classical economists, including Malthus, held a theory in which savings were equated with investment through changes in the ➤ rate of interest (➤ Turgot, A.R.J.). Mill's *Principles of Political Economy* (1848) was used as a school text until the end of the nineteenth century. ➤ Marshall in his *Principles of Economics* (1890) assimilated the old classical economics with the new marginalism of ➤ Jevons, ➤ Menger and ➤ Walras. The great controversy that raged in the years of the Depression of the 1930s between the late classical economists and the advocates of deficit spending on public works was resolved at the time when the classical macroeconomic theory gave way to the new economic revolution set in train by ➤ Keynes. Classical economics continues to influence economists, however (➤ neo-classical economics; new classical economics; ➤➤ economic doctrines).

Classical School The tradition of economic thought that originated in ➤ Smith and developed through the work of ➤ Ricardo, ➤ Malthus and ➤ Mill down to ➤ Marshall and ➤ Pigou (➤ classical economics; neo-classical economics).

classical unemployment A situation in which the number of people able and willing to work at prevailing wages exceeds the number of jobs available. In short, the real wage (the price of labour) is higher than that at which the market clears. Classical unemployment is explained by any operations of the labour market that prevent the unemployed bidding down wages until it is profitable for firms to find jobs for everyone. It contrasts with ➤ structural unemployment or ➤ frictional unemployment that occurs when the prevailing wage is too low to attract some people into employment. Classical unemployment also contrasts with ➤ Keynesian unemployment, although both represent different regimes of ➤ quantity rationing. Under classical unemployment, firms are not rationed at all – they can get all the labour they want and can sell all the goods they produce. Households, however, can neither sell all the labour they wish nor obtain all the goods they could afford to buy. ➤➤ insider–outsider theory.

clearing banks ➤ commercial banks.

clearing house Any institution that settles mutual indebtedness between a number of organizations, e.g. the ➤ commercial banks, ➤ building societies and large corporate customers of the banks. The UK banks, through the *Association of Payment Clearing Services*, have: (a) *Bankers' Automated Clearing System (BACS)*, which provides bulk electronic bank clearing; (b) *Clearing House Automated Payments System (CHAPS)*, which provides instant clearing for electronic transfers through the ➤ Real Time Gross Settlement System (RTGS); and (c) *electronic funds transfer at point of sale (EFT-POS)* (➤ credit card). There are similar institutions in other countries, e.g. the *Clearing House Interbanks Payments System (CHIPS)* in New York. There are also global systems for settling payments that flow through the foreign exchange markets – including CLS Services, set up by the large banks. There are similar arrangements on the ➤ commodity exchanges, the ➤ stock exchanges (➤ CREST), the ➤ futures ➤ markets, and for payments in the euromarkets (➤ eurocurrency). The clearing house is normally financed by membership subscriptions and other dues of the market.

cliometrics The 'new' ➤ economic history in which quantitative techniques including ➤ econometrics are used to make interpretations and reconstructions of the past. Pioneered by ➤ Fogel and ➤ North.

closed economy An economic system with little or no external trade, as opposed to an *open economy*, in which a high proportion of output is absorbed by exports and similarly domestic expenditure by imports. ➤➤ international trade.

closed-end fund An ➤ investment trust or other investment company with a fixed ➤ capitalization.

closing prices Price of a ➤ commodity (e.g. ➤ securities on the ➤ stock exchange) at the end of a day's trading in a ➤ market.

Coase, Ronald H. (b. 1910) Coase, the winner of the Nobel Prize in Economics in 1991, is an economist who was born and educated in the UK but who made his home in Chicago. He graduated from the London School of Economics, then taught at Dundee (1932–4), Liverpool (1934–5) and the London School of Economics from 1935 to 1951. His great contribution to economics during his life in the UK was an article, 'The Nature of the Firm', *Economica* (1937), that had been drafted as an undergraduate essay several years before. It struggled to explain why individuals group together in firms rather than making contracts with each other for the delivery of specified pieces of work. He couched his explanation in terms of ➤ transaction costs and the difficulty that individuals would face in writing contracts and agreeing prices with each other. His ideas opened up a seam of literature as rich today as ever, and now commonly associated with the 2009 ➤ Nobel Prize winner Oliver E. Williamson. In the 1950s, he emigrated to the USA, taking up posts at universities in Buffalo (1951–8) and Virginia (1958–64) before settling at Chicago Law School until 1982. It was in the USA that he made his second great contribution – loosely labelled the ➤ Coase theorem, which relates to the efficiency of property rights as a means of allocating resources.

Coase's other preoccupations were monopoly and pricing, and it was these that laid the foundation of his work on property rights. He wrote *British Broadcasting: A Study in Monopoly* (1950) and 'The British Post Office and the Messenger Companies' (*Journal of Law and Economics*, 1961). His output is best measured in terms of quality rather than quantity. His contribution is to have explained the underpinnings of ➤ market forces more successfully than anyone of his generation.

Coase theorem A theorem stating that ➤ economic efficiency will be achieved as long as property rights are fully allocated and that completely free trade of all property rights is possible, which was published by Professor Coase in an article 'The Problem of Social Cost' in the *Journal of Law and Economics* in 1961. The importance of the theorem is in demonstrating that it does not matter who owns what initially, but only that everything should be owned by someone. Trade will place resources in their highest-value occupation eventually.

The theorem is used to show that a solution to the problem of ➤ externalities is the allocation of property rights. For example, suppose someone wishes to play loud music that disturbs a neighbour. It is unfair to allow the music to be played loudly as this ignores the neighbour's interests; equally, it is unfair to prohibit it altogether as this ignores his/her interest. Social efficiency requires that the music can be allowed only if the pleasure given exceeds the displeasure caused to the neighbour. This efficient outcome can be achieved by giving the right to play the music, but allowing a neighbour to bribe him/her not to play, an option that will be exercised if the necessary bribe is large enough. Alternatively, the neighbour could have the right to enjoy silence, but allow the music to be played for a fee. It does not matter who has the initial prerogative – both arrangements will lead to music being played only when the neighbour's displeasure is sufficiently small. The theorem stands as a classic of modern economics, but has been shown to rely on a number of strong assumptions that render it of limited practical value. ➤➤ compensation principle; environmental economics; welfare economics.

Cobb–Douglas function A ➤ production function or ➤ utility function with special characteristics, proposed by ➤ Wicksell and tested against statistical evidence by Cobb and Douglas in 1928. For production, the function is $Y = A.L^{\alpha}.C^{\beta}$, where Y = output, L = labour input, and C = capital input. A, α and β are constants determined by technology. If α and $\beta = 1$, the production function has constant returns to scale (➤➤ economies of scale), i.e. if L and C are increased by 10 per cent, Y increases by 10 per cent. If $\alpha + \beta$ is less than 1, returns to scale are decreasing; if greater than 1, increasing. Assuming perfect competition in markets, α and β can be shown to be labour's and capital's share, respectively, of the value of output. Cobb and Douglas were influenced by statistical evidence at the time that appeared to show that labour and capital shares of total output (i.e. ➤ national income) were constant over time in ➤ advanced countries. They sought explanations for this by statistical fitting (➤ least-squares regression) of their production function. There is doubt now whether, in fact, such constancy of shares is true. The Cobb–Douglas form can also be applied to ➤ utility. Consumer satisfaction or utility is represented by $U = AX_1^{\alpha}X_2^{\beta})$ where X_1 and X_2 are quantities of commodities or services consumed (➤ Euler, L.).

cobweb model This is a simple dynamic ➤ model of cyclical ➤ demand and

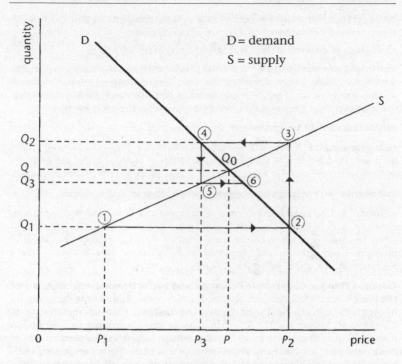

> supply in which there is a time lag between the responses of producers to a change in price. Farming, because of the gap between seed time and harvest, is illustrative of such a model. Consider the diagram (above).

> Equilibrium is represented at the point of intersection of the demand and supply curves at which Q satisfies demand and supply at price P. Suppose in the following period (1), there is a very poor harvest and supply falls to Q_1. At Q_1, prices will rise to P_2 corresponding to (2) on the demand curve. Producers then initiate a new production phase influenced by this high price and in the next period supply Q_2 (point (3) on the supply curve). But prices must now fall to P_3 (point (4) on the demand curve) for all the output to be sold. The process then repeats itself. (Point (5) on the supply curve, point (6) on the demand curve.) It can be seen in the diagram that the path converges to the equilibrium point Q_0, so that the system is stable. However, if the demand and supply curves were drawn such that the latter was steeper than the former (to the P axis), the fluctuations in price and quantity would get wider and wider. If the slopes were equal, the cycle would oscillate around the equilibrium point (>> business cycles; elasticity; rational expectations).

CoCo bond Contingent convertible capital > bonds are a form of debt which converts into > equity in specified circumstances. In 2009 Lloyds Bank, which had been taken over by the UK government the previous year, issued a CoCo bond which pays interest (i.e. a > coupon) unless the bank's core capital falls below 5 per cent of risk-adjusted assets (> capital adequacy) when the coupon is cancelled and the bond is converted into ➤ equity, thus strengthening the capital structure. To attract investors a relatively high coupon has to be paid.

coefficient of determination ➤ multiple correlation coefficient.

coefficient of variation (CV) A statistical measure that can be used to compare the volatility of the prices of ➤ assets that have different rates of return in terms of risk per unit of return. The CV is calculated by dividing the ➤ standard deviation of the asset prices by the average or expected return on the asset. ➤➤ beta.

collateralized debt obligations ➤ derivatives.

collateral security A second ➤ security (in addition to the personal surety of the borrower) for a ➤ loan. ➤ Bank loans, other than ➤ personal loans, are normally made against the security of ➤ stocks and ➤ shares, property or ➤ insurance policies.

collinearity ➤ correlation between two variables. ➤➤ multicollinearity.

collusion Cooperation between independent firms so as to modify competition. Collusion may be tacit or explicit and may involve fixing prices. In *collusive oligopoly* (➤ oligopoly), where two or more firms produce identical or near-identical products, levels of price and output may be similar to those obtaining under ➤ monopoly. ➤➤ cartel; prisoner's dilemma.

Colombo Plan for Cooperative Economic and Social Development in Asia and the Pacific A plan for economic and social assistance in Asia and the Pacific agreed by Australia, Canada, Sri Lanka, India, New Zealand, Pakistan and the UK at Colombo, Sri Lanka, in 1950. The organization has a Secretariat in Colombo. A revision of its constitution in 1977 reflected the increase of its membership to twenty-six. The plan has enabled the development of infrastructure projects in its region and the promotion of the development of skills through training programmes. The organization also provides assistance in the development of public policy on drugs in member countries. ➤ Asian Development Bank.

commercial banks Privately owned banks operating cheque ➤ current accounts, receiving ➤ deposits, taking in and paying out notes and coin, and making ➤ loans, in the UK through a large number of branches (➤ banking; bank loan; branch banking). Sometimes referred to as *retail* (➤ wholesale banking) *banks* or *clearing banks* (➤ clearing house). In the USA, these banks are sometimes referred to as *member banks* (➤ Federal Reserve System) and in Western Europe as *credit banks* to distinguish them from ➤ investment banks. In most countries the commercial banks are concerned mainly with making and receiving payments, receiving deposits and making short-term loans to private individuals, companies and other organizations. The banks increasingly provide a number of other services to their customers: trustee and executor facilities, the supply of foreign currency, the purchase and sale of ➤ securities, ➤ insurance, ➤ credit transfer, ➤ personal loan and ➤ credit card facilities. The banks have also over the years diversified into other financial services in competition with the ➤ finance houses and the investment banks, e.g. venture or ➤ risk capital and the management of ➤ unit trusts (➤ universal banks). In the UK, competition among the retail banks has intensified as technology has rendered the large branch network far less important in the delivery of services, and as the division between different types of financial service has broken down.

commercial paper A ➤ bill or promissory note issued by a large commercial concern and traded in the ➤ money market.

commission A percentage of the ➤ value of a transaction taken by an intermediary as payment for services, e.g. ➤ broker's commission, or estate agency's commission.

commodity 1 In economic theory, a commodity is a tangible good or service resulting from the process of production. Differences between commodities, real or imagined, will determine whether or not they are close ➤ substitutes for one another.
    2 In general usage, a primary product, e.g. coffee, copper, cotton, wool, rubber and tin. ➤ commodity exchange; international commodity agreements.

commodity agreements ➤ international commodity agreements.

commodity control schemes ➤ international commodity agreements.

commodity exchange A ➤ market in which ➤ commodities are bought and sold. It is not necessary for the commodities to be physically exchanged – only rights to ownership need be. The old practice of auctioning commodities from warehouses in which samples could be inspected beforehand has become less important. An efficient system of grading and modern systems of communication have enabled the practice of ➤ 'c.i.f. trading' to develop. A buyer can buy a commodity in the country of origin for delivery c.i.f. to a specified port at which it can be offloaded for direct delivery to his/her own premises. This method saves warehousing costs and auction charges. The market not only enables commodities to be sold 'spot' or for delivery at some specified time and place (➤ spot market), but it also includes a market in ➤ 'futures'. This latter enables merchants to avoid the effect of price fluctuations by buying for forward delivery at an agreed price, which will not be affected by intervening changes in the 'spot' rate (➤ clearing house). Commodity exchanges are now being developed which bring together all the relevant business interests from producer to user into virtual marketplaces online for ➤ electronic commerce transactions.

commodity stabilization agreements ➤ international commodity agreements.

commodity tax A levy on the price of a good or service. ➤ direct taxation.

Common Agricultural Policy (CAP) ➤ farm subsidies.

Common Fund for Commodities (CFC) The Common Fund for Commodities was agreed at Geneva in 1980 by the United Nations Negotiating Conference on a Common Fund and began operations in 1989. The Fund has 106 member countries and 10 institutional members. The Fund promotes through grants and loans the development of the commodity sector, particularly for small-scale operations in the ➤ least developed countries by improvements in ➤ productivity, quality enhancement of outputs, product diversification and ➤ technology transfer. The Secretariat of the Fund is in Amsterdam, Netherlands.

common market ➤ customs union.

Common Market for Eastern and Southern Africa (Comesa) Countries of eastern and southern Africa originally signed a treaty which inaugurated a Preferential Free Trade Area (PTA) in 1982. This treaty envisaged developments leading to the setting-up of a customs and monetary union. Consistent with the terms of that treaty, the PTA was replaced by Comesa in 1993, with a secretariat in Lusaka, Zambia. The aim is to remove all tariffs (➤ tariffs, import) and ➤ quotas on trade between members and to set up a common external tariff, with the ultimate aim of progressing toward the eventual establishment in 2025 of monetary union. Institutions (e.g. the PTA Trade and Development Bank and the Comesa Court of Justice) have been set up. Twenty countries in eastern and southern Africa are members. In 2000, nine member countries – Djibouti, Egypt, Kenya, Madagascar, Malawi, Mauritius, Sudan, Zambia and Zimbabwe – followed in 2004 by Burundi and Rwanda, agreed to the freeing of trade between themselves and the implementation of a common external tariff. These countries eliminated tariffs on goods originating in member countries and planned to abolish quantitative restrictions and other non-tariff barriers to intra-regional trade in preparation for the setting up of a ➤ customs union. (➤ protection)

community charge ➤ local taxation.

company law The law governing the establishment and conduct of incorporated business enterprise. It developed, in the UK, from the ➤ partnership, and has its origins in common law and, from the eighteenth century onwards, in a series of company and other Acts. The first companies were created by royal charter, and the whole basis of company law is that certain benefits are conferred (in many of these first instances, that of a ➤ monopoly) in return for certain obligations. By 1825, the expansion of business had made the creation of companies by separate Acts of Parliament too cumbersome, and in that year a new Act made it possible to form *joint stock companies* by registration with a Registrar of Companies. It was not until 1862, however, that limited liability was extended to certain private as well as public companies.

Company law has continued to evolve under successive Acts as the needs of business have developed and altered. The 1907 Act introduced the distinction between the ➤ private company and the public company. Under present UK law there are three classes of company: (a) limited private companies; (b) unlimited private companies; and (c) public limited companies (plc). Compared with the two other forms of business unit – the ➤ sole proprietorship and the ➤ partnership – ➤ incorporation confers advantages for financing and, in certain circumstances, ➤ taxation, in addition to limited liability where appropriate. (An unlimited private company does not have limited liability, i.e. its owners are responsible for company debt to the full extent of their fortune.) However, companies, unlike individuals or partnerships, are obliged to make public certain information about their business. Both private and public limited companies are obliged to file certain information for public inspection and to circulate accounts to their shareholders. There are exemptions for small- and medium-sized companies which are not public companies. Small- and medium-sized companies are defined in terms of turnover, assets and employment (small having 50 or fewer employees, and medium, 250 or fewer employees).

The amount of information larger companies are required to publish has increased in successive Companies Acts, and the directors' report must now cover, for example, employment, exports, employee aggregate remuneration, payment practices and donations to political causes or charities. Among other provisions, the 1989 Act requires companies to disclose a holding of more than 3 per cent in another company. Quoted companies are public limited companies whose shares are listed on a recognized ➤ stock exchange. Private companies may place certain restrictions on the transfer of shares, but not offer shares to the public. Company law sets out other provisions dealing with the powers, appointment, terms and disqualification of directors (Company Directors Disqualification Act 1986), the protection of investors, including minorities, ownership and control, the regulation of shares, the purchase of its own shares by a company, the disclosure of interest in shares, the preparation of accounts (➤ accounting standards), winding-up and other matters. The Enterprise Act 2002 contained provisions relating to ➤ competition policy, ➤ insolvency, consumer protection and ➤ corporate governance. Company law and corporate governance was consolidated in the Companies Act 2006 which superseded the 1985 Act (➤ corporate governance). Corporate legal requirements are gradually being harmonized in the ➤ European Union, and indeed among other advanced countries, but there remain important differences, especially in the field of company ➤ taxation.

company reserves ➤ Profits retained in the business and set aside for specified purposes. The various UK Companies Acts have drawn distinctions between capital and revenue reserves and undistributable and distributable reserves. Capital reserves are created when new shares are issued at a ➤ premium over par or when the book value of existing assets is revalued to bring it into line with replacement costs or when ➤ capital gains are made. These capital reserves may later be transformed into issued capital (➤ capitalization). Revenue, or distributable reserves, are created by transfers of undistributed profits into special accounts, out of which a dividend may be paid in a later year in which the company makes a loss. Reserves of either type may be converted into capital by a ➤ bonus issue. *Provisions* are not the same as reserves but arise out of ➤ depreciation or allowances made for ➤ liabilities, e.g. provisions for doubtful debts.

company taxation ➤ corporation tax.

comparative advantage   The idea that economic agents are most efficiently employed in activities in which their relative efficiencies are superior to others. The importance of comparative advantage is that it suggests that, even if someone is very bad at some activity, perhaps even worse than anyone else at it, it could still be profitably efficient for him/her to pursue it, if he/she is even more inept at other activities. The idea has been seen as particularly important in explaining ➤ international trade. Countries should specialize in areas in which they have a comparative advantage (➤➤ division of labour; Ricardo, D.).

comparative cost ➤ international trade; Ricardo, D.

comparative static equilibrium analysis The analysis of markets or economies in terms of their different ➤ equilibrium positions, without reference to the process by which adjustment between equilibria is achieved. Most non-mathematical economics is static in this sense. It consists of comparing diagrams which represent snapshots of the state of a market at a single moment, and it aims to assess the characteristics of the equilibrium state and discover the position of a new equilibrium when some variable is changed. Most ➤ demand and ➤ supply analysis, for example, is of this sort. An equilibrium is noted, then the effect of a shift in demand or supply is analysed, its impact on price and quantity sold determined, and the effect of demand or supply curves with different slopes can be assessed.

Such analysis omits any trace of the path or speed of adjustment between different equilibria. In ➤ perfect competition, for example, firms are assumed to have no influence on price and be unable to deviate from the going market rate at all, yet by what process can the market price change? As there is no auctioneer telling every-body what price to set, the price-takers themselves must also be the price-setters, even though this contradicts the basic assumption of the model (➤➤ *tatonnement* process). Comparative statics simply ignores problems such as these. ➤➤ dynamics.

comparative statics ➤ comparative static equilibrium analysis.

compensation principle The principle that total economic welfare increases from a change in the economy, if those who gain from the change could compensate those who lose from it to their mutual satisfaction. It is not necessary for money transfers actually to take place. However, the principle has been criticized in this respect because, without actual transfers, interpersonal comparisons of ➤ utility of money are implied. Actual transfers are required if individuals are to reveal the total worth they place on their gains and losses (➤➤ economic efficiency). ➤➤ Pareto, V.F.D.; social-welfare function; welfare economics.

compensatory finance ➤ United Nations Conference on Trade and Development.

competition ➤ perfect competition.

Competition Act 1980 ➤ competition policy.

competition policy Government measures aimed at stimulating competition and protecting consumers against ➤ monopoly. Policy seeks to achieve these aims by: (a) targeting anti-competitive behaviour such as price-fixing (➤ cartel), ➤ predatory pricing, resale price maintenance and ➤ full-line forcing; (b) regulating ➤ mergers; and (c) regulating 'natural' monopolies such as gas and water utilities. Another element in competition policy is, or should be, the promotion of ➤ contestability by removing ➤ barriers to entry.

There are different views on how competition policy should be handled. On one side are those who believe in an activist competition policy of the type exemplified by the US Department of Justice case against Microsoft in the late 1990s. This view is supported by the followers of the *structure–conduct–performance* (SCP) theory that the performance of an industry follows from its conduct, which in turn is caused by its structure (➤ concentration). On the other side is the more ➤ *laissez-faire* school (associated with economists at the University of Chicago (➤ Chicago School)) which believes that unfettered markets tend to have benign effects, and that even if monopolies emerge, they will tend to do so where they offer real con-sumer benefits and will usually be transient. Recently a synthesis of the different attitudes seems to have emerged in the main jurisdictions: (a) tough penalties for anti-competitive behaviour; (b) a discretionary case-by-case approach to the sanc-tioning of mergers where consumer benefits can be identified; and (c) a midpoint between intervention and non-intervention in the case of ➤ vertical restraints.

In the UK, competition policy is upheld by two main bodies: the Office of Fair Trading (OFT) and the Competition Commission (previously the Monopolies and Mergers Commission). The powers and method of operation of these bodies origin-ally established under the Fair Trading Act 1973 and the Competition Act 1980 were revised and amended in the Enterprise Act 2002. This Act ended ministerial involvement in competition policy, and competition, not the public interest, is the test applied in investigations. Thus, the Competition Commission is able to pro-hibit mergers which fail the competition test or will apply some other remedy such as the sale of assets, in both cases taking account of consumer benefits. The Act also granted new detection powers to the OFT which can investigate anti-competitive practices and if necessary refer them to the Competition Commission. The office of the Director-General of Fair Trading was abolished and the OFT operates as a board of at least four members and a chairman. The Act also established a new independent Competition Appeals Tribunal (CAT).

Other countries have various institutions for upholding competition policy. In the USA, this policy is overseen by the Federal Trade Commission (➤ anti-trust); in Germany by the Federal Cartel Office (Bundeskartellamt) and there is a Monopoly Commission (Monopolkommission) which has an advisory role, and in Italy by the Competition Authority (Autorità Garante della Concorrenza e del Mercato). National laws in the ➤ European Union (EU) incorporate Community law but have yet to be fully harmonized.

At the level of the EU, the European Commission is responsible for competition policy and reserves to itself the power to investigate larger mergers and other competition situations with a 'Community dimension'. The Commission's powers are principally derived from Articles 85 and 86 of the Treaty of Rome (now renumbered 81 and 82), supplemented by subsequent regulation (such as the merger control regulation 4064/89) and interpretation. Article 81 forbids cartel arrangements and Article 82 outlaws the abuse of dominant positions. European competition law is unique in that it covers state aid to commercial enterprises which might distort competition.

The important development of the last decade has been the increasingly international character of competition policy. European Union and USA authorities have dominated, even to the extent of investigating mergers between companies of other jurisdictions (the EU investigated the merger of the American giants Time-Warner and AOL in 2000, for example). Japan enacted an Anti-Monopoly Law in 1947, modelled on US practice. Until 1995 that law was not enforced with any vigour but at that time the powers of the Fair Trade Commission were considerably strengthened. ➤➤ Smith, A.

competitiveness A loose term, popularly used to reflect the ability of a nation to grow successfully, and to maintain its share of world trade. While there have been several government White Papers on the subject in the UK, a wide-ranging debate about it in Europe and the USA and, while league tables of national competitiveness are regularly produced by reputable business authorities, the term has never impressed academic economists. It is used as though it refers to the state of the productive base of the economy, yet attempts to apply a precise definition have foundered. It either reduces to a measure of how rich a country is, measured by its ➤ Gross Domestic Product per head of population, or to a measure of the price of tradable goods expressed in foreign currency (primarily a reflection of the ➤ exchange rate). Yet, those who use the term appear to believe they are talking of a broader concept than either of these. Those who have criticized the growth in usage of the term argue that basic economic theory of ➤ international trade and ➤ comparative advantage makes clear that we should not view the world as a group of nations competing in a ➤ zero-sum game.

complementary goods Pairs of goods for which consumption is interdependent (e.g. cars and petrol, or cups and saucers) are known as *complements* or complementary goods, and changes in the demand for one will have a complementary effect upon the demand for the other. Complements have a negative ➤ cross-price elasticity of demand: if the price of one rises the demand for both may fall. Complementary demand creates difficulties in the application of the theory of ➤ marginal utility, since it cannot be said that the level of utility yielded by a complementary good is yielded directly by that good and in isolation. ➤➤ substitutes.

compliance cost Expenditure of time or money in conforming with government requirements. These costs are of four kinds: (a) *direct costs* such as the cost of installing equipment to reduce emissions; (b) *administrative compliance costs* including the costs of time spent on understanding the law, filling in tax returns and payments to professional advisers such as accountants; (c) *excess burdens or efficiency costs* which result from the effect of ➤ regulation in distorting market outcomes; and (d) the costs of maintaining and enforcing the regulatory system. Various governments now estimate compliance costs on a regular basis and carry out Regulatory Impact Assessments in advance of legislation. These and academic research indicate that the incremental costs of regulation are very substantial, certainly several per cent or more of GDP, and growing. The benefits of regulation are even more difficult to estimate than the costs.

compound interest The calculation of total interest due by applying the ➤ rate of interest to the sum of the capital invested plus the interest previously earned and reinvested. In contrast, *simple interest* is calculated only on the capital invested.

concealed discount ➤ trade discount.

concentration The extent to which a small number of firms account for a high proportion of sales or another dimension of economic importance in an industry. In the USA, the four largest companies accounted, in the early 1990s, for over 80 per cent of output in domestic refrigerators, motor vehicles, electric light bulbs and cigarettes (the four-firm ➤ concentration ratio). In the UK, concentration is high in multiple food retailing, brewing, banking and other sectors. Industry concentration is a key determinant in ➤ competition policy. The two extremes are: (a) ➤ perfect competition, in which products are homogeneous and firms small in relation to the size of the total market (➤ small business) so that they cannot individually influence price; and (b) ➤ monopoly, in which there is a single seller (concentration is absolute). Most markets in the ➤ advanced countries have high (➤ oligopoly) to intermediate levels of concentration and operate under conditions of ➤ monopolistic competition in which prices, in theory, tend to exceed marginal cost, and where, even if there is no ➤ collusion, ➤ barriers to entry may keep concentration high.

Industry concentration, measured by the ➤ concentration ratio, generally increased in the post-Second World War period, at least until the 1970s, though there are a number of practical and conceptual difficulties in measuring concentration and in generalizing about trends over time. Some studies have indicated that ➤ mergers have accounted for about half of increases in concentration.

Attitudes to concentration among economists vary according to their assessment of the relative importance of competition, ➤ contestability and ➤ economies of scale. Where the ➤ optimum scale of output is high relative to the size of the total market, more competitors might lead to higher costs through lower-scale economies.

In general, however, ➤ enterprise concentration in a given market is much higher than ➤ establishment (or plant) concentration, indicating that leading firms have a larger share of markets than would be necessary for them to operate at optimum scales of output (though there may be economies in distribution or other aspects of multi-plant operation (➤ economies of scope)). Larger firms also operate in more than one product market (➤ diversification) and this can result in high levels of *aggregate concentration* in which a small number of firms have a significant share in economic output as a whole. Since the 1970s, there seems to have been some decline in aggregate concentration as increased international competition (➤ globalization) and other factors have encouraged large firms to focus on core activities and subcontract more to smaller firms. In the UK, the share of the hundred largest manufacturing enterprises in total manufacturing net output rose from 16 per cent in 1909 to a peak of 41 per cent in 1970 and then declined from the early 1980s to 30–35 per cent in the 1990s. There is some controversy about how important national concentration is, at least in manufacturing, given the extent of actual and potential competition from imports. Porter has argued that the presence of a number of strong local rivals, however, is a more important factor in promoting ➤ innovation and dynamic efficiency than rivalry from firms abroad. Nations with leading world positions, even in small countries such as Switzerland, often have a number of domestic rivals, even in sectors with substantial economies of scale. ➤➤ Chicago School.

concentration ratio A ratio calculated to show the degree to which an industry is dominated by a small number of large firms or made up of many small firms. There are many ratios that may be calculated, based on turnover, capital employed, employment, etc., e.g. the ratio of the total capital employed of the top five firms as a percentage of the industries' capital employed. However, a comprehensive ratio is the Herfindahl index. This index is given by the sum of the squares of the market shares of each firm in the industry: $H = \Sigma_n (f_n)^2$ where f_n = the market share of firm n, i.e. the sales of firm n divided by industry sales. A pure ➤ monopoly would take the value of 1. At the other extreme, if all the firms in the industry had equal market shares the value would be $1/n$. ➤➤ concentration.

conditional cash-transfer A system of ➤➤ social security payments which allocates money to the poor, but only on condition that they ensure that their children attend school and health clinics.

confidence interval A measure of the likely statistical error in the estimation of a ➤ parameter. It is a term frequently used in ➤ econometrics, where a ➤ sample of data is used to make a generalization of the relationship between different variables, e.g. between the level of consumption and the level of income. A sample may imply, for example, that consumption is equal to 0.8 times the level of income in the economy. But the sample may naturally deviate from the exact relationship across the whole economy. The more variable the relationship in the sample, the less certain one can be about the true relationship. A confidence interval expresses the range of estimates within which it is likely the real relationship lies, e.g. it may be 0.8 ± 0.1.

To estimate the confidence interval, one typically assumes the sample is representative of the whole population, bar some random deviation. Given the variation within the sample, one can calculate how many times such random samples would generate estimates of the parameter outside the confidence interval. Usually, the confidence interval is expressed as the range within which only 5 per cent of samples would generate estimates lying outside the range (a 95 per cent confidence interval). For more precision, one might describe a wider confidence interval, that suggests the range outside of which only 1 per cent of random samples would generate estimates. Clearly, the bigger the sample, the more certain one can be of the estimate, and the smaller the confidence interval. For an estimate of a parameter in any very large sample, the 95 per cent confidence interval can be calculated as the estimate ±1.96 times the ➤ standard deviation of the estimate. ➤ normal distribution.

confirming house An agency in the UK that purchases and arranges the export of goods on behalf of overseas buyers.

conglomerate A business organization generally consisting of a ➤ holding company and a group of subsidiary companies engaged in dissimilar activities. ➤➤ downsizing.

Consolidated Fund Sums standing to a particular account at the ➤ Bank of England into which the proceeds of ➤ taxation are paid and from which government expenditures (➤ budget) are made. Prior to 1787, different funds were maintained for various purposes and taxation receipts divided among them, but after that date the various funds were consolidated, leaving, of major significance, only the National Insurance Fund, which receives ➤ National Insurance contributions and a grant from the Consolidated Fund to meet social security payments. Consolidated Fund standing services is an item in the UK budget which includes expenditure authorized by specific legislation. This expenditure (e.g. the salaries of judges and payments to the ➤ National Loans Fund for service of the ➤ national debt) is paid out of the Consolidated Fund but, unlike ➤ supply services, does not have to be voted annually in Parliament.

consolidated stock ➤ consols.

consols Abbreviation for 'consolidated stock': unredeemable UK government stock first issued in the eighteenth century as a consolidation of the ➤ national debt. Consols bear an interest of 2½ per cent and have a total nominal value of £267 million.

conspicuous consumption A term used by Thorstein Veblen (1857–1929) in his book *The Theory of the Leisure Class* (1899) to identify that ostentatious personal expenditure which satisfies no physical need but rather a psychological need for the esteem of others. Goods may be purchased not for their practical use but as 'status symbols' and to 'keep up with the Joneses' (➤➤ Giffen good).

constant prices ➤ real terms.

constant returns to scale ➤ returns to scale.

consumer behaviour ➤ demand, theory of; indifference curve; indifference-curve analysis; marginal utility; Marshall, A.

consumer credit Short-term ➤ loans to the public by suppliers, including retailers, for the purchase of specific goods. Consumer credit takes various forms but over-drafts, moneylenders and other private sources of borrowing are not referred to as consumer credit, either because they are not tied to the purchase of specific goods or because they are long-term loans facilities, e.g. ➤ mortgages.

Consumer Credit Act A UK Act, passed in 1974 and amended in 2006. The Act tidied up and consolidated legislation in the field of ➤ consumer credit, some of which had existed on the statute books since Victorian times. The Act introduced a licensing system which applied not only to credit and hire firms such as the ➤ finance houses and banks, but to all agencies connected with consumer credit such as credit brokers and debt collectors. Licences are issued by the Office of Fair Trading if it is satisfied that the applicant has in no way infringed any of the con-sumer protection laws. Regulations may be made under the Act with respect to the content and style of advertising material or other documents relating to consumer credit, and also to the way the effective annual ➤ rate of interest is calculated and explained to the consumer (➤ annual percentage rate). ➤ competition policy.

consumer durables ➤ durable goods.

consumer good An ➤ economic good or ➤ commodity purchased by ➤ house-holds for final consumption. Consumer goods include, for example, chocolate or draught beer consumed immediately as well as ➤ durable goods which yield a flow of services over a period of time, e.g. a washing machine. It is the use to which it is put that determines whether a good is a consumer good (sometimes referred to as a *consumption good* or final good), not the characteristics of the good itself. Electricity, or a computer bought for the home, are consumer goods, but the same thing bought for a factory is a ➤ producer good.

Consumer Price Index (CPI) This price index is equivalent to the internationally accepted ➤ harmonized index of consumer prices (HICP) (➤➤ Retail Price Index).

consumers' expenditure A major component of ➤ Gross Domestic Product (GDP), it comprises the total expenditure of households and is equivalent to total personal income after tax (➤ income tax) less personal savings. In 2006–2008, consumers' expenditure accounted for about 70 per cent of Gross Domestic Product of the USA, about 55 per cent in the area of the ➤ European Economic and Monetary Union and about 35 per cent in China.

consumers' preference Attitudes which determine consumer choice between alternative ➤ commodities or groups of commodities. When good X is preferred to good Y it will have greater ➤ utility to the buyer, so that the allocation of expend-iture between these alternatives will, in a ➤ free-market economy, be determined by consumer preference and their relative ➤ prices. These preferences will, in con-junction with the ➤ production function and the prices of the ➤ factors of production, therefore, determine the allocation of scarce resources to the produc-tion of various goods. Consumer preferences may change independently with, say, fashion or may be influenced by ➤ advertising and other forms of sales promotion as well as by the availability of new goods arising from technological progress (➤ technology). Although preferences are something the economist takes as given, and makes no ➤ value judgement about, they are assumed to be consistent and rational in certain ways. ➤ indifference-curve analysis; revealed preference; transitivity; von Neumann-Morgenstern utility function; ➤➤ endogenous preferences.

consumers' sovereignty ➤ Resource allocation determined by ➤ consumers' preference rather than by ➤ state planning. In a ➤ free-market economy consumers vote with their purses for the pattern of production and consumption they want; the outcome, however, will be affected by the ➤ income distribution.

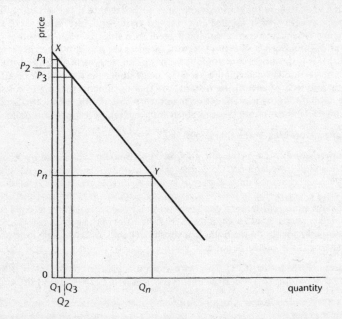

consumer surplus The amount by which consumers value a product over and above what they pay for it. Before the phrase was coined by ➤ Marshall, the idea of a surplus of ➤ utility over the price paid for a good or service was explored by ➤ Dupuit in his study of the benefits arising from the construction of public facilities such as roads and bridges. Marshall explained consumer surplus:

> The price which a person pays for a thing can never exceed and seldom comes up to that which he would be willing to pay rather than go without it: so that the satisfaction which he gets from its purchase generally exceeds that which he gives up in paying away its price: and he thus derives from the purchase a surplus of satisfaction. The excess of the price which he would be willing to pay rather than go without the thing, over that which he actually does pay, is the economic measure of this surplus satisfaction.

Marshall's surplus is illustrated in the diagram of a ➤ demand curve shown above. The consumer buys on the market quantity Q_n at a price P_n. However, following his demand schedule, if only Q_1 were available, he would be willing to pay P_1, if Q_2 to pay P_2, and so on. If the supplier had a ➤ monopoly and could practise ➤ price discrimination, he could extract as revenue the whole of the area under the demand curve, i.e. $XYOQ_n$. However, there is a market price P_n, so that the supplier only obtains P_nYOQ_n and leaves the difference XP_nY as a benefit to the consumer. A difficulty is that as the price falls along Marshall's demand curve, the real income of the consumer increases. To get a more accurate measure of the benefit of the surplus, therefore, an adjustment must be made to offset the effect of the difference in real income at the higher price (P_1) and the lower price (P_n) (➤➤ Hicksian demand function; income effect). Consumer surplus plays an important role in ➤ welfare economics. ➤➤ producer's surplus.

consumption   The use of resources to satisfy current needs and wants. It may be measured statistically by the sum of consumers' and government's current expenditure (including defence expenditure), the remainder of ➤ national income being made up by ➤ investment. However, such statistics may be inadequate in some cases. For example, expenditure on ➤ durable goods such as washing machines may exaggerate consumption, because they have a life of, say, seven years and therefore are not entirely consumed in the current period as implied by simply counting the amount spent on their purchase (➤ consumption function).

consumption function   The relationship between consumption and income. As income increases, other things being equal, consumption will increase, though not at the same rate as income in the short term. As income rises, consumers tend to save proportionately more and spend proportionately less. The exact relationship between income and consumption only holds constant given a number of assumptions. For example, (a) purchases of ➤ durable goods are related to income in the stated way, e.g. they are replaced at a rate related to income and not to other factors; (b) there are no expectations of price changes which might delay or bring forward consumption; (c) no change takes place in the availability or the cost of credit; and (d) there is a constant level of ➤ savings in real terms at any level of income. (➤ Inflation could decrease the real value of savings such that consumers react by increasing their contributions to their savings stock from current income until their real value has been restored; they then revert back to the previous rate of saving.) The consumption function was introduced by ➤ Keynes and applied to his analysis of income determination. ➤➤ average propensity to consume; marginal propensity to consume; multiplier; permanent-income hypothesis.

consumption good   ➤ consumer good.

consumption smoothing   The adjustments that consumers make to their savings in order to protect their expenditure from short- or long-term fluctuations in their income stream. In an advanced country there are many services available such as ➤ insurance, ➤ savings banks and ➤ pension funds which assist consumers to do this. In less developed countries such services may not be available, nevertheless the poor may, for instance, even pay an agent a fee, a negative rate of interest, for taking care of their savings in order to exert a discipline on their expenditure when income is high, to avoid the often very real possibility of starvation in the event of income failure. ➤➤ permanent-income hypothesis.

contango   Synonym for ➤ carry-over.

contestability   The degree of ease with which firms can enter or leave an industry.

A perfectly contestable industry is one in which, as in ➤ perfect competition, there are no barriers to entry at all. Unlike perfect competition, however, perfect contestability implies nothing about how many firms currently exist in the industry – it is possible for an efficient monopolist to exist while no barrier to entry prevents other firms from competing. Contestability theory was stimulated by Baumol in the early 1980s. He showed that the attractive features of perfect competition could be achieved merely by the threat to incumbent firms that entry would occur should large profits be made. The threat of entry should induce ➤ marginal-cost pricing and efficient production. In practice, entry barriers *do* exist and, because incumbent firms can often scare potential entrants away from entering, the discipline that potential competition provides is considered less effective than that of actual competitors. ➤➤ barriers to entry; competition policy; sunk costs.

contingency reserve ➤ public expenditure.

contingent protection The use of anti- ➤ dumping and ➤ countervailing duties as insidious devices to protect domestic industry from foreign competition. The application of ➤ tariffs against products sold by foreign suppliers below their normal prices or against foreign exports that have received government subsidy are generally allowed, the purpose of these tariffs being seen as correcting price distortions in the market without affecting the integrity of free-market principles. There was a considerable growth in the number of applications filed, which reached a peak in 2001, and this led to the suspicion that tariffs were being used in restraint of trade, although the numbers subsequently declined in 2007. Ambiguities can be exploited in the meaning of 'normal' price and in the difficulties of obtaining convincing data.

continuation Synonymous with ➤ carry-over.

contract A statement of the rights and obligations of each party to a transaction or transactions. A contract, as familiarly envisaged, is a formal written statement of the terms of a transaction or relationship, e.g. a house purchase or a pop star's deal with a record company. But most transactions and relationships are conducted without a formal contract: the contractual terms that exist when you buy a newspaper are simple enough to obviate the need for written terms and conditions, and many business relationships are based on implicit contractual terms that are supported not by law but by the mutual interest of the involved parties. An example might be the obligation of a ➤ building society to charge a reasonable rate of interest on a variable rate mortgage. While the formal contract that someone may have with an institution to lend him/her money may not preclude the institution raising its interest rate to above market levels, there is an implicit contract that it would not do so. It is in the interest of the building society not to abuse the implicit contract, for to do so would damage its long-term reputation. ➤➤ incomplete contract; tit-for-tat.

contract curve The curve of exchange between two parties along which their ➤ marginal rates of substitution are the same in relation to the commodities traded. Any bargain concluded at a rate of exchange other than one on the contract curve could be improved (i.e. by making at least one party better off without making the other worse off) by moving to the contract curve. A term introduced by ➤ Edgeworth. ➤ Pareto, V.F.D.; ➤➤ economic efficiency.

contracting out 1 The practice by governments or firms of employing an outside agent to perform some specific task rather than performing it themselves. The practice is defended on the ground that it stimulates competition between companies for contracts to provide services which might otherwise be run less efficiently in-house. The UK Local Government Act 1988 requires authorities either to contract out or to expose to competition a number of services, including refuse collection, vehicle maintenance and general catering (➤➤ vertical integration). But it is proposed that this should be replaced by an obligation simply to ensure 'best value' is obtained. In the public sector contracts are normally awarded after a competitive tender in which bidders state the price and conditions under which they are prepared to supply (➤ private finance initiative).

2 An employee or employer may contract out of the UK State Earnings-Related Pension Scheme (➤ National Insurance) where alternative pension arrangements have been made.

control ➤ separation of ownership from control.

convergence The notion that countries become, or will continue to get, closer in terms of ➤ per capita income (productivity) over time. In principle, one might expect convergence to occur if poorer countries with lower pay rates attract investment and thus raise their productivity. In practice, evidence for convergence is mixed. In the eighteenth and nineteenth centuries Britain, followed by the USA and some other European states, widened the gap between their productivity and that of the rest of the world. Between the latter part of the nineteenth century and the mid 1930s, there was some convergence in the range and variation of output per capita in these countries, although none caught up with the USA. After the Second World War, convergence was resumed, while new members joined the convergence 'club' with some reduction in the USA lead. Since 1970, performance has been variable and more new members of the club have emerged. The convergence hypothesis is controversial and debate has been confused by differences in the period and number of countries covered, as well as by differences in what is meant by convergence. The term can be interpreted to mean a narrowing in the variation between productivity in a group of countries or the catching up of countries on the leader or leaders. The convergence hypothesis is resisted by those economists who emphasize the role of internal factors in a country's development and, therefore, the potential role of government in economic growth, rather than external influences (➤ endogenous growth theory; institutional economics). ➤ economic development; globalization.

convergence criteria The conditions laid out in the ➤ Maastricht Treaty, that were to act as a guide to the suitability of different ➤ European Union nations to enter ➤ European Economic and Monetary Union. The criteria held that: (a) the government deficit should be below 3 per cent of ➤ Gross Domestic Product (GDP), unless any excess over that level should be exceptional, temporary and small; (b) that government debt (➤ national debt) should not exceed 60 per cent of GDP, or it should be approaching that level; (c) ➤ inflation should not exceed the performance of the three best-performing countries by more than 1.5 percentage points; (d) long-term interest rates should not exceed those of the three best-performing countries, in terms of inflation performance, by more than 2 percentage points; and (e) that the ➤ exchange rate shall have respected the normal fluctuation margins of the European Exchange Rate Mechanism for two years, without severe tension. ➤ Stability and Growth Pact.

conversion Issue of a new ➤ stock to replace another. This may arise where a ➤ debenture or ➤ warrant is convertible into ➤ equity shares or where holders of ➤ government stock at or near redemption are offered a new stock in exchange for existing stock.

convertibility A ➤ currency is said to be convertible when it may be exchanged freely for another currency or gold. All foreign ➤ exchange controls were completely removed by the UK in 1979. The convertibility of US dollars into gold was abandoned in 1971. ➤➤ exchange control; foreign exchange market; gold standard.

convexity A characteristic of tastes or technology that a combination of commodities is preferable to any one on its own. If someone prefers half a slice of bread and half a gram of butter to either a whole slice of bread or a whole gram of butter, they have convex preferences. If it is easier to make one car using ten men and ten machines than to make it using twenty men and no machines or using twenty machines and no men, the production technology is convex. Convexity implies that combinations of products are more desirable than extremes. It is itself usually implied by ➤ diminishing marginal utility. It takes its name from the shape of the ➤ indifference curves or ➤ isoquants that convexity generates.

core capital ratio ➤ capital adequacy.

corporate governance The rules by which companies are managed, managers appointed and remunerated and who watches over them have become increasingly important with the ➤ separation of ownership from control and as some businesses have grown to very large size. Although partly determined by ➤ company law, corporate governance in the UK and the USA is largely left to market forces, for example poorly managed companies are open to takeover. There are voluntary codes of practice which require, as another example, that the roles of chairman of the board of directors and the chief executive should not be combined in one person, but these codes of practice are not universally followed.

Germany has a two-tier board structure with a supervisory board (*Aufsichrat*) and a management board (*Vorstand*). This system has been mandatory since 1884 and also includes works councils for employees and representation of trades unions on supervisory boards. Companies in Germany are also required to take account of the wider public interests of stakeholders in their activities, an element which has been introduced into Britain in the Companies Act 2006.

Measures taken by the ➤ European Union to adopt some of these features in harmonized company law illustrate the tendency to convergence of governance systems and have been driven by ➤ globalization to include such matters as ➤ accounting standards. In Japan, although the law does not require employee representation on boards, there is a presumption that companies must exercise responsibility towards them as manifested in the life-long employment system.

The economic consequences of different governance systems are controversial but probably not very great. However, the 2007–9 credit crisis has led to a move towards greater ➤ regulation of companies, particularly banks (➤ banking). (➤➤ Corporate Social Responsibility)

corporate income tax (US) ➤ corporation tax.

Corporate Social Responsibility (CSR) The doctrine of corporate social responsibility holds that companies in their activities should take into account the interests of all their stakeholders, not only of their owners but also employees, suppliers, customers, the environment and the community at large. The UK Companies Act 2006 states that directors should 'have regard' to factors of this kind but the weight given to each of them is left to their 'good faith'. The Act, therefore, does introduce multiple objectives for directors but it does not give any guidance on cases where there may be a conflict between the interests of the owners and other stakeholders. Many, perhaps most, large companies do have CSR programmes of some kind and there is some evidence that such programmes may be associated with above average economic performance. Critics of CSR maintain that it undermines property rights and can lead to an increase in ➤ agency costs as well as distorting the allocation of resources and economic efficiency.

corporate venture capital (CVC) Investment in the ➤ risk capital of smaller firms by larger firms. Companies' CVC activity usually takes the form of minority stakes in ➤ equity ➤ capital for strategic, financial or social responsibility reasons. The motivation of these investments is usually primarily strategic: opening windows on new technologies or markets that might affect the investor's core business. The main force behind CVC has been technological change but, as in information and communications (➤ new economy), the activity is not limited to high-tech industries. Investors may invest directly or via venture capital funds. CVC is one of several types of intercorporate relationships that include trade investments, alliances and ➤ joint ventures.

corporation tax A tax (➤ taxation) levied on the assessable ➤ profits of companies and unincorporated associations.

Corporation taxes can generally be modelled on two main forms. In the *classical system*, tax is paid on the whole of company profits whether distributed to shareholders or not and shareholders are taxed on the dividends they receive. In the so-called *imputation system*, some relief is offered to shareholders to ensure that dividends are not subject to both income tax and corporation tax. The UK and the USA use the classical system. In the UK the imputation system was in force from 1973 to 1999. UK tax is progressive with taxable profits under £300,000 paying 21 per cent and then a tapered rate on profits up to £1.5 million and beyond that level paying 28 per cent (2010–11). Individuals pay a lower rate of ➤ income tax on dividends (10 per cent and 32.5 per cent for higher rate taxpayers) which goes some way to alleviate the double taxation inherent in the classical system. The US corporate income tax also has a progressive element and is levied both at Federal level and by many states. Member states of the ➤ European Union have varied systems for taxing company profits and the European Commission is attempting to harmonize the tax bases employed (no attempt is being made to harmonize rate structures which are the prerogative of national government).

The rationale for corporation tax is not entirely clear since, in principle, company profits are subject to tax in the hands of their owners either by capital gains or income tax rates, and ➤ compliance costs are high under both the main systems in use. However ➤ tax tolerance appears to be greater for multiple taxes than a few at higher rates. Corporation tax was originally introduced in classical form to encourage the retention of earnings by companies in the hope that this would stimulate ➤ investment. The reversion to something closer to the classical system was justified on the same grounds. Some economists argue that the allocation of capital ➤ resources is best determined by the ➤ capital market, and would prefer to see a higher proportion of dividends distributed and then rechannelled back to investment via the capital market. Moreover, the possibility of ➤ tax avoidance by individual investors liable to high rates of tax in close companies has in the past led to the application of special rules to enforce distributions by these companies, so-called *shortfall assessments*.

Companies are also liable to corporation tax on ➤ capital gains in many countries including the UK.

Individuals in business on their own (operating on own account) and members of ➤ partnerships pay income tax on their individual share of total profits (broadly defined in the same way as for companies). In the USA, certain companies can opt to be taxed as unincorporated businesses under *sub-chapter S*.

correlation A statistical measure of the closeness of the variations in the values of one ➤ variable to the variations in the values of another. The 'correlation coefficient' is calculated by the following formula:

$$r = \frac{\Sigma(x_i - \bar{x})(y_i - \bar{y})}{\sqrt{[\Sigma_i(x_i - \bar{x})^2]}\sqrt{[\Sigma_i(y_i - \bar{y})^2]}}$$

in which x_i and y_i are the values of the two variables, $\bar{x}$ and $\bar{y}$ are their means (➤ average); r can take any value between +1 and –1, at which extremes there is perfect correspondence between the variations of the variables. At the value 0, there is no correspondence. It should be noted that a value of r close to unity does not imply a causative connection between the two variables. ➤ multiple correlation coefficient; partial correlation; regression analysis; Slutsky, E.

cost ➤ opportunity cost.

cost, avoidable ➤ prime costs.

cost, overhead ➤ fixed costs.

cost accounting, costing and cost control Procedures by which the expenditure of a firm is related to units of output. Cost accounts, while they can be related directly to financial accounts, are concerned with the detailed elements of ➤ opportunity costs in identifiable output for purposes of pricing, departmental budgeting and the control of manufacturing methods, and material and ➤ labour usage for these products rather than the overall financial results of the firm's operations.

cost–benefit analysis The appraisal of an investment project that includes all social and financial costs and benefits accruing to the project. The techniques adopted in order to evaluate and decide whether a proposed project should proceed – whether, that is, its benefits would exceed its costs – are the same as applied in ➤ investment appraisal (➤ present value). However, the valuation in money terms of the social or welfare costs and benefits (➤ welfare economics) presents special problems, e.g. the costing of the loss of an area of outstanding natural beauty or the valuation of the benefits arising from the reduction in road accidents due to the construction of a motorway. In other cases, the market prices prevailing may not be appropriate. For example, the real cost of labour may be much lower than the going wage rate, because of very high unemployment. The ➤ opportunity cost (which is the cost that matters in cost–benefit appraisals) is lower and, therefore, a ➤ shadow price is used to represent this low opportunity cost in place of the wage rate. Similarly, the rate of interest at which the future time streams of costs and benefits are discounted has to be chosen with care. ➤ interest, time preference theory of; quality-adjusted life years; risk assessment.

cost centre ➤ management accountancy.

cost control ➤ management accountancy.

cost curves The graphical representation of cost schedules, ➤ average costs or ➤ marginal costs, dependent on various levels of output or production.

costing ➤ cost accounting.

cost of capital ➤ capital, cost of.

cost-of-living index ➤ Retail Price Index.

cost-plus A method of setting a price in which the contractor charges the actual cost of the goods he supplies or for the work he carries out, plus either a percentage or an agreed absolute amount for his services. Used for some government contracts, the cost-plus formula provides no incentive for the contractor to keep his costs to the minimum and, where a percentage service charge is applied, he actually has an incentive to inflate them. The justification for the cost-plus system is that for certain kinds of work (e.g. development contracts in large technical projects) it is not possible to estimate costs in advance.

Cost-plus is also often used in business as a method for calculating prices (e.g. in retailing) by adding a ➤ gross margin or mark-up to the bought-in cost of goods, where there may be no simple alternative. This is in contrast to the pricing described by traditional economic theory, which asserts competitive forces should lead ➤ marginal cost to be equal to ➤ marginal revenue. But because if one retailer charges more than another he may lose custom and be obliged to reduce his margins or go out of business, ➤ price theory (➤➤ firm, theory of the) is not invalidated by the widespread use of the cost-plus method.

cost-push inflation ➤ Inflation induced by a rise in the costs of production of goods and services. Such cost increases may arise abroad and be transmitted through higher prices of imported raw materials and then be fed by higher wage costs as workers try to prevent inflation eroding the real value of pay. The rapid escalation in oil prices in the 1970s (➤ Organization of Petroleum Exporting Countries) accelerated price inflation in the period, although the rate of inflation had begun to rise before this. Cost increases may also arise within the domestic economy from firms attempting to increase profits and/or employees to increase their earnings. Success in achieving increases depends on their degree of market dominance (➤ monopoly) and, therefore, bargaining power. Any money gains greater than ➤ productivity will tend to result in price increases. Economists assert that money wage increases exceeding 4.5 per cent annually, on average, are inconsistent with an ➤ inflation target of 2.5 per cent. The cost-push argument for inflation is traditionally held to contrast with ➤ demand-pull inflation and has been associated with the different policy prescriptions (➤➤ prices and incomes policy). However, cost push cannot lead to sustained inflation, in the long run, without monetary growth being sufficient to support it. ➤➤ monetarism.

costs, fixed ➤ fixed costs.

costs, historical or historic Actual costs at the time incurred. An ➤ asset in the ➤ balance sheet at historical cost is shown at the price actually paid for it, even though it might be worth more or cost more to replace. ➤➤ depreciation.

costs, prime ➤ prime costs.

costs, selling The expenses incurred in creating or maintaining the ➤ market for a product. Distribution costs are normally excluded, but ➤ advertising sales staff, sales campaign costs and sales office expenses are included.

cost schedule A table showing the total costs of production at different levels of output and from which ➤ marginal costs and ➤ average costs can be calculated and cost curves drawn. A *price schedule*, in a similar way, would give information about prices at different levels of sales or output. Cost and price schedules are basic tools in economic theory, though in practice they are not easily constructed, especially over wide ranges of output where the ➤ production function may not be linear.

council tax A tax designed to finance a proportion of UK local government spending. It is a tax on the *occupation* of property with the amount to be paid loosely determined by the market price of the occupied property. All dwellings are put into eight bands based on their values, and all homes in each group within a council jurisdiction are charged the same amount. The banding system obviates the need for periodic revaluation of properties. Homes occupied by only one person receive a discount (➤ local taxation).

counterparty risk The risk in securities trading that the other party (counterparty) to a purchase or sale may fail to discharge his obligation.

counter trade A form of ➤ barter in ➤ international trade in which the buyer requires the seller to accept goods (of the buyer's choosing) in lieu of currency. The seller has the task of marketing the goods. Another form of counter trade is the agreement by a seller of plant and machinery to 'buy back' the products produced by the plant and machinery in settlement of the debt.

Counter trade developed rapidly as a favoured trading method by Communist states and by ➤ developing countries with non-convertible currencies (➤ convertibility) and a shortage of foreign exchange. Counter trade may take the form of the exchange of one commodity for another or the exchange of a mixed selection of commodities. Multinational firms and banks have specialist divisions to advise on counter trade and firms have been established specializing in the giving of advice on conducting counter trade.

countervailing duty An additional import duty (➤ tariffs, import) imposed on a

➤ commodity to offset a reduction of its price as a result of an export subsidy in the country of origin. ➤➤ contingent protection; dumping; export incentives.

countervailing power The balancing of the market power of one economic group by another. The concept was advanced by ➤ Galbraith in the first of his books – *American Capitalism* (1952) – on the domination of the modern economic system by large firms along with ➤ economies of scale and technological development (➤ technology) and the need for planning, to meet the criticism that this system of ➤ monopolistic competition is inferior to ➤ perfect competition. The power of large manufacturers was, he suggested, balanced by that of large retailing groups; the power of large employers by that of the ➤ trade unions.

coupon A piece of paper entitling the owner to ➤ money payment (as in ➤ bearer bonds), cut-price or free goods (gift coupons) or rations.

Cournot, Antoine Augustin (1801–77) Cournot was made Professor of Analysis and Mechanics at Lyons in 1834, Rector of Grenoble University in 1835 and of Dijon University in 1854. His main economic work, *Recherches sur les principes mathématiques de la théorie des richesses*, was published in 1838. Other economic works were *Principes de la théorie des richesses* (1863) and *Revue sommaire des doctrines économiques* (1877). In *Recherches*, Cournot set out in mathematical form the basic apparatus of the theory of the firm (➤ firm, theory of the) that, after being refined by ➤ Marshall, appears in elementary economic textbooks today. He was the first to set out: (a) the ➤ variables and functions facing a firm; (b) ➤ demand as a diminishing function of ➤ price; and (c) ➤ cost curves and revenue curves. By the use of calculus he demonstrated that a monopolist will maximize profit at the output at which ➤ marginal cost is equal to ➤ marginal revenue. Cournot traced a direct logical line from the single seller (➤ monopoly) through two (➤ duopoly) or many (➤ oligopoly) sellers to 'unlimited competition'. He showed how, in the last case, 'the marginal cost equals the marginal revenue relationship of the monopolist' becomes 'the price equals the marginal cost relationship of the firm in ➤ perfect competition'. In doing so, he analysed the situation of duopoly and showed that, given that each seller assumed the other's output was unaffected by his own, they would each adjust prices and output until a position of ➤ equilibrium was reached, somewhere between that reflected by the equations for monopoly and that for unrestricted competition (➤ Bertrand competition). In spite of the undoubted significance of his work, he had no influence on the mainstream of economic thought until his ideas were developed by Marshall.

cover The ratio of total to distributed ➤ profit of a limited company. A ➤ dividend is said to be twice covered if it represents half the earnings of the company.

covered bear ➤ bear.

CPP Current purchasing power (➤ inflation accounting).

credibility A measure of the expectation of the population that the government, or monetary authorities, will adhere to policies delivering low ➤ inflation. It is an important article of faith among macroeconomists that where people – particularly those negotiating wage deals – expect inflation to be low, it is much easier to keep inflation low. But if the monetary authorities have little credibility, and inflation is anticipated, then people will factor inflation into their behaviour and will, for example, demand higher pay rises. Those pay rises will be inflationary, or at least make it costly for the authorities to keep inflation low. By sticking to rules on how much money is in the economy, or by delegating authority over ➤ money supply to an independent ➤ central bank with no incentive to print money, credibility can to some extent be enhanced. The usual measure of credibility is taken as the market ➤ interest rate on long-term loans: if that rate is high, then it can be assumed the market anticipates inflation will occur in the future, and hence extra compensation is required for those who are lending. ➤➤ inflation target; monetary policy.

credit The use or possession of goods and services without immediate payment. There are three types of credit: (a) *consumer credit*: credit extended formally and informally by shopkeepers, ➤ finance houses and others to the ordinary public for the purchase of consumer goods (➤➤ consumer credit); (b) *trade credit*: credit extended, for example, by material suppliers to manufacturers, or by manufacturers to wholesalers or retailers (➤➤ trade credit) – virtually all exchange in manufacturing industry, services and commerce is conducted on credit, and firms may provide small discounts on accounts settled within, say, one month; and (c) *bank credit*: credit consisting of ➤ loans and overdrafts to a bank's customers (➤ banking).

Credit enables a producer to bridge the gap between the production and sale of goods, and a consumer to purchase goods out of future ➤ income. Bank and other kinds of credit form part of the ➤ money supply and have considerable economic importance.

credit account 1 An account against which purchases may be made and paid monthly (US = charge account).

2 A form of revolving ➤ instalment credit offered by some retail stores in which the consumer makes fixed regular monthly payments into an account and receives in return credit to purchase goods up to the limit of a certain multiple of the monthly payments, normally eight or twelve. A service charge, which is, in effect, an ➤ interest charge, is normally made as a percentage of the value of each purchase.

3 Bank and agency ➤ credit cards in which the consumer pays his account monthly are also a form of credit account.

credit banks ➤ commercial banks.

credit bureau ➤ rating agencies.

credit card A plastic, personal magnetized card with the name and account number of the holder and the expiry date embossed. Smart cards contain information about the holder in a microchip and can validate the holder's personal identification number (PIN). Purchases up to a prescribed limit may be credited on signature of a voucher franked by the card or on entry of the PIN. The vendor recovers the cash from the issuer of the card (less ➤ commission) and the purchaser pays the issuer on receipt of a monthly statement. For most cards, the purchaser has the option of paying a minimum amount and settling the account in instalments, plus interest. A *debit card* works in the same way as a credit card, but the holder's bank account is debited immediately through Electronic Funds Transfer at a Point of Sale. Credit cards, popularly referred to as 'plastic money', are issued by ➤ banks,

➤ building societies and other organizations, including retailers (*charge cards*). Cards issued by financial institutions often serve also as *cheque cards* and may be used to withdraw cash from an automatic teller machine.

credit default swaps (CDS) These contracts arise where the buyer pays a premium or interest on the value of a financial instrument (such as a loan or security) for which he is buying protection. If there is a default, the seller of the contract pays the amount protected. The buyer is in effect swapping the risk in the financial instrument for the premium paid. It differs, however, from a normal insurance as the buyer of the CDS does not have to own the financial instrument covered.

credit guarantee A type of insurance against default provided by a government, credit guarantee association or other institution to a lending institution. Credit guarantees enable otherwise 'sound' borrowers who lack ➤ collateral security, or are unable to obtain loans for other reasons, to obtain the credit they require through banks in the normal way. A government loan guarantee scheme insuring loans to small firms by the ➤ commercial banks was introduced in the UK in 1980 and is now called the Enterprise Finance Guarantee Scheme. Under this scheme the government guarantees repayment to the bank of 75 per cent of the loan in return for an annual premium of 2 per cent on the outstanding balance. Loans are for a period of up to ten years. All ➤ European Union member states (except Denmark), the USA, Japan and other countries have similar schemes.

creditor One to whom an amount of money is due. A firm's creditors are other firms, individuals and perhaps the government to which it owes money in return for goods supplied, services rendered and taxes for which it is liable, respectively. Antonym of ➤ debtor.

creditor nation A country with a ➤ balance of payments surplus. The ➤ Keynes Plan recognized that ➤ disequilibrium in international payments was as much the responsibility of creditor as of *debtor nations*. Under that plan, the International Clearing Union or international ➤ central bank would have given overdrafts to debtor countries and, by so doing, would have created deposits for the creditor countries in terms of its special ➤ currency called bancor, in a similar way to normal ➤ banking operations. However, ➤ interest would be charged not only on the debtors' overdrafts, but also on the creditors' deposits. Although the Keynes Plan was not accepted at the ➤ Bretton Woods conference, the principle that a surplus country had 'obligations' was accepted and a scarce-currency clause written into the ➤ International Monetary Fund agreement. ➤➤ international liquidity.

credit rating agencies ➤ rating agencies.

credit sale ➤ consumer credit.

credit transfer, or giro A system in which a bank or post office will transfer ➤ money from one account to another on receipt of written instructions. Several accounts (e.g. ➤ households or trade bills) may be included in a list which must state the location and account numbers of the payee. Standing orders for giro transfer of regular payments may be made. Credit transfers – which have been used by post offices in continental Europe for many years – were first introduced into the UK by the ➤ commercial banks in 1961 and the Post Office in 1968. Benefits to the customer include the saving on stamp duty payable on ➤ cheques (since abolished in the UK) and economies in accounting procedures, though banks may make a charge for each item transferred.

credit union 1 A non-profit organization accepting deposits and making loans, operated as a cooperative often run by volunteers aimed at the poorer sections of the community without ➤ bank or ➤ building society support. Credit unions in the UK are regulated by the Credit Union Act 1979 and their activities have remained restricted there with less than 1 per cent of the population being members. They are much more active in other countries, e.g. the Republic of Ireland, the USA and Australia.

2 A mutual ➤ savings bank (➤ mutual company).

CREST Electronic share settlement system introduced in the London ➤ stock exchange in 1996. By recording title to shares electronically it has reduced the cost of the traditional system of ➤ share certificates sent through the post. Title is recorded through nominee companies set up by ➤ stockbrokers and others. CREST is also used for ➤ money market instruments.

critical-path analysis A method of structuring the sequence of work on a project to minimize the duration of work on the whole project. Between the start of a project and its finish there are a number of separate tasks which have to be done in particular sequence: in the construction of a house, for example, the foundations are laid before the walls. The foundations are on the critical path because every extra day spent on them means an extra day on the whole building project. Other tasks may be carried out simultaneously, such as the fitting of window frames as the roof is being tiled. Critical-path analysis attempts to order all tasks, minimizing the time that resources are spent idly waiting for other tasks to be completed. The critical path is the sequence of tasks – mostly those that have to be finished in a particular order – that affect the overall length of the whole project. The window frames, for example, may not be on the critical path, as fitters can install them while other work goes on, and there is probably some flexibility as to when the windows can be fitted. Management is better devoted to focusing on keeping the foundations part of the project working smoothly, rather than on the window frames.

cross-price elasticity of demand The proportionate change in the quantity demanded of one good divided by the proportionate change in the price of another good. If the two goods are ➤ substitutes (e.g. butter and margarine), this elasticity is positive. For example, if the price of margarine increases, the demand for butter will increase. If the goods are complementary (➤ complementary goods) (e.g. pot plants and flower pots), this elasticity is negative. If the price of pot plants rises, the demand for flower pots will fall. ➤➤ elasticity of substitution.

cross-section analysis Statistical analysis of the members of a ➤ population at one moment. It contrasts with ➤ time-series analysis, in which the population is drawn from a number of time periods (generally months, quarters or years). ➤➤ econometrics.

cross-subsidy Financing a loss-making line of business with profits made elsewhere. This may be motivated by private business concerns (to help establish new lines of business, for example), or those of public policy (the provision of rural bus routes at the expense of urban ones). It can be an important object of public policy to prevent it where it provides the means by which ➤ predatory pricing can occur. ➤➤ subsidy.

crowding-out The process by which an increase in government borrowing displaces private spending. If an increase in government borrowing has a large effect on interest rates, private spending will fall as investors slim down their plans. Therefore, overall, spending will not increase much. If the government borrowing has no effect on interest rates, however, then there will be no reduction in private spending and aggregate demand will rise by the full amount of the increase in government spending. ➤➤ IS–LM model; Keynes, J.M.; monetarism; Ricardian equivalence.

cum **dividend** With ➤ dividend; the purchaser of a security quoted '*cum* dividend' is entitled to receive the next dividend when due. The term *cum*, meaning 'with', is also used in a similar sense in relation to ➤ bonus issues, ➤ rights issues, or ➤ interest attached to ➤ securities, etc.

cumulative preference shares ➤ preference shares.

currency Notes and coins that are the 'current' medium of exchange in a country (➤ money supply). Gold and national currencies that act as ➤ reserve currencies (e.g. the dollar) are referred to as *international currency* because they are regarded as acceptable for the settlement of international ➤ debts. ➤➤ banknote; exchange control; exchange rate; soft currency.

currency, trading ➤ trading currency.

currency appreciation The increase in the ➤ exchange rate of one ➤ currency in terms of other currencies. The term is usually applied to a currency with a floating rate of exchange; upward changes in fixed rates of exchange are called *revaluations*. ➤ currency depreciation; devaluation; effective exchange rate.

currency board A national body established to maintain its domestic currency at a fixed ➤ exchange rate with a stronger more stable currency. Under its rules, the domestic currency cannot be increased except in line with a corresponding increase in its reserves of the currency to which it is linked. Unlike a ➤ central bank, it cannot increase the quantity of money in order to finance government deficits. It is a system which gives a very strongly fixed exchange rate regime. Its disadvantage is that, in certain circumstances, an economy could benefit from adjustment in its exchange rate if it has become uncompetitive. Argentina had a currency board from 1991 to 2002 with the peso linked to the US dollar. Latvia and Lithuania have currency boards with their respective currencies linked to the euro.

currency depreciation The fall in the ➤ exchange rate of one ➤ currency in terms of other currencies. Usually applied to floating exchange rates. Downward changes in fixed rates of exchange are called ➤ devaluations. A depreciation makes imports more expensive in terms of domestic currency, and exports cheaper. However, in so far as a currency depreciation simply reflects a relatively high level of domestic inflation (e.g. if a 10 per cent rise in prices leads to a 10 per cent fall in the currency), the ➤ real exchange rate has not changed. Indeed, if inflation occurs without a depreciation of the currency, in real terms the currency has *appreciated* because the price of imported goods will be relatively lower than domestic goods than before the inflation, and the price of exported goods will have risen compared to foreign ones. ➤ currency appreciation; effective exchange rate; J-curve.

currency school ➤ banking and currency schools.

currency union ➤ European Economic and Monetary Union.

current account 1 The most common type of bank account, on which ➤ deposits do not necessarily earn ➤ interest, but can be withdrawn by ➤ cheque at any time (US = demand deposit). The bank charges according to the number of cheques cleared through the account and the credit balance. If the average balance is high, the customer may pay no bank charges.
   2 That part of the ➤ balance of payments accounts recording current (i.e. non-capital) transactions.

current assets ➤ assets.

current balance The net position on the current account of the ➤ balance of payments.

current budget In the UK, a measure of government borrowing that compares total revenues to total spending minus investment spending. If the current budget is in deficit, it means the government is borrowing more than it is investing, which implies that it is borrowing simply to sustain consumption spending. Under the ➤ golden rule of government finances – that government should only borrow to invest – the current budget should be in surplus or in balance.

current-cost accounting ➤ inflation accounting.

current expenditure Expenditure on recurrent (i.e. non- ➤ capital) items in business or private accounts.

current liabilities ➤ liabilities.

current prices ➤ Prices unadjusted for changes in the purchasing power of money. Whether prices are in current or constant terms in historical series of economic statistics is of great importance at times of ➤ inflation or ➤ deflation. ➤➤ real terms.

current purchasing-power accounting ➤ inflation accounting.

current ratio The ratio of the current ➤ liabilities to the current ➤ assets of a business. Current assets normally exceed current liabilities. The difference between the two is ➤ working capital, which is normally financed from long-term sources. The amount of working capital required varies with the type of business and its commercial practices (e.g. the proportions of its output sold for cash and on three months' ➤ credit) so that the current ratio is not a universally useful guide to the solvency of a business. ➤➤ capital; liquidity.

current yield ➤ yield.

Customs Cooperation Council ➤ World Customs Organization.

customs drawback The repayment of customs duties (➤ tariffs, import) paid on imported goods which have been re-exported or used in the manufacture of exported goods.

customs duties ➤ tariffs, import.

customs union A union established within two or more countries in which all barriers (e.g. ➤ tariffs or ➤ quotas) to the free exchange of each other's goods and services are removed and, at the same time, a common external tariff is established against non-members. This contrasts with a ➤ free-trade area in which each member country retains its own tariffs vis-à-vis non-members. At one time, it was generally accepted that customs unions unambiguously yielded economic benefits. Without the distortions imposed by trade barriers, trade was directed in favour of the producer with advantageous costs (➤➤ Ricardo, D.). It was believed that as ➤ free trade was itself beneficial in that it led to the optimal allocation of world resources, so a customs union, which was a step in that direction, must also be beneficial.

However, Viner, in *The Customs Union Issue* (1950), pointed out that in the creation of a customs union there could be two effects: (a) a trade-creating effect, and (b) a trade-diversion effect. Although (a) might be a gain, greater losses might be incurred by (b). Take the example of two countries A and B and the rest of the world C producing a particular commodity for $50, $40 and $30 respectively. If the home market of A is protected by a $25 tariff on the item, then no one in A will find it economic to import from B or C. Production in A will occur, at $50. If A then forms a customs union with B, trade will be created because it is cheaper for A to obtain the commodity from B than to produce it itself. There is a gain in so far as A is $10 better off. On the other hand, if A's original import duty had been $15, trade would then have taken place with the rest of the world C, despite the tariff, as this would be the least-cost source to A. In this example, if A forms a customs union with B it will now switch its trade because it can obtain the commodity for $40 from B compared with $30 + $15 = $45 from C. This trade diversion represents a move away from the optimum of ➤ resource allocation, because B is a higher real-cost source than C (➤➤ second best, theory of). Whether, therefore, a customs union will yield overall gains from shifts in the location of production will depend on the superiority of trade creation to trade diversion.

However, this type of analysis covers only a part of the problem; many other factors must be taken into account in assessing whether a customs union is beneficial. In particular, the removal of trade barriers between countries will change the ➤ terms of trade and therefore the relative volumes of the different commodities demanded, because of the price changes. It will shift the commodity pattern of trade as well as the geographical origins of the commodities traded. Whether a community will finish up better off therefore depends on the price and income elasticities of demand for the commodities traded (➤ elasticity). An added benefit may accrue because the increase in the size of markets may enable ➤ economies of scale to be made. Finally, a protective tariff may initially have been imposed because home costs are high, but home costs may remain high because a protective tariff is imposed. Removal of the tariff may induce more efficient operation and lower costs. ➤ Association of South East Asian Nations; Caribbean Community and Common Market; Central American Common Market; Common Market for Eastern and Southern Africa; European Union; Mercosur.

cycle, trade ➤ business cycle.

cyclically adjusted budget deficit A measure of government borrowing at any period that attempts to strip out any effect of a strong or weak economy on the government's financial position. If the actual deficit is, for example, 3 per cent of national income, but the economy is in a serious recession, the 3 per cent may not be regarded as seriously imprudent. The cyclically adjusted budget deficit, also referred to as the *structural budget deficit*, is a measure of what government borrowing would be in the absence of any ➤ output gap, or in the absence of any ➤ built-in stabilizers.

cyclical unemployment Temporary ➤ unemployment resulting from lack of ➤ aggregate demand in a downswing in the ➤ business cycle.

D

dark pools ➤ stock exchange.

data-mining The practice of searching for ➤ correlations in data with the purpose of generating theoretical hypotheses. The normal pattern of scientific research is for hypotheses to be produced by abstract models and then validated by ➤ empirical testing. Data-mining reverses the procedure. It is not held to be a respectable mode of inquiry because, while any theories it produces will be empirically valid, it is hard to tell whether they are the result of coincidence or not. All data are bound to enclose some coincidences, and the data-miner is likely to have unearthed these. For example, a data-miner might unearth a theory that people whose names start with the letter H tend to be richer than average. But this would not be remarkable if discovered in data, as at least one letter group must have higher than average income. The theory would only be convincing if there was some prior reason for believing it that was subsequently substantiated by data analysis. ➤➤ null hypothesis; regression analysis.

dated securities ➤ bonds, ➤ bills of exchange or other ➤ securities that have a stated date for redemption (repayment) of their nominal value. *Short-dated securities* are those for which the ➤ redemption date is near; *long-dated securities* are those for which it is a long time ahead.

DCE ➤ domestic credit expansion.

d.c.f. Discounted cash flow (➤ present value).

deadweight debt A ➤ debt incurred to meet ➤ current expenditure, or which for any other reason is not covered by a real ➤ asset. Most of the ➤ national debt is deadweight debt since it was incurred to finance war and other current ➤ public expenditure.

deadweight loss 1 A particular loss in ➤ social welfare deriving from a policy or action that has no corresponding gain. Deadweight losses represent economic inefficiency (➤ economic efficiency) and usually result when there is some flaw in the price-setting mechanism. For example, congestion on roads imposes costs on road users, and these costs are deadweight losses, because the inconvenience of congestion to one driver is not matched by a reduction in inconvenience to another. If, on the other hand, road space were allocated by setting high prices for road access, the costs borne by drivers that pay those charges would benefit government revenues, and would thus not be deadweight costs at all. Society often finds it worth bearing certain deadweight losses in order to promote social objectives.

2 The part of the cost of a particular policy that has to be incurred, but that does not further the objective of the policy. For example, the cost of subsidizing those in ➤ long-term unemployment back to work includes some element of subsidy to people who would have returned to work regardless of the subsidy.

death rate The number of deaths occurring in any year for every 1000 of the population (the *crude death rate*). It may be quoted for each sex and each age group. Related to this statistic is the *expectation of life at birth* which is the estimate of the number of years on average a newborn baby will live, with separate estimates for male and female, the latter generally living longer. Experience has shown that life expectancy increases with economic development. According to the United Nations, the life expectancy at birth of males in 2005/2010 was 73.6 years in more developed countries, 63.9 years in less developed countries and 54.7 years in least developed countries. An alternative measure is ➤ *quality adjusted life years* that estimates the number of years a newborn baby may expect to have a healthy life, i.e. a life in which there is no illness severe enough to limit physical mobility or mental acuity. ➤ demographic time bomb; dependency ratio; human development index; poverty.

debentures, debenture stock A little-used term for fixed-interest unsecured ➤ securities issued by companies which are now more commonly called ➤ bonds.

Debreu, Gérard (1921–2004) A graduate in mathematics at the University of Paris, Debreu joined the Cowles Commission (subsequently the Cowles Foundation For Research in Economics) in 1950. In 1960, he was appointed to the Chair of Economics and Mathematics at the University of California at Berkeley. His published works include *Existence of an Equilibrium for a Competitive Economy* (1954) with Kenneth ➤ Arrow, and *Theory of Value, an Axiomatic Analysis of Economic Equilibrium* (1959). Professor Debreu, who was awarded the ➤ Nobel Prize in Economics in 1983, is recognized, with Arrow, as having proved the theoretical consistency of a market economy in which prices can lead to ➤ equilibrium between supply and demand in many different markets simultaneously. Furthermore, by extending the notion of what we mean by a 'good' to something at a particular place, at a particular time under particular conditions, Debreu's work naturally extends itself to the study of location, capital and uncertainty. ➤ general equilibrium; Walras, M.E.L.

debt A sum of ➤ money or other property owed by one person or organization to another. Debt comes into being through the granting of ➤ credit or through raising ➤ loan capital. *Debt servicing* consists of paying interest on a debt. Debt is an essential part of all modern, capitalist economies (➤ capitalism). ➤➤ national debt.

debt conversion ➤ conversion.

debt management The process of administering debt (e.g. the ➤ national debt) by providing for the payment of ➤ interest and arranging the refinancing of maturing ➤ bonds.

debt neutrality The idea that financing spending by borrowing money will have exactly the same effects as financing it through other means. It has been applied in various forms, notably to government spending (➤ Ricardian equivalence) and to corporate investment (➤ Modigliani–Miller theorem).

debt ratio ➤ gearing.

debtor One who owes money to another. A firm's debtors, for example, are those to whom invoices have been sent for goods or services supplied and which remain unpaid. Antonym of ➤ creditor.

decentralized decision-taking ➤ free-market economy.

decile ➤ percentile.

decreasing returns ➤ diseconomies of scale; returns to scale.

deemed disposal The assumed realization of an ➤ asset in the calculation of liability for ➤ capital gains taxation or ➤ inheritance tax. Shares in a company, for example, might be valued and tax charged on the difference between that value and the price originally paid for them, even where the shares did not change hands.

deep discounted bonds ➤ Bonds that are issued at a price much lower than that at which they can be redeemed (➤ redeemable securities) at the specified date. The intention is to provide large ➤ capital gains for the holders and to pay a correspondingly low interest rate. In some countries and especially for higher-rate taxpayers, less tax may be payable on a gain than upon interest income; however, the 'capital gain' on deep discounted bonds is liable to be treated as income by the tax authorities.

deferred rebate A rebate or discount on a purchase which is accumulated for a specified period to encourage customers to remain with a particular supplier. Also called *aggregated rebate.* ➤➤ competition policy.

deferred shares A ➤ share issued where ➤ ordinary shares have a fixed ➤ dividend and which entitle the holders to all ➤ profits after prior charges have been met. Now virtually unknown.

deficit An excess of an expenditure flow over an income flow, e.g. ➤ budget deficit, ➤ balance of payments deficit, or an excess of ➤ liabilities over ➤ assets.

deficit financing The use of borrowing to finance an excess of expenditure over ➤ income. Most often, it refers to governments, who often spend more than they can raise in taxation. The term is normally used in economics to refer to a planned budget deficit (➤ balanced budget) incurred in the interests of expanding ➤ aggregate demand by relaxing ➤ fiscal policy and thus injecting purchasing power into the economy, a policy advocated by Keynes to increase employment in the 1930s. ➤➤ crowding-out; fiscal policy.

defined-benefit pension ➤ pension funds.

defined-contribution pension ➤ pension funds.

deflation 1 A sustained reduction in the general level of prices. Deflation is often, though not inevitably, accompanied by declines in output and employment and is distinct from 'disinflation' which refers to a reduction in the rate of inflation. Deflation can be brought about by either internal or external forces in an ➤ open economy. Although uncommon in the second half of the twentieth century, there was deflation in the USA during the interwar years' ➤ Great Depression and it re-emerged in Japan following its stock exchange crash and collapse of its real-estate bubble after 1990.

The most obvious policy response to a deflation is to stimulate spending, to get demand up, so that prices stop falling and the economy stabilizes. Unfortunately, one of the biggest problems of a deflation is that the normal tool of monetary policy to increase spending and borrowing – lower interest rates – may be ineffective. If there is a deflation of 3 per cent, and if interest rates fall to zero, the *real* interest rate is still 3 per cent. This may not be low enough to promote spending and borrowing. Or, to put it another way, consumers will be inclined to postpone spending as long as they think prices will be lower in future than they are now. Further, they will not be inclined to borrow if they think that the debt they take out will be growing in ➤ real terms over time.

2 A deliberate policy of reducing ➤ aggregate demand and output so as to reduce the rate of ➤ inflation and the quantity of imports and lower the ➤ exchange rate, thus improving export performance and the ➤ balance of payments. Aggregate demand may be reduced by ➤ fiscal policy (increasing taxes or reducing government expenditure) or ➤ monetary policy (increases in the ➤ rate of interest and slower growth or contraction in the ➤ money supply).

3 In economic statistics, the adjustment of index numbers or economic aggregates to eliminate the effects of price changes, as in dividing an index of the ➤ Gross Domestic Product (GDP) at ➤ current prices by a price index (➤ index number) to give an index of GDP in ➤ real terms. In estimating changes in net output in real terms, there are two alternative methods: (a) to deflate the series of the value of net output at current prices by a single index of output prices, and (b) to deflate separately each particular input by its own appropriate price index, and to subtract the sum of these adjustments from the value of gross output deflated in the same way by indices of output prices. Method (b) is called *double deflation*, which has the advantage of capturing changes in the ratio of net to gross outputs in real terms. This may be important where, for example, profit margins are being squeezed by faster increases in input than in output prices. To deflate net output directly by output prices in these circumstances would lead to an overstatement of the real rise in net output.

deflationary gap A state of the economy in which there are unemployed resources and there is no inflationary pressure. It is a state first highlighted by ➤ Keynes, and in more modern literature identified as ➤ Keynesian unemployment, characterized by a chronic shortage of ➤ aggregate demand. More recently, the concept has been revived in mainstream economic policymaking, as the existence of a gap between actual ➤ Gross Domestic Product (GDP), and the economy's potential GDP (➤ output gap). ➤➤ inflationary gap; Keynesian economics.

deflator ➤ GDP deflator.

de-industrialization A decline in the share of manufacturing in ➤ national income. In the UK, the contribution of manufacturing to the ➤ Gross Domestic Product fell from 28 per cent in 1979 to 22 per cent in 1991, and to 12 per cent in 2004 (when it was 13 per cent in the US). Although a decline in the manufacturing ratio is common to most of the ➤ advanced countries and reflects the growth of ➤ services, fears have been expressed that, since manufactures constitute the bulk of exports, the process of decline could continue to the point where a large imbalance on ➤ visible trade could not be offset by the growth of invisible exports (➤ invisibles) without a decline in real income (➤ real terms). However, the decline of manufacturing is to some extent a statistical illusion, reflecting the growth of ➤ productivity in manufacturing compared with slower growth in output per person in the rest of the economy (➤ Baumol effect).

demand The desire for a particular good or ➤ service supported by the possession of the necessary means of exchange to effect ownership. ➤➤ demand, theory of; demand curve; Marshall, A.; money.

demand, theory of The area of economics concerned with the allocation of limited resources to different commodities in the purchasing decisions of rational consumers. Together with the theory of the ➤ firm (which is really a theory of supply), it forms the basis of ➤ microeconomics.

There are several different approaches to consumer behaviour: (a) the cardinal ➤ utility approach associated with ➤ Marshall and other economists of the nineteenth century; this was superseded by (b), ➤ indifference-curve analysis (➤ ordinal utility), which dispensed with the need for an absolute measure of utility; a third approach, (c), ➤ revealed preference, is largely a re-expression of indifference-curve analysis, in which no explicit notion of utility is used at all. All these approaches give rise to the same qualitative analysis of consumer behaviour and support the laws of demand and supply, such as that price rises lead to cuts in demand. ➤➤ demand function.

demand curve The graphical representation of a schedule listing the quantities of a commodity a consumer would be willing to buy at various prices. The schedule is drawn up on the assumption that other economic factors remain the same between the consideration of one price and another. Such factors are: (a) income; (b) prices of ➤ substitutes or ➤ complementary goods; and (c) consumer preferences or

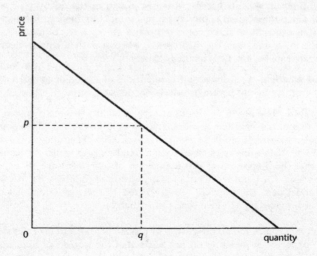

➤ expectations. In most cases, the curve would slope downwards from left to right, reflecting the fact that the higher the price of a commodity the lower the demand for it.

In the diagram, the quantity q would be demanded at the price p for a commodity with the demand curve shown. However, the slope and shape of the demand curve (see diagram) will depend on the response of demand to a change in price (➤➤ elasticity) in specific cases. ➤➤ demand, theory of; endogenous preferences; excess demand; income effect; indifference-curve analysis; substitution effect; supply curve.

demand deposit (US) Money on ➤ current account, i.e. a ➤ bank deposit that can be withdrawn without notice.

demand for labour ➤ labour, demand for.

demand function A mathematical expression of the relationship between the quantity of a good or service that is demanded, and changes in a number of economic factors, e.g. its price, the prices of ➤ substitutes and ➤ complementary goods, income, credit terms, etc. The quantity demanded is the ➤ dependent variable and the other factors are ➤ independent variables. The effect of each independent variable on the dependent variable may be estimated statistically by ➤ time-series analysis or ➤ cross-section analysis of ➤ household expenditure data. Also known as the Marshallian demand function. ➤➤ demand, theory of; demand curve; elasticity; Hicksian demand function.

demand management ➤ fiscal policy.

demand-pull inflation ➤ Inflation induced by a persistence of an excess of ➤ aggregate demand in the economy over ➤ aggregate supply. The balance of aggregate supply and demand does not reach ➤ equilibrium because supply reaches a capacity limit at the ➤ full employment level (➤➤ output gap). The excess demand probably persists because there is growth in the quantity of ➤ money either through the creation of money by government to finance the budgetary gap between its expenditure and income or because the quantity of money is allowed to expand to accommodate the rise in prices. ➤➤ cost-push inflation; Friedman, M.; inflationary gap; Keynes, J.M.; quantity theory of money.

demand schedule A list showing the quantities of a good or service a consumer would be willing to buy at various prices. ➤➤ demand curve.

demographic time bomb A reference to the possibility that many countries could face a crisis in the next few decades, caused by the ageing of their populations (➤ frequency distribution; population). Increased life expectancy and a declining ➤ birth rate, both sometimes allied with a trend towards earlier retirement, have meant that the proportion of the population of retirement age (➤ dependency ratio) is rising. The trend is evident in many advanced countries, e.g. the European Union and Japan. The problem has given rise to the suggestion that pensions should be provided on a funded basis rather than on a pay-as-you-go basis (➤ pension funds).

Governments may look more closely at private pensions to take the burden off public finance. Such measures do not mean that the workers of tomorrow avoid supporting the elderly; it simply means they support them from returns to savings rather than from extra tax revenue. Those who are not working in a society will always be dependent for their income on those who are working.

demography ➤ population.

Denison, Edward F. (1915–92) ➤ growth accounting.

dependency culture The phenomenon by which the granting of benefits to help those in adverse circumstances increases the likelihood of the recipients staying in adverse circumstances. Because such benefits are withdrawn from those whose incomes rise, they penalize those who make an effort to earn their way out of them, and therefore foster a reliance on such assistance. This analysis has been responsible for the introduction of more ➤ active labour-market policies, but the analysis does not simply have to apply to the impact of the benefits system – it can be used as a description of any perverse response by private agents to a well-intentioned government intervention aimed at helping them. Dependency culture can be seen as the application of the ➤ Lucas critique to an area of ➤ microeconomics in that it suggests that the existence of a policy towards a problem affects the relationship between the problem and its causes. ➤ poverty trap.

dependency ratio The dependency ratio is defined as the ratio of the total number of children (0–14 years of age) and/or pensioners to the working ➤ population, i.e. the number of people of non-working age in an economy, relative to those who are of working age. The term is used flexibly, sometimes referring to dependants of old age only, and sometimes to those either too old or too young to work. It is calculated by taking the ratio of non-working to working-age groups, and multiplying by 100 to give a percentage. The inverse is the support ratio.

According to United Nations statistics, Japan had the highest old-age dependency ratio of 35.1 per cent in 2010, compared with 26.2 per cent in the European Union, 11.4 per cent in China, 7.7 per cent in India and a world average of 11.6 per cent. ➤ frequency distribution; population; ➤➤ demographic time bomb.

dependent variable A ➤ variable whose value is conditional on the value of another variable. For example, if the quantity of butter a person buys falls or rises as the price of butter rises or falls, the quantity of butter is a variable depending on the movements in the (independent) variable price. ➤➤ econometrics; endogenous variable.

depletion theory The branch of economics concerned with the rate at which natural resources are consumed over time. Economists view abstinence from using up a resource as a form of investment in that more is available to consume in the future, just as investment in machines today will produce consumer goods tomorrow. For instance, if the price of an asset is expected to rise by 10 per cent over the next year, and the market rate of interest is 5 per cent, it will pay to keep the asset in the ground. If, however, the price is expected to rise by 5 per cent and the interest rate is 10 per cent, it will pay to sell the asset now and invest the proceeds at 10 per cent. The fundamental principle of depletion theory is that consumption should occur at a rate which ensures that profits to be made from not depleting stocks of the resource are equal to those from other forms of investment. In reality, extraction costs and many other factors throw into question whether the principle explains either how quickly stocks of resources do get depleted, or how quickly they ought to (➤ environmental economics; natural resources).

deposit Money placed in an account at a bank and constituting a claim on the bank. The term 'bank deposit' includes deposits on all types of account, including ➤ current accounts. ➤➤ banking.

deposit account An account with a ➤ bank, ➤ building society or other financial institution in which ➤ deposits earn ➤ interest, and withdrawals from which may require notice. Until 1971, interest was paid by the bank at a rate fixed by agreement between the clearing banks and normally 2 per cent below ➤ bank rate. Since that date, banks have been obliged to fix their rates individually and now offer a range of deposit accounts to compete with the remaining building societies and other ➤ financial intermediaries. Deposit accounts are called *time deposits* in the USA and *savings accounts* in France and other continental European countries. ➤➤ banking.

depreciation 1 The reduction in ➤ value of an ➤ asset through wear and tear. An allowance for the depreciation on a company's assets is always made before the calculation of ➤ profit, on the grounds that the consumption of ➤ capital assets is one of the costs of earning the revenues of the business and is allowed as such, according to special rules, by the tax authorities. Since depreciation can be measured accurately only at the end of the life of an asset (i.e. ➤ *ex ante*), depreciation provisions in company accounts require an estimate of both the total amount of depreciation and the asset life. Annual depreciation provisions are normally calculated according to two methods: (a) the *straight-line method*, where the estimated residual (e.g. scrap) value of an asset is deducted from its original cost and the balance divided by the number of years of estimated life to arrive at an annual depreciation expense to set against revenue; and (b) the *reducing-balance method*, in which the actual depreciation expense is set at a constant proportion of the depreciated value of the asset, i.e. a diminishing annual absolute amount.

There are other methods of calculating depreciation and also of dealing with the fact that, in periods of rising prices, the replacement cost of an asset may be very much greater than its original cost. This latter problem is dealt with by revaluing assets at intervals, or even annually, using special capital-cost indices and adjusting depreciation charges accordingly. This is called *replacement-cost depreciation* as opposed to *historic-cost depreciation* (➤ costs, historical or historic; inflation accounting) when the original cost of purchase is retained throughout the period.

It should be noted that ➤ obsolescence is distinct from depreciation in that the former is an unforeseen change in the value of an asset for technological or economic reasons. If an asset becomes obsolescent, its undepreciated value is usually written off (depreciated) completely in the year of replacement. In some cases, the life of an asset may be very difficult to determine because it is specific to the production of a product, the demand for which is subject to rapid changes in taste or fashion, i.e. there is a high risk of product obsolescence. In these cases, the life of the asset is written off over a very short period.

The purpose of depreciation provisions in accounting is to ensure that the cost of the flow of services provided by capital assets is met in the price of the company's products – it is not for the purpose of building up funds for the replacement of these assets to be available at a certain date. In practice, depreciation provisions are treated as part of the net ➤ cash flow of a business and are used to repay ➤ loans, to purchase other fixed assets, or to invest in other businesses, i.e. they are put to the use that will give the highest possible return. Much confusion is caused on this point, since what happens to depreciation provisions – which are, in effect, transfers of funds from fixed assets to current assets and sometimes back again – is not often clear from the ➤ balance sheet. ➤➤ Amortization; sources and uses of funds.

Depreciation is accepted for tax purposes as a charge against profits, but this depreciation has to be calculated according to certain rules and does not necessarily bear any relation to the depreciation actually charged by the business in its accounts. ➤➤ capital allowances.

2 A reduction in the value of a ➤ currency in terms of gold or other currencies under ➤ free-market conditions and coming about through a decline in the ➤ demand for that currency in relation to the supply. ➤ currency depreciation.

depreciation at choice ➤ capital allowances.

depression A severe fall, persisting for more than the two successive quarters, in ➤ Gross Domestic Product which defines a ➤ recession. The most serious was the ➤ Great Depression in the 1930s which saw major declines in output, prices, investment and international trade and the collapse of financial institutions. There was a consequential loss of employment so that, for instance, the ➤➤ unemployment rate in the USA rose to 26 per cent among industrial workers as Gross Domestic Product fell by 30 per cent. Prices and international trade collapsed by over 20 per cent, particularly affecting ➤ developing countries relying on exports of primary products, prices of which in Latin America, for instance, fell by 50 per cent. ➤➤ business cycle; Friedman, M.; Keynes, J.M.

deregulation The process of reducing the burden of government controls in a sector of the economy generally focusing on those that have the effect of creating ➤ barriers to entry. The goal of deregulation initiatives – which were particularly important in the 1990s – is generally to promote competition in areas previously considered to be ➤ natural monopolies, or in areas in which regulation appeared to have long outlived its original rationale (➤ regulated utilities). Deregulation is distinct from ➤ privatization which, especially in the case of the natural monopolies, has to be followed by new ➤ regulation. Deregulation in any of a variety of forms has affected a substantial area of economic life in much of the developed world, from financial services (➤ Big Bang; Glass-Steagall Act) to those manufacturing sectors subject to international competition and to sectors primarily under government ownership. Apparent success in sectors such as telecommunications worldwide, and intercity coach travel in the UK, has not been matched in every area. For example in the case of the deregulated US airline sector, prices are low and activity high but the impact has been marred by a constant flow of bankruptcies. There has been a concern that global deregulation has led producers to operate under such tight competitive constraints that normal social obligations are being neglected, and that jobs are insecure (➤ downsizing). Nevertheless, many economists believe that, although deregulation was seen as a policy complementary to ➤ privatization, it was the more important of the pair.

derivatives A generic term for instruments derived from conventional direct dealings in securities, currencies and commodities. In the markets for derivatives an important distinction is between the ➤ over-the-counter market (OTC) in which tailor-made contracts are made directly between parties and the standardized ones traded on formal exchanges such as the Chicago Mercantile Exchange (CME) and the ➤ London International Financial Futures Exchange. The OTC derivatives, which are largely unregulated, are by far the largest market of the two but both have grown considerably, especially in the 1990s and into the new millennium. The OTC market has become dominated by trade in ➤ swaps and is handled chiefly by a relatively small number of banks. It is estimated by the ➤ Bank for International Settlements that the OTC derivatives business amounted to $604.6 trillion in 2009.

Derivatives are of various kinds and include ➤ futures, ➤ options and ➤ swaps. They are used by large companies, such as airlines, to ➤ hedge against changes in exchange rates, oil prices and other commodities and interest rates, that is to say, to shift risk to others, mainly banks and insurers, that are willing to bear them (at a cost). This is a valuable function and the sellers of derivatives can shift some of the risk to other institutions. However it seems that the risks were underestimated for conditions like those following the collapse of property markets in 2007–8 in which several major financial institutions failed.

One of these failures was American International Group (AIG) which had a vast business in selling protection from credit risk, especially in the form of insuring *Collateralized Debt Obligations* (CDOs). CDOs are asset-based securities backed by bundles of securitized debt obligations, such as home mortgages (➤ securitization). When property prices plummeted, the value of the collateral also fell. Regulators want more derivatives to shift to the formal exchanges and also for greater use to be made of *central counterparties* (CCPs) which would guarantee execution of derivatives contracts, just as they do in the ➤ clearing houses for ➤ stock exchange trading.

derived demand The demand for a ➤ factor of production in which the demand for the factor is derived indirectly from the demand for the finished product to which the factor has contributed in production. ➤➤ labour, demand for.

destination principle ➤ value-added tax.

devaluation The reduction of the fixed official rate at which one ➤ currency is exchanged for another (➤ currency depreciation) in a fixed ➤ exchange rate regime. Currencies were in such regimes for much of the second half of the twentieth century, particularly under the arrangements agreed at the ➤ Bretton Woods conference and in Europe under the European Monetary System. Apart from such general schemes, individual countries may opt to fix their currency's exchange rate. For example, Argentina, in 1991, based its monetary policy on a ➤ currency board and a fixed rate of exchange of 1 peso to 1 $US. This regime lasted until 2002, when the peso was first devalued and then left to float (➤ exchange rate).

There are three basic situations which lead to devaluation: (a) persistent ➤ balance of payments deficits; (b) a period of high ➤ inflation; and (c) diversion between the economic activity of the country and the other members of the fixed rate region. In (a) and (b) the devaluation helps the exporting sector of the economy at the expense of the non-tradable sector. For example, it works to reduce a deficit, because devaluation makes prices (in foreign currencies) of exports cheaper and the domestic price of imports more expensive. (The immediate effect, however, is similar to an unfavourable change in the ➤ terms of trade (➤ J-curve).) Similarly, with high inflation, prices (in foreign currencies) of exports rise and demand for the country's exports falls, unless the exchange rate falls to make the prices competitive again. If a country is a member of a fixed exchange-rate area, economic policy differences lead to devaluation. For example, if one country is ➤ overheating, while another is deflating (➤ deflation), then a looser ➤ monetary policy is required in the former. Under fixed exchange rates, it is not possible for monetary authorities to fix both the ➤ rate of interest and the ➤ exchange rate independently – fixing one implies some rate of the other. The country requiring a looser policy needs to devalue until policies converge. In effect, all three causes of devaluation are the same: a need to restore domestic balance (neither overheating, nor deflation) while also maintaining a reasonable balance between the exporting and non-exporting sector.

developing countries Countries which have not achieved a level of economic development comparable to that of the most advanced or developed countries. There is no specific definition of such a country and it is left to an individual country to choose to be so defined, subject only to the approval of other members of the ➤ World Trade Organization (WTO). On the other hand, there are more specific criteria for membership of the 'least developed' group. To become a member, a country must have a ➤ Gross Domestic Product (GDP) per head below a specified level and must leave the group when its GDP per head passes a specified upper limit. It must record a low Human Assets Index (HAI) (➤ Human Development Index) and a low Economic Vulnerability Index (EVI), which includes variables such as the volatility of agricultural output and trade, the share of primary production in GDP and the frequency of natural disasters. Membership of these groups entitles member countries to benefit from some relaxation in the terms of any WTO international agreements. For instance, an extension of the period of transition for the implementation of internationally agreed import tariff reductions.

After 2000, developing countries benefited from the growth in ➤ international trade supported by a rise in commodity prices and an easing of their tax burden by low ➤ rates of interest and grew on average about two and a half times faster than the developed countries. As a result their share of world output rose from about 36 per cent to about 43 per cent in the decade. ➤➤ economic development; poverty; Rostow, W.W.

development assistance Also referred to as foreign aid. The administered transfer of resources from the ➤ advanced countries for the purpose of encouraging economic growth in the ➤ developing countries (➤ economic growth, stages of). Funds transferred to the developing countries from governments and international institutions (➤ International Bank for Reconstruction and Development) in the form of official aid account for about one third of the total transfer of funds to the developing countries (the rest is accounted for by loans through the ➤ commercial banks and ➤ foreign investment). Official aid from the advanced countries represented in the ➤ Organization for Economic Cooperation and Development's Development Assistance Committee (DAC) amounted to $121 billion in 2008, 0.31 per cent of their total ➤ gross national income (GNI). Aid from the DAC members is expected to reach 0.33 per cent of their aggregate GNI in 2010; the USA and

Japan at 0.20 per cent, the EU at 0.48 per cent and the UK at 0.56 per cent. ➤ export credit insurance; export incentives; foreign direct investment; generalized system of preferences.

development economics ➤ economic development.

Development Finance Institution (DFI) An institution devoted to financing and guiding ➤ economic development such as the ➤ African Development Bank, the ➤ Asian Development Bank, the ➤ Caribbean Development Bank and the Inter-American Development Bank. These are examples of multilateral DFIs but some are also established on a national basis.

differentiation, product Distinguishing essentially the same products from one another by real or illusory means, as in petrol, washing powder, cigarettes. The significance of product differentiation in economic theory is that by relaxing the assumption of product homogeneity under ➤ perfect competition, each supplier may create an opportunity to depart from the market price, charge a premium for his product and make greater ➤ profits. Under perfect competition, this supplier would sell nothing if he raised the price above market levels (he faces a horizontal ➤ demand curve); with product differentiation he may be able to build up some loyalty from his customers (and introduce a downward slope to the demand curve, which is a characteristic of ➤ monopolistic competition). The means by which suppliers differentiate their products may involve improved product performance and ➤ innovation (e.g. radial-ply tyres which, though more expensive initially than conventional tyres, have a longer life) or they may be restricted to ➤ advertising and packaging. In business economics, differentiation is seen as one of two important strategic directions, the other being leadership through volume sales and low cost.

diminishing marginal product ➤ diminishing returns, law of.

diminishing marginal utility The psychological law that, as extra units of a commodity are consumed by an individual, the satisfaction gained from each unit will fall. For example, although for every extra Mars bar someone eats they derive extra pleasure, the more Mars that are eaten, the less pleasure is gained from each incremental one. Eventually, as sickness strikes, subsequently consumed Mars bars will yield disutility.

The approach to consumer theory that uses the notion of diminishing marginal utility is flawed, as there is no single unit or scale by which the utility derived from a wide range of items can be measured (➤➤ ordinal utility). Nevertheless, the concept remains relevant to many issues, especially when applied to consumption in general. For example, it provides a case against a poll tax (➤ local taxation) which, it shows, cuts the utility of the poor (who treasure their every possession) more than the rich (who hardly notice small losses). It also explains why people may like to avoid risk: the utility lost from a $100 cut in income is greater than the utility gained by a $100 increase in income and, consequently, most consumers would reject a fair bet in which they were faced with a 50 per cent chance of either, despite the fact that on average they would lose nothing in cash terms. ➤ behavioural economics; ➤➤ endogenous preferences; marginal utility; risk aversion.

diminishing returns, law of A law that states that, as extra units of one ➤ factor of production are employed, with all others held constant, the output generated by each additional unit will eventually fall. In effect, that the ➤ marginal product of factors declines when they are employed in increasing quantities. For example, a farm owner with one field might find that one man could produce 2 tons of grain; two men 5 tons of grain – more than twice as much – but three men only 7 tons of grain. The extra production gained from adding a worker started at 2, rose to 3, then fell back to 2.

Diminishing returns should not be confused with negative returns. Successively adding workers to a factory can increase its total output but at a falling rate; only when the factory becomes very overcrowded would the presence of an extra worker actually cause production to fall. ➤➤ diseconomies of scale; returns to scale; short-run cost curves; Turgot, A.R.J.

direct costs ➤ variable costs.

direct investment ➤ foreign direct investment.

direct taxation ➤ Taxation on the income and resources of individuals or organizations. In general, direct taxation (➤ income tax, corporation tax, inheritance tax, local taxation, National Insurance) is levied on ➤ wealth or ➤ income and is in contrast to *indirect taxation* (➤ value added tax, ➤ excise duties, betting duties, vehicle licence duties, stamp duty) which is levied on expenditure. Direct taxation accounts for over two thirds of UK general government tax receipts. It was argued that a shift in favour of indirect taxation would improve incentives for higher earnings and capital accumulation; however, that process, which occurred substantially in the UK in the 1980s and 1990s, can make the tax system more regressive (➤ regressive tax) and may also distort ➤ resource allocation. The categorization of direct and indirect taxation is not as precise as it may appear because it tells us nothing about the incidence of taxation (➤ taxation, incidence of). ➤➤ expenditure tax; fiscal neutrality; marginal tax rate.

dirty float ➤ managed currency.

disclosure requirements ➤ private company.

discount Generally meaning a deduction from ➤ face value, i.e. the opposite of ➤ premium. Discount has a number of specific applications in economics and commerce: (a) a discount for cash is a percentage deductible from an invoice as an incentive for the debtor to pay within a defined period; (b) a deduction from the retail price of a good allowed to a wholesaler, retailer or other agent; (c) a charge made for cashing a ➤ bill of exchange or other promissory note before its maturity date; and (d) the difference, where negative, between the present price of a ➤ security and its issue price. ➤➤ discounting; present value.

discounted cash flow (d.c.f.) ➤ present value.

discount house A UK institution, no longer in existence, that dealt in the ➤ money market. The term ceased to be used after 1997 as a result of a new policy of the ➤ Bank of England to influence interest rates via ➤ gilt repos.

discounting 1 The application of a discount or ➤ rate of interest to a ➤ capital sum or title to such a sum. Calculations of ➤ present value or the price of a bill before maturity are made by discounting at the current appropriate rate of interest.
    2 The future effects of an anticipated decline or increase in ➤ profits or some

other event on ➤ security prices, commodity prices, or ➤ exchange rates. These are said to be discounted if buying or selling leads to an adjustment of present prices in line with expected future changes in these prices.

3 The pledging of accounts receivable (i.e. sums owed by debtors), as ➤ collateral security against a ➤ loan. ➤➤ discount.

discount rate ➤ bank rate; discounting.

discriminating duty An import duty (➤ tariffs, import) imposed at a level different from other comparable import duties so as to favour (or discourage) the importation of a particular commodity or imports from a country of origin. ➤➤ customs union; most-favoured nation clause; World Trade Organization.

discriminating monopoly A company with some degree of ➤ market power, and able to charge different prices for its output in the different markets. ➤➤ price discrimination.

diseconomies of scale Increase in long-run ➤ average costs which may set in as the scale of production increases. Although the unit cost of production may fall as plant size increases (➤ economies of scale), there are several reasons why this process is eventually reversed:

(1) The different processes within a plant will probably not have the same optimum scale. For example, a car-body press might be at its most efficient at 150,000 units a year, while an engine transfer machining line may be optimal at 100,000 units a year. When 150,000 cars are produced, it will be necessary either to have a suboptimal engine line with a capacity of 50,000 in addition, or to run a second line at 50 per cent capacity.

(2) As firm size increases, problems of administration and coordination increase and there is a growth of bureaucracy.

(3) If output for a national or international market is concentrated at one large plant in a single location, transport costs of raw materials and finished goods to and from distant markets may offset scale economies of production at the large plant.

These are *internal diseconomies*. *External diseconomies* are said to arise as a geographic region sees larger-scale production – these might include traffic congestion or pollution, for example (➤ externalities). Diseconomies of scale are not to be confused with diminishing returns (➤ diminishing returns, law of). ➤➤ returns to scale.

disequilibrium A state in which the forces influencing a system are not in balance and there is a tendency for one or more ➤ variables in the system to change. The system may be static or dynamic and subject to ➤ stochastic processes. The operation of some mechanism or process is central to the concept of disequilibrium, as it is this that drives the system variables to move. The direction of movement caused by a process in most applications is towards a state of equilibrium, but this need not be the case. ➤➤ business cycles; ➤ dynamics; equilibrium; stability analysis.

disguised unemployment A situation in which more people are available for work than is shown in the ➤ unemployment statistics. Married women, some students or prematurely retired persons may decide to register for work only if they believe opportunities are available to them. Also referred to as *concealed unemployment* and the 'discouraged worker effect'. Disguised unemployment will be revealed in an unusually low ➤ participation rate. The term has become less relevant with the wider use of surveys. ➤ ILO unemployment; Labour Force Survey; minimum wage.

dishoarding The reduction of stocks of goods or money previously accumulated by ➤ hoarding.

disinflation The reduction or elimination of ➤ inflation. ➤➤ deflation.

disintermediation Flows of funds between borrowers and lenders avoiding the direct use of ➤ financial intermediaries. Companies, for example, may lend surplus funds to each other without the use of the banking system or may issue bills guaranteed (accepted) by the banks but sold to non-banks.

Disintermediation may make it more difficult to measure and control the ➤ money supply since the authorities' measures to do so are focused upon financial intermediaries who can avoid controls based upon deposits by lending through parallel ➤ money markets. The use of financial intermediaries for lending and borrowing activities previously carried out outside them (i.e. the opposite of disintermediation) is called *re-intermediation*. ➤➤ securitization.

disinvestment Negative investment which occurs where part of the capital stock is destroyed or where gross ➤ investment is less than ➤ capital consumption, i.e. capital equipment is not replaced as it wears out. Antonym for ➤ investment. ➤➤ divestment.

disposable income Total ➤ income of households less ➤ income tax and employee social security contributions ➤ National Insurance.

dissaving Negative ➤ saving, i.e. ➤ consumption in excess of ➤ income. Dissaving is financed either by the running down of ➤ assets or by borrowing, and results in a reduction in *net worth*. ➤ balance sheet; ➤➤ public sector financial deficit.

distribution, theory of Explanation of the determination of the ➤ incomes of the ➤ factors of production. The theory of distribution is actually part of the more comprehensive theory of production and distribution (➤ production, theory of), since in their determination, output and factor prices are interdependent. It is one of the oldest branches of economic theory (➤ Marx, K.; Ricardo, D.) but today is still dominated by the basic theoretical structure of ➤ neo-classical economics.

In the first part of this theory, the incomes of ➤ land, ➤ labour and ➤ capital are determined by the ➤ supply and ➤ demand for them, which in turn is a ➤ derived demand for ➤ commodities. In the market for the factors of production, the owners of the factors will seek to maximize their incomes and the purchasers (firms) will seek to maximize their ➤ profit from the use of the factors in the production process. Firms will adjust their output and their employment of each factor to the point where the ➤ marginal cost and ➤ marginal revenue of each additional unit of the factor are equal. This equilibrium quantity and equilibrium price will be determined by supply and demand. For example, shortages of computer programmers will tend to push up their incomes. On the other hand, if there are more programmers than jobs, their incomes will fall. The theory does not state, it should be noted, that a computer programmer will receive his/her marginal product (the amount he/she personally adds to the employer's revenue), but the increase in output that would arise from the employment of one additional programmer if inputs of all other factors of production were held constant. Profit maximization and competition between them should, in theory, ensure that factor incomes equate to their marginal products. ➤ marginal productivity theory of wages. This is how the first part of the theory explains the reward to the factors of production.

The second part of the theory describes the share of total output accruing to different groups, e.g. the amount going to workers equals the wage rate multiplied by the number of workers employed. When the number of workers increases, the ➤ marginal product of labour is assumed to fall and the wage level will fall, but as the total number of workers has risen, the share of output going to labour may not fall.

The third part of the theory holds that with total output divided up in this way between the different groups, there will be nothing short and nothing over. This is, in fact, true in conditions of perfect competition with constant returns to scale or zero profits (➤ Euler, L.).

For these reasons, alternative theories to replace each part of the traditional account have been developed. In the first part, wage bargaining is viewed as occurring outside perfectly competitive markets with collective bargaining by ➤ trade unions. In the second part, shares of national income have been explained in terms of the distribution necessary to maintain ➤ balanced growth in a macroeconomic approach associated with Nicholas Kaldor. In the third part, the existence of monopoly profits suggests that some portion of total output does not accrue to workers, investors or property owners, but to those fortunate enough to be in monopoly industries. ➤ bargaining theory of wages; ➤➤ Cobb–Douglas function.

diversification 1 Extending the range of goods and services in a firm or geographic region. The motives for diversification will include declining profitability or growth in traditional markets, surplus capital or management resources and a desire to spread risks and reduce dependence upon cyclical activities. Diversification has accounted for a significant proportion of the growth of ➤ multinational corporations, though more recently competitive pressures have encouraged large corporations to return to core businesses and dispose of unwanted subsidiaries. This process has been called ➤ downsizing or ➤ divestment. The means of diversification are either internal growth or ➤ merger. By definition, a ➤ conglomerate is a diversified firm.

2 The holding of shares in a range of firms in a ➤ portfolio in order to spread the risk. ➤➤ capital asset pricing model; portfolio theory; risk.

divestment The liquidation or sale of parts of a firm. Divestment is, in effect, the opposite of acquisition or ➤ merger.

dividend The amount of a company's ➤ profits that the board of directors decides to distribute to ordinary shareholders. It is usually expressed either as a percentage of the ➤ nominal value of the ➤ ordinary share capital, or as an absolute amount per ➤ share. For example, if a company has an issued ➤ capital of $100,000 in 400,000 25-cent ordinary shares and the directors decide to distribute $10,000, then they would declare a dividend of 10 per cent or 2.5 cents per share. A dividend is only the same as a ➤ yield if the shares stand at their nominal value. Some shareholders may not have bought their shares at ➤ par value and might have paid, say, 50 cents each for them, in which case the yield would not be 10 but 5 per cent.

Dividends are declared at general meetings of the shareholders. Interim dividends are part payments of the annual dividend made during the year. Dividends are paid out of profits for the current year or, if profits are inadequate but the directors consider that a dividend is justified, out of reserves from profits of previous years. The profits after tax from which dividends are paid are those after payments to holders of ➤ preference shares and ➤ debentures have been allowed for, the balance being split between dividends and reserves.

There has been much discussion of whether the rate of ➤ investment could be raised if companies paid out fewer dividends, as that would leave more cash to invest.

dividend cover The number of times the net ➤ profits available for distribution exceed the ➤ dividend actually paid or declared. For example, if a company's net profits are $100,000 and the dividend was $5000, the dividend cover would be 20. It is the inverse of the payout ratio.

dividend warrant The ➤ cheque by which companies pay ➤ dividends to shareholders.

dividend yield ➤ yield.

divisia money ➤ money supply.

division of labour The allocation of labour such that each worker specializes in one or a few functions in the production process. ➤ Smith illustrated the principle in the different stages of pin-making: drawing the wire, cutting, head-fitting, sharpening. The division improved labour productivity: (a) by the more efficient acquiring of specialist skills, and (b) through the saving of time because workers did not have to move from one operation to another. Through the division of labour ➤ economies of scale could be achieved. The exchange economy was essential to its operation. Each worker could so specialize as long as he was assured that he could exchange his output for others to satisfy his needs. The principle applies to firms and countries also: similar benefits may be achieved by the specialization in those activities in which the firm or country has a ➤ comparative advantage. ➤➤ Ricardo, D.

Doha Round of Trade Negotiations Agreement was reached at Doha, Qatar, in 2001 to launch a further round of international trade negotiations, and the first meeting of the ➤ World Trade Organization's Trade Negotiations Committee was held in January 2002. Although many aspects were to be a carry-over of the work of the ➤ Uruguay Round of Trade Negotiations, special consideration was to be given to the needs of the ➤ developing countries. Improvements in market access were to be sought in agriculture, services and industry, through, for example, a reduction in agricultural subsidies and industrial tariffs. No final conclusion to the negotiations had been reached by the beginning of 2011. ➤ farm subsidies; protection; Regional Trade Agreements; trade promotion authority.

dollar certificate of deposit ➤ Eurocurrency.

domestic credit expansion (DCE) A measure of monetary growth that allows for changes in the ➤ balance of payments. It is equal to the public sector borrowing requirement minus public sector borrowing from the domestic non-bank private sector plus the increase in bank lending to the private sector in domestic currency at home and overseas. The significance of the DCE, a measure favoured by the ➤ International Monetary Fund, is that it nets out changes in the ➤ money supply created by overseas capital flows on capital and the current account of the balance of payments. ➤➤ monetary policy.

dominant strategy A course of action that is best pursued whatever it is that other agents choose to do. It is a concept of ➤ game theory, applied to situations in which players choose from a selection of strategies, taking into account the response and behaviour of fellow players. The best-known dominant strategy is to 'confess' in the ➤ prisoner's dilemma game. The strategy to 'not confess' is *dominated*. In most situations, there are no dominant or dominated strategies; the best strategy will depend on what the other side chooses to do. ➤➤ tit-for-tat.

dominated strategy A course of action that would not make sense whatever other agents chose to do. ➤➤ dominant strategy.

Dornbusch, Rudiger (1942–2002) ➤ exchange rate overshooting.

double deflation ➤ deflation.

double-entry bookkeeping The accounting system in which every business transaction, whether a receipt or a payment of ➤ money, sale or purchase of goods or ➤ services, gives rise to two entries – a debit and a corresponding credit – traditionally on opposite pages of a ledger. The credit entries record the sources of finance (e.g. shareholders' ➤ capital, funds acquired from third parties or generated through current operations); the debit entries record the use to which that finance is put, e.g. acquisition of fixed ➤ assets, ➤ stocks, financing of debtors and current operating expenses, etc. Since every debit entry has an equal and corresponding credit entry, it follows that if the debit and credit entries are added up they will (or should) come to the same figure, i.e. balance (➤ balance sheet). Confusion is caused by identifying credits and debits with gains or losses. While this is basically true in the very long run, the profit or loss over a short period of time is measured by selecting from ledger balances items of income and expenditure that are then used to produce a *profit and loss account* (in the USA = *income and earned surplus statement*). ➤➤ balance of payments; business finance.

double option ➤ option.

double taxation The situation in which the same ➤ tax base is taxed more than once. Double-taxation agreements between two countries are designed to avoid, for example, ➤ incomes of non-residents being taxed both in the country they are living in and in their country of origin. Many proponents of an ➤ expenditure tax argue that its main advantage is to avoid double taxation of savings.

Dow-Jones industrial average A daily index (➤ index number) of prices on the principal ➤ stock exchanges in the USA. It is an ➤ average of the prices of thirty shares quoted on the ➤ New York Stock Exchange and ➤ NASDAQ. The ➤ stocks include both manufacturing companies such as IBM and Kraft Foods and service sector companies such as Walmart and McDonald's. It is calculated and published every day the exchange is open. In its present form the index dates from 1928.

downsizing Large-scale shedding of employees by major corporations, sometimes also used to refer to the disposal of subsidiaries and other unwanted activities. Downsizing is generally a response to pressures from competition, or investors, to reduce costs and may in some cases reflect long-delayed reaction to technological change which allows output to be maintained with fewer employees. In a dynamic and changing economy some firms will be reducing and others gaining employment, but redundancies by large firms attract more attention than widespread employment gains among smaller firms. Critics point out that the quality of jobs lost in large corporations, in terms of salaries, pensions and other benefits, is superior to that in employment gained in smaller firms, but this might suggest the existence of ➤ economic rent.

drawback ➤ customs drawback.

duality An area of mathematics, sometimes used in economics, in which essentially the same optimization problem can be framed in two different ways. For example, the problem of maximizing ➤ utility given prices and income can also be seen as a problem of minimizing the cost of obtaining the level of utility that would be achieved. This can be useful for the economist trying to observe consumer behaviour if the cost-minimizing problem is easier to frame than the utility-maximizing one. ➤➤ envelope theorem.

dummy variable A variable in ➤ regression analysis that takes a value of 1 or 0, depending on whether some particular characteristic applies to the observation. For example, in a regression that measured the relationship between weight and height, there might be a gender dummy which takes a value of 1 for men, and 0 for women. This would take account of the possible fact that, on average, a man of the same height as a woman may weigh more.

dumping Strictly, the sale of a ➤ commodity on a foreign ➤ market at a ➤ price below ➤ marginal cost. An exporting country may support the short-run losses of this policy in order to eliminate competition and thereby gain a ➤ monopoly in the foreign market. Alternatively, it may dump in order to dispose of temporary surpluses in order to avoid a reduction in home prices and therefore producers' ➤ incomes. The international trade regulations developed under the ➤ General Agreement on Tariffs and Trade and its successor, the ➤ World Trade Organization (WTO), approves the imposition of special import duties (➤ tariffs, import) to counteract such a policy if it can be established that dumping is taking place and is harming a domestic industry. Under WTO regulations, if products are sold in a foreign market below the price at which they are sold on the home market, dumping is deemed to take place. The number of initiations of new anti-dumping investigations fell from a peak of 366 in 2001 to 163 in 2007 but rose to 208 in 2008. ➤ contingent protection; free trade; protection.

duopoly Two sellers only of a good or service in a market. A decision by one seller, such as the raising or lowering of his price, will be likely to stimulate a response from the other which, in turn, will affect the market response to the first seller's initial decision. Depending on assumptions made about the market and each seller's responses, price ➤ equilibrium may exist at any point between that of a ➤ monopoly and that of ➤ perfect competition (➤ Bertrand competition; Cournot, A.A.). ➤➤ game theory; oligopoly.

duopsony Two buyers only of a good or service in a market.

Dupuit, Arsène Jules Étienne Juvénal (1804–66) A French civil engineer, whose main works relating to economics were *De la mesure de l'utilité des travaux publics* (1844) and *De l'influence des péages sur l'utilité des voies de communication* (1849). His studies of the pricing policy for public services such as roads and bridges led him to the concepts of ➤ consumer surplus and ➤ producer surplus. These terms were, in fact, invented by ➤ Marshall, but the ideas were clearly expounded by Dupuit. He realized that the prices were not the maximum users would be willing to pay for services, except those users at the very margin who found it just worth while to pay. Consumers, therefore, benefited by the difference. Similarly, the producer selling the service obtains a surplus in so far as his fixed charge is related to his cost at the margin (➤ marginal cost) and this is greater than his ➤ average cost.

durable goods Consumer goods like washing-machines, motor cars and TV sets, which yield ➤ services or ➤ utility over time rather than being completely used up at the moment of ➤ consumption. Most consumer goods are, in fact, durable to some degree, and the term is often used in a more restricted sense to denote relatively expensive, technologically sophisticated goods – 'consumer durables' – such as the examples given above. The significance of the durability of these goods is that the conventional apparatus of demand analysis must be supplemented by the modes of analysis developed in ➤ capital theory (➤ demand, theory of).

dynamics Analysis that aims to trace and study the behaviour of variables through time, and determine whether these variables tend to move towards ➤ equilibrium. Although the word 'dynamic' is used rather loosely, it safely describes any analysis which gives an account of the process by which equilibrium is achieved, or disequilibrium sustained. An example of dynamic analysis is ➤ optimal-growth theory, which traces the path an economy should follow to maximize the ➤ present value of consumption over time. In contrast to ➤ comparative static equilibrium analysis, dynamics does not just specify the conditions that prevail when the economy is in equilibrium, or whether it is in a satisfactory equilibrium or unsatisfactory one. It traces the optimal path towards an equilibrium.

dynamic stochastic general equilibrium model A macroeconometric ➤➤ model of the interrelationships between ➤ variables in an economy enabling the long-run implications of particular government interventions to be evaluated. It is dynamic in that it attempts to follow the path of an economy over time and the long-term implications of policy decisions. It is ➤ stochastic in that it allows for the influence of random events. Finally, the assumption of general equilibrium reflects the interrelationships between economic agents and the clearing of markets at accepted prices. These models have been the bases for economic advice to governments and central banks. They have been criticized for their preoccupation with the real or physical structure of economies at the expense of awareness of the implications of the impact of the evolution of financial systems. ➤ Arrow-Debreu general equilibrium model; general equilibrium analysis; ➤➤ macroeconomics.

E

earnings **1** The return for human effort, as in the earnings of ➤ labour and the earnings of management. In labour economics, wage earnings are distinguished from wage rates; the former include overtime, the latter relate only to earnings per hour or standard working week. Earnings may be quoted as pre- or post-tax (gross or net) and other deductions and in ➤ real terms or money terms.

2 The ➤ income of a business, part of which may be retained in the business and part distributed to the shareholders (➤ retained earnings). Earnings per ➤ share (post-tax), which is a measure of the total return earned by a company on its ➤ ordinary share capital, are calculated by taking gross income after ➤ depreciation, ➤ interest, ➤ preference shares and minority interests, deducting tax and dividing the resulting figure by the number of ordinary shares. Note that earnings per share are normally higher than the ➤ dividend per share. For example, a firm may earn 10 cents per share but may only pay a 5-cent or 20 per cent dividend on its 25-cent ordinary shares.

earnings before interest, taxes, depreciation and amortization (EBITDA) One of a number of ➤ financial ratios used in the analysis of company accounts. EBITDA is an approximation to gross corporate ➤ cash flow before payment of ➤ interest on ➤ debt, ➤ taxation, ➤ depreciation and ➤ amortization. It can be easily calculated from income statements.

earnings yield ➤ yield.

East African Community The original East African Community failed in 1977 but was revived by a treaty signed in 1999 and the new Community of Tanzania, Uganda and Kenya came into operation in 2001, with Rwanda and Burundi joining in 2007. A Secretariat, East African Legislative Assembly and Court of Justice have been established. The elimination of import tariffs between members and the setting up of a common external tariff was achieved by 2010. Following the formation of a ➤ customs union and common market, the longer-term aim is for a monetary union. ➤ Common Market for Eastern and Southern Africa; Economic Community of West African States.

EBITDA ➤ earnings before interest, taxes, depreciation and amortization.

e-commerce ➤ electronic commerce.

econometric models The representation of a relationship between economic variables as an equation or set of equations in which statistical precision can be attributed to the ➤ parameters linking the variables. ➤➤ econometrics; model.

econometrics The setting-up of mathematical ➤ models describing economic relationships (e.g. that the quantity demanded of a good is dependent positively on income and negatively on price), testing the validity of such hypotheses (➤ statistical inference) and estimating the ➤ parameters in order to obtain a measure of the strengths of the influences of the different independent ➤ variables. Econometricians most commonly use the techniques of ➤ regression analysis (➤ least-squares regression), in which the relationship between a ➤ dependent variable and an ➤ independent variable is analysed, based on the ➤ correlation in the variation of the two. The more they move together, the more likely it is there is a relationship between them. If the variation analysed is variation over time, then it is referred to as ➤ time-series analysis; if the variation is across a sample of different subjects, it is known as ➤ cross-section analysis. Sets of such models are used to make ➤ macroeconomic forecasts. Although econometrics has dominated all ➤ empirical testing in economics, it has nevertheless had its critics, who point to problems in interpreting causation between variables that are correlated, and in separating out statistical fluke from underlying cause (➤ confidence interval). ➤➤ dynamic stochastic general equilibrium model; Frisch, R.A.K.

economic activity rate ➤ labour force.

Economic Community of West African States (ECOWAS) The member states of ECOWAS agreed, by the Treaty of Lagos in 1975, to develop a ➤ customs union, and in 1981, at Freetown, Sierra Leone, concluded a plan for the elimination of trade restrictions. The treaty was revised in 1993. The aim is for the gradual elimination of all barriers to trade in goods and services, the free movement of people between the fifteen member states, the improvement in inter-regional transport and telecommunications and the eventual establishment of a monetary union. A Fund for Cooperation, Compensation and Development has been established to finance projects and to compensate for losses derived from the implementation of the treaty. In 2001, the West African Monetary Institute – the precursor to the West African Central Bank – the Court of Justice and the West African Parliament began operations. A Secretariat operates from Abuja, Nigeria.

economic complexity Since Adam ➤ Smith, it has been accepted that the essential ingredient for improvement in ➤ productivity is the division of labour and specialization. This structure leads to an increase in complex interrelationships between producers and products which becomes ever more complex as an economy grows, particularly with the expansion of ➤ international trade and ➤ globalization. There is therefore a ➤ correlation between the level of complexity in an economy and its ➤ gross national income, and an economy would be retarded by any barriers to the mutual support and interrelations needed for an increase in complexity to be possible. (➤ economic development; network economics)

economic development The growth of ➤ national income per capita. *Development economics* is concerned with the reasons why ➤ developing countries remain behind ➤ advanced countries, and what can be done about them. Mainstream thinking of development economists, and with it the policies of ➤ bilateral and ➤ multilateral agencies, has changed considerably over the past fifty years. In the early post-Second World War period, there was emphasis on the roles of ➤ investment in ➤ infrastructure and industrial or agricultural projects and the ➤ planned economy. The view then was that poor countries lacked the savings and investment necessary for growth, which created a vicious circle of ➤ poverty. The policy response therefore was for aid agencies to provide loans and grants for large investments in physical capital.

Later, in the face of the intractability of the problem and the influence of ➤ growth accounting studies which found that quantities of inputs of ➤ capital and other factors of production in the advanced countries could not alone explain development, attention turned to the role of ➤ human capital (➤ education). More emphasis was accordingly placed on programmes for improvements in health and education that would not only be of immediate benefit to the poor but which would make growth possible. In the 1980s, there was another shift in emphasis towards freeing up markets and allowing the market to channel resources to growth activities.

Attention therefore turned to ➤ macroeconomics, and the ➤ Bretton Woods institutions created *structural adjustment programmes* to reduce government budget deficits, remove price controls, free exchange rates and privatize (➤ privatization) state assets. Once again, emphasis on a single set of policies, in this case macroeconomic, proved insufficient even in the early 1990s in the economies in transition (➤ transition, economies in) in which education and infrastructure standards were much higher than in developing countries. Meanwhile, many such countries in South and East Asia and China have experienced rapid growth rates without massive foreign aid. Models of development in these ➤ emerging markets have varied, and there is controversy about why their experience has been so different from that of most developing countries.

From the late 1990s onwards, policies were again shifting, this time to emphasize a more broadly based and comprehensive strategy towards poverty alleviation that recognized not only the overriding role of private sector development but also the importance of institutions and the rules and regulations that affect economic activities (➤ institutional economics). There has always been much dissent in development economics and some have argued that there is a development trap in which countries are too poor to invest but cannot grow without that investment and this was a justification for foreign aid. As long ago as the 1950s, Peter Bauer (1915–2002) argued that all countries were once poor and that if there were a vicious circle of underdevelopment the advanced countries would still be in the Stone Age. He also believed that foreign aid was corrupting and ineffective. More recently ➤ Stiglitz has criticized the Bretton Woods institutions and the ➤ International Monetary Fund in particular for placing too much faith in the workings of free markets. ➤ growth theory.

A large proportion of the ➤ labour force in developing countries – as much as 70 per cent or more in some cases – is in the ➤ informal economy. In the informal sector, most people are engaged in agricultural subsistence or in small trading and craft activities. ➤ Direct taxation and most ➤ regulation is not enforced and because land, particularly in Africa, is held under communal arrangements, formal property rights do not exist. De Soto has argued that lack of property rights prevents the use of ➤ savings embodied in buildings as ➤ collateral security for borrowings, thus neutralizing these savings and preventing the development of ➤ capital markets. It has also been argued that the high ➤ compliance cost of regulation in the formal sector acts as a barrier to the integration of the informal economy into the modern formal sector. The importance of the informal sector, where much output may be unreported and is not exchanged in the market economy, means that statistics for developing countries are subject to qualifications.

US dollars	Per cent of urban population	Per cent of GDP in 2007			Per cent of real GDP per capita growth 2006/07
		Agriculture	Industry	Services	
Low incomes <$935	32	25	30	46	4.2
Middle incomes $936–11,455	48	9	37	53	7.2
High incomes >$11,456	77	1	26	72	1.8

Source: World Development Indicators 2009, World Bank.

It can be seen from the above table that development is associated with an increase in the proportion of the population living in urban areas, a decline in the proportion of ➤ Gross Domestic Product (GDP) generated in agriculture, and an increase in that generated in ➤ services. Industrialization first becomes more important as development proceeds, and then declines again as countries reach the advanced stage. Rates of GDP per capita growth per annum also tend to decline as countries develop (➤➤ convergence).

economic doctrines Sets of beliefs about how economies function and their corresponding policy implications. The most interesting modern means of truly defining different mainstream doctrines is in their view of the importance of ➤ aggregate demand in determining output and employment in the economy, and in whether policy to influence demand has any effect (➤ policy ineffectiveness theorem).

(1) ➤ Classical economics was not much concerned with macroeconomics because it accepted ➤ Say's law that supply created its own demand. A supplier would spend the revenue earned and any saved would be invested. Investment and saving would be equated through the interest rate. Almost by assumption, therefore, the economy was in ➤ equilibrium.

(2) Keynesian disequilibrium economics (➤➤ Keynesian economics; quantity rationing) holds that the economy can get stuck in ➤ disequilibrium as the overall level of saving may not be absorbed by the level of investment and, hence, not all output will necessarily be bought by anyone; therefore government *can* influence the economy by increasing demand, most effectively by borrowing (➤➤ fiscal policy).

(3) Neo-Keynesian/➤ neo-classical economics holds that the Keynesian view is broadly right in the short term, but that over long periods of time the economy

did have a natural tendency to find an equilibrium. Policy could be effective in the medium term.

(4) Monetarist economics (➤➤ monetarism; quantity theory of money) holds that it is money, rather than aggregate demand, that matters, and that policies to increase demand using money supply growth would only be effective in the short term, and then at the cost of increasing rates of inflation.

(5) ➤ New classical economics holds that policy won't even work in the short run if private agents anticipate its effect. A policy to increase money supply will simply increase prices immediately if agents spot it coming, and have ➤ rational expectations. New Keynesians (➤ New Keynesianism) revert to the idea that anticipated policy can have short- to medium-term effects, on the grounds that prices are sticky, and therefore that equilibrium is not immediately restored after a shock, by a change in prices.

The doctrines also fall into categories dependent on how far they use the analysis of ➤ microeconomics. Classical economists almost only used microeconomic analysis; the Keynesians, and indeed the monetarists, almost only use ➤ macroeconomics in their analyses. Neo-classicists blend the two, while the new classical and new Keynesian economists have attempted microeconomic rationales for all their macroeconomic findings.

economic efficiency The state of an economy in which no one can be made better off without someone being made worse off. For this to be the case, three types of efficiency must hold: (a) *productive efficiency*, in which the output of the economy is being produced at the lowest cost; (b) *allocative efficiency*, in which resources are being allocated to the production of the goods and services the society most values; and (c) *distributional efficiency*, in which output is distributed in such a way that consumers would not wish, given their ➤ disposable income and market ➤ prices, to spend these incomes in any different way.

In a two-person, two-product economy with two factors of production, the following three types of efficiency are achieved when three conditions hold:

(1) Productive efficiency demands that the ➤ rate of technical substitution for the two products must be equal, to ensure a unit of one factor of production is worth the same amount in terms of the other factor whichever product it is used in. Otherwise, factors could be swapped between products and extra output gained.

(2) The ➤ marginal rate of substitution must be equal for both consumers; otherwise, the consumers could swap commodities to their mutual benefit.

(3) Allocative efficiency requires that the marginal rate of transformation must equal the marginal rate of substitution: if consumers feel one banana is worth two apples, and producers can make one extra banana at the sacrifice of only one apple, it will pay society to produce one apple less and one extra banana, and to go on making that switch, until eventually consumers tire of bananas and value apples more highly than they did; and land suitable for banana production will be so marginal that for every bit of land removed from apples, hardly any bananas will be produced. At this stage, the two rates of substitution will be equal.

Economic efficiency on these criteria will exist in an economy in which perfect competition characterizes every sector. ➤➤ compensation principle; marginal-cost pricing; Pareto, V.F.D.; perfect competition; price system; Ricardo, D.; welfare economics.

economic good Any physical object, natural or manmade, or service rendered, that could command a price in a market.

economic growth The increase in a country's ➤ national income, or sometimes, its per capita national income. Growth is taken as the basis of advancing human welfare, although in fact there are problems in the measurement of national income (some activities – such as do-it-yourself car maintenance rather than buying the services of a garage mechanic, or transactions in the ➤ informal economy – may not take place in a ➤ market, or not in a market for which statistics are collected). Moreover, growth in national income should not be equated necessarily with growth in welfare (➤➤ environmental accounting; welfare economics). The processes of growth (e.g. industrialization, the expansion of the motorway network, the construction of airports) yield disbenefits, e.g. pollution, noise and the destruction of countryside amenity, all of which are costs that are not subtracted from the statistical measures of the national income. Nevertheless, explaining the factors behind economic growth, in order that more of it can be generated, is an important area of economics (➤ growth theory).

Most important is not the growth associated with the ➤ business cycle – which tends to vary to some extent with ➤ aggregate demand – but instead ➤ trend growth, or the growth in the long-term productive potential of the economy. The dominant interest in growth theory post-Second World War has been the degree to which the accumulation of ➤ capital through ➤ investment explains economic performance. Clearly, more capital, like more of any input, should lead to more output (eventually). But does it lead to enough output to justify the sacrifice of saving for it? And how much extra output does it yield? Capital accumulation alone has never been able fully to account for growth – there has always been a residual determinant, typically caught under the heading 'technology'. More recently, growth theory has moved into trying to explain how much capital is accumulated, and how successfully technology translates capital into growth. ➤ endogenous growth theory; ➤➤ economic development; economic growth, stages of.

economic growth, stages of The five stages of economic growth through which all economies are considered to pass in their development from fairly poor agricultural societies to highly industrialized mass consumption economies. These five stages were defined and analysed by ➤ Rostow in his book *The Stages of Economic Growth* (1960), i.e.:

(1) The traditional society, in which adherence to long-lived economic and social systems and customs means that output per head is low and tends not to rise.
(2) The stage of the establishment of the pre-conditions for 'take-off' (see (3) below). This stage is a period of transition, in which the traditional systems are overcome, and the economy is made capable of exploiting the fruits of modern science and technology.
(3) The take-off stage. 'Take-off' represents the point at which the 'old blocks and the resistances to steady growth are finally overcome', and growth becomes the normal condition of the economy. The economy begins to generate its own

➤ investment and technological improvement at sufficiently high rates so as to make growth virtually self-sustaining.

(4) The 'drive to maturity', which is the stage of increasing sophistication of the economy. Against the background of steady growth, new industries are developed, there is less reliance on ➤ imports and more exporting activity, and the economy 'demonstrates' its capacity to move beyond the original industries which powered its take-off, and to absorb and to apply efficiently the most advanced fruits of modern technology.

(5) Stage (4) ends in the attainment of this stage, which is the age of high mass consumption, where there is an affluent population and durable and sophisticated consumer goods (➤ economic good) and ➤ services are the leading sectors of production.

As a broad and imaginative description of the process of economic growth, this characterization of the stages of growth is interesting and possibly useful, having much the same flavour as ➤ Marx's famous theory of the evolution of society from feudalism to bourgeois ➤ capitalism and finally to communism. It also leads directly to a policy conclusion that was already favoured by many, namely that aid should be given to the economies at the pre-take-off stages, in an attempt to get them to the take-off stage. Once this is achieved, these economies will have their own dynamic and momentum, and hence aid becomes much less necessary. The theory has had only limited impact among professional economists concerned with the problem of ➤ economic development. Partly this is because Rostow's analysis of exactly what factors were responsible for take-off and subsequent self-generating growth tended to be vague, ambiguous and incomplete. Also, the theory is framed in such general terms that it can be made consistent with virtually any past growth situation. Partly also perhaps, the broad sweep of the historian's vision, with the implication of the inexorability of the historical processes, is not of very much help in trying to solve the particular development problems of particular economies. ➤➤ economic growth; development assistance.

economic history The study of the subject matter of economics in a historical context. Economic history was originally part of political economy, the antecedent of modern ➤ economics, and was taught in faculties of history and moral philosophy. In the late nineteenth century economic history began to separate off from history and economics and is now a more or less distinct discipline. The first chair in economic history was established at Harvard in 1892 and occupied by W. J. Ashley, an Englishman. A chair at Manchester University in the UK followed in 1910, the first incumbent being George Unwin. ➤ cliometrics.

economic imperialism The exploitation of ➤ developing countries by ➤ advanced countries. ➤ Marx held that the capitalist classes were inexorably driven to overseas economic expansion by falling profit opportunities at home. Later writers in the Marxist tradition have argued that profits from slave trading and other exploitative activities were important in financing the industrial revolution in Britain.

Critics of this view have responded that the amounts of capital involved were small and in any event offset by the costs of empire defence. Certainly after the Second World War, many years later, independence was given to the colonies with some relief by the colonists. Others writing in the Marxist tradition have argued that imperialism prevented balanced ➤ economic development by making the colonies dependent on exports of raw materials developed with imported capital and imports of high value-added goods from the mother countries, buttressed by ➤ tariffs and other restrictions to keep out their exports of cheap manufactured goods, even after independence.

These *dependency theories* – that imperialism can prevent the subject countries from developing balanced economies – have been falsified, by the virile expansion in many ➤ emerging markets. That economic development is facilitated by the establishment of suitable institutions (➤ institutional economics) is illustrated by the development of North America and the settled dominions where immigrants brought knowledge of institutions from other developed countries. The more recent nascent expansion of India and Brazil, both former colonies, shows that early colonization, at least in the long run, is not a bar to development.

economic rent The difference between the return made by a factor of production and the return necessary to keep the factor in its current occupation. For example: (a) for a brain surgeon earning $100,000, whose only other possible occupation is nursing on $20,000, the economic rent is $80,000 (the surgeon would remain in his current job even if it paid only $20,100); and (b) a firm making excess profits (➤ profits) is earning economic rent.

In ➤ perfect competition, no rents are made by any factor, because changes in supply bid prices of inputs and labour down to the level just necessary to keep them employed. In general, economic rents accrue where changes in supply of this sort are not possible, e.g. to a brain surgeon with rare skills, that are difficult to emulate, or to a ➤ monopoly protected by ➤ barriers to entry. True economic rents are among the few returns that can be taxed (➤ taxation) without distorting production decisions. ➤➤ quasi-rent; rent-seeking behaviour.

economics The study of the production, distribution and consumption of wealth in human society. Economists have never been wholly satisfied with any definition of their subject. This one is as good as any. It should not be interpreted as restricting the subject matter of economics to the positive aspects of material welfare alone. Lionel Robbins (1898–1984) criticized this limitation by pointing out, for example, that the economy of war, which may destroy material welfare, is an aspect of choice in the use of resources and therefore a proper subject for economic inquiry. His definition was: 'Economics is the science which studies human behaviour as a relationship between ends and scarce means which have alternative uses.' In fact, no short definition can convey the scope and flavour of the whole subject as it has evolved. The reader will gain a good notion of the scope of economics by examining the coverage of this *Dictionary*, but the borderlines between such other disciplines as psychology, sociology, accounting and geography are not easily defined and it is, perhaps, not particularly productive to attempt to do so. Political economy, an early title for the subject, now sounds old-fashioned but usefully emphasizes the importance of choice between alternatives in economics which remains, despite continuing scientific progress, as much an art as a science. ➤ economic history.

economic sanction A measure, taken in respect of some economic activity, that has the intention of damaging another country's economy, e.g. a complete embargo on trade between countries, or refusal to permit ➤ bank deposits held in a country imposing the sanction to be drawn upon by the government and residents of another country.

Economic Vulnerability Index (EVI) ➤ developing countries.

economies in transition ➤ transition, economies in.

economies of scale Factors that cause the average cost of producing a commodity to fall as output of the commodity rises. For example, a firm or industry that would less than double its costs, if it doubled its output, enjoys economies of scale.

There are two types of such economies:

(1) *Internal* economics, that accrue to the individual firm regardless of the size of its industry. They generally result from technological factors which ensure the optimal size of production is large: (a) with high fixed costs in plant and machinery, the larger its production, the lower the cost per unit of the fixed inputs, e.g. producing steel without a blast furnace is possible but very expensive – once a blast furnace is built it is inefficient only to make small quantities of steel with it and, hence, steel companies tend to be large; (b) large firms can also arrange for the specialization of labour and machines as, for example, in the techniques of the production line which can increase productivity (➤ Smith, A.); and (c) only large firms can afford the high costs of ➤ research and development – non-technological factors are important, too, however, for example by buying inputs in bulk, large firms can get discounts from their suppliers (who grant them because of economies of scale in distributing the supplies); there are also economies of scale in ➤ business finance.

(2) *External* economies, that arise because the development of an industry can lead to the development of ancillary services of benefit to all firms, i.e. a labour force skilled in the crafts of the industry, a components industry equipped to supply precisely the right parts, or a trade magazine in which all firms can advertise cheaply; these can at least partly explain the much observed tendency for firms to cluster geographically more often than would be predicted from random location decisions. ➤ industrial districts.

The existence of economies of scale in most industries is used to explain the predominance of large firms in the world economy, but recently there has been some reassessment of the relative importance of technological economies of scale as such. ➤➤ diseconomies of scale; economies of scope; minimum efficient scale; returns to scale.

economies of scope Factors that make it cheaper to produce a range of related products than to produce each of the individual products on their own. Economies of scope can provide a base for corporate ➤ diversification. ➤➤ economies of scale.

Économistes, les ➤ Physiocrats.

ECOWAS ➤ Economic Community of West African States.

Edgeworth, Francis Ysidro (1845–1926) Professor Edgeworth held the chair of Political Economy at Oxford University from 1891 to 1922 and edited the *Economic Journal* from 1891 to 1926. His published work includes *Mathematical Psychics: An essay on the application of mathematics to the moral sciences* (1881), 'The Pure Theory of Monopoly' (*Economic Journal*, 1897), 'The Theory of Distribution' (*Quarterly Journal of Economics*, 1904) and *Papers Relating to Political Economy* (1925). The last includes the two reports of 1887 and 1889 of the committee on the study of ➤ index numbers set up by the British Association for the Advancement of Science, for which Edgeworth acted as secretary. Apart from economics, he made valuable contributions to statistics and statistical method. In showing the inadequacy of the ➤ value theory of ➤ Jevons, Edgeworth invented the analytical tools of ➤ indifference curves and ➤ contract curves. ➤➤ Pareto, V.F.D.

education Through education, knowledge is transmitted throughout a community and from one generation to another. Resources are devoted to education because its benefits are perceived to surpass the costs and sacrifices it requires whether by the individual or the state. For an individual, education would be expected to yield knowledge and skills that enable him or her to attract higher future income enhanced by the improved quality of life that wider understanding brings. For the state, the incentives range from the inculcation of a desired cultural attitude to the training of its workforce appropriate to the current and expected needs of the economy. Education may be directed, therefore, to improving and widening social understanding and behaviour and the propensity to learn, or it may emphasize the teaching of technical skills specific to particular activities. Investment in education and through education investment in human capital has come to be seen to be as relevant to economic growth as investment in physical capital. (➤ Smith, Adam). Many studies have been carried out to measure the effects of education expenditure on the growth of ➤ Gross Domestic Product. There are difficulties of measurement because its benefits accrue over a long period and expenditure may not be translated directly into an enhancement of human capital because of the poor quality of education.

The ➤ Organisation for Economic Co-operation and Development (OECD) regularly carries out a 'Programme for International Student Assessment' (PISA), an internationally standardized assessment of fifteen-year-old children in schools covering reading, mathematics and science, and publishes comparative tables of achievement by country. A study published by the OECD in 2010 confirmed that it was the quality of education that was significant and that it made an important contribution to long-term economic growth. (➤➤ sow's ear effect; Spence, A. Michael)

effective exchange rate The ➤ exchange rate of a country's currency measured by reference to a ➤ weighted average of the exchange rates of the currencies of the country's trading partners. The weights are chosen to correspond to the relative importance of each trading partner in the country's domestic, as well as overseas, markets. The ➤ International Monetary Fund calculates effective exchange rate indices (➤ index number) for a number of countries. ➤ real exchange rate.

efficiency-wage hypothesis The hypothesis that it may benefit employers to pay their workers wages that are higher than their ➤ marginal revenue product (➤ marginal productivity theory of wages). The idea behind the theory is that the value of a worker may depend on how much he/she is paid. This may be because richer workers are healthier and more productive, or better motivated, or keener to avoid unemployment. It could also apply to those workers who cannot be adequately supervised so that these workers have more to lose if they are sacked. The theory can be used to explain why it is that the ➤ price system may not work in the ➤ labour market, and that wages do not get bid down until there is no unemployment. ➤ Akerlof, G.; Stiglitz, J.; tournament theory.

efficient markets hypothesis (EMH) The idea that in a market which is efficient (that is, the prices fully reflect all available information), it is impossible to earn abnormally large economic profits by trading in that market. The hypothesis which is invariably applied to financial markets, derives from a seminal paper by Eugene F. Fama published in 1970. If, on commonly held information, the price of an asset is expected, for instance, to rise tomorrow, traders, anticipating this, will buy the asset today. This will drive the price of the asset up immediately until tomorrow's price rise has already occurred, and no further rise is expected. Thus no quick capital gain could be made by buying the asset. However, the 2007–9 credit crisis has demonstrated that at times of great stress markets become inefficient. This is because at these times ➤ liquidity may disappear, preventing markets from adjusting instantaneously and because, as ➤ behavioural economics suggest, individuals tend to extrapolate recent trends which leads to the formation of asset bubbles which eventually burst. The Value at Risk (VAR) models used by market operators, which should give warning, fail to do so because at such times ➤ correlations which suggest for example that certain asset price movements are not correlated may break down. ➤ business cycle; capital-asset pricing model; chartist; random walk; rational expectations.

EFTA ➤ European Free Trade Association.

EFTPOS Electronic Funds Transfer at Point of Sale ➤ credit card.

EIB ➤ European Investment Bank.

elasticity The proportionate change in a ➤ dependent variable of a ➤ function, divided by the proportionate change in an ➤ independent variable at a given value of the independent variable. It is a measure of the sensitivity of one thing, e.g. demand for a commodity, to another, e.g. the price of it. In practice, you can have elasticities of anything, with respect to anything else (➤ cross-price elasticity of demand; elasticity of substitution; income elasticity of demand) and not just in the area of consumer demand theory. Government, for example, estimates the elasticity of its tax revenues with respect to economic growth.

Elasticity, being the product of ratios, is independent of the units in which the variables are measured. There are two forms: (a) *arc* elasticity which measures changes over a range and (b) *point* elasticity which measures changes at the margin. Their formulas are:

$$\text{(a)} \quad e = \frac{(\% \text{ change in } y)}{(\% \text{ change in } x)}$$

$$\text{(b)} \quad e = \frac{dy}{dx} \cdot \left(\frac{x}{y} \right)$$

In the case of price elasticity, y would be the quantity demanded, and x would be price. One might have observed market behaviour in order to calculate an elasticity; alternatively, it can be derived from an ➤ econometric model expressing demand as a ➤ function of price in equation form. If an elasticity has an absolute magnitude numerically smaller than unity, the quantity demanded is price-inelastic, i.e. if the price is increased (marginally), the quantity demanded will not fall proportionately as much and, therefore, the total expenditure on the good will increase. If the good is price-elastic (i.e. elasticity is numerically greater than unity), demand will be reduced more than price, and therefore less will be spent on the good than before the price was increased. The term 'elasticity' was invented by ➤ Marshall.

elasticity of substitution The proportionate change in the relative use of a commodity compared with another over the proportionate change in its relative price. It is used to measure the degree to which two commodities can substitute for each other in consumer demand (➤ demand, theory of) or in production. For example, if labour and capital are two inputs in production (➤ factors of production), they would have a high elasticity of substitution if a small increase in the relative price of labour leads firms to switch in large measure to the use of capital. If the elasticity is zero, the two commodities are used in fixed proportions no matter how expensive one of them becomes. If the elasticity is infinity, the two are perfect substitutes. The formula for the elasticity of substitution between two inputs, x and y, with prices p_1 and p_2 respectively, is:

$$e = \frac{(\% \text{ change in } x/y)}{(\% \text{ change in } p_2/p_1)}$$

➤➤ elasticity; rate of technical substitution.

electronic commerce Trading activities carried out wholly or partly using new information and communication technologies (➤ new economy) and principally the internet. It is increasingly possible for consumers (business to consumer, or B2C) or businesses (business to business or B2B) to search for and compare goods and services and order them online. Some items (e.g. computer software) can also be delivered online, but in most cases physical delivery by post or van is necessary. Because of this, and because consumers seem loath to give up the shopping experience involving seeing and handling branded goods and discussing them with a salesperson, the penetration of e-commerce, though widespread, has so far been limited. As a proportion of total retail sales, e-commerce, although expanding rapidly, is still only about 3 per cent in both the USA and the UK. In the USA, 93 per cent of e-commerce is B2B.

Initially, it was thought that new companies would capture most of the business, but what has happened is that old-economy companies with well-known brands have partially adapted their marketing to embrace the new technologies, a phenomenon known as 'clicks and mortar' in the UK and 'bricks and clicks' in the USA. E-commerce should increase customer proximity (and thus favours international trade), price transparency and ➤ contestability and therefore competition ➤ perfect competition).

Emergency Economic Stability Act ➤ Troubled Asset Relief Program.

emerging markets 1 Markets in ➤ securities in *newly industrialized countries* and in countries in central and eastern Europe and elsewhere in transition from ➤ planned to ➤ free-market economies (➤ transition, economies in) and in ➤ developing countries with ➤ capital markets at an early stage of development, e.g. the ➤ stock exchanges in Mexico, Thailand and Malaysia.

2 Although originally used to refer to securities markets, the term now commonly refers to the countries themselves. The economies of these countries have been growing rapidly at rates several times greater than those of members of the ➤ Organisation for Economic Co-operation and Development. How this has been achieved and, in particular, what the role of national governments has been in the process, is controversial. However, common factors have included high rates of savings, the devotion of considerable resources to ➤ education, high levels of ➤ exports and shifts in the labour force from agriculture to industry and services. There is no universally agreed definition of what constitutes an emerging market for which the term *newly industrialized country* is also used. Among countries often listed as emerging are: Brazil; the Chinese economic area (China, Hong Kong and Taiwan); India; Mexico; South Africa and Turkey. ➤ economic development; foreign direct investment.

emigration ➤ migration.

e-money Money can now be transferred electronically from account to account and stored in smart cards (➤ credit cards) and other pre-paid devices such as phone cards. Strictly speaking, e-money is a store of value in electronic form that can be transferred between individuals and organizations without necessarily involving bank accounts.

empirical testing Checking theories against facts. In contrast to the physical sciences, it is rarely possible to conduct controlled experiments in economics, e.g. to see what would happen to exports if the ➤ exchange rate were reduced and all other variables in the international economy remained unchanged. It is possible, however, to test hypothesis with facts, e.g. to verify historically the extent to which changes in the exchange rate have been associated with changes in exports (➤ econometrics). In fact, experiments can be, and are, carried out in economics (e.g. laboratory simulations of market behaviour) and there is a growing interest in experimental economics as an adjunct to historical empiricism and theoretical work. ➤➤ stylized fact.

employee share-ownership schemes Schemes to allow employees to acquire ➤ shares in the company in which they work. These and ➤ profit-sharing are promoted in some countries by various forms of tax relief, e.g. the Employee Share Ownership Plan in the UK and Employees Stock Ownership Plan (ESOP) in the USA. Share-ownership schemes provide partial employee ownership while cooperatives and ➤ mutual companies may be owned from the outset by customers or employees. The effectiveness of these schemes in improving business performance is controversial.

employment, full A situation in which everyone in the ➤ labour force who is willing to work at the market rate for his type of labour has a job, except for those who are switching from one job to another, i.e. it excludes ➤ frictional unemployment. Under full employment there is neither ➤ structural unemployment nor any unemployment arising from a deficiency in ➤ aggregate demand. It does not imply anything about the rate of ➤ inflation (➤ labour force; unemployment; unemployment, natural rate of) but the term does normally apply to a situation in which the ➤ capital stock and the labour force are in balance, i.e. the full employment level of ➤ Gross Domestic Product is one in which capacity is fully utilized. ➤ Beveridge, W.H.

endogenous growth theory A set of economic models and ideas that attempt to explain the rate of ➤ economic growth without recourse to the assumption that technological progress is simply given, and cannot be accounted for. Traditional exogenous growth models did tend to assume that technology – which they interpreted very widely to include everything from new machines to a better understanding of efficient production methods or improved marketing techniques – is exogenous (➤ exogenous variable), that for all intents and purposes it is predetermined.

Models of endogenous growth attempt to explain that technology. The earlier models simply outlined a more important role for ➤ investment – in physical and human capital – than had until then been common. In particular, they questioned the assumption of diminishing returns to investment (➤ diminishing returns, law of). As much investment has appeared to be subject to diminishing returns, these models have been superseded by others that have tended to focus far more narrowly on 'knowledge-based' investment in ➤ education and in research in particular. They have stressed the need for institutions that nurture innovation and provide incentives for individuals to be inventive.

Indeed, ➤ competition policy, industrial relations and the trade regime in place could all be said to be important. In general, these models have supported the conclusion that it may be sensible to subsidize education and research and development. They have also demonstrated that a far wider set of factors can affect growth than was traditionally supposed. But beyond that, they have not yielded a precision sufficient to offer useful prescriptions for policy. ➤➤ education; sow's ear effect; supply-side economics.

endogenous preferences Consumer tastes that are not fixed as a matter of personal character but which are to some extent dependent upon the experiences of the consumer. The clearest example of endogenous preferences follows from addiction – an individual's taste for cigarettes is very much affected by whether the individual happens to have smoked many cigarettes or not. Acquired tastes, habits, the desire to justify to oneself one's past consumption, all provide examples of ways in which yesterday's purchase affects our preferences today. The notion is destructive of much traditional economics, because once the assumption of exogenous (➤ exogenous variable) preferences is removed, life is far more complicated than normal demand theory (➤ demand, theory of) would imply. A cut in the price of a product may lead to a shift of the demand curve. The notion of ➤ diminishing marginal utility may be turned upside down. Unfortunately, it is hard to provide a very constructive and precise theory of endogenous preferences, although study of the subject has fruitfully introduced an element of psychology into economics. ➤ behavioural economics.

endogenous variable A ➤ variable whose value is determined by other variables within a system. The quantity of a good demanded is endogenous within the normal framework of demand theory (➤ demand, theory of) because it is affected by price, while consumer tastes are not usually seen as endogenous. However, in the real world, it can be argued that almost everything is endogenous eventually. Even the weather – always taken as the prime example of a non-endogenous variable – is said to be affected, through climate change, by economic behaviour. Several recent developments in economics have attempted to explain factors that were considered fixed. ➤ endogenous growth theory; endogenous preferences; ➤➤ dependent variable; exogenous variable; parameter.

endowment effect hypothesis The propensity for people to value more highly the property that they own than they would be willing to pay in order to obtain it. (➤ behavioural economics)

Engel, Ernst (1821–96) ➤ Engel's law.

Engel's law A law of economics stating that, with given tastes or preferences, the proportion of income spent on food diminishes as incomes increase. The law was formulated by Engel, the director of the Bureau of Statistics in Prussia, in a paper published by him in 1857.

enterprise One or more firms under common ownership or control. ➤ establishment.

entrepôt A centre at which goods are received for subsequent distribution. An entrepôt port has facilities for the trans-shipment of imported goods or their storage prior to their re-export, without the need to pass through customs control. ➤➤ freeport; free trade zone.

entrepreneur An economic agent who perceives market opportunities and assembles the ➤ factors of production to exploit them in a firm. As the prime mover in economic activity the entrepreneur has received attention from the beginnings of economics (e.g. by ➤ Cantillon and ➤ Say) but, as Casson has recently pointed out, has never been fully integrated into modern economic theory. In the static ➤ neo-classical economics of ➤ perfect competition there is no place for the entrepreneur, since it is assumed that there is perfect information and perfect freedom of entry. After ➤ Knight, the pure function of the entrepreneur is to deal with uncertainty in the dynamic, imperfect, real world in which ➤ profit is a return to uncertainty and entrepreneurship is inseparable from control of his/her firm. The essence of the entrepreneur, therefore, is that he/she should be alert to gaps in the market which others do not see and is able to raise the finance and other resources required by a firm to exploit the market that he initiates. If successful he will make a super-normal ➤ profit that will later reduce to a normal profit as new competitors are attracted into the market.

In this conception, the pure function of the entrepreneur is as a fourth factor of production. Other functions than risk-taking have been attributed by economists to the entrepreneur: invention, the provision of ➤ risk capital and management, for example. Though not part of the pure entrepreneurial function which is remunerated by profit, all these functions may be embodied in the owner-manager of a ➤ small business. His/her remuneration may comprise ➤ rent as an owner of ➤ land, ➤ interest as a return on ➤ capital, a wage or salary for management function and therefore a return for his/her ➤ labour, and profit, a return for entrepreneurship. In the large firm, the entrepreneur is a theoretical abstraction whose functions are divided between the management (the board of directors and senior executives) and the shareholders. Many economists have argued that the ➤ separation of ownership from control has important implications for the behaviour of managers and market performance.

entry ➤ barriers to entry; freedom of entry.

envelope theorem A proposition with numerous applications in the economics and mathematics of ➤ utility and of production (➤ production, theory of) that uses the assumption of optimizing behaviour to simplify the mathematical relationship between different variables. It is best explained by example. Imagine a firm that produces widgets, using only skilled labour and unskilled labour, and that to some extent it can ➤ substitute one type of labour for the other. Now imagine the firm wants to know how the total cost of producing 100 widgets will change if the cost of skilled labour rises by $1 an hour. The answer is that there is a direct effect and an indirect effect. The direct effect is that the cost rises by $1 for every hour of skilled labour employed. The indirect effect emerges because the firm will, in light of the change in relative prices, choose to alter the mix of skilled and unskilled labour it employs. (It will want to replace skilled workers with unskilled ones as far as is possible.)

The envelope theorem says that if the firm is optimizing the mix of skilled and unskilled labour, then for small changes in costs, the indirect effect is effectively zero. Thus, the theorem dramatically simplifies the calculation needed. It does so because the firm could only be optimizing when it mixes inputs such that small changes in how much of each is used have no effect on profit. (After all, if changing the product mix could increase profits, then the firm could not have been optimizing in the first place.)

If the effect of changes in the quantity of the different types of labour can be ignored, so can the indirect effects of the cost change. Thus, the change in total cost, resulting in a unit change to the price of an input, is simply the amount of the input employed. Of course, if the firm were not optimizing, it would not be possible to make the assumption that small changes in the input mix were irrelevant. The theorem is central to ➤ duality theory – the relationship between the ➤ production function and the related function describing the firm's costs, given an optimal input mix. It asserts that the ➤ demand function for inputs is effectively derivable from the firm's cost function. Similarly, in demand theory (➤ demand, theory of), it can be used as a means of obtaining the demand function, from observation of the consumers' expenditure at different prices. The theorem is also known as Shephard's lemma.

environmental accounting The attempt to apply numerical magnitudes to uncosted environmental factors, and to include these in conventional accounts. The goal is to improve those conventional accounts as a measure of overall well-being. For example, at the national level, an environmental disaster (e.g. an oil spill) has the perverse effect of enhancing national income, spawning as it does extensive, fully costed clear-up activity. Obviously, though, the economy is no richer as a result of an oil spill. Environmental accounting can reflect this. It can also introduce rational treatment of depletable resources, deducting their consumption as a cost, rather than adding it as a benefit. Changing the national accounts on this basis would make little difference to international rankings of economic success. Those who propound it do so in the hope that a greater emphasis on environment in the headline measures of success would lead to changes in policy. Attempts have been made to produce accounts reflecting this argument. Daly and Cobb's index of sustainable economic welfare, devised in 1989, appears to have grown at 0.9 per cent a year, in contrast to conventional ➤ Gross Domestic Product (GDP) growth of about 2 per cent a year. Tobin (➤ Tobin, J.) and Nordhaus constructed a measure of economic welfare with more limited accounting (but still with a large number of welfare effects included, e.g. the negative cost of time spent travelling to work) and found an annual per capita growth rate of about 1.1 per cent over a long time period in which GDP had grown at about 1.7 per cent. ➤➤ cost-benefit analysis; depletion theory; environmental economics; social accounting.

environmental economics The area of economics concerned with issues relating to man's use and abuse of ➤ natural resources. Environmental problems are frequently characterized by the existence of ➤ externalities and public goods. In these areas, it is hard for the ➤ price system to operate in such a way as to allocate scarce resources (e.g. clean air and the ozone layer) in an efficient way (➤ economic efficiency). Many of the problems that are faced in this area derive from the lack of clearly defined property rights over natural resources, which makes environmental abuse likely in the absence of governmental control (➤ Coase theorem).

Much of environmental economics has concerned the relative merits of different policy responses to the various flaws of the market mechanism in these areas. For example, should emissions be stopped by regulation, that is direct controls, or should they be taxed i.e. the ➤ polluter-pays principle? Policy responses have been increasing following growing concern about global warming and the impact of human activity. Emissions fees charged by governments on the amount of external damage caused and tradable emissions permits are alternative and theoretically equivalent approaches. Tradable permits in terms of tons of pollutants allowed by the holder are issued by governments so that the market can determine their price as firms buy and sell them to offset the pollution they cause. Firms can choose between investing in the reduction of pollution (abatement) and in acquiring permits. Theoretically, controls are optimized when the marginal private costs of control are equal to the marginal social benefits. In practice, these costs and benefits and indeed, the impact of human activity on climate change, are difficult to determine. There are also problems that derive from the depletable nature of some resources (➤ depletion theory).

equation of international demand The law of comparative cost (➤ Ricardo, D.) sets out the limits of the ➤ terms of trade within which one country will exchange commodities with another. ➤ Mill realized that the point at which exchange actually took place within these limits set by costs would depend on the reciprocal ➤ demand of each country for the other's commodities. The ratio at which one country's commodities exchange for another country's commodities (the terms of trade) will be in equilibrium when the quantity the importer will accept at this ratio equals the quantity the exporter will be willing to deliver. It will depend, *inter alia*, on the ➤ elasticities of demand and ➤ supply of the goods traded. ➤➤ Marshall–Lerner criterion.

equilibrium A situation in which the forces that determine the behaviour of a variable are in balance and thus exert no pressure on that variable to change. It is a situation in which the actions of all economic agents are mutually consistent. It is a concept meaningfully applied to any variable whose level is determined by the outcome of the operation of at least one mechanism or process acting on countervailing forces. For example, equilibrium price is affected by a process that drives suppliers to increase prices when demand is in excess and to undercut each other when supply is in excess – the mechanism thus regulates the forces of supply and demand. It is possible for a short-run equilibrium to exist when some quickly adjusting processes are in balance while other, longer-term, forces are still causing change to occur. For example, in ➤ perfect competition, in the short run firms' profit-maximizing behaviour can lead to a market equilibrium with price equal to marginal cost, yet if abnormal ➤ profits exist at that price new firms might enter the industry – a process quite separate from the price-setting behaviour of those already in it – that will change the long-term equilibrium price.

A distinction can be drawn between a static equilibrium – when the value of the relevant variable is unchanging – and a dynamic equilibrium – when the value of the variable is changing, but in a regular way. Equilibrium growth, for example, might manifest itself in a steady 2.25 per cent rise in ➤ Gross Domestic Product.

The concept of an equilibrium has developed in recent decades with the advance of ➤ game theory. An equilibrium in a game is, loosely, a set of mutually compatible strategies in which, given the strategies of other players, each player will be content with his/her own strategy.

Finally, equilibrium should not be confused with efficiency. Although the efficient level of a variable is sometimes likely to be an equilibrium, there is no guarantee that equilibria are efficient. ➤➤ disequilibrium; Nash equilibrium; *tatonnement* process.

equities ➤ shares in companies.

equity The residual ➤ value of a company's ➤ assets after all outside ➤ liabilities (other than to shareholders) have been allowed for. In a ➤ mortgage, or ➤ hire purchase contract, equity is the amount left for the borrower if the asset concerned is sold and the lender repaid. The equity in a company under ➤ liquidation is the property of holders of ➤ ordinary shares, hence these shares are popularly called *equities*. Equity yields and prices, although fluctuating, have historically delivered returns about 8 per cent higher than risk-free ➤ stocks (➤ capital asset pricing model).

equity/efficiency trade-off The conflict that is traditionally held to arise between maximizing average consumption and making that consumption equal across the population. Under certain conditions, a ➤ free-market economy is generally recognized as exhibiting ➤ economic efficiency, but would have no tendency to result in equality of earnings. To achieve an alternative income distribution, a ➤ progressive tax system is required. However, it is possible that high taxes have a negative effect on work incentives, or create other distortions, and thus depress output. In so far as there is a trade-off, however, a ➤ social welfare function must be defined to derive the optimal combination. ➤➤ Atkinson index; welfare economics.

equity gearing ➤ gearing.

equity-linked assurance ➤ assurance.

ERDF ➤ European Regional Development Fund (➤ European Union).

establishment An operating unit of a business, to be distinguished from a firm or ➤ enterprise, which are controlling units.

estate duty ➤ inheritance taxes.

ethical investing The attempt by lenders or shareholders to influence company behaviour by investing only in companies that observe certain standards of behaviour. The goal – apart from satisfying the conscience of the investors concerned – is to increase the cost of capital (➤ capital, cost of) to firms whose ethical standards are low, and in doing so make capital less available. Where a capital market is dominated by non-ethical investors, however, it is not clear that any small cluster of individuals has the power to affect any company's cost of capital. In so far as they do, the less ethical can pick up investment bargains. Ethical investment funds – and those doing research on their behalf – have influenced corporate behaviour through the publicity they bring to company actions.

Euler, Leonhard (1707–83) Economists have found that certain propositions in pure mathematics developed by Euler, a Swiss mathematician, can be usefully applied to problems in economic theory. The most notable application concerns a theory of distribution based on ➤ marginal productivity of capital. This theory states that ➤ factors of production (i.e. ➤ land, ➤ labour and ➤ capital) will each earn an ➤ income corresponding to the ➤ value of output produced by the last unit of the factor employed. For example, if a firm employs nineteen workers at an average wage of $400 per week, it will be willing to employ an additional worker as long as his/her output is worth more than $400. Moreover, if the twentieth worker yields, say, $410 per week it will be worthwhile to pay him/her more than $400 to attract him/her. The firm cannot, however, pay its workers different wages if they have the same skill, and therefore must pay all of them more than $400 per week. The earnings of each worker are therefore made equal to that at which it is just worthwhile to the firm to employ one more worker.

A similar argument is applied to other factors of production and for the total national output as well as for a single firm. However, total output must, by definition, equal total income (➤ national income). National output is distributed among the three basic factors of production: land, labour and capital. No arithmetical reasons, however, can be given for the different factor incomes, derived from marginal productivities, necessarily adding up to the same figure as total output. Euler's theorem resolved the problem by showing what assumptions about the nature of the ➤ production function (which describes how the factors of production are combined to produce outputs) had to be made in order for the equality between the sum of incomes and the sum of outputs to be achieved. ➤➤ Cambridge School; distribution, theory of; neo-classical economics.

Euler's theorem ➤ Euler, L.

euro ➤ European Economic and Monetary Union.

eurobond ➤ bond; eurocurrency.

eurocurrency ➤ Currency held by individuals and institutions outside the country of issue. The ➤ Bank for International Settlements has described eurodollars as the dollars acquired 'by banks located outside the United States, mostly through the taking of ➤ deposits, but also to some extent through swapping other currencies into dollars, and the relending of these dollars, often after redepositing with other banks, to non-bank borrowers anywhere in the world'. It should be noted, therefore, that the market for eurocurrencies is not confined to Europe. In terms of a simple example, the following happens. A London bank, as a result of a commercial transaction of one of its customers, has, for example, a ➤ credit balance with a US bank in New York. A Tokyo businessman asks his bank for dollars to finance imports from the USA. In order to meet this request, the Tokyo bank accepts the dollar deposit transferred by the London bank from its account in New York. The essential point about this operation is that it creates credit. The London bank still has a claim on Tokyo instead of New York, whereas the Tokyo bank now has a claim on New York that its customer can use to finance his trade. The questions are naturally raised as to why London should be willing to transfer its deposit and why Tokyo should finance its requirements in this way. The US ➤ balance of payments deficits and *dollar certificates of deposit* issued by overseas branches of US banks generate a supply of eurodollars, and interest-rate ➤ arbitrage (New York versus Tokyo) enables a ➤ profit to be made. Relative ➤ rates of interest are a factor in these transactions but, in addition, the existence of national ➤ exchange controls and credit controls may encourage the practice. Of course, there can be many relending transactions between banks in response to differentials in interest rates and in many different currencies.

eurodollars ➤ eurocurrency.

European Bank for Reconstruction and Development An international bank set up in 1991 to assist countries in transition towards open and democratic market economies, through financial assistance to private sector activities (➤ transition, economies in). Sixty-one countries and two institutions, the ➤ European Union and the ➤ European Investment Bank, are members of the bank. Projects in twenty-nine countries from Central Europe to Central Asia have received assistance. Total new investment in 2009 reached €7.9 billion. The bank is located in London.

European Central Bank (ECB) The organization responsible for conducting ➤ monetary policy in the eurozone at the supra-national level (➤ European Economic and Monetary Union (EMU)). It was established in Frankfurt in 1998 and became fully operational on 1 January 1999, when it became responsible for monetary policy in the euro area. The ECB is independent of national governments; it works with the national ➤ central banks of the member states that have adopted the euro. The governing council of the ECB consists of a six-member, full-time executive board and the governors of the central banks participating in EMU. The national central banks in the eurozone have no independent responsibility for monetary policy but do hold the ECB's minimum reserve requirements (➤ capital adequacy) for the commercial banks and assist in implementing the ECB's monetary policy decisions. An important difference between the ECB and some other central banks is that it does not rely solely on interest rates but also on bank reserves and it pays considerable attention to the ➤ money supply. The ECB has the sole right to authorize the issue of euro banknotes. The ECB is not responsible for banking supervision or for regulating other financial institutions; these are functions reserved for national authorities, at least for the present. The objectives of the ECB are laid down in the ➤ Maastricht Treaty and are: (a) to maintain price stability (less than 2 per cent annual increase in the ➤ harmonized index of consumer prices) and (b) subject to price stability, to 'support the general economic policies in the Community'.

European Community ➤ European Union.

European Economic and Monetary Union (EMU) A programme for the establishment of monetary union was agreed under the terms of the ➤ Maastricht Treaty, to establish a single European currency (the euro). Member states of the European Union (EU) judged to have 'converged' sufficiently with other members of the EU, by reference to a number of conditions, are entitled to join (➤ convergence criteria). The euro was launched on 1 January 1999, but initially only used for accounting purposes – until 2002 when it replaced national currencies. By 2011, seventeen countries had adopted the euro, namely Austria, Belgium, Cyprus, Estonia, Finland, France, Germany, Greece, Ireland, Italy, Luxembourg, Malta, Netherlands, Portugal, Slovakia, Slovenia and Spain. Although members of the European Union and qualified to join under the convergence criteria, Denmark, Sweden and the United Kingdom chose not to join.

Member nations are not able to exert an independent monetary policy. A level of interest rate (➤ rate of interest) is set for all members. ➤ European Central Bank). If each member tends to follow the others, and absorb similar shocks to demand and supply, this need not be a problem. However, if member states endure divergent patterns of economic performance and the free internal movement of labour is inhibited, the burden of adjustment will have to fall on domestic prices and employment, rather than on interest rates or exchange rates. ➤ Friedman, Milton; Mundell, R.A.).

European Economic Area ➤ European Free Trade Association.

European Economic Community (EEC) ➤ European Union.

European Exchange Rate Mechanism (ERM) The fixed ➤ exchange rate regime established by the then European Community (➤ European Union) in 1979. The system was designed to keep the member countries' exchange rates within specified bands in relation to each other. Each currency in the system was allowed initially to fluctuate between ±2.25 per cent against any other currency, later widened to up to ±15 per cent. The ERM came to be seen as a precursor to ➤ European Economic and Monetary Union, with membership implicitly representing a condition of entry to EMU according to the ➤ Maastricht Treaty.

European Free Trade Association (EFTA) The Stockholm Agreement of 1959 established a ➤ free trade area between the UK, Norway, Sweden, Denmark, Austria, Portugal and Switzerland. The association was later joined by Finland, Iceland and Liechtenstein. Currently, there are four member states, Iceland, Liechtenstein, Norway and Switzerland, the other countries having left on becoming members of the ➤ European Union (EU). In 1994, the European Economic Area (EEA) came into force which linked EFTA, excluding Switzerland, with the EU into a wider free trade area. This established a single market for the free movement of goods, services, people and capital. The agreement does not extend to the European Common Agricultural Policy nor the Common Fisheries Policy and the group remains a free trade area rather than a ➤ customs union. Meanwhile, Switzerland had concluded a number of bilateral agreements with the EU and it was decided to subsume the EEA and these Swiss–EU agreements into a revised EFTA Convention in 2001. The members of EFTA have the right to consultation in the EU legislative process and the EEA convention is continuously updated to keep it in line with relevant EU legislation. The EFTA has continued a policy of setting up free trade agreements with other countries and these now cover 80 per cent of its foreign trade. ➤ General Agreement on Tariffs and Trade; Regional Trade Agreements.

European Investment Bank (EIB) A bank established in 1958 by the then European Community (➤ European Union (EU)) whose board of governors comprises the ministers of finance of the EU. It is a non-profitmaking institution whose function is to make loans and give guarantees with respect to: (a) projects in the underdeveloped areas of the EU and in support of EU ➤ development assistance; (b) projects of modernization, conversion or development that are regarded as necessary for the development of the EU; and (c) projects in which member countries of the EU have a common interest.

European Regional Development Fund (ERDF) ➤ European Union.

European Union (EU) Six countries of Western Europe (i.e. France, West Germany, Italy, Belgium, the Netherlands and Luxembourg) signed the Treaty of Rome in 1957 for the creation between them of a ➤ customs union or common market. By this treaty the European Economic Community (EEC) came into force on 1 January 1958. The EEC merged with the European Coal and Steel Community and Euratom in 1967 to form the European Community, subsequently referred to as the European Union (EU). All internal import duties were abolished and a common external tariff established by 1 July 1968. For agricultural products, the Common Agricultural Policy (➤ farm subsidies) became effective in 1968. As from 1 January 1973 the Republic of Ireland and two members of the ➤ European Free Trade Association (i.e. the UK and Denmark) became full members of the EU. The elimination of tariffs between the original six and the new members and the adoption by them of the common external tariff was completed on 1 January 1977. Greece became a member in 1981, Portugal and Spain in 1986, Austria, Finland and Sweden in 1995. The German Democratic Republic (East Germany) became a member in 1990 following its merger with the Federal Republic of Germany (West Germany). In 2004, the EU was also joined by Cyprus, Czech Republic, Estonia, Hungary, Latvia, Lithuania, Malta, Poland, Slovakia and Slovenia and, in 2007, by Romania and Bulgaria. In 2010, there were, in addition, three official applications to join from Croatia, Macedonia and Turkey.

The EU was not a complete single market because restrictions existed that prevented free trade, e.g. national differences in technical standards within the Community and differential qualification requirements for the professions (➤ barriers to entry). A programme was embodied in the Single European Act 1986 for the abolition of such restrictions. The programme included the abolition of exchange controls, the recognition of qualifications, the abolition of restrictions on internal transport (➤ cabotage), liberalization of the market in air services, public procurement tendering, life insurance and banking services, and the abolition of frontier controls (➤ Schengen Treaty). The Act also widened the application of qualified majority decision-making in the EU. The Treaty of Rome was subsequently amended by the Treaties of Maastricht in 1992, Amsterdam in 1997, Nice in 2000 and Lisbon in 2007.

The executive management of the EU is vested in the European Commission to which each member country appoints one member in charge of a particular area of policy. The European Commission monitors competition to ensure that no enterprise acts in such a way as to restrict the free movement of goods and services in the EU or to exploit a dominant market position (➤ competition policy).

The Council of the European Union is responsible for setting policy along with the European Parliament. The post of the Council's President is rotated every six months among the member countries. The Council's meetings are attended by a minister, appropriate to the particular subject under discussion, from each member country.

The European Council is composed of the presidents or prime ministers and foreign ministers from each member country. The European Council is responsible for setting the EU's broad policy objectives and agenda. By the Treaty of Lisbon, the post of President of the European Council was created, as was that of a High Representative of the Union for Foreign Affairs and Security to represent the EU overseas.

A European Regional Development Fund has been established with powers to lend and grant money for the development of backward regions of the EU and for ➤ development assistance. ➤ European Economic and Monetary Union; European Investment Bank; migration.

Eurostat ➤ Labour Force Survey.

ex ante Expected or intended before the event, as distinct from *ex post*, which is the result after the event. Since the future is largely unpredictable, expectations and outcomes will often be different. The concepts of *ex ante* and *ex post* are particularly useful in economics because the nature of expectations may help either to realize or to falsify expectations in the process of moving towards ➤ equilibrium. For example, if investors expect security prices to rise today *ex ante*, this will increase demand for them and their price now, so that *ex post* and *ex ante* prices may be similar. If intended aggregate ➤ savings (*ex ante*) are larger than intended ➤ investment, this will set in train forces, via lower incomes, to reduce savings so that *ex post* savings and investment will be equal (➤ income determination, theory of). ➤➤ Myrdal, G.K.

exceptional items ➤ below the line.

excess capacity 1 The difference between the amount produced by a firm or group of firms and the higher amount that could most efficiently be produced. If a firm produces 1000 cars at a cost of $5000 each, but the lowest cost output would be 1300 cars at $4000 each, there is said to be excess capacity of 300 cars. It will exist at any point on an average-cost curve to the left of the lowest point (➤ average cost). Sustained excess capacity is a feature of firms in ➤ monopolistic competition. In ➤ perfect competition, it will exist only in the short term.

2 The difference between actual output and maximum possible output in a firm, industry or economy. Excess capacity exists when there are unemployed resources; for a national economy it implies the existence of a ➤ deflationary gap. ➤ output gap.

excess demand The state of a market for a commodity in which consumers would choose to buy more of the commodity than is available at the prevailing price. Excess demand will be equal to zero at the ➤ equilibrium price; it will be negative (i.e. ➤ excess supply will exist) when the price is higher and will be positive when the price is lower. If price does not ration the available supply, something else must;

usually it will be state-organized rationing or a queuing system coupled with a first-come first-served distribution. The situation can result from price control in which suppliers are legally prevented from raising their prices in response to high consumer demand. ➤➤ repressed inflation.

excess profit ➤ profit.

excess supply The state of the market for a commodity in which more of the commodity is available for purchase than consumers choose to buy at the prevailing price. Usually, such a situation leads to a price fall and excess supply disappears. In a market in which minimum price control is applied it can, however, persist; if, for example, ➤ trade unions prevent wages from falling enough, some argue that there can be an excess supply of labour (or unemployment) at the prevailing wage. ➤➤ excess demand; Keynesian unemployment.

exchange control The control by the state through the ➤ banking system of dealings in gold and foreign ➤ currencies. Exchange control is concerned with controlling the purchase and sale of currencies by residents alone, since governments do not have complete powers to control the activities of non-residents. This must be done through the ➤ market and is a matter of exchange management. Exchange control is required only where a country wishes to influence the international value of its currency. It is not willing to leave the value of its currency in terms of other currencies or gold to be determined in the ➤ free market, as it would be under a system of floating ➤ exchange rates, or to allow the fixed external value of its currency to be the determinant of the domestic price level. In its most extreme form, a country facing a balance-of-payments deficit may use exchange control to restrict imports to the amount earned in ➤ foreign exchange by its nationals. All forms of exchange control are discouraged by the ➤ Organisation for Economic Co-operation and Development and other international organizations concerned with encouraging ➤ international trade. It should be noted that a currency is not fully convertible (➤ convertibility) when exchange control is operated. ➤➤ counter trade; European Economic and Monetary Union; mobility of capital.

exchange economy An economy which has progressed beyond the point at which each household produces goods solely for its own consumption. Exchange, whether by ➤ barter or by the use of ➤ money, enables the benefits of the specialization (➤ division of labour) and the ➤ economies of scale to be realized. ➤➤ economic growth.

exchange equation ➤ Fisher, I.

exchange of shares A means of business combination which can take two forms: (a) the companies retain their separate identities, but exchange a quantity of ➤ shares so that each company holds shares in the other and normally some directors will sit on both boards (➤ interlocking directorates); and (b) two companies will merge, shares of one company being exchanged with or without a cash adjustment for the whole of the issued share ➤ capital of the other. ➤➤ merger; reverse takeover.

exchange rate The price (rate) at which one ➤ currency is exchanged for another. Transactions in foreign exchange occur spot or forward (➤ spot market; forward market) in the ➤ foreign exchange markets. The actual rate at any one time is determined by ➤ supply and ➤ demand conditions for the relevant currencies in the market. An economy has an internationally traded sector and a domestic sector. The prices obtained by the former are determined by the prevailing prices on the international market and the exchange rate, whereas prices in the latter are not determined so directly.

A fall in the exchange rate will increase demand and make the internationally traded sector relatively more attractive compared with the domestic sector and therefore there will tend to be a redirection of resources in its favour. The reverse would happen with an increase in the exchange rate. Often when the economy receives a 'shock', the relative size and profitability of the two sectors need to adjust, and the exchange rate is one means by which the relative price changes needed to induce the adjustment can be transmitted to the two sectors. For example, a shock might include a big rise in domestic savings, without a rise in domestic investment. In this event, as domestic demand falls, exports may be expanded to offset this loss of demand by a fall in the exchange rate.

The exchange rate is simply a component of the ➤ price mechanism, albeit an important one, responding to the pressures set by preferences for domestic and foreign goods and services, and the flows of savings and investment funds across currencies. It follows that the value of the currency is also determined by domestic ➤ monetary policy – more inflation tends to mean a lower exchange rate as, without a depreciation, inflation hits the tradable sector more harshly than the non-tradable sector because it has to accept the world prices for its products. Given the importance of such an economic variable, governments have often sought to control exchange rates such as pegging them at a fixed rate to another currency (➤ protection ➤➤ carry trade; currency appreciation; currency board; effective exchange rate; European Economic and Monetary Union; exchange-rate overshooting; fixed exchange rate; Mundell, R.; purchasing-power parity; real exchange rate.

exchange-rate overshooting The idea, promulgated by Rüdiger Dornbusch, in his paper 'Expectations and exchange rate dynamics', published in 1976, that when governments make a domestic monetary policy shift, for a short time the exchange rate will adjust further than the changed monetary stance merits. For instance, under plausible assumptions about the ➤ mobility of capital, if a government orchestrates a rise in interest rates, money will flow into its currency from other lower-interest-rate jurisdictions. This will lead the currency to appreciate in value, and it will go on appreciating until it has risen beyond its market equilibrium level until it readjusts at the rate at which it is expected to fall again. ➤ exchange rate; impossible trinity; law of one price.

Exchequer The account of the UK central government kept at the ➤ Bank of England. ➤➤ Consolidated Fund.

excise duties Indirect taxes levied upon goods produced for home consumption, as distinct from customs duties (➤ tariffs, import) which are levied on goods entering or leaving the country (➤➤ taxation).

exclusive dealing A 'tie' under which a retailer or wholesaler contracts to purchase from a supplier on the understanding that no other distributor will be appointed or receive supplies in a given area, e.g. tied petrol-filling stations and public houses.

Exclusive dealing may be a ➤ barrier to entry, but it can be defended on grounds of benefits to the consumer, such as after-sales service. ➤➤ Chicago School; competition policy; vertical restraints.

ex-dividend Without ➤ dividend. The purchaser of a ➤ security quoted ex-dividend does not have the right to the next dividend when due. The term 'ex-', meaning 'excluding', is also used in a similar sense in relation to ➤ rights issue, capitalization issue (➤ bonus issue), etc.

exempt company ➤ private company.

exogenous growth theory ➤ endogenous growth theory.

exogenous variable A ➤ variable whose value is not determined within the set of equations, or ➤ models, established to make predictions or test a hypothesis. ➤➤ endogenous variable; parameter.

expectation of life ➤ death rate.

expectations The views held by economic agents as to the future behaviour of relevant economic variables. Although expectations have some role in the theory of ➤ microeconomics (in particular, the ➤ cobweb model and in pricing behaviour in ➤ oligopoly) their primary importance is in ➤ macroeconomics. In almost all models of the economy, in-built assumptions are made as to what views individuals hold about the future. For example, when future rates of return in asset markets are uncertain, the expectations of investors will determine the prevailing rate of interest more than the actual return made on any asset; when wage bargainers target a real wage, (➤ real terms) they must have a view of expected inflation to know what money wage to seek, and under the ➤ acceleration principle of investment, it is the expectations of firms about future demand that determines their investment behaviour. In any model where uncertainty is prevalent, the expectation-forming process of individuals will be important.

There are various different assumptions that can be made about expectations: (a) they could be an ➤ exogenous variable – in this case they are not influenced by any events in the model, but are just imposed from outside; (b) they could be backward-looking, made by economic agents on the basis of past values of the variables in question (➤ adaptive expectations); and (c) they can be so-called ➤ rational expectations, in which case agents are assumed not to make systematic errors in their forecasting of variables. In certain economic models, by assuming rational expectations, very strong conclusions can be reached about how the economy should be controlled. ➤➤ Lucas critique; policy ineffectiveness theorem.

expected utility A measure of the welfare accruing to a consumer from an asset which yields an uncertain flow of benefits. Suppose, for example, a consumer takes part in a lottery, in which there is a 50 per cent chance of winning $10 and a 50 per cent chance of winning nothing. The consumer's expected ➤ utility will be 50 per cent of the utility of winning $10 and 50 per cent of the utility of winning nothing. An important distinction should be made between the expected utility of a lottery and the utility of the expected outcome. In the example above, the expected utility of $5 may not be the same as the average of the utility of $10 and the utility of zero dollars. ➤ von Neumann–Morgenstern utility function. ➤➤ diminishing marginal utility; risk; risk aversion.

expenditure tax A form of ➤ direct taxation on spending. Advocated by Nicholas Kaldor and ➤ Meade and others on the ground that it would eliminate the necessity to define ➤ income, which is a source of complexity and, many would argue, inequity in the common form of ➤ income tax. In practice, an expenditure tax would be just like income tax, either with full tax deductibility of all income that is saved, or with a zero rate of tax on all income from savings. Each of the two systems involves removing ➤ double taxation from income that is invested. With so many forms of savings now subject to generous tax treatment, we already have a rather complex hybrid income/expenditure tax mix. Among the advantages claimed for a full expenditure tax are that it: (a) would encourage saving and not discriminate between alternative savings media (eliminating one set of distortions in ➤ capital markets), and (b) would reduce ➤ compliance costs, and close loopholes in the present system that allow the avoidance of income tax by converting income into ➤ capital. It should be understood that indirect taxes such as ➤ value-added tax, although taxes on expenditure, are quite different from the proposed expenditure tax both in the method of collection and in their inability to take the individual financial circumstances of the spender into account.

experimental economics ➤ empirical testing.

export credit insurance The granting of ➤ insurance to cover the commercial and political risks of selling in overseas markets. Concern about the use of government export credit agencies to subsidize export markets led to the Export Credit Arrangement, agreed between a number of member states of the ➤ Organisation for Economic Co-operation and Development (OECD). This arrangement established minimum ➤ rates of interest and maximum repayment periods for specified categories of borrower. These guidelines were revised in 1991 following concern about the growth of the use of a mix of credits with direct aid tied to a requirement that the recipient country must buy the goods and services of the donor country. The terms are regularly updated by the OECD. ➤➤ Multilateral Investment Guarantee Agency.

export incentives Preferential treatment for firms that sell their products abroad, compared with firms that sell to the home market. They may take the form of direct ➤ subsidies, special ➤ credit facilities, grants, concessions in the field of ➤ direct taxation, benefits arising from the administration of indirect taxation, and ➤ export credit insurance on exceptionally favourable terms. Various international associations discourage the practice of artificially stimulating exports by any of these methods. The ➤ World Trade Organization lays down special provisions relating to export subsidies, direct or indirect, in an attempt to limit them. In the field of 'tied aid' (➤ development assistance), the rules of the ➤ Organisation for Economic Co-operation and Development determine that a minimum proportion of the finance must be grant aid where the finance is not conditional on the donor country receiving the contract for the project being financed.

export multiplier The ratio of the total increase in a country's ➤ national income to the increment in export revenue generating the increase. The size of the multiplier depends on the propensities to save (➤ average propensity to save; marginal propensity to save) of the recipients of the increases in incomes derived from the increase in export revenue and the country's ➤ propensity to import. The export multiplier can be regarded as a special case of the general ➤ multiplier.

export processing zone ➤ free trade zone.

export rebates ➤ customs drawback; export incentives.

exports The goods and ➤ services produced by one country that are sold to another for gold, or ➤ foreign exchange or in settlement of ➤ debt, or in exchange for the second country's own goods and services. Countries tend to specialize in the production of those goods and services in which they can be relatively most efficient, given their indigenous factor endowments (➤ factors of production). Countries devote home resources to exports because they can obtain more goods and services by international exchange than they would from the same resources devoted to home production directly. According to the ➤ World Trade Organization, China was the leading exporter of goods in 2009, accounting for 9.6 per cent of the world total, followed by Germany with 9.0 per cent and the USA with 8.5 per cent. The USA had the lead in exports of services with 14.2 per cent followed by the UK at 7.3 per cent and Germany at 6.5 per cent. ➤➤ balance of payments; international trade; mercantilism; Ricardo, D.

export surplus ➤ balance of payments.

ex post ➤ *ex ante*.

external deficit A synonym for ➤ balance of payments deficit.

external diseconomies ➤ diseconomies of scale.

external effects ➤ externalities.

externalities Consequences for welfare of ➤ opportunity costs not fully accounted for in the ➤ price and ➤ market system. *External diseconomies* of production include traffic congestion and pollution created by a manufacturing plant. These cause reductions in the welfare of people living near the factory and perhaps increased costs to adjacent factories that might need to purify water taken from a river bordering both plants. Because the third parties receive no compensation (do not charge) for these external diseconomies, there are costs of production not accounted for in the price system. External diseconomies also arise in ➤ consumption, e.g. where people eating ice-cream leave litter on the pavement or cigarette smokers pollute the air in a public building. Both production and consumption externalities can occur simultaneously where, for example, a restaurant creates noise, congestion and smell.

External economies of production may arise where the existence of several factories stimulates the availability of skilled labour, shopping facilities or component supplies. External economies of consumption include a garden at the front of a house that gives pleasure to passers-by as well as to the occupants and increases the value of adjoining property. Defence or other public expenditure on research and development is sometimes justified on the additional ground that it stimulates the development of new ➤ technology that may become freely available to all. This is usually called a *spillover effect*, an alternative term for externality.

Externalities are important in determining the efficient allocation of resources. In a ➤ free-market economy, individuals typically only attempt to maximize their own private utility or profit, and external costs and benefits will not be reflected in the prices of things. A firm may make perfumes very cheaply but nevertheless be polluting the atmosphere in the process, to the detriment of non-perfume buyers. Unless the cost of this pollution is reflected in the price of the perfume, people will buy more of it than they would choose to if they had to pay for the entire cost to society of its production. In short, it is full *social* costs that are important in determining an efficient resource allocation, and *private* costs that determine prices.

There are two means of dealing with externalities: (a) a structure of taxes and subsidies can be designed to *internalize* the externalities and ensure that the full costs or benefits of production are reflected in the prices charged; in this case, even if a factory causes pollution, it can carry on producing as long as it properly compensates society for the damage caused; and (b) to put restrictions on certain unsocial activities and make other beneficial activities compulsory. This will, however, usually not be as efficient as the optimal taxes or subsidies could be, because you may restrict activity that, despite its negative external effects, still benefits the performer more than its restriction helps society. ➤ social welfare. ➤➤ Coase theorem; environmental economics; polluter-pays principle.

extraordinary items ➤ below the line.

F

face value Nominal as distinct from market value. The face value of a ➤ security is the price at which it will be redeemed: (a) of an ➤ ordinary share, its ➤ par value or issued price; (b) of a coin, the amount stamped on it which might, for a silver or gold coin, be less than its market value.

factor **1** ➤ factors of production.
   2 ➤ factoring.
   3 An agent who buys and sells goods on behalf of others for a ➤ commission called 'factorage'.

factor cost A term used in the national accounts (➤ social accounting) to describe the valuation of output at market prices less taxes on expenditure plus subsidies.

factor endowment The relative availability of the different ➤ factors of production in a country. An important determinant of the pattern of international trade. ➤ Heckscher-Ohlin principle; ➤➤ comparative advantage.

factoring The business activity in which a company takes over the responsibility for the collecting of the ➤ debts of another. It is a form of asset-based finance primarily intended to meet the needs of small and medium-sized firms (➤ small business; ➤➤ lease). Typically, the client debits all his sales to the factor and receives immediate payment from him less a charge of about 2–3 per cent and interest for the period of ➤ trade credit given to the customer, thus improving the client's cash flow considerably. There are a number of different types of factoring; the simplest is known as 'invoice discounting'. In its most elaborate form the factor maintains the company's sales ledger and other accounting functions, and does not seek recourse to its client if unable to obtain payment from that client's customers (non-recourse factoring). The customer need not know that a factor is being used. The factor generally has some control over sales either by imposing a maximum ➤ credit limit that he is willing to meet or by vetting specific prospective clients. Through international factoring companies, the factor can offer a service to exporters by protecting his customers from bad debts overseas and by giving, for example, expert advice on ➤ foreign exchange transactions.

factor markets The ➤ labour market, the ➤ capital market and other ➤ markets in which the ➤ factors of production are bought and sold. The theory of distribution (➤ distribution, theory of) attempts to explain how the ➤ prices of factors are determined and how they are allocated between alternative uses.

factor payments Payments made to the owners of the ➤ factors of production in return for their use in the production process.

factor price equalization theorem ➤ Samuelson, P.A.

factors of production The inputs or resources used in the process of production. ➤ Land, ➤ labour and ➤ capital are the three primary groups used in analysis of factors, with entrepreneurship (➤ entrepreneur) often counted as a fourth. ➤➤ factor endowment; natural resources; Say, J.-B.

Fair Trading Act ➤ competition policy.

Fama, Eugene F. (b. 1939) ➤ efficient market hypothesis.

famine Improvements in agricultural productivity and the national and international development of transport infrastructure meant that by the last quarter of the nineteenth century Western Europe no longer had to endure recurrent famines. Major famines, however, afflicted parts of the rest of the world throughout the twentieth century in China, India, North Korea and Russia and continue to do so in sub-Saharan Africa. Famines may be initiated by natural disasters such as droughts and floods but are exacerbated by maladministration and inadequate transport links which inhibit the flow of produce from one region to another. Famine does not necessarily lead to death by starvation as such but by the loss of integrity of the immune system, leading to fatal disease. Shortage of food leads to high prices if supplies cannot be transported quickly to the stricken region. The poor cannot afford such prices and therefore are the most susceptible (➤ farm subsidies; foreign aid; protection).

Fannie Mae The Federal National Mortgage Association (FNMA) or Fannie Mae, one of a number of US government-sponsored enterprises (GSEs) aimed at promoting housing finance. The Government National Mortgage Association (GNMA or Ginnie Mae) buys mortgages from banks and other financial institutions for ➤ securitization and sale to investors with a government guarantee. The Federal Home Loan Mortgage Corporation (FHLMC or Freddie Mac) also purchases and securitizes mortgages. Fannie Mae performs a similar function in competition with Freddie Mac and these two institutions together account for about half of US housing finance. The Federal Home Loan Bank System (FHLBS), founded in 1932, provides credit reserves and loans to mortgage-lending institutions and holds public quoted stock in Freddie Mac. With the sharp fall in house prices and the credit crisis after 2007, Freddie Mac and Fannie Mae got into difficulty and were given financial support by the Federal Government and taken into 'conservatorship' in 2008.

FAO ➤ Food and Agriculture Organization.

farm subsidies Financial assistance granted by governments to support and protect their agriculture from foreign competition. ➤ Protection may take the form of import ➤ tariffs, import ➤ quotas, export subsidies, guaranteed commodity prices or direct payments to farmers. Arguments for farm subsidies are: (a) the perceived need to have a secure domestic food supply; (b) to limit the effect of wide fluctuations in farm prices (➤ cobweb model); and (c) to maintain the rural environment. According to the ➤ Organisation for Economic Co-operation and Development

(OECD), the value of subsidies supporting farm production as a proportion of farm revenues between 2006 and 2008 ranged on average from a low of 1 per cent in New Zealand to a high of 62 per cent in Norway, with 10 per cent in the USA and 27 per cent in the ➤ European Union. However, the total value of support granted by the members of the OECD in 2008 amounted to $375 billion, of which $168 billion was by the European Union, $97 billion by the USA and $52 billion by Japan, accounting together for 85 per cent of the total. Such subsidies distort international trade and are detrimental to the economies of the ➤ developing countries. Improvements in market access for agricultural products of the developing countries are included in the ➤ Doha Round of Trade Negotiations. ➤ General Agreement on Tariffs and Trade; protection.

f.a.s. Free alongside ship. The term in a contract by which the seller is required to deliver the goods to a quay or to lighters alongside the vessel at the seaport of shipment specified in the contract of sale. The seller is not obliged to obtain ➤ insurance cover. ➤➤ c.i.f.; f.o.b.

Fed ➤ Federal Reserve System.

Federal Deposit Insurance Corporation (FDIC) (US) An independent US federal government agency founded in 1933. The FDIC insures bank deposits (including those of ➤ savings banks) up to $250,000 per depositor per bank. It is funded by premiums paid by the banks themselves. The FDIC is the primary regulator of banks which are not members of the ➤ Federal Reserve System and monitors compliance with consumer protection laws and assists in consumer financial education. Finally, the FDIC is helping in the implementation of recent reforms of ➤ financial services regulation.

Federal Home Loan Bank System (FHLBS) ➤ Fannie Mae.

Federal Reserve Banks ➤ Federal Reserve System.

Federal Reserve Board ➤ Federal Reserve System.

Federal Reserve System The central banking system (➤ central bank) of the USA, established by the Federal Reserve Act 1913 and organized on a regional basis, given the large area involved and the multiplicity of small- and medium-sized banks. The system is composed of twelve regional Reserve Banks, twenty-five branches and eleven offices under the control of a board of governors located in Washington, DC (the Federal Reserve Board). The board of governors consists of seven governors appointed by Congress on the nomination of the President, each serving for fourteen years, with one reappointment falling due every two years. The chairman of the board of governors is the head of the Federal Reserve System, appointed for a term of four years.

The board approves the Federal funds rate and other ➤ rates of interest of the system, supervises foreign business and generally regulates the operation of the ➤ banking system, including the review of applications for ➤ mergers. It has proved a formidable force in controlling inflation through tight ➤ monetary policy, and its independence in decision-making has been much admired – indeed, partly copied in the reform of the ➤ Bank of England announced in 1997.

The Fed (like other central banks) has been subject to criticism at times. In the 1930s ➤ depression the Fed lost control of the ➤ money supply, allowing it to fall too far and in the 1970s it allowed the money supply to rise too much, resulting in accelerating ➤ inflation. More recently the Fed has been criticized for keeping interest rates too low at the expense of asset inflation and the credit crisis which emerged in 2007–9.

The regional Reserve Banks are controlled by boards of nine directors, of whom three are commercial bankers, three represent local labour and commerce, and three are appointed by the board of governors; the president and vice-president of each Reserve Bank are drawn from the last three. The regional Reserve Banks supervise banking practice and management, act as ➤ lenders of last resort, provide common services in cheque clearing, statistics and research, and apply monetary policy at the instance of the board of governors. Monetary control is exercised chiefly through open market operations and is determined by the board of governors' Federal Open Market Committee (FOMC), day-to-day transactions in pursuance of this being handled by the Reserve Bank of New York. These operations are supplemented by variations in the reserve requirements which the Fed imposes on banks and which include a cash ratio and contractual clearing balances which they hold at the Fed (➤ capital adequacy). By discount window-lending the Fed also extends credit to depository institutions as necessary. In 2004 there were 7,709 ➤ commercial banks of which some 2,900 (national and state banks) were members of the Federal Reserve System.

The Fed's board of governors' constitutional independence is guaranteed by the long-term appointment of the governors and by the fact that the system generates a surplus (mostly paid as a dividend to the Treasury), relieving it of financial dependence on Congress, though it is subject to oversight by that body. The chairman, members and staff of the board frequently explain Federal Reserve policy to congressional committees and maintain close contact with the US administration, but retain final responsibility for their policy. ➤➤ Federal Deposit Insurance Corporation.

Federal Trade Commission ➤ anti-trust.

fertility rate ➤ birth rate.

fiat money Currency that is legally decreed a valid means of financing transactions. It is, in short, ➤ legal tender, in contrast to other forms of paper (e.g. cheques) that carry credibility but no legal support. ➤➤ fiduciary issue; monetary base.

fiduciary issue Paper ➤ money (➤ banknote) not backed by gold or silver. The term has its origins in the Bank Charter Act 1844 in the UK, that fixed the fiduciary issue limit at £14 million. Any notes issued in excess of this amount had to be fully backed by gold. The fiduciary limit has been successively raised and the monetary authorities are now free to alter the note issue as they wish; effectively the note issue is now entirely fiduciary. ➤➤ banking and currency schools.

final consumption ➤ final goods.

final expenditure ➤ final goods.

final goods Goods that are produced for ➤ consumption rather than as an ➤ intermediate product used in the process of production. *Final consumption* (i.e. consumption of final goods alone) is included in the totals of national output in ➤ social accounting. (If intermediate goods were also included there would be double counting of output.) Only government final consumption (that excludes ➤ transfer payments), consumers' expenditure (all of which, by definition, is final) and investment goods enter into *final expenditure* and thus into the ➤ Gross Domestic Product.

finance The provision of ➤ money when and where required. Finance may be short-term (usually up to one year), medium-term (usually over one year and up to 5–7 years) or long-term. Finance may be required for ➤ consumption or for ➤ investment. For the latter, when provided, it becomes ➤ capital. ➤➤ business finance; consumer credit; public finance.

finance company An imprecise term covering a wide range of ➤ financial intermediaries; most commonly a synonym for ➤ finance house.

finance house A financial institution engaged in the provision of ➤ instalment credit. Also called finance companies, hire-purchase finance companies and industrial banks. There are several hundred finance houses in the UK that, together with ➤ credit card companies, account for the bulk of ➤ instalment credit debt, the remainder being owed to retailers. Some of the instalment finance debt of retailers is purchased by the finance houses under what are known as 'block discounts'. The funds of the finance houses come from interest-bearing deposits, not only from the general public but from industrial and commercial companies and other financial institutions, including the ➤ commercial banks (the interest paid is generally higher than that offered by the commercial banks); other sources of funds are capital reserves, ➤ bills discounted and bank overdrafts. The largest source of finance house funds is the commercial banks, however, and most of the larger finance houses are subsidiaries of the banks. Similarly, several finance houses are subsidiaries of manufacturing companies and advance instalment credit only for their parent company's products, e.g. Ford Motor Credit Co. Although advances for cars and other consumer durables represent a major proportion of their business, a huge proportion of the outstanding balances of the finance houses is for business purposes. Hire purchase is not the sole, although it is the main, activity of the finance houses; they also make loans for other purposes, including bridging finance, leasing and ➤ factoring, stocking loans for motor dealers and second mortgages.

financial assets ➤ assets.

financial intermediaries Institutions that hold ➤ money balances of, or borrow from, individuals and other institutions in order to make loans or other ➤ investments. Hence, they serve the purpose of channelling funds from lenders to borrowers. In standing between lenders and borrowers, intermediaries provide services to each, often at little or no cost compared with direct investment. By virtue of their size and expertise, financial intermediaries are able to reduce risks for lenders by enabling them to spread their investments widely, e.g. through ➤ assurance or ➤ investment trusts. They also provide *maturity transformation*. ➤ Building societies, for example, allow depositors to withdraw their money on demand but provide long-term funds for ➤ mortgage lending. It is usual to distinguish between banks in the banking sector and so-called non-bank financial intermediaries. The importance of this distinction arises from the fact that the ➤ liabilities of banks are part of the ➤ money supply, and this may not be true of the non-bank financial intermediaries (➤ banking). The most important of the non-bank financial intermediaries are the building societies, ➤ finance houses, ➤ insurance companies, ➤ savings banks, ➤ pension funds and investment trusts.

financial ratios 1 Specifically, measures of creditworthiness. The principal measures are: (a) the ➤ current ratio; (b) the ➤ debt or *net worth* ratio (long-term debt to net worth); (c) ➤ dividend cover; (d) ➤ interest cover; and (e) the net tangible ➤ assets ratio (total tangible assets less current ➤ liabilities and minority interests to long-term debt). All these ratios are measures of the asset or income cover available to the suppliers of ➤ capital to the business.

2 Generally calculations based on company accounts and other sources, e.g. ➤ stock exchange share prices, designed to indicate the profitability or other financial aspects of a business, e.g. return on net assets, ➤ price–earnings ratio and stock sales ratio (➤ inventories). ➤➤ rate of return.

Financial Services and Markets Act ➤ financial services regulation.

Financial Services Authority (FSA) ➤ financial services regulation.

financial services regulation There are various approaches to the regulation of financial services which is thought to be necessary because of the importance of these markets and because consumers are often not well informed about the nature and risks of financial products. There is some tendency towards the adoption of unitary regulators covering the whole financial service industry but in many countries central banks (➤ central bank) play a role, especially in relation to ➤ banking and there are separate regulators for different branches of the industry.

In the UK the Financial Services Authority (FSA) is a unitary body covering virtually all financial services. The FSA was established under the Financial Services and Markets Act (2000) and replaced the Securities and Investments Board (SIB) and various self-regulating organizations. The operational scope of the FSA has now widened to include: banking; ➤ building societies; ➤ insurance; housing finance; the recognition of domestic and overseas investment exchanges (➤ stock exchange); and independent financial advisers. The ➤ Bank of England and the Treasury have surrendered their authority over the banking system and insurance respectively. The objectives of the FSA, as set out in the Act, are to maintain confidence in the financial system, to protect consumers and to reduce financial crime. It is expected to maintain competition and innovation and to minimize burdens on the industry. In 2009–2010 it had a budget of £415 million and employed about 3,000 people. The budget is sourced by fees charged to regulated firms.

The USA has multiple regulators both at federal and state levels. These regulators include: the ➤ Federal Reserve System; the Office of the Comptroller of the Currency, which supervises the national banks; the ➤ Federal Deposit Insurance Corporation; the Office of Thrift Supervision (➤ savings banks); the Federal Housing

Finance Agency (the mortgage markets); the National Credit Union Administration (➤ credit union) and the ➤ Securities and Exchange Commission. Insurance companies in the USA are regulated by state insurance regulators and each state has a banking department.

In Europe, financial services regulation is by central banks, unitary bodies and separate bodies covering securities and insurance. At pan ➤ European Union level there is a Systemic Risk Council. Following the failure, virtually everywhere, of regulatory institutions to foresee or forestall the 2007–2009 credit crisis, regulatory systems are being reformed.

Financial Stability Board (FSB) The FSB was established in 2009 as a successor to the Financial Stability Forum set up by the ➤ G-7 finance ministers ten years earlier. Its aim is to promote international financial stability by coordinating the work of national regulatory and supervisory financial authorities and standard-setting bodies. The Secretariat is located in Basle and hosted by the ➤ Bank for International Settlements.

financial trusts ➤ trust.

financial year The period of account used for financial purposes. These often do not coincide with calendar years, and are hence referred to as financial years. A financial year 2009–2010, for example, might run from 1 September 2009 to 31 August 2010. The UK government fiscal or tax year runs from 6 April of one year to 5 April in the following year. In the USA the fiscal year runs from 1 July to 30 June.

firm, theory of the The study of the behaviour of firms with respect to: (a) the inputs they buy; (b) the production techniques they adopt; (c) the quantity they produce; and (d) the price at which they sell their output. Two basic approaches to the theory can be identified:

(1) The traditional approach assumes that producers aim to maximize profits; whether they are monopolists or perfect competitors, they produce at a point where ➤ marginal cost equals ➤ marginal revenue, and employ inputs to a point at which their ➤ marginal revenue product is equal to the cost of employing them (➤ labour, demand for; perfect competition).

(2) Other theories attempt to represent the complications of the large institutions which characterize society today, especially the ➤ separation of ownership from control of firms which, it is suggested, may lead to objectives other than profit maximization. These alternative theories postulate the aim as being the maximization of sales, growth or management utility – with profit merely held to some minimum level (➤ satisficing). The ➤ behavioural theory of the firm postulates the existence of a multiplicity of conflicting objectives. It is not clear whether the alternative theories actually contradict the claim of the traditional approach that firms maximize profits because in the long run the maximization of, for example, sales growth might merely amount to the maximization of profit. Moreover, as a single goal, profit maximization perhaps better and more simply approximates to the behaviour of firms than any other single objective. It is thus usually accepted that the insights of traditional theory are useful despite their dependence on apparently unrealistic assumptions.

More recently, ➤ game theory has been influential in analysis of firms, with concepts like the ➤ principal–agent problem increasingly deployed to explain behaviour. ➤➤ Cournot, A.A.; Galbraith, J.K.; Simon, H.A.

first-mover advantage The notion that countries or firms that create new industries or products first may establish a competitive advantage that makes it hard or impossible for other countries or finish to follow in the same area. The advantage is most likely to prevail in sectors with large ➤ economies of scale, and especially in cases where the most efficient scale represents a high proportion of the global market. It would certainly be difficult for, say, China or Japan to enter wide-bodied aircraft manufacture in competition with Boeing and Airbus. The frequency with which airframe manufacture is quoted as an example of potential first-mover advantage suggests it may be one of very few special cases requiring a large supplier chain and technological depth. It is not difficult to think of examples of other first movers (e.g. motorcycles in the UK) that have failed to sustain an early advantage. The argument is not new; it is a variant of the ➤ infant-industry argument for protection against imports. It re-emerged in the late 1980s under the guise of *strategic trade theory* associated with the 2008 ➤ Nobel Prize winner Paul Krugman. He suggested the traditional arguments for nations to allow ➤ free trade were undermined. In practice, however, he has argued that so few industries meet the right conditions to justify strategic trade policy, and the gains are so small, that a presumption in favour of free trade is justified.

fiscal drag The effect of inflation upon effective tax rates, or the effect of growth in ➤ nominal Gross Domestic Product on tax revenues. Under progressive ➤ income tax systems, increases in earnings may push taxpayers into higher tax brackets. In a tax system that is not indexed for inflation (➤ indexation), this has the result that increasing earnings to keep pace with inflation will generate higher tax revenues. With the decline in inflation rates since the 1980s, the term 'fiscal drag' has loosely been used to refer to the fact that, even in an indexed tax system, if earnings grow more quickly than prices (and indeed, they typically do), then the government again ends up with extra revenues without having to raise tax rates in explicit policy changes. Fiscal drag could result in an unintended shift in ➤ fiscal policy, with a depressing effect upon the growth of demand and output. A similar process can work in reverse and under conditions of ➤ deflation, e.g. if prices fall, tax rates will also fall even though real incomes have increased. Fiscal drag, therefore, can have the effect of a ➤ built-in stabilizer; ➤➤ fiscal illusion.

fiscal federalism The system of sharing tax revenues and public expenditure between central and regional government (➤ public sector). Revenue may be raised by the upper level of government and grants given to lower levels on the basis of population or other criteria, or revenues from specific national taxes may be shared in agreed proportions, e.g. a small proportion of national ➤ value-added tax revenues in the ➤ European Union goes to help finance community institutions. Another possibility is that certain ➤ tax bases (e.g. property in the UK) may be reserved for local government, with or without freedom on the part of local authorities to determine their own tax rates. For the division of expenditure between central and regional government, the main principle is that local governments should confine their expenditure to uses which have limited spillovers outside their areas, e.g. roads and schools. ➤ externalities; ➤➤ subsidiarity.

fiscal illusion The lack of transparency in taxation that allows governments to raise extra revenue without the population fully understanding the extent of the tax burden. Fiscal illusion is often a consequence of ➤ fiscal drag. Some economists in the area of ➤ public-choice theory have worried that governments have found it too easy to grow as a result of public ignorance, and have advocated constitutional limits on the size of Western governments' spending. However, the need has diminished with the emergence of pressures from sovereign bond holders and popular resistance to unlimited growth in the tax burden. ➤➤ Buchanan, J.M.; hypothecation; sovereign risk; tax tolerance.

fiscal neutrality The idea that the tax system should be designed so that as few distortions are caused to economic behaviour as possible. It is not fiscally neutral, for example, to apply ➤ value-added tax to some items but not others, for this causes consumers to switch spending from taxed items to untaxed ones. This distortion of behaviour is economically inefficient. Despite the ➤ economic efficiency of applying the principle of fiscal neutrality, it is often argued that distributional or other objectives are served by manipulating different taxes. For this reason, ➤ lump-sum taxes, which are the most neutral, are rarely applied in practice and fiscal neutrality is seen as only one of a number of desirable features of a tax system. ➤➤ deadweight loss; double taxation.

fiscal policy The budgetary stance of central government. Decisions to lower taxation or increase ➤ public expenditure in the interests of stimulating ➤ aggregate demand are referred to as 'loosening fiscal policy'. Higher tax rates or reductions in public expenditure will tighten fiscal policy. There is considerable controversy about the appropriate weight of fiscal policy in economic management, relative to ➤ monetary policy. It is generally left to monetary policy to regulate economic activity in the short term, and the recent goal of fiscal policy has been directed at maintaining a prudent level of borrowing (➤ structural budget deficit), preferably according to certain rules (➤ golden rule; stability and growth pact). This is because tax changes can take too long to be effective in fine-tuning the ups and downs of the economy, and changing tax rates can distort the timing of economic decisions. However, the economic cycle does bring about changes in government borrowing, as tax revenues follow economic activity up and down, and government borrowing thus tends to swing counter-cyclically. This is automatically stabilizing of the economy. ➤➤ balanced budget; Keynesian economics; policy ineffectiveness theorem; quantity theory of money; reflation.

fiscal year ➤ financial year.

Fisher, Irving (1867–1947) A mathematician by professional training, Fisher was Professor of Political Economy at Yale University from 1898 to 1935. His main works on economics are *Mathematical Investigations in the Theory of Value and Prices* (1892), *The Nature of Capital and Income* (1906), *The Rate of Interest* (1907), *The Purchasing Power of Money* (1911), *The Making of Index Numbers* (1922) and *The Theory of Interest* (1930). *The Rate of Interest*, which was substantially revised in 1930, developed the theory of ➤ interest from ➤ Böhm-Bawerk towards the modern theory of ➤ investment appraisal. The ➤ rate of interest is governed by the interaction of two forces: (a) the 'willingness or impatience' of individuals with respect to the giving up of ➤ income now compared with income in the future (Fisher invented the term ➤ 'time preference'), and (b) the 'investment opportunity principle', the technological ability to convert income now into income in the future. He called the latter the 'rate of return over cost', which ➤ Keynes said was the same as his 'marginal efficiency of capital' (➤ internal rate of return). He defined this 'rate of return over cost' as that discount rate (➤ discounting) that equalized the ➤ present value of the possible alternative investment choices open.

Fisher showed how the ranking of investment choices depended on the rate of interest used. He emphasized the distinction between the nominal rate of interest and the real rate of interest, the nominal rate adjusted for ➤ inflation.

Fisher clarified economists' ideas on the nature of ➤ capital, distinguishing between a stock and a flow of ➤ wealth. A house is capital stock, but its use is a flow of income. He was the author (1911) of the 'quantity of money' (exchange) equation $MV = PT$, in which M = the stock of money, V = the ➤ velocity of circulation, P = the ➤ price level and T = the output of goods and ➤ services (➤ quantity theory of money). Fisher developed the theory of ➤ index numbers and established a set of conditions which an ideal index should satisfy.

Fisher equation ➤ Fisher, I.; quantity theory of money.

fixed asset ➤ assets.

fixed capital ➤ business finance; capital.

fixed charge ➤ floating charge.

fixed costs ➤ Costs that do not vary with output, e.g. the ➤ rent on a factory ➤ lease. Also called *overheads,* although in accounting terminology all costs except direct labour and materials are usually regarded as overheads and some of these overhead costs (e.g. electricity and postage) may vary with output. In the ➤ long run all costs are variable, and the ➤ short run is defined as the period of time in which all the ➤ factors of production cannot be varied. ➤➤ average costs; sunk costs.

fixed debenture ➤ floating debentures.

fixed exchange rate A rate of exchange of a currency which is fixed in relation to a foreign currency or a group of foreign currencies. ➤ exchange rate; floating exchange rate; International Monetary Fund.

fixed interest ➤ securities.

fixed-point theorem A theorem stating that for certain types of functions, $y = f(x)$, there is at least one value of x such that $y = x$. That is, that x maps on to itself, or x is a fixed point. These theorems are used in ➤ equilibrium analysis to help prove the existence of a ➤ general equilibrium. If a simple economy can be modelled as a system of functions that conform to the types described in a fixed-point theorem, the fact that a fixed point must exist can be turned into proof that a market equilibrium exists.

fixed trust ➤ flexible trust.

flags of convenience The regulations applicable to merchant ships are those of the country in which it is registered and whose flag it flies. The term 'flags of convenience' refers to those of countries which have set up registries solely to produce revenue. Shipowners are attracted to them rather than the countries of their home ports as they offer benefits from less stringent regulation in, for instance, the employment of crews.

flat tax A tax (➤ taxation) on incomes at a fixed rate, i.e. one that does not alter with income levels beyond a threshold. Flat taxes can reduce ➤ compliance costs and advocates argue that they may increase revenue by raising tax compliance (➤➤ Laffer curve). Such a tax is likely to be regressive but it has been adopted in Russia and in ➤ transition economies in some other Eastern European countries.

flat yield A ➤ yield on a fixed-interest ➤ security, calculated by expressing the annual ➤ interest payable as a proportion of the purchase price of the security. It omits any allowance for the difference between purchase price and redemption price. ➤➤ redeemable securities.

flexible trust The most common form of ➤ unit trust, in which the ➤ portfolio of ➤ securities purchased by the trust can be varied at the discretion of the managers. Also called a 'managed' trust. Flexible trusts were developed in the 1930s to overcome the problems raised by the inflexibility of *fixed trusts*, in which the investment portfolio is fixed in the trust deed.

floating asset ➤ floating capital.

floating capital ➤ Capital that is not invested in fixed ➤ assets (e.g. machinery) but in work in progress, wages paid, etc. Synonymous with ➤ working capital. ➤➤ current ratio.

floating charge An assignment of the total ➤ assets of a company or individual as ➤ collateral security for a ➤ debt, as opposed to particular assets, when such an assignment is called a *fixed charge*.

floating debentures A type of debenture (➤ bond) in which the ➤ loan is secured by a charge on the assets of a firm generally. Where specific assets secure a debenture loan, it is known as a *fixed debenture*.

floating debt 1 Generally, any short-term ➤ debt as opposed to ➤ funded debt.
   2 Specifically, that part of the UK ➤ national debt that consists of short-term borrowing, i.e. ➤ Treasury bills. Treasury bills form an important part of the ➤ liquid assets of the money market, so that the size of the floating debt has considerable influence over the total ➤ money supply.

floating exchange rate A rate of exchange of a currency which is determined by market forces in relation to foreign currencies. ➤ exchange rate; fixed exchange rate; International Monetary Fund.

flotation Raising new ➤ capital by public subscription. A private company issuing ➤ shares to the public for the first time is said to be 'going public' or making an *Initial Public Offering*. ➤➤ stock exchange; unlisted securities markets.

f.o.b. Free on board. The term in a contract under which the seller's contract

includes the delivery to and loading of the goods for sale on board ship at the seaport of shipment, at which point the buyer takes over the title (ownership) for the
goods.

Fogel, Robert William (b. 1926) A joint winner of the ➤ Nobel Prize for Economics in 1993, an economic historian and director of the Center for Population
Economics at the University of Chicago, Fogel has been a pioneer in the area of
'new economic history'. This attempts to analyse the past on the basis of new, or
reconstructed databases. Fogel has applied this approach in controversial ways, e.g.
to argue that slavery was an economically efficient social order that ultimately collapsed on account of political decisions. He has also reassessed the role of the
railways in American economic development, in *Railroads and American Economic
Growth* (1964), arguing that the sum of many changes, rather than a few great innovations, determines economic advance. ➤ cliometrics; North, D.

FOMC ➤ Federal Reserve System.

Food and Agricultural Organization (FAO) An organization set up in 1945, with
headquarters in Rome, within the framework of the United Nations. It conducts
research and offers technical assistance with the aim of improving the standards of
living of agricultural areas. It is concerned with the improvement of ➤ productivity
and distribution networks for the agricultural, forestry and fishing industries. It
conducts surveys, issues statistics, produces forecasts of the world food situation
and sets minimum nutritional standards.

forced saving A situation in which expenditure falls short of ➤ disposable income
because goods are not available for ➤ consumption, rather than because consumers
have voluntarily decided to accumulate ➤ saving. Under these circumstances,
➤ prices of goods would rise and supply would increase in a ➤ free-market economy so that forced saving would be a temporary symptom or ➤ disequilibrium.
If for any reason there were ➤ long-run constraints on the increase in output,
the increase in prices would reduce demand and stimulate the development of
➤ substitutes. Forced saving does occur in ➤ planned economies and, at a ➤ macroeconomic level, democratic governments can enforce saving by increasing ➤ taxation
while holding ➤ public expenditure constant. ➤➤ quantity rationing; repressed
inflation.

foreign aid ➤ development assistance.

foreign balance ➤ balance of payments.

foreign bill of exchange ➤ foreign exchange market.

foreign direct investment (FDI) Investment in a foreign country through the
acquisition of a local company or the establishment there of an operation on a new
('greenfield') site. Direct investment implies control and managerial, and perhaps
technical, input. According to statistics collected by the ➤ United Nations Conference on Trade and Development, the total world inflow of foreign direct investment
grew from US$1,270 billion in 2000 to US$1,697 billion in 2008 but in the following year dropped to about US$1,040. In 2009, the ➤ developing countries received
about US$621 billion, ➤ transition economies US$114 billion and the ➤ advanced

countries US$ 962 billion. ➤ development assistance; foreign investment; globalization; multinational corporation.

foreign exchange Claims on another country held in the form of the currency of that country or interest-bearing ➤ bonds. ➤➤ exchange control; foreign exchange market; gold and foreign exchange reserves.

foreign exchange market The ➤ market in which transactions are conducted to effect the transfer of the ➤ currency of one country into that of another. The need to settle accounts with foreigners gave rise to the *foreign bill of exchange*, which was accepted by banks or other institutions of international standing (accepting house). These bills were traded at discount, and in this way the foreign exchange market was established, the bills reflecting actual international trade flows. However, the market has developed in modern times and is now dominated by financial institutions that buy and sell foreign currencies, making their ➤ profit from the divergences between the ➤ exchange rates and ➤ rates of interest in the various financial centres. In April 2001, the ➤ Bank for International Settlements estimated that average daily world turnover in foreign exchange dealing was US$1,200 billion compared with a turnover of US$1,490 billion recorded in its previous survey for April 1998. Within the total, dollar–euro transactions accounted for 30 per cent, dollar–yen 20 per cent and dollar–sterling 11 per cent. ➤ forward exchange market; ➤➤ convertibility; Tobin tax.

foreign exchange reserves ➤ gold and foreign exchange reserves.

foreign investment The acquisition by governments, institutions or individuals in one country of ➤ assets in another. Foreign investment covers both ➤ foreign direct investment and ➤ portfolio investment, and includes public authorities, private firms and individuals. For a country in which ➤ savings are insufficient relative to the potential demand for ➤ investment, foreign capital can be a fruitful means of stimulating rapid growth. In addition, foreign investment may be a means of financing a ➤ balance of payments deficit.

forward exchange market A ➤ market in which contracts are made to supply ➤ currencies at fixed dates in the future at fixed ➤ prices. Currencies may be bought and sold in the ➤ foreign exchange market either 'spot' or 'forward' (➤ forward market; spot market). In the former case, the transaction takes place immediately, and it is in this market that ➤ exchange rates are kept at their managed levels by government intervention. In the forward exchange market, currencies are bought and sold for transacting at some future date, i.e. in three months' or six months' time. The difference between the 'spot' rate of exchange and the 'forward' rate is determined by the ➤ rate of interest and the exchange risk, i.e. the possibility of ➤ appreciation or ➤ depreciation of the currencies transacted. Therefore, the size of the ➤ premium or ➤ discount of, for example, forward dollars compared with spot dollars indicates the strength of the market's expectation of an appreciation or depreciation of the dollar and its extent. ➤ exchange-rate overshooting.

forward market Any ➤ market in ➤ futures, i.e. a market in which promises to buy or to sell ➤ securities or ➤ commodities at some future date at fixed ➤ prices are bought and sold. An example of a forward market is the ➤ forward exchange market.

franchising A contractual arrangement under which an independent franchisee produces or sells a product or service under the brand name of the franchiser and to his/her specifications and with marketing and other support. The franchisee pays a royalty to the franchiser and may purchase supplies from him/her. The franchisee provides his/her own ➤ capital and is legally an independent ➤ enterprise that is none the less highly dependent upon the franchiser, though, as Curran and Stanworth have pointed out, many ➤ small businesses (e.g. with a high proportion of sales to a single customer) may enjoy no greater degree of independence than many franchised enterprises. Franchising is growing rapidly in the UK but is less important than in the USA.

franked investment income ➤ Income, normally of a company, on which ➤ taxation has already been paid at source, i.e. income received as a ➤ dividend by one company from another (➤ corporation tax).

Freddie Mac ➤ Fannie Mae.

free depreciation ➤ capital allowances.

freedom of entry Absence of ➤ barriers to entry preventing new suppliers entering a ➤ market. One of the assumptions of ➤ perfect competition. ➤➤ contestability.

free-enterprise economy ➤ free-market economy.

free goods ➤ Commodities that have no ➤ price because they are not scarce and do not require the use of scarce ➤ factors of production to create them, e.g. fresh air and sunshine (in certain parts of the world). Things that are given away without charge (e.g. a book of matches or government services) are not free goods because they have ➤ opportunity costs.

free market A ➤ market in which ➤ supply and ➤ demand are not subject to ➤ regulation other than normal ➤ competition policy, but in which property rights are allocated and upheld so that trade can occur. The definition of a free market becomes blurred in cases where free trade and competition are incompatible. Most economists would be loath to describe the world diamond market as completely free, given its dominance by an international cartel arrangement. ➤➤ Chicago School; Coase theorem.

free-market economy Strictly, an economic system in which the allocation of ➤ resources is determined solely by ➤ supply and ➤ demand in ➤ free markets, though in practice there are some limitations on market freedoms in all countries. Moreover, in some countries governments intervene in free markets to promote competition that might otherwise disappear. Usually used as synonymous with ➤ capitalism.

free on board ➤ f.o.b.

freeport A seaport or airport that is able to accept cargo without the imposition of any import ➤ tariff or some specified ➤ taxes. In addition, freeports may be granted special dispensation regarding legislation affecting businesses in the domestic market outside the port, e.g. employment conditions, health and safety regulations and development planning. There are several hundred such ports throughout the world. ➤➤ free trade zone.

free reserves ➤ company reserves.

free rider problem The problem, arising in many situations, that no individual is willing to contribute toward the cost of something when he/she hopes that someone else will bear the cost instead. The problem arises whenever there is a ➤ public good, e.g. everybody in a block of flats may want a faulty light repaired, but no one wants to bear the cost of organizing the repair themselves – they would each rather free-ride on the effort of someone else. Examples of the problem abound. For example, shareholders take little interest in the management of their companies, hoping someone else will monitor what the executives are doing (➤ separation of ownership from control); rude taxi drivers free-ride on the reputation of the profession as a whole; nations who contribute nothing to disaster-relief efforts are said to free-ride on the efforts of others. Obtaining satisfactory levels of managerial monitoring, politeness or disaster relief in these situations is difficult in the absence of compulsory enforcement measures. ➤ stability and growth pact.

free trade The condition in which the free flow of goods (➤ economic good) and ➤ services in international exchange is neither restricted nor encouraged by direct government intervention. In practice, all governments are involved in regulating overseas trade in some way. The most common means of affecting the distribution and levels of international trade are import ➤ tariffs, import ➤ quotas and export subsidies (➤ export incentives). It has been broadly accepted among economists that an international free trade policy is desirable to optimize world output and ➤ income levels in the long run.

The ➤ Organisation for Economic Co-operation and Development and the United Nations (➤ World Trade Organization) are committed to freeing world trade. Towards the end of the eighteenth century there was a reaction against ➤ mercantilism, which had advocated government intervention to obtain surpluses on ➤ visible trade. This reaction was consolidated in a new economic liberalism and the doctrine of ➤ *laissez-faire*. The ➤ classical economists' support of a free trade policy was not so much based on specific economic analyses of international trade as simply part of their general belief in what ➤ Adam Smith called the 'hidden hand': the greatest good is achieved if each individual is left to seek his own ➤ profit. (➤➤ Ricardo, David).

The free trade era lasted in England for almost a century. After the First World War, economic nationalism reached its peak and free trade was abandoned for ➤ protection. However, since the end of the Second World War, there has been a general acceptance internationally of the dangers of protectionism and considerable reduction in barriers to ➤ international trade, especially for manufactured goods. Progress has paradoxically been associated with the growth of regional ➤ customs unions and regional trade areas. Some economists have advocated unilateral free trade (countries can help themselves by freeing up imports, regardless of other countries' behaviour). Other economists have seen the problem as that of the ➤ prisoner's dilemma – with gains for nations individually if they restrict trade but a collective net benefit if all nations should pursue it. In practice, the latter view is reflected in the several international negotiations pursued through the ➤ General Agreement on Tariffs and Trade, culminating in the setting up of the World Trade Organization and continuing in the ➤ Doha Round of Trade Negotiations.

free trade area An association of a number of countries between which all import ➤ tariffs and ➤ quotas and export subsidies and other similar government measures to influence trade (➤ export incentives) have been removed. Each country, however, continues to retain its own international trade measures vis-à-vis countries outside the association (➤ certificate of origin). There has been an increase in recent years in the number of trading areas being formed worldwide (➤ regional trade agreements).

free trade zone A customs-defined area in which goods or services may be processed or transacted without attracting taxes or duties or being subjected to certain government regulations. A special case is the ➤ freeport, into which goods are imported free of customs ➤ tariffs or taxes. According to the ➤ International Labour Organization, there are about 850 free trade zones throughout the world, employing about 30 million people, almost all of them women.

frequency distribution A tabulation showing a (statistical) ➤ population allocated numerically into sub-categories of a specified classification (➤➤ income, distribution of). For example, the following table shows the frequency distributions of populations in different age groups compared between countries in 2005. ➤➤ demographic time bomb

Age group	Number (millions)				
	China	India	USA	Europe[a]	World
0–14 years	279	350	62	49	1809
15–64 years	925	687	198	210	4153
65 and over	99	58	36	56	476
Total	1304	1095	296	314	6438

[a]European Economic and Monetary Union (EMU).
Source: World Bank, 2009.

frictional unemployment The ➤ unemployment that results from the process of jobseeking. It will exist under conditions of so-called full employment (➤ employment, full), but it is not precisely clear what proportion of total unemployment can be called 'frictional'. Frictional unemployment arises in the functioning of ➤ labour markets because of inevitable time lags in a ➤ free-market economy – there are search delays involved, for example, in moving from one job to another. Frictional unemployment is conceptually distinct from ➤ structural unemployment, which results in heavy local concentrations of unemployment, and from unemployment arising from a deficiency of demand. ➤➤ classical unemployment; labour, mobility of.

Friedman, Milton (1912–2006) Professor of Economics at the University of Chicago and leading member of the Chicago School. After a short period with the Natural Resources Commission in Washington, Professor Friedman joined the research staff of the National Bureau of Economic Research in 1937. During the Second World War, he served in the Tax Research Division of the US Treasury. In 1946, he was appointed Associate Professor of Economics and Statistics at the University of Chicago, becoming Professor of Economics there from 1948 until he retired in 1977. There followed the appointment as senior research fellow at the Hoover Institution at Stanford University, a post he held until his death in 2006. In 1976, he was awarded the ➤ Nobel Prize in Economics 'for his achievements in the fields of consumption analysis, monetary history and theory, and for his demonstration of the complexity of stabilization policy'. His main published works in economics include *Taxing to Prevent Inflation* (1943), *Essays in Positive Economics* (1953), *A Theory of the Consumption Function* (1957), *A Program for Monetary Stability* (1960), *Price Theory* (1962), *A Monetary History of the United States 1867–1960* (1963), *Inflation: Causes and Consequences* (1963), *The Great Contraction, 1929–1933* (1965), *The Optimum Quantity of Money* (1969), *A Theoretical Framework for Monetary Analysis* (1971), *An Economist's Protest: Columns on Political Economy* (1975), *Free to Choose. A Personal Statement* (1980) and *Monetary Trends in the United States and the United Kingdom* (1982).

Friedman made contributions to the theory of distribution (➤ distribution, theory of), arguing for an approach in which high incomes are regarded as a reward for taking risks. He was a leading defender of the Marshallian tradition in ➤ microeconomics (➤ Marshall, A.) and made a methodological defence of classical economics that stimulated controversy for a decade. His ➤ permanent-income hypothesis was also an important contribution to the theory of the ➤ consumption function. His main work, however, was on the development of the ➤ quantity theory of money and its empirical testing. He extended the Fisher equation (➤ Fisher, I.) to include other variables such as ➤ wealth and ➤ rates of interest, and made statistical tests to attempt to measure the factors determining the demand for money to hold. Friedman advocated strict control of the ➤ money supply – preferably in accordance with a simple rule as to how much growth will be allowed year by year – as a means for controlling ➤ inflation. His view that it was not desirable to fine-tune the economy using ➤ stabilization policy (an early adherent to the ➤ policy ineffectiveness theorem) has, to a large extent, been accepted, but in the world of economic theory Friedman's findings have been overshadowed by the more elegant route to similar conclusions based on ➤ rational expectations associated with ➤ new classical economics. He expressed doubts about the stability of the ➤ European Economic and Monetary Union, being concerned about structural inflexibilities in and between the labour markets of the member countries in the event of a serious ➤ recession (➤ Chicago School; economic doctrines; liquidity preference; unemployment, natural rate of.)

fringe benefits Non-wage or salary rewards provided for employees, e.g. pensions and company cars. Some fringe benefits, within certain limits (e.g. pension arrangements, private use of company e-mail, or subsidized canteens) are not assessed for ➤ income tax, while others (e.g. cars and low-interest loans) are. Holidays (in excess of any legal minimum requirement), private health insurance and discounts on goods purchased through the employer are other examples of fringe benefits. In England, a series of laws from 1749 onwards, culminating in the Truck Acts in the nineteenth century, made it illegal to pay workers wholly in kind, because of abuse by employers of rights given, for example, in 'company stores'.

Frisch, Ragnar A.K. (1895–1973) Born in Norway, Professor Frisch graduated in economics at the University of Oslo. He was appointed to the Chair of Economics at that university in 1931, a post he held until he retired in 1965. His published works include *Statistical Confluence Analysis by Means of Complete Regression Systems* (1934), *Planning for India* (1960), *Theory of Production* (1965), *Maxima and Minima* (1966) and *Economic Planning Studies: A collection of essays* (1976). He won the ➤ Nobel Prize in Economics (jointly with Tinbergen) in 1969.

Professor Frisch pioneered work in the application of mathematics and statistics in the testing of hypotheses in economics. He invented the word ➤ 'econometrics' and founded the Econometric Society. He contributed to the analysis of the dynamics of ➤ trade cycles and the application of econometrics to economic planning.

FTC Federal Trade Commission (➤ anti-trust).

full employment ➤ employment, full.

full-line forcing The exercise of market power to oblige a buyer to take a whole range of products rather than only one of them. Also known as ➤ tie-in sales, that more strictly means that the sale of a product carries with it a condition that some other item will be purchased at the same time. ➤➤ competition policy; vertical restraints.

function A description of the relationship which governs the behaviour of two or more related ➤ variables. Functions can be expressed in different ways. If consumption C is $0.9 \times$ income Y, we can represent this information as either: an equation ($C = 0.9Y$), a graph (C on one axis, Y on the other), or a tabulation (with certain values of C in one column and the corresponding values of Y in the other). The function is an important feature of many different areas of economics. For example, the ➤ utility function maps the quantities of different goods consumed against corresponding levels of consumer utility. A ➤ demand function maps different price levels against the corresponding quantities demanded. ➤➤ production function.

fundamental analysis ➤ chartist.

fundamental-equilibrium real exchange rate That ➤ real exchange rate which would be consistent with an economy in full employment and with a stable current ➤ balance of payments. The concept was explored in a paper in 1983 by John Williamson of the Peterson Institute for International Economics, and methodologies have been developed on its premise to estimate whether a country's current exchange rates appear to be over- or under-valued.

funded ➤ pension funds.

funded debt Generally, short-term ➤ debt that has been converted into long-term debt (➤ funding). Specifically, the funded debt was originally that consisting of ➤ consols, the ➤ interest on which was paid out of the ➤ Consolidated Fund. Then it came to mean all government perpetual ➤ loans where there is no obligation on the part of the government to repay (e.g. consols 2½ per cent war loan) but it is sometimes taken to include all government ➤ securities quoted on the ➤ stock exchange.

funding The process of converting short-term to long-term ➤ debt by the sale of long-term ➤ securities and using the funds raised to pay off short-term debt. Funding may be carried out by a company because its ➤ capital structure is inappropriate, i.e. to take advantage of the fact that long-term ➤ capital is normally cheaper and less likely to be withdrawn than short-term capital. Companies or governments may also take advantage of a period of low ➤ rates of interest to repay long-term ➤ stocks at the earliest possible date and replace them with new stocks at lower rates of interest.

Funding has also been used as an instrument of ➤ monetary policy by the government as well as for ➤ national debt management. By selling long-dated securities and purchasing ➤ Treasury bills (which are treated as part of the ➤ cash reserves of the ➤ commercial banks), the ➤ liquidity of the ➤ banking system is reduced. *Overfunding* occurs when the government is selling more debt to the non-bank sector than is necessary to meet the ➤ public sector borrowing requirement. ➤➤ pension funds.

funding operations The conversion of short-term fixed-interest ➤ debt (➤ floating debt) to long-term fixed-interest debt (➤ funded debt). It is normally used in relation to the management of the ➤ national debt, but the ➤ Bank of England's operations in ➤ Treasury bills and government ➤ bonds approaching maturity are also covered by the term. Private companies with bank overdrafts or other short-term sources of ➤ capital may also decide to convert them to long-term debt by funding operations. ➤➤ funding.

futures Contracts made in a 'future ➤ market' for the purchase or sale of ➤ commodities or financial ➤ assets, on a specified future date. Futures are negotiable instruments, i.e. they may be bought and sold. Many commodity exchanges (e.g. wool, cotton and wheat) have established futures markets that permit manufacturers and traders to ➤ hedge against changes in the ➤ price of the raw materials they use or deal in. ➤➤ forward exchange market; London International Financial Futures Exchange; options; speculation.

G

G-7 Originally a forum of the world's largest five industrial economies: the USA, Japan, Germany, France and the UK; the group became G-7 in 1986 when Italy and Canada joined and G-8 in 1997 when Russia also joined the group. Their finance ministers have met regularly. In 2002, in Halifax, Canada, the group confirmed action plans for the control of potential international financial crises and for international cooperation in the policing of the financing of terrorism.

G-20 A group of ➤ advanced and ➤ developing countries whose finance ministers and ➤ central bank governors meet regularly to agree international cooperative measures to maintain international growth. The group is composed of nineteen countries and the ➤ European Union. Following the financial crisis in 2008, the G-20 agreed to implement coordinated macroeconomic policies, embracing both fiscal and monetary expansion, to counter a severe fall into recession.

Galbraith, John Kenneth (1908–2006) He was born in Canada and, after graduating at Toronto in Agriculture, took a Ph.D. in Agricultural Economics at the University of California. In 1949, he became Professor of Economics at Harvard University and was, from 1961 to 1963, US ambassador to India. His major books include *A Theory of Price Control* (1952), *American Capitalism* (1952), *The Great Crash, 1929* (1955), *The Affluent Society* (1958), *The New Industrial State* (1967), *A Contemporary Guide to Economics, Peace and Laughter* (1971), *Economics and the Public Purpose* (1973), *The Nature of Mass Poverty* (1979), *A Short History of Financial Euphoria* (1990) and *The Culture of Contentment* (1992).

He was critical of current economic theory because of its preoccupation with growth (➤ growth theory), and argued that in modern advanced economies the problems of the distribution of the total product to the different sectors of society should be given more attention. In *American Capitalism* (1952) he argued that modern society bred monopolistic power systems. ➤ Monopoly in industry induces a countervailing monopoly or ➤ monopsony in distribution, in ➤ labour and even in government purchasing agencies.

In *The New Industrial State* (1967) he argued that the 'technostructures' (managers) of the largest corporations in modern industrial society were motivated primarily by a desire to remain secure and to expand their corporation rather than to maximize ➤ profits. The highly capitalized nature of the industrial system required a considerable extension of planning and control, notably of the capital supply through ➤ self-financing, and of demand through advertising and distribution techniques. Under these conditions the assumption of ➤ consumers' sovereignty that underlay modern microeconomic theory (➤ microeconomics) was invalid.

Galbraith's views have been challenged by many economists as an overstatement of monopolistic power but are none the less sometimes accepted as an accurate statement of tendency in the modern economy. He was critical of the advocates of the strict control of the supply of ➤ money as a means of reducing ➤ inflation (➤ consumption; countervailing power; firm, theory of the; Friedman, M; Keynes, J.M.; Mill, J.S.; oligopoly; quantity theory of money.)

Galiani, Ferdinando (1728–87) A Neapolitan priest who wrote a number of treatises on economic subjects, in particular *Della moneta* (1751) on ➤ money and exchange, and *Dialogues sur le commerce des blés* (1770) on ➤ free trade in cereals. He resolved the so-called ➤ paradox of value (e.g. water is useful but cheap, whereas diamonds are useless but expensive), by analysing the ➤ price of a ➤ commodity in terms of its ➤ scarcity on the one hand and its ➤ utility on the other – utility being not only a reflection of a commodity's usefulness, but also its pleasure-giving potential. He explained how price both influences, and is influenced by, ➤ demand. Much of his work in ➤ value theory was original, though part of a long tradition of ecclesiastical thought. However, he was not familiar to English economists of the early nineteenth century, and much of the ground covered by Galiani was revisited by them. ➤➤ marginal utility.

game theory The branch of economics concerned with representing economic interactions in a highly stylized form, with players, pay-offs and strategies. Much of economic theory is concerned with the processes and conditions under which individuals or firms maximize their own benefits or minimize their own costs in markets in which their individual actions do not materially influence others (➤➤ perfect competition). There are, however, many cases in which economic decisions are made – often in situations of conflict – where one party's action induces a material reaction from others, e.g. wage bargaining between employers and unions. A more simple case is that of ➤ duopoly, in which the price set by one seller will be based on his/her view of that set by the other in reply. The mathematical theory of games has been applied to economics to help elucidate problems of this kind. The theory of games is concerned with the study of the optimal strategies to maximize pay-offs, given the risks involved in judging the responses of adversaries and also the conditions under which there is a unique solution, i.e. that the optimum strategy for X and that of Y are both possible and not inconsistent.

Games may be classified into ➤ zero-sum games, in which one player's gain is another player's loss; *non-zero-sum games*, in which one player's decision may benefit (or hurt) all players; *cooperative games*, in which collusion between players is possible, and *non-cooperative games*, when it is not. The application of the theory of games to economics was first introduced by John von Neumann and Oskar Morgenstern in *Theory of Games and Economic Behaviour* (1944). It has since risen to become perhaps the most important source of new ideas in ➤ microeconomics, and the mindset of game theory now dominates almost any analysis of interactions between economic agents. Game theory was at the heart of the design of the rules applied in the ➤➤ auction of telecommunications licences in the UK in 2000. ➤➤ bargaining; battle of the sexes; mixed strategy; Nash equilibrium; prisoner's dilemma; repeated game; tit-for-tat.

GATT ➤ General Agreement on Tariffs and Trade.

GDP ➤ Gross Domestic Product.

GDP deflator An index of prices (➤ index number) that can be applied to the value estimates of the ➤ Gross Domestic Product (GDP) over a time period in order to remove the effects of changes in the general level of prices. The resultant revised estimates give a more accurate picture of movements during the period in the physical or real output of goods and services. In practice, the components of GDP are deflated (➤ deflation) separately to constant prices and then added together to give an estimate for a given year in ➤ real terms. The advantage of the GDP deflator, as a measure of domestic ➤ inflation, is that it strips out the effect on prices of a change in the price of ➤ imports, on account of, say, a change in the ➤ exchange rate. It is argued that it represents the best measure of underlying inflation. It is not used as the basis for the ➤ inflation target, as publication of the deflator is less frequent than the ➤ consumer prices index, and often subject to late revision.

gearing The relative importance of ➤ loans in the ➤ capital structure of a firm. Also called the *debt ratio* and, in the USA, *leverage*. There are several ways of measuring gearing. The usual way is the ratio of fixed-interest ➤ debt to shareholder's interest plus the debt (➤ net worth). *Equity gearing* is the ratio of borrowings to ➤ equity or risk capital. *Capital gearing* may be defined as bank borrowings and other debt as a percentage of *net tangible assets* (➤ assets; financial ratios). A corporation may borrow ➤ capital at fixed interest, and if it can earn more on that capital than it has to pay for it in interest, then the additional earnings accrue to the ➤ equity shareholders.

A firm with high gearing will be able to pay higher ➤ dividends per ➤ share than a firm with lower gearing earning exactly the same return on its total capital, provided that return is higher than the rate it pays for ➤ loan capital. However, the contrary is also true, so that the higher the gearing, the greater the risk to the equity shareholder. Roughly speaking, if a firm's initial capital consists of $7000 subscribed by ordinary shareholders and $3000 borrowed at fixed interest (e.g. through ➤ debentures) it would be said to have a gearing of 30 per cent. The tax system (➤ taxation) encourages gearing, since interest is deductible for ➤ corporation tax but dividends are not. ➤➤ Modigliani-Miller theorem.

General Agreement on Tariffs and Trade (GATT) An international organization that came into operation in 1948. Its Articles of Agreement pledged its member countries to: (a) the expansion of multilateral trade (➤ multilateralism) with the minimum of barriers to trade; (b) the reduction in import tariffs (➤ tariffs, import) and ➤ quotas; and (c) the abolition of preferential trade agreements. There have been successive negotiations between the contracting parties, aimed at reducing the levels of tariffs, from the first meeting in Geneva in 1947, up to the eighth, so-called ➤ Uruguay Round of trade negotiations that began in 1986 and was concluded in 1993. In 1965, a revision came into force that laid emphasis on the special problems of the ➤ developing countries and a committee on trade and development was given the responsibility for progress on the elimination of barriers on the trade in products of particular interest to the developing nations. This enabled the ➤ most-favoured nation clause to be waived in relation to agreements entered into with developing countries (➤ generalized system of preferences).

A ministerial meeting of GATT was held in 1982 to reaffirm the ➤ free trade principles upon which GATT was founded. The ministers affirmed that they would 'make determined efforts to resist protectionist measures and refrain from taking or maintaining any measures inconsistent with GATT'. Agreement was reached, at Punta del Este, Uruguay, in 1986, on an agenda for the Uruguay Round of trade negotiations. The GATT became the responsibility of the ➤ World Trade Organization from 1 January 1995. A further round of trade negotiations was agreed at Doha in 2002. ➤ Doha Round of trade negotiations.

General Agreement on Trade in Services (GATS) Following from decisions made at the ➤ Uruguay Round of trade negotiations, rules were established for the liberalization of international trade in ➤ services, e.g. banking, insurance, transport, telecommunications, health and education provision. The aims of the GATS were confirmed at the ➤ Doha Round of trade negotiations that were begun in 2002.

general equilibrium The state of a set of interrelated markets when there is no ➤ excess demand or supply in any market. In a world of two commodities, increase in demand for one must lead to a decrease in demand for the other if all consumers spend what they have and no more. Given this interrelation, it is not as obvious that equilibrium can prevail in all markets simultaneously as it is that it can prevail in one market at a time. ➤ Arrow-Debreu general equilibrium model; Walras, M.E.L.

general equilibrium analysis 1 The study of the behaviour of economic variables, taking full account of the interaction between those variables and the rest of the economy. For example, a general equilibrium approach to the study of waiters' wages would concentrate both on demand and supply in the market for waiters *and* the effects of wages or unemployment in other markets more generally. In this it contrasts with partial equilibrium analysis.

2 The study of simultaneous equilibria in a group of related markets. The prime focus is whether there is a set of prices that would ensure that equilibrium exists in each market. If so, is such an equilibrium stable – if disruptions occurred, would there be a tendency to return to equilibrium? And is such an equilibrium unique, or are there any sets of prices at which all markets clear? The analysis is attributable to ➤ Walras, who limited his consideration to a theoretical economic system in which all consumers were utility-maximizers and firms perfectly competitive. A unique, stable equilibrium can exist in such an economy. ➤ Arrow-Debreu general equilibrium model; dynamic stochastic general equilibrium model; Leontief, W.W.; Walras, M.E.L.

general government Term used as an overall heading for the central and local government sectors, but which excludes public corporations. General government is thus a more restrictive notion of the state than that defined as the ➤ public sector.

generalized system of preferences The elimination or reduction of import ➤ tariffs by the ➤ advanced countries on specified products exported by approved ➤ developing countries. The scheme was first introduced in 1971. The intention is to encourage the development and diversification of developing countries' exports. ➤ Doha Round of trade negotiations; World Trade Organization; ➤➤ most-favoured nation clause.

generational accounting A system for assessing the differential impact of government tax and spending decisions on the welfare of different generations. It starts by calculating the present value of all government spending and taxes on an average person born in each year, over his/her whole lifetime. If governments did not make pension promises that have differential impacts on the generations, and if governments could not borrow money (which can transfer a burden from one generation to the next), one would expect that each generation of citizens would more or less finance the spending from which they benefit. As it happens, though, governments *can* transfer burdens from one generation to the next. Studies for the USA and Japan indicate that those over age 60 in 1995 were net recipients of government policy, while the generation below them were likely to be net contributors, i.e. to pay more tax over their lifetime than they would receive in spending.

geometric progression A sequence of numbers in which the ratio of each number to the preceding one is a constant, e.g. 2, 4, 8, 16 . . . ➤➤ arithmetic progression.

German stock exchanges There are numerous stock exchanges in Germany including Berlin-Bremen, Munich and Stuttgart, but Frankfurt is by far the largest. Deutsche Börse AG, which itself floated (➤ flotation) in 2001, owns the exchange in Frankfurt as well as part of Eurex, the derivatives exchange which in 2007 merged with the New York Options Exchange to create the International Securities Exchange (ISE). Deutsche Börse differs from most stock exchanges in that it also owns Clearstream, a clearances and settlement service (➤ clearing house). The Neuer Markt (New Market), an ➤ unlisted securities market, opened in 1997 but closed in 2001 following the puncturing of the dot.com boom.

Gerschenkron, Alexander (1904–1976) ➤ universal bank.

GFCF Gross fixed capital formation (➤ capital formation).

Gibrat's law If each firm in a population of a fixed number of firms is subjected to a growth rate randomly derived from a distribution of potential growth rates, with the same mean and standard deviation as applies to each other firm in the population, the distribution of firms will be of a ➤ log-normal distribution, the skewness of which will increase with repeated applications of the rates of growth. The law is derived from the work by Gibrat in *Les inégalités économiques*, published in 1931.

Giffen good A commodity for which demand increases at higher prices and falls at lower prices. This odd feature of basic commodities in the budgets of the nineteenth-century poor was observed by Robert Giffen (1837–1910). As the price of bread rose, the poor, who relied on it as their staple diet, could no longer afford to buy other relatively more luxurious food items that they had to replace with increased purchases of bread. Similarly, because bread constituted the bulk of their spending, they enjoyed such an increase in their ➤ real income when its price fell that they could afford to substitute other more palatable food than bread in their diet.

The 'Giffen paradox' is explained within the normal framework of demand and supply analysis. When the price of any good rises, it has two effects: (a) it changes the relative attractiveness of other goods, increasing the desire of consumers to buy more of the items with prices that have not risen – the ➤ substitution effect; and (b) it has an effect on the spending power of consumers, who can do less with their money than they could before prices rose, as though their income had fallen and no prices had changed – the ➤ income effect. Two features explain the characteristics of a Giffen good: (a) demand for it rises as the income of consumers falls (it is an ➤ inferior good), and (b) what essentially accounts for its perverse behaviour is the fact that this income effect on the demand for the Giffen good outweighs the substitution effect which causes consumers to switch purchases from items that have rising prices.

The Giffen good should not be confused with items that enjoy 'snob value'. These, too, can enjoy simultaneously rising prices and demand, accounted for by the fact that some consumers delight in paying for the knowledge that certain of their possessions are expensive. Such behaviour can be explained as a form of ➤ signalling. The usual way of viewing this 'snob effect' is to treat a change in the price of an item to which it applies as a change in the fundamental characteristics of the product sold, making it wholly incomparable to the same physical object sold at a different price and not, therefore, an item for which a single demand curve can be constructed. ➤ price theory.

gift tax A levy on the ➤ value of certain property given away to others and paid by the donor, i.e. on *inter vivos* gifts. There is also an estate tax on the wealth of deceased persons. Charitable donations are exempt from both taxes and gift-tax transfers between spouses are also exempt. ➤ inheritance tax.

gilt-edged securities Fixed-interest British ➤ government securities traded on the ➤ stock exchange. They are called gilt-edged because it is certain that ➤ interest will be paid and that they will be redeemed (where appropriate) on the due date. For individuals, no ➤ capital gains tax arises on disposal of gilts. Some gilt-edged securities are ➤ dated securities, some are ➤ undated securities and some are index-linked (➤ indexation). Gilt-edged securities are not, of course, a risk-free investment, because of fluctuations in their market value. Gilt-edged securities do not include ➤ Treasury bills. ➤➤ yield.

gilt repos The market in agreed sales and repurchase of ➤ gilt-edged securities (➤ repo) introduced by the ➤ Bank of England in January 1996. Within two months of its launch, the open gilt repo market was already much larger than the ➤ bill market (➤ money market), the restricted size of which has recently hampered ➤ open-market operations. The gilt repo market was launched to increase the attractiveness of gilts to foreign investors and to reduce the cost of funding the government ➤ deficit, but may be used by the Bank of England for open-market operations, just as repos are used by the ➤ Bundesbank and the ➤ Federal Reserve System.

gilt stripping The creation of two tradable financial securities out of a single ➤ gilt-edged security, with one security taking the ➤ interest, and the other left with the principal. The facility for strippable gilts was introduced by the ➤ Bank of England in 1997 but has long been available in the USA for US Treasury and other securities.

Gini coefficient A coefficient, developed by the Italian statistician Corrado Gini (1884–1965), showing the degree of inequality in a ➤ frequency distribution, e.g. personal income. Based on the ➤ Lorenz curve, it can be measured as:

$$G = \frac{\text{area between Lorenz curve and the } 45° \text{ line}}{\text{area above the } 45° \text{ line}}$$

At G = 0, the frequency distribution is equal (the Lorenz curve coincides with the 45° line). At G = 1, its maximum value, there is complete inequality. ➤➤ Atkinson Index; concentration ratio.

Ginnie Mae ➤ Fannie Mae.

giro system ➤ credit transfer.

glass ceiling An expression referring to the relative lack of women in the highest levels of management whether in the public or private sectors, implying that women are prevented by an invisible ceiling constructed by a cultural prejudice that prevents them from achieving their full potential (➤➤ labour force; inequality).

Glass-Steagall Act 1933 US legislation prohibiting ➤ commercial banks from acting as ➤ investment banks or owning a firm dealing in securities. The Act was repealed in 1999.

global corporation ➤ multinational corporation.

globalization Geographical shifts in domestic economic activity around the world and away from nation-states. The ➤ Organisation for Economic Co-operation and Development has defined globalization as 'the geographic dispersion of industrial and service activities (for example ➤ research and development, sourcing of inputs, production and distribution) and the cross-border networking of companies (for example through ➤ joint ventures and the sharing of assets)'. The most obvious manifestations of this process are that the annual rate of growth in ➤➤ international trade has been consistently higher than that of world production, while ➤ multinational corporations have continued to extend their operations. However, globalization no longer necessarily requires a physical presence in other countries, or even ➤ exports and ➤ imports, e.g. activity can be shifted abroad by licensing, which only needs information and finance to cross borders. Although not new, the pace of globalization has accelerated, facilitated by improvements in transport and communications, the promotion of ➤ deregulation in different sectors, the removal of trade restrictions and ➤ exchange controls (➤ convertibility; World Trade Organization).

The motives for globalization include lower labour costs and other favourable ➤ factor endowments abroad and the circumvention of remaining ➤ tariff and non-tariff barriers to trade (➤ protection). Evidence indicates that the result of firms in the ➤ advanced countries outsourcing to countries with lower labour costs has resulted in the dampening of wage rates in the advanced countries, which has only partially been offset by the resulting increase in productivity, so that the share of profits in their ➤ Gross Domestic Product has increased at the expense of the share of wages.

Nevertheless the theory of international trade and past experience suggest that all nations in the globalization process will gain in the long run. That has not allayed concerns that the opportunities for employment of the unskilled in the labour force in richer countries will diminish. ➤➤ balance of payments; compensation principle; convergence; immiseration; weightlessness.

GNP ➤ Gross National Product.

gold This precious metal ceased to have a significant monetary role in 1971, when the USA abandoned its commitment to buy or sell gold at a fixed price (➤ International Monetary Fund). However, the non-monetary role of gold, especially in jewellery, has expanded rapidly and gold also remains in demand as a store of value as well as a means of adornment. Gold is a sanctuary in times of trouble. In the 1970s, during which inflation in some countries reached double digits, gold rose in three weeks from $110 per oz to $850 per oz (equivalent to over $2,000 per oz at 2009 prices). It reached a new peak in March 2008 of $1030 at the beginning of a severe recession in the world economy. ➤ gold and foreign exchange reserves; gold standard.

gold and foreign exchange reserves The stock of gold, foreign ➤ currencies and Special Drawing Rights (SDRs) (➤➤ International Monetary Fund) held by a country to finance any calls that may be made from its creditors for the settlement of ➤ debt. Reserves used to be held primarily to finance the ➤ balance of payments. Pressure on the reserves, therefore, tended to reflect underlying trading problems of the country in question, or sometimes the expectation of a fall in the ➤ exchange rate which led people to sell their holdings in the currency. Today, however, currencies are more freely traded than they used to be (➤ convertibility) and the national reserves are not relied upon to finance private transactions. As a result, the reserves are primarily seen as a tool for influencing the exchange rate. The authorities can use them to influence supply and demand on the ➤ foreign exchange market. Such intervention is bound to be of limited duration, but can serve a role as a ➤ signalling device, letting the markets know the intention of the authorities.

The official published figures of reserves, however, do not necessarily reflect the total amount of gold and foreign currency that could be used to meet obligations any more than does an individual's ➤ current account at the bank. The reserves exclude, for example, the ➤ credit facilities available through the ➤ International Monetary Fund and ➤ portfolio foreign investments (➤ foreign investment; reserve currency).

golden rule **1** The idea that government should borrow each year only to finance ➤ investment, not to finance ➤ current expenditure. This implies that the ➤ current budget should be in balance. Meeting the golden rule across the economic cycle (➤ business cycle) became official UK government policy in 1997. At that time, net ➤ public sector investment spending represented a little under 1 per cent of ➤ Gross Domestic Product – the government's rule could be interpreted as saying there should be a ➤ structural budget deficit no higher than that in any year. The ambiguity in the 'golden rule' is that it is impossible to be precise about the end and beginning of the business cycle and this does allow politicians to be flexible as it did in the case of the UK.

2 The level of savings and investment that an economy enjoying ➤ balanced growth would need to support in order to maximize the long-term value of consumption per head (➤ optimal-growth theory). The rule holds, under a number of restrictive assumptions, that the growth rate of population, output and capital stock should equal the real ➤ rate of interest. This is sometimes referred to as the *biological interest-rate rule*, as it stipulates that projects should be discounted (➤ discounting) at the rate of population growth. It implies that the share of profits in the economy should equal the share of savings and investment.

Note: Definitions **1** and **2** above are clearly related. If the rule in definition **2** holds, it will be the case that a government subscribing to the rule in definition **1** will have interest payments on its debt equal to the value of its borrowing. So such a government would be in a sustainable and balanced position. It will be borrowing to invest, and the returns it makes on investment will just finance its debt. Conduct of government in definition **1** is therefore consistent with the golden rule in definition **2**.

gold exchange standard A special form of the ➤ gold standard. In this system the ➤ central bank did not exchange its ➤ currency for gold on demand (as is the case under the gold standard), but exchanged it for a currency which was itself on the gold standard. The central bank held the parent country's currency in its reserves along with gold itself. The Scandinavian countries adopted this system in respect of sterling up until 1931, when the UK came off the gold standard.

gold points ➤ specie points.

gold standard A country was on the gold standard when its ➤ central bank was obliged to give gold in exchange for any of its ➤ currency presented to it. When the UK was on the gold standard, anybody could go to the ➤ Bank of England and exchange ➤ banknotes for gold. The gold standard was central to the ➤ classical economists' view of the equilibrating processes in ➤ international trade. The fact that each currency was freely convertible into gold fixed the ➤ exchange rates between currencies (➤ specie points), and all international debts were settled in gold. A ➤ balance of payments surplus caused an inflow of gold into the central bank's reserves. This enabled the central bank to expand the ➤ money supply without fear of having insufficient gold to meet its ➤ liabilities. The increase in the quantity of money raised prices, resulting in a fall in the demand for ➤ exports and therefore a reduction in the balance of payments surplus. The reverse happened in the event of a ➤ deficit. The UK was the first country to go on to the gold standard in 1817 and eventually the spread of countries on the gold standard was worldwide and included both ➤ advanced and ➤ developing countries. The gold standard was suspended during the First World War but fifty countries later returned to it. The ➤ Great Depression forced the end of the worldwide gold standard by 1933.

good ➤ economic good.

Goodhart's law The phenomenon that when regulatory policy focuses on a particular variable with which it is expected to have a close relationship (e.g. the quantity of money in circulation (➤ money supply) and bank deposits) the relationship will alter, thus frustrating the exercise of policy. The law, credited to Professor Charles Goodhart of the London School of Economics, in a paper published in 1975, was originally applied to the targeting of ➤ monetary policy but has since been accepted to have wider applicability. ➤➤ Lucas critique.

goodwill The value of a business to a purchaser over and above its ➤ net asset value. It is normal practice to show goodwill in the ➤ balance sheet but to write it down for ➤ depreciation.

Gossen, Hermann Heinrich (1810–58) Born in Düren, near Aachen, in Germany, Gossen studied law and went into government service in deference to his father's wishes. It was not until after his father's death in 1847 that he dedicated himself to the study of economics. His major economic work is *Die Entwicklung der Gesetze des menschlichen Verkehrs und der daraus fliessenden Regeln für menschliches Handeln* (1854) (*The Development of the Laws of Human Intercourse and the Consequent Rules of Human Action*). In this book, Gossen set out a theory of consumer behaviour based on theories that were subsequently to be independently rediscovered and enshrined in the theory of ➤ marginal utility by ➤ Jevons, ➤ Menger and ➤ Walras. The first edition of his book was completely ignored and Gossen's recognition had to wait until after his death. It was Jevons who, in the preface to his own *Theory of Political Economy* (1871), drew attention to the significance of Gossen's achievement, admitting that Gossen had 'completely anticipated him as regards the general principles and methods of economics'.

Gossen's first law states that the pleasure obtained from each additional amount consumed of the same ➤ commodity diminishes until satiety is reached. Gossen's second law states that once a person had spent his entire ➤ income, he would have maximized his total pleasure from it only if the satisfaction gained from the last item of each commodity bought was the same for each commodity. Gossen's third law, derived from the first two, states that a commodity has a subjective ➤ value, and the subjective value of each additional unit owned diminishes and eventually reaches zero. ➤➤ Bernoulli's hypothesis.

government expenditure ➤ public expenditure.

government securities All government fixed-interest paper, including ➤ funded debt and ➤ Treasury bills. The government does not, of course, issue ➤ equity capital. ➤➤ gilt-edged securities.

government stocks Fixed-interest ➤ securities issued by the government, often known as ➤ 'gilt-edged'. ➤➤ funded debt.

Granger, Clive W.J. (1934–2009) ➤ Granger causality.

Granger causality A technique for testing whether information in one ➤ time series can be applied to another time series. The concept of such causality was explored by Sir Clive Granger (➤ Nobel Prize) and Paul Newbold in the *Forecasting Economic Time Series*, published in 1977.

If we observe that money-supply increases are followed by inflation, we cannot say that increases in money supply *cause* inflation. It may be that both money-supply increases and inflation are caused by something else. Under the Granger test of causation, a time series of both money supply and inflation is taken, and each is stripped of any independent long-term trends they may exhibit. Then the values of money supply and inflation are regressed against each other (➤ regression analysis). Money-supply changes can be said to cause inflation if in such analysis (a) values of inflation are explained by previous values of money supply, *and* (b) values of money supply are explained by future values of inflation.

gravity model A model of ➤ international trade first described by Jan ➤ Tinbergen in *Shaping the World Economy; Suggestions for an International Economic Policy* published in 1962. The formula derives its name from a similar structure describing Newton's Law of Gravitation.

$$Y_{ij} = kX_i^\alpha X_j^\beta / D_{ij}^\gamma$$

in which trade between two countries Y_{ij} is determined by the economic size of the two countries given by X_i and X_j divided by the transport costs between them, given by D_{ij}. k is a constant.

Great Depression The Great Depression refers to the deep and rapid collapse in national and international economic activity between the First World War and the Second World War. There were major declines in output, prices, investment, profits and ➤ international trade. The USA and Germany were the most affected of the advanced nations. Between 1930 and 1938, the average unemployment rate in the USA was 26 per cent, in Germany 22 per cent, in the UK 15 per cent and 10 per cent in France. In the USA, ➤ Gross Domestic Product (GDP) fell 30 per cent between 1929 and 1933 and wholesale prices fell by 27 per cent in two years. International trade fell by over 40 per cent in current prices between 1929 and 1932 and ➤ developing countries, which relied on exports, suffered accordingly with falls in GNP of over 33 per cent.

There were many bank failures. In 1931, the largest private bank in Austria failed and the second largest in Germany also failed. In 1932 Germany defaulted on its foreign debt. Bank failures also occurred in the USA and in France. In the USA, output had begun to decline in 1929 and the ➤ stock market crashed in 1929 and, to support domestic agriculture, the Smoot-Hawley Tariff Act was passed in 1931 which increased import ➤ tariffs and encouraged protectionism (➤ protection). The ➤ Federal Reserve Bank raised ➤ interest rates from 1.5 per cent to 3.5 per cent and the USA left the ➤ gold standard (➤ New Deal).

There was an underlying assumption in ➤ classical economic theory that economies tended to full employment ➤ equilibrium, which was not successfully challenged until ➤➤ Keynes did so in 1936. There were two basic issues at the time: whether expenditure on public works was useful in increasing employment, and with or without a budget deficit, or merely diverted expenditure away from the private sector (➤ Pigou); and the advantages of reducing wages to encourage recruitment (➤ Hayek).

Gresham's law The law states that if two coins are in circulation, the relative ➤ face values of which differ from their relative ➤ bullion content, the 'dearer' coin will be extracted from circulation for melting down (➤ 'bad money drives out good'). The law is named after Sir Thomas Gresham (1517/18–79), a leading Elizabethan businessman and financial adviser to Queen Elizabeth I.

grey imports ➤ parallel imports.

gross cash flow ➤ cash flow.

Gross Domestic Product (GDP) A measure of the total flow of ➤ goods and ➤ services produced by the economy over a specified time period, normally a year or a quarter. It is obtained by valuing outputs of goods and services at ➤ market prices, and then aggregating. Note that all intermediate goods are excluded, and only goods used for final ➤ consumption or investment goods (➤ capital) or changes in ➤ inventories are included. This is because the ➤ values of intermediate goods are implicitly included in the ➤ prices of the final goods. The word 'gross' means that no deduction for the value of expenditure on capital goods for replacement purposes is made. Because ➤ income arising from ➤ investments and possessions owned abroad is not included, only the value of the flow of goods and services produced in the country is estimated; hence, the word 'domestic' to distinguish it from the ➤ Gross National Product and ➤ Gross National Income. Since no adjustment is made for indirect taxes (➤ direct taxation) and ➤ subsidies, the measure here defined is often referred to as 'GDP at market prices'. ➤ gross value added at basic prices.

The ➤ World Bank Group has calculated the global distribution of Gross Domestic Product in 2005, compared with ➤ population, to have been the following:

	GDP	Population
	%	%
Low income countries	7	35
Middle income countries	32	48
High income countries	61	17
	100	100

➤ developing country; ➤➤ human development index.

gross fixed capital formation (GFCF) ➤ capital formation.

gross investment ➤ Investment expenditure inclusive of replacement of worn-out and obsolescent equipment, i.e. inclusive of ➤ depreciation. ➤➤ net investment.

gross margin In a retail business, the margin on a sale that is the difference between the purchase ➤ price of a good and the price paid by the retailer, i.e. it makes no allowance for ➤ fixed costs, ➤ stock appreciation or ➤ tax. The gross margin is sometimes loosely referred to as *gross profit*, but this term has a different, strictly defined, meaning in accounting (➤ profit).

gross national expenditure ➤ national income.

Gross National Income (GNI) ➤ Gross Domestic Product plus the ➤ income accruing to domestic residents arising from ➤ investment abroad less income earned in the domestic market accruing to foreigners abroad. ➤ national income.

Gross National Income at market prices ➤ Gross National Income with all flows valued at ➤ market prices. Since market prices include indirect taxes (➤ direct taxation) and ➤ subsidies, and since taxes and subsidies are regarded simply as ➤ transfer payments, it is often preferable to measure national income and output excluding these. This gives the measure of national income, net of ➤ taxation and subsidies, known as ➤ gross value added at basic prices. Valuations may be at prices obtaining in the current year (current prices) or in a specified year, e.g. 1995 prices. ➤ real terms.

Gross National Product (GNP) ➤ Gross Domestic Product plus the income accruing to domestic residents arising from investment abroad less income earned in the domestic market accruing to residents abroad.

gross profit ➤ profit.

gross trading profit Gross ➤ profit before allowing for ➤ depreciation, ➤ interest and stock ➤ appreciation.

gross value added at basic prices The measure of ➤ Gross Domestic Product (GDP) that makes an adjustment for the impact of taxes and subsidies. In the measure of 'GDP at market prices', the prices used to value outputs and aggregate them include indirect taxes, i.e. ➤ value added tax, and ➤ subsidies. As a result, the ➤ value of output will not equal the value of ➤ incomes paid out to ➤ factors of production. This is because it is the revenue received by firms after indirect taxes (➤ direct taxation) that is distributed as factor incomes. So, by subtracting the total of indirect taxes (and, since subsidies have the opposite effect of taxes, by adding in subsidies) from the GDP we arrive at the estimate of the gross value added at basic prices, which is consistent with the value of incomes paid to factors of production. This is the measure of GDP from which growth rates are conventionally drawn. ➤ national income.

growth accounting Quantitative analysis of economic growth rates that seeks to disaggregate the sources of growth: (a) changes in inputs of the ➤ factors of production (➤ labour and ➤ capital); (b) changes in the quality of labour; and (c) *total factor productivity*, a residual intended to capture the contribution of knowledge, technological progress and other exogenous factors (➤ endogenous growth theory). Growth accounting, which is a statistical imputation of the ➤ production function, originated with ➤ Solow and has been elaborated statistically by Edward Denison (1915–92), Maddison and others. Denison's first book on this subject appeared in 1962. In *Accounting for United States Economic Growth 1929–1969* (1974), he calculated that the annual growth of real ➤ national income of 3.3 per cent over the period was composed of growth of labour input of 1.31 per cent, capital of 0.50 per cent and a residual, sometimes called the Solow residual, of 1.52 per cent attributable to advances in knowledge and other causes. Labour inputs were split down into employment, average hours worked, ➤ education of workers and other. Since it is not actually possible to separate out the contributions of all the various factors to growth, growth accounting is based on assumptions, e.g. Denison weighted the factors of production according to their shares in the national accounts (➤ Gross Domestic Product; Human Development Index; social accounting).

growth theory The area of economics concerned with the development of models that explain the rate of ➤ economic growth in an economy. The most important questions in growth theory post-Second World War were about: (a) the optimal level of growth (➤➤ optimal-growth theory), and (b) whether the economic system has a natural tendency to achieve ➤ balanced growth, a position in which all variables grow at the same rate. If growth in the economy is balanced, it can be shown that $n = s/v$ where n is the rate of growth of the labour force, s the ➤ average propensity to save and v the ratio of capital in the economy to output produced (➤ capital–output ratio). For balanced growth to be sustained with ➤ investment equal to savings and with constant full employment, some mechanism has to exist to cause one of these three factors to change when one of the other two moves out of balance. In the neo-classical (➤ neo-classical economics) approach to growth, it is the capital–output ratio, v, that alters. If, for example, the labour force was growing too fast to maintain full employment with the given level of savings and stock of capital, the capital–output ratio would fall as entrepreneurs switched from employing capital to labour in response to the lower wages that the excess supply of labour caused. The fixed relationship between the three factors would thus still hold.

In the ➤ Harrod–Domar model, none of the three variables is endogenous (➤ endogenous variable) and thus there is no tendency for balanced growth to occur at all. The capital–output ratio is assumed to be fixed by technological factors or by sticky interest rates (➤➤ liquidity trap). In models associated with the ➤ Cambridge School, it is the *propensity to save* which is the endogenous variable; in particular, if there is a difference between the inclination for profit-earners and wage-earners to save, growth can lead to redistributions from one group to the other in such a way as to alter the savings necessary to maintain a full-employment steady-state growth path. In recent years, economics has become less concerned with ➤ steady-state growth, and more with the factors that explain why some economies grow faster than others. ➤ endogenous growth theory; inequality; optimal-growth theory.

GSE Government-sponsored enterprise. ➤ Fannie Mae.

H

Haavelmo, Trygve (1911–99) Norwegian economist and winner of the ➤ Nobel Prize for Economics in 1989, Haavelmo's contribution to the subject was made during the Second World War in the USA. His most important paper, 'The Probability Approach in Econometrics', in *Econometrica* (1944), was path-breaking in introducing the ideas of ➤ probability theory into ➤ econometrics, explicitly accounting for uncertainty in the estimation of variables. Haavelmo argued that economists' models were necessarily simplistic, and thus could not hope to explain fully the factors affecting a piece of economic data, representing the behaviour of many individual agents. There would inevitably be a degree of randomness in the real world as economists observed it, and he pioneered the use of statistical techniques to make assumptions about the pattern of that randomness and draw inferences from the data. He also had a huge effect on how econometric models are drawn up, where systems of different variables interact upon each other. He argued that econometricians need to look at relationships between variables that are autonomous, in the sense that the relationships are not affected by other parts of the system being estimated.

hard currency A ➤ currency traded in a ➤ foreign exchange market for which ➤ demand is persistently high relative to the ➤ supply. ➤➤ soft currency.

harmonized index of consumer prices A standardized measure of inflation introduced in 1997 by the ➤ European Union (EU). It is used in the assessment of performance against the criteria for convergence for prospective candidates for membership of the ➤ European Economic and Monetary Union and is used by the ➤ European Central Bank as its measure of ➤ inflation in determining ➤ monetary policy. It is designed to be consistent throughout the EU member countries and does not, therefore, have the same structure of goods and services or weights (➤ index number) as those in, for example, the UK ➤ Retail Prices Index (RPI) (for instance, it does not include mortgage interest payments or local authority taxes which are included in the RPI). It is calculated using a geometric mean, as opposed to the arithmetic mean in use in the RPI. ➤ average; hedonic price index.

Harrod, Sir Roy Forbes (1900–1978) Educated at New College, Oxford, Professor Harrod began his career in 1922 as a lecturer at Christ Church, Oxford, and continued teaching there until 1952. From 1940 until 1942, he served under Lord Cherwell and in the Prime Minister's office and then held the post of Statistical Adviser to the Admiralty until 1945. In 1952, he was appointed Nuffield Reader of International Economics. His publications include *The Trade Cycle* (1936), *Essay in Dynamic Theory* (1939), *Towards a Dynamic Economics* (1948), *The Life of John Maynard Keynes* (1951),

Policy Against Inflation (1958), *The British Economy* (1963), *Reforming the World's Money* (1965), *Towards a New Economic Policy* (1967), *Dollar–Sterling Collaboration* (1968), *Money* (1969) and *Economic Dynamics* (1973).

His *Essay in Dynamic Theory* (1939) brought together in a mathematical framework the accelerator and the ➤ multiplier (➤➤ accelerator–multiplier model). Professor Harrod shifted economic theory away from its preoccupation with the conditions of stationary ➤ equilibrium towards the analysis of the problems of growth (➤➤ growth theory). He investigated the implications for growth of the interactions of the ➤ acceleration principle and the multiplier (➤➤ Harrod–Domar model).

Harrod–Domar model A theory of economic growth (➤ growth theory) that suggests there is no natural tendency for an economy to enjoy ➤ balanced growth. In the model, developed by ➤ Harrod in 1939 and independently by Evsey Domar (1914–97) shortly afterwards, there are three concepts of growth: (a) *warranted* growth: the rate of output growth at which firms believe they have the right amount of capital and don't feel it necessary to increase or decrease investment, given their expectations of future demand (➤ capital–output ratio); (b) *natural rate* of growth, which corresponds to the increase in the labour force – if the labour force rises, growth must rise to maintain full ➤ employment; and (c) *actual* growth: the change in aggregate output that finally materializes.

In the model, two problems are seen to arise in the growth pattern of an economy – the relationship between actual and natural growth, and the relationship between actual and warranted growth. The first problem is that the factors determining actual growth are quite independent of the factors determining natural growth, and so there is no reason that an economy will achieve a level of growth necessary to maintain full employment. The natural rate of growth is determined by factors such as attitudes to birth control and the tastes of the population with respect to family size. Actual growth, however, is affected by the *propensity to save* (the more ➤ saving, the more ➤ investment, and the more growth) and the increase in output caused by each pound's worth of investment. Neither the capital–output ratio nor the propensity to save will adjust to meet the requirements of the labour market, however.

The second problem is that, in the model – if entrepreneurs expect output to grow – they will increase their investment to meet the anticipated demand. If the increase in demand is forthcoming, the aspirations of firms will be met and warranted growth will be equal to actual growth and no problem arises. If, however, actual growth exceeds expectations, then entrepreneurs will discover they have not invested as much as they would have wanted to if they had known what was coming. In response, they will increase their investment to the level warranted by actual growth, *but this increase in investment will cause actual growth to rise even more*. A reverse story can be told when actual growth falls short of warranted growth: entrepreneurs, in the model, set up a vicious circle, by which any discrepancy between their expected growth and actual growth magnifies as they attempt to change the level of their investment to the level warranted. The result is instability.

The conclusion of the Harrod–Domar model (i.e. that the economy does not naturally find a full-employment, stable-growth rate) is analogous to the Keynesian (➤➤ Keynes, J.M.) belief that it need not find a full-employment equilibrium level of output. However, the model's results can be criticized because of the severity of the assumptions built into it. The first problem suggested by the model – that there is no reason for growth to equal the level necessary to maintain full employment – is created largely because it assumes that the relative price of labour and capital is fixed, and that they are always employed in equal proportions. It is quite possible, however, that increases in labour supply might drive down wages and lead to an increase in the amount of labour used relative to capital. Secondly, the model naively assumes that investors are influenced by only one thing: the level of output. This is the ➤ acceleration principle. It explains the way in which discrepancies between warranted and actual growth may lead to spiralling increases or decreases in growth. ➤➤ economic growth; optimal-growth theory; steady-state growth; trend growth.

Harsányi, John C. (1920–2000) Hungarian-born, Harsányi made a major contribution to ➤ game theory in 1967–8 with his paper 'Games with Incomplete Information Played by "Bayesian" Players'. He was a joint winner of the ➤ Nobel Prize for Economics in 1994. He extended an understanding of game theory to situations in which players had incomplete and differing amounts of information. He showed that for every game characterizing such a situation, there was an equivalent game that could be defined with complete information. Those equivalent games could be studied using conventional methods. ➤➤ Nash, J.F.; Selten, R.

Hayek, Friedrich August von (1899–1992) Born in Vienna, Hayek was director of the Austrian Institute for Economic Research from 1927 to 1931 and lectured at Vienna University. In 1931, he was appointed Tooke Professor of Economic Science and Statistics at the London School of Economics, a post he held until 1950. From 1950 until 1962 he was Professor of Social and Moral Science at Chicago University. He was Professor of Economics at the University of Freiburg until 1969, when he was appointed Visiting Professor of Economics at the University of Salzburg. In 1974, he received the Alfred Nobel Memorial Prize (➤ Nobel Prize) in Economics jointly with ➤ Myrdal. His published works include *Monetary Theory and the Trade Cycle* (1929), *Prices and Production* (1931), *Profits, Interest, Investment* (1939), *The Pure Theory of Capital* (1941), *The Road to Serfdom* (1944), *Individualism and Economic Order* (1948), *The Constitution of Liberty* (1960), *Studies in Philosophy, Politics and Economics* (1967), *Law, Legislation and Liberty* (3 volumes, 1973–9), *Denationalisation of Money* (1976), *New Studies in Philosophy, Politics, Economics and the History of Ideas* (1978) and *The Fatal Conceit: The Errors of Socialism* (1988).

A member of the ➤ Austrian School, Hayek elaborated the ➤ business-cycle theory of von ➤ Mises by integrating it with von ➤ Böhm-Bawerk's theory of ➤ capital. In a boom, ➤ real wages fall because of the rise in prices, and so firms switch to less 'roundabout' (➤ capital-intensive) methods of production. In consequence, ➤ investment in total is reduced. In ➤ recession, the reverse situation induces 'roundabout' production methods, and investment is stimulated. Professor Hayek believed that a very severe restriction on the growth of the ➤ money supply was necessary in order to control the growth of ➤ inflation, even if such a policy led to very high levels of ➤ unemployment. Hayek criticized socialist planning (➤ planned economy), advocating free markets which, he argued, were more accommodating to the propagation and dissemination of the knowledge required for efficient economic systems. Open markets gave proper opportunities to the expression of personal incentives and the freedom to work and save. ➤➤ acceleration principle; Keynes, J.M.; Ricardo effect.

Heckman, James J. (b. 1944) Economist from the University of Chicago and a pioneer in the area of *microeconometrics*, the study of large sets of data on groups of individuals, firms or households. Professor Heckman jointly won the Nobel Prize for Economics in 2000 for his work on statistical techniques for coping with samples that are not randomly selected. The problem is ubiquitous, not just because administratively data-collation agencies may have their own impediments to random sampling, but because there are innate obstacles to unbiased samples. For example, when looking at wages and labour supply, data can only include the wages of those in work, and yet those out of work are, of course, an important component of analysis that looks at the motivations for work participation. Another example is work that assesses the effectiveness of government schemes to get the unemployed into work. Entry into these schemes is non-random, and thus you can't just compare people in the schemes to those outside them to see how successful the schemes are.

Professor Heckman's published works include 'Sample Selection Bias as a Specification Error', *Econometrica* (1979). But he has not just been a theoretician in econometrics – he has also practised empirical economics, most notably in the study of labour supply decisions and racial discrimination. His works include 'Shadow Prices, Market Wages and Labor Supply', *Econometrica* (1974), and with Brook S. Payner, 'Determining the Impact of Federal Antidiscrimination Policy on the Economic Status of Blacks: A study of South Carolina', *American Economic Review* (1989). Apart from Chicago, his career has involved periods at Columbia and Yale Universities.

Heckscher–Ohlin principle The principle that a country will export those commodities that are intensive (➤ capital-intensive; labour-intensive) in the factor (➤ factors of production) in which it is most well endowed. The law of ➤ comparative advantage (➤➤ Ricardo, D.) had been established by economists as an explanation for the existence and pattern of international trade based on the relative ➤ opportunity-cost advantages between different countries producing different commodities. The principle says nothing about why or how a comparative advantage exists. The Heckscher–Ohlin principle states that advantage arises from the different relative factor endowments of the countries trading.

The principle was first put forward by Eli F. Heckscher (1879–1952) in an article published in 1919 and reprinted in *Readings in the Theory of International Trade* (1949). It was refined by ➤ Ohlin in his *Interregional and International Trade* (1933). The principle has been developed further by Paul ➤ Samuelson in his factor price equalization theorem.

hedge Action taken by a buyer or seller to protect his business or assets against a change in ➤ prices. A flour-miller who has a contract to supply flour at a fixed price in two months can hedge against the possibility of a rise in the price of wheat in two months by buying the necessary wheat now and selling a two-month ➤ future in wheat for the same quantity. If the price of wheat should fall, then the loss he will have sustained by buying it now will be offset by the gain he can make by buying in the wheat at the future price and supplying the futures contract at higher than this price, and vice versa. In practice, perfect hedging may not be possible because spot (➤ spot markets) and future prices will not balance one another out after the event, but a significant reduction in risk is normally possible. Hedging in this form is, in effect, shifting risk on to specialized futures operators. The purchase of ➤ equities, or other things for which prices are expected to move at least in line with the general price level, is often referred to as a 'hedge' against ➤ inflation.

hedge fund The distinguishing characteristic of hedge funds, which are privately owned investment vehicles, is that they are not open to smaller private investors. Hedge funds take positions in bankrupt or merging companies and on the direction of markets, including ➤ equities, ➤ debt, currencies and commodities. They take their name from their frequent use of hedging (➤ hedge) and also make use of ➤ short-selling, ➤ derivatives and ➤ gearing. These funds are lightly regulated on condition that the numbers of investors are strictly limited and must be 'qualified investors'. There are no centrally collected statistics on them.

hedonic price index An ➤ index number for prices adjusted for changes in the quality of the goods for which market prices are being measured, i.e. *quality adjusted price indices*. The rationale for these adjustments is that products are not homogeneous over time. For example, motor cars now frequently have radios or assisted-braking systems, or even air-conditioning, fitted as standard equipment, features which at one time were optional extras. If car list prices have not changed, then effectively there has been a price reduction. For personal computers, prices have actually fallen considerably but at the same time processing power has increased so that a price for a given standard of product has fallen even faster. In a hedonic price index, the price-relatives (➤ index number) are adjusted downwards to allow for product improvements.

The use of hedonic indices has important implications because ➤ Gross Domestic Product (GDP) in ➤ real terms will be higher if the ➤ GDP deflator is quality adjusted than if it is not. The ➤ harmonized index of consumer prices of the ➤ European Union and official statistics in the USA make extensive use of hedonic indexes. While theoretically defensible, in practice quality adjustments involve judgements by statisticians and may not necessarily reflect market-determined prices (➤ Human Development Index).

hedonism The theory that all human action is motivated by pleasure and the avoidance of pain or the ethic that it should be so motivated.

Herfindahl index ➤ concentration ratio.

heteroscedasticity The problem encountered in ➤ regression analysis when the ➤ variance of the error term in a regression is not constant for every observation. It may be in a ➤ time-series analysis, for example, that while the relationship between the ➤ dependent variable and the ➤ independent variable remains constant on average, it becomes more and more variable around that average as time progresses. In this case, ➤ least-squares regression will not be the most efficient method of measuring that relationship; instead, it is better to give more weight to those observations that have the smallest expected error. ➤➤ econometrics.

Hicks, Sir John Richard (1904–89) Educated at Balliol College, Oxford, Hicks lectured at the London School of Economics from 1926 until 1935, when he became a Fellow of Gonville and Caius College, Cambridge. In 1938, he was appointed to the Chair of Political Economy at the University of Manchester. In 1946, he was made Official Fellow of Nuffield College, Oxford, and in 1952, Drummond Professor of Political Economy at Oxford, a post he held until 1965. In 1972, he was awarded the ➤ Nobel Prize for Economics jointly with Kenneth ➤ Arrow. His major published works include *The Theory of Wages* (1932), *Value and Capital* (1939), *The Social Framework* (1942), *A Contribution to the Theory of the Trade Cycle* (1950), *A Revision of Demand Theory* (1956), *Capital and Growth* (1965), *Critical Essays in Monetary Theory* (1967), *A Theory of Economic History* (1969), *The Crisis in Keynesian Economics* (1974), *Capital and Time: A neo-Austrian theory* (1973), *Economic Perspectives: Further essays on money and growth* (1977), *Causality in Economics* (1979) and *A Market Theory of Money* (1989).

In an article in *Economica* in 1934, Hicks and Allen showed how the ➤ indifference curve could be used to analyse consumer behaviour on the basis of ➤ ordinal utility. Their exposition gave an important impetus to the development of this tool of analysis in economic theory (➤➤ Slutsky, E.). In his work on the ➤ business cycle, Hicks demonstrated by means of mathematical ➤ models how the *accelerator* could induce several types of fluctuation in total output. In an article in *Econometrica* in 1937, 'Mr Keynes and the Classics', he expounded the analytical tool of the ➤ IS–LM model that he had invented in order to explore the assumptions relating to the equilibrium between the supply and demand for ➤ money, ➤ savings and ➤ investment, the rate of ➤ interest and ➤ income. ➤➤ Harrod, R.F.; Keynes, J.M.

Hicksian demand function The relationship between the consumer's demand for a commodity and the price of that commodity, when the total level of consumer ➤ utility is held constant. Hicksian demand curves are also known as 'compensated demand curves' as, when the price of a product changes, it is assumed that the consumer is compensated so that he/she feels no less satisfied than before; they contrast with Marshallian (➤ Marshall, A.) demand functions (➤ demand function). ➤➤ substitution effect.

hidden economy ➤ informal economy.

hidden hand ➤ 'invisible hand'; Smith, A.

hire purchase ➤ instalment credit.

historical costs ➤ costs, historical.

hoarding The accumulation of idle money balances, ➤ inactive money. ➤➤ liquidity preference.

holding company A company that controls one or more other companies, normally by holding a majority of the ➤ shares of these ➤ subsidiaries. A holding company is concerned with control and not with ➤ investment, and may be economically justifiable where one holding company can perform financial, managerial or marketing functions for a number of subsidiaries; most large companies in the UK are holding companies exercising a greater or lesser degree of control over their subsidiaries. The holding company form of organization also has a number of practical advantages, e.g. it is a simpler and less expensive way of acquiring control of another company than by purchasing its ➤ assets, and the original company can retain its name and goodwill. It is possible for a holding company to control a large number of companies with a combined ➤ capital very much greater than its own, since it needs to hold only half or even less of the shares of its subsidiaries. Abuse of this possibility of 'pyramiding', as it is sometimes called, is now limited by company legislation (➤ company law). Diversified holding companies, or ➤ conglomerates, are tending to become less important than they once were. ➤ downsizing.

homogeneous of degree *n* The characteristic of a function that, when all the ➤ independent variables are multiplied by λ, the ➤ dependent variable rises by λ to the power *n*. It is commonly referred to in describing the characteristics of a ➤ production function, e.g. $y = f(x,z)$ where y is output and x and z are inputs to production. This function, for example, would be homogeneous of degree 2 (λ = 2) if $4y = f(2x,2z)$ (➤➤ Cobb–Douglas function).

homogeneous products Goods and services purchased by consumers that the latter consider to be perfect substitutes (➤ perfect competition). It is mostly in ➤ commodity markets that homogeneity can be assumed and, indeed, the characterization of something as a commodity frequently simply means different producers are selling more or less homogeneous outputs. In some markets, the differentiation of their products by producers (➤ product differentiation) is criticized as wasteful. On the other hand, the tendency for markets to generate uniform products may be a form of market weakness (➤ Hotelling's law).

horizontal integration ➤ merger.

hot money Funds that flow into a country to take advantage of favourable ➤ rates of interest in that country, influencing the ➤ balance of payments and strengthening the ➤ exchange rate of the recipient country. These funds are highly volatile and will be shifted to another ➤ foreign-exchange market when relative interest rates favour the move. ➤➤ arbitrage; Bank for International Settlements.

Hotelling, Harold (1895–1973) Associate Professor of Mathematics at Stanford University from 1927, Hotelling became Professor of Economics at Columbia University in 1931. He held this post until 1946, when he was appointed Professor of Mathematical Statistics of the University of North Carolina. In 'Stability in Competition', *Economic Journal* (1929), he showed how profit maximization can lead retail outlets or competing companies to locate close to each other (➤ Hotelling's law). In 'The General Welfare in Relation to Problems of Taxation and of Railway and Utility Rates', *Econometrica* (1938), he put forward the case for ➤ marginal-cost pricing by public utilities, arguing that, even if by so doing such industries ran at a loss that had to be financed by lump-sum payments by the state, total economic welfare would be increased by such a pricing policy (➤ welfare economics).

Hotelling's law The observation by Hotelling that in many markets it is rational for all the producers to make their products as similar as possible. Suppose, for example, there are two newsagents in a street, each of which wanted to maximize its share of local business by locating its shop so that it is the nearest newsagent for as much of the trade visiting the street as possible. In this situation, both newsagents will position themselves in the middle of the street, guaranteeing themselves half the market. It would be socially more desirable for them to separate themselves, and sit a third of the way along the street from different ends. Unfortunately, if one newsagent did this, the other could position himself so as to capture more than half the total market. Too little variety results from the process. Hotelling's law manifests itself in numerous markets, e.g. competing bus operators scheduling their buses to run at the same times. ➤➤ Nash equilibrium.

household An economic unit defined for the purpose of a ➤ census of population as a single person living alone or a family or group voluntarily living together, having meals together and benefiting from housekeeping shared in common. Because of the fact of shared use – which is a household's characteristic – it is an important economic statistic. For instance, the percentage of households having certain consumer products (e.g. computers, television sets, refrigerators and broadband connection) is critical to the growth of the future sales of these products. In the initial introductory period, sales grow quickly as households buy for the first time, but then slow down rapidly when a high proportion of householders own the product (➤ logistic curve). Thereafter, without innovation, sales can only be for replacement.

human capital The skills and knowledge embodied in the ➤ labour force. A metallurgist can expect to earn more than a laboratory assistant because he/she has invested more in education and training, and these higher earnings are a return on the investment he/she (or his/her parents, or the state) has made in school fees and foregone earnings. Investment in human ➤ capital should increase labour ➤ productivity in the same way as investment in machinery. ➤➤ Becker, G.; education; sow's ear effect.

Human Development Index (HDI) An index published by the United Nations (UN) Development Programme in its annual Human Development Report that lists countries in order of human achievement. The measures included in calculating the index are life expectancy at birth (➤ death rate), adult literacy rate and the school attendance rate (➤ education; sow's ear effect) and ➤ Gross Domestic Product per capita, measured in US dollars at ➤ purchasing power parity. The UN Development Programme also publishes a Gender Development Index, based on the HDI but adjusted for inequalities between men and women in the population (➤ glass ceiling).

The development of these indexes reflects growing concern that the Gross Domestic Product (GDP) is an inadequate measure of human welfare. There have been proposals for calculating instead a 'Gross Domestic Happiness (GDH)' measure. The GDH would cover, for instance, pollution, public order, good governance, education, ➤ inequality, life expectancy, health care and leisure. The expectation would be that it would redirect government policies away from viewing the GDP as an end in itself to seeing it as a means towards promoting human welfare (➤➤ utilitarianism).

Hume, David (1711–76) Scottish philosopher whose systematic treatment of economics is contained in several chapters of his *Political Discourses* (1752). He exposed as unwarranted the mercantilist fear (➤ mercantilism) of a chronic imbalance of trade and loss of gold. He argued that the international movement in ➤ bullion responded to the rise and fall of prices and in so doing kept national price differences within limits and prevented permanent ➤ balance of payments surpluses or deficits. He also foresaw how this mechanism could be distorted by the growth of domestic ➤ banking and of paper money. He accepted a ➤ quantity theory of money but distinguished between ➤ short-run and ➤ long-run effects. By tracing the course of the effects of a rise in the quantity of ➤ money, he came to the conclusion that money was not neutral (➤ neutrality of money) but could affect employment, although only in the short run. His belief that the level of the ➤ rate of interest depended on the rate of business profits became the basis of classical interest-rate theory. ➤➤ interest, classical theory of.

Hurwicz, Leonid (1917–2008) ➤ mechanism design.

hyperinflation Very rapid growth in the rate of ➤ inflation in which ➤ money loses its value to the point where alternative mediums of exchange (e.g. ➤ barter or foreign currency) are commonly used. There have been periods of hyperinflation in a number of ➤ developing countries, one of the most recent being in Zimbabwe between 1997 and 2009. It has been less usual in ➤ advanced countries, although it occurred in Germany in the 1920s and in a number of countries in Eastern Europe after the Second World War.

hypothecation Earmarking of particular sources of finance to particular uses. The idea of hypothecating tax to particular forms of spending has been much discussed – although in the UK, the Treasury has tended to oppose the idea on the grounds that it introduces an element of inflexibility into spending and sometimes makes it hard to cut programmes once they are underway. Nevertheless, the principle was adopted with respect to the revenues of the National Lottery and, with decreasing ➤ tax tolerance, many believe it is a good way of ensuring revenue for popular programmes and overcoming public mistrust of the way politicians use tax revenue.

hypothesis A theoretical explanation of the behaviour of phenomena that can be tested against the facts. A hypothesis can be refuted – unlike a tautology, which is true by logical form but may not be capable of proof that it is correct. An example of a hypothesis is that ➤ saving is a function of ➤ disposable income such that when disposable income doubles, savings will also double (the ➤ savings ratio is a constant). The statement that saving equals income minus expenditure, however, is a tautology. ➤➤ empirical testing.

hysteresis A term derived from more common use in the physical sciences, to describe a lag between the behaviour of a variable and a change in the factors that influence the variable. It is a characteristic of viscous liquids, for example, that when inverted in an open jar they do not pour out immediately. In economics, hysteresis has acquired a life of its own, to describe the idea that the history of a variable – the path it has followed over time – can have an effect on where it settles. In its most common manifestation, hysteresis is the idea that a high level of unemployment is self-reinforcing because the unemployed become less and less suited to work as they stay out of work longer. A burst of high unemployment tends to solidify into a permanently high level of unemployment, notwithstanding the removal of the original cause. It enjoyed preponderance as a possible explanation of the rising levels of unemployment in the 1980s across Western Europe. Hysteresis has also been taken as having broader implications for economic method. It holds that the ➤ equilibrium of a variable is dependent on the path it follows, so conventional analysis explaining the equilibrium entirely in terms of the factors that normally influence things is impoverished. ➤ long-term unemployment; unemployment, natural rate of.

IADB ➤ Inter-American Development Bank.

IBMBR Interbank market bid rate (➤ interbank market).

IBOR Interbank offered rate (➤ interbank market).

IBRD ➤ International Bank for Reconstruction and Development.

IDA ➤ International Development Association.

idle money ➤ inactive money.

IEA ➤ International Energy Agency.

IFC ➤ International Finance Corporation.

illiquidity A situation in which ➤ assets cannot easily and quickly be turned into ➤ money. Antonym of ➤ liquidity.

ILO ➤ International Labour Organization.

ILO unemployment A standard definition of ➤ unemployment agreed through the ➤ International Labour Organization for the purpose of statistical measurement. It covers people above a specified age who, at the time of survey, are without work, available for work, actively taking steps to get work or waiting to start work that has been offered. ➤ Labour Force Survey.

IMF ➤ International Monetary Fund.

immigration ➤ migration.

immiseration In a paper published in 1958, Jagdish N. Bhagwati drew attention to the possibility that, in certain cases, ➤ economic growth could lead to a reduction in a country's economic welfare unless there is appropriate countervailing government intervention – an effect he called 'immiseration'. For instance, if a country's growth is generated by the expansion of the export of a product dominant on the international market, the increase in supply could lead to a reduction in its price and therefore a fall in the country's ➤ terms of trade, causing a loss greater than the gain from growth. Again, if an innovation can be exploited only by producers with access to capital, those producers without such capital would suffer a loss of income and there would be a corresponding increase in income ➤ inequality (➤ globalization; welfare economics).

impact effect The first effect of a change in a variable before any secondary responses can be made to the change. It amounts to the very short-run effect. For example, when demand in a market increases, prices rise because output is fixed in the short period involved by more than they do once producers have had time to respond to the increases in demand. ➤➤ J-curve.

imperfect competition ➤ monopolistic competition.

imperfect market A market in which the forces that tend to ensure productive and allocative efficiency are thwarted (➤ economic efficiency). In a perfect market, three characteristics predominate: (a) price equals ➤ marginal cost (or ➤ marginal revenue equals marginal cost); (b) there are no abnormal ➤ profits (i.e. ➤ average cost equals ➤ average revenue); and (c) production takes place at the minimum cost, i.e. at the bottom of the average-cost curve, where average cost equals marginal cost. Although price acceptance by consumers and firms, and free entry and exit of firms, are the important features to ensure these hold, underlying them are a number of other conditions. These include rational consumers, profit-maximizing firms, ➤ homogeneous products made without ➤ economies of scale, a smooth pattern of ➤ demand without peaks, a smooth pattern of ➤ supply where the quantity of output is easily adjusted, no collusion between producers, and the existence of complete and costless market information. In the absence of any of these, imperfect markets exist and the efficiency result no longer necessarily holds. The most important developments in economics in recent years have concerned the role of information in explaining deviations from perfect markets (➤ asymmetric information; screening; signalling). ➤ Pareto, V.F.D.; ➤➤ perfect competition.

implementation theory ➤ mechanism design.

implicit contract ➤ contract.

import deposits A system of ➤ import restrictions under which importers are required to deposit, with a government-nominated institution, a percentage of the value of their ➤ imports. This ➤ deposit is held for a period of time, after which it is repaid to the importer. The system restricts imports because it reduces the ➤ liquidity of importers and also imposes an extra charge on them, inasmuch as they are, in effect, forced to give an interest-free loan to the government. However, the impact of import deposits may be weakened if there is sufficient liquidity generally in the economy to enable importers to obtain loans at favourable ➤ rates of interest against the ➤ collateral security of their import-deposit receipts. Again, foreign exporting companies may be willing to finance the deposits themselves rather than lose their market position, especially if it is expected that the scheme is only a temporary one. ➤ protection.

import duties ➤ tariffs, import.

import licence A document that gives the importer authority to import the commodity to which the licence applies. It is a device to enable the government to regulate and supervise the flow of ➤ imports, e.g. under its import ➤ quota regulations.

import quota ➤ quotas.

import restrictions Restrictions on the importation of products into a country may be effected by means of ➤ tariffs, ➤ quotas or ➤ import deposits, and are

generally imposed to correct a ➤ balance of payments deficit. Their purpose, as with
➤ devaluation, is to divert expenditure away from foreign-produced goods in favour
of goods produced at home. The magnitude of this diversionary effect will depend
on the ➤ elasticity of demand for the ➤ imports in question, i.e. the degree to which
acceptable ➤ substitutes are available on the home market. In addition, import
restrictions could be used to increase a country's economic welfare (➤ welfare economics) at the expense of foreign countries to the extent that it has power to exploit
its foreign suppliers, e.g. as a monopolist (➤ monopoly), without fear of retaliation.

Finally, import duties may be applied to protect the market of a domestic industry while it is being established (➤ free trade; infant-industry argument; protection).
Non-tariff barriers to trade include revenue duties (e.g. value added tax) which,
being imposed as a percentage on landed (i.e. duty-paid) ➤ value, increase the cost
of imported goods more than locally produced goods and thus discriminate in
favour of the latter. Other examples are domestic taxes applied according to the
technical characteristics of goods (e.g. on engine capacity) which may subtly discriminate against imports. ➤ General Agreement on Tariffs and Trade; protection;
World Trade Organization.

imports The flow of goods and ➤ services that enter for sale into one country and
that are the products of another country. About 30 per cent of ➤ Gross Domestic Product in the UK was spent on imports in 2007, compared with, for example, the USA,
where the proportion was about 17 per cent. ➤ balance of payments; exports; international trade; invisibles; parallel imports.

import surcharge A temporary increase in import tariffs (➤ tariffs, import) designed
to correct a short-term ➤ balance of payments deficit and to stabilize the ➤ exchange
rate.

import tariffs ➤ tariffs, import.

impossibility theorem A proof that it is impossible to devise a constitution or voting system, complying with certain reasonable conditions, that can guarantee to
produce a consistent set of preferences for a group from the preferences of the individuals making up the group. Suppose, for example, that a society wants to vote on
whether to spend the proceeds of a national lottery on education, the arts or sport.
If resources are to reflect public tastes, it would be desirable that the public's individual rankings of the three options could be combined by some voting system to
produce an overall ranking to determine which option was the choice of the society
as a whole. ➤ Arrow showed in the impossibility theorem that no system could be
found that was both rational and egalitarian. For example, a simple majority voting
system, although giving equal weight to everybody's opinion, gives rise to the
➤ paradox of voting, allowing the possibility of an inconsistent ordering of preferences. A system that may be consistent would be to allow one individual – a
dictator – always to determine what choice to make, but this lacks the feature of
equality.

It has since been shown that a democratic system can at least meet a weaker
rationality condition, but only by abandoning a third desirable property of a voting
system – decisiveness. Such a system would allow every individual a personal veto
over any decision so that society would simply be unable to do anything unless
there was no one opposed to it. ➤ social-welfare function.

impossible trinity The proposition that government economic policy cannot at the same time (a) allow the free international mobility of ➤ capital; (b) maintain a fixed ➤ exchange rate; and (c) conduct ➤ monetary policy independently. One or other of these must give way–either fixed to free exchange rates or controls on the short-run movement of capital or an unfettered monetary regime. Also referred to as the trilemma. (➤ Mundell, R.)

imputation system ➤ corporation tax.

imputed cost The cost attributed to using an asset owned by the user. The ➤ opportunity cost of not putting an asset to its best alternative use. For example, a shopkeeper who owns his/her own shop forgoes the rent if the shop was not used for his/her own business. This loss of income is an imputed cost, which the owner would compare against the revenue from the business when considering whether it were truly profitable. Similarly, an imputed income is the amount an owner would pay not to put the asset to an alternative use. If the shopkeeper had to pay $10 a day to rent an alternative to his own shop he would willingly forgo $10 to keep it, and he thus enjoys an imputed income of $10 from his shop. ➤➤ income.

imputed income ➤ imputed cost.

inactive money ➤ Money that is not in circulation, i.e. not on ➤ deposit or invested in other financial ➤ assets or being used for transactions. Inactive money is also referred to as *idle money* or idle balances. According to ➤ Keynes' theory of ➤ liquidity preference, the amount of idle balances will depend, among other things, upon the ➤ rate of interest. ➤➤ velocity of circulation.

inactivity rate The percentage of the ➤ labour force that is neither employed nor looking for work. ➤ ILO unemployment.

incentive compatibility A system of behaviour in which each individual has a personal incentive to act in accordance with some overall interest. A classic example of an incentive-compatible system is that used by parents to divide a cake between two hungry children, in which one is allowed to slice the cake in two and the other allowed to choose which slice to take. The first child then has the incentive to split the cake into two equal halves, which is the fairest division. Incentive compatibility is important throughout economics, but has more recently become a preoccupation, because it is an ingredient in the economics of ➤ screening and ➤ signalling, where there are types of behaviour, e.g. the giving of an engagement ring, that are used to distinguish certain types of individual from certain other types, e.g. people who are serious about getting married from those who are not. These systems work only if the types of individuals being distinguished do not have the incentive to behave like the other type, e.g. it must not be the case that the benefits of pretending you were going to marry someone were so great that you would be willing to buy them an engagement ring, even if you were not intending to wed. This condition is known as the incentive-compatibility condition. The same notion is important in the areas of ➤ public-choice theory, where voting systems are designed to obtain true indications of people's preferences, undistorted by tactical considerations. Another example is the ➤ Vickrey ➤ auction, in which participants have the incentive to bid their true valuation of an item. ➤➤ mechanism design; moral hazard.

incidence of taxation ➤ taxation, incidence of.

income A flow of money, goods or services to any economic agent or unit. Such flows can take a variety of forms. At the level of individuals, income is usually a return to a ➤ factor of production – ➤ labour yields wages, ➤ capital yields ➤ interest, land yields ➤ rent and entrepreneurship yields ➤ profit. Otherwise, income can be a ➤ transfer payment in the form of a state benefit or receipt from a private-sector source, e.g. alimony payments. At the level of the firm, income can be seen as either total sales receipts (turnover) or receipts minus costs. For a country, ➤ national income is taken as the sum of all incomes.

Economists do not view income in conventional ways. First, their concept of income extends more widely than a cash receipt – the person who lives in his own house effectively derives an income in the form of housing consumption worth the rental value of his property. Secondly, great importance is attached to the concept of 'permanent income' – the flow of resources that is sustainable in the long term. For example, North Sea oil provides the UK with sale receipts but these will expire when the oil runs out. The permanent income deriving from the oil is therefore the money that would be earned from investing those receipts and making a return on them that lasts for ever. This would be lower than the actual flow of receipts while the oil is still being tapped but it would provide a flow of income after the oil has gone. ➤ income, distribution of; permanent-income hypothesis.

income, circular flow of ➤ circular flow of income.

income, distribution of A ➤ frequency distribution showing numbers of persons, taxpayers or households classified by levels of annual income. A feature of this distribution is that it is skewed – a greater number appear in the low-income classifications than in the high income ones. ➤ Atkinson index; Gini coefficient; inequality; Kuznets curve; Lorenz curve; Pareto, V.F.D.; poverty.

income and earned surplus statement (US) ➤ double-entry bookkeeping.

income determination, theory of The body of theory that describes the factors affecting ➤ national income. The term is usually used to describe specifically Keynesian models of the economy, in which ➤ aggregate demand is the primary factor explaining output and employment. ➤➤ Keynesian economics.

income effect The change in demand for a product caused by the impact of a change in its price on the spending power of consumers. The change in price of a product leads to a change in the ➤ real income of individuals, who either can no longer afford the 'basket' of goods that they previously bought or who can afford the old basket with cash over to spend on extra items. The *income effect* is the impact of this change in spending power on the demand for the product with the price that has changed. It is equivalent to some change in income with all prices remaining constant. It can be added to the ➤ substitution effect to derive the total effect of the price change on the demand for the product.

The main factor in determining the size of the income effect of a product is the proportion of total spending that item comprises. The effect on total spending of a change in the price of matches, for example, is trivial, but it is large for a change in the price of food. Unlike the substitution effect, the income effect can move in either direction. If a product is demanded more as incomes fall (e.g. second hand clothes) it is called an ➤ inferior good. If, as is more usual, it is demanded more as income rises, it is called *normal.* ➤➤ income elasticity of demand; Giffen good.

income elasticity of demand The proportionate change in the quantity of a commodity demanded after a unit proportionate change in the income of consumers with prices held constant. For example, a product that has an income ➤ elasticity of 2 will enjoy demand growth of 2 per cent for every 1 per cent growth in consumer income. Commodities can be grouped by their income elasticities: (a) luxury items that comprise a high proportion of the spending of the rich have income elasticities in excess of 1 and enjoy growth in demand above that of average incomes; (b) basic items (e.g. food) enjoy some increased demand when the economy grows, but proportionately not as much as the growth in average incomes; and (c) ➤ inferior goods have negative income elasticities – as soon as people can afford to stop buying them they do, e.g. secondhand clothes and certain cheap but unsavoury foods.

Income elasticities can be measured at the level of individual consumers or at that of the economy as a whole, and can be assessed for individual commodities or groups of commodities taken together. In the most general case, the income elasticity of all spending in the long term must be equal to 1 (i.e. spending must rise in the same proportion as income), otherwise savings would have to be unsustainably growing or contracting. The income elasticity is of practical importance to business and policymakers because any product that has an income elasticity below 1 in a growing economy will have a falling share of total spending, and countries that export commodities with low-income elasticities will suffer worsening ➤ terms of trade in the long term if world economic growth occurs. The income elasticity of a commodity is equal to the negative of the sum of the elasticity of demand of a commodity with respect to its own price and all other prices.

incomes policy ➤ prices and incomes policy.

income tax A ➤ tax on ➤ income. For example, in the UK, which has income tax broadly similar to that in other countries, individuals are taxed on their income from employment or ➤ investment in the ➤ fiscal year (including some ➤ fringe benefits but not including gifts (➤ inheritance tax); ➤ capital gains are taxed separately). Deductions (e.g. married couple's allowances or age allowance) are allowed in arriving at taxable income. Income tax is progressive in its effect, and successive slices of assessable income are taxed at ascending rates. There are special rates for capital gains, dividends and other savings income. Persons in employment are normally taxed under the ➤ pay-as-you-earn system. Company income is taxed under a different system (➤ corporation tax). Federal Income Tax was introduced in the US from 1913 and is also levied by most states.

There is some disagreement among economists on the effects of income tax on incentives to work and save and these effects are difficult to verify empirically. On equity grounds, a progressive income tax places a higher burden on those with the means to bear it, but this may discourage effort through the ➤ substitution effect or encourage people to work harder (and encourage sophisticated tax avoidance) to make up their income (➤ income effect). The system of income tax reliefs for particular types of saving (e.g. pension contributions) distorts savings decisions and this is one of the reasons why many economists advocate an ➤ expenditure tax in place of income tax. ➤ supply-side economics. The complexity of tax systems and high ➤ costs are universal problems. The US Tax Reform Act 1986 simplified the system by widening the tax base and reducing tax rates but complexity has crept back in again as a result of political pressures for 'fairness'. Such measures are often self-defeating, since complexity favours those with access to the best tax advice.

income velocity of circulation ➤ velocity of circulation.

incomplete contract A formal or written ➤ contract that fails to outline the rights and duties of each party in all situations. The difficulty of framing complete contracts – even in quite straightforward situations – is increasingly seen as an economic problem in that it can inhibit individuals from trading with each other. A builder may not wish to enter a contract to build a wall for someone at a given price in a given time unless he knows exactly what will happen if the ground is found to be hard to build on, or if the weather is bad. It is very costly to draw up a contract that specifies every eventuality, and this may force the builder to charge a high price to cover the risks. Or it may be that certain features of the best contract would be unenforceable. ➤➤ principal–agent problem; transaction costs.

incorporation The action of forming a company by carrying out the necessary legal formalities. ➤➤ company law.

increasing returns ➤ economies of scale.

independent commodity ➤ complementary goods.

independent variable ➤ dependent variable.

indexation The introduction of automatic linkage between monetary obligations and the price level. It can apply to wages, prices or government tax charges. In practice, it should mean that the money value of a long-term loan would be increased in line with inflation measures by some index, such as the ➤ Retail Prices Index, so that the borrower would have to repay the loan in ➤ real terms. In the absence of indexation, unanticipated ➤ inflation, by eroding the real value of loans, shifts resources from lenders to borrowers and therefore disrupts the credit mechanism and the ➤ capital market. While indexation reduces the costs of inflation, some economists believe it entrenches inflationary expectations and makes it harder to get inflation down. General indexation has been used in some countries (e.g. Brazil) to help cope with inflation in the past. The UK government introduced an index-linked ➤ gilt-edged security in 1981 for financial institutions and has subsequently issued others for private investors as well as institutions, e.g. a 2½ per cent Index-linked Treasury Stock 2011.

indexed ➤ indexation.

index-linked ➤ indexation.

index number A ➤ weighted average of a number of statistical observations of some economic attribute as a percentage of a similar weighted average calculated for the attribute at an earlier, or base, period. Important economic attributes for which index numbers are calculated are prices (➤ harmonized index of consumer prices; ➤ Retail Prices Index). The price of each commodity or service included in the index is recorded in the current period (e.g. 2010) and divided by its price in the base period (e.g. 2000), to obtain a *price relative* for each item. Each price relative is then multiplied by a weight. The weights used may be either the amount spent on each item in the current period (a *current-weighted* index or ➤ Paasche index) or the amount spent on each item in the base period (a *base-weighted* index, or ➤ Laspeyres index). The average may be either an arithmetic or geometric mean. ➤ average; hedonic price index; index-number problem.

index-number problem This problem arises from the use of ➤ index numbers, that are summary single numbers encapsulating a range of values and used to describe succinctly changes in values over time. The ➤ Retail Prices Index, for example, could equally rationally, for the above purpose, be calculated as a *base-weighted* or a *current-weighted* index, but the two types of index do not necessarily give the same answer. For example, consider a simple example of two goods X and Y that have the following prices and quantities purchased in the base year 1 and the current year 2:

	Year 1		Year 2	
	Price	**Quantity**	**Price**	**Quantity**
X	10c	5	8c	6
Y	20c	5	25c	1

The current-weighted index is given by:

$$\text{Year } 2 = \left[\left(\frac{8}{10}\right) \times 6 + \left(\frac{25}{20}\right) \times 1\right] \div 7 = 0.86 \ (\text{Year } 1 = 1.00)$$

The base-weighted index is given by:

$$\text{Year } 2 = \left[\left(\frac{8}{10}\right) \times 5 + \left(\frac{25}{20}\right) \times 5\right] \div 10 = 1.025 \ (\text{Year } 1 = 1.00)$$

According to the base-weighted index, the general level of prices rose in year 2 compared with year 1 (by 2.5 per cent), but according to the current-weighted index, prices fell in year 2 (by 14 per cent). The problem of choice is that if base weights are not updated, items will continue to be included that are no longer relevant in household expenditure. On the other hand, changing weights in order to keep them current could lead to the index being influenced by changes in quantities and therefore not being properly representative of price movements only. Further, a Consumer Price Index may fail to reflect in its weights technological changes enhancing product quality. A new computer launched in 2011 could have benefits unknown to its five-year-old predecessor that are not reflected in its price. ➤➤ hedonic price index.

indifference curve A graphical representation of sets of different combinations of commodities which each yield to the consumer the same level of satisfaction (see diagram). Indifference curves can be plotted on graphs called 'indifference maps', on each axis of which is represented the quantity of some commodity. To produce such a curve, any point can be taken to start with, representing a basket of two goods (though the analysis can be extended to more than two). One unit of the first commodity (e.g. books) could be removed from the basket and units of the second commodity (e.g. CDs) added until a point is found at which the consumer feels that the new CDs exactly compensated for the loss of the book. This new basket, with perhaps two more CDs in it but one less book, is the second point on the same indifference curve as the first basket. The exercise can be repeated with steadily fewer books and increasing numbers of CDs and then again with increasing numbers of books and correspondingly falling numbers of CDs. A new indifference curve altogether could be derived by taking a starting-point with both more CDs and books than the previous basket and repeating the whole process again.

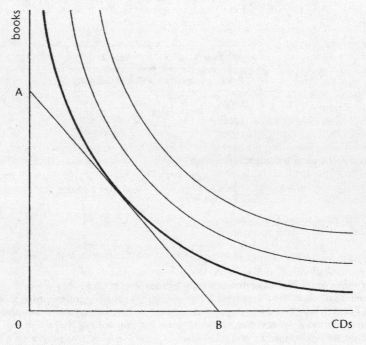

Indifference curves can never intersect. If a point X lies on two intersecting indifference curves, then all the points on each curve must have the same utility as point X, and the two curves must both represent bundles of goods of equal utility. It is then logically impossible for them to be separate indifference curves. As a result of this, every point on the indifference map lies on one and only one indifference curve. Normally, various assumptions are made about consumers and their tastes, with the result that indifference curves have the following properties:

(1) *They slope downward.* As the consumer loses some of one commodity, he/she must receive more of another if satisfaction is to be maintained. Similarly, a

consumer should always prefer a basket with more of both commodities than another.

(2) *They are convex to (i.e. bulge towards) the origin* (➤ convexity). This is because, as units of the first commodity are removed from the basket, increasing amounts of the second commodity will be required to compensate. A consumer may start off valuing CDs and books equally, but after accumulating a basket of books with only a tiny selection of CDs remaining, there will be a requirement for a large number of extra books in return for one CD.

In the diagram, the line AB is the ➤ budget line. The consumer would buy a combination of CDs and books given by the point at which the budget line is tangential to the indifference curve. Any other combination would either be above the budget line and therefore unaffordable, or on a lower indifference curve and therefore give less satisfaction.

Various extreme forms of indifference curve can be drawn without the usual properties described above. Perfect ➤ substitutes (two identical brands of washing powder, for example) have indifference curves that are straight downward-sloping lines. At no stage will the consumer change the rate at which one item is swapped for the other. Perfect complements (➤ complementary goods), on the other hand, have L-shaped indifference curves; increasing quantities of a left shoe will derive for a consumer no extra utility at all unless extra right shoes are found to match. If a consumer actively hates one commodity, his indifference curves will slope upwards. Indifference maps are used extensively in theoretical economics. By plotting money against any commodity, the individual's demand curve for that commodity can be derived. If leisure is compared to money on an indifference map, analysis of the decision of individuals on how much to work (and earn) and how much to relax can be analysed. ➤➤ convexity; demand, theory of; indifference-curve analysis; marginal rate of substitution; ordinal utility.

indifference-curve analysis The study of consumer demand in terms of ranked combinations of commodities consumed subject to the constraints of price and income. Under this approach, there is no need for an absolute measure of utility or satisfaction; consumers merely need to be able to choose between different bundles of goods (➤➤ ordinal utility). One can view the basic task of the consumer as ranking all the combinations of items that can be bought with the income available and choosing the bundle at the top of the resulting list. The tools for this analysis are the *indifference map* (built of ➤ indifference curves), that expresses the consumers' tastes, and the ➤ budget line, that shows the combinations of items that can be bought for a given income and set of prices.

Indifference-curve analysis suggests that people should consume items such that the rate at which they are prepared to swap them with complete indifference equals the ratio of the prices of the two items. For example, if two glasses of milk cost the same as one glass of wine and a consumer values one glass of each equally, he can enhance his utility by reducing his wine consumption by a glass and increasing his milk consumption by two glasses, without any extra cost. This process can go on until the consumer has so much milk and so little wine that he would actually enjoy a single glass of the one rather than two glasses of the other. On the indifference map, this corresponds to the point at which the budget line is tangential to the indifference curve. ➤➤ marginal rate of substitution.

indirect taxation ➤ direct taxation.

indirect utility function A *direct* utility function maps the relationship directly between the consumption of commodities and the utility gained by the consumer. However, a rational consumer will maximize utility by consuming the optimum mix of commodities subject to their relative prices and, in addition, to the constraint of available income.

The *indirect* utility function incorporates both the effects of prices and incomes in the determination of utility. ➤➤ ordinal utility.

induced investment That part of ➤ investment that is determined by changes in output, as opposed to *autonomous investment*, e.g. government expenditure on infrastructure capital.

industrial districts Geographical clusters of firms in the same and related activities, e.g. Silicon Valley near San Francisco and Route 128 near Boston in the USA, and Cambridge in the UK. In these three instances, the firms are predominantly in new ➤ technology-based industries that are ➤ research and development-intensive. There are many other examples of industrial districts in traditional sectors, e.g. ceramic goods in Sassuolo, Emilia-Romagna, Italy. The existence of industrial districts has long been noted by economists – indeed, they are sometimes referred to as 'Marshallian districts' after ➤ Marshall, who first gave them extended analysis. Firms in industrial districts benefit from ➤ externalities in the availability of suppliers, reserves of skilled labour, specialized distribution, training facilities and information that seems to promote ➤ innovation. It has been suggested that industrial clusters allow ➤ small businesses to enjoy some of the ➤ economies of scale (via market coordination under conditions of low ➤ transactions costs) available to large firms within their own organizations. The origin of industrial districts cannot be attributed to similar causes. In Cambridge and on Route 128, proximity to centres of academic scientific research has played a major role. In some traditional industries, the origin of clusters can be traced to putting-out systems, trade routes, markets and other factors.

industrial organization Branch of applied ➤ microeconomics dealing with the performance of business enterprises and especially with the effects of ➤ market structures on market conduct (e.g. pricing policy, restrictive practices and ➤ innovation) and how firms are organized, owned and managed. ➤➤ concentration; firm, theory of the; game theory.

industrial zone ➤ free trade zone.

industry concentration ➤ concentration.

inequality The degree to which the distribution of economic welfare among a country's population differs from a situation in which they all had equal shares. The attributes most commonly adopted are those of the distribution of personal incomes (before or after tax) and of wealth. Inequality may be measured within countries or between countries and over time. People have inequality of opportunity because of their initial endowments and they may not be able to escape the inequality of outcomes. Excessive inequality threatens the stability of society, hence the supply of free ➤ education by the state. Inequality of opportunity is more pernicious when it exists not in the natural endowment of inherited personal characteristics but in society where it may be manifested in class, racial or sexual prejudice that prevents people gaining their full potential (➤ glass ceiling).

The most common measure of inequality is the ➤ Gini coefficient which takes a value of zero for perfect equality and a maximum of unity for the extreme of inequality. The distribution of wealth is more unequal than that of income. In 2000, whereas income distribution within countries worldwide had a Gini coefficient ranging from 0.35 to 0.45, that for the distribution of wealth ranged from 0.65 to 0.75. The USA had a wealth distribution Gini coefficient of 0.8 compared with Japan, for instance, of 0.55. The top 10 per cent of the world adult population owned 85 per cent of the world total of household wealth and the bottom 50 per cent owned 1 per cent. The ownership of wealth per head ranged from $181,000 in Japan and $144,000 in the USA to $1400 in Indonesia and $1100 in India (➤ developing countries; poverty).

infant-industry argument An argument in support of the retention of a protective import ➤ tariff to promote the creation of a local industry. It is held to apply in cases in which an industry cannot operate at an optimum least-cost output until it has reached a sufficient size to obtain significant ➤ economies of scale. A new industry, therefore, in, for example, a ➤ developing country will always be in a competitively vulnerable position vis-à-vis an established industry in an advanced country. It follows that the stage of growth at which the industry (or country) can 'take off' (➤ Rostow, W.W.) industrially will be postponed indefinitely. The argument concludes that ➤ protection is necessary until the industry has reached its optimum size (➤ first-mover advantage).

inferior good A good, the demand for which falls as income rises, i.e. its ➤ income elasticity of demand is negative, e.g. the demand of married couples for small apartments. A good that is not inferior is called a *normal good*. ➤➤ Giffen good; income effect.

inflation Persistent increases in the general level of prices. It can be seen as a devaluing of the worth of money. Inflation is a recurring but only intermittent historical phenomenon. A serious appearance occurred during the 1970s in the wake of the quadrupling of oil prices in 1973, when annual inflation rates in the developed world rose as high as 25 per cent, but for the rest of the post-Second World War period it has not been unusual for the inflation rate to be exceeded by the real growth rate. A crucial feature of inflation is that price rises are sustained. A once-only increase in a consumption tax, for instance the ➤ value added tax, will immediately put up prices, but this does not represent inflation, unless the indirect effects of the rise have repercussions on prices in periods after the direct effects.

Accounts of the causes of inflation are numerous. The most popular arguments are that it is caused by ➤ excess demand in the economy (➤ demand-pull inflation); that it is caused by high costs (➤ cost-push inflation) or excessive increases in the money supply (➤ monetarism). These causes often amount to the same thing. The mechanism by which the increase in money supply causes inflation is by creating excess demand, making monetarism compatible with the demand-pull argument. The demand-pull and cost-push theories are also linked. An excess of demand causes producers to raise their prices, but this leads workers to demand higher wages to maintain their living standard, causing higher demand, and the process begins again. Similarly, if under the cost-push argument the cost increases stimulating price rises are wage costs, firms can still only raise their prices if there is demand for their goods – if not, high costs merely bankrupt them. All three of these causes amount to an attempt by a nation to enjoy a living standard higher than that consistent with its output and borrowing. This implies that inflation can rarely be cured by a measure that does not suppress these attempts at maintaining living standards which are too high. Controlling inflation by restricting demand has costs, however. If wages are growing rapidly, and the government squeezes demand in the economy, unemployment may result because employers will not be able to afford to pay their staff if they cannot raise their sales prices because of low demand. In the short term, it appears that allowing higher demand may be inflationary, but unemployment can be kept lower than otherwise.

The inverse relationship between money wages and unemployment was described by the *Phillips curve* (➤ Phillips, A.W.H.). However, the Phillips relationship did not persist and the role of ➤ expectations in pre-empting rises in prices was stressed, mainly on account of the work of ➤ Friedman. Inflation could not act as a break on real wages, it was asserted, unless it outstripped the expectations of wage bargainers. If, in the longer term, inflation rates could be anticipated, inflation would have no effect on unemployment (➤ unemployment, natural rate of). The Friedman view that the inflation–unemployment trade-off was only short term was superseded in theoretical economics by ➤ new classical economics, which held that there was no trade-off even in the short term (➤ policy ineffectiveness theorem). Now, policymakers tend to accept the idea that there is no trade-off but, equally, they tend to believe policy can have a positive effect on demand without necessarily provoking inflation. They act on the assumption that if the economy is operating below its potential (➤ output gap), inflation will tend to fall; if the economy is above its potential, inflation will tend to rise. The task is simply to manage ➤ aggregate demand. In its effects, inflation probably disrupts investment, by causing interest rates to rise, shortening pay-back periods, and affecting company cash flow. It arbitrarily distributes wealth away from those whose incomes are fixed in money terms or rise more slowly than inflation. It generates ➤ menu costs. To allow inflation to develop carries the risk of incurring rates high enough to disrupt economic life. ➤ hyperinflation; indexation; inflation target; prices and incomes policy; superneutrality of money.

inflation accounting Methods of keeping a record of financial transactions and analysing them in a way that allows for changes in the purchasing power of money over time. Until recently, solely *historic-cost accounting* methods have been used, i.e. accounts were derived more or less directly from bookkeeping records of actual expenditures and receipts. For example, ➤ assets (e.g. buildings) were recorded in the balance sheet at their actual (depreciated) cost (➤ depreciation). In a period of rapidly rising prices, the replacement cost of these assets is likely to be much higher than their recorded cost, and historic-cost accounting, therefore, may understate depreciation and costs in ➤ real terms and overstate profits. Over a period of time this may lead to a situation where ➤ capital is not being maintained in real terms at all but distributed as 'illusory' money profit in dividends and tax payments. *Current cost accounting* (CCA) is a form of replacement-cost accounting that involves revaluing assets from historic costs to current costs (➤ mark-to-market).

inflationary gap A situation in which aggregate demand is at an equilibrium level in excess of the full employment level of output. If it exists, all resources in the economy are fully utilized and prices have to rise to eliminate the excess demand. Based on Keynesian (➤ Keynesian economics) models of the economy, the inflationary gap leads to a ➤ demand-pull inflation that can be removed by ➤ deflation. Because persistent inflation has been combined with high unemployment (something that should not occur in the inflationary gap view of the world) the concept faded from view. In recent years, however, it has been revived in all but name with the growth in popularity of the ➤ output gap as a basis for analysing economic policy. ➤➤ inflation; stagflation.

inflation target The adoption of an explicit level of inflation to which ➤ monetary policy is geared towards steering the economy. Inflation targets rose to prominence in the early 1990s as national authorities grew disenchanted with the effectiveness of targeting growth of ➤ money supply. The UK's inflation target was introduced in 1992 as a range of 1–4 per cent, subsequently to fall to 'below two and a half per cent'. In 1997, the target was set at 2.5 per cent precisely for the ➤ Retail Prices Index, later the ➤ Consumer Price Index, with policy *ex post* (➤ *ex ante*) considered satisfactory if it actually delivered inflation within one percentage point either side. The recent 'point target' is a more useful guide to policy – if inflation is heading above the target, policy should be tightened and vice versa if it is below. The range around the target is more useful for judging whether the authorities have succeeded or failed reasonably to control inflation. In New Zealand, Canada and the UK, inflation targets came to have an explicit role in setting the relationship between national government and the ➤ central banks, who were given responsibility for setting monetary policy. The objective of policy – the target – is then an explicit political choice, while the operation of policy is delegated. The ➤ Federal Reserve System does not have inflation targeting and such a system can be criticized as being overconstraining to the freedom of the central bank. However, targeting is really mainly concerned with communication and does not prevent central banks from concerning themselves with issues such as financial stability and asset inflation. The ➤ European Central Bank, which was established on the setting up of the ➤ European Economic and Monetary Union, has a similar inflation target based on the ➤ harmonized index of consumer prices. ➤➤ Taylor Rule.

inflation tax A form of incomes policy (➤ prices and incomes policy) under which firms granting pay rises above a set level are taxed on those pay rises.

informal economy 'Underground', 'black' or 'popular' economic activity which avoids taxes and government regulations, such as health and safety, employment laws and property rights. According to a 2009 report by the ➤ Organisation for Economic Co-operation and Development, the share of the informal sector worldwide falls generally into a range between 10 per cent and 50 per cent of ➤ Gross Domestic Product with that in developed economies being generally less than 20 per cent but considerably higher in ➤ developing countries. In developing economies, such activity can make a major contribution to employment, reaching up to 90 per cent of the total labour force. In these countries, the impetus to this activity is often simply the need to generate income for survival in a situation in which the formal sector fails to generate sufficient employment opportunity. It is argued, however, that it retards economic growth because of its low productivity. The firms in the sector remain small, having no incentive to grow and therefore lack innovation and the benefits of ➤ economies of scale. The consequential loss of taxes increases the tax burden on the formal economy.

information, economics of The area of economics concerned with the impact of information, or lack of it, on the functioning of markets and economies. Until the 1960s, economists were happy to assume that economic agents were more or less perfectly informed. While this was obviously simplistic, it was not appreciated that deviations from this assumption could make an enormous difference to the functioning of markets. In particular, ➤ asymmetric information, in which one party has more knowledge than another, turns out to be crucial to market performance. Many economic institutions can be explained by a need for gaps in information to be filled, for example, by ➤ signalling and ➤ screening. In ➤ macroeconomics, it is possible to rewrite much of ➤ Keynesian economics as a form of information deficiency in the functioning of a modern economy. ➤ principal–agent problem; Stigler, G.; Stiglitz, J.; ➤➤ quantity rationing.

information and communication technologies (ICTs) ➤ new economy.

infrastructure Roads, airports, sewage and water systems, railways, telecommunications and other public utilities. Also called *social overhead capital*, infrastructure is basic to economic development and improvements in it can be used to help attract industry to a disadvantaged area.

inheritance taxes Almost all ➤ advanced countries tax transfers of wealth arising on death and gifts made during lifetimes. Some countries, for example France and some cantons in Switzerland, levy annual taxes on net wealth, although several European countries have abolished *wealth taxes* in recent decades (for example Spain and Germany).

Taxes arising on death may be paid either out of the estate (*estate tax*) or by the beneficiary (*inheritance tax*). Almost everywhere there are complex reliefs, exemptions and thresholds to these death taxes. In the UK, 'inheritance tax' is payable on the transmission of wealth on death and on gifts made in the seven years before death (the objective being to discourage lifetime avoidance of the tax after death). All transfers to a spouse living in the UK are exempt. Business property qualifies for relief of up to 50 per cent. This tax is not a true inheritance tax because it is levied on the donor or his/her estate, not on the recipient.

In the USA, estate taxes are levied at both federal and state levels. There is also a *gift tax*, which is a levy on the value of certain property given away to others and paid by the donor, i.e. on *inter vivos* gifts. Charitable donations are exempt from both taxes and, for the gift tax, transfers between spouses are exempt.

initial allowances ➤ capital allowances.

initial public offering ➤ flotation.

innovation Putting new products and services on to the market or a new means for producing them. Innovation is preceded by research that may lead to an invention that is then developed for the market (➤ research and development). Innovation is an important source of economic expansion and ➤ productivity. It is central to the new theories of economic growth (➤ endogenous growth theory) although it has long been taken as important – ➤ Schumpeter gave a central role to it in his theory of economic growth. Long before, ➤ Smith drew attention to the way in which specialization through the ➤ division of labour stimulates technological invention, and ➤ Marx emphasized the embodiment of technological innovation in ➤ capital goods. Interest in innovation grew with the much later recognition that the expansion of physical and human capital left a major proportion of growth to be explained by other factors, including technological progress (➤ growth accounting). For these reasons there is intense interest in how innovation comes about and what can be done to promote it.

A.N. Whitehead announced in his book *Science and the Modern World* (1925) that 'the greatest invention of the 19th century was the invention of the method of invention'. Research, development and innovation became more strongly institutionalized in the twentieth century and Schumpeter believed that ➤ monopoly favoured innovative development because research and development (R&D) required large resources and large markets. This view can no longer be fully sustained. Studies show that ➤ small businesses account for a disproportionate share of innovations (disproportionate to their share in output or R&D expenditure, although the latter may not be fully captured in the statistics). There is also some evidence that rivalry stimulates innovation.

The determinants of innovation are now recognized as being very complicated and operating through *national innovation systems*, increasingly on a global scale (➤ globalization). The term 'innovation system' is perhaps misleading because its operations are not planned or systematic and it has three main elements: government, higher educational and research establishments, and business. Early theories of innovation saw it as a linear process driven either by 'technology push' from research establishments or 'need pull' by the market, which transmitted consumer needs to firms and technology needs to the research community. The role of government in these models was to invest in research. This was necessary because, since technology and other forms of knowledge are not fully appropriable by the firm, the social return on investment in R&D is much greater than the private return. Other firms will benefit from knowledge of technology privately developed in a business even where an adequate system for the protection of intellectual property is in place. There are many innovations that cannot be patented. The idea of telephone banking, for example, has been widely copied. That replication is an important development for the benefit of consumers, but does it diminish the likelihood that such ideas will flow in the future? The existence of a ➤ first-mover advantage may be important, however; allowing the innovator to capture profits from an early start can be an important incentive. ➤ weightlessness.

The linear theories could not be supported empirically since there is not a clear relationship between inter-country and inter-regional R&D investment and rates of economic growth. It is now generally accepted that the absorptive capacity of the innovation system – the ability of businesses to make use of scientific developments – is an important factor in innovation. Moreover, technology is not perfectly mobile; much knowledge is 'embedded' in people and groups in their tacit knowledge and acquired skills. The linear models of innovation have therefore given way to circular and dynamic models with multiple paths and feedbacks.

input ➤ factors of production.

input–output analysis The analysis of an economy in terms of the relationship between all ➤ inputs and outputs. The output of a good or service in an economy is used either in the production of goods and services (including itself) or it goes into final consumption, e.g. households, exports, government. Each output in an economy can be represented by an equation, with output equal to its final consumption plus the sum of its inputs used in all production activity throughout the economy. The amounts used in production will depend on the ➤ production functions for each. Consider the simplified ➤ model of two commodities, Y_1 and Y_2:

$$Y_1 = C_1 + a_{11}Y_1 + a_{12}Y_2$$
$$Y_2 = C_2 + a_{21}Y_1 + a_{22}Y_2$$

Y_1 and Y_2 are total outputs, C_1 and C_2 are the final consumptions for each and a_{11}, a_{12}, a_{21} and a_{22} are the input–output coefficients representing the amounts of Y_1 and Y_2 required to produce one unit of Y_1 and Y_2. These equations may be put in ➤ matrix form:

$$Y = C + AY \text{ or } Y = (1-A)^{-1}C$$

where Y is the ➤ vector Y_1Y_2, C the vector C_1C_2 and A the matrix

$$\begin{bmatrix} a_{11} & a_{12} \\ a_{21} & a_{22} \end{bmatrix}$$

AY is the total of intermediate demands and A is the matrix of input–output coefficients or *technology matrix*. By structuring the production functions of an economy in this way, it is possible to trace the effects of a change in final demand, or change in output, of one good or service, throughout its inter-industry linked relationships, so that the knock-on effects on other industries may be measured. ➤ Leontief, W.W.; ➤➤ non-substitution theorem.

input–output matrix ➤ input–output analysis; Leontief, W.W.

insider–outsider theory The division of participants in a market – usually it is the labour market – into a privileged core with a certain amount of market power, and a less privileged periphery with almost no market power. For example, there might be insiders who have good union jobs (➤ trade unions), with full employment rights, and outsiders who find it difficult to get any job at all. The crucial feature of this kind of segmentation is that the outsiders are not in a position to influence the market conditions of the insiders, e.g. they cannot credibly offer themselves as alternative employees at a lower wage. As a result, the mechanism normally assumed to bring about increased employment – a falling wage reducing the cost of taking more people on – simply doesn't work. The gap between the two types of worker, of course, has to be explained to be meaningful. It may result from a difference in the perceived employability or skills of the different types, or from powerful unions who can use industrial muscle to prevent non-union labour from displacing union labour. The idea has been seen both as a cause and an effect of ➤ long-term unemployment. ➤ hysteresis; unemployment.

insolvency The state of a firm when its ➤ liabilities, excluding ➤ equity capital, exceed its total ➤ assets (➤➤ bankruptcy). A less stringent definition would be that a firm is insolvent if it is unable to meet its obligations when due for payment.

Insolvency Act 1985 ➤ bankruptcy.

installment credit (US), **instalment credit** (UK) A form of ➤ consumer credit provided by vendors in which the purchaser pays a deposit on a good and the balance of the purchase price, plus interest, over a period of six to twelve months or more. Typically, the goods remain the property of the vendor until the final instalment is paid. Usually referred to as 'hire purchase' in the UK. This form of credit originated with retailers in the USA during the nineteenth century but is now supplemented for consumers principally by ➤ credit cards and other forms of non-vendor credit. Businesses also use instalment credit for the purchase of certain types of machinery and equipment (➤ finance house; ➤➤ lease).

institutional economics A school of economic thought that first flourished in the 1920s in the USA. Economists holding institutional views criticize orthodox economists for relying on theoretical and mathematical models that not only distort and oversimplify even strictly economic phenomena but, more importantly, ignore their non-economic, institutional environment. The political and social structure of a country may block or distort the normal economic processes (➤ economic development). Institutionalists believe that there is a need for economists to recognize the relevance of other disciplines (e.g. sociology, politics, law) to the solution of economic problems. ➤ Veblen, ➤ Mitchell and ➤ Myrdal have been the leading economists sympathetic to institutionalism. Institutional economics has been strengthened and renewed by the work of a number of economists and economic historians. ➤ North, D.C.; Olson, M.

institutional investor An organization, as opposed to an individual, that invests funds arising from its receipts from the sale of ➤ securities from ➤ deposits and other sources, i.e. ➤ insurance companies, ➤ investment trusts, ➤ unit trusts, ➤ pension funds and trustees. Institutional investors own three-quarters of all quoted securities.

institutions Established forms of law, accepted practice and organization which govern social and economic relationships. More explicitly, they include, for example, property rights, the rules governing political behaviour, commercial transactions and the organizations that conduct them, such as the judiciary. It is widely agreed that institutions are of great importance in governing economic performance (➤ economic development) and the term is much used but rarely defined. ➤➤ institutional economics; North, D.C.

instrumental variable A method applied in the evaluation of cause and effect in ➤ regression analysis. If a ➤ correlation is found between changes in an independent variable and those in a ➤ dependent variable, it is necessary to be sure, before assuming that the changes in the independent variable are caused by the changes in the dependent variable, that there is not an unobserved variable which is affecting the result. This is illustrated in a study by Joshua D. Angrist and Alan B. Krueger to determine the effect of years of schooling on subsequent earned income. The problem was that the years someone stays at school could be related to his innate ability which could not be measured. Their solution was to use the instrumental variable of the schoolchildren's date of birth. The earlier in the year children are born, the older they are when they start school and therefore the less time is spent at school when they reach the statutory leaving age. Birth date is uncorrelated with innate ability, therefore can be clearly used to relate time spent at school to earnings.

insurance A contract to pay a ➤ premium in return for which the insurer will pay compensation in certain eventualities, e.g. fire, theft and motor accident. The premiums are so calculated that, on average in total, they are sufficient to pay compensation for the policyholders who will make a claim, together with a margin to cover administration costs and profit (➤ actuary; underwriting). In effect, insurance spreads risk, so that loss by an individual is compensated for at the expense of all those who insure against it, and as such it has an important economic function. The traditional forms of insurance are *general insurance* (i.e. marine and other property insurance against theft, fire and accident) and *life insurance*, the last-named strictly being ➤ assurance, because the cover is given against the occurrence of an event that is inevitable. There are also many other kinds of insurance, including public or professional liability, sickness and unemployment insurance, some of which, like ➤ National Insurance and insurance for private medical treatment, may not be carried out by the traditional insurance companies but by specialist firms, especially in the USA where medical insurance is highly developed.

Traditional insurance is carried out by a large number of companies in both the USA and the UK. The UK is an important centre for the world insurance industry and about half of the premium income of British insurance companies is derived from their overseas operations. The bulk of their ➤ assets consist of ➤ investments made out of premium income against their ➤ liabilities to 'pay out' on life policies – only about 10 per cent of their assets are in respect of general funds. Life insurance is a popular way of providing for old age and purchasing a house or even ➤ equity shares, as well as protecting the financial positions of dependants. ➤➤ adverse selection; moral hazard; pension funds; unit trust.

intangible assets ➤ assets.

integration ➤ merger; vertical integration.

intellectual property rights ➤ patents.

Inter-American Development Bank (IADB) The bank was established in 1959 to give financial assistance for the encouragement of economic and social development to the ➤ developing countries of Latin America and the Caribbean. The head office is in Washington. Membership now covers twenty-six borrowing countries in Latin America and the Caribbean and twenty non-borrowing countries including Canada, Europe, Israel, Japan and the USA. In 1994, the authorized capital of the bank was increased to $101 billion, the bank was given authority for the first time to lend to the private sector, and shares of the member countries readjusted. The main effect was an increase to 5 per cent for Japan and reductions for the USA down to 30 per cent, and of the Latin American and Caribbean countries to 50 per cent. Bank assistance reached $15.5 billion in 2009. ➤ Asian Development Bank.

inter-bank market The ➤ money market in which banks (➤ banking) borrow or lend among themselves for fixed periods either to accommodate short-term ➤ liquidity problems or for lending on. The interest rate at which funds on loan are offered to first-class banks is called the *inter-bank offered rate* or, in London, the *London inter-bank offered rate*. The corresponding rate for deposits is known as the *inter-bank market bid rate*.

inter-company loans market The ➤ money market in which large companies borrow or lend money among themselves to accommodate short-term ➤ liquidity problems or for the lending on of surplus funds.

interest 1 A charge made for the use of borrowed money, levied as a percentage of the amount of the ➤ debt (➤ rate of interest; usury).

2 More generally, a right, privilege or share in something, as in common grazing land or in shareholders' interest (➤ balance sheet).

interest, abstinence theory of An explanation of ➤ rates of interest in terms of a reward for choosing to abstain from consumption. ➤➤ interest, classical theory of; Senior, N.W.; time preference.

interest, classical theory of In the early tradition of classical theory (e.g. that of ➤ Smith and ➤ Ricardo) interest was regarded as simply the ➤ rate of return on ➤ capital invested. It was considered to be an ➤ income to capital rather like ➤ rent to land. With the subsequent development of the classical system (➤ classical economics), the nature and the determinants of the rate of interest came to be regarded in terms of a more complex pattern. The rate was arrived at by the interaction of two forces operating on the supply of, and the demand for, funds. On the one hand, the strength of demand was related to businessmen's expectations regarding ➤ profits. This was connected with the marginal productivity of ➤ investment. On the other hand, the supply was dependent upon the willingness to save. This willingness was in turn related to the marginal rate of ➤ time preference. People judge how much a pound is worth to them today compared with a pound in the future. They make their decision of whether or not to save by comparing this 'rate of exchange' between now and the future with the current rate of interest. In the classical system, therefore, it was the rate of interest that brought ➤ savings into balance with investment. ➤ Keynes attacked this assumption in his *General Theory of Employment, Interest and Money* (1936). The balance was brought about, he argued, by means of changes in income and output. The rate of interest was itself more closely identified with monetary factors. ➤➤ Hume, D.; liquidity preference; loanable funds.

interest, natural rate of The ➤ rate of interest at which economic activity is neither driving ➤ prices higher nor lower. One of the conditions put forward by ➤ Wicksell for monetary ➤ equilibrium (i.e. a situation in which there are no forces tending to make prices rise or fall) was that the money rate of interest should be equal to the 'natural rate'. The owner of a forest has a choice between two alternatives in any one year. Either the trees can be cut down and the money obtained from them lent out, or they can be allowed to grow for another year. The ➤ rate of return obtained from lending is the 'money rate'; the return from letting the trees grow heavier is the 'natural rate'. Wicksell thought of the natural rate, therefore, in terms of a physical investment. However, ➤ Myrdal, in developing this theme, pointed out that the natural rate should also take into account the price at which the timber was expected to be sold. ➤➤ Fisher, I.; Keynes, J.M.

interest, productivity theories of Theories that place the emphasis of the explanation for the existence of a ➤ rate of interest on the ➤ yield from ➤ investment. ➤ Böhm-Bawerk, in particular, developed this theory as one of his reasons for the existence of a positive interest rate. It was built upon his theory of 'roundabout' production methods. A direct method of obtaining drinking water, for example, is to go to a stream and drink. A more roundabout method is to manufacture a bucket and use it to fetch water. An even more roundabout method is to build a water-pipe, pump and tap. Each stage involves more ➤ capital, and also more time, but nevertheless yields increased product. Goods available today, therefore, have more value than goods available tomorrow, for two reasons: (a) goods today can be used in a time-consuming roundabout process to yield benefits tomorrow that are greater than could be obtained by the same goods applied to direct production tomorrow; and (b) they also yield greater benefits over the same goods applied to roundabout production tomorrow. This is because there are ➤ diminishing returns to the extension of roundabout methods. Present goods are, therefore, always technically superior to future goods, and it follows that there must exist a positive rate of interest by which future goods are equated to present goods. ➤➤ interest, classical theory of; interest, natural rate of; Keynes, J.M.

interest, time preference theory of A psychological theory of the existence of ➤ rates of interest. An individual prefers consumption now to consumption in the future for two reasons: (a) awareness of the possibility that death may occur before the benefits from postponing consumption can be enjoyed; and (b) less rationally, there exists a tendency for people to undervalue future benefits – a 'deficiency of the telescopic faculty'. ➤➤ Böhm-Bawerk, E. von; Fisher, I.; interest, classical theory of; interest, natural rate of; interest, productivity theories of; time preference.

interest cover The number of times the fixed-interest payments made by a company to service its ➤ loan capital are exceeded by ➤ earnings. This ratio shows the decline in earnings that could take place before interest payments could not be met out of current income and is therefore a useful guide for the prospective fixed-interest investor.

interest rate ➤ rate of interest.

interim dividend ➤ dividend.

interlocking directorate The holding by an individual of directorships in two or more separate companies.

intermediate goods, intermediate products Something that is used in the production of other goods, e.g. sheet steel used in the production of car bodies. Also called producer goods.

intermediate products ➤ intermediate goods.

intermediate technology The use of simple, labour-intensive means of production, utilizing non-traditional techniques incorporating modern science and technology. Intermediate technology was advocated notably by Ernst Friedrich Schumacher (1911–77) in a number of publications including the popular book of essays '*Small is Beautiful': A Study of Economics As If People Mattered* (1973). Schumacher founded the Intermediate Technology Development Group, a non-governmental organization that works in ➤ developing countries. His ideas were based on the belief that modern large-scale ➤ capital-intensive industry is not an appropriate vehicle for economic development in backward societies that lack capital and skilled personnel but have a surplus of labour. Intermediate technology is, moreover, less environmentally intrusive, is consistent with ➤ sustainable development and minimizes dependence on external assistance, allowing citizens in developing countries more control over their lives.

internal markets The adoption of market-like mechanisms as a reform strategy in public services. Central to the principle of internal markets is the idea that there should be a division between those who deliver services (e.g. hospitals) and those who purchase them, e.g. general practitioners or health authorities. Reforms in the UK National Health Service and at the BBC did appear to deliver productive efficiency, as cost-conscious purchasers applied pressure to the service providers to keep prices low. But the reforms were criticized as generating a great deal of extra bureaucracy – inevitable in a world in which all output is measured and accounted for. And they were also criticized for failing to deliver the benefits of genuine market mechanisms – providers have not been subject to the real budget constraints of private firms and have been cushioned by long-term contracts ensuring comfortable levels of business. ➤➤ private finance initiative; privatization; resource accounting and budgeting.

internal rate of return That ➤ rate of interest necessary in discounting the flow over time of net revenue generated by an investment such that the ➤ present value of the net revenue flows is equal to the capital sum invested. The internal rate of return, therefore, is the discount rate at which the net present value of a project is zero. It may be used in ➤ investment appraisal to determine whether a prospective investment is viable. For example, if the internal rate of return is higher than the rate of interest at which a firm can borrow, the investment would be worth pursuing. However, the internal rate of return has two disadvantages: (a) if the period (e.g. annual, quarterly) costs and revenues of the project being considered change sign more than once (costs exceeding revenues give negative flows and revenues exceeding costs give positive flows) during the life of the project, a solution cannot be found giving a unique internal rate of return; and (b) in ranking alternative investment proposals in priority order, the internal rate of return procedure could give a different ranking from that of net present value. For example, consider the following two investment projects:

	(1)	(2)
Capital cost	$100	$300
Net revenue per year	$40	$40
Project life (years)	3	12
Net present value at 5 per cent	$8.9	$54.5
Internal rate of return (per cent)	9.7	8

According to the ranking by net present value, (2) is preferable to (1), whereas by ranking according to the internal rates of return, (1) is preferred to (2). The net present value calculation always gives the correct answer because it shows the absolute amount of profit to be made on the investment. The internal rate of return is also the *marginal efficiency of capital* and *investor's yield*.

International Bank for Reconstruction and Development (IBRD) A part of the World Bank Group (➤ International Development Association; International Finance Corporation; Multilateral Investment Guarantee Agency). The establishment of the IBRD, like the ➤ International Monetary Fund, was agreed by the representatives of forty-four countries at the United Nations Monetary and Financial Conference at ➤ Bretton Woods in July 1944. It began operations in June 1946, and has its head office in Washington, DC. The purpose of the bank is to encourage ➤ capital investment for the reconstruction and development of its member countries, particularly ➤ developing countries, either by channelling the necessary private funds or by making ➤ loans from its own resources. Originally, 20 per cent of each member's subscription was paid into the bank's funds in ➤ currency and gold, but this has been progressively reduced to 4.4 per cent; the remainder is retained but available to meet any of the bank's ➤ liabilities if required. The bank also raises money by selling ➤ bonds on the world market. Generally speaking, the bank makes loans either directly to governments or with governments as the guarantor. Contributions of member countries to its capital are made in proportion to that member's share of world trade. Members' voting rights are allocated in the same way. The five leading member countries in terms of their voting rights are the USA (16.4 per cent), Japan (7.9 per cent), Germany (4.9 per cent), France (4.3 per cent) and the UK (4.3 per cent). The total of loans outstanding at 2007–2008 was $99 billion. In 2010, there were 186 member countries.

International Clearing Union ➤ Keynes Plan.

international commodity agreements Several international commodity agreements have been signed in the past. They have included cocoa, coffee, olive oil, rubber, sultanas, sugar, timber, wheat and tin. It has been a feature of the ➤ markets in primary commodities that imbalance between supply and demand gives rise to wide fluctuations in prices. Primary commodities often have long production cycles that are difficult to bring into ➤ equilibrium with relatively short-run fluctuations in demand (➤ cobweb model). At the same time, the development of the economies of the primary producing countries can depend heavily on the export earnings of these commodities, with the result that, in response to a fall in demand, there can be a tendency to increase supply to maintain total earnings in the face of intensified competition, thereby forcing prices down even further.

There are two features of commodity agreements. They could be concluded for: (a) the stabilization of prices, or (b) the increase or maintenance of prices. The first International Coffee Agreement signed in 1962 was designed to halt the long decline in prices by fixing export ➤ quotas for each producing country. Agreements were regularly renewed until the last agreement attempted to raise prices by stockpiling 20 per cent of each country's output but failed to do so and was abandoned in 2001. The International Tin Agreement was an example of a 'price stabilization' agreement. The first operated from 1956. A 'buffer' stock of tin was created and a manager appointed who had the responsibility of buying and selling tin so as to keep the price within a 'ceiling' at which point he sold, and a 'floor' when he bought, tin. This too was abandoned. At the end of 1976, an agreement was concluded among producers for the stabilization of the prices of natural rubber by means of a buffer stock and controls on production. It was the last agreement that regulated price by selling and buying from a buffer stock. The agreement was abandoned in 1999. ➤ developing countries; Organization of Petroleum Exporting Countries; United Nations Conference on Trade and Development.

International Development Association (IDA) Part of the World Bank Group (➤ International Bank for Reconstruction and Development; International Finance Corporation; Multilateral Investment Guarantee Agency), established in 1960. It gives long-term ➤ loans to governments, at little or no interest, and grants for projects in the poorer of the ➤ developing countries. It is intended for ➤ investments for which finance cannot be obtained through other channels without bearing uneconomically high interest charges. The repayment period for the loan may be up to forty years with repayments being delayed by up to ten years. In 2010, loans were averaging at about $14 billion per year.

International Energy Agency (IEA) An organization established in 1974 by the ➤ Organisation for Economic Co-operation and Development. Its original aims were to: (a) reduce the member countries' dependence on oil supplies; (b) maintain an information system relating to the international oil markets; (c) develop a stable international energy trade; and (d) through cooperative sharing, prepare and protect member countries against a disruption of oil supplies. These aims have been widened to the development of alternative energy sources, environmental protection, energy research and international technological cooperation. There were twenty-eight member countries in 2010. ➤ Organization of Petroleum Exporting Countries.

International Finance Corporation (IFC) A part of the World Bank Group (➤ International Bank for Reconstruction and Development (IBRD); International Development Association; Multilateral Investment Guarantee Agency). In the early 1950s, it was recognized that the requirement that IBRD loans should have a government guarantee was a significant handicap to the attraction of private ➤ investment to ➤ developing countries. The IFC was created in 1956 so that greater advantage could be taken of private initiative in the launching of new ➤ capital projects. Until 1961, when its charter was amended, its activities were restricted because it had few resources and could not participate itself in ➤ equity holdings. Since that time its activities have developed rapidly. The IFC can invest directly and give ➤ loans and guarantees for private investors. It is financed by subscriptions from the 182 countries that make up its membership. In 2008–2009, the IFC had a borrowing programme of $8 billion.

international investment ➤ foreign investment.

International Labour Organization (ILO) An organization established in 1919 under the Treaty of Versailles that became affiliated to the United Nations in 1946. Its aims are the improvement of working conditions throughout the world, the spread of social security and the maintenance of standards of social justice. It has drawn up a labour code based on these aims. The ILO offers technical assistance to ➤ developing countries, especially in the field of training. Its budget is financed by contributions from its 183 member countries. The organization was awarded the Nobel Peace Prize in 1969. ➤ ILO unemployment.

international liquidity The amount of ➤ gold, ➤ reserve currencies and ➤ special drawing rights available for the finance of international trade. Broadly, if sufficient reserves were not available, a fall in prices and world trade could follow (➤ quantity theory of money). Gold has lost some of its appeal as a reserve asset in a world of comparatively low inflation. Preference is given to the holding of interest-bearing assets denominated in stable reserve currencies such as the US dollar, the euro, Japanese yen and sterling. ➤➤ creditor nation; eurocurrency; United Nations Conference on Trade and Development.

International Monetary Fund (IMF) The organization set up by the ➤ Bretton Woods conference of 1944 that came into operation in 1947. The IMF was established to encourage international cooperation in the monetary field, and the removal of ➤ foreign exchange restrictions, to stabilize exchange rates and to facilitate a multilateral (➤ multilateralism) payments system between member countries. Under the IMF's articles of agreement, member countries were required to observe an ➤ exchange rate, fluctuations in which should be confined to 1 per cent around its par value. This par value was quoted in terms of the US dollar, which was in turn linked to ➤ gold. In 1969, the creation of an international unit of account was ratified. The system proposed was that annual increases in international credit would be distributed to IMF members by means of ➤ special drawing rights (SDRs). These credits are distributed among member countries in proportion to their quotas and may be included in their official reserves; the first, $3.5 billion, was distributed in this way in 1970. An agreement in 1976 led to a major revision of the IMF's articles. First, it was no longer required for member countries to subscribe 25 per cent of their quotas in gold, and gold was no longer the unit of account of the SDRS. The IMF was authorized to sell its gold holding. Second, the commitment to fixed par values contained in the original articles was abolished.

Member countries finance the IMF through subscriptions based on their quotas that reflect their economic standing. Subscriptions are made up of 25 per cent of SDRs and major foreign currencies and 75 per cent in the country's own currency. Borrowing ability and voting rights are determined by quota. Quotas were revised in 2009 and the financial resources available to the IMF were increased from $250 billion to $750 billion and approval given for the issue of $250 billion in SDRs. In 2002, the IMF had 186 members. ➤ gold standard.

International Organization of Securities Commissions (IOSCO) A body representing the primary regulators of ➤ securities and ➤ futures markets.

International Settlements, Bank for (BIS) ➤ Bank for International Settlements.

international trade The exchange of goods and ➤ services between one country and another, which arises because of differences in relative costs of production between countries, and because it increases the economic welfare of each country by widening the range of goods and services available for ➤ consumption. ➤ Ricardo showed with the law of comparative advantage that it was not necessary for one country to have an absolute cost advantage in the production of a commodity for it to find a partner willing to trade. Even if a country produced all commodities more expensively than any other, trade to the benefit of all could take place provided only that the relative costs of production of the different commodities were favourable. Differences in costs of production exist because countries are differently endowed with the resources required. Countries differ as to the type and quantity of raw materials within their borders, the climate, the skill and size of the labour force, the stock of physical ➤ capital and their institutions (➤ institutional economics). Countries will tend to export (➤ exports) those commodities the production of which requires relatively more than other commodities of those resources (➤ factors of production) it has most. (➤ Heckscher–Ohlin principle.) By increasing the scope for the specialization of labour (➤ division of labour) and for achieving ➤ economies of scale by the enlargement of ➤ markets, there is a presumption that international trade should be free from restrictions (➤ free trade). The classical economists (➤➤ classical economics) condemned ➤ mercantilism for its advocacy of government control over trade in order to achieve export surpluses, and from the nineteenth to the early twentieth century there was a presumption in favour of free trade. This philosophy gave place to economic protectionism (➤ protection) in the 1930s but it was revived again in the ➤ General Agreement on Tariffs and Trade in 1948. The latter had some success in reducing tariffs on ➤ imports (➤ tariffs, import), culminating in the creation of the ➤ World Trade Organization. However, many trade restrictions still remain (➤ protection). At the same time, there has been an increase in the number of ➤ customs unions and ➤ free trade areas (➤ Regional Trade Agreements). World trade has been growing at about 6 per cent per annum, twice the rate of world Gross Domestic Product (GDP), so that its share in total world output has reached about 30 per cent.

International Trade Commission (ITC) A US government agency set up by the Trade Act 1974; it replaced the US International Trade Organization that had previously operated since 1916. The ITC has judicial powers to investigate cases in which ➤ imports are alleged to materially damage domestic industry and to make recommendations to the President. Such damage need not be due to unfair trading practices (e.g. ➤ dumping), although the ITC does carry out studies to determine whether dumping has taken place. It has the power to overturn anti-dumping duties imposed by the US Department of Commerce if it finds that no injury is caused to the USA from the imports under suspicion. The ITC also investigates cases in which imports might be undermining US agriculture-support schemes or infringing intellectual property rights. It collects and disseminates information and statistics on US international trade and domestic production (➤ international trade; protection).

intervention Any form of government interference with ➤ market forces to achieve economic ends. Intervention may be in the area of ➤ macroeconomics (➤➤ policy ineffectiveness theorem), or may be applied to one sector or market. In the latter case, it may take the form of ➤ regulation, ➤ taxation (e.g. a tax on environmentally destructive behaviour, ➤ polluter-pays principle) or ➤ subsidy. There are numerous problems with interventions. They may have: (a) *unforeseen costs* (e.g. a regulation designed to improve food hygiene in restaurants may result in the closure of many local restaurants); (b) *side-effects* (e.g. the provision of subsidized child care may undermine the provision of informal, unpaid child care); (c) *revenge effects* (in which they achieve the opposite of the intended result, e.g. the building of a road to reduce traffic congestion may create extra traffic and increase congestion); (d) deadweight costs (➤ deadweight loss) (the intervention ends up affecting many more people than it needed to to achieve its end, e.g. a job subsidy for those in ➤ long-term unemployment may go to many people who would have found jobs anyway); and (e) they may create *perverse incentives* (e.g. a job subsidy to help the long-term unemployed gives the short-term unemployed an incentive to become long-term unemployed). ➤➤ cost–benefit analysis; risk assessment.

invention The creation of ideas for new products and processes that lead to ➤ innovation that makes them available on the ➤ market. Inventions that may be subject to ➤ patents may be made by one individual or organization and developed for the market by others, or the whole process may be carried out by one organization. There may be a long gap between invention and innovation, e.g. between the Wright brothers' flight in 1903 and the development of scheduled intercity flights thirty years later.

inventories Term for ➤ stocks of raw materials, work in progress and finished goods. Inventories represent ➤ capital tied up in unsold goods and require storage space, insurance and other incurred costs, but are an inevitable part of the process of production and distribution. This is because: (a) in most cases, customers are not willing to wait while goods are produced, but expect delivery off the shelf; (b) it is not possible to forecast sales accurately and sales might be lost if stocks were not held, while it may be uneconomic to interrupt production to match short-term fluctuations in sales because of loss of ➤ economies of scale; (c) while production may be continuous, deliveries of components and raw materials arrive in batches; and (d) transport arrangements may be such that finished goods also need to be dispatched in batches, e.g. by the lorry-load. *Inventory investment* may be intentional, e.g. where stocks are built up to meet an anticipated seasonal peak in demand, or unintentional, e.g. when demand falls sharply. Since increasing the level of stocks is an ➤ investment, running them down is ➤ disinvestment. The management of inventories, in particular the goal of minimizing the capital tied up in them, is seen as an important task (➤ just-in-time). As the change in inventories each year varies so much, and Gross Domestic Product so little, inventories can affect ➤ aggregate demand significantly. ➤➤ inventory investment cycle.

inventory investment ➤ inventories.

inventory investment cycle Fluctuations in economic activity caused by changes in ➤ inventories. Although firms may increase or run down stocks to maintain a steady rate of production, there will be upper and lower limits to inventory accumulation determined by the need to hold a minimum stock and the cost of excessive stocks. For these reasons, many firms will try to keep stocks at so many days of sales or output. Since production will increase faster than sales when inventories are increasing (and vice versa), changes in inventories tend to accelerate the effect on production of changes in sales, thus contributing to ➤ business cycles. ➤➤ acceleration principle.

inverse elasticity rule The rule that, if prices are to deviate from marginal cost (➤ marginal-cost pricing), it is best for the mark-ups to be highest for those products that have the most inelastic demand. By this argument, first articulated by

Ramsey and also known as *Ramsey pricing*, if we were to tax certain goods, the tax should be highest on goods that people will continue to buy anyway and low on those items that are very price-sensitive. Keeping to these rules will minimize the distorting effect of the tax, because it means that consumers will behave very much as they would have without the tax. The same principle can also be applied to allocating fixed costs to different consumers when ➤ marginal cost is below ➤ average cost in a particular industry. Although this idea has achieved wide currency, it does not stand up to ➤ general equilibrium analysis. If all commodities are going to be taxed, for example, the inverse elasticity rule will not apply.

investment 1 Real ➤ capital formation (e.g. the production or maintenance of machinery or the construction of dwellings) that will produce a stream of goods and services for future consumption. Investment involves the sacrifice of current ➤ consumption and the production of investment goods that are used to produce ➤ commodities (➤ producer goods) and includes the accumulation of ➤ inventories. In the national accounts (➤ social accounting), investment is the sum of gross fixed capital formation and the physical change in inventories and work in progress. Investment contributes to higher output. Investment may be stimulated by changes in ➤ demand or ➤ technology, by high ➤ profits or by low interest rates (since much *investment expenditure* is financed by borrowing). The theory of ➤ income determination shows how ➤ savings and investment are brought into equilibrium. (➤➤ capital; depletion theory; gross investment; net investment).
2 In common usage, expenditure on the acquisition of financial or real ➤ assets. To the economist, this is not investment but simply a shift of savings from one form (cash) to another.

investment, inward ➤ foreign investment.

investment allowances ➤ capital allowances.

investment appraisal The evaluation of the prospective costs and revenues generated by an investment in a capital project over its expected life. Such appraisal includes the assessment of the risks of, and the sensitivity of the project's viability to, forecasting errors. The appraisal enables a judgement to be made whether to commit resources to the project. ➤➤ internal rate of return; present value.

investment bank A ➤ financial intermediary which assists companies floating or raising capital on ➤ stock exchanges by ➤ underwriting ➤ share issues. Investment banks also advise on mergers and deal in securities and through subsidiaries provide ➤ risk capital, ➤ instalment credit, manage retail investment funds such as ➤ unit trusts, and provide other financial services, including accepting ➤ bills of exchange. In the UK, the alternative terms 'merchant bank' and 'issuing house' are falling out of use. Many investment banks are members of financial ➤ conglomerates which, although common in Europe (➤ universal banks), were not permitted in the USA where banks were not allowed to carry out investment-banking functions before the repeal of the ➤ Glass-Steagall Act in 1999. Following the ➤ Big Bang, most of the investment banks in London are foreign-owned or subsidiaries of banks.

investment function ➤ acceleration principle.

investment goods ➤ investment.

investment incentives Government assistance designed to encourage firms to invest in physical or other ➤ assets in total, in particular industries or in particular locations. The incentives may take the form of ➤ capital allowances for tax relief, special reliefs for ➤ research and development, for ➤ corporate venture capital or they may be in the form of special regional incentives. ➤➤ enterprise zones; free trade zone; regional policy.

investment trust A company, the sole object of which is to invest its ➤ capital in a wide range of ➤ securities, i.e. a ➤ closed-end fund. An investment trust issues ➤ shares and uses its capital to buy shares in other companies. A ➤ unit trust, on the other hand, issues units that represent holdings of shares. Unit holders thus do not share in the ➤ profits of the company managing the trust. Although sharing the advantages of widespread investment with unit trusts, investment trusts pay their management expenses out of taxed ➤ income and not out of shareholders' incomes. The price of a share in an investment trust may be above (at a ➤ premium) or below (at a ➤ discount) the ➤ net asset value per share of the underlying holdings. There are various types of investment trusts, one of which is the Real Estate Investment Trust (REIT). REITs can be free of ➤ corporation tax provided they distribute 90 per cent of their earnings. Originating in the USA, REITs first appeared in the UK in 2007. Many ➤ quoted companies have converted to REITs. Investment trusts can raise part of their capital by fixed-interest ➤ securities, and the ➤ yield on their ➤ ordinary shares can thus benefit from ➤ gearing.

investor's yield ➤ internal rate of return.

invisible balance ➤ invisibles; balance of payments.

'invisible hand' The idea, postulated by ➤ Smith, that society is best served by individuals being free to pursue their own self-interest. Smith said that each individual was 'led by an invisible hand to promote an end which was no part of his intention'. ➤ Mandeville, B. de; price system; resources.

invisibles A term used to describe those items included in the current ➤ balance of payments accounts that are distinct from physically visible ➤ imports and ➤ exports of goods. Invisibles include government grants to overseas countries and subscriptions to international organizations; financial transfers (➤ remittances), interest, profits and dividends and income and expenditure on commercial ➤➤ services.

involuntary saving ➤ forced saving.

inward investment ➤ foreign investment.

IRR ➤ internal rate of return.

irredeemable security A ➤ security that does not bear a date at which the ➤ capital sum will be paid off or redeemed, e.g. 2½ per cent ➤ consols or certain ➤ debentures. Sometimes called 'undated securities'. Possession of an irredeemable security entitles the owner to ➤ interest payments but not to repayment of face-value capital. This affects the price at which the security is marketable. For example, 2½ per cent consols, which are irredeemable £100 stock bearing 2½ per cent interest, might, depending on prevailing interest rates, fetch only about £50, i.e. the price at which they will give a 5 per cent yield. If this stock were redeemable in one year, its price would obviously be very much higher.

Islamic finance The Koran, the sacred scripture of the religion of Islam, is the main basis of Islamic law (*sharia*), which forbids usury and the borrowing or lending of money at interest (*riba* in Arabic), as did other religions and secular law until the seventeenth century and the rise of ➤ capitalism. It is, however, acceptable for Islamic banks to share profits and losses with depositors and borrowers, where they share the risks. Sharia-compliant bonds (*sukuk*) may also be issued where the 'interest' paid varies with the profits or losses of the issuer.

IS–LM model A model developed by ➤ Hicks shortly after the publication of ➤ Keynes' *General Theory of Employment, Interest and Money* (1936), providing a framework for analysing the factors determining the level of demand in an economy. It became the standard framework for studying ➤ macroeconomics, primarily because it appeared to be able to encompass widely differing views of how the economy works. The strength of the model is that it combines events in the market for cash with events in the market for goods and services to establish an equilibrium level of overall demand. Two variables – aggregate expenditure and the ➤ interest rate – determine whether: (a) equilibrium exists in the two markets; (b) the demand for ➤ investment goods matches the supply of ➤ savings; and (c) the demand for cash (or liquid assets) matches the supply.

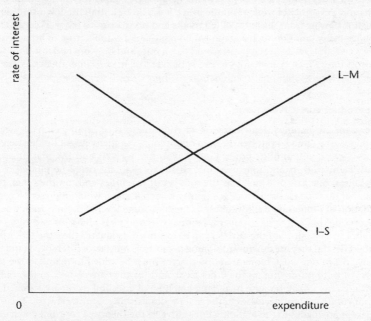

On a graph (see diagram) with the interest rate on the vertical axis and the level of spending on the horizontal axis, two curves can be plotted. The I–S (investment–savings) curve slopes down from left to right depicting the set of combinations of interest rate and spending that ensure equilibrium in the investment and savings market. For each level of the interest rate, there is a unique level of spending, ensuring that planned investment equals planned saving. The second curve, L–M (liquidity–money supply), plots combinations of interest rates and income levels, ensuring that the demand for money (➤➤ liquidity preference) is equal to the supply. A high interest rate suppresses the demand for cash and thus may be combined with a high level of national income (stimulating the demand for cash) if equilibrium is to be maintained. This curve usually slopes upwards. Where the two curves intersect, there is an equilibrium level of both ➤ aggregate demand and the interest rate.

Much of the dispute between ➤ Keynesian economics and ➤ monetarism can be interpreted as arguments over the relative slopes of the I–S and L–M curves. However, the IS–LM model says nothing of the factors determining the ➤ aggregate supply of goods and services, and in recent years more attention has been paid to this area of analysis than the level of demand. ➤ supply-side economics; ➤➤ economic doctrines; transmission mechanism.

isocost line A graphical representation of combinations of inputs, each of which may be purchased for a given cost. It may be that by spending $1000 per week a firm could hire ten workers or ten robots or any combination in between. In this case, the isocost line could be plotted on a graph with a quantity of robots on one axis and a quantity of workers on the other. It would be a straight, downward-sloping line passing from the point of ten robots and no workers to ten workers and no robots. Every point on such a graph would represent a combination of inputs costing a certain level and each point would be on one, and only one, isocost line. The isocost line, which is analogous to the ➤ budget line in consumer theory, is useful for analysing the optimal combination of inputs firms should employ. ➤➤ isoquant.

isoproduct curve ➤ isoquant.

isoquant A graphical representation of combinations of inputs, each of which produces the same output (see diagram opposite). A company might be able to produce a given output of its product either with five workers and five machines, or with eight workers and four machines. If so, an isoquant could be plotted on a graph, on one axis of which was the number of machines and, on the other, the number of workers employed. Each point on such a graph would represent a combination of inputs and each would thus produce some level of output. Each would be on one, but only one, isoquant. Normally, economists allow for two inputs – capital and labour – but the analysis can be extended. Isoquants have the following properties: (a) they are downward sloping because, as one factor is removed (and we move down one axis), more of another factor must be added to maintain the old level of output (moving up the other axis), and (b) they are convex to (i.e. bulge towards) the origin, because increasing amounts of a second factor are required to compensate for unit decreases in the first (➤ diminishing returns, law of). The isoquant is analogous to the ➤ indifference curve in the theory of consumer demand. ➤➤ convexity; isocost line; rate of technical substitution.

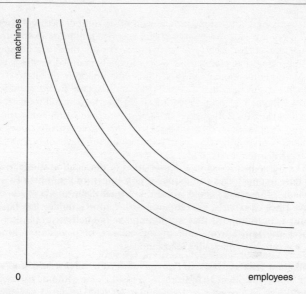

issued capital That part of a company's ➤ capital that has been subscribed to by shareholders. It may or may not be paid up (➤ paid-up capital).

issuing broker A ➤ broker acting as an agent for a new issue of ➤ securities.

issuing house An ➤ investment bank, or ➤ stockbroker, that organizes the raising of ➤ capital by new issues of ➤ securities on behalf of clients. The issuing house will advise the client on the timing and form of the issue, and investment banks, in return for a commission, will underwrite all or part of the issue (➤ underwriting). The sponsorship of an issue by an established issuing house greatly affects the confidence of the investor and success of the issue. Increasingly, and especially in ➤ unlisted securities markets, other securities dealers and firms of accountants are sponsoring new issues while other financial institutions will also underwrite issues. ➤ new-issue market.

J

J-curve The immediate effect of a depreciation or devaluation of the ➤ exchange rate is to raise import prices and reduce export prices. In the short run, therefore, the ➤ balance of payments could worsen. Eventually, the effects of the change in the relative price of exports, as compared with imports, induce the expansion of exports and a cut in imports that would improve the balance of payments. The J-curve traces the initial worsening in the balance of payments followed by a recovery. ➤➤ international trade; 'leads and lags'.

Jevons, William Stanley (1835–82) Jevons studied natural science and worked as an assayer to the Australian Mint from 1853 to 1859. He became Professor of Logic at Owens College, Manchester, in 1866, and in 1876 at University College London. His main theoretical economic work is *The Theory of Political Economy* (1871). Other aspects of his work are collected together in *Investigations in Currency and Finance* (1884). He was one of the three economists to put forward a ➤ marginal utility theory in the 1870s. He argued that one ➤ commodity will exchange for another such that the ratio of the ➤ prices of the two commodities traded equals the ratio of their marginal utilities.

➤ Edgeworth criticized the way Jevons developed these ideas, and in so doing invented the ➤ indifference curve. Jevons also made an important contribution to the theory of ➤ capital, many aspects of which were, in fact, taken up by the ➤ Austrian School. He superimposed on the ➤ classical economics theory the idea that capital should be measured in terms of time as well as quantity. An increase in the amount invested is the same as an increase in the time period in which it is being employed. Output can be increased by extending the period in which the investment is available by, for example, reinvesting the output instead of consuming it at the end of the production period. With given levels of ➤ labour and capital, output becomes a function of time only. He derived from this a definition of the ➤ rate of interest as the ratio of the output gained by an increase in the time capital remains invested divided by the amount invested (➤ Böhm-Bawerk, E. von; internal rate of return).

Jevons was also one of the founders of ➤ econometrics – he invented ➤ moving averages. He also propounded a theory of the ➤ business cycle based on sunspots, but this is of little importance except for the stimulus it gave to the study of statistics for economic empirical work. ➤➤ Gossen; Menger; Walras.

jobber ➤ market maker.

joint costs ➤ Costs arising simultaneously in the production of two or more

➤ commodities that cannot be precisely allocated to each product. ➤➤ economies of scope.

joint demand ➤ Demand for two or more ➤ commodities or ➤ factors of production that are used together so that a change in demand for one will sooner or later be reflected in a change in demand for the other, e.g. cloth and thread. Another term for complementary demand (➤ complementary goods).

joint products ➤ Commodities that are produced in such a way that a change in the output of one of them necessarily involves a change in the output of the other. For example, in refining crude oil into petrol, fuel oil and other heavier oils, limits are set to the relative proportions of each product that can be achieved. Leather and beef are joint products. Under conditions of joint production, the allocation of costs between the products will be arbitrary. ➤➤ economies of scope.

joint-stock company The now usual arrangement in which the share capital of a company is subscribed by shareholders who receive ➤ equity in proportion to their share of the capital raised. The two other forms of business unit are the ➤ sole proprietorship and the ➤ partnership. ➤ company law.

joint supply ➤ joint products.

joint venture A business arrangement in which two companies invest in a project over which both have partial control. It is a common way for companies to collaborate – especially on risky high-technology ventures – without engaging in full-scale ➤ merger. The growth of international joint ventures has been striking and raises many public policy issues analogous to those raised by acquisitions, for which joint ventures may often be a strategic substitute.

Juglar, Clément (1819–1905) ➤ Juglar cycle.

Juglar cycle A ➤ business cycle identified by Clément Juglar of about 9 or 10 years in length. Juglar was one of the first analysts to use ➤ time-series data effectively to elucidate an economic problem. His work was published in 1862 in *Des crises commerciales et leur retour périodique en France, en Angleterre et aux États-Unis*. Through his work he came to the conclusion that 'The only cause of ➤ depression is prosperity.' ➤ Kondratiev cycle; Kuznets, S.S.

junk bond A high-yield, fixed-interest ➤ security of low quality which is rated below investment grade by credit ➤ rating agencies. Junk bonds were pioneered in the mid-1970s by the New York house Drexel Burnham Lambert and were issued as such, though other ➤ bonds may descend to junk bond status when their security deteriorates. ➤➤ toxic assets.

just-in-time A form of production management, originating in Japan, in which companies do not obtain stocks of components until they are actually needed. Traditionally, companies kept large quantities of parts ready for use in production. Just-in-time management can cause the production process to be held up if a certain part is short but, as this exposes which parts of the production process are going wrong most often, this is not seen as a disadvantage. It also lowers the costs of maintaining stocks of parts. ➤➤ inventories.

K

Kahneman, Daniel (b. 1934) Israeli-American psychologist from Princeton University, who jointly won the Nobel Prize for Economics in 2002 for pioneering work in combining the study of human economic behaviour with insights from cognitive psychology. Kahneman is seen as one of a handful of pioneers in the discipline of ➤ behavioural economics. This attempts to analyse human decision-making and its deviations from the traditional economic assumption of 'rationality'. Economists always understood that people were not fully rational, but hoped that deviations were not very systematic in any particular direction. In practice, there are systematic deviations. Kahneman and his late colleague Amos Tversky have documented different biases in behaviour. The two have written many influential papers, e.g. 'Subjective Probability: a judgment of representativeness', *Cognitive Psychology* (1972), 'On the Psychology of Prediction', *Psychological Review* (1973), 'Prospect Theory: an analysis of decision under risk', *Econometrica* (1979), and edited *Choices, Values and Frames* (2000).

Kantorovich, Leonid (1912–86) An economist of the then USSR, and joint winner of the ➤ Nobel Prize for Economics in 1975. Based at the Academy of Sciences in Moscow, Kantorovich's subject was the optimal allocation of resources. His book, *The Best Use of Economic Resources*, was published in 1965. He was keen to improve the planning system adopted by his country, and developed mathematical techniques – notably ➤ linear programming and the use of ➤ shadow prices – as a means to that end. His work was concerned with the decentralization of planning, and the need for a rational price system to make decentralization work.

Keynes, John Maynard (1883–1946) Educated at Eton, Keynes won prizes there in mathematics as well as in English and Classics before going up to King's College, Cambridge. At university he graduated with a first in mathematics. During his stay at Cambridge, he studied philosophy under A.N. Whitehead and G.E. Moore and economics under ➤ Marshall and ➤ Pigou. He was granted a fellowship at King's College, Cambridge, for his *Treatise on Probability*, which was subsequently published in 1921, and after a period in the Civil Service, he accepted a lectureship in economics there. In 1911, he became editor of the *Economic Journal*. During the First World War he held a post in the UK Treasury, but resigned because he believed that the figure for German war reparations was set too high (*The Economic Consequences of the Peace* (1919)). He was also a severe critic of the decision of the government to return to the ➤ gold standard at the prewar ➤ exchange rate (*The Economic Consequences of Mr Churchill* (1925)). In 1930, he published *A Treatise on Money*, and in the same year was appointed a member of the Macmillan Committee on Finance and Industry. His major work, *The General Theory of Employment, Interest and Money*, appeared in 1936. He served a second spell in the Treasury during the Second World War, and was responsible for negotiating with the USA on Lend-Lease. He took a leading part in the discussions at ➤ Bretton Woods in 1944 that established the ➤ International Monetary Fund.

➤ Unemployment during the interwar period persisted in the UK, never falling below 5 per cent, and reaching 14 per cent of the total ➤ labour force. The failure of the economy to recover from such a long depression was unprecedented in the economic history of industrial society (➤➤ Great Depression). The policy recommendations of the classical economists (➤ classical economics) were that the unions should be persuaded to accept a wage cut. Keynes argued that, although this policy might make sense for a particular industry, a general cut would lower ➤ consumption, income and ➤ aggregate demand, and this would offset the encouragement to employment by the lowering of the 'price' of labour relative to the price of capital, e.g. plant and machinery. Why, said Keynes, should not the government take over the businessman's function and spend money on public works? Current opinion upheld the belief that government budget-deficit financing would bring more hardship than already existed. The UK government view was that public works would merely divert ➤ savings and labour from the private sector and, as the former was less productive, the net effect would be a worsening of the situation (➤ crowding out). It was not until after Keynes had written his *General Theory* and crystallized his arguments into a coherent theoretical framework that his views were accepted.

Keynes did not deny the classical theory. He agreed that a reduction in wage rates could be beneficial, but it would operate only through the ➤ liquidity preference schedule. A fall in prices would increase the value of the stock of money in people's hands in real terms. This would make available an increase in the amount that people were willing to lend, with a consequent drop in the rate of interest to the benefit of investment. However, if this is so, why not operate directly on the rate of interest or the quantity of money in the economy? Moreover, Keynes argued that there exists a level of interest rate below which further increases in ➤ money supply are simply added to idle balances (➤ inactive money) rather than being used to finance investment. Wage cuts or not, the economy would stick at this point with chronic unemployment. In the classical system, the national product (➤ national income) was determined by the level of employment and the latter by the level of real wages. The quantity of money determined the level of prices. Savings and investment were brought into balance by means of the rate of interest. In Keynes' system, the equality of savings and investment was achieved by adjustments in the level of national income or output working through the ➤ multiplier. The rate of interest was determined by the quantity of money people desired to hold in relation to the money supply. The level of output at which savings equals investment does not necessarily correspond to full employment.

The innovation in the Keynesian system was that the rate of interest was determined by the quantity of money and not the level of output, as in the classical system. In the Keynesian model, if you increased the propensity to invest or consume, you did not simply raise the rate of interest, you raised output and employment (➤ consumption function). Keynes' study of monetary aggregates of investment, savings, etc., led to the development of national accounts. Keynes'

General Theory is now criticized for its reliance on special cases (the insensitivity of investment to the rate of interest, and the idea of a minimum rate of interest at which the demand for money became infinitely elastic), its preoccupation with ➤ equilibrium and the fact that, despite its presentation as a radical new departure, it nevertheless embodies many of the analytical limitations of the Classical School of economics. However, the transformation which Keynes brought about, in both theory and policy, was considerable. In effect, he laid the foundations for what is now ➤ macroeconomics. ➤➤ behavioural economics; Keynesian economics; Keynesian unemployment; new Keynesianism; Pigou effect.

Keynesian economics The branch of economic theory, and the doctrines, associated with ➤ Keynes. In general, Keynesian economics tends to support the following propositions: (a) ➤ aggregate demand plays a decisive role in determining the level of real output; (b) there is no automatic tendency for the level of ➤ savings and ➤ investment to be equal, as the level of investment is not primarily determined by the ➤ rate of interest; (c) as a result, economies can settle at positions with high unemployment and exhibit no natural tendency for unemployment to fall; and (d) governments, primarily through fiscal policy, can influence aggregate demand to cut unemployment.

It would be wrong, however, to consider Keynesian economists to be a single, united body of theorists. Since 1945, two predominant Keynesian schools have emerged. First the *Neo-Keynesians* reached a consensus view with more classically oriented economists. Under what is known as the *neo-classical synthesis* (➤ neo-classical economics), it was largely accepted that the practical conclusions of Keynes were correct but that, at least in theory, the market *did* have a theoretical tendency towards full employment (other than possibly in the very exceptional circumstances of a ➤➤ liquidity trap). It was on account of price rigidities and institutional inflexibility that unemployment could persist. This neo-Keynesian view used the ➤ IS–LM model to describe the determination of aggregate demand, and the ➤ Phillips curve acted as a description of the behaviour of ➤ aggregate supply. The synthesis dominated ➤ macroeconomics until it was challenged by ➤ Friedman and ➤ monetarism.

At the same time, a second strand of Keynesian thought emerged. This held that economists were mistaken in considering the behaviour of an economy only in ➤ equilibrium. It was possible that because of interactions between different sectors of the economy, a state of ➤ disequilibrium could persist. When the economy left an equilibrium state, no amount of price flexibility could guarantee its return to full employment. This branch of disequilibrium economics is associated with Clower, Leijonhufvud and Malinvaud (➤➤ Keynesian unemployment; quantity rationing).

More recently, another variant – ➤ new Keynesianism – has been concerned to find foundations for Keynesian findings in ➤ microeconomics. It arrives at certain Keynesian implications, using the assumption of ➤ rational expectations. ➤➤ information, economics of.

Keynesian unemployment A situation in which the number of people able and willing to work at prevailing wages exceeds the number of jobs available and, at the same time, firms are unable to sell all the goods they would like. ➤ Excess supply thus exists in both the labour and goods markets. Keynesian unemployment is one of four possible regimes in an economy in which ➤ quantity rationing exists, i.e.

that markets are not in equilibrium. Its important distinguishing feature is in its possible cures. For ➤ classical unemployment, a cut in wages should make it profitable for employers to take on new workers. In the Keynesian case, however, firms are already unable to sell all their output. This induces them to cut their prices at the same time that workers will be trying to price themselves into jobs by accepting lower wages. When both prices and wages fall, ➤ real wages remain constant, and it is real wages that determine the level of employment. Thus, when both the labour market and goods market are in excess supply, even if prices and wages are flexible, there will be no natural tendency for the economy to lift itself out of recession. In this case, the most obvious solution is for the government to inject some demand through higher borrowing. ➤➤ Keynesian economics; unemployment.

Keynes Plan Proposals by the UK Treasury, submitted for the establishment of an International Clearing Union (ICU) for discussion at the ➤ Bretton Woods conference in 1944. These proposals were primarily the work of ➤ J.M. Keynes, and became known as the Keynes Plan. The ICU would have basically the same functions as a domestic ➤ bank and ➤ clearing house. International ➤ debts would be cleared on a multilateral basis between its members. It would give overdraft facilities to a member running a temporary ➤ balance of payments deficit and would create its own unit of ➤ currency – called bancor – in which the overdraft facility would be made available. Bancor would have a gold ➤ exchange rate in the initial phases of the scheme, though it was expected that it would eventually break its gold connection and replace gold in international finance. Each member would have a quota that determined the limits of its credit facilities with the ICU. There was a set of suggested safeguards and penalties to encourage the elimination not only of deficits but also of persistent surpluses. The plan did not win approval at Bretton Woods and the less radical ➤ International Monetary Fund was established, which was more in line with the ideas put forward by the USA.

Klein, Lawrence R. (b. 1920) Professor Klein studied at Berkeley, the University of California, and obtained his Ph.D. at the Massachusetts Institute of Technology. After working for the Cowles Commission, he was at Michigan University from 1949 to 1954 and at Oxford University until 1958. Professor Klein was then appointed Professor of Economics and Finance at the Wharton School of Finance, University of Pennsylvania. He was awarded the ➤ Nobel Prize for Economics in 1980. His major publications include *The Keynesian Revolution* (1947), *Economic Fluctuations in the United States, 1921–1941* (1950), *An Econometric Model of the United States, 1929–1952* (1955), *An Essay on the Theory of Economic Prediction* (1971) and *The Economics of Supply and Demand* (1983).

Professor Klein pioneered the design, construction and application of large-scale ➤ econometric models for forecasting ➤ Gross National Product and its components in the 1950s and 1960s, capitalizing on the emergent computer technology of the time. His work has contributed to the development of applied ➤ econometrics and stimulated the development of statistical information about macroeconomic fluctuations (➤ macroeconomics).

Knight, Frank Hyneman (1885–1972) Appointed Associate Professor of Economics at the University of Iowa in 1919 and Professor in 1922; after studying at Cornell and Chicago Universities, Knight returned to Chicago as Professor of Economics in

1928. His major published works include *The Economic Organization* (1933), *The Ethics of Competition and Other Essays* (1935), *The Economic Order and Religion* (1945), *Freedom and Reform* (1947), *On the History and Method of Economics: Selected essays* (1956) and *Intelligence and Democratic Action* (1960). His most influential work has been *Risk, Uncertainty and Profit* (1921). In this work, he made a clear distinction between insurable ➤ risk and uninsurable uncertainty. It was the latter that gave rise to ➤ profit. A businessperson must guess future demand and selling prices and pay in advance the ➤ factors of production amounts based on his/her guesses. The accuracy of the guesses is reflected in the profit made. It follows that profits are related to uncertainty, the speed of economic change and business ability.

knowledge economy A characterization of modern economies in which 'knowledge-intensive' activities (i.e. those that involve the creation, processing and interpretation of information) account for a substantial and growing proportion of employment and output. Examples of these activities are education, professional services, the media, communications and ➤ research and development. The term first came into common use in the 1960s and had its roots in the observations that services accounted for more employment than agriculture, manufacturing and mining, and that rates of economic growth were considerably higher than could be explained by the combined growth of inputs of ➤ capital and ➤ labour, a difference that in part was attributed to advances in knowledge (➤ growth accounting). The preponderance of service activities and the role of knowledge has given rise to another term – *post-industrial economy* – which can be a synonym for knowledge economy. However, all production, whether in manufacturing, agriculture or services, requires knowledge and always has, and there is no novelty in the importance of knowledge. ➤➤ innovation; new economy.

Kondratiev cycle A ➤ business cycle of very long duration – ➤ Schumpeter applied the term to a cycle of fifty-six years. Named after the Russian economist Nikolai Kondratiev (1892–1938), who made important contributions in the 1920s to the study of long-term fluctuations. Kondratiev studied US, UK and French wholesale prices and interest rates from the eighteenth century through to the 1920s and found peaks and troughs at regular intervals. Similar work has been carried out at Harvard, confirming a fifty-four-year cycle in UK wheat prices since the thirteenth century. ➤➤ Juglar cycle; Kuznets, S.S.; Schumpeter, J.A.

Koopmans, Tjalling C. (1910–86) Professor Koopmans was born in the Netherlands and studied physics and mathematics at the Universities of Utrecht and Leiden. After four years with the League of Nations in Geneva, he went to the USA in 1940 to take up a post as statistician with the Allied Combined Shipping Adjustment Board. He moved to the Cowles Commission at Chicago in 1944, where he was appointed Director in 1961. He was a Professor of Economics at Yale University from 1955 until his retirement in 1981.

Professor Koopmans was awarded, in 1975, the ➤ Nobel Prize in Economics (jointly with ➤ Kantorovich). His publications include *Linear Regression Analysis of Economic Time Series* (1937), *Statistical Inference in Dynamic Economic Models* (1950), *Analysis of Production as an Efficient Combination of Activities* (1951), *Three Essays on the State of Economic Science* (1957) and *The Scientific Papers of Tjalling C. Koopmans*, vol. 1 (1970). Professor Koopmans introduced the mathematical procedures of ➤ linear programming (or *activity analysis*) to economics. He demonstrated the application of linear programming to the solution of transportation problems, to general ➤ equilibrium analysis and to problems in ➤ investment appraisal. He has made important contributions to the theory of ➤ econometrics.

Kuznets, Simon S. (1901–85) Professor Kuznets, who was born in Russia, went to the USA in 1922 where he studied economics at Columbia University, receiving his Ph.D. in 1926. After a number of years at the National Bureau of Economic Research, he went in 1930 to the University of Pennsylvania where he was later to be appointed Professor of Economics, a post he held until 1954. There followed a period as Professor of Economics at Johns Hopkins University until 1960 when he accepted a Chair in Economics at Harvard, where he remained until his retirement in 1971.

Professor Kuznets was awarded the ➤ Nobel Prize for Economics in 1971. His publications include *Secular Movements in Production and Prices* (1930), *National Income, 1929–1932* (1934), *National Income and Capital Formation, 1919–1935* (1941), *National Product Since* 1869 (1946), *Six Lectures on Economic Growth* (1959), *Economic Growth and Structure* (1965), *Modern Economic Growth: Rate, structure and spread* (1965), *Economic Growth of Nations* (1971) and *Population, Capital and Growth* (1979). Professor Kuznets made important contributions to the development of applied ➤ econometrics through the compilation of macroeconomic statistics. His analysis and statistical identification of fifteen to twenty year fluctuations in time series of production and prices initiated a continuing debate in the analysis of ➤ business cycles. He completed major studies in income distribution, exploring the relationship between growth in income per head and the distribution of income (➤ Kuznets curve). ➤ Juglar cycle; Kondratiev cycle.

Kuznets curve A proposition put forward by ➤ Kuznets in 'Economic Growth and Income Inequality', *American Economic Review* (1955), which suggested that ➤ inequality in ➤ income distribution increased during the early rapid phase of economic growth and subsequently diminished, thus tracing an inverted U-shape. There was a view that increasing inequality not only resulted from growth but encouraged it, reflecting the fact that the savings rate of the rich was higher than that of the poor. However, subsequent studies of more extensive data sets have been inconclusive.

L

labour A ➤ factor of production. The term not only includes the numbers of people available for, or engaged in, the production of goods or services but also their physical and intellectual skills and effort. ➤➤ employment, full; human capital; labour force; sow's ear effect; unemployment.

labour, demand for The amount of labour that firms will employ at different wage levels. In a simple model of the structure of the ➤ labour market, firms employ labour as long as it is profitable for them to do so. It will be profitable as long as the selling price of the output of the marginal worker is greater than the cost of that worker. To maximize profits, therefore, firms employ additional workers until the ➤ marginal revenue product (i.e. the marginal revenue of the firm's output times the number of extra units produced by taking on one more worker) is equal to the wage costs. In this situation, when: (a) the price of the firm's output rises, its demand for labour rises; (b) the physical output of workers rises (from more developed skills or harder work), the demand for labour rises; (c) the wage rate falls, the demand for labour rises; and (d) the amount of capital employed increases, the demand for labour will either increase – as the capital enhances the productivity of each worker – or it will fall, if the capital displaces workers.

This account, in which all workers are assumed to be identical, has been developed in many directions: (a) complications can be added, e.g. the influence of ➤ trade unions and industries in which there is only one employer (➤ monopoly); (b) alternative models have been developed to account for the stickiness of wages and to describe alternatives to fixed-wage contracts (➤ efficiency-wage hypothesis; profit-sharing). Finally, the whole subject can be viewed in a macroeconomic perspective (➤ macroeconomics), in which the demand for labour is viewed as a function of ➤ aggregate demand only. In this case, high wages can be portrayed as stimulating employment through their effect on maintaining high aggregate demand. ➤➤ marginal productivity theory of wages.

labour, division of ➤ division of labour.

labour, mobility of The degree to which workers are able and willing to move between jobs in different occupations and areas. A lack of ➤ labour mobility may manifest itself in high ➤ frictional unemployment or high ➤ structural unemployment and it has been an object of policy to encourage workers to move to areas in which jobs are available and to take on jobs in new occupations, requiring skills different from those in which they were first trained. Policies to this end could include (a) a faster rate of housebuilding, making it easier for people to find homes in different areas; (b) the removal of taxes like stamp duty on house transfer; (c) the provision of full information on what jobs are available and where; (d) the provision of training courses for the unemployed; and (e) the abolition of restrictions on entry to different jobs. In practice, it has been found that, for a multitude of social and economic reasons, labour may be geographically and occupationally immobile. Moreover, it is recognized that social costs could be incurred by an itinerant population, from regional overcrowding or depopulation. These factors have been used to justify ➤ subsidies to jobs in regions of high unemployment. The Treaty of Rome of the ➤ European Union (EU) guarantees the free movement of labour throughout the Union. Such movements are, however, constrained in Europe by the lack of a common language and it has been found that interstate mobility in the USA is six times higher than intercountry mobility in the EU. ➤➤ active labour-market policies.

labour, specialization of ➤ division of labour.

labour force The economically active population. The total number of people in a country who are either in work or unemployed but looking for work. According to the ➤ International Labour Organization, the total labour force of the ➤ advanced countries was 622 million in 2009, having grown by 5 per cent since 2000, compared with a labour force of 2.6 billion and a growth of 18 per cent in the ➤ less developed countries. *Activity rate (or participation rate)* is defined as the proportion of the labour force of a specified group in the total population of that group. In 2009, the activity rate for women was 53 per cent and for men was 68 per cent in the developed countries, compared with 51 per cent and 80 per cent in the less developed countries. The labour force is significantly younger in the less developed countries in which 47 per cent is in the age group between 15 and 35, compared with 36 per cent in the developed countries. ➤ glass ceiling.

Labour Force Survey (LFS) A quarterly survey of households in Great Britain. Similar surveys are carried out in all ➤ European Union member states under the auspices of Eurostat, the statistical office of the European Communities. It collects data on employment, including self-employment, and persons seeking employment. It uses the measure of unemployment as defined by the International Labour Organization (➤ ILO unemployment) in contrast to the ➤ claimant count measure. It counts everyone who wishes to work, and has looked for work in the previous four weeks, as unemployed, whether or not he/she is eligible for benefits. It includes many unemployed people who live with working partners and are thus excluded from obtaining benefits. It excludes people who are on benefits but admit to not having looked for work in the previous four weeks. The net effect is that the LFS measure of unemployment has followed the same trend as the claimant count, but is higher. ➤ unemployment.

labour-intensive A production technology for which relatively more labour value is required as input per unit of output than other ➤ factors of production. ➤➤ capital-intensive; production function; productivity.

labour market The ➤ market in which wages, salaries and conditions of employment are determined in the context of the supply of labour (➤ labour force) and the demand for ➤ labour. Most economists believe that lack of labour market flexibility is an important cause of ➤ unemployment and a drag on ➤ economic growth. Many factors can reduce incentives for the unemployed to move to available jobs, e.g. deficiencies in training and ➤ education, the availability of housing and transport and generous unemployment benefits. The ➤ regulation of labour markets, restrictions on temporary workers, hiring and firing and, possibly, ➤ minimum wages, if set at a high level, can reduce labour market flexibility. There is little direct evidence that employers are deterred from hiring the unemployed by these 'employment protection' measures, but various measures of labour market flexibility have been found to be negatively correlated (➤ correlation) with unemployment rates across a wide range of countries. Neo-classical economic analysis certainly indicates that anything that raises the cost of employment will reduce the demand for labour and encourage ➤ capital-intensive methods of production. Lack of labour market flexibility could help to explain (and many economists think it mainly explains) the loss of the growth advantage that Europe had over the USA before the early 1970s. Superior US growth since then has been made possible not by a greater productivity increase (which has been lower than in Europe) but by higher labour utilization rates, i.e. lower unemployment. The USA seems to have been more able to employ its low-skilled workers and this can be explained by greater labour market flexibility. ➤➤ active labour-market policies; labour, demand for; labour, mobility of.

labour theory of value ➤ value, theories of.

labour turnover The number of employees who leave a firm within a year as a percentage of the firm's total employment.

Laffer curve A graphical illustration of the argument that there exists an optimum rate of tax at which government tax revenue is maximized. If tax rates are low, revenues will be increased if tax rates are increased; however, if rates are raised beyond the optimum point, the loss of incentives caused by the resultant low net incomes discourages production and tax revenues fall. The curve is named after the American economist Professor Arthur Laffer, who argued that the economy could be expanded without government budget deficits. Lower taxes lead to lower prices, higher output and, therefore, higher government revenues. This argument has yet to find full empirical justification. ➤➤ supply-side economics.

LAFTA Latin American Free Trade Association (➤ Latin American Integration Association).

Lagrange multiplier A technique, devised by the French mathematician Joseph Louis Lagrange (1736–1813), for calculating the optimal value of a variable subject to some constraint, in order to maximize or minimize another variable. It is a technique pervasive in economics, where so many problems relate to the best use of scarce resources. In demand theory (➤ demand, theory of), for example, the consumer is assumed to maximize utility subject to prevailing prices and income by choosing the right combination of goods to buy. Firms are assumed to maximize profits subject to the constraints of technology and the ➤ production function by setting their output and price at the right levels. The Lagrangian technique allows the method of maximizing a ➤ function *without* a constraint – using calculus to set the derivative of the function with respect to the variable that can be controlled equal to zero – to be used in those cases where there is a constraint. It does this by expanding the function to be maximized – the *objective function* – to include the constraint, multiplying the constraint by a new parameter – the Lagrange multiplier – and then setting the derivatives of the new function equal to zero. For example, suppose we wish to set X and Z at a level that maximizes Y, where the objective function is:

$$Y = X \times Z$$

and is subject to the constraint that $(X + Z)$ is equal to 10, or:

$$X + Z - 10 = 0$$

We construct a new, artificial objective function of this form:

$$L = X \times Z + \lambda(X + Z - 10)$$

This is, in fact, the same as the old one, but it has had the constraint added on. It has been added on, however, in such a way that it equals zero, if it holds. We could just as well have subtracted it. The constraint is also multiplied by λ, called the Lagrange multiplier.

Maximizing this new objective function is the same as maximizing the old one, subject to the constraint. So we then maximize L by controlling X, Z and λ in the normal way. We set the partial derivatives of these three equal to zero and solve them as a system of simultaneous equations. The resulting values of X and Z are the values we want. Note that the partial derivative of the equation with respect to λ is the constraint itself, thus ensuring that it will hold when the solution is found. We can also interpret λ as the value by which the objective can be advanced for a one-unit relaxation of the constraint. It can thus be seen as the ➤ shadow price of the constrained variables. In this case, the values of X and Z will each be 5, and the value of λ will be –5. ➤➤ calculus of variations; linear programming.

LAIA ➤ Latin American Integration Association.

laissez-faire '*Laissez-faire, laissez-passer*' was the term originally used by the ➤ Physiocrats. They believed that only agriculture yielded wealth. Consequently, they condemned any interference with industry by government agencies as being inappropriate and harmful, except in so far as it was necessary to break up private ➤ monopoly. The principle of the non-intervention of government in economic affairs was given full support by the classical economists (➤ classical economics), who inherited the theme from ➤ Smith (*Wealth of Nations*, Book IV, chapter 2):

> The Statesman, who should attempt to direct private people in what manner they ought to employ their capitals, would not only load himself with a most unnecessary attention, but assume an authority which could safely be trusted, not only to no single person, but to no council or senate whatever, and which would nowhere be so dangerous as in the hands of a man who had folly and presumption enough to fancy himself fit to exercise it.

More recently, *laissez-faire* economics has been associated with the ➤ Chicago School, who not only believe in ➤ free-market economics, but have also promoted the idea that some privately imposed restrictions on trade are socially efficient. ➤➤ Manchester School; Mandeville, B. de; Sismondi, J.C.L.S. de.

land Taken to include, in economics, all ➤ natural resources, including the sea and outer space. One of the ➤ factors of production, land is distinguished from the others in that its supply is more or less fixed. Since the productive power of land is conceptually distinct from that of ➤ capital, land is a factor of production only in its natural, unimproved state. ➤➤ depletion theory.

Laspeyres index An ➤ index number whose weights (➤ weighted average) are derived from values obtaining in a base year. For example, the UK producer price index of output in 2000 was calculated on weights reflecting the pattern of sales of the different industries making up the index in 1995. Because the weights are constant from one year to another, indices can be constructed to give a consistent time series. On the other hand, the weights do get significantly out of date eventually and have to be revised. The above index was previously based on 1990 weights. A base-weighted index formula was first published in 1864 by Etienne Laspeyres (1834–1913). ➤➤ index-number problem; Paasche index.

latent variables A variable in ➤ regression analysis that is, in principle, unmeasurable. Examples of variables that might be wanted for inclusion in a ➤ model would be intelligence or permanent income (➤ permanent-income hypothesis). These cannot be measured directly, and have to be replaced by proxy variables.

Latin American Free Trade Association (LAFTA) ➤ Latin American Integration Association.

Latin American Integration Association (LAIA) The Latin American Free Trade Association (LAFTA), which had been set up in 1960, was replaced by the LAIA through a new treaty agreed in 1980. Under this treaty, the member countries Argentina, Bolivia, Brazil, Chile, Colombia, Ecuador, Mexico, Paraguay, Peru, Uruguay and Venezuela agreed to continue the encouragement of economic integration through regional tariffs and other measures. The intention of the LAIA is to reduce tariffs between member countries but on a pragmatic industry-by-industry approach, rather than by across-the-board tariff reductions following a fixed timetable, as attempted by LAFTA. Cuba joined the Association in 1999. ➤➤ Mercosur.

Lausanne School The Chair of Economics in the Faculty of Law at Lausanne University was founded in 1870 with ➤ Walras as the first incumbent. He retired in 1892 and was succeeded by ➤ Pareto. The school was noted for the development of a ➤ general equilibrium theory.

Law, John (1671–1729) A Scottish financier who put his monetary theories into practice in France through such institutions as the Banque Royale and the Compagnie des Indes. His most significant publication appeared in 1705 under the title *Money and Trade Considered, with a Proposal for Supplying the Nation with Money.* He was in favour of the replacement of specie coin by paper money (➤ banknote). Not only would this save expensive precious metals, but it would enable the state to manage the ➤ currency more effectively by making it independent of the ➤ market for precious metals. Moreover, it would facilitate increasing the quantity of money in circulation and therefore the stimulation of economic activity. ➤➤ Hume, D.; quantity theory of money.

law of comparative advantage ➤ Ricardo, D.

'law of demand' ➤ demand curve.

law of diminishing returns ➤ diminishing returns, law of.

law of large numbers ➤ probability.

law of one price The law, articulated by ➤ Jevons, stating that 'In the same open market, at any moment, there cannot be two prices for the same kind of article.' The reason is that, if they did exist, ➤ arbitrage should occur until the prices converge. ➤➤ price system.

LDC Less developed country. ➤ developing country.

'leads and lags' The differences in timing in the settlement of ➤ debts in ➤ international trade. These differences could cause a deficit or surplus for a short period in the ➤ balance of payments, even though the underlying trade was in balance. The effect may be particularly acute when there is an expectation of a change in the ➤ exchange rate. Importing countries will delay payment to their supplying country if it is expected that the latter's rate of exchange will fall. ➤➤ devaluation; J-curve.

lease An agreement between the owner of property (lessor) to grant use of it to another party (lessee) for a specified period at a specified ➤ rent, payable annually, quarterly or monthly. The rental may be subject to review, e.g. every five years. It is possible to lease cars, office equipment, machinery, etc., as well as buildings or land, and a recent development has been the rapid growth of leasing arrangements for business requirements. In most cases, these include servicing and maintenance. In some cases, the title of the property passes to the lessee at the end of the lease for a nominal charge. In effect, this is a form of hire purchase without a down payment, and is subject to differences in tax treatment that may be advantageous.

leaseback An agreement in which the owner of property sells that property to a person or institution and then leases it back again for an agreed period and rental. Leaseback is often used by companies that want to free for other uses the ➤ capital tied up in buildings.

least developed countries In 1971, the General Assembly of the ➤ United Nations Conference on Trade and Development drew up a list of twenty-five countries that it defined as least developed, each having a ➤ Gross Domestic Product below a minimum. By 2009, fifty countries were classified as 'least developed' and the criteria for inclusion in the group include such measures as literacy rates, life expectancy, population and the dominance of agriculture in Gross Domestic Product. ➤ convergence; developing country; poverty.

least-squares regression A statistical technique for estimating the relationship between a ➤ dependent variable and ➤ independent variables. The method derives estimates for the ➤ parameters and constants in the equation postulated as representing the nature of the relationship between the variables (➤ model). For example, a ➤ demand function may take the form $D = a + bP$, in which D is the quantity demanded of a good and P its price. The observed values of D and P (i.e. how much was actually demanded at each of a number of price levels) may be plotted on a graph, with D on the x-axis (horizontal) and P on the y-axis (perpendicular) (called a 'scatter' diagram). We would expect in this case that the points on the graph would be grouped so as generally to slope downwards from left to right (the lower the price, the higher the demand). The least-squares regression finds that line so that the difference between the actual observations and those traced by the line along its length is at a minimum. The slope and position of the line yields the estimates for b and a, respectively. ➤➤ beta; dummy variable; heteroscedasticity; latent variables.

legacy costs The ➤ social costs inherited from past economic activity. An ➤ enterprise might incur such costs through legislation requiring it to clean up the site of an abandoned chemical plant or through damages awarded to users of a product that has had unintended consequences. These are examples applying mainly to large firms, but any firm may, if it goes into voluntary ➤ liquidation, be left with large costs for compensating redundant employees. Some legacy costs will have to be met by the public sector, but in the case of an otherwise still viable enterprise they may be an obstacle to the acquisition of the firm and the redeployment of its ➤ assets. ➤ sunk costs.

legal tender That which must be accepted in legal settlement of a money ➤ debt. In the UK only, ➤ Bank of England notes and £1 and £2 coins are legal tender up to any amount. Cheques and postal orders are not legal tender. In the USA, all coins and currency issued by the government under federal law are legal tender and therefore cannot be refused in settlement of a debt. However, unless state law determines otherwise, organizations are free to make conditions about the currency acceptable in the course of ordinary affairs, for example a bus company could refuse to accept a $100 bill in payment of a 50-cent fare. ➤ fiat money.

Leibenstein, Harvey (1922–1994) ➤ X-efficiency.

lemon problem ➤ adverse selection.

lender of last resort The essential function of a ➤ central bank in its willingness to lend to the ➤ banking system at all times (➤ bank rate). Because it can do so on its own terms, it is this function that permits the bank (a) to influence the level of ➤ rates of interest and the ➤ money supply, and (b) to provide a basis of confidence for the banking system, since it stands ready to lend to solvent but illiquid banks. In the UK, the ➤ Bank of England traditionally acted as a lender of last resort only to the ➤ discount houses, and would not lend to the ➤ commercial banks, as part of its exercise of monetary policy (the first function). Since March 1997, the bank uses ➤ gilt repos as a means of influencing the interest rate structure and deals directly with counterparties which include commercial banks. One of the motives for these changes was to prepare the way for ➤ European Economic and Monetary Union and it has brought the UK into line with other countries in which the central bank deals directly with the commercial banks.

Leontief, Wassily W. (1906–99) Born in St Petersburg, Leontief obtained a post at the University of Kiel in Germany in 1927. In 1931, he moved to Harvard and was appointed Professor of Economics there in 1946. In 1973, he was awarded the ➤ Nobel Prize for Economics. His publications include *Studies in the Structure of the American Economy* (1953), *Input–Output Economics: Collected Essays* (1966) and *The Future of the World Economy* (1977). The interdependence of the various sectors of a country's economy has long been appreciated by economists. The theme can be traced from ➤ Cantillon and ➤ Quesnay and the ➤ *Tableau économique* through

➤ Marx and ➤ Walras. The sheer complexity of the interactions and interrelation-ships between the different sectors of a modern economy was a Gordian knot that had to be cut before the theoretical structure could be translated into a practical reflection of an actual economy and serve as the basis for policy recommendations. Leontief's achievement was to see the solution of this problem in ➤ matrix algebra, and modern computers have made ➤ input–output analysis a practical proposition. His book *The Structure of the American Economy, 1919–1929* was first published in 1941, and a second edition, *1919–1939*, appeared in 1951. He attempted, with the limited statistical facts available to him, to establish in these studies a *tableau économique* (➤ Physiocrats) of the USA. The economy was described as an integrated system of flows or transfers from each activity of production, ➤ consumption or ➤ distribution to each other activity. Each sector absorbs the outputs from other sectors and itself produces ➤ commodities or ➤ services that are in turn used up by other sectors, either for further processing or for final consumption. All these flows or transfers were set out in a rectangular table – an input–output matrix. The way in which the outputs of any industry spread out through the rest of the economy could be seen from the elements making up the rows. Similarly, the origins of its ➤ inputs could be seen directly from the elements of the appropriate column. Given such a structure, the implications of a specific change in one part of the economy could be traced through to all the elements in the system. ➤➤ social accounting.

Lerner, Abba Ptachya (1903–82) ➤ Marshall–Lerner criterion.

less developed countries (LDCs) ➤ developing country.

letter of credit A non-negotiable order from a bank to a bank abroad, authorizing payment to a person named in the letter of a particular sum of ➤ money or up to a limit of a certain sum. Letters of ➤ credit are often required by exporters who wish to have proof that they will be paid before they ship goods, or who wish to minim-ize delay in payment for the goods. Letters of credit, unlike ➤ bills of exchange, are not negotiable, but being cashable at a known bank are immediately acceptable to the seller in the exporting country. A confirmed letter of credit is one that has been recognized by the paying bank. Letters of credit may be irredeemable or revocable, depending on whether or not they can be cancelled at any time.

leverage ➤ gearing.

Lewis, Sir William Arthur (1915–91) Professor Lewis was born in St Lucia in the Caribbean. He received his university education at the London School of Econom-ics and the University of Manchester. He was appointed to a Chair of Economics at Manchester University in 1948 where he remained until he took up the post of Principal of the University College of the West Indies in 1959. He was subsequently appointed Professor of Public and International Affairs at Princeton University in 1963. Professor Lewis was awarded (jointly with ➤ Schultz) the ➤ Nobel Prize for Economics in 1979. His published works include *Overhead Costs* (1949), *Economic Survey, 1919–1939* (1949), *The Principles of Economic Planning* (1950), *The Theory of Economic Growth* (1955), *Development Planning* (1966), *Some Aspects of Economic Development* (1969), *Tropical Development, 1880–1913* (1971), *The Evolution of the International Economic Order* (1977) and *Growth and Fluctuations, 1870–1913* (1978).

Professor Lewis made fundamental contributions to the theory and application of economics in the context of the problems of the growth of ➤ developing countries. Developing countries were characterized by dual economies of urban growth centres within large areas of traditional agriculture in which the latter was the source of a supply of labour that kept urban wages low. Wages remained low until urban industrialization had absorbed the surplus labour from the agricultural sector.

liabilities Sums of ➤ money for which account has to be made. The liabilities of a company include its ➤ bank loans and overdrafts, short-term ➤ debts for goods and ➤ services received (*current liabilities*) and its ➤ loan capital and the ➤ capital subscribed by shareholders. ➤➤ balance sheet.

life-cycle hypothesis A theory that suggests that consumers during their lifetime will save when their income is high and spend more than they earn when their income is low. In this way, they smooth their consumption flow, despite the fact that income varies over a lifetime. The theory, attributable to ➤ Modigliani, complements the ➤ permanent-income hypothesis. ➤➤ consumption function; product life-cycle.

life expectancy ➤ death rate; Human Development Index.

LIFFE ➤ London International Financial Futures Exchange.

limited liability The restriction of an owner's loss in a business to the amount of ➤ capital that he has invested in it. If a limited public company is put into ➤ liquidation because it is unable to pay its ➤ debts, for example, the individual shareholders are liable only for the nominal ➤ value of the ➤ shares they hold (unless they have provided personal guarantees to the bank or other ➤ creditors). Before the principle of limited liability was recognized, investors could be made liable for the whole of their personal possessions in the event of ➤ insolvency. The extension of limited liability to private as well as public companies that wished to register for it in the second half of the nineteenth century greatly increased the flow of capital, and today the limited liability company is the predominant form of business organization. There are also limited liability ➤ partnerships. ➤➤ company law.

linear expenditure system ➤ Stone, Sir J.R.

linear programming A mathematical technique for the solution of problems in which a maximum or minimum of a function is to be determined, subject to a set of constraints. Examples of such problems are:

1 Stocks of a commodity are located at a number of ports and need to be shipped to meet a demand for specific quantities at a number of other ports. The cost per tonne for shipping differs between the various ports of loading and discharge. The problem is to find the minimum cost of shipment, subject to the constraints that no more than the stock available can be loaded at a port and the total amount discharged at a port should equal the demand at that port.

2 A firm able to produce a range of commodities, each of which would require a different mix of inputs (➤ factors of production). Given the selling prices of the commodities and the costs per unit of the various inputs, the firm chooses the mix of output which maximizes profits, subject to the technical constraints of its ➤ production function and restrictions on the availability of the different inputs.

As its name implies, the technique is applicable only to problems in which all the relationships are linear (➤ linear relationship). In problems of resource allocation of the firm and the economy as a whole (➤ input–output analysis), linear programming is also synonymous with *activity analysis*.

linear relationship A mathematical ➤ function that traces a straight line on a graph. The ➤ independent variables, of which there may be one or more, are additive. The simplest example is $y = ax + b$, in which x is the independent variable, a and b are constants. These functions are such that any given absolute increase in an independent variable (e.g. x), will give an absolute increase in the ➤ dependent variable (e.g. y), which will always be the same whatever the size of x on which it is based. Many non-linear relationships can be transformed into linear ones by converting the values of the variables into logarithmic form.

liquid In economics, the description of an ➤ asset which can easily be converted into ➤ money. In practice, it applies to ➤ cash or anything that can be quickly converted into cash at little loss. Assets are said to possess degrees of ➤ liquidity that are their nearness to cash. Highly liquid assets other than cash and bank deposits are Post Office ➤ savings, ➤ Treasury bills, ➤ money at call and short notice. ➤➤ liquidity preference.

liquidation The termination, dissolution or winding-up of a limited company (➤ limited liability). Liquidation of a company may be initiated by the shareholders, the directors (voluntary liquidation) or by its creditors, or by a court order if the company is insolvent (➤ insolvency). Where initiated by the creditors, a liquidator is appointed to realize the company's ➤ assets and to pay the creditors. In case of insolvency, these functions are performed, initially at least, by the Official Receiver. If the company is solvent, the ordinary shareholders will receive any surplus after the company's liabilities have been met. ➤➤ bankruptcy.

liquidity 1 The degree to which an ➤ asset can be quickly and cheaply turned into ➤ money that, by definition, is completely liquid. A ➤ current account bank deposit is a liquid asset because it can be withdrawn immediately at little cost; an office building, by contrast, will take a considerable time to dispose of and estate agent's fees and other costs will be incurred. A company or individual is said to be liquid if a high proportion of its or his/her assets are held in the form of cash or readily marketable securities.

➤ **2** International liquidity consists of the total of ➤ gold and foreign exchange reserves and ➤ special drawing rights of all countries.

liquidity preference The desire to hold ➤ money rather than other forms of ➤ wealth, e.g. ➤ stocks and ➤ bonds. It can be thought of as stemming from the ➤ transactions motive, ➤ speculative motive and ➤ precautionary motive for holding money, and so will be influenced by the levels of ➤ income and wealth, ➤ rates of interest, ➤ expectations and the institutional features of the economy. A high degree of liquidity preference implies that a given supply of money flows relatively slowly through the economy, resulting in a low ➤ velocity of circulation. ➤➤ Keynes, J.M.

liquidity ratio 1 The proportion of the total ➤ assets of a bank which are held in the form of ➤ cash and ➤ liquid assets. These assets consist, in general, of money lent out to the ➤ money market at call and short notice, short-term ➤ bonds issued by the government and other borrowers and balances at the ➤ Bank of England. Many central banks have mandatory liquidity ratios, including the ➤ Bank of China and the ➤ Federal Reserve System. In the UK this is no longer so although all larger banks (over £500 million in eligible assets) are required to deposit 0.11 per cent of eligible liabilities with the Bank of England. However, this *cash ratio deposit* (CRD) earns no interest and is effectively a tax to provide income for the bank – it has no significance for credit control or ➤ monetary policy (➤➤ capital adequacy).

2 The ratio of liquid assets to the current ➤ liabilities of a business. Also called the ➤ cash ratio, it is a very crude test of solvency.

liquidity trap A situation in which the ➤ rate of interest is so low that no one wants to hold interest-bearing assets (i.e. ➤ bonds) and people only want to hold cash. The interest rate can fall far enough for everybody to expect it to rise. Bond prices fall when interest rates rise and, because no one wants to hold an asset whose price will fall, everyone will hold cash rather than bonds. In this situation, the interest rate can fall no further – ➤ liquidity preference is absolute. If the government expands the money supply, instead of the usual fall in interest rates occurring, there is no effect at all. There is no need for the interest rate to drop to entice people to hold the extra cash available. Although best described in terms of the simplifying assumptions of the ➤ IS–LM model, the liquidity trap can also be applied to a world in which wealth is stored in forms other than merely cash or bonds. It was first described by ➤ Keynes as an example of a case where, at least theoretically, changes in the money supply did not affect ➤ aggregate demand. ➤➤ transmission mechanism.

listed company A company, the shares of which are listed on the main market of the ➤ stock exchange.

listed security A ➤ security listed and tradable on the ➤ stock exchange. ➤➤ quotation.

loan The borrowing of a sum of ➤ money by one person, company, government or other organization from another. Loans may be secured or unsecured (➤ securities), ➤ interest-bearing or interest-free, long-term or short-term, redeemable or irredeemable. Loans may be made by individuals and companies, banks, ➤ insurance and ➤ hire-purchase companies, ➤ building societies and other ➤ financial intermediaries, pawnbrokers, or by the issue of securities. ➤➤ bank loan; finance; term loans.

loanable funds Money available for lending in financial markets. It consists of current ➤ saving, ➤ dishoarding and any increase in the ➤ money supply, e.g. credit creation by the banks. The *loanable funds theory* holds that the rate of interest (like any other ➤ price) is determined by the supply and demand for loanable funds in the capital market. This theory has its origins in classical theory (➤ interest, classical theory of) but was developed by ➤ Wicksell.

loan capital Fixed-interest borrowed funds. Alternative term for ➤ debentures.

loan guarantee scheme ➤ credit guarantee.

loan stock Synonym for ➤ bond. ➤ stock.

local taxation ➤ Taxation levied by (or for) local rather than central government. The design of local tax systems is not straightforward. ➤ Income tax is not easy to administer, at least in small jurisdictions where people may work and live in different jurisdictions. In any event, governments have been reluctant to let local authorities determine a variable as important as the basic rate of income tax. Corporate taxes do not work well at all, given the extensive nature of most large companies. ➤ Sales taxes suffer from the fact that varying rates of tax encourage cross-boundary shopping, and distort trade. Property taxes have the advantage that at least property cannot move between jurisdictions.

In the UK, the local tax is levied on occupants of dwellings valued in one of eight bands at rates set by local councils. *Non-domestic rates* are based on estimated rentable value and set by the government on a uniform basis. Local government finance has two major problems. The varying nature of property prices in different authorities means that a central government subsidy to poorer authorities is necessary to equalize the effective tax base (➤ fiscal federalism). At the same time, even in affluent authorities, because government has been reluctant to see council taxes rise to very high levels, a substantial proportion of local authority spending has to be financed nationally. This undermines the relationship and accountability that should exist between voters and their local politicians.

Internationally there are greater differences in the forms of local than of national taxation. In the USA, the states levy a ➤ sales tax which in most cases is the largest single source of revenue, followed by personal and corporate income taxes and property tax. In France, the principal local taxes paid by individuals are the residence tax paid by occupiers and land taxes paid by owners. There is a tax on self-employment, while incorporated businesses pay corporate taxes to central government. In Germany, regional government levies local business profits, assets and property taxes. Everywhere, local authorities also derive revenue from other sources and especially from parking and other motor-related services.

location theory The area of economics concerned with the factors that determine where producers choose to locate and the effects of the location of a piece of land on the use made of it. The starting-point of this area of theory was developed by ➤ Thünen in 1826. Thünen held that farmers near a market would tend to grow things that would be relatively expensive to transport, while those further away from towns would produce lighter items that were cheap to carry. Thus, the location of land would have a significant effect on the ➤ economic rent that could be derived from it.

A second important theory, of industrial location, attributable to Weber, established that firms producing goods less bulky than the raw materials used in their production would settle close to the raw-material source. Firms producing heavier goods would settle near their market. The firm minimizes the weight it has to transport and, thus, its transport costs. These two theories primarily treated transport costs as the main factor in influencing location. However, many other factors have been identified as having an important role:

(1) Being able to capture monopoly power in the local market.

(2) The possibility of gaining external ➤ economies of scale, by settling in an area where firms requiring similar inputs have settled.

(3) The influence of non-profit-maximizing behaviour – notably the ➤ behavioural theory of the firm – suggests that location could be dependent on where a firm's management considers it pleasant to live.

(4) The possibility of attracting public assistance in the form of grants or subsidies paid out as part of a country's regional policy.

(5) The influence of ➤ local taxation and provision of ➤ public goods. An area that has good roads, efficient refuse collection or low business taxation will be more attractive than a high-tax or low-service area. Firms will choose the combination of service provision and taxation that most suits their needs. Those producing a lot of refuse will perhaps value refuse-collection services more highly than low taxes, while the reverse might be true for a firm requiring no refuse collection at all.

(6) The location and cost of labour. Because workers are geographically quite immobile – especially across international borders on account of, for example, immigration controls – wages are not equal across countries. This makes it attractive for some labour-intensive firms to settle in areas in which wages are low. This has particularly manifested itself in the high investment that has occurred in South-East Asia. ➤ labour, mobility of.

(7) Other international influences. Political and social factors have a particularly strong effect on the expectations multinational firms have as to the profits they can make. Local tariff regimes can also induce firms to produce domestically where otherwise they would be unable to sell in the local market at all. ➤ globalization; multinational corporation.

logistic curve A curve traced on a graph by the function, $y = a/(1 + be^{-cx})$, in which a, b and c are constants (➤ parameters), $x =$ ➤ independent variable, $e =$ approximately 2.71828, which is a constant with many applications in the analysis of growth (e can be defined as follows: if \$1 were invested at 100 per cent per annum, its worth at the end of the year would get closer and closer to \$$e$, the more frequently interest was added and compounded (➤ compound interest) for shorter and shorter periods during the year). The logistic function takes the following values: if $x = 0$, $y = a/(1 + b)$; if $x \to +\infty$, $y \to a$; and if $x \to -\infty$, $y \to 0$; as can be seen by substituting these values in the above equation.

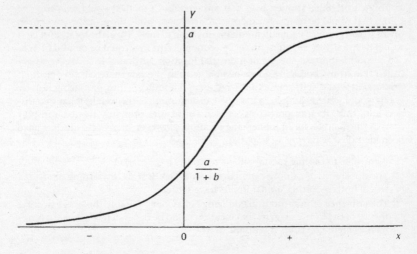

The curve is illustrated opposite. It is often used to describe the sales growth of a new product – an initial learning period when sales are low, rising rapidly as sales spread through the population and then slowing down as new demand for the product reaches ➤ saturation point.

log-normal distribution A ➤ frequency distribution that is skewed towards the higher values of the ➤ independent variable, as in an ➤ income distribution, which is transformed into a ➤ normal distribution when the independent variable is converted into logarithms.

London inter-bank offered rate (LIBOR) ➤ interbank market.

London International Financial Futures Exchange (LIFFE) A ➤ market to trade in financial ➤ futures and ➤ options, set up on 30 September 1982. Futures traded include an equity index contract based on the FT/SE 100 Share Index. In 2001, LIFFE introduced futures in single stocks and made an arrangement to merge (➤ merger) with Euronext, which in turn in 2006 merged with the ➤ New York Stock Exchange.

London Stock Exchange ➤ stock exchange.

long-dated securities ➤ dated securities.

long-end of the market That part of the market for ➤ bonds that is concerned with dealings in long-term issues.

Longfield, Samuel Mountifort (1802–84) An Irish lawyer who became the first incumbent of the Chair of Political Economy at Trinity College, Dublin. His most important work in economics was *Lectures on Political Economy*, which was published in 1834. He argued convincingly against the labour theory of value (➤ value, theories of) and developed a marginal revenue productivity theory (➤ marginal revenue product) of ➤ labour and ➤ capital. Some of his ideas on capital and ➤ interest foreshadowed the work of the ➤ Austrian School.

long rate The ➤ rate of interest on long-term ➤ bonds. Because purchasers of bonds take a risk that ➤ inflation may erode the value of their investment over a long time period, the market rate that is observed is often held to be a good indicator of inflationary expectations. Long rates tend to drop when the authorities gain ➤ credibility, and appear to be more committed to low inflation.

long run A period of time in which all variables are able to settle at their equilibrium or final disequilibrium levels and all economic processes have time to work in full. Its most common application is in the theory of the firm (➤ firm, theory of the), in which it is the period of time in which the quantities of all ➤ factors of production employed are allowed to vary and all entry and exit that can occur into or from an industry have occurred. The duration of the 'long term' will clearly vary with the context in which the term is applied, depending on the speed with which the variables spoken of change. ➤➤ short run.

long-term capital ➤ business finance.

long-term unemployment Joblessness for a period in excess of six months, a year or two years. There has been increasing concern that long-term unemployment is a different problem from that of unemployment generally. It has a self-reinforcing character – the longer a period of unemployment, the harder it is to find work. This may be explained by demotivation on the part of the unemployed, or by lack of trust on the part of potential employers. The existence of long-term unemployment may be associated with the protection afforded by the benefit system, particularly the indefinite persistence of unconditional benefits. Policymakers have started to give increasing attention to ➤ active labour-market policies. These concentrate on ensuring the unemployed are trained and motivated and may involve a temporary employment subsidy. Long-term unemployment is usually a form of ➤ structural unemployment. ➤➤ hysteresis; insider–outsider theory.

Lorenz curve A graphical representation, constructed by the American economist Max O. Lorenz (1880–1962), showing the degree of inequality of a ➤ frequency distribution in which the cumulative percentages of a population (e.g. taxpayers, firms) are plotted against the cumulative percentage of the variable under study, e.g. incomes, employment.

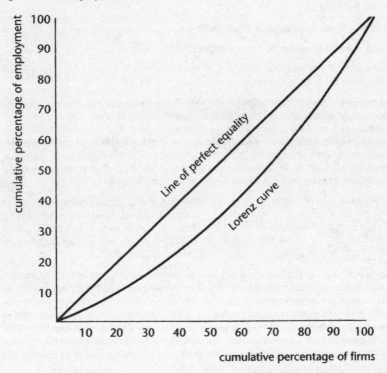

A straight line rising at an angle of 45° from the start on the graph will indicate perfect equality, e.g. if 10 per cent of firms employ 10 per cent of the total labour force, 20 per cent of firms employ 20 per cent of the total labour force and so on

(➤ linear relationship). However, if there are a large number of small firms that employ few people and a small number of large firms employing many people, the distribution will be unequal. When such a distribution is plotted, a curve will be traced below the 45° line (see diagram) and the degree of curvature will be greater the greater the inequality (➤➤ Atkinson index; Gini coefficient).

Lucas, Robert E. (b. 1937) An economist from the University of Chicago, Lucas probably had more influence than anyone else in the 1970s on research in ➤ macroeconomics. He was the man who took ➤ rational expectations, first devised as an assumption by John Muth in 1961, and investigated their rich implications for economic policy. He also did more to promote the rational expectations hypothesis than anyone else. His name was put to the ➤ Lucas critique, the argument that relationships that appeared to characterize the fundamental features of an economy could not be relied upon to last, were policy to change. In particular, the Phillips curve (➤ Phillips, A.W.H.) would break down as soon as one attempted to exploit that apparent trade-off between inflation and unemployment. It is now virtually taken for granted that in assessing a change in policy, the authorities must take into account any change in expectations and behaviour consequent upon the policy change. For these contributions, Lucas won the ➤ Nobel Prize for Economics in 1995. ➤ new classical economics; policy ineffectiveness theorem.

Lucas critique An argument put forward by ➤ Lucas in the 1970s that economists were mistakenly assuming that relationships they observed to hold would continue to hold even when conditions changed. The critique was an important component of the move towards accepting ➤ rational expectations as a significant development in ➤ macroeconomics. In essence, Lucas argued that, although economic agents may act in a certain way, you should not assume that they would continue to act in that way if you changed economic policy. For example, if consumers believed that inflation was to be 5 per cent next year, they might only demand 5 per cent wage increases. But suppose that a government, failing to understand the Lucas critique, expands the money supply, causing inflation to be 10 per cent in the hope that this would cut the ➤ real income of consumers and make it cheaper for firms to employ new staff to make higher-priced goods. This would increase output by effectively exploiting people's expectation that inflation would be 5 per cent and cutting their real wage. Lucas claimed that such policies may work once or twice, but that if a government tried to exploit that, people would come to anticipate the 10 per cent inflation and set their wage demands accordingly. Thus, the expansionist policy would not work at all. Exploiting the trade-off between unemployment and inflation is rather like employers getting two minutes' of extra work out of employees by setting the clocks two minutes slow and fooling them into staying a little longer than they wanted to stay. Observing that the workers do work more when the clocks are slow would not imply at all that, by setting the clocks ten minutes or an hour slow, you would get ten minutes or an hour of additional work from them. ➤➤ Goodhart's law; new classical economics.

lump-of-labour fallacy Advocates of a statutory maximum of hours that a worker can work in order to reduce ➤ unemployment imply the belief that there is a limited, fixed amount of work available to spread among the ➤ labour force. Similar is the argument against the introduction of innovative production methods in that these displace labour and therefore increase unemployment. It is a fallacy because there is always work to be done, and increases in ➤ productivity through innovation increase opportunities for workers through the generation of higher incomes.

lump-sum tax A tax that must be paid irrespective of the behaviour of an economic agent, e.g. a tax of $100 on blue-eyed people that bore no relation to their income or spending. While usually considered impractical on political grounds, economists see lump-sum taxes as efficient in that they do not have any tendency to affect the incentives of individuals to work, save, purchase goods or services, etc. These are all things that other taxes will necessarily distort. ➤➤ fiscal neutrality; local taxation; marginal tax rate.

M

Maastricht Treaty Treaty signed in Maastricht, the Netherlands, in February 1992, more formally entitled Treaty on European Union. The Maastricht Treaty was simply a large package of amendments to the Treaty of Rome, with the effect of creating the ➤ European Union (EU) out of the European Economic Community. It plotted the path towards ➤ European Economic and Monetary Union, enshrined for the first time the principle of ➤ subsidiarity into the EU's affairs and contained the Social Charter. It also built the foundations of intergovernmental cooperation on foreign policy, and on certain domestic policy matters.

Macmillan gap ➤ risk capital.

macroeconomics The study of whole economic systems aggregating over the functioning of individual economic units. It is primarily concerned with ➤ variables that follow systematic and predictable paths of behaviour and can be analysed independently of the decisions of the many agents who determine their level. More specifically, it is a study of national economies and the determination of ➤ national income. It focuses on sectors of the economy – not those that function as separate units like the 'car-production sector', but those that run across the entire economy – the industrial, personal, financial, government and overseas sectors. In classical macroeconomics (➤➤ classical economics) there is a presumption of the efficiency and effectiveness of free markets, and all macroeconomic variables are seen as the sum of the variables as they applied to individual firms or consumers. Macroeconomic mechanisms are largely embedded in the theory of ➤ microeconomics. Since ➤ Keynes, however, economists have allowed for ➤ disequilibrium in macroeconomic variables as such, and therefore collective outcomes distinct from those implied by individual behaviour (➤➤ paradox of thrift).

The main topics covered by macroeconomics are: (a) the determination of national income (➤➤ income determination, theory of), prices (➤➤ inflation) and ➤ employment; (b) the role of ➤ fiscal and ➤ monetary policy, analysed through different ➤ models, each containing its own assumptions and emphasis; (c) the determination of ➤ consumption and ➤ investment; (d) the ➤ balance of payments; and (e) ➤ economic growth. In recent years, the tendency in academic economics has been for macroeconomic models to be laid on ➤ microeconomic foundations. ➤➤ circular flow of income; economic doctrines; information, economics of.

macro-prudential regulation Regulatory measures to reduce ➤ systemic risk for the financial system as a whole. One such measure might be to make ➤ capital adequacy requirements counter-cyclical, i.e. raising them in boom times and relaxing them in ➤ recession. *Micro-prudential regulation* is concerned with the financial stability of individual financial institutions.

mainstream corporation tax ➤ corporation tax.

Malthus, Thomas Robert (1766–1834) Educated at St John's College, Cambridge, Malthus became a Fellow there after studying mathematics and philosophy. He was ordained and became a country parson. He was subsequently Professor of History and Political Economy at the East India Company's Haileybury College. His *Essay on the Principle of Population as It Affects the Future Improvement of Society* was published in 1798, with a revised edition in 1803. His other works include *An Inquiry into the Nature and Progress of Rent* (1815), *The Poor Law* (1817), *Principles of Political Economy* (1820) and *Definitions in Political Economy* (1827).

Malthus is remembered for his essays on ➤ population. Population had a natural growth rate described by a ➤ geometric progression, whereas the natural resources necessary to support the population grew at a rate similar to an ➤ arithmetic progression. Without restraints, therefore, there would be a continued pressure on living standards, both in terms of room and of output. He advocated moral restraint on the size of families. Malthus also carried on a long argument with ➤ Ricardo against Say's law (➤ Say, J.-B.). Briefly, Say's law stated that there could be no general overproduction or underproduction of ➤ commodities on the ground that whatever was bought by somebody must have been sold by somebody else. (➤ Keynes found some affinity between Malthus' conclusions and his own in his *General Theory of Employment, Interest and Money* (1936).) Malthus, however, was arguing strictly within the basic assumption of the equality of planned ➤ savings and ➤ investment in ➤ classical economics, and was a long way away from Keynes' revolutionary assumption that they are made equal only by movements in total ➤ income. Saving to Malthus was investment. His argument for under-consumption was simply that an increase in savings necessarily diminished consumption on the one hand, and on the other increased the output of consumer goods through increased investment. At the same time, because the ➤ labour supply was inelastic (➤ elasticity), wages rose and, therefore, so did costs. ➤ Sismondi, J.C.L.S. de.

Malynes, Gerard de (1586–1641) An English merchant and government official and a leading exponent of ➤ mercantilism. His publications include *A Treatise of the Canker of England's Commonwealth* (1601), *Saint George for England, Allegorically Described* (1601), *England's View in the Unmasking of Two Paradoxes* (1603), *The Maintenance of Free Trade* (1622) and *The Centre of the Circle of Commerce* (1623). He showed how an outflow of precious metals could lead to a fall in prices at home and a rise in prices abroad. This was an important clarification of the economic thought of the time. He suggested that higher import ➤ tariffs should be levied and ➤ exports of ➤ bullion prohibited, because he believed that a country's growth was related to the accumulation of precious metals. He thought that ➤ exchange control should be used to improve the ➤ terms of trade, supporting his policy with the belief that exports were price inelastic (➤ elasticity). ➤➤ quantity theory of money.

managed bond ➤ bond.

managed currency A ➤ currency is said to be managed if the ➤ exchange rate is not determined by ➤ free-market forces, i.e. if government influences the rate by buying and selling its own ➤ money or by other means. Most currencies are managed in some sense today, even when they are allowed to float. ➤➤ exchange control; impossible trinity; International Monetary Fund.

managed trade ➤ protection.

management accountancy Business accounting practice concerned with the provision of information to management for policymaking purposes, as opposed to financial accounting. Management accountancy techniques have developed considerably since the nineteenth century, when firms had few locations and products. Modern multinational enterprises may have hundreds of *profit centres* in which managers have operational discretion and are evaluated on the basis of their financial results. Not only are financial accounts produced for these centres, but also, for example, return on investment (➤ rate of return) used for the purpose of allocating capital between them. These large enterprises may have thousands of *cost centres* that are established where output and related inputs can be measured. In *cost accounting* for these centres, costs are related to outputs for the purposes of pricing, departmental budgeting and the control of production methods, material and labour usage.

Some costs vary with output (e.g. material or labour costs), while others (e.g. overheads) do not. Overheads may be allocated to outputs using the measures of *standard costing* or *absorption costing*, where unit overheads are costed at levels that will cover total overhead costs at budgeted output by means of, for example, percentages of direct labour cost. In *activity-based costing*, more sophisticated methods are used to allocate overheads in a way that reflects cost-drivers. For example, the cost of the after-sales service overhead is allocated to products according to the number of guarantee claims received or the number of sales engineer-related visits in connection with the product in question.

Management accountancy may be concerned simply with the production of management accounts prepared on a more frequent basis (e.g. quarterly) than financial accounts and show gross profits for profit centres, i.e. their contribution to overheads and the overall financial result for the enterprise after overheads. Or management accounts may be very similar to the audited financial results, with adjustments for ➤ depreciation, work in progress, foreign-exchange gains and losses, etc. With modern information technology and full data capture throughout the organization it should be possible to produce management accounts at shorter intervals – indeed, at least one large IT company claims to produce them on a daily basis!

management buy-in ➤ management buy-out.

management buy-out (MBO) The acquisition of all or part of the ➤ equity capital of a company by its directors and senior executives, usually with the assistance of a financial institution (➤ risk capital). Competitive pressures upon large companies in the 1980s led to the disposal of many weak or peripheral subsidiaries in this way. In a *management buy-in*, an outside team of managers acquires a company in the same way. In a *BIMBO*, some existing management is retained. Developing in the early 1970s in the USA, buy-outs were virtually unknown in the UK before 1980 but have become more common since then.

Manchester School 'Manchesterism' was an epithet applied in Germany to those who subscribed to a political-economic philosophy of ➤ *laissez-faire*. It was applied, in particular, to the movement in England from 1820 to 1850 which was inspired by the propaganda of the Anti-Corn Law League. This was headed by Richard Cobden and John Bright, and supported by the economics of ➤ Ricardo. The 'school' believed in ➤ free trade and political and economic freedom with the minimum of government restraint.

Mandeville, Bernard de (1670–1733) Born at Dort in Holland, Mandeville obtained an MD at Leyden and established himself in London as a general practitioner. In 1705, he published a poem called *The Grumbling Hive*, which was reissued in 1714 and 1729 under the title of *The Fable of the Bees or Private Vices, Publick Benefits*. In this pamphlet he showed how, although individuals indulge in unholy vices in their private behaviour, nevertheless in the aggregate they contributed to the public good and therefore could be excused. ➤ Smith was severely critical of the satirical nature of the work (➤ 'invisible hand').

marginal analysis The study of ➤ variables in terms of the effects that would occur if they were changed by a small amount. For example, rather than analyse whether or not it is in the interest of an individual to spend money on food at all, attention can sensibly be focused on whether or not welfare could be enhanced by spending slightly more or less on food. Nothing better demonstrates the concept than the paradox of value: although water is more necessary to man than diamonds, it has a much lower price. This is because man usually has so much of it that extra water is worthless. This is not true of diamonds (➤➤ marginal utility). The marginal value of a variable is equivalent to its rate of change or, mathematically, its first derivative. For example, a firm's sales revenue rises as sales increase and this can be plotted on a graph as total revenue. By taking the gradient of the total revenue curve, ➤ marginal revenue can be derived, depicting how much extra revenue is gained, from an extra sale, at each different level of total sales. If the marginal revenue is plotted on a graph, total revenue can be derived by finding the area under the marginal-revenue curve up to a given level of sales. The marginal value of a variable lies below the average value of that variable if the average is falling. The marginal value lies above it if the average is rising.

The margin is important in economics as it is the impact of small changes in variables rather than their level per se that determines whether rational economic agents change them. It is the average level of utility, costs or revenues that tends to determine whether things are consumed or produced at all, but the marginal utility, costs or revenues that determine how much is consumed or produced once a decision to do so at all has been taken. ➤➤ Gossen, H.H.; Jevons, W.S.; marginal cost; marginal-cost pricing; marginal product; Menger, C.; Thünen, J.H. von; Walras, M.E.L.

marginal cost The increase in the total costs of a firm caused by increasing its output by one extra unit. If all costs are fixed, the marginal cost of the first unit of output will be very high, but all subsequent units can be made for nothing. Economists normally assume firms to be producing at a point at which marginal costs are positive and rising. ➤➤ firm, theory of the.

marginal-cost pricing The setting of the price of an item equal to the cost of producing one extra unit of the item. ➤ Marginal cost represents the ➤ opportunity cost, or the total sacrifice to society from producing an item. The price represents the cost to consumers of buying a unit of it, and they will ensure therefore that they will buy it if and only if they value it at least as much as the money it sells for. If the price is below the marginal cost, consumers will be happy to buy an item even if they perhaps value it less than the goods that could have been made if it had not been produced. If, on the other hand, the price is greater than the marginal cost, some consumers who value the item more than it costs to make will still be deterred from buying it. For an efficient allocation of ➤ resources (➤ economic efficiency), therefore, marginal-cost pricing is considered essential.

There are, however, factors that undermine the case for marginal-cost pricing. Primarily, any company enjoying ➤ economies of scale will have average costs in excess of marginal costs (➤ marginal analysis), and with marginal-cost pricing, average costs will exceed price. A company in such a position will therefore make a loss. Only if production is at a point at which marginal and average costs are equal will marginal-cost pricing be sustainable. Marginal-cost pricing provides a major advantage of ➤ perfect competition over ➤ monopoly or ➤ monopolistic competition, and attempts to impose it on firms outside competitive markets – especially ➤ nationalized industries – have been made, with limited success. ➤➤ Hotelling, H.; peak pricing.

marginal efficiency of capital ➤ internal rate of return.

marginal efficiency of investment ➤ internal rate of return.

marginal product The output created by the employment of one additional unit of a ➤ factor of production. In general, it is believed that the marginal product of a factor rises when the factor is employed in small quantities, but eventually falls as the amount of the factor employed increases. Marginal product is measured in the physical units of the output produced and it is thus sometimes called *marginal physical product*. ➤➤ diminishing returns, law of.

marginal productivity of capital The value of the output that would be created by the employment of one extra unit of capital. As a major part of the cost of capital is the interest that has to be paid to buy the capital, the marginal productivity of capital can be measured by the ➤ internal rate of return, the interest rate at which the marginal productivity has a ➤ present value of zero.

marginal productivity theory of wages The doctrine that the demand for labour is determined by the value of the output created by the employment of an extra worker. In this account of the determination of wages, firms employ workers as long as the revenue generated by the output of the marginal worker exceeds the cost of that worker, i.e. until the worker's ➤ marginal revenue product is equal to the market wage rate. From this account of a firm's behaviour, a curve depicting the demand for labour at different wage levels can be derived, and the wage rate determined by the interaction of this curve with that of the supply of labour at different wage levels. As more workers are employed at a given level of capital stock, the ➤ marginal product of labour will decline and the wages of all workers will fall (➤ diminishing returns, law of). This fall in wages occurs because any new workers entering the labour market cannot profitably be employed at the going wage rate as the value of their output would be less than that of the workers already employed.

If they are keen for work, therefore, they will offer themselves to employers at lower rates of pay than the current employees, and all wages will be bid down. At the new lower wage level, all workers can profitably be employed.

The theory is part of the *neo-classical theory of distribution* (➤ distribution, theory of) that attempted to explain the share of total output accruing to labour, investors and landowners (➤ bargaining theory of wages; efficiency-wage hypothesis; neo-classical economics).

marginal product of labour The output created by the employment of one extra worker with all other ➤ factors of production held constant. It is a measure of the physical increase in output that occurs in a firm or in the economy as a whole when one extra person starts work. It is generally assumed that the marginal product of ➤ labour rises initially, and then diminishes. In a hypothetical factory manned by a single worker, adding helpers would allow at first for specialization and the ➤ division of labour. Eventually, however, all such gains would be realized and the gains from employing additional staff would diminish. ➤➤ diminishing returns, law of.

marginal propensity to consume (MPC) The proportion of a small increase in income that would be spent rather than saved. The most important variable determining expenditure on consumption is income (➤➤ consumption function). The ➤ average propensity to consume is the proportion of total income that is spent, rather than saved. In principle, the MPC should really depend on whether the income is assumed to be permanent or a temporary windfall. ➤➤ Keynes, J.M.; multiplier; ➤ permanent-income hypothesis.

marginal propensity to save (MPS) The proportion of a small increase in income that is saved. It is equal to 1 minus the ➤ marginal propensity to consume. ➤➤ savings ratio.

marginal rate of substitution (MRS) The rate at which a consumer needs to substitute one commodity for another in order to maintain constant total ➤ utility from the commodities taken together. If a consumer values two bags of apples equally to one bag of pears, the marginal rate of substitution between them is two, because if one bag of pears were taken away from the consumer, two bags of apples would have to be provided to compensate. The marginal rate of substitution between commodity A and commodity B usually diminishes as consumption of commodity A increases. If at consumption of twenty oranges and twenty bananas the consumer is indifferent between one of either, at consumption of thirty oranges and ten bananas the consumer is likely to start demanding more than a mere one orange before giving up a scarce banana. Graphically, the MRS is the slope of an ➤ indifference curve and it is in ➤ indifference-curve analysis that the concept is important. Mathematically, it is the ratio of the ➤ marginal utilities of two items. As long as the MRS declines with increased consumption of an item, the indifference curves are convex (➤ convexity) to the origin of an indifference map. ➤➤ rate of technical substitution.

marginal revenue The increase in the total revenue received by a firm from the sale of one extra unit of its output. For a small firm that cannot influence market price (➤➤ perfect competition), the extra revenue gained is equal to the price of the sale. For a firm with a large share of the total market (➤ monopoly), however, putting an extra item on sale drives down the market price slightly, so that the revenue gain equals the cash gained on the new sale *minus* the loss that occurs on all the sales that would otherwise have been made at the previously higher price. ➤➤ market power.

marginal revenue product The revenue gained by a firm when it sells the output generated by the employment of one additional unit of a ➤ factor of production. It is influenced by three factors: (a) the physical output of the extra factor; (b) the sale price of the product made; and (c) the rate at which that price falls when the extra supply of the new factor is put on to the market. To calculate it, ➤ marginal product must be multiplied by ➤ marginal revenue (➤ marginal productivity theory of wages; marginal value product).

marginal social product The effect on ➤ social welfare of employing one additional unit of a ➤ factor of production. When new workers are taken on, for example, the physical output they produce has a private value to their employer, measured as the ➤ marginal value product, or the price at which the output is sold. However, to measure the value of their output to society, two other factors must be taken into account: (a) ➤ consumer surplus: the amount by which consumers value something in excess of what they pay for it, and (b) any ➤ externalities that may be present: a benefit (or cost) that accrues to other than the purchaser of the item.

marginal tax rate The rate of tax paid on extra units of income. An individual may pay no tax on the first $1000 of income, and 50 per cent tax on all dollars earned thereafter. Those individuals earning more than $1000 will thus face a marginal tax rate of 50 per cent even though their overall tax rate will be less than 50 per cent. Someone earning $1001, for example, will only pay 50 cents of tax – a tiny proportion of his total income. The marginal tax rates facing economic agents are often considered important in determining how far taxation impinges on incentives to work, save or spend money. They are of only limited importance in determining whether a tax is progressive or not (➤ progressive tax). The fact that poor people may lose 80 per cent of any marginal earnings (➤➤ poverty trap) and the rich only 60 per cent is irrelevant in assessing whether the tax system is borne more heavily by either group – an assessment that depends not on the tax paid on incremental pounds of earnings but on tax paid on all actual earnings. ➤➤ lump-sum taxes; taxation.

marginal utility The extra satisfaction gained by a consumer from a small increment in the consumption of a commodity. More formally, it is the partial derivative of the ➤ utility function with respect to the quantity of some commodity that is consumed. It is a concept of central importance to demand theory (➤ demand, theory of), one approach to which holds that marginal utility diminishes as consumption of an item increases (➤ diminishing marginal utility). Rational consumers will equalize the marginal utility gained from a unit of spending on all the different things they consume, because not to do so would imply that costless extra utility could be derived by switching spending from items yielding low marginal utility to those for which it is higher. Such a theory can explain why a price rise causes consumers to cut demand of an item. As consumers, however, do not possess an objective scale of utility measurement (➤ ordinal utility), in more modern theory (➤ indifference-curve analysis) no meaning is attached to the numerical magnitude of the marginal utilities themselves, but only to their ratios and signs.

marginal utility, diminishing ➤ diminishing marginal utility.

marginal utility of money The pleasure or satisfaction gained by a consumer from an extra unit of money. The rational consumer should ensure that the marginal ➤ utility of money with respect to the different things consumed is the same: if someone would get more utility from spending an extra pound on clothes than they would get from spending it on books, by transferring some of their budget from books to clothes they would costlessly increase their utility. They should go on transferring until they have so many clothes that they no longer value them, pound for pound, more than books. The marginal utility of money diminishes the greater the quantity of money available to a consumer. ➤➤ demand, theory of; marginal utility; Marshall, A.; ordinal utility.

marginal value product The market value of the output generated by the employment of one additional unit of a ➤ factor of production. It is equal to the ➤ marginal product of a factor multiplied by the unit selling price of the extra output produced. It is thus comparable to the ➤ marginal revenue product, which is marginal product multiplied by ➤ marginal revenue; in ➤ perfect competition, where price is equal to marginal revenue, the two are identical.

market A collection of homogeneous transactions. A market is created whenever potential sellers of a good or service are brought into contact with potential buyers and a means of exchange is available. The medium of exchange may be ➤ money or ➤ barter. Exchange agreements are reached through the operation of the laws of ➤ supply and ➤ demand. In traditional economics (➤ Marshall, A.) a market is characterized by a single prevailing price for commodities of uniform quality (➤ law of one price). This is not necessarily the same as the business view (the market is a collection of selling opportunities) or the legal view (the market is a trading zone free of artificial restrictions on transactions). ➤➤ price system; single market; two-sided market.

marketable securities ➤ Securities dealt in on the ➤ stock exchange.

market capitalization ➤ capitalization.

market economy ➤ free-market economy.

market failure An outcome deriving from the self-interested behaviour of individuals in the context of ➤ free trade, in which ➤ economic efficiency does not result. Market failures provide a ubiquitous argument for ➤ intervention of some form or other. But they have two main sources:

1   They derive from the fact that many transactions that would need to occur for the sake of economic efficiency simply do not occur. This may be on account of ➤ transaction costs. Or there may be a deficiency of information to the parties involved, or ➤ asymmetric information (with its corresponding problems of ➤ adverse selection, ➤ moral hazard and ➤ agency costs). Or the necessary transaction may be deterred by the fact that the efficient price is not set – on account of ➤ menu costs. Or there may be *strategic behaviour* by the individuals involved, who fail to engage in a trade in the hope that they might extract a

better deal from their adversary if they 'play it tough'. A large number of 'missing trades' are those involving the many resources over which no properly defined property rights exist (such as clean air) and thus over which no trade can occur (➤ Coase theorem).

There are sometimes collective interests that are unable to be served by self-interested, individual behaviour. There are goods or services that have to be consumed collectively, e.g. ➤ public goods like defence. There can be ➤ free-rider problems in which, for example, citizens hope to avoid paying for a service on the ground that someone else will pay (why should I invest in ➤ innovation, if someone else will do it for me?). There can be ➤ prisoner's dilemma-type situations, in which selfish behaviour leads to sub-optimal outcomes (particularly apt in areas in which ➤ utility is a function of relative position, rather than absolute position). There can be industries subject to increasing ➤ returns to scale, in which ➤ monopoly is inevitable, that carries large efficiency costs unless there is a collective effort to regulate.

The two sources of market failure – missing trades and collective interests – can be used to describe certain market failures that are commonly discussed. For example, ➤ externalities are a combination of lack of allocation of property rights, and a lack of trade in the externality itself. Or deviation of price from ➤ marginal cost tends to occur as a result of increasing returns to scale.

market forces The application of self-interested, individual behaviour in a ➤ free-market economy that, through ➤ supply and ➤ demand in different ➤ markets, determines ➤ price and the allocation of resources. (➤ two-sided market)

marketing Broadly, the functions of sales, distribution, ➤ advertising and sales promotion, product planning and market research. That is, those functions in a business that involve direct contact with the consumer and assessment of his/her needs, and the translation of this information into outputs for sale consistent with the firm's objectives.

market maker A ➤ broker-dealer who is prepared to quote buy and sell (bid- and offer) prices, and to buy and sell specified ➤ securities at all times at these prices, and is thus 'making a market' in them. Prior to the ➤ Big Bang, this function was carried out by the jobbers, who were not allowed to deal with the public. Since the Big Bang, all members of the ➤ stock exchange have been able to deal with the public as broker-dealers, some of whom specialize as market makers and others as ➤ stockbrokers. Market makers help to provide ➤ liquidity on the stock market, particularly for less frequently traded ➤ shares.

market power The degree to which a firm exercises influence over the price and output in a particular market. Under ➤ perfect competition, all firms are assumed to have zero market power: they have to take the going price, and cannot hope to alter it on their own. Wherever firms represent a non-negligible portion of the whole market, however, instead of facing a flat ➤ demand curve, they will face a downward-sloping one. This means that, in contrast to the perfect competitor, they do not lose all their sales if they raise their price. It also means, however, that if they wish to increase their sales they have to lower their price. The stronger this relationship, the greater the market power. Where market power exists, the producer has such influence on the market that the amount he/she produces affects the market price, and so price is not equivalent to ➤ marginal revenue. Market power is related to the availability of substitute items. Those items that are highly differentiated from those of competitors will give more market power to the producer than those that are standard. ➤➤ monopoly; two-sided market.

market share Either, (a) the sales of the product or products of a firm as a proportion of the sales of the product or products of the ➤ market as a whole, e.g. sales of Ford motor cars compared with total US motor car sales, or (b) the sales of a particular ➤ commodity compared with the total sales for the class of commodity of which the particular commodity is a member, e.g. sales of mobile telephones compared with sales of all telephones. The presumption is that the firm's product in (a) and the particular commodity in (b) are faced with competitive ➤➤ substitutes in their respective markets. Market shares may also be calculated in terms of the proportion of the product in the total existing stock of that class of products, as opposed to its share of the flow of new sales. ➤➤ saturation point.

market structure The organizational and other characteristics of a ➤ market and in particular those that affect the nature of competition and pricing. Traditionally, the most important features of market structure are the numbers and size distributions of buyers and sellers, which reflect the extent of ➤ monopoly or ➤ monopsony; this, in turn, will be affected by the existence or absence of ➤ barriers to entry. ➤➤ concentration.

Markowitz, Harry M. (b. 1927) Markowitz, from the City University of New York and a joint winner of the 1990 ➤ Nobel Prize for Economics, is credited with the pioneering contribution in the field of financial economics. His insight was to recognize that the risk of an asset that was relevant to assessing its price was its risk relative to the market generally. Other risks more specific to particular assets can be diversified away in a moderately sized ➤ portfolio. With his contribution, the massive problem of designing the optimal portfolio, with maximum expected return for minimum risk, could be seen to be reduced to a two-dimensional problem of looking at the mean and the variance of the portfolio returns. That laid the foundation to the ➤ capital-asset pricing model.

mark-to-market Valuing ➤ assets and ➤ liabilities for accounting purposes at market values as distinct from at ➤ costs, historical. From the 1990s increasingly, ➤ accounting standards have required *fair value accounting*, which means marking-to-market, but it remains controversial. Not only are some assets and liabilities difficult to value but changes in these values can introduce unwelcome volatility in the profitability of companies including banks (➤ profit) at times of market stress as in 2007–9. Some argue that the vulnerability of banks is increased by the use of fair value accounting.

Marshall, Alfred (1842–1924) Educated at Merchant Taylors' School, Marshall graduated in mathematics at St John's College, Cambridge. In 1868, he was appointed to a lectureship in moral science at Cambridge, and it was during this period that he began to study economics. In 1882, he moved to the Chair of Political Economy at Bristol. In 1885, he returned to Cambridge as Professor of Political Economy, a post he retained until his retirement in 1908. His most important works include *The Pure Theory of Foreign Trade* (1879), *Principles of Economics* (1890), *Industry and*

Trade (1919) and *Money, Credit and Commerce* (1923). Marshall was in the long tradition of the English ➤ Classical School, which was founded by ➤ Smith and
➤ Ricardo, and his influence on succeeding generations of economists has been
very great. His achievement was to refine and develop ➤ microeconomic theory to
such a degree that much of what he wrote is still familiar to readers of the elementary economic textbooks today. His theory of ➤ value brought together the diverse
elements of previous theories. On the one hand, he showed how the demand for a
➤ commodity is dependent on a consumer's ➤ utility or welfare. The more of a
commodity a consumer has, the less extra utility or benefit accrues to him/her from
an additional purchase (➤ Gossen, H.H.). Consumers will not go on buying a commodity until this extra benefit falls to zero, but rather will stop buying extra when
finding that the ➤ money to pay for it is worth more to them than the gain from
having an extra unit of the commodity. At this point of ➤ equilibrium, a fall in the
➤ price, therefore, will mean that it becomes worthwhile to exchange his/her
money for more of the commodity. In general, a fall in price will increase the quantity of the commodity demanded, and in theory a schedule could be drawn up
which shows how much would be demanded at each price. The resultant graph
would show a downward-sloping ➤ demand curve. Marshall invented the expression ➤ 'elasticity' to describe his measure of the response of demand to small
changes in price. Similarly, on the supply side, higher prices are necessary to bring
forward increased outputs, and a supply schedule with its corresponding supply
curve can be drawn up. The price of the commodity is determined at the point at
which the two curves intersect. These work like a pair of scissors, neither blade of
which cuts without the presence of the other.

  Marshall recognized that his consumer utility theory was in some ways an over-
simplification. It does not take account of complementary or competitive goods
(➤ complementary goods), and assumes that the ➤ marginal utility of money is
constant. However, he argued that his analysis applied to small price changes and
to goods upon which only an insignificant proportion of income was spent. It was
within this framework that Marshall discussed the idea of ➤ consumer surplus
(➤ Dupuit, A.J.E.J.). For a given quantity of a commodity purchased on a competitive market, the price will be the same for each unit of the commodity sold.
However, for any individual purchaser the price is equal to the utility of the last
unit of the total quantity purchased, the last but one being worth more, the last but
two worth more again, and so on. These utilities can be added up and the extra,
over the price and quantity paid out, is the consumer's surplus. Marshall was aware
of the shortcomings of the 'stationary state' of the typical classical analysis and
emphasized the importance of the production period. He recognized the element
of time as the chief difficulty of almost every economic problem, and considered:
(a) a market period in which supplies are all fixed; (b) a short period in which supplies can be increased, but only to the extent possible by better use of current
capacity; and (c) a long period in which capacity itself can be increased.

  The classical economists had shown how ➤ rent is received by landowners as a
surplus. As land was a ➤ factor of production in fixed supply, it differed from other
factors of production in that its returns were not related to work done. Marshall
extended the concept by pointing out that, in the short run, manmade ➤ capital
was in fixed supply also and, during the period it took to manufacture, earned a
➤ quasi-rent. ➤➤ Cournot, A.A.; Marshall–Lerner criterion; Mill, J.S.

Marshall Aid At the end of the Second World War, only the USA had the necessary productive capacity to make good the losses experienced by other countries. European countries had heavy ➤ balance of payments deficits vis-à-vis the USA. In 1946, in order to alleviate the resultant shortage of dollars, the USA and Canada made substantial ➤ loans, including £1 billion to the UK. It was hoped that these loans would be sufficient to cover requirements over the short period that was expected to be necessary for the world economies to recover. However, in 1948 a general ➤ liquidity crisis was avoided only by further loans made under the European Recovery Programme, through which Europe received $12 billion between 1948 and 1951. This programme was called Marshall Aid or the Marshall Plan, after the then US Secretary of State, General George Marshall. The loans were allocated under the direction of the Organisation for European Economic Co-operation (➤ Organisation for Economic Co-operation and Development) set up for this purpose. Marshall Aid in total amounted to the equivalent of one or two years' ➤ Gross Domestic Product of the recipient European countries. The aid allowed imports, particularly of capital goods, to continue despite payments deficits, though half of it was spent on imports of food and raw materials. It is no longer considered that Marshall Aid was crucial to triggering European economic recovery which had already begun in 1948 when the aid began. However it did promote financial stability and encouraged the development of international economic cooperation.

Marshall–Lerner criterion A rule stating the ➤ elasticity conditions under which a change in a country's ➤ exchange rate would improve its ➤ balance of trade. Lerner set out the appropriate formulae in his book *The Economics of Control* (1944) on the basis of the elasticity concepts developed by ➤ Marshall. In its simplest form, the rule states that the price elasticities of demand for ➤ imports and ➤ exports must sum to greater than unity for an improvement to be effected. The volume of exports increases and the volume of imports decreases in response to a fall in the ➤ price of the former and rise in the price of the latter when a ➤ currency is devalued (assuming, for the sake of the argument, that there are no other factors influencing the ➤ market, e.g. ➤ supply restrictions). There would, therefore, be an improvement in the balance of trade in volume terms, i.e. in terms of the prices ruling prior to ➤ devaluation. However, what is important for the ➤ balance of payments is the impact of devaluation on the value of trade. If the price elasticity of exports plus the price elasticity of imports is less than unity, it means that the increased cost of imports in terms of the domestic currency outweighs the value of the growth in exports. Putting it another way, the improvement in the volume of the balance of trade is not sufficient to offset the fall in the value of the balance of trade occasioned by the devaluation. ➤➤ J-curve; terms of trade.

Marx, Karl (1818–83) Born in Trier in Prussia, Marx studied philosophy and law at the Hegelian Centre at Berlin University, and took a doctorate at Jena. At Berlin, Marx was influenced profoundly by Hegel's ideas of dialectical progress. In any evolutionary development, contrary forces emerged which eventually reached breaking point into a violent resolution. It was only through this process of conflict and resolution that any advance through history could be achieved. For a time, he was editor of the *Rheinische Zeitung*, but the paper was suppressed and in 1843 he went to Paris to edit the *Deutsch-Französische Jahrbücher*. There he began his friendship and close association with Engels, who encouraged in him an interest in political economy and helped to support him and his family throughout his life.

After a brief return to Germany he was banished, and in 1849 he settled in London where he remained until his death in 1883. The *Communist Manifesto*, written jointly by Marx and Engels, was published in 1848. In 1859, the first fruits of his long, painstaking research at the British Museum appeared in his *A Contribution to the Critique of Political Economy*. The first volume of *Das Kapital* appeared in 1867. The remaining volumes, edited by Engels, were published posthumously in 1885 and 1894.

Marx's economics was essentially that of the ➤ Classical School, especially of ➤➤ Ricardo, to whom he owed a great debt. However, he shifted economics away from its preoccupation with agriculture and stationary states. For Marx, ➤ capitalism was a stage in the process of evolution, removed from the primitive agricultural economy and moving towards the inevitable elimination of private property and the class structure. Marx attempted a synoptic view of the development of the whole structure of human society. His economics was only a part, though a fundamental part, of his all-embracing sociological and political theories. Marx postulated that the class structures of societies, their political systems and, indeed, their culture were determined by the way in which societies produced their goods and ➤ services. Moreover, the whole structure was evolutionary. The class structure of a capitalist state was a reflection of the split between owners and non-owners of ➤ capital, which division characterized the manner in which production was carried out, and that already had within it the necessary ingredients of change through the Hegelian dialectic of conflict and resolution.

Marx developed from ➤➤ Smith and Ricardo their labour theory of value (➤ value, theories of) which held the central place in his economic theory. For Ricardo, the amount of labour used in the production of commodities was a rough determinant of relative prices in the long run. For Marx, however, the quantity of labour used up in the manufacture of a product determined value, and this value was fundamental and immutable. He did not satisfactorily explain any connection with relative prices. Labour consumption determined exchange value, which differed from use value. The distinction between the two in the case of labour, regarded in itself as a commodity, was a vital one in Marx's analysis. The capitalist pays wages that are determined by the exchange value of workers. This exchange value is, in turn, determined by the socially necessary labour time required to 'produce' the worker, i.e. labour inputs required to rear, feed, clothe and educate him/her. However, in return, the capitalist receives the labourer's use value. The value of the labourer to the capitalist who uses him/her is greater than the value the capitalist paid in exchange for his/her services. This difference Marx called 'surplus value' (s). Only labour yields surplus value. Other ➤ factors of production (e.g. plant and machinery and raw materials) reproduce only themselves in the productive process. (These ideas have some affinity with the ➤ Physiocrats' *'produit net'*, although in their case it was land that was the only factor which produced a surplus.) The amount of capital required to pay wages Marx called variable (v) (➤ wage-fund theory), and the remainder he called constant (c). ➤ Gross National Product in the Marxian system therefore is given by $c + v + s$. The ratio of constant capital in total capital $c/(c + v)$ he called the organic composition of capital. The 'exploitation rate' was s/v. The rate of profit was $s/(c + v)$.

The desire for further wealth, coupled with competition and technical change, induced capitalists to invest from the surplus (which they expropriated from the workers) and in labour-saving machinery. The organic composition of capital, therefore, rose over time as more was spent on plant and machinery (c) compared with wages (v), with the result that, as only variable capital produced a surplus (and assuming that the exploitation rate remained constant), the rate of profit tended downwards (➤ profit, falling rate of). On the one hand, diminishing profits and stronger competition would lead to ➤ monopoly and the concentration of wealth in a few hands, and on the other there would be an increasing squeeze on the real incomes (➤ real terms) of workers by the capitalists in their attempt to maintain ➤ profits and the emergence of a large 'reserve army of unemployed' arising from mechanization (➤ Ricardo). The class conflict would become increasingly acute until the environment was such that the change inherent in the economic structure would be made manifest by the overthrow of capitalism.

Maskin, Eric S. (b.1950) ➤ mechanism design.

matrix An array of numbers displayed in rows and columns. For instance:

$$\begin{bmatrix} 2 & 1 \\ 7 & 3 \end{bmatrix}$$

The numbers are called the *elements* of the matrix and are generally denoted by a_{ij} in which i refers to the row and j to the column. In the example above, $a_{21} = 7$. The order of a matrix is given by the product of the number of rows times the number of columns. The above matrix is of order 4. An algebra exists for the manipulation of matrices, with rules for addition, subtraction, multiplication and division. Matrix algebra has found many useful applications in ➤ econometrics, and in particular in ➤ input–output analysis and ➤ linear programming. ➤➤ vector.

maturity The date upon which the principal of a redeemable security becomes repayable. ➤ redeemable securities; securities.

maturity transformation ➤ financial intermediaries.

maximin strategy A decision rule in the theory of games (➤ game theory). The rule states that a 'player' with a number of optional strategies to choose from considers first the minimum pay-offs that could be gained from each depending on the reaction of his 'opponent'. The 'player' should then choose that strategy corresponding to the maximum of all the possible minimum pay-offs. In other words, it is a selection of the best possible worst-case scenario. For example, consider a decision-maker faced with two optional strategies, each of which could have two pay-offs. They can be summarized in a ➤ matrix:

$$\begin{matrix} (1) \\ (2) \end{matrix} \begin{bmatrix} 2 & 5 \\ 4 & 3 \end{bmatrix}$$

Strategy (1) could have a pay-off of 2 or 5, strategy (2) a pay-off of 4 or 3. The minimum pay-off of strategy (1) is 2 and that of strategy (2) is 3. The maximum minimum pay-off is therefore 3 and strategy (2) would be chosen under the rule. There is no obvious rationale for choosing a maximin rule. Most of us would focus attention on likely outcomes, not just worst-case outcomes. However, since ➤ Rawls, the rule has almost developed into a political philosophy, with the argument that it justifies increased attention to the poor in society (➤➤ prisoner's dilemma).

maximum-likelihood estimation Estimation of a ➤ parameter by choosing the value which is statistically most likely, given observed data. In ➤ regression analysis, under certain assumptions, it can be shown that ➤ least-squares regression yields the maximum-likelihood estimate of the ➤ beta coefficient in an equation. Once the simple assumptions are removed, maximum-likelihood approaches may diverge from other statistically plausible methods.

MBO ➤ management buy-out.

McFadden, Daniel L. (b. 1937) Economist from the University of California at Berkeley and joint winner of the Nobel Prize for Economics in 2000 for his work in microeconometrics, the analysis of large datasets of households, firms or individuals. In particular, Professor McFadden was instrumental in improving the statistical techniques that economists use to study decisions that are necessarily drawn from limited choices, e.g. whether to buy a car, how many children to have, whether to marry, what occupation to take. These contrast with such decisions as how much food to buy, because the range of options is 'discrete'. You can't have 2.4 children. McFadden edited, with C. Manski, and contributed to *Structural Analysis of Discrete Data With Econometric Applications* (1981), and has written a long list of papers on transport, economic development and production. McFadden has also taken an interest in the empirical implications of ➤ behavioural economics, studying, for example, how people answer survey questions. He has held academic appointments at Pittsburgh, Yale, the Massachusetts Institute of Technology and the California Institute of Technology as well as at Berkeley.

Meade, Sir James Edward (1907–95) Educated at both Oxford and Cambridge Universities, Professor Meade was appointed Professor of Commerce at the London School of Economics in 1947. He was appointed to the Chair of Political Economy at Cambridge University in 1957, a post he held until 1969. Professor Meade was awarded the ➤ Nobel Prize for Economics (jointly with ➤ Ohlin) in 1977. His published works include *The Theory of International Economic Policy* (1951), *A Geometry of International Trade* (1953), *The Theory of Customs Unions* (1955), *A Neo-Classical Theory of Economic Growth* (1961), *Efficiency, Equality and the Ownership of Property* (1964), *Principles of Political Economy* (1965, 1976), *The Inheritance of Inequalities* (1974), *The Intelligent Radical's Guide to Economic Policy* (1975) and *Stagflation* (1981, 1983). Professor Meade made important advances in the theory of international trade, in the study of equilibrium conditions in domestic and external economies. In his work on the welfare effects (➤➤ welfare economics) of tariffs and customs unions (➤ customs union), he introduced the concepts of the theory of the ➤ second best. Professor Meade contributed much to the analysis of income distribution and in the field of ➤ growth theory, being an advocate of a ➤ prices and incomes policy. ➤➤ nominal Gross Domestic Product.

mean ➤ average.

means test ➤ The assessment of wealth or income as, for example, when determining the eligibility of a claimant for welfare benefits. Means-tested benefits contrast with *universal* benefits given to all families irrespective of income, e.g. state pensions. ➤➤ dependency culture; marginal tax rate; poverty trap.

measure of economic welfare (MEW) ➤ environmental accounting.

mechanism design The classical economists (➤➤ classical economics) held that, although individuals were motivated by self-interest, free competition ensured that the community as a whole benefited. Scarce resources would be allocated in accordance with relative prices in such a system more efficiently (➤➤ economic efficiency) than they would be if allocated by government planning (➤➤ planned economy). In practice, however, free markets may fall short of reaching an optimum because it may be in the interests of the participants to conceal information because they think it in their own interests to do so (➤➤ asymmetric information). For instance, in a transaction between a buyer and a seller, the buyer does not know the seller's minimum price and the seller does not know the buyer's maximum price. The price arrived at depends on the differential negotiating skills of the two. In an auction, the highest bid may not be the highest that a seller could have obtained. It could help towards this if the auction was designed so that the highest bidder wins but pays the next lowest bid.

Mechanism design has been developed to find solutions to this type of problem and in 2007 Leonid Hurwicz (1917–2008), Eric S. Maskin (b.1950) and Roger B. Myerson (b.1951) shared the ➤ Nobel Prize for Economics for their work on mechanism design theory. Hurwicz argued that the key was the lack of incentives to induce people to share information and share it honestly. The solution, therefore, was to design a mechanism in which the individuals or institutions in the system were given incentives so they each benefited if they shared information and shared it truthfully in order for the system to attain an optimum allocation of resources through the transparency of information. Myerson's work on this 'revelation principle' was on mathematical modelling for the evaluation of the appropriate rules for mechanism design for optimum efficiency. Maskin's contribution was in 'implementation theory', which is concerned with the compatibility of social objectives of institutions with the incentives of the agents interacting within the system. ➤➤ incentive compatibility; moral hazard.

median ➤ average.

medium of exchange ➤ money.

member banks ➤ commercial banks.

Memorandum of Association The document forming the basis of registration of a company. As required by the Companies Acts, the Memorandum of Association must list the subscribers to the ➤ capital of the company and the number of ➤ shares they have agreed to take, the name and address of the company and, where appropriate, the powers and objects of the company, and that the ➤ liability of its members is limited (➤ company law). The *Articles of Association* set out the rules by which the company will be administered, e.g. the voting of directors, the calling of meetings.

Menger, Carl (1840–1921) Professor of Economics in the Faculty of Law at Vienna

University from 1873 to 1903. His major work, in which he develops his marginal-utility theory, *Grundsätze der Volkswirtschaftslehre* (*Principles of Economics*), was published in 1871. He was one of the three economists in the 1870s who independently put forward the theory of ➤ value based on ➤ marginal utility and whose work had a profound influence on the subsequent evolution of economic thought (➤ Gossen, H.H.; Jevons, W.S.; Walras, M.E.L.). Exchange takes place, he argued, because individuals have different subjective valuations of the same ➤ commodity. Menger saw commodities in terms of their reverse order in the productive process, i.e. bread is prior to flour and flour prior to wheat. The ➤ price of the first-order commodities, which is determined by their exchange for ➤ consumption, is imputed back through to the higher-ordered commodities. The theory of diminishing ➤ utility was the catalyst that eventually unified the theories of production and consumption. Menger himself, however, overemphasized consumption demand in the theory of value, just as the ➤ classical economists had overemphasized production supply (➤ Marshall, A.).

menu costs The practical costs incurred by producers in having to change their prices – costs of relabelling products, or re-entering prices into computer systems. Menu costs are one factor in support of keeping ➤ inflation relatively low. They also explain why prices may move in moderate-sized jumps, rather than in smooth, small increments. The existence of menu costs can explain why money may not be neutral (➤ neutrality of money). ➤➤ new Keynesianism.

mercantilism The growth of ➤ international trade and the establishment of the power of the merchant after the medieval era led to the emergence of a body of thought, between the mid sixteenth and late seventeenth centuries, that was primarily concerned with the relationship between a nation's wealth and its balance of foreign trade. The mercantilists recognized the growing power of the national economy and were in favour of the intervention of the state in economic activity to maximize national ➤ wealth. Partly because the monetary system was very primitive in relation to the growing needs of economic expansion, mercantilist writing was often overburdened with the identification of national wealth with precious metals. Its leading writers, however, did make important progress in developing economic thought and made significant contributions to the analysis of ➤ international trade problems. ➤➤ Malynes, G.; Misselden, E.; Mun, T.; Serra, A.

Mercosur A ➤ customs union of Argentina, Brazil, Paraguay and Uruguay. By the Treaty of Asunción in 1991 and a final protocol signed in 1994, they agreed to establish the Mercosur – or Southern Common Market – between their four countries from January 1995. Tariffs were abolished on intra-Mercosur trade and a Common External Tariff (CET) established. However, economic crises in Argentina and Brazil in 2000–2001 led to the relaxation of the CET. In 2009, Bolivia, Chile, Colombia, Ecuador and Peru were associate members and Bolivia and Venezuela were being considered for full membership. ➤ Andean Pact; free trade area; Latin American Integration Association; Union of South American States.

merger The fusion of two or more separate companies into one. In current usage, merger is a special case of combination, where both the merging companies wish to join together and do so on roughly equal terms, as distinct from a ➤ takeover, which occurs against the wishes of one company. However, 'merger', 'takeover', 'amalgamation', 'absorption' and 'fusion' are sometimes used as synonyms. Where two firms in the same business (i.e. competitors) merge, this is known as 'horizontal integration'. Where two firms that are suppliers or customers of one another merge, this is known as ➤ 'vertical integration'.

Acquisitions and mergers – which research suggests frequently do not benefit the shareholders of the acquiring company – have been an important cause of increasing ➤ concentration, and some economists have argued that major mergers should be controlled more closely by the authorities, even when they do not threaten to reduce competition directly (➤ competition policy; Takeover Panel). This is because pressures to maintain high short-term earnings, and hence share prices to avoid the risk of a takeover bid, may inhibit investment in research and development. Against this it is argued that mergers are the only way of transferring assets to more capable hands when existing management has proved deficient.

The value of merger activity has fluctuated roughly in line with stock-market prices. Not all acquisitions involve takeovers of independent companies. In recent years between one-fifth and one-third of total expenditure has been accounted for by sales of subsidiaries between company groups. ➤ Management buy-outs have also been growing. ➤ conglomerate; holding company; reverse takeover.

merit goods ➤ Commodities, the consumption of which is regarded as socially desirable, irrespective of ➤ consumers' preferences. Governments are readily prepared to suspend ➤ consumers' sovereignty by subsidizing the provision of certain goods and services, e.g. education.

Merton, Robert C. (b. 1944) Professor Merton is a finance specialist at the Harvard Business School, and joint winner of the 1997 Nobel Prize for Economics, for his work in deriving methods for the valuation of complex financial instruments, e.g. ➤ options. The work was also crystallized by Black and Scholes in one particular and path-breaking equation (➤ Black–Scholes formula), but Professor Merton found means of generalizing their formula and expressing it in a widely applicable form. Their work led to the development of a significant new financial market that enables traders to diversify risk and allocate it in far more flexible ways than had hitherto been possible. In addition, insurance and guarantees comprise forms of option, and thus these can now also be valued more accurately. Professor Merton's most famous paper is 'Theory of Rational Option Pricing', *Bell Journal of Economics and Management Science* (1973). His career has primarily centred around Cambridge, Massachusetts, first at the Massachusetts Institute of Technology, then at Harvard.

microeconometrics ➤ McFadden, Daniel.

microeconomics The study of economics at the level of individual consumers, groups of consumers or firms. No very sharp boundary can be drawn between microeconomics and the other main area of the subject – ➤ macroeconomics – but its broad distinguishing feature is to focus on the choices facing, and the reasoning of, individual economic decision-makers. It is a long-standing requirement of microeconomics that it can justify the behaviour it ascribes to individuals as being logical, given their preferences or objectives. The general concern of microeconomics is the efficient allocation of scarce resources between alternative uses (➤➤ resource allocation), but more specifically it involves the determination of

➤ price through the optimizing behaviour of economic agents, with consumers maximizing ➤ utility and firms maximizing ➤ profit. It covers both the behaviour of individual sectors and the way the sectors interact in ➤ equilibrium and disequilibrium in individual markets. The main areas of microeconomics are: (a) demand theory (➤ demand, theory of); (b) the theory of the firm (➤ firm, theory of the); (c) the demand for labour (➤ labour, demand for), and other ➤ factors of production; (d) ➤ welfare economics; and (e) the study of the interactions between markets in ➤ general equilibrium analysis.

micro-finance Financial services for the poor who do not have access to the formal banking system. In its origins micro-credit began with the rediscovery that poor people can save and repay loans, especially women in rural areas, perhaps by means of rotating credit in which regular savings can earn the right to borrow at a multiple of the amount saved and perhaps making use of peer pressure when the finance is gathered in small communities. It has developed into a large-scale phenomenon – mostly for credit rather than saving – with many thousands of institutions in developing countries financed by non-governmental organizations such as charities and international aid organizations. There are some institutions that provide micro-finance on a purely commercial basis but there are acute difficulties in reducing costs per loan down to viable levels.

micro-prudential regulation ➤ macro-prudential regulation.

migration The movement of people outwards (emigration) and inwards (immigration) between one location and another, either within a country or between countries. There has been a continuing increase in international migration. According to the United Nations, the estimated number of the world stock of migrants grew at 1.8 per cent per annum from 2000 to 2010 and reached 213.9 million; 3 per cent of world population. In the ➤ advanced countries the proportion was 10 per cent compared with 1.3 per cent in the ➤ least developed countries. Migration is beneficial in so far as it eases the problems of a static, declining or ageing ➤ population that exists in many advanced countries, and satisfies the demand for skilled and unskilled workers that could not otherwise be met. The sources of this migration are the ➤ developing countries from which people are attracted by the opportunities for work not available in their own countries. This outflow, through the loss particularly of skilled workers, could inhibit the economic growth of the developing countries, although emigrants often provide an important source of income through remittances home. According to the United Nations, remittances to the developing countries in 2010 are estimated to be $322 billion in a world total of $425 billion. ➤ globalization; Samuelson (factor price equalization theorem).

Mill, John Stuart (1806–73) Mill was subjected as a child to a regime of severe educational discipline by his father, James Mill. He was acquainted with the major works of economics of the day by the age of twelve, and was correcting the proofs of his father's book, *Elements of Political Economy*, when he was thirteen. He learnt Ricardian economics and Benthamite ➤ utilitarianism from his father. In 1823, he joined the East India Company, where he remained for thirty-five years. For three years, before moving to France to spend his retirement there, he was a Member of Parliament. He was an extraordinarily prolific writer, especially when it is remembered that he had a full-time job. His reputation was made by *A System of Logic, Ratiocinative* *and Inductive; Being a Connected View of the Principles of Evidence and the Methods of Scientific Investigation*, which was published in 1843. His essay *On Liberty* appeared in 1859, and his *Examination of Sir William Hamilton's Philosophy* in 1865. His two most important works on economics are *Essays on Some Unsettled Questions of Political Economy* (which came out in 1844, though he actually wrote it in 1829 when he was only twenty-three) and *Principles of Political Economy with Some of Their Applications to Social Philosophy* (1848). The latter was intended to be a comprehensive review of the field of economic theory at the time, and was, in fact, an up-to-date version of ➤ Smith's *Wealth of Nations* (1776). It succeeded so well that it remained the basic textbook for students of economics until the end of the century. The work is regarded as the apogee of the ➤ Classical School of Smith, ➤ Ricardo, ➤ Malthus and ➤ Say. Mill himself said the book had nothing in it that was original, and indeed it is basically an eclectic work, intended simply to bring together the works of others.

However, it is not true to say that Mill lacked originality altogether. He analysed the forces that lead to increasing ➤ returns to scale, arguing that as a result there will be a tendency for industries to become more and more concentrated in a few firms. The advantages this gave should be set against the disadvantages that will accrue in the form of higher prices from the loss of competition. Recognition of this tendency led him to support strike action by ➤ trade unions. Trade unions were a necessary counterweight to the powerful employer (➤ Galbraith, J.K.). In his exposition of the theory of ➤ value, Mill showed how ➤ price is determined by the equality of ➤ demand and ➤ supply, although he did not demonstrate the relationship by means of graphs or schedules. Mill recognized as a distinct problem the case of ➤ commodities with ➤ joint costs. He showed also how reciprocal demand for each other's products affected countries' ➤ terms of trade. Mill brought in the idea of ➤ elasticity of demand (though the actual expression was invented later by ➤ Marshall) to analyse various alternative trading possibilities. His father had suggested that ➤ rent, being a surplus according to Ricardian theory, was ideally suited to ➤ taxation. Mill took up this idea, and it became quite popular. He proposed that all future increases in unearned rents should be taxed.

Miller, Merton H. (1923–2000) An economist from the University of Chicago, and joint ➤ Nobel Prize winner in 1990. Miller's great contribution was in the theory of finance, with ➤ Modigliani, F. (➤ Modigliani–Miller theorem). Even though the pair's findings were based on a large number of simplifying assumptions, Miller had been pre-eminent in analysing the effect of taxation and bankruptcy costs on optimal company financial structure.

minimum efficient scale (m.e.s.) The scale of production at which further increases in scale would not lead to lower unit costs (➤ average costs). ➤ Economies of scale are measured in terms of unit costs versus plant size or output. The resulting long-run cost curve is generally thought to be L-shaped. The m.e.s. is the point on this curve at which it flattens out. Where the m.e.s. is large and requires large ➤ capital expenditure, it may act as a ➤ barrier to entry, especially where the m.e.s. is large in relation to total market size. Often, however, many firms may operate profitably below m.e.s. (a) because: the cost disadvantage of doing so is small, (b) they expect to grow, (c) because of product differentiation (➤ differentiation, product), or (d) because of other departures from the theoretical conditions of ➤ perfect competition. It should also be remembered that technological economies of scale revealed in plant size are only one of the forces determining the efficiency of firms. ➤ transaction costs; X-efficiency.

minimum wage The setting of wage rates at a minimum level either economy-wide or for specific industries by state legislation or by collective bargaining. The aim is to boost the incomes of the low paid to prevent employers exploiting the existence of government benefits for the low paid by cutting wages or passing company taxes on to their employees. As a means of helping the poor, minimum wages are of limited efficiency – many poor households have no worker in them and are thus not affected; yet reasonably well-off households which have a second earner on low pay are affected. A minimum wage could price labour out of the workforce, and create unemployment. Differential minimum wages should be set at one level to be high enough to help someone supporting a family and at another to give employers sufficient incentive to employ single eighteen-year-olds. In defence of such laws, it has been argued that the demand for labour is in practice very inelastic (➤ elasticity) and that minimum wage laws do not give rise to the problem of the ➤ poverty trap. They give an incentive to the 'discouraged worker' (➤ disguised unemployment). Moreover, they encourage employers to nurture their staff more carefully and make them more productive (➤ efficiency-wage hypothesis). It has also been argued that in some circumstances, because of the inflexibility of a labour market, an employer could in effect behave as a ➤ monopsonist and restrict demand for labour to keep wages down. A minimum wage, therefore, rather than reducing employment would increase it as the incentive to restrict labour take-up would have been removed. The setting of minimum wages has a long history, the first being applied in New Zealand in 1894. The USA introduced a federal minimum wage in 1938. In 2007, the ➤ Organisation for Economic Co-operation and Development (OECD) recorded that there were twenty-one OECD countries which had minimum wage schemes in one form or another and on average gross minimum wage earnings were about 38 per cent of average wages.

minorities, minority interest Elements shown in the consolidated accounts of groups of companies in which one or more of the ➤ subsidiaries is not wholly owned by the parent. Where a company owns 95 per cent of the ordinary ➤ capital of a subsidiary, for example, and its accounts are consolidated, then the whole of the assets and income of the subsidiary will be included in the consolidated accounts. In showing net assets attributable to shareholders of the parent company, 5 per cent in this case belongs to the minority shareholders and must be deducted. Similarly, in calculating ➤ net income attributable to the same shareholders, earnings will be shown after minority interest.

Mirlees, James A. (b. 1936) A Scottish-born economist, Mirlees has been a Professor at both Oxford and Cambridge Universities (at the latter since 1995). He received the joint ➤ Nobel Prize for Economics in 1996. His main area of study has been in the economics of taxation. His achievement has been to analyse the trade-off between equity and efficiency in a tax system, and to derive rules and conditions to govern the imposition of efficient taxes. For example, he is credited with the finding that, under certain assumptions, it is inefficient to impose any tax that affects business production decisions. It is always better to levy taxes on final consumption and to maintain efficient production. He also investigated the role of marginal tax rates, and the idea that it is better to have higher marginal rates lower down the income spectrum in order that the rich pay more tax on that middle slice of their income, but themselves face a low marginal rate. He found that that particular advantage was outweighed by the fact that more people were affected by marginal rates in the middle-income spectrum than at the top. He also posited the problem of designing an income tax in terms of ➤ asymmetric information, in that the government does not know how hard people could work in the absence of a tax, and hence initiated a discussion of an old issue – the design of tax systems – in terms of a new area of economic thinking – the economics of information.

Mises, Ludwig Edler von (1881–1973) Professor at Vienna University from 1913 until he joined the Graduate Institute of International Studies at Geneva in 1934. In 1940, he left Europe for the USA and was appointed five years later to a professorial Chair at New York University, where he stayed until 1969. His published works include *The Theory of Money and Credit* (1912), *The Free and Prosperous Commonwealth* (1927), *Geldwertstabilisierung und Konjunkturpolitik* (Monetary Stabilization and Economic Policy) (1928), *Bureaucracy* (1944), *Omnipotent Government: The Rise of Total State and Total War* (1944), *Human Action: A Treatise on Economics* (1949), *Theory and History: An interpretation of social and economic evolution* (1957) and *The Ultimate Foundation of Economic Science* (1962).

Von Mises argued in favour of the ➤ price system as the most efficient basis of ➤ resource allocation. A ➤ planned economy must be wasteful, because it lacks a price system and cannot institute such a system without destroying its political principle. He applied the ➤ marginal utility theory of the ➤ Austrian School to develop a new theory of ➤ money, and pointed out that ➤ utility could be measured ordinally only and not cardinally (➤ Hicks, J.R.). He also outlined a ➤ purchasing-power parity theory comparable to that of ➤ Cassel. His ➤ business-cycle theory explained fluctuations in terms of an expansion of bank credit in the upturn which caused a fall in the ➤ rate of interest and surplus ➤ investment with a consequent reversal when the ➤ money supply was reduced. ➤➤ Hayek, F.A. von.

Misselden, Edward (1608–54) A leading member of the merchant adventurers and a member of the group of writers referred to as ➤ mercantilists. He argued that international movements of specie and fluctuations in the ➤ exchange rate depended on international trade flows and not the manipulations of bankers, which was the popular view. He suggested that trading returns should be established for purposes of statistical analysis, so that the state could regulate trade with a view to obtaining ➤ export surpluses.

Mitchell, Wesley Clair (1874–1948) ➤ institutional economics.

mixed economy A market economy in which both private and ➤ public enterprise participate in economic activity, though not necessarily in all sectors, some of which may be reserved for public ➤ monopoly. Mixed ownership of the means of production is, in fact, characteristic of all contemporary economic systems. ➤➤ free-market economy; planned economy.

mixed strategy A means of making one choice from a set of options by random selection, on the basis of pre-assigned probabilities attached to each option. It is a concept used in ➤ game theory where, in certain situations and in order to prevent an opponent guessing your behaviour, your best strategy is to behave unpredictably. It is the opposite of a *pure strategy*, in which there is no random element. A mixed strategy is beneficial when, given your opponent's action, you are indifferent between two pure strategies, and when your opponent can benefit from knowing what your next move is. It is best to adopt a mixed strategy in the game tic-tac-toe (sometimes referred to as paper-scissors-stone), for example. An important finding in game theory is that anyone facing a mixed strategy will always find a pure strategy to be among the best responses.

MNC ➤ multinational corporation.

mobility of capital The ability of investment funds to flow across international borders. Impediments to capital mobility may take the form of restrictions on the inflow of investment funds to a country (restrictions on the rights of foreigners to buy property or companies, for example) or ➤ exchange control, limiting the ability of domestic citizens to invest overseas. If capital is mobile, investors can lend money to those borrowers who are willing to pay the highest rate of return (after taking into account any expected changes in exchange rates). If they do this enough, and if the ➤ purchasing-power parity theory holds, real interest rates should converge across countries. In practice, they deviate but not by very much. ➤➤ exchange-rate overshooting.

mobility of labour ➤ labour, mobility of.

mode ➤ average.

model A representation of an economic system, relationship or state, that takes any of a variety of forms. At its most informal, a model can be said to consist of a *verbal description* or *analogy* of some real-world phenomenon. It may take the form of a *diagram* (e.g. the graph of the ➤ cobweb model), or a *set of equations* setting out the relationship between ➤ variables (e.g. ➤ consumption as a ➤ function of income). In applied economics, a model is likely to be expressed in a computer program or *spreadsheet* in which data (the 'input') are processed and manipulated to produce results (the 'output'). Model-building usually consists of two main stages: (a) inspired by economic reasoning, the development of the structure of the model (setting out what factors affect which variables) – this is often as far as construction goes, and (b) estimation of the actual strength (➤ parameters) of the relationship postulated, often by using ➤ econometrics.

Models have a variety of uses: (a) they can illuminate and describe systems clearly by stripping them of all unnecessary complications; (b) computer models in particular are useful for ➤ simulation – a variable (e.g. ➤ unemployment) is defined in terms of the values of a set of other variables and, by simulating a change in these, the effect of different policies on unemployment can be estimated; (c) forecasts of the behaviour of variables can be made, based on past observations; and (d) the specification of models is a prerequisite to the testing of different theories. ➤ empirical testing; hypothesis.

Modigliani, Franco (1918–2003) Born in Rome, Professor Modigliani studied at the University of Rome. Moving to the USA, he obtained his Ph.D. at the School of Social Research in New York in 1944. He was appointed to a Chair of Economics at the University of Illinois in 1949 and in 1952 to the Chair of Industrial Administration at the Carnegie Institute. From 1962, he held the post of Professor of Economics and Finance at the Massachusetts Institute of Technology. Professor Modigliani was awarded the ➤ Nobel Prize for Economics in 1985. His many published articles in the professional journals have been assembled in *Collected Papers of Franco Modigliani* (1980). He put forward an explanation of the constancy of the aggregate ➤ average propensity to save: (a) in the face of rising incomes in the economy, and (b) in terms of the balance between the high savings of the employed workforce and the dissavings of the retired population (➤ life-cycle hypothesis). He also contributed to financial economics. ➤➤ Modigliani–Miller theorem.

Modigliani–Miller theorem The proposition that the market value of a firm is – under certain assumptions – independent of the way it chooses to finance its investment or distribute ➤ dividends. If a firm wants to expand, it can choose between three methods of financing its investment: borrowing, issuing shares and spending profits rather than giving them to shareholders in the form of dividends. ➤ Modigliani and ➤ Miller showed that under a number of assumptions (e.g. an absence of taxes) the method of financing a firm chooses in a perfectly functioning capital market will ultimately not affect the cost of capital (➤➤ capital, cost of) or the value of the firm. It is the risk and expected rate of return of the expanded firm that will determine how attractive investors find it, not the way the firm raises the money. Any attempt to attract low-cost capital will probably have the effect of raising the cost of other capital in the company. ➤➤ investment appraisal; Ricardian equivalence.

monetarism The name applied to a theory of ➤ macroeconomics which holds that increases in the ➤ money supply are a necessary and sufficient condition for ➤ inflation. Two strands of thought underlie this doctrine and distinguish it from its main theoretical antagonist, ➤ Keynesian economics (➤➤ Keynes, J.M.):

(1) That changes in the money supply have a substantial effect on ➤ aggregate demand. Two separate reasons are given for this: (a) that the demand for money is stable and insensitive to the ➤ rate of interest, and (b) that the demand for goods in the economy, particularly ➤ investment, is sensitive to the interest rate. Together, these determine the monetarists' ➤ transmission mechanism – the way in which increases in the money stock affect spending in the economy. Under the monetarist account, if the authorities printed some crisp $10 notes and dropped them over the country from a helicopter, people would find they had more cash in this liquid form (➤➤ liquidity; liquidity preference) than they wanted. They would therefore spend much of the cash on goods and services, increasing aggregate demand. The rest might be invested in interest-bearing ➤ securities; the increase in demand for these would drive the price up and the interest rate down. Under the monetarist account, even the smallest cut in interest rate would cause a large increase in investment, again boosting aggregate demand. The contrary account holds that the helicopter money would not be spent at all, but invested in financial assets. The interest rate would fall a great deal, but that investment is insensitive to interest rates, so this would have

no effect on the demand for investment goods. In effect, all that happens from expanding the money supply is that interest rates drop, and people hold more cash, without spending it, implying that the speed with which cash circulates has slowed down to offset the extra cash (➤ velocity of circulation).

(2) That any change in aggregate demand the government succeeds in bringing about will manifest itself (in the long run at least) in higher prices and not higher output. The economy will tend to an equilibrium position with all markets clearing: all that money can do is raise all prices equally, leaving all relative prices constant (➤ neutrality of money). Increases in the stock of money can, however, have a short-term effect on the economy, but only as long as the inflation created outstrips people's expectations of inflation. Once inflation is built into people's expectations, increases in the money supply only result in increases in the level of prices.

In terms of the ➤ quantity theory of money, of which monetarism can be seen as a revival, the above propositions are equivalent to holding that the velocity of circulation of money and the level of output are exogenous (➤ exogenous variable), and fixed independently of the money stock.

Monetarists advocate ➤ supply-side economics, and deny a role for ➤ stabilization policy. Instead, greatest stability can be achieved by adhering to a rule for money-supply growth in line with the growth of real output (➤ real terms). The emergence of monetarism in the 1960s and among policymakers in the 1970s can mainly be attributed to ➤ Friedman (➤➤ economic doctrines). The doctrine has been somewhat superseded by the theoretically more elegant theory deriving similar results from ➤ new classical economics. ➤ policy ineffectiveness theorem.

monetary base The stock of an economy's most liquid financial assets (➤ liquidity). The monetary base is usually taken as the stock of notes and coins and the banks' own deposits at the ➤ central bank. It has often been suggested that the ➤ money supply as a whole could be controlled by strict rationing of the monetary base. However, the base is very small relative to the total money supply, so rather sensitive changes to the base could lead to instability in the money supply as a whole.

monetary policy Central government policy with regard to the quantity of money (➤ quantity theory of money) in the economy, the ➤ rate of interest and the ➤ exchange rate. Monetary policy is now broadly accepted as having the predominant role in the control of ➤ aggregate demand, and therefore of ➤ inflation. This owes much to the rise of the doctrine of ➤ monetarism and to the defeat of the popular interpretation of ➤ Keynes, who was held to believe that ➤ fiscal policy was more important, and that monetary policy matters only in so far as it affects fiscal variables, e.g. the level of government borrowing.

Monetary policy in most advanced economies is executed primarily by the authorities engaging in ➤ open market operations to set a level of short-term interest rates that encourage the banks to let their deposits grow at a level consistent with the objectives of policy. This being said, there are still plenty of important decisions to be made over what those objectives are:

(1) Is the ultimate objective simply to control inflation? Or are there other motives for changing policy as well, e.g. preventing asset prices from changing too rapidly even if there are no consequences for the general price level?

(2) Is there an intermediate objective of policy, e.g. constraining growth of ➤ money supply (broad or narrow money) or stability of the exchange rate? It is not possible to set up targets individually for the money supply and the exchange rate because the two are often simultaneously determined. If the money supply is increased, for example, the exchange rate tends to fall unless interest rates are raised. Exchange-rate targets (e.g. those that existed for members of the ➤ European Exchange Rate Mechanism) encourage trade by reducing the risk of exchange-rate fluctuations, while targeting money supply, it is argued, can have an impact on ➤ credibility and, hence (somewhat implausibly) on wage demands; plus, money-supply targeting can better reflect domestic economic needs.

(3) Should policy be run on the basis of preset rules or on discretion?

(4) Who conducts policy in the absence of a rule? Should control be in the hands of elected politicians, or an independent ➤ central bank?

While monetarists appear to have essentially won the battle over the importance and objectives of monetary policy, they lost the battle over the conduct of policy. They supported the use of simple money-supply growth rules, yet the experiences of the UK and USA in following such rules were unhappy. Even the ➤ European Central Bank, which explicitly includes money supply in deciding policy action, has used a heavy dose of discretion in responding to changes in money-supply growth. ➤➤ inflation target; Taylor rule.

Monetary Policy Committee The nine-person committee of the ➤ Bank of England, charged with setting interest rates in the UK. The committee consists of the bank's governor, the two deputy governors, two other officials of the bank, plus four economists nominated by the government. It is accountable to the Court of the Bank of England, and to Members of Parliament through the House of Commons Treasury and Civil Service Select Committee. It meets monthly, and the minutes of its proceedings are published. The committee is charged with setting interest rates to meet the government's explicit ➤ inflation target. ➤➤ credibility; monetary policy.

monetary sector (UK) Defined by the ➤ Bank of England to include its own banking department, the retail banks, accepting houses, and other UK and foreign banks. Other ➤ financial intermediaries (e.g. the ➤ building societies, insurance companies and ➤ pension funds) are not counted as part of the monetary sector.

monetary union ➤ European Economic and Monetary Union.

money Something that is widely accepted in payment for goods and services and in settling ➤ debts. In primitive economies, goods and services were exchanged wholly through ➤ barter. Exchanging goods for one another or using property (e.g. cows, sheep) as money was cumbersome and inconvenient and inhibited the ➤ division of labour. Later, coins made of valuable metals came into use as intermediate commodities, but in the modern economy ➤ banknotes and coins have little or no intrinsic value, while ➤ bank deposits are simply book entries (➤ banking): their use as money depends on confidence that they can be exchanged for things of value. In addition to its use as a medium of exchange, money acts as a store of value, making ➤ saving convenient, as a measure of value (or unit of account), and as a standard of deferred payments that facilitates the granting of ➤ credit, though all these functions can be threatened by ➤ inflation. ➤➤ money supply; transactions motive.

money, demand for ➤ liquidity preference.

money, inactive ➤ inactive money.

money, neutrality of ➤ neutrality of money.

money, superneutrality of ➤ superneutrality of money.

money at call and short notice In the UK, ➤ money loaned to the ➤ money market on a short-term basis by the ➤ commercial banks. These ➤ loans are regarded as part of the ➤ liquid assets of the banks because they can be withdrawn immediately or at periods of notice of up to fourteen days. They also include overnight loans. The terms of the loans vary, and in practice the money may not be called in for long periods. The commercial banks are willing to loan their liquid funds to the money market in this way, because they know that the ➤ Bank of England will act as a ➤ lender of last resort. In most other countries the major commercial banks invest directly in short-term paper and have direct access to the ➤ central bank for loans, e.g. ➤ Federal Reserve System. ➤➤ discount market.

money illusion The confusion arising from changes in money values and changes in real values. If an employee's wages increased by 3 per cent over a period during which consumer prices rose 3 per cent, they would be suffering from money illusion, if they thought they were any better off. ➤ behavioural economics; real terms.

money in circulation ➤ Money in use to finance current transactions as distinct from idle money (➤ inactive money).

money market The financial institutions that deal in short-term ➤ securities and ➤ loans, gold and ➤ foreign exchange. ➤ Money has a 'time value', and therefore the use of it is bought and sold against payment of ➤ interest. Short-term money is bought and sold on the money market, and long-term money on the ➤ capital market. Neither the money market nor the capital market exists in one physical location. In the money market most transactions are made by telephone or electronically. In the UK, the money market sometimes refers only to the ➤ commercial banks dealing in ➤ Treasury bills, ➤ bills of exchange and ➤ money at call and short notice, with the ➤ Bank of England acting as a ➤ lender of last resort. In a wider context, the money market also includes the ➤ foreign-exchange market and the ➤ bullion market.

money supply The stock of liquid assets in an economy that can freely be exchanged for goods or services. Money supply is a phrase that can describe anything from notes and coins alone (➤ monetary base) to the sum of all cash, plus bank deposits, because by writing cheques, individuals exchange bank deposits for goods or services. There is a spectrum of assets of differing ➤ liquidity in the economy, and any degree of liquidity may be chosen to define an asset as money. A set of very liquid assets is known as *narrow money*. A set includes also less liquid assets, known as *broad money*. In general, the wider the definition, the harder it is for the authorities to control the money supply, but the more direct the relationship between money supply and other economic variables. For example, the quantity of notes and coins in the economy – a narrow definition – is easy to control, but is of little importance in influencing the spending of individuals.

In the UK, several definitions of money supply are used for monitoring the money supply. 'M0' is the stock of sterling notes and coins in circulation, plus the banks' deposits at the ➤ Bank of England. 'M4' is a much broader definition, embracing notes and coins, plus the value of all UK sterling bank (➤ banking) and ➤ building society accounts held by private citizens and companies. Because some of these are not really used to support transactions, they are more a form of savings. Since 1993, the Bank of England has also published an index of growth in *divisia money*. This simply takes the elements of M4, and weights them by the degree to which they are used for financing transactions. It is, in essence, a measure of M4, adjusted to give more importance to the more liquid part. At times of rapid financial innovation or change, particular definitions can exhibit rather erratic behaviour, compounding the problems of control and interpretation of the money supply. ➤➤ domestic credit expansion; monetary policy.

money terms ➤ real terms.

Monopolies and Mergers Commission ➤ competition policy.

monopolistic (imperfect) competition Competition in an industry in which there are many firms each producing products that are close, but not perfect, ➤ substitutes. Three features characterize such an industry. (a) The firms make products between which consumers slightly differentiate (they may have different coloured packets, for example) and consequently, the demand for any individual firm's product is not perfectly elastic (➤ elasticity). Some consumers will prefer one product to those of its competitors sufficiently to exhibit a limited amount of loyalty to that brand when its price rises. This means that each firm has a small amount of ➤ market power (➤ monopoly) and is thus not a price-taker in the market for its own product. In this regard it is similar to a monopoly, but not a perfect competitor (➤ perfect competition). (b) Firms are able to enter the industry if the level of ➤ profits is attractive. This is a feature shared with the perfectly competitive industry, but not the monopoly. (c) Like both perfectly competitive and monopolistic firms, producers in monopolistic competition are assumed to maximize profits.

In monopolistic competition, firms set output to equate ➤ marginal cost and ➤ marginal revenue. Price at the specified output is determined by demand. Profits are zero in the long term, on account of entry occurring whenever they are positive, driving up ➤ supply in the industry and cutting the ➤ demand for each company's product. While monopolistic competition shares this with perfect competition, its output will be rather lower than it would be under perfect competition and its price above marginal cost and thus rather higher. Moreover, production will not take place at the lowest cost point as it does under perfect competition. Each firm operates with some ➤ excess capacity. The theory of such markets, which lie between monopoly and perfect competition, was simultaneously developed by ➤ Chamberlin in the USA and ➤ Robinson in the UK.

monopoly A market in which there is only one supplier. Three features characterize a monopoly market: (a) the firm in it is motivated by ➤ profits; (b) it stands alone and barriers prevent new firms from entering the industry (➤ barriers to entry); and (c) the actions of the monopolist itself affect the market price of its output (➤ marginal revenue) – it is not a price-taker. The output of the monopolist will be set at the point at which marginal revenue is equated with ➤ marginal cost. If marginal revenue were any higher it would pay the monopolist to increase production because the additional costs generated would be lower than the revenue and profits would rise. The reverse would be true if marginal revenue were any lower than marginal cost (➤➤ marginal-cost pricing). The price of the monopolist is determined by ➤ demand as the firm cannot set both output and price. For its chosen output, the monopolist can read price off a market ➤ demand curve, which will lie above the marginal revenue curve.

The monopoly will make profits in excess of those merely necessary to stay in business, and no pressure exists for the price to fall and reduce these. Theory suggests that, under monopoly, prices are higher and output lower than they would be under ➤ perfect competition. The power of the monopolist derives from the fact that demand for his/her product is not perfectly elastic (➤➤ elasticity) so that, when the price rises, sales largely hold up. This is not so for a perfect competitor, who will sell nothing on raising price even a fraction above the going rate. The degree of *monopoly power* a firm enjoys can be measured by how inelastic demand for its product is. The more inelastic demand is, the more the monopoly can raise its prices without losing sales.

Monopoly is held to be inefficient because, under it, the price will be higher than marginal cost so that, even if some consumers value an item more than it costs to make, they may not choose to buy it. Moreover, there is no tendency for costs to be at their lowest possible level in the long term, because the pressure of more efficient, incoming competitors does not exist. It is not surprising, given these results, that most nations choose to control monopolies, which are usually defined as any firm dominant in a particular industry, e.g. with a market share in excess of 25 per cent. However, in some industries, efficient production requires a single dominant supplier (➤ economies of scale; natural monopoly; regulation). Moreover, a distinction has to be made between a monopoly that has earned its dominance, and one that has not. It is possible that consumers benefit from monopoly in the long run if the profits generated act as a spur to ➤ innovation (➤ Schumpeter, J.A.). And in any event, defining monopoly is a more subtle process than it looks – almost no company really has a monopoly. Even what appears to be a monopoly gas company faces some competition from electricity suppliers. ➤➤ bilateral monopoly; competition policy; contestability; monopsony.

monopoly, discriminating A ➤ monopoly that charges different prices for the same product to different consumers. ➤ price discrimination.

monopsony A market in which there is only one buyer of the item sold. Unlike individual consumers in most markets, a monopsonist will have an impact on the market price. When he/she purchases an extra unit of the item, market demand perceptibly increases and the market price rises. This means that to buy one extra item costs the monopsonist not only the price of that item, but also the extra price that has to be paid for all the items that were previously being bought at the lower price. In some markets, therefore, it could pay a monopsonist to restrict demand. ➤➤ bilateral monopoly; monopoly.

Monte Carlo method A technique for estimating ➤ probabilities. The method involves the construction of a ➤ model and the ➤ simulation of the outcome of an activity a large number of times. Probabilities are then estimated from an analysis of the range of outcomes from the model.

moral hazard The presence of incentives for individuals or institutions to act in ways that incur costs that they do not have to bear. A typical example is that of insurance. In insuring property, there is less incentive to be as careful in protecting it than there is without insurance. Similarly, the state support for a bank to prevent its collapse could encourage banks to pursue more risky business practices. Moral hazard is one of those important market distortions based upon imperfect information, as it is the inability of, say, the insurer to distinguish the well-behaved claimant from the badly behaved one, and the benefits of a particular business policy accrue to the institution but not any costs arising from failure of the policy. ➤➤ dependency culture; incentive compatibility; mechanism design; principal–agent problem.

mortality ➤ death rate.

mortgage A legal agreement conveying conditional ownership of ➤ assets as ➤ security for a ➤ loan and becoming void when the ➤ debt is repaid. ➤ Building societies, banks (➤ banking) and ➤ insurance companies (*mortgagees*) loan a proportion of the purchase ➤ price of houses to individuals or companies (*mortgagors*), the property being mortgaged to the lender until the loan is repaid.

mortgage debenture ➤ bond.

most-favoured nation clause The clause in an international trade treaty under which the signatories promise to extend to each other any favourable trading terms offered in agreements with third parties. ➤➤ General Agreement on Tariffs and Trade; generalized system of preferences.

moving average A ➤ time series derived from another by the calculation of a sequence of ➤ averages. The averages are calculated in sequence from a consecutive group in the series; for each average, the next value in the series is added and the earliest value in the group dropped. The number of values in the group to be averaged may be two or more, depending on the time series from which they are to be derived. Moving averages are calculated to eliminate seasonal variations from a series and to highlight the longer-term trends.

MPC ➤ marginal propensity to consume.

MPS ➤ marginal propensity to save.

MRS ➤ marginal rate of substitution.

multicollinearity ➤ Correlation between the ➤ independent variables in a regression (➤ regression analysis) equation. If such correlation exists, the application of

➤ least-squares regression for estimation of the parameters in an equation is difficult, because it is hard to determine which of several correlated variables is truly influential.

multilateral agencies International organizations for aid (➤ foreign aid) and economic cooperation funded by several or many countries, as distinct from ➤ bilateral agencies. The ➤ International Bank for Reconstruction and Development, the ➤ Asian Development Bank, the ➤ European Bank for Reconstruction and Development and the ➤ Inter-American Development Bank are multilateral agencies.

Multilateral Investment Guarantee Agency An agency of the World Bank (➤ World Bank Group) which was established in 1988 and is open to all members of the World Bank. The agency gives guarantees and ➤ insurance cover for private direct investment in ➤ developing countries (➤ foreign investment) against non-commercial risks (e.g. the imposition of ➤ foreign-exchange restrictions, war and the expropriation of assets) and is financed from incomes received from insurance premiums and financial contributions made available by member countries. In 2008–2009, the Agency issued $1.4 billion in insurance guarantees. ➤ export credit insurance.

multilateralism ➤ International trade and exchange between more than two countries without discrimination between those involved. In contrast to ➤ bilateralism. ➤➤ General Agreement on Tariffs and Trade; most-favoured nation clause; Regional Trade Agreements.

multinational corporation, multinational enterprise (MNC, MNE) A company, or more correctly an ➤ enterprise, operating in a number of countries and having production or service facilities outside the country of its origin. A commonly accepted definition of an MNE is an enterprise producing at least 25 per cent of its world output outside its country of origin. There were, according to estimates by UNCTAD (➤ United Nations Conference on Trade and Development), 64,000 parent corporations engaged in international production with 866,000 affiliates located abroad and employing 53 million in 2002. Most of the largest MNEs come from Europe, the USA and Japan, but recently numbers have emerged from ➤ developing countries. Switzerland and the Netherlands are represented amongst the larger MNEs, which shows that a large domestic market is not essential. The multinational corporation takes its principal decisions in a global context and thus often outside the countries in which it has particular operations. In some countries these corporations account for a very significant proportion of total manufacturing ➤ value-added, for example 40 per cent in the Republic of Ireland, 24 per cent in Hungary and 6 per cent in China. The rapid growth of these corporations, and the possibility that conflicts might arise between their interests and those of the individual countries in which they operate, has provoked much discussion among economists. MNEs possibly account for over one-quarter of world trade and have played a major role in ➤ globalization, but earlier fears that they would come to dominate the world economy now seem misplaced and the general view is that they have been a beneficial influence on ➤ economic development, for example by diffusing new technology, and ➤ foreign direct investment.

In their book *Managing Across Borders* (2002) Christopher A. Bartlett and Sumantra Ghoshal make distinctions between three types of international company which are widely accepted as useful. They argue that neither the decentralized types of business with strong local presence (*multinational*), nor the more central-ized types of business building cost advantages through centralized production (*global*) or exploiting the parent company's ➤ research and development and systems capability (*international*) are now sufficient to maximize competitiveness. The authors claim that the *transnational* company (TNC), which somehow blends these approaches by differentiating contributions by national units to a none the less highly integrated worldwide operation, has the most successful approach.

multi-plant operations Firms that produce at more than one plant or location. Most small firms operate from a single establishment. Large firms serving a national market (e.g. in the brewing industry) may find that lower transport costs to the final consumer from multiple plants outweigh the ➤ economies of scale in a single large plant. ➤➤ enterprise.

multiple correlation coefficient A statistical measure of the accuracy by which a known ➤ variable is estimated by an equation, or ➤ model, containing two or more ➤ independent variables (➤➤ correlation). It can take values between 0 and 1. At 0, there is no correspondence at all between the predicted and actual variable, and at unity the coefficient indicates a perfect correspondence. Also called the *coefficient of determination* and *R-squared* (➤ partial correlation; regression analysis).

multiplier An increase in ➤ national income divided by the increase in expenditure generating that increase in income. In simple models, the size of the multiplier depends on the ➤ marginal propensity to consume. For example, if the government increased its investment expenditure by $100, this sum would be paid out in wages, salaries and profits of the suppliers. The households and firms receiving these incomes and profits will, in turn, save a proportion and spend the remainder. These expendi-tures will in turn again generate further incomes and profits and so on. At each round, therefore, a proportion of receipts will be paid and a proportion spent, the latter being the marginal propensity to consume, denoted, for example, by c. We have, therefore:

	Expenditure	**Saving**
Round 1	$100	
2	$100c$	$100(1 - c)$
3	$100c^2$	$100(1 - c)^2$
.	.	.
.	.	.
.	.	.
n	$100c^n$	$100(1 - c)^n$

and, therefore, the total increase in national income generated by the $100 is the sum of the infinite number of expenditures:

$$\$100 + \$100c + \$100c^2 + \$100c^3 + \ldots \$100c^n$$
$$= \$100(I + c + c^2 + c^3 + \ldots c^n)$$

This series is the sum of a ➤ geometric progression whose sum can be shown to be equal to $100[(1 - c^n) / (1 - c)]$. The marginal propensity to consume is less than unity, so that as n gets larger, c^n becomes smaller. Therefore, the series converges to $100/(1 - c)$ and the multiplier is, therefore, equal to $1/(1 - c)$ or $1/s$, where s is the ➤ marginal propensity to save. ➤ accelerator–multiplier model; Keynes, J.M.

multi-product firm A business producing two or more different ➤ commodities or products. Most large firms produce more than one product and are often engaged in more than one industry (➤ diversification), although for simplicity the basic theory of the firm (➤ firm, theory of the) is couched in terms of a single-product firm.

Mun, Sir Thomas (1571–1641) An English mercantilist (➤ mercantilism) and a director of the East India Company. His publications include *A Discourse of Trade From England unto the East Indies* (1621) and *England's Treasure By Forraign Trade* (1664). He attacked the idea that ➤ exports of ➤ bullion should be completely prohibited and other restrictions put on trade, pointing out that restrictions on trade invited retaliation in foreign ➤ markets and raised domestic ➤ prices. He did emphasize, however, that an export surplus should be sought in the ➤ balance of trade for the country as a whole, although it was unnecessary to seek to achieve this with each trading partner.

Mundell, Robert A. (b. 1932) A Canadian economist at Columbia University in New York, Professor Mundell was awarded the ➤ Nobel Prize for Economics in 1999 for his work on fiscal and monetary policy in different ➤ exchange rate regimes, and on optimum currency areas. His contribution was primarily generated in the 1960s (for some of this period he was at the University of Chicago) where he more or less transformed the study of international macroeconomics, and is perhaps primarily associated with the Mundell–Fleming model (with the late Marcus Fleming) of an open economy that demonstrates a paradox: in a fixed exchange rate regime ➤ fiscal policy is powerful and ➤ monetary policy impotent, while the reverse is true in a floating rate regime. The reason for the paradox is that with a floating exchange rate, fiscal policy enacted through, for example, extra government borrowing, either pushes up the interest rate (thus reducing investment) or simply sucks in foreign capital, which drives up the exchange rate (thus reducing exports). Either way, any stimulatory effect is negated. Monetary policy can work through changing interest rates by increasing the money supply and by affecting the exchange rate. In the fixed rate regime, monetary policy is powerless, as it has to accommodate any exchange rate target. Fiscal policy can work, though, as no offsetting exchange rate or interest rate effects can undermine it. (➤➤ impossible trinity)

Professor Mundell was also prescient in analysing the nature of optimal currency areas (➤ European Economic and Monetary Union). He asked when countries should combine their currencies. He concluded that there are benefits in terms of transaction costs in so doing, but that if asymmetric shocks occurred to the different countries, policy would be difficult to manage unless labour was mobile and could migrate from a high unemployment zone to a low unemployment one. (➤ migration)

His two most prominent publications are probably 'Theory of Optimum Currency

Areas', *American Economic Review* (1961), and 'Capital Mobility and Stabilization Policy under Fixed and Flexible Exchange Rates', *Canadian Journal of Economics* (1963). He has also written several books, including *The International Monetary System: Conflict and reform* (1965), *International Economics* (1968), *Monetary Theory: Inflation, Interest and Growth in the World Economy* (1971), *Debts, Deficit and Economic Performance* (1991) *Building the New Europe* (1992) and *Inflation and Growth in China* (1996).

Mundell–Fleming Model ➤ Mundell, R.A.

mutual company A company without issued ➤ capital stock, owned by those members doing business with it. The ➤ profits of a mutual company, after deductions for reserves, are shared out among members or used to reduce prices of services for members. Some ➤ savings banks, ➤ building societies and ➤ insurance companies were formerly mutual companies but have demutualized and incorporated (➤ incorporation). These companies have sought ➤ flotation to facilitate ➤ mergers and capital raising. Since mutual companies are owned by their members (e.g. depositors and policy holders), in these cases members have received ➤ shares in the newly floated enterprises and in some cases a distribution of cash. In the USA, the term 'mutual' is also used to refer to open-ended ➤ trusts or *mutual funds*, which correspond to ➤ unit trusts in the UK.

mutual funds ➤ mutual company.

Myerson, Roger B. (b.1951) ➤ mechanism design.

Myrdal, Gunnar Karl (1898–1987) Born in Sweden, Professor Myrdal graduated in law at Stockholm University in 1923. After a period in private practice, he obtained a degree in economics in 1927 and took a post as lecturer in Political Economy at Stockholm University, eventually succeeding ➤ Cassel to the Chair of Political Economy and Financial Science in 1933. From 1936 to 1938, he was a Member of Parliament as a Social Democrat. After a period as Economic Adviser to the Swedish legation in the USA, he was appointed Minister of Commerce in the Swedish government, a post he held from 1945 to 1947. He resigned from this post to become Secretary-General of the UN Economic Commission for Europe at Geneva, where he stayed until 1957. In 1957, he was appointed Professor at the Institute for International Economic Studies of Stockholm University and in 1974 was awarded the ➤ Nobel Prize for Economics jointly with von ➤ Hayek.

His published work includes *Price Formation under Changeability* (1927), *Vetenskap och Politik i Nationalekonomien* (1929) (*Science and Politics in Economics* (1953)), *Om Penningteoretisk Jamvikt* (1931) (*Monetary Equilibrium* (1931)), *An American Dilemma: The Negro Problem and Modern Democracy* (1944), *Economic Theory and Underdeveloped Regions* (1957), *Value in Social Theory* (1958), *Beyond the Welfare State* (1960), *Challenge to Affluence* (1963), *Asian Drama: An Inquiry into the Poverty of Nations* (1968), *Objectivity in Social Research* (1969), *The Challenge of World Poverty* (1970) and *Against the Stream – Critical Essays in Economics* (1973).

Professor Myrdal invented the terms, and formulated the distinction between, ➤ *ex ante* and *ex post*, in particular in relation to the equality of aggregate savings and investment in equilibrium. He emphasized the need to study the dynamics of ➤ macroeconomic processes. His book *Monetary Equilibrium* (1931), which developed the economics of ➤ Wicksell, foreshadowed many aspects of ➤ Keynes' *General Theory of Employment, Interest and Money* (1936). He argued that economists should accept the need to make explicit value judgements, without which their theoretical structures were unrealistic. He became an advocate of ➤ institutional economics. Professor Myrdal believed that such a framework was necessary in any economic studies of the ➤ developing countries.

N

NACE ➤ Standard Industrial Classification.

NAIRU Non-accelerating inflation rate of unemployment (➤ unemployment, natural rate of).

NASDAQ National Association of Securities Dealers Automated Quotations system (➤ over-the-counter market).

Nash, John F. (b. 1928) A mathematician from Princeton University in New Jersey and the Massachusetts Institute of Technology, John Nash gave his name to the most important concept of ➤ equilibrium as applied to ➤ game theory. For that, he won the ➤ Nobel Prize for Economics in 1994 (jointly with ➤ Harsanyi and ➤ Selten, who refined his work). Nash drew the important distinction between *cooperative games* and *non-cooperative games,* where players have incompatible interests and are unable to make binding agreements to maximize joint welfare. He outlined the equilibrium position for non-cooperative games, in which all players' expectations are fulfilled and all players' strategies are optimal. While this remains the foundation of most discussion in game theory, it is not sufficiently limiting to be universally interesting as a tool of analysis. Moreover, it relies on each player having complete information about the other players' options. ➤ Nash equilibrium.

Nash equilibrium A concept central to ➤ game theory, which characterizes any situation where all the participants in a game are pursuing their best possible strategy given the strategies of all the other participants. A game is any situation in which there are participants, strategies for each participant, and pay-offs for each player associated with the combination of strategies chosen. One might imagine a simple 'game' in a two-person country in which both the people have to decide on which side of the road to drive. The pay-offs are either 'no crash' (when both drive on the left or right) or 'crash' (when one drives on the left and the other on the right). In this situation, two possible Nash equilibria exist: (a) both driving on the left, or (b) both driving on the right. If one drives on the left and the other on the right, it is not a Nash equilibrium because, given the choice of the other, each would change his/her own policy. Popular examples of Nash equilibria arise in ➤ Hotelling's law and the ➤ prisoner's dilemma (➤➤ equilibrium).

The Nash equilibria are considered a rather weak basis for determining the likely outcome of a game, as in some cases Nash equilibria can involve players choosing ➤ dominated strategies, i.e. strategies that can easily be bettered. In other cases, the Nash equilibria can be upheld by the use of implausible threats by one player. Even though the threat would not be likely to be carried out, it can influence a Nash equilibrium. For these reasons, economists have searched for other notions of 'solving' games. Nash nevertheless represents the starting-point for all discussion on the subject. ➤ Nash, J.; Selten, R.

national accounts ➤ social accounting.

National Association of Securities Dealers Automated Quotations system (NASDAQ)(US) ➤ over-the-counter market.

national debt The total outstanding borrowings of the central government ➤ Exchequer. It represents the stock of borrowing as opposed to the annual increase in total borrowing, represented by the government deficit (➤ public sector net borrowing). Under the provisions of the ➤ Maastricht Treaty, countries in the ➤ European Economic and Monetary Union are expected to keep debt below, or falling towards, 60 per cent of GDP. Although the UK has not participated in monetary union, in February 2010 the public sector net debt (see below) was within the Maastricht guidelines despite massive expenditure on bailing out financial institutions during the credit crisis of 2007–9.

Two different definitions of the debt are in common use: (a) *net public sector debt*, which measures the ➤ public sector financial liabilities to the private sector and abroad, net of short-term financial assets, and (b) *gross general government debt* – the variable used in the Maastricht Treaty – which excludes ➤ nationalized industries and measures total financial liabilities, before netting off short-term financial assets.

The UK national debt as a proportion of GDP, which was exceptionally high at the end of the Second World War (180 per cent), declined almost continuously from 1945 until 1990. In 2001–2002 public sector net debt as a percentage of the GDP was 30 per cent, but had doubled to almost 60 per cent in early 2010. These levels are not exceptional in recent conditions: US budgeted gross Federal debt for 2010 was 94 per cent of GDP (local and state debt amounts to about 8 per cent of Federal debt). In Japan the national debt had risen to some 160 per cent of GDP in 2008 as a result of its long battle to counter deflation.

The national debt is of great importance in the financial system of the private sector and plays quite an important role in the interdepartmental accounting of government. Government securities provide convenient investments for ➤ insurance companies, for example, and these securities form an important part of the reserve assets of banks and other financial institutions. Although it is spoken of as a burden, the interest paid on the national debt held by residents is not a burden on the nation as a whole, since the interest payments are actually transfers between those residents who pay taxation and those who also receive the interest. The willingness of non-residents, however, to hold sovereign debt affects the interest rates that have to be paid and places limits on the extent to which governments can borrow to pursue ➤ Keynesian economic policies during a ➤ depression.

national income The total incomes of residents of an economy in a given period after providing for ➤ capital consumption. Also referred to as *net national product at factor cost* (➤ factor cost). Incomes in this calculation include: (a) all payments for the use of the ➤ factors of production, i.e. wages, salaries, ➤ profits in the form of ➤ dividends and retained profits, ➤ rents and net income from abroad but excluding ➤ transfer payments; or (b) the sum of ➤ value added in all sectors of the economy at factor cost; or (c) as the sum of expenditure on final consumption and ➤ investment goods, plus ➤ exports and minus ➤ imports. These three methods should, in theory, yield the same figure since all incomes should equal total expenditure plus net ➤ saving or ➤ investment, which in turn should also equal the value of output (provided output is defined as value added, i.e. intermediate expenditure is excluded). In practice, each of the three methods involves estimation and the totals can diverge significantly, so often an averaging procedure is used. Comparisons of output and expenditure will be affected, among other things, by the extent of evasion (➤ informal economy). National income before capital consumption is equal to the Gross National Product and, if net income from abroad is also excluded, it is equal to the Gross Domestic Product. Comparisons between the national incomes of various countries are subject to many qualifications: the distribution of income will differ and so too may methods of estimation; moreover, the exchange rates used may not reflect purchasing-power parities (➤ purchasing-power parity theory).

National income or other aggregates from the national accounts are regarded as indicators of national welfare in the market economy, but they are not unambiguous in this respect. One reason is that some activities that contribute to national welfare are not included because they are not valued in markets, e.g. the work done by mothers in bringing up their own children. Environmental costs (e.g. pollution and the depletion of natural resources) are not included in the accounts (➤➤ environmental accounting).

national innovation system ➤ innovation.

National Insurance (NI) A social security scheme in the UK that provides unemployment and sickness benefits, flat-rate pensions, maternity benefits and other grants or benefits on widowhood or incapacity in return for regular contributions paid by employees, employers and others.

The US social security scheme provides retirement and unemployment and other benefits. Based on ➤ payroll taxes (Federal Insurance Contributions), like the UK system, it is a pay-as-you-go scheme in which current contributions pay the benefits, but there are important differences. Basic state pension benefits in the UK are calculated on a fixed sum tied to the cost of living, for example, whereas US state pensions, within limits, are related to average earnings. The US system in its present form dates from 1935 under the ➤ New Deal. ➤ demographic time bomb; pension funds.

nationalized industries State-owned enterprises in the market sector of an economy (e.g. a post office), as distinct from state activity in ➤ public goods, e.g. defence. In the UK, most nationalized industry was literally private industry that was taken into public ownership (i.e. nationalized), for example, British Steel, British Leyland and Rolls-Royce. In the UK, as in other European countries, most of the public utilities (electricity, water, coal, transport and communications) undertakings are, or were, in state ownership, although several countries, led by the UK, have engaged in a programme of denationalization (➤ privatization). The growth of nationalization largely began after the Second World War and has always been a subject of controversy in the UK; the steel industry, for example, was nationalized in 1951, denationalized in 1953 and renationalized in 1967. The heads of these industries have often complained of political interference – in the interests of broader ➤ macro-economic objectives. Whatever the relative merits of state versus private enterprise, some form of ➤ regulation in many nationalized industries is inevitable given their economic importance and ➤ monopoly powers.

National Loans Fund A UK government account opened in 1968 for the domestic lending of government and all the transactions relating to the ➤ national debt. The *payments* of the fund include interest, management and expenses of the national debt, deficit on the ➤ Consolidated Fund and loans to the nationalized industries and public corporations, local authorities and the private sector. *Receipts* include interest on loans, profits of the Issue Department of the ➤ Bank of England, interest transfer from the Consolidated Fund and borrowings.

national product ➤ national income.

natural monopoly An industry in which technical factors preclude the efficient existence of more than one producer (➤ monopoly). Examples are the public utilities such as water, gas and electricity, where there is a requirement for a network of pipes or cables. In order to derive the efficient (➤ economic efficiency) results of ➤ perfect competition from a market that is necessarily monopolistic, various suggestions of control have been made, notably government regulation if the firm is in private ownership, ➤ public ownership and ➤ franchising. Under any of these, control is enhanced if the monopoly can be divided regionally, allowing performance comparison between different regions (➤ yardstick competition). Alternatively, licensing arrangements can be set up so that a dominant supplier runs a network (e.g. pipes or cables), but is obliged to lease the use of it to competing suppliers. ➤➤ privatization; regulation.

natural rate of growth ➤ growth theory; Harrod–Domar model.

natural resources Commodities or assets with some economic ➤ value that exist without any effort of mankind. The value they have is usually only realized, however, when they are exploited, i.e. dug out of the ground, processed or refined. Natural resources are necessary ingredients of all economic activity. Natural resources can be of three types: (a) *non-renewable*, e.g. oil and coal, stocks of which will eventually run out (➤ depletion theory); (b) *renewable*, e.g. water and fish, which are reproducible; and (c) *non-expendable*, i.e. not used up in the consumption process as, for example, in the case of a landscape of outstanding beauty that yields ➤ utility for those seeing it, and tourist income for the owner. ➤➤ environmental economics.

near money An ➤ asset which, like ➤ money, acts as a store of value but which is not immediately acceptable as a medium of exchange, for example a ➤ building society deposit. What constitutes money and what does not, however, is controversial and important for defining the ➤ money supply.

neo-classical economics A school of economic thought imbued with behaviour consistent with ➤ microeconomic theory, constructed to explore conditions of ➤ static equilibrium (➤ comparative static equilibrium analysis). Neo-classical models are based around maximizing behaviour of individual firms and consumers, with decisions at the margin (➤ marginal analysis) often most important. Statements about macro-events are often derived from the aggregation of micro-relationships, and this has led to criticism, particularly from the ➤ Cambridge School. In contrast to ➤ Keynes, the neo-classical economists consider that savings and investment naturally balance as the rate of interest changes; and full employment is achieved in the labour market by changes in ➤ factor prices. Essentially, the Neo-classical School has been concerned with the problems of equilibrium and growth at full employment, again in contrast to Keynes, who was primarily concerned with the underemployment of resources. ➤➤ Keynesian economics; Samuelson, P.A.

neo-classical synthesis Description given to the dominant economic consensus in ➤ macroeconomics during the 1960s, between those supporting ➤ Keynesian economics, and those basing their opinions on ➤ neo-classical economics. The compromise doctrine essentially held that, in principle, the economy did have natural mechanisms to ensure full employment, but that, in practice, ➤ Keynes' analysis of the potential persistence of unemployment without government action was well founded. In principle, the economy can find full employment, because even if there is a spiral of falling demand and falling prices (the Keynesian case of the ➤ liquidity trap) people should eventually feel richer as their wealth becomes worth more, and that should lead them to spend. In practice, Keynes receives credit under the synthesis, as market frictions imply that the wait for natural mechanisms to work can be interminable. ➤ economic doctrines.

net assets The ➤ capital employed in a business. It is calculated from the ➤ balance sheet by taking fixed ➤ assets plus current assets less current ➤ liabilities. Often used as a basis for calculating ➤ rate of return on capital.

net capital employed ➤ capital employed.

net capital formation ➤ capital formation.

net cash flow ➤ cash flow.

net domestic product ➤ Gross Domestic Product less capital consumption.

net income Net ➤ profit on earnings after tax and, where appropriate, after ➤ minority interest.

net investment Gross expenditure on ➤➤ capital formation minus the amount required to replace obsolete and worn-out plant and equipment. It measures the change in the ➤ capital stock.

net national product ➤ national income.

net output ➤ value added.

net present value ➤ present value.

net profit ➤ profit.

net tangible asset ratio ➤ financial ratios.

net tangible assets (NTA) Fixed ➤ assets plus current assets minus intangible assets such as goodwill and minus current ➤ liabilities.

network economics The study of industries which are characterized by their internal interconnections, such as telecommunications and computer internet applications. These industries are defined by a structure in which each consumer derives increasing benefit as more consumers join the network. Consumers benefit from the system's 'network externalities' (➤ externalities) and producers from its ➤ economies of scale as they recruit more and more consumers. A mature network, however, creates a ➤ barrier to entry against any potential competitors because of the costs to a consumer of switching to a new supplier with a more limited network. ➤ two-sided market.

net worth ➤ balance sheet.

net worth ratio ➤ financial ratios.

neuro-economics From Adam ➤ Smith, it was a fundamental assumption in ➤ Classical Economics that the welfare of society as a whole was best achieved by individuals being left to pursue their own interests and that individuals behaved rationally. Practical observations, however, have shown that people did not always behave rationally. For instance, in the 'ultimatum game', one person is given $20 and told he or she can share any amount with a second person. However, if the second person rejects the offer, both of them get nothing. Experiments have shown that offers below a particular level are rejected, which appears not to be in the best interests of the second person. A 'rational' person would take the view that something was better than nothing. The inference is that the second person punishes the first for being selfish, even at his or her own expense. Neuro-economics is a development from ➤ behavioural economics and combines economics with psychology and the recent discoveries in neuroscience of the processes of the brain. Decisions are reached by a resolution of the conflict in an individual between the rational calculation of personal benefit and costs of a decision made in one part of the brain and a contrary emotional reaction arising in another part. It has been argued that the latter activity arises from social evolution and the need to be accepted in a society and to protect that society from disruption. Hence the instinct to punish what is viewed as unfair behaviour in the ultimatum game. It may be inferred from this that the emotional check is the weighing of the long-term benefits and costs arising from a decision against the rational short-term benefits and costs. ➤ Allais, M.; Kahneman, D.

neutrality of money The inability of changes in the stock of ➤ money in an economy to affect anything except the general level of prices. If money is neutral, a 10 per cent increase in the ➤ money supply causes a one-off 10 per cent rise in all prices but stimulates no growth in the real level of output. The issue of whether money is neutral or not is central to debates in ➤ macroeconomics. In ➤ Classical Economics and under ➤ monetarism, money *is* held to be neutral. ➤ Keynes and his followers, however, have had a more complicated attitude to monetary neutrality. On the one hand, they have downgraded the importance of money in influencing ➤ aggregate demand; on the other, they have argued that aggregate demand has an important role in influencing real ➤ variables. Because of this latter belief, modern Keynesian economics is associated with asserting that money is *not* neutral. It would be more accurate, however, to say that it asserts aggregate demand is not neutral.

In order to explain why money might have some real impact on the economy, it is easiest to assume that certain prices or wages are fixed in nominal terms. For example, imagine what happens if the money-supply authorities print extra cash, expanding the money supply by, for example, 10 per cent. People will have high money balances that they may attempt to spend on, for example, computers. First, if all prices are flexible, the growth in money supply leads to a shift in the ➤ demand curve for computers which leads to an immediate rise in computer prices. This should encourage firms to deliver more computers. However, the increase in the money supply pushes up prices throughout the economy, so the suppliers' costs also rise. This causes a shift in the computer suppliers' ➤ supply curve, so leading to a reduction in supply. This also increases prices and so takes the quantity sold back to where it started. The story ends with higher prices, and the same output as before, so money is neutral. Suppose, however, that computer manufacturers are contractually obliged to provide goods to retailers at pre-set prices. In response to extra demand, the computer retailers this time increase their prices, but *can* supply more without suffering higher costs. There is no shift in their supply curve. In this case, the extra money leads prices up less than before, and output rises. The economy grows.

Even without the pre-set prices, money could have a real impact if retailers and their suppliers react very slowly in adjusting their prices to the extra demand. An increase in the money supply could also have a real effect if there is ➤ money illusion. Even though all prices and wages increase, consumers would spend more. There would also be an increase in the supply of labour in response to the apparent increase in wages, thereby reducing real costs and raising the computer supply curve. The view that money is neutral stems from a belief that market forces function reasonably effectively and fast (i.e. that computer suppliers do not fix their prices in advance), and that economic agents are rational (suffer no money illusion). ➤➤ economic doctrines; menu costs; monetarism; policy ineffectiveness theorem; rational expectations; superneutrality of money; supply-side economics.

new classical economics A theory of ➤ macroeconomics that emphasizes the role of ➤ rational expectations in decision-making and the natural rate of unemployment (➤➤ unemployment, natural rate of) in ➤ equilibrium growth. The central view of new classical economists is the ➤ policy ineffectiveness theorem that argues governments can only have an impact on the economy in so far as their policies are unanticipated.

Unlike the monetarists, therefore, proponents of this view argue that government demand-management intervention is ineffective even in the short run. Growth can only be enhanced by influencing ➤ supply. This has been an influential doctrine in ➤ macroeconomics in the past two decades. Its prime advantage over other accounts of the economy is that it is well founded in ➤ microeconomics, using the economic tradition of assuming individuals are rational. This means that, unlike other approaches, its principal conclusions do not rely on the assumption that people are systematically fooled into behaviour counter to their own true desires. Contrast it with, for example, the notion that prices are sticky, accounting for money having some effect on real output (➤ neutrality of money). While the assumption of rational expectations may appear extreme, it is perhaps best to think of new classical economics as arguing that, although policy may have a short-term effect, in the long term the short term becomes very short indeed as people see the way policy operates. ➤➤ Akerlof, G.; economic doctrines; Lucas critique; supply-side economics.

New Deal The US Federal government under President Roosevelt began, in 1933, a number of projects designed to give financial assistance and work to the large number of people thrown out of employment by the ➤ Great Depression that followed the stock market collapse on Wall Street in 1929. These measures were aimed at countering the Depression by structural reform and by promoting ➤ reflation. For example, farm output was restricted to push up prices and an industrial policy also aimed at higher prices. The overriding aim was to achieve a better social balance, not a Keynesian approach to higher public expenditure which came later; though public expenditure did go up and this caused controversy. Some of the measures taken to extend regulation of financial markets, such as the establishment of the ➤ Securities and Exchange Commission, have endured. The New Deal did not get the USA out of the depression, this was to be achieved by rearmament from 1940. (➤ Keynes, J.M.)

new economy Narrowly, new activities created by information and communication technologies (ICTs), including computer hardware and software, telecommunications and other aspects of the digital revolution, notably the internet. These new activities are seen to be distinct from those of the *old economy* (steel, cars, food processing, services etc.), though for the present they are only a very small part of total output. The borderline between the new and old economies is increasingly hard to draw as the old economy adopts the technology of the new, e.g. online ordering by consumers from food multiple retailers. The driving force behind ICTs is the rapidly declining cost of semiconductor chips. In the past thirty years the processing power of these chips has doubled about every eighteen months and this is expected to continue for some time (Moore's Law, named after Gordon Moore, founder of INTEL). The average US cost of semi-conductors fell from $50 to $2.33 per circuit and has continued to fall rapidly.

In a wider sense, the term 'new economy' is used to encapsulate multiple trends in the world economy, including ➤ globalization, a shift to more flexible methods of production and the attempt to make the economy ecologically sustainable in response to evidence of global warming. It was expected that ICTs would generate considerable ➤ productivity growth. There are some signs of this in some sectors but little evidence of a global impact on productivity. Despite these caveats, ICTs will undoubtedly have profound long-term effects on the economy, perhaps comparable to those resulting from the adoption of electricity from the 1920s. ➤➤ electronic commerce; knowledge economy.

new-issue market That part of the ➤ capital market serving as the market for new long-term ➤ capital. Those institutions needing capital (industrial, commercial and financial companies and public authorities) offer ➤ shares and ➤ securities that are then purchased by each other and the general public. Internally generated funds provide about 70 per cent or more of the capital required by business and the new-issue market is not large, accounting on average for about 5 per cent, although it is of some importance. The new-issue market does not include certain other sources of new long-term external finance, e.g. ➤ mortgages and other ➤ loans from financial institutions. Borrowers in the new-issue market may be raising capital for new ➤ investment, or they may be converting private capital into public capital; this is known as 'going public' (➤ flotation).

The largest concerns are able to issue stocks and shares direct to the public. These stocks and shares will normally be quoted on the ➤ stock exchange. Other concerns will raise their new capital through an ➤ issuing house that will either underwrite the issue or first purchase the securities and then offer them for sale to the public (➤ unlisted securities markets). In all cases the issues will actually be handled by an ➤ issuing broker. A full prospectus describing the company and its prospects as well as public advertising are necessary and, for smaller issues, costs can be reduced by private placing, i.e. by selling the shares to ➤ insurance companies or other investors.

Quoted companies may issue unquoted shares in this way. Rather larger amounts are raised by private placing by other public companies that have no quoted securities, but ➤ private companies have no access to the new-issue markets, since they cannot achieve quotations while retaining their private status. Well-established companies can greatly reduce the cost of raising new capital by offering shares to their existing shareholders by what are known as 'rights issues' (➤ rights issue). Rights issues save the cost of advertising, issuing brokers and underwriting commissions, although the shares will normally have to be offered at well below market price to ensure the issue is fully taken up. The difficulty that smaller quoted and unquoted companies experience in raising new long-term capital in the UK was noted in the 1931 Macmillan Report, although unlisted securities markets have developed further and a number of new institutions have since emerged to meet this need outside the new-issue market (➤ risk capital). The ➤ commercial banks have also greatly increased their lending to ➤ small business.

The new-issue market, sometimes called the *primary market* (➤ secondary market), like the rest of the capital market, is increasingly becoming an international one and public companies and the public sector raise money in overseas capital markets.

New Keynesianism The economics of those who combine the assumption of ➤ rational expectations with the stickiness of prices and wages much discussed in ➤ Keynesian economics. New Keynesians stress the existence of institutions that may quite rationally lead to sticky prices, e.g. ➤ menu costs, or long-term contracts in which prices are fixed well in advance and cannot thus be changed in response to economic events. They do not believe that money is neutral (➤ neutrality of money) and believe that the ➤ business cycle can partially be explained by changes in ➤ aggregate demand. The sticky nature of prices means any change in demand does not lead to an automatic or rapid change in prices; it can lead to a change in output or employment. This position is distinct from the ➤ new classical economics, which shares the rational expectations assumption, but assumes prices adjust more quickly and as a result that only *unanticipated* changes in aggregate demand have a real effect. ➤➤ Akerlof, G.; economic doctrines; policy ineffectiveness theorem.

newly industrialized country ➤ emerging markets.

New York Stock Exchange (NYSE) The leading New York stock exchange and largest in the world in terms of domestic ➤ market capitalization (➤ stock exchange). The NYSE is a self-regulating body, though it has to secure compliance with the requirements of the ➤ Securities and Exchange Commission. The NYSE is also referred to as the 'Big Board' and as 'Wall Street'. *Euronext*, which integrates the stock exchanges in Amsterdam, Brussels and Paris, was taken over in 2006 to form NYSE-Euronext.

NIC Newly industrialized country ➤ emerging markets.

NNP Net national product ➤ national income.

Nobel Prize The sixth Nobel Prize, for Economics, in memory of Alfred Nobel (1833–96), the Swedish chemist, was introduced in 1969 and is financed by the Swedish National Bank. The following economists have been awarded this prize in each year: 1969, Tinbergen and ➤ Samuelson; 1971, ➤ Kuznets; 1972, ➤ Hicks and ➤ Arrow; 1973, ➤ Leontief; 1974, von ➤ Hayek and ➤ Myrdal; 1975, Kantorovich and ➤ Koopmans; 1976, ➤ Friedman; 1977, ➤ Meade and ➤ Ohlin; 1978, ➤ Simon; 1979, ➤ Schultz and ➤ Lewis; 1980, ➤ Klein; 1981, ➤ Tobin; 1982, ➤ Stigler; 1983, ➤ Debreu; 1984, ➤ Stone; 1985, ➤ Modigliani; 1986, ➤ Buchanan; 1987, ➤ Solow; 1988, ➤ Allais; 1989, ➤ Haavelmo. In 1990 the prize was won by three American finance economists, ➤ Markowitz and ➤ Sharpe for their development of the ➤➤ capital asset pricing model, and ➤ Miller (➤➤ Modigliani–Miller theorem). ➤ Coase won the prize in 1991. ➤ Becker won it in 1992. ➤ Fogel and ➤ North collected it jointly in 1993. Three ➤➤ game-theory pioneers won it in 1994: ➤ Harsanyi, ➤ Selten and ➤ Nash. ➤ Lucas won it in 1995, and in 1996 ➤ Mirlees and ➤ Vickrey. For their work on option pricing models, ➤ Merton and ➤ Scholes won in 1997. ➤ Sen won it in 1998 for his work on development economics and ➤ Mundell for international macroeconomics in 1999.

In 2000, the prize was shared between ➤ Heckman and ➤ McFadden for advances in microeconometrics. In 2001, ➤ Akerlof, ➤ Spence and ➤ Stiglitz shared the award for their work on the analysis of markets. In 2002, the prize was shared between ➤ Smith and Kahneman for their work on the analysis of the rationality of human behaviour. In 2003, the prize was shared between Robert F. Engle III and Clive W.J. ➤ Granger for their analyses of time series (➤➤ Granger causality). In 2004, the prize was divided between Finn E. Fydland and Edward C. Prescott for their work on dynamic macroeconomics, time series, consistency of economic policy and ➤ business cycles. In 2005, the prize was shared between Robert J. Aumann and Thomas C. Schelling for the application of ➤ game theory to conflict and cooperation situations. In 2006, Edmund S. Phelps won the prize for his work on inter-temporal trade-offs in macroeconomic policy. In 2007, the prize was shared between Leonid Hurwicz, Eric S. Maskin and Roger B. Myerson for their pioneering work on ➤ mechanism design theory. In 2008, Paul Krugman received the prize for his analysis of trade patterns and the location of economic activity (➤ first mover advantage). In 2009, the prize was shared between Elinor Ostrom and Oliver E. Williamson for their work on economic governance, and in 2010 between Peter A. Diamond, Dale T. Mortensen and Christopher A. Pissarides for their analysis of markets (such as the labour market) with search frictions.

nominal Gross Domestic Product The value of the ➤ Gross Domestic Product (GDP) at ➤ current prices. Many economists, notably ➤ Meade, have suggested that the government should set a target for nominal GDP; if workers take low pay rises, this target will be reached by real output increases; if workers take high pay rises, then the nominal GDP rise will almost entirely consist of ➤ inflation.

nominal value The ➤ face value of a ➤ share or ➤ bond, which may be more or less than its market price. ➤➤ par value.

nominal yield The return or ➤ yield on a ➤ security in which ➤ dividend or ➤ interest is expressed as a percentage of the ➤ nominal value of the security as opposed to its market price.

non-accelerating inflation rate of unemployment (NAIRU) ➤ unemployment, natural rate of.

non-domestic rates ➤ local taxation.

non-price competition Attracting or attempting to attract business from rivals by means other than selling at lower prices, e.g. by the use of ➤ advertising or product differentiation (➤ differentiation, product). Non-price competition is found commonly under conditions of ➤ oligopoly, where price-cutting could lead to a damaging price war, thus the use of free gifts, coupons and special offers.

non-substitution theorem A theorem that states that, if there are no economies or diseconomies of scale in an economy, if there are no ➤ joint products and if all inputs that are not themselves produced are used equiproportionately in production of everything, then competitive prices will reflect only technology and cost, and demand will have no impact on them.

non-tariff barriers ➤ protection.

normal distribution Also referred to as the *Gaussian distribution*. It was first discovered by de Moivre in 1763 but remained unnoticed until it was independently discovered again by Gauss. It is a continuous, symmetrical, bell-shaped curve (see diagram) at the heart of ➤ probability and sampling (➤ sample) theory. If, for example, a random sample of tax returns were taken from a population and the mean (➤ aver-

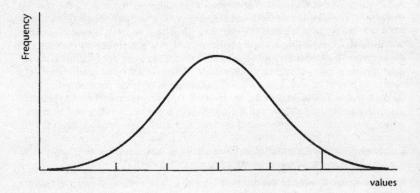

age) income of the sample were calculated, then these tax returns were returned and another sample taken and the mean income of these calculated and so on, a series of mean incomes would be derived that would eventually generate a normal curve when plotted against the frequencies with which each mean occurs. This mathematical fact (i.e. that a normal curve emerges from the continuous random, unbiased, sampling of a population variable) is used to test whether a given value has been derived from a particular population. In a normal distribution, 5 per cent of the observations are more than 1.96 times the ➤ standard deviation away from the mean. If a new income observation falls into this area of the curve, it can be said that the sample has a ➤ probability of 5 per cent of having been drawn from the same population as the previous samples. ➤➤ chi-squared test; log-normal distribution; Student's t-test.

normal good ➤ inferior good.

normal profit ➤ profit.

normative economics Economics concerned with judgements about 'what ought to be' in contrast to ➤ positive economics, which is concerned with 'what is'. A normative statement would be that 'industry should be more concentrated'. Such a statement should rest upon a positive assertion about the existing level of ➤ concentration and a ➤ value judgement that fewer firms would lead to greater efficiency or some other benefit.

North, Douglass C. (b. 1920) Economic historian at Washington University, St Louis, Missouri, and a joint winner of the ➤ Nobel Prize for Economics in 1993. North, like his fellow winner, ➤ Fogel, has been important in promoting the importance of, and explaining, the ➤ institutions in which an economy operates. He maintains that new institutions are created when groups see an opportunity for profit that cannot be realized under prevailing conditions. Attaching some weight to the context in which economic mechanisms operate, as much as to the mechanisms themselves, became fashionable in the context of former Eastern-bloc nations (➤ transition, economies in) and their attempts to emulate Western nations. North himself was an adviser to the government of the Czech Republic.

North American Free Trade Agreement A ➤ free trade area set up from 1994, comprising Canada, the USA and Mexico. ➤ Import tariffs, ➤ quotas and other trade barriers (➤ non-tariff barriers) between the member countries were phased out by 2008. The agreement also includes environmental provisions relating to the use of renewable resources, health and pollution.

NTA ➤ net tangible asset.

NTB ➤ non-tariff barrier.

null hypothesis A proposition assumed to be valid, unless evidence is found to the contrary. A common null hypothesis used in ➤ econometrics is that there is no relationship between two variables, i.e. that a ➤ parameter being estimated has the value zero. The null hypothesis will be *accepted* if the statistical evidence is weak for the relationship; it will be *rejected* if the relationship is convincingly found to exist in the data provided that is within acceptable bounds of statistical likelihood, given that the study is usually based on a ➤ sample. A null hypothesis has always to be set against an alternative hypothesis, with the null hypothesis usually representing the 'status quo'. The legal equivalent would be the proposition that someone is innocent unless proven guilty. It is generally incumbent on those trying to demonstrate the validity of a new theory to show it to be true, rather than for those doubting the point having to show it not to be true. ➤➤ beta; confidence interval.

NYSE ➤ New York Stock Exchange.

O

objective function ➤ Lagrange multiplier.

obsolescence A reduction in the useful life of a ➤ capital good or consumer durable (➤ durable goods) through economic or technological change or other external changes, as distinct from physical deterioration in use (➤ depreciation). For example, a new process or machine may be developed that renders existing equipment uneconomic because a firm could significantly reduce its costs by scrapping its existing machinery even though it might still have many years of physical life. Then the old equipment has become obsolescent.

occupational pension schemes ➤ personal pension.

OECD ➤ Organisation for Economic Co-operation and Development.

Office of Fair Trading ➤ competition policy.

OFT Office of Fair Trading (➤ competition policy).

Ohlin, Bertil (1899–1979) Born in Sweden, Professor Ohlin studied at the University of Lund and the Stockholm School of Economics. He was appointed to a Chair of Economics at Copenhagen University in 1925. In 1930, Professor Ohlin moved to the Stockholm School of Economics where he remained until his retirement in 1965. He was a Member of Parliament from 1938 until 1970 and Chairman of the Swedish Liberal Party for many years. He was awarded the ➤ Nobel Prize for Economics in 1977 (jointly with ➤ Meade). His major contribution – to ➤ international trade theory – was published in *Interregional and International Trade* (1933). Professor Ohlin refined the theory of ➤ comparative advantage by building on the work of Heckscher (➤➤ Heckscher–Ohlin principle). He also made important contributions to ➤ macroeconomic theory, in many ways anticipating in the 1930s the work of ➤ Keynes.

Okun, Arthur M. (1928–80) Professor Okun graduated from Columbia University in 1956 and became Professor of Economics at Yale in 1963. From 1969 until his death he was Senior Fellow at the Brookings Institution. His major publications include *The Political Economy of Prosperity* (1970) and *Prices and Quantities: A macroeconomic analysis* (1981). Professor Okun argued that ➤ supply and ➤ demand are not necessarily brought into ➤ equilibrium by lowering prices but they are by adjusting output. Excess capacity may not lead to lower prices in an economy. In *Potential GNP, Its Measurement and Significance* (1968), he analysed US gross national product (GNP) for the 1950s and 1960s. He discovered that a 1 per cent increase in unemployment was associated with a 3 per cent drop in the ratio of actual GNP to full-capacity GNP. This relationship has become known as Okun's law.

Okun's law ➤ Okun, A.M.

oligopoly A market which is dominated by a few large suppliers (➤ concentration). Oligopolistic markets are often characterized by heavy ➤ product differentiation through advertising and other marketing ploys, with long periods of price stability intermittently disrupted by keen price competition. Petrol sales and soap powder are notable oligopoly industries in which free offers, competitions and advertising are more heavily used than price competition for attracting custom.

There is no single theory of oligopoly equivalent to that of ➤ perfect competition or ➤ monopoly because the behaviour of oligopolistic firms is determined by the reaction and behaviour of their rivals, and the assumptions they make about those reactions. Instead, there are several alternative theories.

1   A theory developed by ➤ Cournot assumed that each firm sets its price and output on the assumption that its rival does not react at all. In such a situation, each firm will leap-frog past the other, lowering price and increasing output to gain a higher market share. The result is, nevertheless, a market in which prices are higher and output lower than each would be if the firms behaved as perfect competitors.

2   That of ➤ Bertrand competition, in which keen price competition drives firms to the perfectly competitive outcome.

3   That firms recognize their interdependence, and one among them leads in price setting with others following. In this case, the leader enjoys higher profits than any followers, but all firms benefit from the stability and predictability of the industry.

4   That all firms attempt to act as leader; then they all earn lower profits than they would under Cournot's solution (➤➤ prisoner's dilemma).

5   That firms assume their rivals will follow their prices down but not follow their price if it rises; in this situation, firms will be very reluctant to change their prices. It could account for the fact that prices are often stable in oligopolistic industries despite large changes in costs.

6   That in which firms collude and between them achieve the outcome that would occur if a ➤ monopoly existed in the industry. However, if one firm colludes, it always pays another to cheat and sell more than agreed, so that maintaining collusive agreements may be difficult in situations where firms cannot monitor each other's behaviour. Otherwise, hefty state penalties for collusion can deter oligopolists from making agreements that have negative effects on consumers.

Other approaches to oligopoly exist, notably ➤ game theory, which has been used to simulate the reactions of firms to each other's behaviour. ➤➤ anti-trust; Nash equilibrium; Organization of Petroleum Exporting Countries.

Olson, Mancur (1932–98) Economist who investigated the workings and implications of how collective action can frustrate the public interest. Born in North Dakota, USA, he graduated from the State University in 1954. After two years as a Rhodes Scholar at Oxford, followed by military service, he became Assistant Professor at

Princeton. In 1969 he joined the University of Maryland where he was Distinguished Professor of Economics until his death. In 1990, he founded the Center for Institutional Reform and the Informal Sector (IRIS) that carries out research, training and consultancy in ➤ developing countries and former Communist countries (➤ transition, economies in).

The kernel of all Olson's subsequent work lies in his first book, *The Logic of Collective Action: Public goods and the theory of groups* (1965), which was based on his doctoral dissertation. The book explores the relationships between members of special interest groups, their size and the interaction of their incentives and actions on each other and the wider public welfare, effectively a rich exercise in ➤ game theory. In *The Rise and Decline of Nations: Economic growth, stagflation and social rigidities* (1982), Olson showed how distributional coalitions could secure benefits for the group (e.g. by lobbying successfully for ➤ subsidies or tariff ➤ protection) at the expense of those outside the group. Special interest groups proliferate and become more deeply entrenched over time. The longer a society goes without an upheaval, the more powerful these organizations become and the more they slow down economic expansion. The disruption of these institutions following the Second World War was a more important factor in explaining the rapid postwar growth of Germany and Japan than the replacement of physical plant and infrastructure with state-of-the-art equipment. According to Olson, the formation of dense networks of collusive, cartelistic (➤ cartel) and lobbying organizations helps to explain the slow growth of the American north-eastern and older mid-western regions, and of the UK, and the faster growth of the American south and west.

A Not-So-Dismal Science (2000), a collection of articles edited by Olson and Kälikönen, a director of IRIS, appeared posthumously. The theme of the book is that it is the economic policies and organizational arrangements of a society that mainly determine how innovative and prosperous it is. In Olson's words, 'goods and services can be obtained not only by making, but also by taking, and that makes societies less efficient'. In an article by Olson, 'Dictatorship, Democracy and Development', *American Political Science Review* (1993), reproduced in the book, it is shown that in a world of roving banditry there is little incentive for anyone to produce or accumulate anything that may be stolen. It is in the interest ('encompassing interest') for the banditry to settle down, provide law and order and other ➤ public goods and incentives for production so that output and the 'take' can be maximized. By extension, the same emphasis on individual rights that is necessary for lasting democracy is also necessary for securing rights to property and enforcing contracts. Democracies, however, help to prevent an excessive extraction of the social surplus by their leaders. Olson was committed to a multidisciplinary approach to economic problems using sociology, law and politics and worked in the tradition of ➤ institutional economics.

on-cost The contribution of the ➤ cost of ➤ overheads added to the direct costs of production.

OPEC ➤ Organization of Petroleum Exporting Countries.

open economy A situation in which foreign trade (➤ exports and ➤ imports) and payments and movements of labour and capital into and out of a country are unrestricted.

The term is also used to refer to countries for which foreign trade is a large percentage of the ➤ Gross Domestic Product. The degree of openness of an economy may act as a constraint on the freedom of governments to pursue particular types of economic policy, e.g. the reduction of interest rates to stimulate expansion may, in an open economy, lead to a flight of capital to other countries, depressing the ➤ exchange rate with adverse consequences for ➤ inflation.

open-ended fund An investment company in which units may be purchased from, or sold to, the fund manager, as in a ➤ unit trust. The fund is open in the sense that its size continuously depends on its success in selling units, in contrast to a ➤ closed-end fund like an ➤ investment trust.

open-ended investment company (OEIC) An ➤ open-ended fund, listed on a ➤ stock exchange at a single unit price; like an ➤ investment trust, but it can issue or redeem ➤ shares to match demand in a similar way to a ➤ unit trust.

open-market operation The purchase or sale of ➤ securities by the ➤ central bank to influence the supply of funds in the ➤ capital market, and so interest rates and the volume of credit.

operating cost A term for prime or ➤ variable costs.

operating profit 1 Profit on current activities.
2 The difference between total revenue and total operating costs (or ➤ variable costs) and before deduction of ➤ fixed costs. ➤➤ inflation accounting; profit.

operating ratios Various measures of the efficiency of a business, e.g. the operating rate or ➤ capacity utilization rate, the stock–sales ratio, ➤ labour turnover ratio, the creditor–debtor ratio and other ➤ financial ratios.

operations research (OR) A multidisciplinary approach to the solution of quantifiable business or administrative problems, e.g. the determination of ➤ optimum levels of ➤ inventories, quality control and vehicle routing. Operations research usually involves the use of computer models to test alternative solutions and the basic discipline of OR personnel may be mathematics, engineering or economics. A number of techniques used in economics are of this type, e.g. ➤ critical-path analysis, discounted cash flow (➤ present value) and ➤ linear programming.

opportunity cost The value of that which must be given up to acquire or achieve something. Economists attempt to take a comprehensive view of the cost of an activity. If a firm invests undistributed ➤ profits to spend $1000 on new machinery that requires less electricity than the equipment it replaces, the cost of that machinery is not the *outlay* of $1000 alone: what could be earned from the best alternative use of the money also has to be taken into account. If, for example, the firm is paying 12 per cent interest on an overdraft and the saving in electricity is less than $120 a year, it would be better for the firm to pay off its overdraft than to invest in the new machinery. If self-employed people make a ➤ profit of $20,000 a year without a wage, they need to consider the alternative use to which their time could be put. They might, for example, be able to earn $25,000 a year working for someone else: this is the *opportunity cost* of their time. Accounting costs, as in these examples, normally allow only for cash outlays, but cash outlays will only approximate to opportunity costs when competition ensures that the prices of all ➤ factors of production are equal to those for their best alternative use (➤ Wieser, F. von). (Under the assumptions of ➤ perfect competition, self-employed people would be aware that they could earn more in employment and, since we assume profit maximization, would do so.) Economists also distinguish between private costs and ➤ social costs and costs in ➤ real terms and money terms. ➤➤ average cost; imputed cost; prime costs; shadow price.

optimal-growth theory The area of economics concerned with analysing the level of ➤ economic growth that maximizes social welfare. The starting point is known as the *golden rule of capital accumulation* (➤ golden rule) which, under a large number of assumptions, suggests that the optimal-growth path will be the one that maximizes consumption per worker over time. To vary consumption per worker, society can vary its stock of capital per worker: if there is too much capital, maintaining the capital–labour ratio will require such high levels of investment that workers would have to save a lot and refrain from consumption. If there is too little capital, however, while it is easy to maintain the stock, the product of workers is low because they are poorly equipped. The rule suggests that the optimal position is one in which the rate of growth of population equals the ➤ marginal productivity of capital, or which, in a perfectly competitive economy, equals the rate of profit. An alternative way of expressing the same rule is to say that the rate of saving should equal the rate of profit. The golden rule is limited in its application to a society in which ➤ balanced growth is achieved from an ideal starting point. It does not suggest how growth should proceed in the absence of an optimal starting point or whether balanced growth is itself desirable.

Alternative rules and principles have been developed, notably that of Frank P. Ramsey in 1928 that the ➤ marginal productivity of capital should equal the proportionate decline in the marginal utility of consumption. Other theoreticians have attempted to show that it is sometimes optimal to adopt the maximum or near maximum possible balanced growth path; this allows an economy to move from an unsatisfactory state to a more satisfactory one very quickly even if consumption is lower in the interim than it is at either the starting or finishing point. Known as *turnpike theorems* (turnpike being an American term for motorway), such theorems imply that the quickest route between two states of the economy may not be the shortest in distance terms, as is the case with many motorway journeys. Optimal-growth theory is an area of economics grounded in complicated mathematics, in contrast to the more popular debate about whether growth is desirable at all. ➤➤ economic growth theory.

optimum A position in which the aim of any economic unit is being served as effectively as it possibly can be, within the constraints applying. Where a situation is not optimal, gains in welfare (➤➤ welfare economics) can be made for some without any sacrifice by others. Essential to the meaningful application of the concept of an optimum is the existence of some *objective* (e.g. the maximization of ➤ utility) and some *constraint* on the pursuit of that objective, e.g. a specified set of prices and a given income. While it is possible to have two conflicting objectives (e.g. money and leisure), an optimum can only be attained with respect to both of them if some desired trade-off between them can be expressed; this is roughly equivalent to finding a single criterion by which both can be judged and optimizing with respect to that criterion. Individuals, ➤ trade unions, firms and countries are generally assumed to be rational in economic theory and thus exhibit optimizing behaviour. ➤➤ economic efficiency; linear programming; Lagrange multiplier.

optimum currency area ➤ Mundell, R.

option An agreement with a seller or buyer permitting the holder to buy or sell a financial instrument or ➤ commodity at a given ➤ price within a given period. In the ➤ stock exchange, an option may be purchased from a dealer, giving the right to purchase a certain number of ➤ shares at a certain price within a certain time, e.g. a three-month option. If, in the mean time, the price falls by more than the cost of the option, then the dealer will lose and the purchaser gain, and vice versa. An option to buy is a ➤ *call option*, an option to sell is a *put option*, and one to buy or sell is a *double option*. Trade in option contracts (hence *traded options*) in ➤ securities markets, ➤ money markets and commodity exchanges has expanded enormously in recent years (➤ London International Financial Futures Exchange). There are major options markets in Chicago and other financial centres. ➤➤ Black–Scholes formula; derivatives.

OR ➤ operations research.

ordinal utility A measure of consumer satisfaction expressed in terms of rankings of preferred combinations of commodities rather than through the assignment of values to them of some absolute ➤ utility measure (➤➤ Marshall, A.). Until the beginning of the nineteenth century, economists assumed that individuals had a cardinal measure of utility, with the consumer able to give a mark to each basket of products to reflect the pleasure it generates. It came to be realized, however, that no sensible meaning could be given to statements of the form: 'This apple provides me with twice as much utility as it provides you.' Fortunately, no such scale was necessary for a consumer theory to be derived. All that is required is that consumers list bundles of commodities in order of preference and group bundles between which they have no preference. The difference between the two approaches can be highlighted by contrasting the way in which they show that a rise in the price of a product leads consumers to ➤ demand less of it. The cardinal approach holds that rational consumers will equalize the utility derived from the marginal unit of cash spent on each item. A rise in the price of eggs thus implies that consumers raise the marginal utility they derive from eggs. Given the assumption of ➤ diminishing marginal utility, the only way to effect such an increase is to cut consumption to a point at which eggs are more appreciated than they were and their marginal utility rises. The ordinal approach is only concerned with the *relative* attractiveness of items. It is the ratio of marginal utilities that is important and neither the consumer nor the economist needs to rely on a concept of utilities of some absolute value. In this approach, consumers will ensure that the ratio of prices of items equals the ratio at which the consumer would choose to swap the items with indifference. ➤➤ indifference-curve analysis; marginal rate of substitution; Pareto, V.F.D.; Pigou, A.C.; Slutsky, E.; social welfare function.

ordinary least-squares estimation ➤ least-squares regression.

ordinary share Shares in the ➤ equity capital of a business entitling the holders to all distributed ➤ profits after the holders of ➤ debentures and ➤ preference shares have been paid.

Organisation for Economic Co-operation and Development (OECD) The convention establishing the OECD was signed in Paris by twenty countries in 1961. In 2009, there were thirty member countries, the latest country to join being the Slovak Republic in 2000. The aims of the OECD are: (a) to encourage economic growth and high employment with financial stability among member countries, and (b) to contribute to the economic development of the less advanced member and non-member countries and the expansion of world multilateral trade (➤ multilateralism). The OECD carries out its functions through a number of committees (i.e. the Economic Policy Committee, the Committee for Scientific Research, the Trade Committee and the Development Assistance Committee), serviced by a secretariat. It publishes regular statistical bulletins covering the main economic statistics of member countries and regular reviews of the economic prospects of individual members. It also publishes *ad hoc* reports of special studies covering a wide range of subjects. The OECD has been particularly important as a forum for countries to discuss international monetary problems and in promoting aid and technical assistance to ➤ developing countries. In 2007, an enlargement process began to extend membership to Chile, Estonia, Israel, Russia and Slovenia. ➤ International Energy Agency; International Monetary Fund.

Organization of Petroleum Exporting Countries (OPEC) A group of twelve countries that are major producers and exporters of crude petroleum. The OPEC, set up in 1960, acts as a forum for discussion of, and agreement on, the level at which the member countries should fix the price of their crude petroleum ➤ exports by production quotas. The OPEC also acts as a coordinator for determining the level of aid to ➤ developing countries granted by the members. In 2010, the member countries were Algeria, Angola, Ecuador, Iran, Iraq, Kuwait, Libya, Nigeria, Qatar, Saudi Arabia, the United Arab Emirates and Venezuela. These countries account for about 80 per cent of total world crude oil reserves. ➤➤ international commodity agreements; International Energy Agency.

origin ➤ certificate of origin.

origin principle ➤ value added tax.

OTC ➤ over-the-counter market.

output gap The difference between the actual level of activity in an economy, and the sustainable amount of activity given the capacity of the economy. An output gap is measured as a percentage. It may be negative (equivalent to a ➤ deflationary gap) or it may be positive, implying that the economy was operating unsustainably fast – that it was ➤ overheating (in an ➤ inflationary gap). The output gap is expressed as a percentage of the *level* of ➤ Gross Domestic Product (GDP). Unfortunately, it is not possible to observe potential activity; it is only the actual activity we can record. So, proponents of output-gap analysis typically have to estimate potential output. This is usually extrapolated as follows:

1 Find a year in the past when the economy was neither booming nor in recession. Assume that the output gap then was zero and that, in that year, potential GDP was the same as actual GDP.

2 To derive potential GDP in subsequent years, assume that it grows from the base year by a constant rate. That constant rate is ➤ trend growth. In any sub-

sequent year, actual GDP can then be compared to the extrapolated potential GDP measure, to derive the gap.

Proponents of the output gap make one additional plausible assumption: that when companies operate in excess of their capacity, they attempt to raise their real prices; and when they operate below their capacity, they tend to cut their real prices (➤ real terms). The inflation rate tends to rise when actual output is above potential. It tends to fall when actual output is below potential. The gap is useful in assessing ➤ monetary policy, because it assumes that any increase in ➤ aggregate demand in the economy will generate extra output if actual GDP is below potential, and will generate inflation if actual output exceeds potential. The gap is useful in explaining why an economy can grow fast for several years with falling inflation. If output started well below potential, then even if growth is fast, it might remain below potential and thus inflation should still be coming down. It is also useful in assessing how much a government can reasonably borrow. Borrowing tends to go up or down across the ➤ business cycle (➤ built-in stabilizers). Estimating the output gap can give a clue as to the ➤ structural budget deficit. Estimates of the output gap for all main developed economies are produced by the ➤ Organisation for Economic Co-operation and Development. ➤➤ unemployment, natural rate of.

overfunding ➤ funding.

overheads ➤ fixed costs.

overheating A situation in which ➤ aggregate demand in the economy is growing at a rate likely to lead to ➤ inflation. It refers to a situation in which the ➤ output gap is close to zero, or is positive. ➤➤ recession; stabilization policy.

overseas aid ➤ foreign aid.

overseas banks **1** Banks operating in, say, the UK, but which are incorporated outside the UK and not UK-controlled. There are over 600 overseas banks represented in the UK.
2 Banks from, for example, the UK, that conduct their business mainly abroad. Many of these banks are subsidiaries of the ➤ commercial banks.

overseas investment ➤ foreign investment.

over-subscription Where a new issue of ➤ shares is made and the demand for the shares exceeds the number on offer, the issue is said to be over-subscribed. It is, of course, extremely difficult for the ➤ issuing house to estimate precisely the price at which a share issue will be fully taken up, and new issues are usually either over- or under-subscribed. It is very common for an attractive issue to be ten times or more over-subscribed, especially because of purchases by *stags*, i.e. speculators who subscribe to new issues in the expectation that they will be over-subscribed and that dealings will begin at a ➤ premium. Very often, new issues that start at a premium fall back to below the issue price as a result of ➤ profit-taking by stags.

over-the-counter (OTC) market **1** A group of licensed dealers who provide two-way trading facilities in company ➤ securities outside the ➤ stock exchange. The term originated in the USA in the 1870s when stocks were first purchased across bank counters. Today the OTC in the USA is an elaborate electronic dealing system, with ➤ market makers across the country, called the National Association of Securities Dealers Automated Quotations (NASDAQ) system. ➤➤ unlisted securities markets.

2 More generally, any securities trading activity carried out outside stock exchanges, e.g. OTC ➤ options written by a single seller for a single buyer under a private and confidential arrangement, as distinct from traded options.

overtrading A firm is said to be overtrading when it has insufficient ➤ working capital to meet the needs of its present level of business. For example, a firm that doubled its production, and then found that it could not meet all its current expenditure because too much ➤ capital was tied up in stocks and work in progress, would be overtrading, even though it had correctly forecast the demands for its products. In such circumstances, the firm's ➤ current ratio would probably be less than unity.

overvalued currency ➤ undervalued currency.

ownership ➤ Coase theorem; separation of ownership from control.

P

Paasche index An ➤ index number, compiled by Hermann Paasche (1851–1925), that employs weights (➤ weighted average) derived from current statistics rather than from those of some past period (➤ Laspeyres index). As an example, an annual Paasche price index would calculate the price change (the *price relative*) of each commodity or service included in the index between the current year and a base year, and then derive the weighted average of these *price relatives*, each weight being the amount spent on each commodity in the current year. ➤ index-number problem.

paid-up capital That part of the ➤ issued capital of a company that has been paid up by the shareholders. Except for partly paid ➤ privatization issues, it is rare among shares dealt with on the London ➤ stock exchange for the issued capital not to be paid up, and the phrase is sometimes used loosely as a synonym for issued capital to distinguish it from ➤ authorized capital.

panel data Data that consists of both ➤ time series and cross-section values (➤ cross-section analysis), e.g. a dataset that consists of spending by a large sample of households for several years. ➤➤ econometrics; regression analysis.

paper profit An unrealized ➤ money increase in the ➤ value of an ➤ asset or assets. An individual, for example, will have made a paper profit on his/her house if it is worth more now than when it was bought.

paradox of thrift The phenomenon that if too many people try to increase their saving simultaneously, spending and national income can fall, with the effect that people have less income to save. In the extreme case, the volume of savings could even fall. In principle, under models built around ➤ neo-classical economics, there should be no paradox, as any extra supply of savings should drive down interest rates and encourage extra investment spending, thus keeping national income up. However, under the assumptions of ➤ Keynesian economics, there is little reason to expect investment to grow in response to higher saving.

paradox of value The paradox that certain items that are very valuable to mankind (e.g. water) are very cheap to buy, while other less useful items (e.g. diamonds) are expensive. The supposed paradox is a widely used illustration of some key principles in economics. The reason prices do not reflect our intuitive notion of value is that they are set by conditions of supply as well as demand: water may be very important, but there is an awful lot of it, so it does not have to be highly priced. This is to repeat the conclusion that prices are set by the *marginal* value of an item –

the value of consuming yet more of it – not by the value of consuming it all. If we had to give up all consumption of either diamonds or water, we would clearly choose to give up diamonds.

paradox of voting The paradox (also referred to as 'Condorcet's paradox', after the eighteenth-century French philosopher) that a majority voting system can produce a set of inconsistent social preferences from a set of individually consistent preferences. Suppose electors Anne, Bill and Caroline rank three options – defence, education and social security – as follows:

	Anne	Bill	Caroline
Defence	1	2	3
Education	2	3	1
Social security	3	1	2

When the options, taken in pairs, are voted on, defence beats education, education beats social security, but social security beats defence. In each case, two of the voters rank the winning option higher than its opponent, thus ensuring its victory. As a result, the electors could either never determine which of the three options to put first, or their choice will merely depend on the order in which voting takes place – the social ranking does not possess ➤ transitivity. As transitive preferences are a precondition for the meaningful derivation of ➤ indifference curves, the paradox is one indication that the theory of optimal behaviour for individuals cannot easily be extended to 'democratic' societies. ➤➤ impossibility theorem; social welfare function.

parallel imports ➤ Imports of a product into a country and its sale outside the existing franchised sales network for the product and without the approval of its manufacturer. This occurs when the price at which the product is sold in one country is higher than in another. There is then an opportunity for ➤ arbitrage. This ➤ arbitrage would eventually reduce the differences in prices between countries, unless there were technical, legal or other obstacles to this trade.

parameter The values in a mathematical function that remain constant against movements in the *variables* of the function. For example, in the demand equation $d = aY + bp + c$, d (quantity demanded), Y (disposable income) and p (price) are *variables*, and a, b and c are *parameters* (constants). ➤ beta; ➤➤ regression analysis.

Pareto, Vilfredo Federico Damaso (1848–1923) An Italian born in Paris, Pareto was trained as, and practised as, an engineer. He succeeded his father to a post in the Italian railways, and in 1874 was appointed Superintendent of Mines for the Banca Nazionale, Florence. He succeeded ➤ Walras to the Chair of Economics in the Faculty of Law at Lausanne University in 1892. His publications include *Cours d'économie politique* (1896–7) and *Il Manuale di Economia Politica* (1906). He retired in 1907.

He developed analytical economics from the foundation laid by Walras and pointed out the shortcomings of any theory of ➤ value in so far as it rested upon assumptions of measurable or 'cardinal' rather than ➤ ordinal utility. He demonstrated that an effective theory of consumer behaviour and exchange could be constructed on assumptions of ordinal utility alone. Exchange would take place in a competitive ➤ market between individuals so that the ratios of the ➤ marginal utilities of the goods traded equalled the ratio of their prices. An optimum point of exchange could be defined without the need to compare one individual's total ➤ utility with another's. He defined an increase in total welfare as occurring in those conditions in which some people are better off as a result of the change, without at the same time anybody being worse off (➤ compensation principle). Pareto's work in this field, coupled with the development of ➤ indifference-curve analysis, invented by ➤ Edgeworth, became the foundation upon which modern ➤ welfare economics is based.

A study of the distribution of personal incomes in an economy led him to postulate what became known as *Pareto's law*, i.e. that whatever the political or ➤ taxation conditions, ➤ income will be distributed in the same way in all countries. He noted that the distribution of the number of incomes is concentrated heavily among the lower income groups, and asserted that the number of incomes fell proportionately with the size of income. Pareto's law has not, in fact, proved valid in its strict sense but it has given rise to the realization that a relatively small proportion of a firm's customers generate the most profit and firms have designed their marketing strategy accordingly. ➤➤ economic efficiency; income, distribution of; Slutsky, E.

Pareto-optimal ➤ economic efficiency.

Pareto's law ➤ Pareto, V.F.D.

partial correlation The ➤ correlation between two variables, after having adjusted for any correlation either or both the variables may have with a third variable. For example, observations of the quantity of a commodity sold over a number of years may be highly correlated with consumers' disposable income over the period. A simple correlation between the two would be misleading if, during the same period, there was a substantial fall in price, so that there was also a strong simple correlation between quantity and price. The correlation between income and quantity is calculated, after having deducted the correlation between quantity and price, to obtain the *partial correlation*.

partial-equilibrium analysis The study of the behaviour of ➤ variables that ignores the indirect effects that changes in the variables have on themselves through the impact they have on the rest of the economy. When we study, for example, the market for pet dogs, we do not consider the impact that a change in the number of dogs sold has on the profits of pet-food manufacturers. This and other effects will have an impact on prices, income and taxation and, through these, have a feedback effect on the demand for dogs. The usual partial-equilibrium approach is considered adequate for the study of most markets because such feedback effects are swamped by the direct effects of events in any individual market and are considered negligible. This approach contrasts with ➤ general equilibrium analysis. ➤➤ Marshall, A.

participation rate ➤ labour force.

partnership An unincorporated business formed by the association of two or more persons who share ➤ risks and ➤ profits. Except in a limited partnership, each partner is liable for the ➤ debts and the business actions of the others, to the full extent of their own ➤ resources (although taxed as an individual). Partnerships are a common form of organization in the professions and in businesses in which ➤ capital requirements are relatively small, e.g. retail shops and other service trades. Partnerships, with sole traders (➤ sole proprietorship) (i.e. self-employed persons working on their own), account for about 85 per cent of the total number of businesses. For the tax treatment of partnerships, ➤ corporation tax. The UK Limited Liability Partnership Act 2000 offers ➤ limited liability to members of partnerships in return for similar treatment in disclosure of financial information and other matters.

par value   The ➤ price at which a ➤ share or other ➤ security is issued, i.e. the ➤ face value of the ➤ investment. A share is said to be standing above par if its quoted price on the ➤ stock exchange is greater than that at which the share was issued. The term was also used to describe the official fixed ➤ exchange rate of currencies in terms of gold and US dollars, as declared to the ➤ International Monetary Fund.

patents   A temporary ➤ monopoly conferred on an inventor by government for the exploitation of the product or process. Inventors may use the results of their work exclusively themselves, usually for a period of twenty years, or they may license their use to others for a lump sum or against royalties. For example, a biotechnology company may license the rights to manufacture and distribute a product to a large pharmaceutical firm. By providing inventors with economic rewards safe from others who might simply copy inventions, it is hoped that ➤ research and development (R&D) and invention will be encouraged to the benefit of society at large. In practice, there are many problems: the patenting process, particularly if international protection is to be achieved, is costly, and not all countries observe patent conventions. Not all patents are 'watertight' and in any event the legal costs of recovering damages for the unauthorized use of an invention may be prohibitive, especially for an individual inventor or a ➤ small business. There is also a growing conviction among some economists that patents restrict competition and the diffusion of new products and processes. Patents are a form of *intellectual property rights* analogous to copyrights for the arts but, unlike these, patented ideas must have novelty, not be obvious and have an industrial application. Patent statistics are often used as proxies for the rate of innovative activity (➤ innovation) and can be used, for example, to analyse the results of R&D by ➤ multinational corporations.

pay-as-you-earn (PAYE)   System of collecting ➤ income tax in the UK through regular deduction by the employer from employees' weekly or monthly earnings. Confidentiality of the taxpayer's private circumstances is preserved through the use of code numbers which, in conjunction with tax tables, enable the employer to calculate the amount of tax to be deducted. The system was introduced in 1944 and had been recommended by ➤ Keynes. It is thought to be a stabilizing factor in the economy, since the tax yield automatically varies directly and rapidly with ➤ income and employment, whereby the government tends to spend proportionately more tax yield in recession (➤ depression) and less in time of high demand and employment. ➤➤ built-in stabilizers.

pay-as-you-go ➤ pension funds.

pay-back The period over which the cumulative net revenue from an ➤ investment project equals the original investment. It is a commonly used but crude method for analysing ➤ capital projects. Its main defects are that it takes no account of the ➤ profits over the whole life of the investment, nor of the time profile of the ➤ cash flow. ➤➤ investment appraisal.

PAYE ➤ pay-as-you-earn.

payment in kind Payment in goods or services instead of money. ➤➤ fringe benefits.

payments, balance of ➤ balance of payments.

payroll tax A ➤ tax levied on employers' wage bills. It is now regarded by many economists in developed economies as a means of encouraging capital intensiveness (➤ capital-intensive) at the expense of employment. This type of tax as such is not used in the UK, although ➤ National Insurance contributions are a form of payroll tax. A flat-rate employment tax (*selective employment tax*) was introduced in 1966 and abolished in 1973 on the introduction of ➤ value added tax.

peak pricing The setting of higher prices than average when supplying services during a period of peak demand. For example, enough electricity capacity must be installed to satisfy demand at peak times because electricity cannot be stored. At off-peak times the cost of electricity is lower at the margin than at the peak times at which less efficient power stations have to be switched in to meet the demand. ➤ marginal-cost pricing.

peg ➤ exchange rate.

pendular arbitration ➤ arbitration.

pension funds Sums of money laid aside and normally invested to provide a regular ➤ income on retirement, or in compensation for disablement, for the remainder of a person's life. Nearly all developed countries have state pension schemes. Unlike state schemes – which operate on a pay-as-you-go basis with contributions from those in employment paying for the pensions of the retired – private pension schemes, for which contributions attract favourable tax treatment, are usually *funded*, i.e. placed in managed invested funds.

Occupational pension schemes may be contributory or non-contributory by the employee; the benefits of private schemes may be related to the length of service of the employee and the level of salary or contributions, i.e. they are *defined pension benefits* of, for example, 50 per cent of final salary. In *defined pension contribution* schemes, employers and/or employees pay regular contributions, but the pension finally paid is determined by the performance of the fund in which contributions are invested. On maturity, these funds may be (in the UK where tax relief is given, *must* be) used to purchase an ➤ annuity. Pension funds allocate most of their investments to ➤ ordinary shares and ➤ bonds with a small proportion in property and other assets. In recent years, in the face of tighter regulatory requirements, increasing life spans and market volatility, pension funds in the UK and the USA and indeed everywhere have been phasing out defined benefit schemes. ➤ personal pension.

per capita income Income per head, normally defined as the ➤ national income divided by the total population. ➤ purchasing-power parity; real exchange rate.

percentile The xth percentile is that value of a distribution of numbers below which are x per cent of the number of observations. For example, the 50th percentile is the value below which there are 50 per cent of the observations (this is called the *median*) (➤ average). The *quartiles* are at 25 per cent and 75 per cent. Similarly, *deciles* subdivide the distribution into 10ths.

perfect competition A model of industrial structure in which many small firms compete in the supply of a single product. Three primary features characterize a perfectly competitive industry: (a) there is a multitude of firms (buyers as well as sellers) that are all too small to have any individual impact on market price, resulting in ➤ marginal revenue and ➤ price being equal; (b) all firms aim to maximize ➤ profit; and (c) firms can without incurring prohibitive costs enter and exit the industry. Also, it is assumed that the outputs traded are homogeneous.

Perfect competition is economically efficient in three ways (➤➤ economic efficiency):

(1) In the ➤ short run, profit maximization ensures that each firm will set its output so that its ➤ marginal cost is equal to its ➤ marginal revenue (➤ firm, theory of the). To produce when marginal costs exceed marginal revenue implies that cutting back production would save more than the revenue lost, and to produce when marginal revenue exceeds marginal costs implies that expanding production would increase revenue more than costs. Thus, marginal revenue will equal marginal cost. Moreover, under the price-taking assumption, the effect is that marginal cost equals price. This is efficient for the allocation of resources because it ensures that no consumer will be deterred from buying something which he/she values more than it cost to make.

(2) In the long run, freer entry and exit ensures new entrants will be attracted into any industry in which high profits are made. The effect of these new entrants is to increase supply and bid down price until no profit is made (apart from a normal entrepreneurial return), i.e. when average revenue equals average cost. The zero profit result means that no entrepreneur or factor of production earns more than it needs to be persuaded into an industry.

(3) Again, in the long run, as average revenue equals marginal cost (from the profit maximization assumption) and average revenue equals average cost (from the free entry and exit assumption), we can deduce that average cost equals marginal cost. The only point on the average cost curve for which this is true is at the bottom of it, i.e. at the lowest cost point. Finally, therefore, perfect competition ensures minimum-cost production.

Although the features of perfect competition make it look a poor description of modern industry, it is a realistic description of world commodity markets where many traders deal in a homogeneous product. Moreover, its very powerful results indicate that the achievement of even a partially competitive market can be advantageous. Thus, the simple perfect competition model provides a good starting point for illuminating the forces underlying the real behaviour of firms. ➤➤ contestability; imperfect market; marginal-cost pricing; monopoly.

permanent-income hypothesis The theory proposed by ➤ Friedman that suggests that, however variable their income, consumers will attempt to smooth out the pattern of their consumption (➤ consumption function). If, for example, someone's income varies between zero and $20,000 a year, averaging $10,000, they will spend at a constant rate equivalent to a constant $10,000. Given that the ➤ marginal utility of money declines with the increasing amounts of spending, it is sensible to transfer spending from bountiful times to those when one is poor. By saving in some periods and 'dissaving' in others, this can be achieved. The theory has several implications.

1 If one has a permanent increase in income, the ➤ marginal propensity to consume out of it will equal the ➤ average propensity to consume.

2 A large increase in short-run ➤ incomes will not lead to corresponding increases in consumption. Any extra pound a consumer gets will be treated not as a cause for a quick spending spree but as a temporary bonus that should raise lifetime consumption by the value of the pound spread over a lifetime.

3 This explains why high-income households save more than low-income households: the high-income group is likely to contain the very people who are enjoying transient high incomes that they are thus storing away for the day when their income drops.

➤ consumption smoothing.

perpetual preferences shares ➤ preference shares.

personal disposable income ➤ disposable income.

personal loan A ➤ bank loan made without ➤ collateral security to a private customer for specific purposes.

personal pension 1 A regular income after a certain age and usually after retirement from work, provided by a state or private scheme. There are two broad types of private pension schemes which exist in most countries: occupational and defined benefit (➤ pension funds).
  2 A private pension scheme of the personal ➤ annuity kind. Under these schemes, individuals pay contributions into a fund managed by an ➤ insurance company or other ➤ institutional investor, which provides a cash lump sum at retirement age, part of which, if it is to qualify for tax relief on the premiums, must be used to purchase an annuity.
  Up to stated limits, UK pension contributions by individuals and employers qualify for ➤ income tax and ➤ corporation tax relief. Pension schemes may be *funded* – a capital-reserve system, in which contributions are paid into a fund that is invested in ➤ securities and other ➤ assets and from which pensions are ultimately paid – or *unfunded*, where pensions for retirees are paid out of the contributions of those in work (pay-as-you-go system). Because of extended life spans, pension schemes are being modified in most countries, principally by changes to retirement ages but also by the withdrawal of private sector defined benefit pension schemes (➤ pension funds).

personal sector Households and individuals. In the national accounts this sector includes unincorporated businesses. ➤➤ private sector.

Petty, Sir William (1623–87) The pioneer of numerical economics. His main interest lay in public finance, and he made important contributions to monetary theory and ➤ fiscal policy. His approach to these subjects contributed to the development of ➤ classical economics and from his work in the field of comparative data has emerged the modern field of economic statistics. His best-known work is *Political Arithmetic* (1690). The so-called Petty's law was a remarkably far-sighted statement of the tendency for the proportion of the working population engaged in ➤ services to increase as an economy develops.

Petty's law ➤ Petty, Sir W.

PFI ➤ private finance initiative.

Phillips, Alban William Housego (1914–75) After a number of jobs in electrical engineering, and after serving in the Royal Air Force during the Second World War, Phillips began lecturing in economics at the London School of Economics in 1950. From 1958 until 1967, he was Tooke Professor of Economics, Science and Statistics at the University of London. In 1968 he accepted the Chair of Economics at the Australian National University. Professor Phillips published many articles exploring the relationships between the ➤ multiplier and accelerator in mathematical ➤ models (➤➤ accelerator–multiplier model) with various time lags, and applied the engineering technique of closed-loop control systems to the analysis of ➤ macroeconomic relationships.

In 'The Relation between Unemployment and the Rate of Change of Money Wage Rates in the United Kingdom, 1861–1957' (*Economica*, 1958), Phillips set out empirical evidence to support the view that there was a significant relation between the percentage change of money wages and the level of ➤ unemployment – the lower the unemployment, the higher the rate of change of wages. This relationship, which became known as the *Phillips curve*, has attracted considerable theoretical and empirical analysis. Its main implication is that, since a particular level of unemployment in the economy will imply a particular rate of wage increase, the aims of low unemployment and a low rate of ➤ inflation may be inconsistent. The government must then choose between the feasible combinations of unemployment and inflation, as shown by the estimated Phillips curve, e.g. 3 per cent unemployment and no inflation, or 1.5 per cent unemployment and 8 per cent inflation, etc. Alternatively, it may attempt to bring about basic changes in the workings of the economy, e.g. a ➤ prices and incomes policy, in order to reduce the rate of inflation consistent with low unemployment. However, the relation between unemployment and inflation has not been sufficiently stable in practice to permit exact judgements to be made.

Phillips curve ➤ Phillips, A.W.H.

physical controls Direct controls on production and ➤ consumption, licensing of buildings or ➤ imports, and the rationing of goods are examples of physical controls. These controls are alternatives to the use of monetary or fiscal measures (➤ fiscal policy), that control production and consumption through the price mechanism (➤ price system). ➤➤ quotas.

Physiocrats A group of eighteenth-century French economists, led by ➤ Quesnay, who later became known as the Physiocrats or '*les Économistes*'. They believed in the existence of a natural order and regarded the state's role as simply that of preserving property and upholding the natural order. They held that agriculture was the sole source of ➤ wealth and therefore this sector only should be taxed by *l'impôt unique*. In this, and in their advocacy of free trade, their views were directly opposed to those of the mercantilists (➤ mercantilism). In their belief in ➤ *laissez-faire*, they had much in common with, and certainly influenced, British ➤ classical economics, and especially ➤ Smith. Quesnay's *Tableau économique* (1758) has in it the origins of modern ideas on the circulation of wealth and the nature of interrelationships in the economy. ➤➤ Cantillon, R.; Leontief, W.W.; Mill, J.S.

Pigou, Arthur Cecil (1877–1959) A pupil of ➤ Marshall, whom he succeeded to the Chair of Political Economy at Cambridge University in 1908 until he retired in 1944. His major publications include *Principles and Methods of Industrial Peace* (1905), *Wealth and Welfare* (1912), *Unemployment* (1914), *The Economics of Welfare* (1920), *Essays in Applied Economics* (1923), *Industrial Fluctuations* (1927), *The Theory of Unemployment* (1933) and *Employment and Equilibrium* (1941).

His work on monetary theory, employment and the ➤ national income, which was in the tradition of the ➤ Classical School, led him into controversy with ➤ Keynes. He was the first to enunciate clearly the concept of the real balance effect, which as a consequence became known as the *Pigou effect*. The Pigou effect is a stimulation of employment brought about by the rise in the real value of ➤ liquid balances as a consequence of a decline in prices – as the real ➤ value of ➤ wealth increases, so ➤ consumption will rise, thus increasing income and employment. This was one of the processes by which the classical ➤ model envisaged that full-employment ➤ equilibrium could be obtained as a result of a reduction in real wages.

Although his work on ➤ macroeconomics was partly superseded by Keynes, Pigou made a lasting contribution with his original work in ➤ welfare economics. He resisted strongly the belief that practical policies based on propositions from welfare economics were impossible because interpersonal comparisons of ➤ utility cannot be made. He argued that, though this may be true for individuals, it was possible to make meaningful comparisons between groups. His distinction between private and social product now plays an important role in the formation of government economic policy in the field of ➤ public expenditure.

Pigou effect ➤ Pigou, A.C.

placing The sale of a new issue of ➤ shares or ➤ stock (➤ new-issue market), usually to ➤ institutional investors, by a financial intermediary (e.g. a firm of stockbrokers) acting on behalf of the company issuing the shares. This method of 'private placing' of shares minimizes the cost of a new issue, since it does not involve the advertising and other costs associated with an offer for sale or subscription. For shares that are to be quoted on the ➤ stock exchange there are limitations on the total market ➤ capitalization of shares that can be issued by this method.

planned economy An economy in which state authorities rather than market forces directly determine prices, output and production. Although planned economies can take a variety of forms, their most important features usually include: (a) production targets for different sectors of the economy that determine the ➤ supply of different commodities; (b) rationing of certain commodities to determine ➤ demand for them; (c) price- and wage-fixing by state bodies; and (d) sometimes, a conscripted ➤ labour market in which workers take jobs assigned to them.

When all or nearly all economic activity is governed by the state, two advantages can prevail: (a) the external costs and benefits of all activities that are not reflected in prices and are ignored by the market economy can be taken into account by the authorities (➤ externalities), and (b) a distribution of income (➤ income distribution) nearer to many people's view of that which is just can be achieved. There are, however, disadvantages of planning: (a) the practical problem of setting optimal prices in all markets (➤➤ price system) – too often, the authorities set excessively low prices, resulting in queues which ration goods to the earliest in line; (b) the lack of worker and management motivation that attends a system in which earnings are not performance-related and ➤ profits not retained by the companies making them; and (c) when wages and prices differ from their market levels, substantial control of individual activities is required. ➤➤ free-market economy; state planning; transition, economies in.

ploughing back ➤ self-financing.

point elasticity ➤ elasticity.

poison pill A damaging action (e.g. sales of ➤ assets) which a company threatens to inflict on itself in the event of ➤ takeover by another firm. A poison pill serves to deter other firms from attempting an acquisition in the first place, because to do so would immediately lower the value of the company they are attempting to buy. ➤ merger.

policy ineffectiveness theorem The idea that if there are flexible prices and wages, and if the public hold ➤ rational expectations, then any government policies to stimulate ➤ aggregate demand can have no real effect on output or employment unless the policy measures are unanticipated by the public. Increasing demand only generates extra ➤ inflation. The theorem is the basis of ➤ new classical economics and can be thought of as positing that money is neutral in its effects (➤ neutrality of money) *when a change in money supply is anticipated*. Academic economists are divided on whether monetary and fiscal policies are ineffective, or have some effect in the short or long term. Economists are almost unanimous in believing that *unanticipated* injections of demand can increase output and employment in at least the short term. ➤➤ economic doctrines; new Keynesianism.

political economy ➤ economics.

poll tax ➤ local taxation.

polluter-pays principle The idea that polluting emissions should be taxed in order that those who create them bear the costs of their actions. The principle of allowing pollution to occur, but taxing it, derives from ➤ Pigou in 1932. It is an approach that contrasts with banning pollution outright or allowing it within certain limits. The advantage of taxing it is that if the tax rate covers the damage or suffering caused by the pollution, it will pay firms to pollute only if the benefits of them so doing outweigh the costs. The tax will also generate revenue that can be used to compensate those who suffer most. An example of a pollution tax would be a tax on the carbon content of fossil fuels to offset the atmospheric warming effect of the carbon dioxide they produce – a carbon tax. While, under perfect information, pollution taxes can produce ➤ economic efficiency, it may be difficult to set the tax level correctly, and the cost of making mistakes – of allowing too much pollution, for example – may be very high.

Ponzi scheme An investment swindle in which the perpetrator pockets the investment and pays interest or profits out of new money flowing into the scheme. The name comes from a 1920s scandal in the USA involving Charles Ponzi. In 2009, Bernard Madoff, a US stockbroker, was brought to trial and found guilty of carrying out a similar scheme, probably the largest fraud of its type in history.

pooled equilibrium ➤ Stiglitz, J.

population 1 In statistics, a term applied to any class of data of which counts are made or samples taken, e.g. a car population.

2 The number of people living in any specified geographical area, e.g. New York or India or the world. The study of the characteristics of human populations is called *demography*. The United Nations (UN) estimated that the total world population in 2010 was 6.9 billion. Although the rate of growth is falling, the UN expects that world population will reach 9.1 billion by 2050. The fall in the rate of growth is a reflection of the combined effect of a drop in *fertility rates* (➤ birth rate) and the rise in life expectancy (➤ death rate). The population of today's ➤ less developed countries will increase from 5.7 billion (82 per cent of the total) in 2010 to 7.9 billion (86 per cent of the total) in 2050. The population of the more developed countries will peak in 2035 at 1.3 billion. The UN expects the population of Europe to peak at 734 million in 2015 and then fall to 691 million in 2050. In contrast, the population of the USA will grow from 318 million in 2010 to 403 million in 2050. The population of China will peak in 2030 at 1.5 billion and thereafter decline to 1.4 billion in 2050. The population of India will grow from 1.2 billion in 2010, overtaking that of China in 2030 to reach 1.6 billion in 2050.

The increase in world population not only raises the issue of the ability of agriculture and fisheries to continue to meet the demand for food (➤ Malthus, T.R.) but also highlights the effect of increasing pressure on other resources, e.g. water and the environment. Further, the change in the age structure of population has important implications for economic growth with the increase in the ➤ dependency ratio and the relative decline in the ➤ labour force. ➤ demographic time bomb; dependency ratio; migration; population, census of.

population, census of A direct count of the number of inhabitants in a country. It is not possible to obtain information accurately by other means. Calculations based on births, deaths and migration are not sufficiently accurate, except as a means of interpolation between censuses. Recognizing the importance of census data, the United Nations Economic and Social Council in 2005 adopted the 2010 World Population and Housing Census Programme to encourage and give technical assistance to countries for census enumeration. The United Nations reported that by early 2010 censuses of population had been completed or were scheduled in 222 countries and 21 per cent of world ➤ population had been enumerated.

portfolio The collection of ➤ securities held by an investor.

portfolio theory A branch of financial economics that analyses the most efficient amounts of different assets an investor should hold. Underlying portfolio theory is the assumption that investors like high returns and dislike risk (➤➤ risk aversion). Risk represents a likelihood of the actual return on an asset deviating from the expected return. In general, therefore, investors will have to expect a higher return from a risky asset than a safe one in order to be persuaded to hold it, although, of course, a risky asset may actually deliver a return either higher or lower than it was expected to yield in advance.

An *efficient* ➤ portfolio is one that delivers the highest expected possible return for a given amount of risk, or the smallest possible risk for a given expected return. In general, by holding a variety of assets, the risk of a portfolio can be reduced, because when one asset happens to perform badly, it may be that others will be doing well. Thus, ➤ diversification does pay, and this explains the popularity of ➤ unit trusts. However, diversification can succeed in reducing risk only if the performances of the assets in a portfolio do not coincide: in so far as the assets' returns move together (because, for example, they are all affected by the state of the national economy) there will always be some systematic risk remaining that cannot be diversified away. It is the development of these basic principles that is the concern of portfolio theory. ➤➤ capital asset pricing model.

positional goods Goods that are necessarily scarce and the scarcity of which cannot be reduced by increased productivity. They were described by Fred Hirsch in his book *Social Limits to Growth* (1977). He distinguished those positional goods, the value of which derives from their intrinsic usefulness but which are limited in their supply, e.g. holiday homes in beautiful places, and those not yielding pleasure from their absolute qualities but from their scarcity, e.g. original paintings by famous artists. Allocation of these goods is a ➤ zero-sum game. They can explain why we still have high levels of material frustration even as our affluence grows.

positive economics The study of economic propositions that can, at least in principle, be verified by observation of events or states of the real world, i.e. without reference to ➤ value judgements. Broadly, positive economics is descriptive and can either consist of statements like 'unemployment is very high' or conditional statements like 'if the economy is reflated, unemployment will fall'. Prescriptive statements, in contrast, like 'unemployment *ought* to be cut', fall into the sphere of ➤ normative economics. In practice, the distinction between the two is not a sharp one, because those who make what sound like prescriptive statements may reasonably claim that, in fact, they are implicitly making conditional statements, e.g. 'unemployment ought to be cut if overall welfare is to be enhanced'. This has the form of a descriptive statement but is no more devoid of opinion than the first clause taken alone.

poverty Poverty can either be defined by some *absolute* measure (income below some specified minimum level) or in *relative* terms, e.g. the number of the poorest 10 per cent of households or a mix of the two methods. Poverty may be measured by the ability of a person to satisfy his or her basic subsistence need for food, clothing and housing but may also take into account a person's perception of poverty because of awareness of the average standard of living of the society in which he or she lives. The US Bureau of the Census defined the *poverty line* as $11,201 for a single-person household and as $21,834 for a four-person household with two children in 2008. A World Development Report in 1990 of the ➤ World Bank Group surveyed measures used in a number of countries, such as India, which defined a person as being in poverty if eating less than 2250 calories per day, and converted them into an average level equivalent to $1 per day. The rate has been subsequently revised and updated and in 2005 was set at $1.25 per day at 2005 prices. At this level there were 1.4 billion people in poverty, or 25 per cent of the population, in the ➤ developing countries, compared with 1.9 billion or 50 per cent in 1981. ➤ inequality; minimum wage; Sen, A.; social security.

poverty line ➤ poverty.

poverty trap The combination of losing state benefit entitlement and paying tax that can ensure that poor families keep very little of any extra money they earn. Under any social security system using ➤ means tests, as the poor earn more, they lose state benefits. For example, a poor family may lose 60 cents of benefit for every extra $1 it earns, and it may also pay 20 cents in tax on that dollar. In this case, the family benefits by only 20 cents of the extra dollar. Apart from the inefficiency of suppressing the incentive for people in the poverty trap to work, concern exists over the debilitating psychological effects of removing individuals' power to alter their own living standards. ➤➤ income, distribution of; marginal tax rate; poverty; social security; unemployment trap.

precautionary motive The factor that causes individuals or firms to hold a stock of ➤ money to finance unforeseen expenditures. It is one of the three motives for holding money outlined by ➤ Keynes.

1 A firm may know what its average pay-outs are each month but, if these payments fluctuate, given that there are costs to being short of the cash necessary to finance them, firms will keep money in excess of what they need for the average month. The amount they keep will first depend on the ➤ interest rate. This represents the cost of keeping money that would earn a return if it was invested.
2 It will depend on the probability of overshooting the foreseeable expenditures – the higher the probability the more money firms will hold.
3 It will depend on the size of the firm's average spending – a big firm will keep more than a small firm.
4 It will depend on the cost of not having cash to meet unforeseen pay-outs – the higher the cost, the more precautions a firm will take.

➤➤ liquidity preference; speculative motive; transactions demand for money.

precautionary principle The precautionary principle may be invoked by countries for the protection of the environment and human, animal and plant health. It was first established as an acceptable argument by the United Nations Charter for Nature in 1982 and has subsequently been incorporated in other international agreements, for example as by the ➤ World Trade Organization (WTO). The European Commission (➤ European Union) has set out guidelines for the appropriate procedures to be carried out based on the precautionary principle. The WTO accepts that each member country has the right to impose restrictions to protect the environment and health from perceived threats as it sees fit. The precautionary principle may be employed where the scientific evidence of a threat is sufficient to give concern, although with significant uncertainty, and any restrictions should be non-discriminatory. Arguments for the imposition of restrictions based on the precautionary principle should be sufficiently robust to avoid the charge of using the precautionary principle as a concealed means of trade ➤ protection. ➤ risk assessment.

predatory pricing Setting ➤ prices at very low levels with the objective of weakening or eliminating competitors or to keep out new entrants to a ➤ market. Since prices will be raised again once these objectives have been achieved there is no permanent benefit to the consumer. Predatory pricing is a means of establishing or maintaining ➤ monopoly power.

preference shares Holders of preference shares precede the holders of ➤ ordinary shares, but follow ➤ bond holders, in the payment of ➤ dividends and in the return of ➤ capital if the issuing company is liquidated (➤ liquidation). Preference shares normally entitle the holder only to a fixed rate of dividend, but participating preference shares also entitle the holder to a share of residual ➤ profits. Preference shares carry limited voting rights and they may be redeemable or not (➤ redeemable securities); when irredeemable they are known as *perpetual preference shares*.

Cumulative preference shares carry forward the right to preferential dividends, if unpaid, from one year to the next. From the investor's point of view, preference shares lie between ➤ bonds and ordinary shares in terms of ➤ risk and ➤ income, while to the issuing company they permit some flexibility in distribution policy at a lower cost than bonds. Preference shares now account for a very small proportion of issues (➤ new-issue market), but are frequently used in the provision of ➤ risk capital.

preferential duty ➤ tariffs, import.

premium 1 The difference, where positive, between the current ➤ price or ➤ value of a ➤ security, or ➤ currency, and its issue price or ➤ par value.
2 A regular payment made in return for an ➤ insurance policy.

prepayments Payments for services (e.g. rent and rates) made in one accounting period for consumption wholly or partly in a following period and written into the balance sheet as a current ➤ asset.

present value The discounted value of a financial sum arising at some future period. For example, if the *discount rate* is 10 per cent per annum, the present value this year of $110 earned next year is $100. $100 this year is equivalent to $110 next year because $100 invested at the going ➤ rate of interest of 10 per cent yields $110 in one year. If there are financial flows over a number of years, the discounted sums are additive. For example, if $110 were earned in each of two years, the present value would be: $110 earned in year 2, discounted to year 1 = $110/1.10; this sum is then to be discounted, again, to the base year = $110/(1.10 × 1.10) = $110/(1.10^2). Finally, to this sum must be added the discounted value of the sum earned in year 1, i.e. $110/1.10. The present value, therefore, is $110/(1.10^2) + $110/1.10. In general:

$$\text{present value (PV)} = \frac{X_1}{(1+r)} + \frac{X_2}{(1+r)^2} + \frac{X_3}{(1+r)^3} + \cdots \frac{X_n}{(1+r)^n}$$

where X^n is the financial flow in year n, and r is the rate of interest (discount rate). The *net* present value is the difference between the present value of a future flow of profits arising from a project and the capital cost of the project. ➤➤ investment appraisal.

price What must be given in exchange for something. Prices are expressed usually in terms of a quantity of ➤ money per unit of a ➤ commodity (a good or service) but in ➤ barter the price of a good is what another good or other goods it can be exchanged for. Price changes are the means by which the competitive process determines the allocation of resources in the ➤ free-market economy. ➤➤ price system; price theory; shadow price.

price discrimination The selling of the same commodity to different buyers at different prices. Several conditions must prevail for it to be profitable: (a) there must be a separation between markets that does not allow buyers in one to resell the item in another (no ➤ arbitrage must be possible); (b) the seller must possess some degree of monopoly power (➤ monopoly) in at least one market for, under competitive conditions, prices will be driven down to the level of costs in all markets; and (c) buyers in different markets must have a different level and elasticity of demand for the good.

The monopolist who discriminates will set output for each market where ➤ marginal cost is equal to the ➤ marginal revenue in that market. Sales will be at a higher price in markets where elasticity is generally low than where it is high. The monopolist, in effect, takes advantage of the fact that in one market consumers are prepared to pay more for his/her item than in the other, without losing sales in the other market.

In *perfect price discrimination* the monopolist charges a different price to every individual consumer and effectively has a sales revenue equivalent to the area under the ➤ demand curve for the product. ➤➤ anti-trust.

price–earnings ratio (P/E ratio) The quoted price of an ➤ ordinary share divided by the most recent year's ➤ earnings per share. The P/E ratio is thus the reciprocal of the earnings ➤ yield and a measure of the price that has to be paid for a given income from an ➤ equity share. A company whose 25-cent ordinary shares were quoted at $1 on the ➤ stock exchange and which, in the previous year, had earnings of 10 cents per share, would have a P/E ratio of 10 to 1, i.e. the price of every cent in earnings would be 10 cents, or the earnings yield would be 10 per cent. The price of earnings will vary with the stock market's assessment of the growth potential involved. Thus, a company with good growth prospects might have a P/E of 15/1 or more, but a company with a poor record might have a P/E ratio of considerably less than that.

price elasticity of demand ➤ elasticity.

price elasticity of supply ➤ elasticity.

price index ➤ index number.

price level, average A term used in ➤ macroeconomics to refer to a base from which changes in the exchange value of ➤ money can be measured (➤ index number). It is a useful concept, but not literally calculable: an ➤ average of the unit ➤ prices of all goods and services on offer in the economy would, in itself, be a meaningless number.

price mechanism ➤ price system.

price regulation A form of regulation in which the prices of the supplier are not allowed to rise above a certain level. The regulation is designed to prevent the abuse of a ➤ monopoly position. In the UK, price regulation has applied to telephone, gas, electricity and water providers. In each case the design has shared certain common features: (a) allowed price rises are set out for a few years in advance, typically four or five; (b) there is a *review* at the end of each period, at which the regime governing the next period is decided; and (c) allowed price rises are specified relative to the ➤ retail prices index (RPI), and might, for example, be RPI minus 4.5 per cent each year (this protects the regulated firm against ➤ inflation).

Under price regulation, if firms can keep their costs low they can earn big profits. This gives them an incentive to be efficient that does not exist under ➤ rate-of-return regulation. But it has been suggested that, in each periodic review, the regulator looks at the rate of return to decide what new price formula should be applied, thus reducing the difference between the two types of scheme. ➤➤ Averch–Johnson effect; monopoly; natural monopoly; regulation.

prices and incomes policy A policy of restraining price or wage increases by regulated limits on the increases that are allowed. In most developed countries, it was used in some form or another to counter the problem of ➤ stagflation that emerged in the 1970s. Sometimes it was used in conjunction with price controls.

In the UK, an incomes policy was in force for almost the whole period 1965–79. For the first few years it was legally enforced, but later pay increases were limited by voluntary agreement of the unions. By the 1980s, prices and incomes controls were abandoned in favour of ➤ free markets.

Limiting wage increases is seen as a means of reducing the problem of ➤ inflation associated with a given level of ➤ unemployment. The difficulty faced by those trying to implement incomes policy is that it distorts the market for labour. Pressure for pay rises can also build up at the end of a period of controls. The long-term effectiveness of limiting increases in the prices of goods in the shops is to be doubted. The problem with price freezes is that of empty shelves, as illustrated in the price freeze in Zimbabwe in 2007. Either producers reduce the goods they sell or consumers buy up everything available as the prices of things no longer adequately ration the supply. ➤➤ indexation; repressed inflation.

price schedule ➤ cost schedule.

price support A system of agricultural support by which market prices are fixed at above ➤ free-market levels and the government buys unsold surpluses, thus supporting the price and raising farmers' incomes. ➤ farm subsidies.

price system The mechanism that sends prices up when ➤ demand is in excess and prices down when ➤ supply is in excess (➤ resource allocation). The mechanism referred to is not some coordinated control from a central authority but relies on the disparate decisions made by independent agents; it is the mechanism that makes a butcher reduce the price of a leg of lamb he/she is unable to sell, or an ice-cream salesperson raise the price of cornets on a hot day. It is usually assumed that one price eventually settles in each market until some disturbance in costs or demand occurs (➤ equilibrium). The importance of the price system is: (a) that it serves as a means of rationing limited supplies among consumers, and (b) that it signals to producers where money is to be made and thus what they ought to be producing. ➤➤ comparative static equilibrium analysis; economic efficiency.

price theory The area of economics concerned with the determination of prices in individual markets. It is an area of ➤ microeconomics and is not directly connected to the study of ➤ inflation. The two components of price theory are the ➤ demand side and the ➤ supply side; it is the interaction of the two that determines ➤ equilibrium output and price in any market. On the demand side, the theory of demand (➤➤ demand, theory of) explains consumer behaviour in terms of rational agents maximizing ➤ utility. On the supply side, various alternative market structures are investigated: ➤ perfect competition, ➤ monopolistic competition, ➤ oligopoly and ➤ monopoly. There are also alternative theories, of the behaviour of firms, that do not assume that profit maximization is the sole goal of producers (➤ behavioural theory of the firm). ➤➤ firm, theory of the; Marshall, A.; resource allocation.

pricing policy The method used by firms for determining their prices. In this area, there appears to be a discrepancy between the suggestions of theory and the observed practice of firms:

1   In theory, firms in ➤ perfect competition take the market price as given – which will equal the marginal cost of production – without being able to influence that price. A ➤ monopoly or any firm in ➤ monopolistic competition first determines its output and only then sets a price at the level that just sells the output chosen.

2   In practice, firms appear to use 'rules of thumb' rather than accurate assessments of ➤ marginal revenue and costs. ➤ Cost-plus pricing, for example, involves charging the average cost of producing an item, plus a profit margin, the size of which is loosely determined by market conditions.

Much debate on pricing policy has surrounded the appropriate policy for ➤ nationalized industries, in particular whether they should attempt to emulate the ➤ marginal-cost pricing of perfect competition (➤➤ Hotelling, H.; menu costs; peak pricing).

primary market ➤ new-issue market.

prime costs Strictly, ➤ variable costs plus administrative and other ➤ fixed costs that can be avoided in the short or long term if there is no output, even while the firm remains in business. Often used loosely as a synonym for variable costs.

prime rate The ➤ rate of interest charged by ➤ commercial banks to first-class-risk corporate borrowers for short-term ➤ loans in the USA. Other borrowers pay more. The prime rate is normally about three percentage points over the Fed Funds Target Rate which is reviewed every six weeks by the FOMC (➤ Federal Reserve System). The prime rate is the rate at which commercial banks lend to each other or pay the Fed for overnight loans. The prime rate is the result of a survey of the ten largest banks: it is published in the *Wall Street Journal* and changes when the Fed Funds Target Rate changes.

principal–agent problem The problem that arises in many spheres of economic activity, when one person (the principal) hires an agent to perform tasks on his/her behalf but cannot ensure that the agent performs them in exactly the way the principal would like. The efforts of the agent are impossible or expensive to monitor and the incentives of the agent differ from those of the principal. The problem does not arise if an enforceable ➤ contract can be drawn up to specify all the duties of the agent (➤ incomplete contract). Examples of the problem include: (a) the management of assets on behalf of investors; (b) the management of companies on behalf of shareholders by executives; and (c) the running of public services by private firms under ➤ regulation by government authorities. The principal–agent relationship is characterized by ➤ asymmetric information. ➤ information, economics of; ➤➤ mechanism design; moral hazard.

prior charges ➤ Bond and ➤ preference shareholders have a prior claim over ➤ ordinary shareholders to ➤ profits or ➤ capital repayments. The amount of these claims is known as 'prior charges on the company'.

prisoner's dilemma A situation in which it pays each of several economic agents individually to behave in a particular way, even though it would pay them as a group to behave in some other way. The prisoner's dilemma is a classic and fundamental concept in ➤ game theory. It is best exemplified by the story from which it derives its name: a sheriff picks up two suspected criminals and puts them in separate cells. He gives each the chance to confess to having committed the crime with the other, and tells them that their fate would be as follows:

(1) If you don't confess and your partner doesn't confess, you will get three years in jail.
(2) If you confess and your partner confesses, you will get four years in jail.
(3) If your partner confesses and you don't, you will get twelve years in jail.
(4) If your partner doesn't confess and you do, you will get two years in jail.

		Criminal B	
		Confess	Don't confess
Criminal A	*Confess*	4,4	2,12
	Don't confess	12,2	3,3

These results are summarized in the table, where the left-hand number in each pair is criminal A's sentence, and the right-hand number is criminal B's. Given these four choices, the optimal one is for them not to confess and get three years each. However, if they each believed the other was to behave in this way, it would pay them to confess in the hope of getting two years. Indeed, scrutiny of the choices shows that if someone believes their partner is going to confess, they ought to confess also (avoiding the twelve years), and if that person believes the other is not going to confess, they still ought to confess in order to get two years instead of three. This compelling logic will drive both criminals to confess unless they genuinely have as much concern for each other as they do for themselves.

Although it recurs in many contexts, the prisoner's dilemma is usually seen as a way of characterizing ➤ oligopoly. Here, it may pay firms to collude and act jointly as a monopolist, but it will also pay individual firms to cheat on the colluding deal and produce more than they agreed to. ➤➤ Nash equilibrium; repeated game; tit-for-tat.

private company A type of business organization that permits a limited number of shareholders to enjoy ➤ limited liability and to be taxed as a company. Unlike the public company – the only other incorporated form of business – a private company may not offer ➤ shares for public subscription but, unlike a ➤ partnership, and if it requires the protection of limited liability, it is obliged to file accounts. Smaller private companies are exempted from certain of the so-called *disclosure requirements*. (➤ small business; ➤➤ company law)

private enterprise Economic activity in the private, as distinct from the public, sector (➤ public enterprise). ➤➤ capitalism; mixed economy.

private equity ➤ risk capital.

private finance initiative (PFI) A policy introduced by the UK government in 1992 to harness private sector capital and expertise in the delivery of public services by ➤ contracting out. It is one of a range of cooperative ventures between government and the private sector that are called public–private partnerships. In a few cases contractors enjoyed large gains and the Treasury's objective is that the public sector should share gains on new contracts 50:50. Since 2008 private finance for PFIs has been difficult to obtain and the government has even provided funds itself. The PFI approach is used in many countries, including the USA. A criticism of PFI is that it shifts what would otherwise have been a capital outlay, clearly registering in a government's current budget, to a cost stream in a distant future.

private net product A term first used by ➤ Pigou for the net ➤ national income or product to distinguish it from the ➤ social net product.

private sector That part of the economy in which economic activity is carried on by ➤ private enterprise as distinct from the ➤ public sector. The private sector includes the ➤ personal sector and the corporate sector.

privatization Principally, the sale of government-owned ➤ equity in ➤ nationalized industries or other commercial enterprises to private investors, with or without the loss of government control in these organizations. From 1981, the UK government embarked on a major programme of asset sales. Companies in public ownership accounted for 12 per cent of ➤ Gross Domestic Product in 1979 but only about 2 per cent by 1997. UK government revenue from sales of equity in state-owned enterprises rose from £377 million in 1979/80 to £7.1 billion in 1988/9, though it fell back later as fewer enterprises were available for sale (➤ public sector financial deficit). In all, between 1979 and 1995, over £50 billion of state assets were sold, according to research at Manchester University. Similar policies were pursued in many other countries worldwide including Russia, China and especially in countries in transition (➤➤ transition, economies in) but not on the same scale as in the UK.

Other types of privatization may take the form of deregulation of a state-supported ➤ cartel or the subcontracting to the private sector of work previously carried out by state employees. Where public utilities have been privatized, leaving them in a monopoly position, new forms of ➤ regulation have been introduced (➤ regulated utilities). ➤ contracting out; natural monopoly.

probability The average number of times an event occurs as a proportion of the number of times it could occur. For example, the probability of a 6 turning up in any given throw of a dice is 1 in 6. All probabilities take a value from 0 (impossible) to 1 (certain). Probability is important in several areas of economics. There is a whole theory associated with consumers and ➤ risk (➤ expected utility), and in the economics of ➤ finance the notion of risk is important in explaining asset prices (➤ capital asset pricing model). In ➤ econometrics, probability theory underlies the statistical tests used to ascertain the significance of the results derived from ➤ empirical testing.

There are two major ways of viewing probability: (a) that it represents the random element of a process, and (b) the view more associated with the Bayesian School (➤ Bayes' theorem) that it represents a degree of ignorance about a process. In this view, when we ascribe a probability to something, we do so given a certain level of knowledge about it. The probability we specify says as much about our knowledge of the event as it does about the event itself. ➤ normal distribution.

producer good A ➤ commodity used in the production of other goods and services, as distinct from final or consumer goods. Whether or not a good is a producer or consumer good will depend not on the good itself but on the use to which it is put. For example, a pencil bought for use in a drawing office is a producer good, but one bought for a child is a consumer good. Producer goods are also known as 'intermediate goods'.

producer's surplus The excess of the revenue received by a supplier of a ➤ commodity over the minimum amount he/she would be willing to accept to maintain

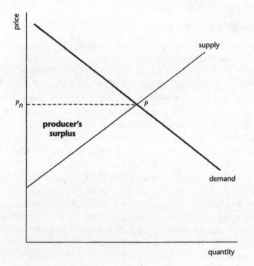

the same level of supply. It is a similar concept to ➤ consumer surplus (see graph on previous page). ➤➤ economic rent; quasi-rent.

product differentiation ➤ differentiation, product.

production, factors of ➤ factors of production.

production, theory of The economic analysis of the transformation through a ➤ production function of ➤ inputs (e.g. ➤ labour and ➤ capital) into outputs. Production possibilities (➤➤ isoquant; transformation curve) will depend on technology, the mix and level of factor prices and marginal productivities, and the level and price of output demanded. ➤➤ economies of scale; firm, theory of the.

production function The mathematical relationship between the output of a firm or economy and the inputs (➤ factors of production) used to produce that output. In mathematical notation it is written $q = f(L, C, t \ldots)$ where q is the dependent ➤ variable (output) and $L, C, t \ldots$ etc. are independent variables (inputs). The amount of inputs (e.g. labour, capital, raw materials) required to produce a given output depends on technology and this will be reflected in the form of the function. For example, it may be linear (➤ linear relationship) or non-linear. An example of the latter is the ➤ Cobb–Douglas function. A production function of the form $q = aL^{\beta} \cdot C^{1-\beta}$ describes a technology with *constant returns to scale*, i.e. if inputs are increased by x, output is increased by x. Similarly, a function may exhibit *increasing returns to scale* (e.g. $q = aC.L$ in which if inputs are, for example, doubled, output increases by $2 \times 2 = 4$ times), and *diminishing returns to scale* (e.g. $q = aC^{\frac{1}{2}}L^{\frac{1}{2}}$, in which, if inputs are increased by, for example, eight times, output increases by only four times). The above functions are termed 'homogeneous of degree n'; a given increase (x) in each of the inputs (independent variables) increases output (dependent variable) by x^n. If n is greater than 1, the function reflects *increasing returns to scale*; if it is less than 1, *diminishing returns to scale*; if it is equal to 1, *constant returns to scale*. ➤➤ homogeneous of degree n.

production possibility curve ➤ transformation curve.

productivity The relationship between the output of goods and services and the inputs of resources (➤ factors of production) used to produce them. Productivity is usually measured by ratios of changes in inputs to changes in outputs using ➤ index numbers. For example, changes in labour productivity – the most common measure – are measured by an index of man-hours divided into an index of output. If the production index stands at 150 (2000 = 100) and the index of man-hours worked stands at 125, then the labour productivity index stands at 120, i.e. labour productivity has increased by 20 per cent over 2000 levels. This is known as a *partial productivity index*, and it does not, in fact, measure changes in the productivity of labour alone unless inputs of land and capital have remained constant.

The calculation of *total factor productivity* is difficult in practice since the proportions of the different factor inputs do not remain constant over time and their individual contribution to output change is difficult to disentangle. Comparisons between labour productivity in different sectors of the economy (e.g. between ➤ capital-intensive manufacturing and ➤ labour-intensive services) need to be interpreted with care for the same reason. Another problem in productivity calculations is that the quality of unit inputs may vary, e.g. the use of more highly trained labour may lead to higher output without any increase in the number of man-hours. Since changes in productivity are affected by the level of capacity utilization, the underlying trend of productivity growth may be very different from that indicated by short-term movements in productivity indices. In the long run, productivity advance is the main cause of increases in real ➤ per capita income. (The measures mentioned relate to average productivity; marginal productivity is the change in output caused by an increase or decrease of one unit of the factors of production.) ➤ interest, productivity theories of.

product life-cycle The theory that new manufactured products are first developed in high-income countries that have large markets for technologically advanced products and the scientists and engineers to develop them. After a time, the products are exported and later produced abroad, perhaps by subsidiaries, then imitated by less advanced countries, the labour costs of which enable them to export to the original first mover (➤ first-mover advantage). This does not mean that the first mover suffers, because it can develop new products that begin their own cycle.

The product life-cycle theory was first put forward by Raymond Vernon to explain leadership and decline by US ➤ multinational corporations in the 1960s. Although subject to criticism, the theory does reflect experience in the production of some products (e.g. motor cars) that began on a large scale in the USA and that are now manufactured in many countries, some of which export to the USA. However, in some cases (e.g. DVD recorders and players from Japan) the first-mover advantage has been retained, while in others (motorcycles from the UK) it has been lost. The real significance of the theory is that it recognizes the interactions between domestic and international markets and the roles of new technology and technological diffusion among nations. ➤ international trade.

profit 1 The residual return to the ➤ entrepreneur. In traditional economic theory, profit does not include any of the return to ➤ land, ➤ labour or ➤ capital (the ➤ factors of production), but is the surplus remaining after the full ➤ opportunity costs of these factors have been met, formally total sales revenue minus total costs. Two types of profit are distinguished in economics: (a) *normal profit* which is the opportunity cost of the entrepreneur, i.e. the minimum amount necessary to attract him/ her to an activity or to provide inducement to remain in it, and (b) *super-normal profit* or *economic profit*, which is any profit over and above normal profit, will be earned only in the ➤ short run, and is a return to ➤ monopoly power which, unless there are ➤ barriers to entry, will be eroded by new entrants. ➤➤ economic rent.

2 In the accounting sense of the term, *net profit* (before tax) is the residual after deduction of all ➤ money costs, i.e. sales revenue minus wages, salaries, rent, fuel and raw materials, etc., ➤ interest on ➤ loans and ➤ depreciation. Net profit after tax is after deduction of ➤ corporation tax or, in the case of a ➤ sole proprietorship or ➤ partnership, ➤ income tax. (However, ➤ assessable profits.)

Gross profit is net profit before depreciation and interest. Accounting profit and economic profit will be the same only where all the factors of production have been credited with their full opportunity costs. The reported profits of quoted companies consist mainly of the return on capital for the shareholders that is not profit in the economic sense of the term. If a company is receiving a subsidized loan from the government, for example, or is paying ➤ rent below the market rate because it has a long leasehold interest, it would also be necessary for the economist to deduct full

➤ imputed costs for these returns to factors of production, rather than simply the actual money outlays from revenue in arriving at profit. A firm may, therefore, be making an accounting profit while operating at an economic loss.

profit, falling rate of The early classical economists (➤ classical economics) believed that it was a feature of the economic system for the general rate of ➤ profit to decline. ➤ Smith argued that ➤ capital accumulation took place at a faster rate than the growth of total output. Although the absolute level of profits rose, competition lowered the ➤ rate of return on capital. For ➤ Ricardo, the decline of the general rate of profit was induced by the decline in the marginal productivity of ➤ land, to which all profits were linked. ➤ Marx took up ideas similar to Smith's, and predicted a fall in the rate of profit because of an intensification of competition between capitalists (➤ capitalism). There would follow, he concluded, a strong pressure to reduce real wages (➤ real terms).

profit-and-loss account ➤ double-entry bookkeeping.

profit-related pay (PRP) ➤ employee share-ownership schemes.

profit-sharing The name given to describe any scheme under which workers in a firm receive a remuneration that is explicitly conditional upon the future ➤ profits of the firm. Typical profit-sharing schemes would give workers a profit-related bonus at the end of the year or would pay workers an amount based on a formula in which profit was a component. Two primary motivations underlie arguments for profit-sharing: (a) the desire for workers' wages to be flexible and reflect the performance of their company – if remuneration automatically falls when profits fall, the need for redundancies will be minimized – and (b) the desire for workers to identify their interests with those of their employer – to feel that they have a personal stake in the success of the company.

Against profit-sharing, it can be argued that: (a) workers desire stable ➤ income and that any risk of company failure should be borne by the shareholders, and (b) that, in a properly functioning free ➤ labour market, wages would be flexible anyway. ➤➤ employee share-ownership schemes.

profit-taking The sale of ➤ shares on the ➤ stock exchange in order to realize ➤ capital appreciation. When share prices rise and then fall back again as sellers appear (including those who bought the shares in the expectation that the price would rise), the fall-off in prices is said to be the result of profit-taking. ➤➤ stag.

progressive tax A ➤ tax that takes an increasing proportion of ➤ income as income rises.

propensity to import A relationship between ➤ income and ➤ import levels. The ➤ demand of a ➤ household for foreign goods depends on its income as does its demand for domestically produced goods. Similarly, we would expect firms' demands for foreign goods (e.g. raw materials, machine tools, components) to depend on their output. The whole economy's demand for imports thus depends on ➤ national income:

(1) *The average propensity to import*: the ratio of the total value of imports to national income. It is the proportion of national income spent on imports.

(2) *The marginal propensity to import*: the proportion of an increase in national income that is spent on imports. For example, if national income increased by $100, and imports increased by $20, then the marginal propensity to import would be 20/100 = 1/5. The marginal propensity to import is a useful concept in two ways: (a) if it can be accurately measured and it is relatively constant over time, it can be used to predict the increase in imports which will result from an increase in income – to continue the above example, if the marginal propensity to import is estimated as 1/5 and national income is expected to increase by $10 billion, we can predict that imports will increase by $2 billion, and this may be very useful from the point of view of control of the economy and the ➤ balance of payments; and (b) the marginal propensity to import determines, among other things, the value of the ➤ multiplier, and an estimate of it will therefore be required to estimate the effects on national income of a change in ➤ investment, government expenditure (➤ budget), exports or ➤ taxation.

Though, in the short run, the average and marginal propensities to import may be taken as relatively constant, it must be remembered that they reflect demands for foreign goods from firms and households, and are therefore influenced by: (a) relative prices of foreign and domestic goods, and (b) the willingness of domestic agents to borrow from abroad to finance their spending.

propensity to save ➤ average propensity to save.

property bond ➤ bond.

proportional tax A ➤ tax which is levied at the same rate at all ➤ income levels. Hence, it is intermediate between a ➤ progressive tax and a ➤ regressive tax.

proprietorship ➤ sole proprietorship.

protection The imposition of ➤ tariffs, ➤ quotas, or other non-tariff barriers, to restrict the inflow of ➤ imports. Non-tariff barriers have included restrictive licensing requirements, discriminating government procurement programmes, ➤ subsidies, customs clearance delays, health and safety and environmental regulations and export quotas to maintain supplies to the domestic market. Arguments in favour of protectionism and against ➤➤ free trade have their origin in the earliest periods of economic discussion (➤ mercantilism).

The arguments take many forms. Domestic industries, especially agriculture, should be maintained at a high level to ensure security of supply. Key industries that have a significant defence role should be protected to avoid reliance on foreign suppliers. In conditions of ➤ excess capacity, protection increases employment by switching demand away from foreign to domestic production and, through an increase in the surplus on the ➤ balance of payments, enables aggregate ➤ income to be raised through the ➤ multiplier effect. Protection also enables new industries to develop to an optimum size – the ➤ infant-industry argument. Protection may be used as a counter to ➤ dumping (➤ contingent protection) and as a retaliatory measure against other countries' restrictions.

Protection has also been proposed as a means by which the ➤ advanced countries could prevent a fall in the real incomes of their unskilled labour occasioned by low-cost imports from ➤ developing countries (➤ income, distribution of). ➤ barriers to entry; customs union; General Agreement on Tariffs and Trade; Great Depression; precautionary principle; World Trade Organization.

PRP Profit-related pay (➤ employee share-ownership schemes).

prudential regulation ➤ capital adequacy.

public-choice theory The area of ➤ welfare economics concerned with the ways in which society makes – and ought to make – decisions on issues such as regulation and public goods. For ➤ economic efficiency, it is important that there is an appropriate level of provision of ➤ public goods (e.g. defence), but it is not possible for individual consumers to make those decisions. It is not easy to turn everybody's individual preferences for defence into a single figure for society as a whole, or to charge people for defence in proportion to their strength of preference (➤ free-rider problem). Some state institutions will make these decisions, using some kind of rules to translate public desires into an overall social decision. Public-choice theory is concerned with voting mechanisms and constitutions that might be more or less efficient in delivering public desires.

But the theory is most closely associated with the Public Choice School and Buchanan (➤➤ Buchanan, J.). This views government *not* as some kind of benevolent agent of the public, doing its best to serve, but instead as some kind of Leviathan, aiming to maximize its revenue, exploit its monopoly power and expand its own power. Buchanan supports constitutional limits on the ability of governments to tax, borrow and print money. ➤➤ impossibility theorem; paradox of voting; social-welfare function; welfare economics.

public debt ➤ national debt.

public enterprise Economic activity in the market carried on by ➤ enterprises owned or controlled by the state. ➤➤ nationalized industries.

public expenditure Spending by governments (➤ public sector) or by central and local government or both combined (i.e. ➤ general government). Quite apart from the practicalities of public spending, economists have been concerned with the principles justifying it (➤ public goods), the mechanisms for allocating it (➤ public-choice theory) and the authorities responsible for it (➤ fiscal federalism). Total public expenditure can be measured in several ways, for example by including or excluding expenditure by public corporations and transfers to supra-national bodies, such as the European Union.

Government final expenditure on goods and services is much lower than total general government expenditure which includes transfers to the private sector in the form of subsidies and social security benefits which in European countries account for about half of the total. Public expenditure is financed mainly by ➤ taxation and borrowing (➤ national debt).

public finance A branch of economics concerned with the identification and appraisal of the means and effects of government financial policies. It attempts to analyse the effects of government ➤ taxation and expenditure on the economic situations of individuals and institutions, and to examine their impact on the economy as a whole. It is also concerned with examining the effectiveness of policy measures directed at certain objectives, and with developing techniques and procedures by which that effectiveness can be increased. ⯈⯈ budget; cost–benefit analysis; fiscal policy.

public goods Commodities, the consumption of which has to be decided by society as a whole, rather than by each individual. Public goods have three characteristics: (a) they yield *non-rivalrous* consumption – one person's use of them does not deprive others from using them; (b) they are *non-excludable* – if one person consumes them it is impossible to restrict others from consuming them, e.g. public television is non-excludable although, if devices are made for scrambling television pictures, except to those who own picture-decoding cards, television becomes an excludable service; and (c) public goods are often *non-rejectable* – individuals cannot abstain from their consumption even if they want to. National defence is a public good of this sort, although television is not. Non-excludability and non-rejectability mean that no *market* can exist and provision must be made by government, financed by ⯈ taxation.

Many items are partly public and partly private goods. A developed patent system, for example, has public-good properties, benefiting not only the community as a whole, but especially inventors who take out patents. ⯈ impossibility theorem; paradox of voting; ⯈⯈ externalities.

public ownership ⯈ nationalized industries.

public–private partnerships ⯈ private finance initiative.

public sector Comprises central government and local authorities (*general government*), together with the nationalized industries or public corporations. *Central government* in the UK includes all those departments and other bodies for whose activities a minister of the Crown or other responsible person is accountable to Parliament. ⯈⯈ privatization.

public sector borrowing requirement (PSBR) ⯈ public sector net borrowing; public sector net cash requirement.

public sector financial deficit (PSFD) The excess of ⯈ public sector spending over ⯈ taxation revenues and other receipts. It differs from the ⯈ public sector borrowing requirement in that it includes the proceeds of capital transactions, e.g. the sale of assets (⯈ privatization).

public sector net borrowing A broad measure of the government's deficit, that includes the deficits of central government, local government and public corporations. Public sector net borrowing is similar to ⯈ public sector net cash requirement (PSNCR), but it is more in line with principles of accruals accounting (⯈ accrued expenses), ⯈ resource accounting and budgeting. For example, whereas the PSNCR is improved if the government sells an asset (as the sale proceeds count as income just as taxation does), public sector net borrowing is not flattered by such an action.

public sector net cash requirement (PSNCR) Formerly called the public sector borrowing requirement. A measure of the government deficit, in terms of the cash needed to fill the gap between receipts and spending. This was seen as the primary measure of fiscal policy in the UK during the 1980s and much of the 1990s, especially during the period when the impact of public borrowing on money supply was considered an important component of anti-inflation policy. The measure was downgraded in 1998, replaced by ➤ public sector net borrowing and the ➤ golden rule.

public utility An industry supplying basic public services to the market and possibly enjoying ➤ monopoly power. Usually, electricity, gas, telephones, postal services, water supply and rail and often other forms of transport are regarded as public utilities. These services all require specialized capital equipment and elaborate organization. ➤➤ natural monopolies; regulation.

pump priming The injection of small amounts of government spending into a depressed economy with the aim of boosting business confidence and encouraging larger-scale private-sector investment. It was the policy pursued by Roosevelt in the USA during the 1930s before ➤ Keynesian economics was accepted by policymakers. ➤➤ multiplier.

purchasing-power parity (PPP) An ➤ exchange rate between two currencies such that the same basket of goods and services could be bought for the same amount in each country if the cost were converted at that exchange rate. For example, if a loaf of bread cost £1 in the UK and $2 in the USA the purchasing-power parity exchange rate would be £1 to $2. The ➤ Gross Domestic Product (GDP) of countries, measured in their national currencies, has to be converted into a common currency in order to be able to make comparisons between them. Market exchange rates between currencies are not an accurate measure because they are influenced by a variety of forces acting through the ➤ foreign exchange markets, but also because many goods and services, from construction to hairdressing, are not traded internationally. The use of PPP is a preferred alternative. In 2005, the International Comparison Program (ICP) of the World Bank completed a study based on data for over 1000 goods and services from which they calculated PPPs for 146 countries, including China for the first time, and from which they were able to produce estimates for GDPs for countries worldwide. Previous estimates had had to rely on data from 1993 and earlier. A further survey to update the necessary data is scheduled for 2011 (➤ purchasing-power parity theory).

purchasing-power parity theory A theory that states that the ➤ exchange rate between one ➤ currency and another is in ➤ equilibrium when their domestic purchasing powers at that rate of exchange are equivalent. For example, the rate of exchange of £1 = $1.70 would be in equilibrium if £1 will buy the same goods in the UK as $1.70 will buy in the USA. If this holds true, purchasing-power parity exists.

The theory has its source in the mercantilist (➤ mercantilism) writings of the seventeenth century, but it came into prominence in the early 1900s through the writings of the Swedish economist Gustav Cassel. The basic mechanism implied is that, given complete freedom of action, if $1.70 buys more in the USA than £1 does in the UK, it would pay to convert pounds into dollars and buy from the USA rather than in the UK. The switch in demand would raise prices in the USA and lower them in the UK, and at the same time lower the UK exchange rate until equilibrium and parity were re-established. Cassel interpreted the theory in terms of changes in, rather than absolute levels of, prices and exchange rates. He argued that the falls in the ➤ foreign exchange markets in the postwar period were a result of ➤ inflation due to unbalanced ➤ budgets increasing the quantity of ➤ money.

In practice, the theory has little validity because exchange rates, which are determined by the ➤ demand and ➤ supply of currency in the foreign exchange markets, are related to such forces as ➤ balance of payments disequilibria, ➤ capital transactions, ➤ speculation and government policy. Many goods and ➤ services do not enter into international trade, and so their relative prices are not taken into account in the determination of the exchange rate. ➤ Balassa–Samuelson effect; index-number problem; Mises, L.E. von; real exchange rate.

pure strategy ➤ mixed strategy.

put option ➤ option.

pyramiding ➤ holding company.

Q

q theory A theory of ➤ investment behaviour which suggests that firms invest as long as the value of their ➤ shares exceeds the replacement cost of the physical assets of the firm. Developed by ➤ Tobin, q theory is attractive because it encompasses other theories of investment in a simple framework. The q referred to is the ratio of two numbers: (a) the value of a firm to its shareholders – this is equivalent to the expected future profits of the firm, and (b) the replacement cost of the assets of the firm, machines, buildings, etc. If (a) exceeds (b) (i.e. q is greater than 1) the firm should want to expand as the profits it expects to make from its assets are greater than the cost of its assets. If q is less than 1, the shares of the firm are worth less than the assets and it will pay the firm to engage in ➤ divestment to sell the assets rather than try to use them. Firms should invest or divest until q is approximately equal to 1.

quality adjusted life years (qalys) A calculation of benefit to assist in determining the optimum allocation of resources in medicine. In considering the outcome of any particular medical procedure, consideration is given not only to the number of years life is prolonged but also its quality. The costs of alternative procedures are compared with their qalys and other benefits that are expected to be gained from the different procedures (➤➤ cost–benefit analysis) to help to choose the preferred option. The use of qalys does not imply that other aspects of decision-making in medicine are not included in the assessment, e.g. the question of the need for procedures to be seen to be equitable between different classes of people. ➤ death rate.

quality adjusted price indices ➤ hedonic price index.

quantitative easing A method of boosting the ➤ money supply in which the central bank buys assets from institutions – mainly from banks, but also from other financial and non-financial institutions. This increases the ➤ money supply by increasing the reserves of the commercial banks by buying debt instruments from them, usually government securities, against a book entry in its own accounts or more directly by buying, for instance, company ➤ bonds.

Quantitative easing has the same effect as the more traditional method of 'printing money'. It has been used on a large scale by the ➤ Bank of England and the ➤ Federal Reserve System in an effort to stimulate their economies during the 2007–2009 banking crisis at a time when interest rates were already as low as was practicable. It was also used by the authorities in Japan between 2001 and 2006, though with little apparent effect in stimulating the economy. The risk is that the practice will create inflation, but this did not happen in any of these cases because inflationary pressures were so small. Quantitative easing may have helped to prevent a deeper depression and it has had the incidental advantage of keeping down government borrowing costs. In theory it can be reversed by the central bank selling the assets it purchased, thus withdrawing money from the system. ➤➤ quantity theory of money.

quantitative restrictions ➤ quotas.

quantity rationing The name given to one of four states of an economy that can exist when ➤ excess demand or ➤ excess supply persist in the ➤ labour market or in the markets for goods and services. Quantity rationing is an area of ➤ macroeconomics in the tradition of ➤ Keynes (➤ Keynesian economics). It focuses on the study of ➤ disequilibrium, in contrast to ➤ neo-classical economics or ➤ new classical economics (➤ economic doctrines) which are predominantly concerned with the behaviour of economies in which all markets are free to clear without restraint. In quantity rationing theory, markets that have become dislodged from an equilibrium may not find that equilibrium again, even if prices are generally flexible. The reason is that when one market is out of equilibrium, the price mechanism in other markets may not work properly. For example, unemployed workers may be willing to work for $300 a week, and employers may be willing to employ them for $300 a week, but to do that, employers need to know that the workers will spend their new-found income. But as the workers have no work and no income, they cannot signal to employers that they would be buying new products if only they could be employed. The disequilibria are mutually reinforcing. Another way of expressing the same point is that in a market out of equilibrium, buyers or sellers are rationed in how much they can buy or sell, and in this case, quantity signals matter as well as price signals.

Four different possible regimes are held to apply: (a) ➤ *repressed inflation*: excess demand exists in both the labour and goods markets (buyers are rationed in both); (b) ➤ *Keynesian unemployment*: excess supply exists in both the labour and goods markets (sellers are rationed in both and don't sell everything they would like to sell); (c) ➤ *classical unemployment*: excess supply exists in the labour market, and excess demand in the goods market; and (d) ➤ *underconsumption*: excess demand exists in the labour market, and excess supply exists in the goods market. ➤ information, economics of.

quantity theory of money The theory that changes in the ➤ money supply have a direct influence on prices and nothing else. The theory is derived from the identity $MV = PT$ (called the ➤ Fisher equation) where M = stock of money, V = velocity with which the money circulates (➤ velocity of circulation), P = average ➤ price level, and T = the output of goods and ➤ services. All this equation says is that the amount of money spent equals the amount of money used.

The theory itself has two key elements: (a) that the velocity with which money circulates is stable, at least in the short term, and (b) that the number of transactions (which is closely related to the level of physical output) is fixed by the tastes of individuals, and the real behaviour of firms in equilibrium. In this case, increases in M can only lead to increases in P, i.e. money supply increases cause ➤ inflation. The theory provided the basis for ➤ macroeconomics prior to ➤ Keynes' *General Theory of Employment, Interest and Money* (1936), and had a plausibility about it in the eyes of early proponents of ➤ neo-classical economics, who strongly believed in the power of markets to settle at equilibrium points. It was largely superseded by ➤ Keynesian economics, under which both elements of the theory came under attack. Increases in M were held to lead to falls in V – and, in some circumstances, increases in real income.

However, in the 1960s the quantity theory re-emerged in a more sophisticated form through the work of Milton ➤ Friedman. He accepted the Keynesian view that V could alter when M altered, but said that it did so only in stable and predictable ways. On the second postulate, whereas Keynes said that unemployment could exist at an equilibrium of the national economy and therefore an increase in the money supply could increase real output, Friedman, although admitting unemployment could persist, held that this was caused by structural factors in the economy (➤ unemployment, natural rate of) and could not be influenced by ➤ aggregate demand measures, at least not for very long. ➤➤ economic doctrines; monetarism.

quartile ➤ percentile.

quasi-money ➤ near money.

quasi-rent A term applied by ➤ Marshall to the earnings of capital, the supply of which is fixed in the short run. It is the excess made in the short run by a firm from the difference between the selling price and the ➤ prime cost of the product. For example, suppose that a firm can make pens at a cost of 10 cents each in labour and raw materials, and it can sell them at 40 cents. A quasi-rent of 30 cents is earned. This is not, however, the profit of the firm, because there are costs of fixed inputs that have to be covered by sales, even though they don't add to the cost of making extra pens. A loss-making firm can also earn quasi-rents.

Quasi-rent is analagous to ➤ economic rent because it represents a return in excess of that necessary to keep the firm in production – whenever price exceeds avoidable costs. It differs from economic rent, however, in that it is a temporary phenomenon. It can exist because, in the short run, competing firms do not have time to enter an industry, and firms do not have time to exit an industry either, and may have irretrievable ➤ sunk costs. ➤ barriers to exit.

Quesnay, François (1694–1774) A surgeon by profession, Quesnay held the post of secretary of the French Academy of Surgery and edited its official journal. He became physician to Madame de Pompadour. His major economic works appeared in various articles in the *Encyclopédie* (1756, 1757), and in the *Journal de l'agriculture, du commerce et des finances* (1765, 1767). The ➤ *Tableau économique* and *Maximes* (1758), a commentary on the *Tableau*, set out three classes of society, and showed how transactions flowed between them. The three classes were: (a) landowners, (b) farmers and (c) others, called the 'sterile class'. Only the agricultural sector produced any surplus value, the rest merely reproducing what it consumed (➤ Marx, K.). He anticipated ➤ Malthus' fear of underconsumption arising from excessive ➤ savings. Net ➤ income would be reduced if the flows in the *Tableau* were interrupted by delays in spending. This was the first attempt to construct a ➤ macroeconomic input–output ➤ model of the economy (➤ input–output analysis). In fact, progress in this field had to await the application of ➤ matrix algebra and computerization (➤ Leontief, W.W.). Quesnay suggested a single tax, *l'impôt unique*, on the net income from land, arguing that the nation would thereby save tax-collecting costs. Only agriculture yielded a surplus, and therefore ultimately it bore all taxes anyway

(➤ Mill, J.S.). He was a central figure in the group of economists called the ➤ Physiocrats, who flourished in France between 1760 and 1770.

quotas In ➤ international trade the quantitative limits placed on the importation of specified ➤ commodities. The ➤➤ protection afforded by quotas is more certain than can be obtained by raising import ➤ tariffs as the effect of the latter will depend on the price ➤ elasticities of the imported commodities. Quotas, like tariffs, can also be used to favour a preferred source of supply (➤ General Agreement on Tariffs and Trade; imports). The term also applies to quantitative restrictions on production which may be set by ➤ cartels or colluding oligopolists (➤ collusion; oligopoly).

quota sample A method of sampling (➤➤ random sample) in which interviewers are given a quota of interviews to carry out with people or households with specified characteristics. For instance, in a travel survey an interviewer may be instructed to interview ten Americans, five Europeans and four Japanese. In this case, the sample is stratified (➤➤ stratified sample) by country of origin. The interviewer is free to choose, within the constraint of the quota, the person to be interviewed and, because of this freedom, bias can easily be introduced, so that the sample is not truly random. For example, the interviewer may select people who are both willing and able to speak English. Quota sampling is cheap, but can lead to misleading results, because of conscious or unconscious bias.

quotation The privilege granted to the issuer of a ➤ security by a ➤ stock exchange of placing the price of that security on the official list. A quoted security is for this reason referred to as a ➤ listed security. Only public companies fulfilling certain requirements designed to safeguard the investing public are granted quotations. Lesser standards apply in the ➤ unlisted securities markets, but companies for which ➤ market makers post prices in these markets are not properly described as *quoted companies*; in the UK, this term is reserved for those on the official list of a recognized ➤ stock exchange.

quoted company ➤ quotation.

R

R&D ➤ research and development.

Ramsey pricing ➤ inverse elasticity rule.

random sample A ➤ sample in which every member of the ➤ population (*simple random sample*) or some subset of the population (➤ stratified sample) being tested has an equal chance of being included in the sample. The purpose of sampling is to be able to infer, from the sample taken, the attributes of the population as a whole. Only if the sample is random can the ➤ probability be calculated that a sampled attribute applies to the population as a whole. ➤ normal distribution; ➤➤ Heckman, J.; quota sample.

random walk The path of a variable over time that exhibits no predictable pattern at all. For example, if a price, p, moves in a random walk, the value of p in any period will be equal to the value of p in the period before, plus or minus some random variable. That random variable is normally distributed (➤ normal distribution) with a constant ➤ variance and is entirely independent of the value of p. To predict the value of p tomorrow, we can do no better than look at its value today. Certain variables (e.g. share prices) are held to follow a random walk because, if anyone could predict that prices were going to rise tomorrow, they would buy shares today in order to sell them tomorrow at the higher price. They would go on buying them until today's price had been driven up so high that it was no longer expected that prices would rise tomorrow. The only thing that will affect the price of a share is news about the firm which could not have been anticipated, and is thus random. ➤➤ efficient markets hypothesis; rational expectations.

rate of exchange ➤ exchange rate.

rate of interest The proportion of a sum of money that is paid over a specified period of time in payment for its loan. It is the price a borrower has to pay to enjoy the use of cash he/she does not own, and the return a lender enjoys for deferring consumption or parting with liquidity. The rate of interest is a price that can be analysed in the normal framework of ➤ demand and ➤ supply analysis. It may be seen as a price in two different markets:

(1) *The market for ➤ investment funds*. It equalizes the *demand* for such funds, which is for investment, and the *supply*, which is ➤ saving. If investors believe that they can earn a return of 10 per cent on borrowed money by building a factory, and the rate of interest is 5 per cent, they will demand all the funds that are available, indeed, will eventually offer more than 5 per cent to obtain cash

which will earn them a profit at any rate up to 10 per cent. Savers, on the other hand, have a rate of ➤ time preference reflecting the compensation they require for putting money aside for the future and not spending it in the present. If they need only 4 per cent to be induced to save, and the rate of interest is 8 per cent, there will be so much money put into savings that the rate will be driven down. The rate of interest thus adjusts to ensure that investment equals saving, with saving reflecting the weight people attach to current consumption over future consumption, and investment the amount of extra future production that can be expected to result from building new plant and machinery.

(2) *The market for liquid assets (*➤ *liquidity).* Firms and consumers may prefer their assets to be in a readily available form – they would prefer money worth $1 million to a factory worth the same. However, most borrowers will need cash for long-term use, and will need the certainty that they won't have to pay it back at short notice. Thus, to compensate people for giving up ready access to the money they lend (their loss of liquidity), interest is paid. This means that the interest rate has an important influence on the demand for money, and on very liquid assets.

The interest rate is thus affected by ➤ liquidity preference and ➤ time preference. ➤ Keynes introduced the idea of its importance in the demand for money and emphasized it in this role. Classical economists ignored liquidity preference, believing that it was in the market for investment that the rate of interest was determined. The problem of bringing the money market and the investment market to equilibrium with one price was at the heart of Keynesian economics. It would be surprising if a satisfactory equilibrium was achieved in both markets simultaneously.

In simple theory, only one interest rate should prevail in the economy – if, for example, one bank offers a lower return than another, investors would move their cash from the first until it has so little money that it is forced to raise its rate (➤ arbitrage). However, for two main reasons, many rates prevail at any one time:

(1) ➤ Financial intermediaries charge for their services by adding to the interest rate they charge borrowers or subtracting from the rate they pay lenders. This means there is an interest rate differential: lenders get less than borrowers pay if a financial intermediary arranges the loan.

(2) Interest rates also carry a risk premium: those lending money will want a higher-than-market rate of return if their investment has an uncertain return (➤ risk).

➤➤ capital asset pricing model; interest, abstinence theory of; interest, classical theory of; interest, natural rate of; interest, productivity theories of; interest, time preference theory of; liquidity trap; term structure of interest rates.

rate of return Usually, net ➤ profit after ➤ depreciation as a percentage of average ➤ capital employed in a business. This is the ➤ return on capital employed and is one of a number of ➤ financial ratios used to measure the efficiency of a business as a whole, or of particular ➤ investment projects. The rate of return may be calculated using profit before or after ➤ tax, and there are a number of other variations of the concept. Profit may be defined as net of tax but not of depreciation and interest, i.e. profits available for ➤ equity shareholders, or as operating profit, i.e. to exclude investment income and ➤ capital gains. Capital employed may be defined to exclude ➤ loan capital, in which case the return measured is that on equity capital; sometimes ➤ working capital is excluded.

The use of simple rates of return in the analysis of alternative investment projects is open to the serious criticism that it does not take account of the timing of capital outlays and earnings, and hence does not allow for the time value of money (➤ investment appraisal). Strictly speaking, the rate of return on capital employed in a business does not measure the return to capital alone or the efficiency of the use of ➤ resources by that business, since the returns to each of the ➤ factors of production cannot be separated out. However, in normal circumstances, a firm that is earning a long-term rate of return lower than its cost of capital (➤ capital, cost of) could be said to be using resources inefficiently.

rate of technical substitution (RTS) The increase in production of one commodity an economy can achieve by cutting the production of another commodity by one unit. If a country could transfer resources from making one spoon to make two forks, the rate of technical substitution between spoons and forks is two. The rate of technical substitution between commodity A and B usually diminishes as production of A increases. If, at production of twenty aircraft and 20 million loaves of bread, society can produce a million loaves with equal ease to one aircraft, at production of thirty aircraft and 10 million loaves the production of one aircraft will require a much larger sacrifice in terms of loaves.

Graphically, the RTS is the slope of the ➤ transformation curve. Mathematically, it is the ratio of the ➤ marginal products of producing two items. ➤➤ economic efficiency; marginal rate of substitution.

rates ➤ local taxation.

rating agencies Organizations which assess the credit-worthiness of ➤ securities issued by corporations and governments, e.g. Standard and Poor's (S&P) and Moody's Investor Services. For S&P, 'AAA' represents the highest quality investment grade, in which the risk of default is minimal; 'BBB' represents the medium grade; 'Bb' the predominantly speculative; 'C' the lowest quality. The 'DDD' rating applies to borrowers in default or in arrears. Other agencies offer similar ratings.

Ratings are often self-fulfilling where investors move out of securities when assessments change. Rating agencies were heavily criticized following the 2007–2009 credit crisis for issuing misleading ratings, especially for certain ➤ derivatives, and there have been calls for regulation or reform. It is also argued that banks and other institutions should rely more on their own research and judgement. The agencies may be paid by the issuers of the securities they are rating as well as by investors and therefore may suffer from conflicts of interest. *Credit bureaux*, or credit reference agencies, provide credit assessments of individuals.

rational expectations The assumption that the behaviour of economic agents is based on an understanding of the economy, and a forecast of future events, that are not systematically falsified by actual economic events. Nobody can predict the future with perfect foresight because unforeseen, random happenings are bound to occur. However, someone with rational expectations will construct their expectations so that on average they are correct, i.e. they will be wrong only because of random, non-systematic errors. The disadvantage of other ways in which individuals may be assumed to predict the future is that they allow them to make systematic errors. ➤ Adaptive expectations, for example, postulate that individuals predict next year's price inflation on the basis of last year's, and the rate of change up to last year. At a time of increasing inflation, their expectation will perpetually lag behind the actual inflation rate – but despite this, under the hypothesis of adaptive expectations, everybody carries on using this predictive method although it produces biased forecasts.

The theory of rational expectations has stimulated debate in economics because it has controversial implications.

(1) It appears to demolish any case for government policy aimed at stimulating demand in the economy: if the government expands the money supply by 5 per cent, everybody will believe that prices will rise as a consequence. This will make them add 5 per cent to their wage demands or prices and a 5 per cent price inflation occurs without there being any positive effect on output or employment (➤ policy ineffectiveness theorem).

(2) Markets behave efficiently (➤ efficient markets hypothesis). The price of the shares of a company reflects the profits the company is expected to make. If expectations are rational, the price at any time is based on expectations that have taken into consideration all possible information about the company. This means that if some 'news' arrives that indicates the company's fortunes are likely to change, that information will cause the price to change immediately. Moreover, as the 'news' that arrives can reflect only random, not systematic, events, the price of the company's shares must follow a random path (➤ random walk).

The interesting implications of rational expectations should not necessarily make them appear a plausible description of people's behaviour. Nevertheless, like ➤ perfect competition in ➤ microeconomics, rational expectation provides an extreme but simple assumption that provides a benchmark against which the behaviour of people in the real world can be judged. Moreover, in the very long term, the hypothesis that systematic forecasting errors are not made appears by no means implausible. ➤➤ expectations; Lucas critique; new classical economics.

Rawls, John (1921–2002) American political theorist, whose main work, *A Theory of Justice* (1971), outlined a basis for ranking social outcomes – an implicit ➤ social-welfare function. His notion was that social welfare should simply be defined in terms of the welfare of the least well off, a so-called ➤ maximin strategy. The welfare of the rest of the population should only be treated as a tie-breaking rule for ranking different outcomes that were irrelevant to the least well off. Rawls derived this idea by postulating that it is the principle we would choose to live by, if we were asked to make such a choice before finding out whether we ourselves were to be rich or poor.

real balance effect ➤ Pigou, A.C.

real business cycle theory The argument that the ➤ business cycle is caused not by fluctuations in ➤ aggregate demand, as generally supposed, but by shocks in the conditions under which producers supply their products (➤ supply-side economics). It is associated with ➤➤ rational expectations, and the idea that markets generally function very smoothly; thus, any ups and downs in economic activity must reflect the outcome of rational decisions made by many individuals.

In real business cycle theory, the ups and downs are caused by technology or some other shock to the supply side of the economy. Suppose a new productivity-enhancing device comes along; employers will want to invest, expand output and employ more people. That will lead to a boom. There may be other times when new advances are lacking, or productivity is low, and at that point employers will rationally choose not to produce as much and there will be a recession. The downturn is simply the optimal reaction of individuals to the lack of productive opportunities. For proponents of the theory, the economy will be busier in high productivity times than low productivity times, just as construction workers do more work in the summer than the winter. Of course, booms are nicer than recessions, but there is no need to react to either as they represent the best use of the opportunities available. While influential and controversial, real business cycle theory has not attracted much empirical support.

real exchange rate An ➤ exchange rate between two currencies calculated by valuing a given basket of goods and services in terms of the two currencies and dividing the two resulting sums. Suppose there is a 10 per cent increase in prices in the UK, no ➤ inflation in the USA and a 10 per cent depreciation of the pound against the dollar; then the real exchange rate between the pound and the dollar is constant. ➤➤ effective exchange rate; purchasing power parity.

real income ➤ real terms.

real terms A ➤ money value adjusted for changes in ➤ prices. The nominal value of the ➤ national income may rise by 10 per cent over a year with a similar increase in personal expenditure, but if consumer prices have risen by 8 per cent, the quantity of goods and services that are purchased by the consumer will have increased only by about 2 per cent. Thus, to convert money values to *constant prices* or real terms it is necessary to deflate (➤ deflation) data at current prices by an appropriate ➤ index number. In the same way, money wages or other forms of income can be adjusted to *real wages* or *real income* to allow for changes in the purchasing power of earnings. ➤➤ money illusion.

real time gross settlement (RTGS) A settlement system based on the immediate payment for a transaction, which is not reduced to take account of offsetting payments in the reverse direction. Its principal merit is that it protects against default by the debtor and hence ➤ systemic risk. The system is used for large-value payment transfers between organizations such as ➤ central banks.

real wages ➤ real terms.

receiver ➤ bankruptcy.

recession An imprecise term used to denote a sharp slowdown in the rate of economic growth or a modest decline in economic activity, as distinct from a slump or ➤ depression which is a more severe and prolonged downturn. Recessions are a feature of the ➤ business cycle. Two successive declines in seasonally adjusted (➤ seasonal adjustment), quarterly, real ➤ Gross Domestic Product would constitute a recession.

reciprocal demand ➤ equation of international demand.

recursive model A system of equations in which ➤ endogenous, or ➤ dependent, variables in one equation appear as ➤ exogenous, or ➤ independent, variables in others, but in which there are no subsets of equations which each cross-refer to endogenous variables. For example, the following two-equation system is recursive:

$$a = f_1(z)$$
$$b = f_2(a)$$

while the following system is not:

$$a = f_1(b)$$
$$b = f_2(a)$$

The significance of the recursive model is the ease with which it can be solved in terms of exogenous variables: values for all the endogenous variables can be found straightforwardly if the equations are solved in the right order. In the above example, the first equation gives a value for the endogenous variable a given a value of the exogenous variable z. The resulting value for a then becomes the value of the now exogenous variable a in the second equation to obtain the value of the endogenous variable b.

redeemable securities ➤ Stock or ➤ bonds that are repayable at their ➤ par value at a certain date, dates or specified eventuality. Most fixed-interest ➤ securities are redeemable, though ➤ consols bear no redemption date. ➤ Ordinary shares and some ➤ preference shares are irredeemable. ➤➤ redemption date.

redemption date The date at which a ➤ loan will be repaid or release given from other obligations. ➤➤ redeemable securities.

redemption yield ➤ yield.

red tape ➤ compliance costs.

reducing balance A means of recording ➤ depreciation expenses in which the original ➤ cost of an ➤ asset is 'written down' by a fixed fraction each year. In this way, the amount of depreciation allowed falls each year, e.g. a machine costing $500 could be written down by 20 per cent per annum (i.e. $100 in the first year) and then 20 per cent on its written-down value of $400 (i.e. $80 in the following year) and so on. A rate can be chosen to write down an asset to an expected residual value in a chosen period of years (e.g. five years and $50), which in our example would require an annual depreciation rate of about 37 per cent. Although the reducing-balance system gives a lighter depreciation charge in later years when maintenance and repair costs as well as risk of ➤ obsolescence may be higher (as opposed to the straight-line method, where equal depreciation is charged every year), it is unlikely to accord very closely with actual depreciation. However, the taxation authorities in many countries base ➤ tax allowances for certain ➤ capital investment on a reducing balance (➤ capital allowances).

reflation A ➤ macroeconomic policy of increasing ➤ aggregate demand in the economy in order to reduce unemployment. The argument for reflation can most clearly be seen in terms of ➤ Keynesian interpretations of the economy. When a ➤ deflationary gap exists, unemployment exists, indicating that there is spare capacity in the economy. Additional demand leads to a rise in spending, itself boosted by the ➤ multiplier, with a consequential rise in the number employed. Criticisms have been made of reflation as a policy prescription, however, often associated with the doctrine of ➤ monetarism. The argument is as follows: the reflation is generated by either printing money or by increased borrowing (➤ public sector borrowing requirement). If it is through printing money, no non-monetary variables can change. The level of aggregate demand rises; prices rise; more labour is sought to produce the extra demand, so wages rise; at the end of the process real wages (➤ real terms) are constant, as are all relative prices. Nothing changes except the absolute price level.

If, on the other hand, the reflation is financed by borrowing, every dollar the government borrows the private sector lends, and thus for every extra dollar of government spending there is a dollar less of private spending. This is called ➤ crowding out, and it occurs because, when the government borrowing increases, ➤ interest rates rise, squeezing private investment (➤➤ classical economics). These criticisms rely on a belief that market forces work effectively and that unemployment is at its natural rate (➤ unemployment, natural rate of), suggesting that a deflationary gap could never exist. They also imply that private investment is highly responsive to interest rate changes and that interest rates themselves are highly sensitive to changes in the supply of government bonds. ➤➤ Keynesian unemployment.

regional policy The framework for measures taken in the attempt to reduce disparities between economic development in general and ➤ unemployment in particular among different parts of the country. All countries have prosperous and depressed regions, though in some the disparities are greater than in others. In most cases, depressed areas result from the decline of once important industries or other economic activities. Governments have attempted to restore prosperity by creating incentives for new industry to move into these areas and by improvements in local ➤ infrastructure, though these policies have had only limited success. More recently, attention has shifted towards the scope for stimulating self-regeneration capacity by the promotion of ➤ small business. ➤ assisted areas.

Regional Trade Agreements (RTA) Agreements between countries to reduce barriers to trade between them have increased rapidly in the last decade or so and now dominate international trade. According to the World Trade Organization, there were about 400 RTAs in 2010, most of which were ➤ free trade areas, ➤ customs unions accounting for only 10 per cent of the total. Most countries have entered into some form of Regional Free Trade Agreement (➤ Association of South East Asian Nations; Caribbean Community and Common Market; Central American Common Market; Common Market for Eastern and Southern Africa; East African Community; Economic Community of West African States; European Union; European Free Trade Association; Mercosur; North American Free Trade Agreement).

regression analysis A mathematical technique for estimating the ➤ parameters of an equation from sets of data of the independent and ➤ dependent variables. For example, in the demand equation $q = aY + bP + c$, in which q = quantity bought of a good, Y = income and P = price, the parameters a, b and c can be estimated, provided there is a sufficient number of actual observations of the variables, q, Y and P. Regression analysis finds the values of a, b and c, which when substituted in the expression $aY + bP + c$ yields the least error in estimating q. Regression analysis is used widely in ➤ econometrics. ➤➤ auto-correlation; beta; dummy variable; heteroscedasticity; latent variable; least-squares regression; multicollinearity.

regression model ➤ regression analysis.

regressive tax   A ➤ tax which takes a decreasing proportion of ➤ income as income rises.

regulated utilities   Privately owned utilities such as water or telephone companies which have an actual or potential ➤ monopoly are regulated in the United States by public service commissioners and their pricing is generally determined on the basis of cost plus a reasonable rate of return.

In the UK, pricing is generally determined on the basis of a ➤ retail prices index, minus an x factor, to take account of ➤ productivity improvements; this system is intended to provide incentives for greater efficiency. The British system is also mostly based on single-person regulators instead of multi-person commissions, as in the USA.

regulation   The supervision and control of the economic activities of ➤ private enterprise by government in the interest of economic efficiency, fairness, health and safety. Regulation has a long history, pre-dating the Industrial Revolution, and takes many different forms. ➤ Externalities such as noise and pollution have made it necessary (among other reasons) to regulate road and air transport. The temptation for producers to collude (➤ oligopoly) or exploit other instances of ➤ monopoly power also requires intervention (➤ competition policy). More recently, economists have been interested mostly in the regulation of private ➤ natural monopolies, e.g. utilities. This has become the predominant model of ensuring the public interest, replacing public ownership (➤ nationalized industries). The choices between different regulatory regimes – ➤ price regulation, ➤ regulated utilities or sometimes ➤ yardstick competition – are all different approaches to the task. The system of regulation of financial services has also been under review and there has been recent interest in the justification for, and consequences of, a broader range of regulatory instruments. These other forms of regulation include measures to safeguard the rights of employees, to regulate the ➤ trade unions, the financial system, personal privacy, health and safety at work, town and country planning, food and drugs, industrial training, the licensing of street traders and taxi-cabs. (➤ Consumer Credit Act)

Regulation may be imposed simply by enacting laws and leaving their supervision to the normal processes of the law, by setting up special regulatory agencies or by encouraging self-regulation by recognizing, and in some cases delegating powers to, voluntary bodies. Though regulation may be regarded as necessary to prevent the abuse of monopoly power, or for preserving health and safety, or to correct ➤ externalities or other instances of ➤ market failure, there may yet be a risk that the ➤ compliance costs and other costs of regulation may exceed the ➤ social benefits. These other costs include administration costs in government or regulatory agencies and what economists call *excess burdens*. Excess burdens are costs imposed on society as a whole through regulatory obstruction of the workings of markets, e.g. by the creation of ➤ barriers to entry and reduction in competition and ➤ innovation. The measurement of excess burdens is necessarily imprecise. Attempts have been made to measure consumer prices and innovative activity before and after deregulation, which indicate that these costs may be substantial. The rapid growth of regulation has led to increasing concern about the costs of regulation and a call for the reform and even abolition of regulatory requirements (➤ deregulation). ➤➤ compliance cost; free trade; regulatory capture.

regulatory capture The situation that occurs when regulators advocate the interests of the producers they are intended to regulate. ➤➤ regulation.

re-intermediation ➤ disintermediation.

relative-income hypothesis A theory of ➤ consumption and ➤ saving which suggests that individuals are more concerned with their consumption relative to other people's than they are with their own absolute living standard. If everybody wants to 'keep up with the Joneses' in their consumption, the poor will spend a higher proportion of their income than the rich. This is observed to be the case. However, as society as a whole gets richer, no one will feel able to consume less, because everybody will also be getting richer. This too has been observed.

The relative-income hypothesis, developed by Duesenberry, is an alternative, and rather less widely accepted theory for reconciling the results from ➤ time series and cross-section analyses on consumption within different countries, compared to the ➤ permanent-income hypothesis and the ➤ life-cycle hypothesis. Nevertheless, the insight that relative income matters to ➤➤ utility is not to be disregarded. Most people would consider that someone today on the average ➤ real income of 1930 would genuinely be poorer than his 1930s counterpart, if only because certain types of important social interaction (such as joining in the daily chat at the office) require possession of the means to share experiences (such as having a TV to watch and DVDs to discuss). ➤➤ consumption function.

remittances ➤ migration.

rent 1 The income accruing to the owner for the services of a ➤ durable good, e.g. a piece of land, property or computer (➤➤ Ricardo, D.).
    2 ➤ economic rent.

rentier Someone who receives his income in the form of ➤ interest and ➤ dividends rather than in wages or salary and who does not otherwise participate in the process of production. A provider of ➤ capital and person of independent means.

rent-seeking behaviour Behaviour that improves the welfare of someone at the expense of the welfare of someone else. The most extreme example of rent-seeking behaviour is that of a protection racket, in which one group betters themselves without creating any welfare-enhancing output at all. Not all examples are criminal, however: the behaviour of labour or management when they put more effort into increasing their share of ➤ turnover, rather than into increasing the total volume of turnover, can be described as rent-seeking.

repeated games A strategic interaction between a small number of players that occurs in the same form many times. The distinguishing features of repeated games are that the players can learn about the strategies of the other players by looking at what they do in earlier rounds, and that the players can punish or reward cooperative behaviour in early rounds by adopting certain strategies in later rounds, substantially changing the nature of the game. This is of more significance in games that go on being repeated indefinitely than those that are played a known number of times. ➤➤ game theory; prisoner's dilemma; tit-for-tat.

replacement-cost accounting ➤ inflation accounting.

replacement rate ➤ unemployment trap.

repo Sale and repurchase agreement under which funds are borrowed through the sale of short-term securities (➤ money market) on condition that the instruments are repurchased at a given date. Used between ➤ central banks and the money market as part of ➤ open-market operations. First developed in the USA, repos are also used widely as a borrowing method by large corporations, banks and non-banking institutions. ➤➤ gilt repo.

repressed inflation The state of a set of markets or an economy in which there is persistent ➤ excess demand for goods and services. If prices are below their market-clearing levels, demand will outweigh the available supply; this should drive prices up, causing ➤ inflation. If, however, prices are prevented from rising (e.g. because of price controls (➤ prices and incomes policy)), the inflation can be prevented but consumers will not be able to obtain as many of the things as they want. Features of markets suffering repressed inflation will thus be queues, explicit state rationing, constant shortages or black markets.

While the term can be used to refer to a state of any set of markets in which excess demand is not removed by price increases, more specifically it is one of four forms of ➤ quantity rationing in the macroeconomy; the others are ➤ Keynesian unemployment, ➤ classical unemployment and ➤ underconsumption. In terms of these models of the economy, repressed inflation is one in which buyers in both the labour and goods markets are rationed: households cannot get the goods they want and firms the labour they want. It can be cured by freeing prices and wages and letting them rise, so that they meet equilibrium prices, or by cutting aggregate demand so that the equilibrium price in each market moves down to the level of the actual price. ➤➤ planned economy.

research and development (R&D) Activity that includes: (a) basic or pure research intended to increase knowledge without any particular application in view, e.g. research into the properties of materials; (b) applied research directed at a particular objective, e.g. searching for a new material for a product; or (c) experimental or development work on new inventions or the improvement of existing products and processes. All three types of R&D are carried out by government research laboratories, universities, research institutes and company research establishments. About 2 per cent of the employed ➤ labour force is engaged in R&D work in the USA and about half that percentage in Europe. However, these figures relate to professional, recorded R&D workers only; a substantial amount of R&D is carried on by amateurs and in small firms and goes unrecorded. Research and development activity is important because of its role in defence policy and commercial ➤ innovation. While it is the case that some countries may have an interest in avoiding the costs of R&D while enjoying the benefits of investments in it by other countries (➤ free-rider problem), academics in the area surmise that a minimum national investment in R&D is necessary even to adopt or replicate other nations' technology. That basic minimum may be seen as an 'entry-ticket' to the modern world.

reserve asset ratio ➤ capital adequacy.

reserve currency A ➤ currency governments and international institutions are willing to hold in their ➤ gold and foreign exchange reserves and that finances a significant proportion of ➤ international trade. These two conditions normally require that: (a) the value of the currency must be stable in relation to other currencies; (b) the currency is that of a country holding an important share of world trade; (c) there exists an efficient ➤ foreign exchange market in which the currency may be exchanged for other currencies; and (d) the currency is convertible (➤ convertibility). According to the ➤ International Monetary Fund, the major reserve currency at the end of 2009 was the US dollar (a position it has held since 1944) which accounted for about 62 per cent of the total, followed by the euro at 27 per cent, the Japanese yen at 5 per cent and UK sterling at 4 per cent (➤ international liquidity; special drawing rights).

reserve ratio ➤ capital adequacy.

reserve requirement ➤ capital adequacy.

resource accounting and budgeting The initiative launched in the UK ➤ budget of November 1993 designed to recast the accounting practices of the public sector. The system of resource accounting and budgeting was finally fully implemented in April 2001, and brings the public sector more into line with private sector accounting practice, most notably in accounting for resources at the time they are used, rather than when cash relating to resources changes hands. Formerly, government departments had just produced information and planned its activities on the basis of the ➤ cash flow. The most important distinction between the two relates to capital assets, which incur a large cash flow in one year but a smaller real flow of resources. The hope is that the bulk of such assets in the public sector can be valued in order that an annual charge can be levied for the ➤ cost of capital incurred by the department over time. ➤➤ private finance initiative; public expenditure.

resource allocation The choices made about how scarce ➤ factors of production should be used in an economy. It is the fact that resources are scarce (➤ scarcity) that leads to the need for allocation. Any allocation of inputs determines the composition and size of an economy's output, so each allocation therefore can be defined in two ways: either (a) by the use made of inputs, or (b) by the mix of total output. In a world consisting of only two goods, e.g. milk and honey, each possible allocation may be represented by a point on a graph with output of one of the commodities on each axis. Society, probably through a ➤ price mechanism, or through central planning (➤➤ planned economy), chooses one of the combinations. If, in such an economy, no more milk could be produced without a fall in the output of honey, the allocation is efficient and lies on the ➤ transformation curve of the economy. If it were possible to allocate resources in a different way so that there was more milk and more honey produced, resources would be being used inefficiently. ➤➤ economic efficiency.

resources Scarce inputs that can yield ➤ utility through production or provision of goods and services (➤ depletion theory; factors of production; natural resources; production function; resource allocation).

restriction, exchange ➤ exchange control.

retail banking ➤ wholesale banking.

retail prices index (RPI) An index (➤ index number) of the prices of goods and services purchased by consumers to measure the rate of ➤ inflation or the cost of living. The weights used in the index are revised annually and based on the proportion of household expenditure spent on each item, information on which is obtained in the UK from the Family Expenditure Survey. The prices of these items are collected, and the index updated, monthly. Changes in the index have an important effect on the UK economy because they influence wage and salary awards and the value of index-linked assets and pensions. Government social benefit payments are related to changes in this index or the Consumer Price Index. ➤ harmonized index of consumer prices (➤ indexation).

retail trade The final link in the chain of distribution from the manufacturer to the final consumer. The economic functions of the retailer are to hold stocks at a location convenient to consumers so as to provide them with choice, guidance, after-sales service and, where appropriate, credit facilities (➤ consumer credit). In providing these services, retailers add value to the goods they purchase from wholesalers or direct from the manufacturer (➤ value added). The number of small retailers has fallen substantially in many countries, mainly as a result of competition from the large multiple retailers that enjoy ➤ economies of scale in operation and in purchasing from their suppliers (➤ countervailing power; wholesale trade).

retained earnings Undistributed ➤ profits. ➤➤ self-financing.

retentions Undistributed ➤ profits. ➤➤ self-financing.

return on capital employed ➤➤ rate of return.

return on investment (ROI) ➤➤ rate of return.

returns to scale The proportionate increase in output resulting from proportionate increases in all inputs. If the number of workers, raw materials and machines used by a firm are all doubled, three situations can result: (a) *decreasing returns to scale* would hold if output less than doubled; (b) *constant returns to scale* would exist if output exactly doubled; and (c) *increasing returns to scale* would hold if output more than doubled. Decreasing returns to scale should not be confused with the law of ➤ diminishing returns, which traces the response of output to an increase in one individual input with all others held constant. ➤➤ economies of scale; production function.

revaluation ➤ devaluation; exchange rate.

revealed preference An approach to demand theory that derives the traditional laws of demand using only information on the choices the consumer makes in different price and income situations, coupled with the assumption that such choices are made rationally. It can be seen as a third approach to consumer behaviour, in contrast to the cardinal approach (➤ marginal utility) – which requires there to be an absolute, single, measure of utility – and the ➤ ordinal utility approach (based on ➤ indifference-curve analysis) – which requires there to be some measure of relative utility, albeit one that does not require actual magnitudes of utility to be ascribed to bundles of commodities.

The revealed-preference approach holds that only two types of information are theoretically necessary to predict the behaviour of consumers and derive the laws of demand: (a) the observed spending of a consumer in different price–income situations – this reveals which bundles of commodities are preferred to others; and (b) the assumption that the consumer's behaviour accords to certain axioms of 'rationality' – to predict how someone will spend their money we must know that they will not behave erratically (➤ transitivity). It can be shown that, if such information were available in full, an indifference map could be constructed for the consumer. Implicitly, therefore, the approach does construct at least a partial indifference map of the form used in indifference-curve theory and should be seen as an alternative expression of this theory rather than a replacement for it. ➤➤ demand, theory of; Samuelson, P.A.

revenue reserves ➤ company reserves.

reverse takeover The acquisition or ➤ takeover of a public company by a private one. Often also used to refer to the acquisition of a company by another, smaller, one.

reverse yield gap ➤ yield gap.

Ricardian equivalence The idea originally expounded by ➤➤ Ricardo, and developed by Robert J. Barro in his paper '*Are Government Bonds Net Worth?*', published in 1974, that government deficits have little real economic effect because private citizens anticipate the fact that any borrowing now has to be repaid later and thus increase their saving with that in mind. If governments issue bonds to finance a deficit, the private sector will buy them from the income received from the deficit. The essence of the proposition is that individuals can unravel the effect of government policy. If the government consumes more and borrows the money to do so, and if the private sector did not want overall consumption to rise, the private sector would save more now so that, when the debts had to be repaid, the money was available. The government might as well have taxed people rather than have borrowed the money. Ricardian equivalence can be seen as part of a thread of economic thinking which holds that only decisions about real variables (e.g. consumption and production) matter, and that decisions about financing will, in perfectly functioning markets, never have an effect. ➤➤ crowding-out; deficit financing; Modigliani–Miller theorem; rational expectations.

Ricardo, David (1772–1823) The son of Jewish parents who were connected with the ➤ money market, first in the Netherlands and later in London, Ricardo had little formal education. At the early age of fourteen, however, he was already working in the money market himself. It was James Mill (the father of ➤ Mill, J.S.) who persuaded Ricardo, himself diffident about his own abilities, to write. Nevertheless, Ricardo succeeded in making a fortune on the ➤ stock exchange, sufficient for him to be able to retire at forty-two. Not surprisingly, many of his earlier publications were concerned with money and banking. In 1810, he published a pamphlet on *The High Price of Bullion, a Proof of the Depreciation of Bank Notes*; in 1811 appeared the *Reply to Mr Bosanquet's Practical Observations on the Report of the Bullion Committee*, and in 1816 *Proposals for an Economical and Secure Currency*.

However, his work on monetary economics did not have the originality or exert the influence of his studies in other branches of economics. His *Essay on the Influence of a Low Price of Corn on the Profits of Stock* (1815) was the prototype for his most important work, *The Principles of Political Economy and Taxation* (1817), that was to dominate English ➤ classical economics for the following half-century. In his *Principles*, Ricardo was basically concerned 'to determine the laws which regulate the distribution (between the different classes of landowners, capitalists and labour) of the produce of industry'. His approach was to construct a theoretical ➤ model which was abstracted from the complexities of an actual economy so as to attempt to reveal the major important influences at work within it. His economy was predominantly agricultural. With ➤ demand rising as a result of increasing ➤ population, and a level of subsistence which tended, by custom, to rise also over time, more and more less fertile ➤ land had to be brought into cultivation. The return (in terms of the output of corn) of each further addition of ➤ capital and ➤ labour to more land fell (➤ diminishing returns, law of). This process continued until it was no longer considered sufficiently profitable to bring any additional plots of land under cultivation. However, ➤ opportunity costs and ➤ profits must be the same on all land, whether or not it was marginal. Labour cost the same wherever it was applied. If profits were higher at one place than at another, it would encourage capital to be invested at the place of high return until, by the process of diminishing returns, profit fell into line with profits elsewhere. Therefore, as costs and profits were the same throughout, a surplus was earned on the non-marginal land, and this was ➤ rent (see the diagram).

The consequence of this was that, as the population expanded and more less fertile land was brought into cultivation, profits became squeezed between the increasing proportion of total output that went in rent and the basic minimum level of subsistence allocated to the wages of labour. Ricardo assumed that prices

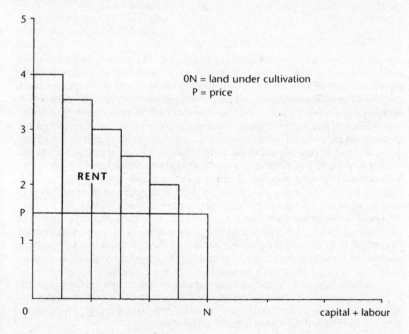

were determined principally by the quantity of labour used during production (➤ value, theories of). However, he recognized that capital costs did, nevertheless, also have an influence on prices and that the effect of a rise in wages on relative prices depended on the proportion of these two ➤ factors of production in the various ➤ commodities. With a rise in wages, ➤ capital-intensive goods became cheaper relative to ➤ labour-intensive goods, with a consequent shift in the demand and output in favour of the former (➤ Ricardo effect).

In the theory of ➤ international trade, Ricardo stated explicitly for the first time the law of comparative advantage. This law can best be illustrated by means of the example of two countries A and B producing two commodities, e.g. cloth and wine. If the relative cost of cloth to wine is the same in both countries, then no trade will take place because there is no gain to be had by exchanging wine (or cloth) for cloth (or wine) produced abroad for that produced at home. Trade will take place where cost differences exist. These can be of two kinds: (a) if wine is cheap in country A and cloth in B, A will specialize in wine and B in cloth, and exchange will take place to their mutual advantage; and (b) the law of comparative advantage states the condition under which trade will take place, even though both commodities may be produced more cheaply in one country than another.

Man-hours per unit of output

Country	Wine	Cloth
A	120	100
B	80	90

Country B exports one unit of wine to A, and imports in exchange 120/100 units of cloth. If country B had devoted the 80 man-hours employed in making wine for exports to making cloth instead, it would have produced only 80/90 units of cloth. Country B therefore gains from trade by the difference ((120/100) – (80/90)) units of cloth. As long as country B can exchange wine for cloth at a rate higher than 80/90, it will therefore gain from the trade. If country A exports a unit of cloth to B, it will obtain in exchange 90/80 units of wine. If the 100 man-hours required by A to produce a unit of cloth had been devoted to the home production of wine, only 100/120 units of wine would be obtained. The gain from trade therefore is (90/80) – (100/120) units of wine. Provided, therefore, country A can exchange cloth for wine at a rate higher than 100/120, it will gain from the trade. Within the range of exchange of wine for cloth of 120/100 and 80/90, both countries therefore benefit.

The law of comparative advantage survives as an important part of the theory of international trade today. The law of comparative advantage is accepted by most economists of all economic doctrines, but like all classical economists (➤ classical economics) Ricardo assumed full employment (➤ employment, full). In circumstances of less than full employment and where ➤ technology is mobile, the law may not apply in certain cases. Ricardo also made an important contribution to the analytical approach of theoretical model-building that has contributed substantially to economists' methodological toolkits. ➤➤ equation of international demand; Heckscher–Ohlin principle; Ricardian equivalence.

Ricardo effect The idea, supported by von ➤ Hayek that, if the ➤ prices firms received for their outputs increased more than the ➤ opportunity costs of their raw materials and wages, the average rate of ➤ profit on ➤ capital employed per year increased more for those firms with a short turnover period, rather than for those with a long one. This can best be illustrated by a simple arithmetical example. If the rate of profit per year is 5 per cent, $100 of capital will yield $5 in one year and $10 in two years (approximately, ignoring ➤ compound interest). If output prices rise by, say, 1 per cent, the ➤ yield rises to $6 for one year and to $11 in two years. The rate of profit, therefore, rises to 6 per cent per annum for the capital that can be turned over in one year, but only to 5½ per cent per annum for capital with a two-year turnover period. Consequently, in a boom, when ➤ commodity prices rise faster than wages, firms are discouraged from investing in capital goods industries because of the long production time required. This reaction is called the Ricardo effect because of its affinity to Ricardo's argument that, if ➤ real wages fall, firms tend to substitute ➤ labour for machinery. This conclusion contrasted sharply with ➤ Keynes' views based on the principle of the accelerator (➤ acceleration principle).

rights issue An offer of new ➤ shares to existing shareholders. A company will offer the 'rights' in a certain proportion to existing holdings, depending on the amount of new ➤ equity capital it wishes to raise. Thus, in a 'one for one rights issue', each shareholder would be offered a number of new shares equal to the number already held. To ensure that the issue is taken up, the new shares are typically offered at well below the market price of the existing shares. The choice of the discount below the ruling price is not as critical in normal circumstances as is often supposed, because when the rights issue is announced, the market price of the shares will adjust to the market's view of the value of the rights price. Rights issues are a relatively cheap way of raising ➤ capital for a quoted company since the costs of preparing a brochure, ➤ underwriting commission or press advertising involved in a new issue are avoided. Moreover, because existing shareholders are given the right of first refusal, they ensure that companies cannot issue new shares at a price that effectively reduces the value of existing shares. ➤➤ new-issue market.

risk A state in which the number of possible future events exceeds the number of events that will actually occur, and some measure of ➤ probability can be attached to them. This definition distinguishes risk from ➤ uncertainty, in which the probabilities are unknown. A gambler, for example, faces risk because he/she could either be very much richer tomorrow or (more likely) slightly poorer, depending on whether a roulette wheel spins the ball into the right hole – and the odds of the roulette wheel are known. ➤➤ Bernoulli's hypothesis; probability.

It is normally assumed that economic agents dislike risk (➤➤ risk aversion) and in the market for financial assets the riskier an asset, the higher the expected return investors will require of it (➤ expected utility; portfolio theory). ➤➤ sovereign risk; systemic risk.

risk adjusted assets ➤ capital adequacy.

risk assessment A measure of the risks of a course of action, and the costs and benefits of reducing those risks. Risk assessment has been promoted as a means of preventing economic activity that creates more dangers than are reasonable. But perhaps more importantly, it can prevent the error of creating 'too much safety' – the imposition of costly safety mechanisms that reduce risks less than is worthwhile, given the cost. Economists argue that it is not worth investing millions of pounds in, for example, a rail safety system, if it is expected to save one life a year, if the money could have saved more lives invested elsewhere. ➤➤ cost–benefit analysis; precautionary principle; quality-adjusted life years.

risk aversion The placing of a higher value on a prospect arriving with certainty than on an uncertain prospect that has the same expected outcome but with some ➤ risk or ➤ uncertainty attached. If you would prefer to be given $10 with certainty than to have a 50 per cent chance of $15 and a 50 per cent chance of $5 (which gives an average of $10) then you are risk-averse. Economists normally assume that consumers are risk-averse on account of ➤ diminishing marginal utility. The displeasure of losing $5 outweighs the pleasure of winning an extra $5 because the richer we are, the less we probably value $5 (➤➤ Bernoulli's hypothesis). Risk aversion explains why people normally insure against disaster. Gambling, on the other hand, is risk-loving behaviour; people at casinos on average pay out more than they win back. ➤➤ Allais, M.; expected utility.

risk capital Medium- and long-term funds invested in enterprises particularly subject to ➤ risk, as in new ventures, and almost entirely in companies which are not listed on a ➤ stock exchange. Sometimes used as a synonym for ➤ equity capital, it is also used instead of the term *venture capital*, a somewhat more precise term meaning equity and ➤ loan capital provided for a new or ➤ small business undertaking by persons other than the proprietors. Neither term is unambiguous, since all capital except that secured by fixed assets is at risk. Venture capital is provided by financial institutions which invest in funds operated by specialized venture-capital institutions, sometimes owned by banks or other financial institutions (*captives*). Much external risk capital is provided by private individuals known as *business angels*. In the USA, the term 'venture capital' is restricted to seed or development capital for new or young enterprises and does not include capital for ➤ management buy-outs, as in the UK. In the USA, and increasingly in Europe also, venture capital plus capital for buy-outs (known there as *leveraged buy-outs*) is known as *private equity*.

Robbins, Lionel (1898–1984) ➤ economics.

Robinson, Joan Violet (1903–83) Professor of Economics at Cambridge University from 1965 to 1971, Robinson believed there was doubtful validity in the assumption of ➤ perfect competition that there were so many firms supplying a commodity that none of them individually could affect the ➤ price – in the face of the existence of the economies of large-scale output. Professor Robinson built up her analysis on the basis of firms in 'imperfect competition' (➤ monopolistic competition). Each firm had a ➤ monopoly in its products in so far as it could, through marketing, relate it to the particular preferences of sub-sets of consumers (➤ consumer preference) in spite of the existence of very close substitutes produced by other firms. (➤ Chamberlin, who developed similar ideas simultaneously and independently.) These ideas were set out in her book *Economics of Imperfect Competition* (1933). She played a prominent role in the ➤ Cambridge School of economic thought, with the development of post-Keynesian ➤ macroeconomics linked to the early classical period of ➤ Ricardo and ➤ Marx.

Robinson–Patman Act ➤ anti-trust.

ROCE Return on capital employed. ➤ rate of return.

ROI Return on investment. ➤ rate of return.

roll-over ➤ corporation tax.

Rostow, Walt Whitman (1916–2003) Educated at Yale, and at Oxford as a Rhodes Scholar, Rostow served during the Second World War in the Office of Strategic Services, and was the assistant chief of the Division of German–Austrian Economic Affairs of the US Department of State from 1945 to 1946. He was Pitt Professor of American History at Cambridge University for 1949–50, Professor of Economic History at Massachusetts Institute of Technology from 1950 to 1965, and finally Professor of Economics and History at the University of Texas. He was appointed special assistant to the US President in 1966. His major publications include *Essays on the British Economy of the Nineteenth Century* (1948), *The Processes of Economic Growth* (1952), *The Growth and Fluctuations of the British Economy 1790–1850* (1953), *The Stages of Economic Growth* (1960), *Politics and the Stages of Growth* (1971), *How It All Began – Origins of the Modern Economy* (1975), *Why the Poor Get Richer and the Rich Slow Down* (1980) and *British Trade Fluctuations 1868–1896* (1981). He postulated that societies pass through five stages of economic development: (a) the traditional society; (b) the pre-conditions for take-off; (c) the take-off, when growth becomes a normal feature of the economy; (d) the drive to maturity; and, some sixty years after take-off begins, (e) maturity, reached in the age of high mass ➤ consumption. ➤➤ economic growth, stages of; growth theory.

'roundabout methods of production' ➤ Böhm-Bawerk, E. von; capital.

rounding error The discrepancy that sometimes arises when numbers are shown to fewer digits than those in which they were calculated. When suppressing a decimal place it is usual to round down when a number is below 0.5 and to round up when it is above 0.5. The same principle applies to the rounding of whole numbers. For example, the following numbers total 6.68 to two decimal places or 6.7 to one decimal place. If each is rounded to the nearest whole number the total of 7 is still retained, although the rounded numbers add up to 8.

1.64	2
1.66	2
1.69	2
1.69	2
6.68	8

RPI minus X ➤ price regulation.

r-squared ➤ multiple correlation coefficient.

RTGS ➤ real time gross settlement.

RTS ➤ rate of technical substitution.

S

saddle point 1 A combination of values of the ➤ independent variables in a function such that the resulting value of the function is a maximum in one dimension and a minimum in another. Imagine a function $Y = f(X,Z)$. If Y rises, then falls as X rises, and if it falls and then rises as Z rises, the function could have a saddle point where it is at its peak with regard to X, and its trough with regard to Z (see diagram in which the saddle point is indicated by SP).

2 An ➤ equilibrium that is stable (➤ stability analysis) in some directions, but not in others. For example, we can ask whether there is a tendency for the price in an industry to converge towards the equilibrium price. If it is true that it converges only when it starts at certain levels, but does not converge if it starts from other points, the equilibrium is known as a saddle point.

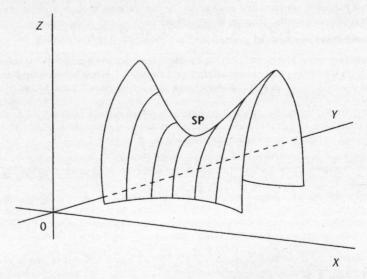

sales promotion ➤ advertising.

sales tax A tax levied as a proportion of the retail ➤ price of a ➤ commodity at the point of sale. An indirect tax (➤ direct taxation), the term is sometimes used to refer to all taxes on expenditure, i.e. to include ➤ value added tax, which is levied at all levels of production and distribution. There are no single-stage sales taxes as such in the UK, though they are levied in the USA and some other countries. Sales taxes may be general (i.e. levied on all sales) or targeted, i.e. levied on a selective basis. ➤➤ fiscal neutrality; taxation.

sample The study of a few members of a ➤ population for the purpose of identifying attributes applicable to the population as a whole. The advantage of sampling is that it is cheaper than a study covering the entire population. Moreover, testing the entire population may be impractical, e.g. when the test procedures are destructive as, for example, in food-tasting. Provided the sampling procedures are designed properly, the margin of error in the estimates may be calculated, and the degree to which the error may be reduced by increasing the sample size. ➤ normal distribution; ➤➤ quota sample; random sample; stratified sample.

Samuelson, Paul Anthony (1915–2009) Professor Samuelson was appointed to the Chair of Economics at Massachusetts Institute of Technology in 1947. He served in the US Treasury for seven years after the end of the Second World War. In 1970, he received the ➤ Nobel Prize for Economics for his development of static and dynamic economic analysis. His publications include *Foundations of Economic Analysis* (1947), *Economics* (1948) and *Linear Programming and Economic Analysis* (with R. Dorfman and ➤ Solow) (1958).

Samuelson developed the ➤ Heckscher–Ohlin principle by showing how an increase in the price of a commodity can raise the income of the ➤ factor of production used most intensively in producing it (➤ capital-intensive). This led to his formulating the *factor price equalization theorem*, which states the conditions under which, as ➤ free trade in commodities narrows differences in commodity prices between countries, the prices (incomes) of factors of production are also brought into line, i.e. free trade is a substitute for the free mobility of factors of production.

Professor Samuelson made important contributions to the development of mathematical economics, general ➤ equilibrium theory and the theory of ➤ consumer behaviour. To free the last from what he considered to be the constraint of the traditional concept of ➤ utility, he invented ➤ revealed preference. In macroeconomic theory (➤ macroeconomics), he was (in 'Interactions between the Multiplier Analysis and the Principle of Acceleration', published in *Review of Economics and Statistics* (1939)) the first to formulate the interaction between the accelerator and the multiplier. He was a leading figure on the side of ➤ neo-classical economics in the debate with the ➤ Cambridge School regarding the integration of classical (➤ classical economics) microeconomics and modern macroeconomics in growth theory. He made significant early contributions in the formulation of the ➤ efficient markets hypothesis and in options pricing (➤ Black–Scholes Formula) (➤ accelerator–multiplier model; social-welfare function; turnpike theorem).

satisficing Behaviour that attempts to achieve some minimum level of a particular ➤ variable, but which does not strive to achieve its maximum possible value. The most common application of the concept in economics is in the ➤ behavioural theory of the firm, which, unlike traditional accounts, postulates that producers do not treat ➤ profit as a goal to be maximized, but as a constraint. Under these theories, although at least a critical level of profit must be achieved by firms, thereafter priority is attached to the attainment of other goals. ➤➤ bounded rationality; optimum; Simon, H.A.

saturation point A level beyond which the *relative* absorption of a product or service is not expected to increase. It is defined in terms of a ratio, e.g. ownership of videos per household or per hundred persons. Once the saturation point is reached, the growth of demand slows down to levels determined by population growth and replacement, although in some cases predictions of saturation points have been falsified by the emergence of multiple ownership, e.g. of cars and television sets. ➤➤ logistic curve; market share.

saving ➤ Income not spent. At the end of any period, saving is equal to income in that period minus ➤ consumption, and could be negative if expenditure exceeds income (➤ dissaving). Note that paying off debt is a form of saving in the economic sense of the term. Saving can occur in the ➤ public sector when tax revenues exceed final consumption by government, plus ➤ transfer payments and ➤ subsidies, and in the company sector where ➤ profits are not distributed (➤ self-financing), as well as in the ➤ household, though typically the public sector is a net borrower (➤ public sector borrowing requirement) while the personal sector and industrial and commercial companies are net lenders.

For the economy as a whole, if total saving is equal to total ➤ investment, then expenditure by firms and individuals will be in ➤ equilibrium (for simplicity we ignore the public sector and foreign trade); if saving exceeds investment, expenditure from wages, salaries and dividends will not return to firms in the form of payments for goods and services (including investment goods) and output will have to fall, thus reducing incomes and bringing saving and investment into balance (➤ circular flow of income).

What determines the level of saving is, therefore, important in ➤ macroeconomics. There are several interpretations of this problem, e.g. that saving will be a function of the level of income (➤ consumption function) (this assumption underlies the mechanism of ➤ income determination just outlined), and that changes in saving will be used to maintain a steady rate of consumption (➤ permanent-income hypothesis). ➤➤ savings ratio.

savings and loan (S&L) associations (US) ➤ savings bank.

savings bank A bank that accepts interest-bearing ➤ deposits of small amounts. The earliest savings banks were established in the private sector but later were set up or supported by governments, to encourage individual ➤ savings. In the UK, the ➤ building societies share the basic objectives of savings banks elsewhere.

In the USA, savings banks are also called 'thrift institutions' or *savings and loan associations*, many of which are ➤ mutual companies. Deregulation of interest rates, tax changes and other factors led to a major crisis for S&Ls in the 1980s and large numbers failed. The Federal government had to intervene at the cost of well over $100 billion and the Financial Institutions Reform, Recovery and Enforcement Act of 1989 created a new Office of Thrift Supervision in the Department of Treasury.

savings function ➤ savings ratio.

savings ratio The proportion of household income that is saved (➤ saving), usually expressed as a percentage of total household ➤ disposable income. It may be calculated gross or net. In the latter case, a deduction is made for the ➤ depreciation of household fixed assets. The savings ratio differs significantly between countries as well as over time. The ratio will depend on: (a) the proportion of old people in the ➤ population, as young people have more incentive and greater means to save; (b) the rate of ➤ inflation, as expectations of rising prices encourage people to spend or invest in fixed assets; and (c) the tax regime. The *savings function* gives the relationship between aggregate savings, that include non-personal savings, and ➤ income, and is the inverse of the ➤ consumption function. (➤ liquidity preference).

Say, Jean-Baptiste (1767–1832) A practical businessman, Say developed an interest in economics and began lecturing in the subject in 1816. In 1819, he was appointed to the Chair of Industrial Economy at the Conservatoire National des Arts et Métiers. In 1831, he was appointed Professor of Political Economy at the Collège de France. His most important published works are *Traité d'économie politique* (1803) (*A Treatise on Political Economy* (1971)) and *Cours complet d'économie politique pratique* (*Complete Course in Practical Political Economy*) (1828–9). Although he can claim some credit for the introduction of the concept of an ➤ entrepreneur into economic theory, and also the division of the fundamental ➤ factors of production into three – ➤ land, ➤ labour and ➤ capital – his fame and notoriety spring from his '*loi des débouchés*', or 'law of markets'.

It is probable that his 'law' would not figure so prominently in economics today had not ➤ Keynes accused the ➤ Classical School of being gravely misled by accepting it as the pivot of their macroeconomic theory (➤ macroeconomics). According to Keynes, the law said that the sum of the values of all ➤ commodities produced was equivalent (always) to the sum of the values of all commodities bought. By definition, therefore, there could be no under-utilization of ➤ resources – 'supply created its own demand'. However, there is some considerable doubt about what Say actually meant. Several versions have been put forward, and some are incontrovertible platitudes, e.g. 'in barter a seller must also be a buyer', and 'if a good is sold somebody must have bought it'. Probably the most meaningful interpretation is that of Keynes, but only as a condition that must be satisfied for ➤ equilibrium to exist. ➤➤ Walras, M.E.L.

Say's law of markets ➤ Say, J.-B.

scarce currency ➤ hard currency.

scarcity A situation in which the needs and wants of an individual or group of individuals exceed the resources available to satisfy them. In the presence of scarcity, choices have to be made between those wants that can be satisfied and those that cannot be; the available resources must in some way be rationed, either through price or some central distribution system. In the absence of scarcity, no difficult choices would need to be made, no prices would need to be attached to anything, and the study of economics would be rendered entirely unnecessary. As an economist uses the term, scarcity is present in any society in which there is anyone whose desires are not all completely satisfied; it is not a concept of any more relevance to a poor society, where want and deprivation are rife, than a rich one in which even a scarcity of Rolls-Royces is considered a shortcoming worthy of attention. ➤➤ price system; resource allocation; resources.

Schengen Treaty A treaty signed at Schengen, Luxembourg, in 1990, the terms of which were subsequently embodied in the Treaty of Amsterdam, agreed by the member countries of the ➤➤ European Union (EU) in 1997. The member countries agreed: (a) to abolish customs and immigration border controls at their common frontiers; (b) to establish a common list of countries, the nationals of which would require visas for entry; and (c) to grant their police the right of pursuit across their common frontiers. At the same time, they promised to tighten controls on their external frontiers and to cooperate in judicial and police matters. All members of the EU, except the UK and Ireland, are parties to the agreements and, in addition, Iceland, Norway and Switzerland. The number of countries within the Schengen border has increased as the EU has expanded its membership and by 2009 there were twenty-four countries in the group.

Scholes, Myron S. (b. 1941) Professor Scholes is a finance specialist and joint winner of the 1997 Nobel Prize for Economics for his work in deriving methods of valuing complex financial instruments, e.g. ➤ options. His work, the result of collaboration with Black, produced the path-breaking ➤ Black–Scholes formula, that itself was generalized by Merton (➤ Merton, R.). Their work led to the development of a significant new financial market that enables traders to diversify risk and allocate it in far more flexible ways than had hitherto been possible. In addition, insurance and guarantees comprise forms of option, and thus these too can be valued more accurately. Professor Scholes' most famous paper is 'The Pricing of Options and Corporate Liabilities', *Journal of Political Economy* (1973), with Fischer Black. Scholes' career has been spent at the Massachusetts Institute of Technology, Chicago University and Stanford University.

Schultz, Theodore W. (1902–1998) After graduation in economics at the South Dakota State College, Professor Schultz obtained a Ph.D. at the University of Wisconsin. In 1943, he accepted a Chair in Economics at the University of Chicago, where he remained until his retirement in 1974. He was awarded the ➤ Nobel Prize for Economics in 1979 (jointly with ➤ Lewis). His major publications include *Agriculture in an Unstable Economy* (1945), *The Economic Organization of Agriculture* (1953), *The Economic Value of Education* (1963), *Transforming Traditional Agriculture* (1964), *Economic Crises in World Agriculture* (1965), *Economic Growth and Agriculture* (1968) and *Investment in Human Capital: The role of education and research* (1971).

Professor Schultz developed the ideas of human capital theory in his work on the economics of education and made major contributions to the analysis of agriculture in ➤ developing countries. He highlighted the distortion of policy in taxation and trade that biases development against agriculture, condemning the sector to subsistence farming.

Schumacher, Ernst Friedrich (1911–77) ➤ intermediate technology.

Schumpeter, Joseph Alois (1883–1950) In 1919, Schumpeter was appointed Professor of Economics at Czernowitz, subsequently moving to Graz in Austria. He was appointed Minister of Finance in the Austrian Republic for a short period after the First World War. From 1925 until 1932 he held the Chair of Public Finance at Bonn. From 1932 until his death he was at Harvard University. His major publications include *Theory of Economic Development* (1912), *Business Cycles: A theoretical, historical and statistical analysis of the capitalist process* (1939) (in which he reviewed the work of Kondratiev (➤ Kondratiev cycle), *Capitalism, Socialism and Democracy* (1942) and *History of Economic Analysis*, which was unfinished and appeared posthumously in 1954.

Schumpeter constructed a theory of the ➤ business cycle that was based on three time periods – short, medium and long – to each of which he attributed different causes. He tested his theory against actual fluctuations from the eighteenth to the twentieth century. Although it was reasonably successful, he was doubtful of the predictive efficiency of his theory for future periods. He attempted to work out a theory of economic growth and fluctuation around an explicit recognition of the contribution of technical ➤ innovation and tried to argue that, without the latter, an economy would reach a static ➤ equilibrium position of a 'circular flow' of goods with no net growth. He emphasized the evolutionary nature of the capitalist system (➤ capitalism) and argued that, under ➤ monopoly capitalism, firms would place less emphasis on ➤ price competition but would increasingly compete in technical and organizational innovation, thus sending 'gales of creative destruction' through the economic system. Furthermore, he predicted that capitalism would evolve gradually into socialism.

Scitovsky, Tibor de (1910–2002) Tibor Scitovsky was born of a noble family in Budapest (he dropped the 'de' when he went to the USA). He obtained his first degree in Hungary and followed it by a Masters degree at the London School of Economics in 1938. He emigrated to the USA and served in the Army (1943–6), spending much of his subsequent career at Stanford and the University of California, Berkeley. From 1966 to 1968 he was seconded to the OECD Development Centre.

Scitovsky was a pioneer in welfare economics and it was his first book on that subject, *Welfare and Competition* (1951), which first established his reputation, though he also made contributions to the theory of international trade and the concept of externalities. From about 1959 he began questioning the rationality of consumer behaviour in the light of developments in behavioural psychology (➤ behavioural economics). His 1976 book, *The Joyless Economy*, argued that individuals want and need risk and novelty and that the volume of consumption could not be equated with progress unless quality of life (joy) were taken into account. His arguments differentiated him from most mainstream economists at the time but are now coming back into fashion (➤ Human Development Index; quality adjusted life years).

screening The use of a mechanism that allows someone to judge the characteristics of someone or something even though they cannot see those characteristics directly. In situations of ➤ asymmetric information, one party to a transaction may wish to know about some feature of the other party (e.g. how hard-working they are) which cannot easily be judged before employing them. A screening device is one that can be observed directly, and correlates with the unobservable characteristics. For example, if hard-working people enjoy school and spend many years there, and lazy people hate it and leave as soon as possible, the number of years spent at school may provide a device for screening hard-working from lazy people. However, the device can work only as long as the extra pay that hard-working people get is not so attractive to lazy people that they choose to endure more time at school anyway. This is known as ➤ incentive compatibility. ➤➤ information, economics of; signalling; Stiglitz, J.

scrip issue An issue of new ➤ shares to shareholders in proportion to their existing holdings, made, as distinct from a ➤ rights issue, without charge. A scrip or bonus issue does not raise new ➤ capital. It is merely an adjustment to the capital structure that capitalizes reserves, usually consisting of past ➤ profits. The word 'scrip' is an abbreviation of 'subscription certificate'. ➤➤ capitalization.

SDR ➤ special drawing rights.

seasonal adjustment The elimination from a ➤ time series of fluctuations that exhibit a regular pattern at a particular time during the course of a year that are similar from one year to another. For example, unemployment rises in the winter months because of the interruption of work by cold weather conditions. From a study of a series of winter periods, the percentage effect this has on the numbers unemployed may be estimated, and the time series of unemployment statistics may be offset by this percentage. The resultant, adjusted, series gives a clearer picture of the underlying trend in unemployment. ➤➤ moving average.

seasonal unemployment ➤ Unemployment that varies with the season as in the construction, tourist and agricultural sectors. ➤➤ seasonal adjustment.

secondary bank A financial institution that accepts deposits and makes loans but has relatively few branches and therefore does not play a major role in the payments system as far as the general public is concerned. Included in the term are the ➤ investment banks, and other money-market banks, ➤ overseas banks, consortium banks, and some ➤ finance houses. There was a secondary-banking crisis in 1973 when a number of minor banks (mainly deposit-taking finance houses and other institutions heavily lent to the property sector) got into difficulties when ➤ monetary policy was tightened following the oil crisis. ➤➤ banking.

secondary market A ➤ market in which ➤ assets are resold and purchased, as distinct from a primary market in which assets are sold for the first time. The ➤ stock exchange is a secondary market in which financial ➤ securities are traded, although it is also a primary market where these securities are issued for the first time (➤ new-issue market). Another example is the secondary ➤ mortgage market in the USA, in which holders of mortgages who need funds can dispose of their holdings before maturity. Secondary markets are typically larger than primary markets and perform an important function, since purchasers of new issues of securities would be reluctant to purchase and would offer a lower price for them (a bigger ➤ discount) unless they were confident that they could, if necessary, dispose of them in the secondary market.

second best, theory of A theory formulated by R.G. Lipsey and K.J. Lancaster of the London School of Economics in 'The General Theory of Second Best', *Review of Economic Studies* (1957), that postulates that, in the absence of being able to attain all the conditions necessary for the existence of the most desirable possible economic situation, the second-best position is not necessarily one in which the remaining conditions will hold. In an efficient economy, for example, price will equal ➤ marginal cost in all industries. This will ensure that no consumer who values a commodity more than it costs society to produce it will be deterred from buying it (➤ marginal-cost pricing). If in one industry, however, price is higher than marginal cost, the theory of the second best suggests that it is not efficient for price to be equal to marginal cost in all the other industries, for this would encourage too much consumption of those items relative to the more highly priced one. In the second-best world, all other items would be taxed so that everything was priced in excess of marginal cost, and consumers would allocate their budgets closely to that in a world of full marginal-cost pricing. ➤➤ welfare economics.

secular trend A long-term directional movement in the trend of an economic ➤ time series, as distinct from effects generated by the fluctuations of the ➤ business cycle or seasonality (➤ seasonal adjustment). Such movements could, for example, be due to changes in tastes or technology or the contraction of an industry due to the growth of overseas competitors.

securities **1** In the widest sense, documents giving title to property or claims on ➤ income that may be lodged, e.g. as security for a ➤ bank loan.
   2 Income-yielding and other paper traded on the ➤ stock exchange or in ➤ secondary markets; usually a synonym for ➤ stocks and ➤ shares. An essential characteristic of a security is that it is saleable. The main types of security are: (a) *fixed interest*: ➤ preference shares, stocks and ➤ bonds (including all ➤ government securities and local authority securities) – sometimes a distinction is made between ➤ gilt-edged securities and other fixed-interest securities, though in both cases the holder normally receives a predetermined and unchanging rate of interest on the ➤ nominal value of the stock, which is what is meant by fixed interest; (b) *variable interest*: ➤ ordinary shares; and (c) *other*: ➤ bills of exchange, ➤ assurance policies, ➤ warrants. Securities may be ➤ redeemable or ➤ irredeemable, quoted or unquoted (➤ quotation). ➤➤ bond; equities.

Securities and Exchange Act (USA) 1934 ➤ Securities and Exchange Commission.

Securities and Exchange Commission (SEC) The US Federal agency for the ➤ regulation of the markets in ➤ securities, set up in 1934 to administer the Securities and Exchange Acts 1933 and 1934 which require most securities offered for sale to be registered. The SEC also enforces the Investment Company Act 1940, the Investment Advisers Act 1940, the Securities Investor Protection Act 1970 and other legislation.
   The SEC has a chairman and four commissioners, all appointed by the President with the advice and consent of the Senate for five-year terms. The SEC has five main divisions: (a) corporation finance (corporate new issues, registration, disclosure, etc.); (b) market regulation (overseas brokers, self-regulating organizations and other market participants, e.g. ➤ commercial banks); (c) investment management (➤ institutional investor and investment adviser supervision); (d) enforcement; and (e) compliance inspections and examinations. The SEC has eleven district offices in addition to the headquarters in Washington, DC.

securitization The substitution of ➤ securities for ➤ loans. Banks and other ➤ financial intermediaries, for example, have packaged house mortgages and ➤ credit card loans in this way so that borrowers continue to pay interest that is received by the investor in the security representing the underlying loans. Securitization converts unmarketable assets (e.g. long-term bank loans) into readily saleable paper. ➤➤ derivatives.

seignorage The profit margin on issuing coins and currency which derives from the difference between the value of the materials (the *assay value*) and the *face value* of the coins or paper money.

self-financing Generating ➤ capital from ➤ income. A firm that is self-financing is generating its ➤ investment funds from internal sources, i.e. the ploughing back of retained ➤ profits (or retentions), and ➤ depreciation, as opposed to external borrowing. A quoted company has the choice of financing fixed capital formation or increasing its stocks and work in progress or acquiring other companies or ➤ shares in them, either by borrowing on the ➤ stock exchange (or from other sources, including banks) or by using undistributed income. If it borrows, it will have to pay ➤ interest or ➤ dividends and issuing costs on new issues. If it uses undistributed income, it is choosing to pay its ordinary shareholders a lower dividend, i.e. to distribute less of its income. Unquoted companies do not have the alternative of new issues of shares, although they may take further ➤ equity from private, and borrow from other, sources.

In fact, the bulk of capital expenditure is financed from internal sources. Of total sources of funds of UK industrial and commercial companies, over 70 per cent in recent years has been provided from internal sources. The remainder comes from new issues, ➤ bank loans, ➤ mortgages, inward investment (➤ foreign investment) and capital transfers.

self-financing ratio ➤ Investment funds derived from undistributed ➤ income as a proportion of total investment funds in any accounting period. ➤➤ self-financing.

self-liquidating A term used to describe a low-risk financial transaction or ➤ loan that incorporates a procedure for simultaneous termination and clearing indebtedness. A hire-purchase transaction is self-liquidating in that regular payments culminate in a final instalment that clears the ➤ debt. More generally, the term is applied to any form of finance to fill a temporary shortfall of funds, e.g. ➤ bills of exchange, or a bridging loan by a bank to a customer in the process of selling one house and buying another.

selling costs ➤ Opportunity costs incurred in ➤ marketing and distributing a product, including the costs of advertising, sales promotion, packaging and sales staff.

selling short Selling a stock in the expectation of being able to buy it back more cheaply later on. It may take the form of a commitment to supply an amount of stock at a future date at a price below the current rate, for example in the sale of a ➤ futures contract.

Selten, Reinhard (b. 1930) A German economist, who has specialized in ➤ game theory, and jointly won the ➤ Nobel Prize for Economics in 1994, with John C. ➤ Harsányi and John F. Nash. Selten has been one of the economists most concerned with defining the characteristics of an ➤ equilibrium in a game. ➤ Nash had developed one such equilibrium (➤ Nash equilibrium), but Selten was the first to refine the concept for analysing dynamic situations. One problem with Nash's equilibrium concept had been its inclusion of intuitively unsatisfactory strategic combinations. In particular, if one party to a game makes an untenable threat to the other, and the other is deterred by that threat from some course of action, it is a Nash equilibrium even if the threat was unlikely to be carried out. That did not seem a likely outcome to an interaction. Selten introduced the refined notion of *sub-game perfection*, which essentially counted only those Nash equilibria that would also be Nash in each and every segment of a game taken on its own. In effect, only credible threats should be taken into account. He also devised the notion of the *trembling hand* equilibrium, which is a Nash equilibrium that still holds, even if the players assume that one of the players may have a 'trembling hand' and make a mistake as to which rational strategy to follow.

Sen, Amartya (b. 1933) The world's most celebrated welfare economist, Master of Trinity College, Cambridge, and winner of the Nobel Prize for Economics in 1998, Professor Sen has held posts at the Universities of Delhi and Calcutta, and at the London School of Economics, Oxford and Harvard. Among his main works are *Collective Choice and Social Welfare* (1970), *On Economic Inequality* (1973) and *Poverty and Famines: An essay on entitlement and deprivation* (1981). He is perhaps best known for his work on famines and the finding that they are not always associated with shortages of food, but that sometimes they reflect the economic predicament of particular groups.

Sen has also contributed to the study of ➤ social welfare functions, and has devised measures of ➤ poverty and welfare, in both cases taking into account inequalities (➤ inequality) among the poor, or across society generally. He has also tried to cast individual welfare not in terms of goods consumed, but in terms of capabilities enjoyed. In this view, goods are welfare-enhancing because they provide capabilities. Owning a DVD player, for example, gives us the capability of being able to interact with our friends, having some common interests to talk about. Therefore, someone who does not have a DVD player in a rich country where most people do have one is poorer than a person without a DVD player in a country where no one owns one. All Sen's work has been characterized by a concern for the least well-off, and a strong inclination to philosophical methods of inquiry.

Senior, Nassau William (1790–1864) Educated at Oxford University, Senior was called to the Bar in 1819 and became a Master in Chancery in 1836. In 1825, he was appointed the first Drummond Professor of Political Economy at Oxford. He held this position twice, the first time until 1830, and the second from 1847 to 1852. He served on many royal commissions. His major work on economics was *An Outline of the Science of Political Economy* (1836). He is remembered mainly for his abstinence theory of ➤ interest. Interest was a reward for abstaining from the unproductive use of ➤ savings. The creation of new capital involved a sacrifice. A positive return must therefore be expected to make the sacrifice worthwhile. Senior can be regarded as one of the first pure theorists in economics. He attempted to elaborate economic theory on the basis of deductions from elementary propositions.

separating equilibrium ➤ Stiglitz, J.

separation of ownership from control The situation in which the owners of a corporation do not actively participate in its management. In its earliest form, business was owned and managed by the same people. Economic and technological development led to the advent of the joint-stock company in the seventeenth century to meet the need for larger amounts of ➤ capital. This began the process of the separation of ownership from control that continued with the introduction of ➤ limited liability for both public companies and ➤ private companies, and the gradual emergence of the modern giant corporation in which none of the directors or managers has more than a minority financial interest. This process has given rise to the possibility that the interests of those who control business and those who own it may conflict, a subject of continuing controversy among economists since the publication by Adolf Berle and Gardiner Means of *The Modern Corporation and Private Property* (1932). ➤➤ firm, theory of the; Galbraith, J.K.; moral hazard; principal–agent problem.

serial correlation ➤ auto-correlation.

Serra, Antonio (15?–16?) A Neapolitan writer in the mercantilist tradition (➤ mercantilism), who was the first to analyse and fully use the concept of the ➤ balance of trade, both visible and ➤ invisible. He explained how the shortage of precious metals in the Neapolitan kingdom was a result of a deficit on the ➤ balance of payments. In so doing, he rejected the idea, current at the time, that the ➤ scarcity of money was due to the unfavourable ➤ exchange rate. The solution was to be found in the encouragement of ➤ exports.

services Intangible economic goods as distinct from physical commodities. Services are difficult to define unambiguously. The output of some services from, for example, a bank may take a physical form (a cheque or bank statement) while – although many services are consumed at the point of sale and are not therefore transferable (e.g. a concert or a haircut) – a service in which knowledge is imparted (e.g. a medical consultation or tax advice) may be transferable freely from one consumer to another. Moreover, many manufacturing companies enhance their product attraction by offering services in support of their product, e.g. computer suppliers who offer online software advice to their customers.

The intangible nature of much of the output of the service sector creates difficulties in the calculation of unit ➤ productivity. Generally speaking, the service sector of the economy is more ➤ labour-intensive than the manufacturing sector, but even this generalization is misleading because, with computerization and the development of telecommunications, automated warehouses, special-purpose buildings and other plant and equipment, much of the service sector now employs more ➤ capital per worker than manufacturing industry.

The service sector also contributes proportionately less to exports compared with its domestic market than does manufacturing, but invisible exports (➤ invisibles) are of growing importance and world trade in services is growing faster than that in physical commodities. Some parts of the service sector and the sector as a whole have, on average, lower levels of ➤ concentration than the manufacturing or extractive industries, but some (e.g. ➤ banking) are highly concentrated. Parts of the sector, notably distribution, banking, business services and communications, have been growing very rapidly. The relative decline of agriculture and manufacturing has given rise to fears of ➤ de-industrialization, though these fears are probably misplaced. The relative faster growth of services compared with other sectors of the economy has been characteristic of all ➤ advanced countries. Exports of commercial services have about a quarter of total international trade and an increasing share. ➤ Baumol effect; General Agreement on Trade in Services; Petty, Sir W.

servicing debt ➤ debt.

shadow economy ➤ informal economy.

shadow price The ➤ opportunity cost to a society of engaging in some economic activity. It is a concept applied to situations in which actual prices cannot be charged, or where actual prices charged do not reflect the real sacrifice made when some activity is pursued. Suppose, for example, there is unemployed labour in the economy: the cost of using that labour to society is virtually zero – by employing it no sacrifice is made in terms of other goods produced. The shadow price of labour is zero, even though the workers, if employed, would have to be paid a wage. Alternatively, suppose there is an ➤ excess demand for labour: at the going wage rate, labour is in short supply. In this case, employing a worker may cost a firm only the going wage, but the cost to society of that firm employing that worker is the output the worker could have produced in an alternative occupation; this will be worth more than the wage rate if labour is in excess demand. The shadow price of labour in this case is higher than the wage rate. In effect, it reflects the benefit that would result from relaxing the constrained supply of workers by one unit.

Of course, in a perfectly functioning economy, market prices will be equal to ➤ marginal cost (➤ perfect competition), and marginal cost itself represents the true cost to society of producing one extra unit of a commodity; it is equivalent to the value of the items that could have been made as alternatives to the last unit of the commodity produced, with the same resources. In the competitive economy, therefore, the market price of an item is equal to the opportunity cost of producing that item. There is no shadow price, distinct from actual prices.

Shadow prices are used in valuing any item that is implicitly rationed or constrained in some way. Shadow prices can be derived using ➤ linear programming techniques and can be used in social ➤ cost–benefit analysis, which attempts to achieve an optimal ➤ resource allocation in the absence of an effective ➤ price system.

Shanghai Stock Exchange In terms of domestic ➤ equity ➤ market capitalization, the Shanghai Stock Exchange was number six in the world in 2009, after the London Stock Exchange, and third in terms of the value of share trading, according to the World Federation of Exchanges. It began operating in the 1860s but ceased trading in the early Communist era. In 1990 the exchange reopened and now foreign access is being progressively extended. There are also exchanges in Shenzhen and Hong Kong.

share One of a number of equal portions in the nominal ➤ capital of a company entitling the owner to a proportion of distributed ➤ profits and of residual ➤ value if the company goes into ➤ liquidation; a form of ➤ security. Shares may be fully ➤ paid-up or partly paid, ➤ voting or non-voting (sometimes called 'A' shares). ➤➤ bearer bonds; ordinary shares; preference shares; stocks.

share certificate A document proving ownership of ➤ shares in a company. ➤➤ CREST; transfer deed.

shareholders' interest ➤ balance sheet.

share indices ➤ Index numbers indicating changes in the average prices of ➤ shares on the ➤ stock exchange. The indices are constructed by taking a selection of shares and 'weighting' (➤ weighted average) the percentage changes in prices together as an indication of aggregate movements in share prices. Roughly speaking, a share index shows percentage changes in the ➤ market value of a ➤ portfolio compared with its ➤ value in the base year of the index. Index numbers are published in several daily papers and weekly journals.

share options ➤ option.

Sharia ➤ Islamic finance.

Sharpe, William F. (b. 1934) An economist at Stanford University in California, William Sharpe was a pioneer of the ➤ capital asset pricing model, encapsulated in his article 'Capital Asset Prices: A theory of market equilibrium under conditions of risk', *Journal of Finance* (1964). He jointly won the ➤ Nobel Prize for Economics in 1990 for that achievement, which built on the foundations laid in ➤ portfolio theory by one of his fellow winners, ➤ Markowitz. ➤➤ envelope theorem.

Shephard's lemma ➤ envelope theorem.

Sherman Act ➤ anti-trust.

shipping conference A group of shipping companies operating scheduled services along specific trade routes. They were first established in the nineteenth century following a period of intense price competition as sailing vessels gave way to steam. A conference may set prices and capacity and share revenue or profits. The argument in their favour is that they are necessary to maintain prices to prevent destructive competition and a consequential loss of scheduled services. However, they could exert ➤➤ monopoly power over the routes along which they operate. The USA grants shipping conferences a block exemption from ➤ anti-trust legislation. The ➤ European Union (EU) also issued shipping conferences that operated to and from EU ports such a block exemption but this was repealed in 2008.

shock therapy ➤ transition, economies in.

short-dated securities ➤ dated securities.

short run A period of time in which only some ➤ variables change or economic processes work. It is a concept that can be defined strictly only in the particular context in which it is applied, because its meaning depends on which variables or processes the user of the term considers flexible. Its most common use is in the theory of the firm (➤ firm, theory of the), where it is defined as the period in which the quantity of certain ➤ factors of production employed (e.g. plant and machinery) is fixed and, for example, only the number of workers hired can be changed. The specific period of time being referred to as the 'short run' also varies with every application of the term, because it may take varying periods of time to build the plant and machinery for different industries. ➤➤ impact effect; long run; Marshall, A.

short-run cost curves A graphical representation of the relationship between the output of a firm and the cost of producing that output with the firm's given level of fixed assets. For example, a company making CDs may have one factory capable of producing any number up to 1 million. The short-run cost curve shows how much it would cost to make any number of CDs with that plant up to its maximum capacity, taking into account the extra labour and raw materials required to produce a given quantity (➤ firm, theory of the). Another factory would have a different short-run cost curve.

Any short-run cost curve can be broken down into two elements: (a) short-run *fixed costs*: the payments incurred independently of the level of production, and (b) short-run *variable costs*: e.g. raw materials and labour costs which vary with the level of output. The sum of these produces short-run *total costs*. This cost function may be depicted as an average cost curve (in which case it is generally assumed that as production rises it falls to a minimum, and then rises). ➤➤ marginal analysis.

short-selling ➤ selling short.

short-term capital ➤ business finance.

short-term gains ➤ capital gains.

signalling The use of a mechanism by which someone indicates to someone else that he/she has certain characteristics, even though these characteristics are not directly observable. A signal is the converse of a screen (➤ screening). Advertising is seen as signalling the quality of a product to consumers, because it is only those with faith in their product, and who think it will be in production for many years, who will find it worth engaging in expensive advertising. An engagement ring is a signal of commitment to a fiancée because – as long as it is expensive enough – it would not pay a man to buy the ring unless he was serious about getting married. A technical or academic qualification is a signal to a prospective employer of the suitability of a job applicant (➤ education). Economists have been increasingly inclined to explain economic and non-economic phenomena as signals. ➤➤ asymmetric information; information, economics of; Spence, M.

Simon, Herbert A. (1916–2001) A graduate of the University of Chicago, Professor Simon held the post of Director of Administrative Measurement Studies at the Bureau of Public Administration of the University of California from 1939 to 1942, in which year he moved to the Illinois Institute of Technology, becoming a professor of political science there in 1947. In 1949, Professor Simon was appointed Professor of Administration and Psychology at the Carnegie Mellon University, becoming Professor of Computer Science and Psychology in 1955. He was awarded the ➤ Nobel Prize for Economics in 1978 for his research into decision-making processes within organizations. His major publications include *Administrative Behaviour* (1947), *Public Administration* (1950), *Organizations* (1958), *The New Science of Management Decision* (1960), *The Shape of Automation (for Men and Management)* (1965), *Models of Discovery* (1977) and *Models of Bounded Rationality and Other Topics in Economics* (1982).

Simon argued that the central assumption in economic theory of a rational 'economic man', who maximizes benefits and minimizes costs, is unrealistic. Any decision faced by an individual, in a household or in a firm, is bounded by uncertainties and ignorance. Individuals 'satisfice' (➤ satisficing), that is, they adjust their behaviour and ambitions continually in the light of experience. More importantly, large organizations that combine many different interests and groups will not generally pursue one goal as consistent or as simple as profit-maximization, as economic theory usually assumes.

simple interest ➤ compound interest.

simple random sample ➤ random sample.

simulation The construction of a ➤ model that describes mathematically the structure and processes of a real-world situation to be studied and the inputting of values of ➤ variables in the model in order to generate appropriate out-turns. The model enables the results of a process to be simulated without the need to test the process in an actual situation. ➤➤ Monte Carlo method; operations research.

Single European Act The legislation passed into law by each member state of the ➤ European Union (EU) in 1987. By this Act, each state agreed to the aim of a single market throughout the EU. The programme involved the abolition of exchange controls, the recognition of qualifications, the abolition of restrictions on internal transport (➤ cabotage), liberalization of the market in air services, public procurement tendering, life insurance and banking services, and the abolition of frontier controls (➤ Schengen Treaty). The Act also widened the application of qualified majority decision-making, as against unanimity, in the EU. However, in a number of areas (e.g. taxation) a unanimous decision was still required from member states for any policy changes to be made. The European Commission monitors competition to ensure that no enterprise acts in such a way as to restrict the free movement of goods and services in the EU or to exploit a dominant market position (➤ competition policy).

single market A trading zone in which roughly homogeneous items are traded in roughly uniform conditions of supply and demand. It is likely that in a single market the ➤ law of one price will prevail. ➤➤ market.

sinking fund ➤ amortization.

Sismondi, Jean Charles Léonard Simonde de (1773–1842) A Swiss historian and economist who, after a period in exile in England, began lecturing at Geneva Academy in 1809 on history and economics. His economic works include *De la richesse commerciale* (1803), *Nouveaux principes d'économie politique* (1819) and *Études sur l'économie politique* (1837).

Sismondi argued against the doctrine of ➤ *laissez-faire* in favour of state intervention. He recommended ➤ unemployment and sickness benefits and pension schemes for workers. With ➤ Malthus, he attacked ➤ Ricardo for not recognizing the possibility of economic crisis developing from underconsumption. He tried to emphasize the dynamic nature of the economic process, compared with the comparative statics of Ricardo (➤ comparative static equilibrium analysis), and was the first to use sequence analysis as an analytical device. Increased output in one period, he argued, is faced with a level of ➤ income generated by a lower level of output in the previous period. Total demand falls short of the available supply. Lags in the economic system, therefore, could give rise to underconsumption.

size distribution of firms ➤ concentration ratio.

Slutsky, Eugen (1880–1948) Slutsky was appointed a professor at Kiev University in 1918, where he stayed until 1926. In 1934, he accepted a post at the Mathematics Institute of the Academy of Sciences of the USSR, where he remained until his death. He published an article ('Sulla teoria del bilancio del consumatore') in the Italian journal *Giornale degli Economisti* in 1915 on consumer behaviour in which he showed how the concept of ➤ ordinal utility could be used to build a theory of consumer behaviour of the same scope as that of ➤ Marshall, but without the underlying assumption of the measurability of ➤ utility. However, the article lay unnoticed until ➤ Hicks and Allen rediscovered it in 1934. In *Value and Capital* (1939), Hicks applied Slutsky's name to the mathematical formulae that illustrate how a consumer would react to ➤ price and ➤ income changes (➤ consumer behaviour; Pareto, V.F.D.).

Slutsky did little further work in economic theory, but made important contributions to statistics and ➤ probability theory that are of relevance to economics. He emphasized the danger of assuming causes for observed fluctuations in ➤ time series by showing how regular cycles could be generated in the derivation of ➤ moving averages from a series, even though the latter was made up of random numbers. He also made important advances in the study of ➤ auto-correlation.

small and medium enterprises (SME) ➤ small business.

small business A firm, managed in a personalized way by its owners or part-owners, that has only a small share of its market and is not sufficiently large to have access to the ➤ stock exchange in raising ➤ capital. Given that *small and medium enterprises* (SMEs) typically have little recourse to institutional sources of finance other than the ➤ commercial banks and rely heavily on the personal savings of the proprietors, their families and friends, the long-term growth in ➤ taxation on income and wealth is believed by some economists to have inhibited the growth of the small-firm sector.

SMEs play important roles in the economy, in a dynamic as well as a static sense, and create a disproportionate number of new jobs. A few SMEs grow to challenge existing large firms (cf. ➤ Schumpeter's 'gale of creative destruction'), change and renewal being an essential feature of the ➤ free-market economy. In the European Union (EU-19) as a whole there were over 19 million enterprises in 2003. SMEs (fewer than 250 employees) accounted for 70 per cent of private sector employment. The balance was accounted for by the 40,000 large firms. ➤➤ enterprise; entrepreneur; establishment.

SME ➤ small business.

Smith, Adam (1723–90) A Scotsman brought up by his mother at Kirkcaldy, he became a student under Francis Hutcheson at Glasgow University at the age of fourteen and won a scholarship to Oxford, where he spent six years until 1746. He lectured at Edinburgh University from 1748 to 1751. From 1751 until 1763 he was at Glasgow, first in the Chair of Logic and a year later the Chair of Moral Philosophy, which he took over from Hutcheson. From 1764 to 1766 he toured France as tutor to the Duke of Buccleuch.

His major work on economics, *An Inquiry into the Nature and Causes of the Wealth of Nations*, appeared in 1776. This work became the foundation on which was constructed the whole subsequent tradition of English ➤ classical economics, which can be traced from ➤ Ricardo through ➤ Marshall to ➤ Pigou. Smith was primarily concerned with the factors that led to increased ➤ wealth in a community and he rejected the ➤ Physiocrats' view of the pre-eminent position of agriculture, recognizing the parallel contribution of manufacturing industry. He began his analysis by means of a sketch of a primitive society of hunters. If it cost twice the labour to kill a beaver as it does a deer, one beaver would exchange for two deer. ➤ Labour was the fundamental measure of ➤ value, though actual ➤ prices of ➤ commodities were determined by ➤ supply and ➤ demand on the ➤ market (➤ Marx, K.; Ricardo, D.). There were two elements in the problem of increasing wealth: (a) the skill of the ➤ labour force (➤ sow's ear effect), and (b) the proportion of productive to unproductive labour. (According to Smith, the ➤ service industries did not contribute to real wealth.) The key to (a) was the ➤ division of labour. To illustrate his point, he quoted the example of the manufacture of pins. If one man were set the task of carrying out all the operations of pin manufacture – drawing the wire, cutting, head-fitting and sharpening – his output would be minimal. If, however, each man specialized in a single operation only, output would be increased a hundredfold. The size of the output need only be limited by the size of its market. The key to (b) was the accumulation of ➤ capital. Not only did this enable plant and machinery to be created to assist labour, but it also enabled labour to be employed. Capital for the latter was the wages fund (➤ wage-fund theory). The workers must be fed and clothed during the period of production in advance of the ➤ income earned from their own efforts.

Smith believed that the economic system was harmonious and required the minimum of government interference (➤ *laissez-faire*). Although each individual was motivated by self-interest, they each acted for the good of the whole, guided by a 'hidden hand' (➤ 'invisible hand') made possible by the free play of competition (➤ Mandeville, B. de). Free competition was the essential ingredient of the efficient economy. However, from his *Wealth of Nations* it is clear that not only did his scholarship range widely over the fields of history and contemporary business, but that, at the same time, he was a very practical man. He was quite aware, for example, of the forces that were at work to limit competition:

> People of the same trade seldom meet together, even for merriment and diversion, but the conversation ends in a conspiracy against the public, or on some contrivance to raise prices. It is impossible indeed to prevent such meetings, by any law which either could be executed, or would be consistent with liberty and justice. But though the law cannot hinder people of the same trade from sometimes assembling together, it ought to do nothing to facilitate such assemblies, much less render them necessary (Book I, chapter 10, part 2).

In his discussions of ➤ public finance, he laid down four principles of ➤ taxation: (a) equality (taxes proportionate to ability to pay); (b) certainty; (c) convenience; and (d) economy. ➤➤ Hume, D.

Smith, Vernon L. (b. 1927) Professor of Economics and Law at George Mason University in Virginia, Smith was a pioneer of experimental economics, the branch of the subject concerned with setting up laboratory trials to test particular propositions. For advancing good experimental method in economics, and actually carrying out some interesting tests, Smith won, jointly with ➤ Kahneman, the ➤ Nobel Prize in 2002. His methods involve repeated experiments (so that subjects can familiarize themselves with the 'rules of the game'), and generous monetary incentives (to induce subjects to treat tests as though they matter and to impose the exact incentives being tested). He has found that the predictions of economic theory hold up rather well. He has also tested different designs of ➤ auction in carefully controlled conditions, and found that some predictions of economic theory do not hold up, perhaps because factors like suspense of waiting in an auction affect behaviour. Smith has also tested different designs of market mechanism for deregulated or privatized industries.

He has held academic posts at Purdue University, the University of Massachusetts and at the University of Arizona, among others. His publications include 'An Experimental Study of Competitive Market Behaviour', *Journal of Political Economy* (1962) and 'Experimental Economics: Induced value theory', *American Economic Review* (1976).

Smithsonian Agreement An agreement concluded in December 1971 between the Group of Ten of the ➤ International Monetary Fund at the Smithsonian Institute, Washington. Under the agreement, the major currencies were restored to fixed parities but with a wider margin, ±2.25 per cent of permitted fluctuation around their par values. The dollar was effectively devalued by about 8 per cent and the dollar price of gold increased to $38 per ounce. Sterling was set at $2.6057 (➤ exchange rate).

Smithsonian parities ➤ Smithsonian Agreement.

social accounting The presentation of the ➤ national income and expenditure accounts in a form showing the transactions during a given period between the different sectors of the economy. The tabulations are set out in the form of a ➤ matrix showing the source of ➤ inputs of each sector or part of a sector and the distribution of their outputs. The production sector, for example, shows for an industry how much of its inputs were bought from other home industries, how much it imported and how much it spent on wages, salaries and ➤ dividends. At the same time, it shows how much of its output it sold to other industries, how much it exported and how much was consumed by private individuals or the government sector. These transactions of the producers' sector are counterbalanced by corresponding transactions of the other sectors. For example, the personal sector shows the value and sources of ➤ incomes earned from the producers' sector and others, as well as the way these incomes are saved or spent on the outputs of the various industries or on ➤ imports. ➤➤ input–output analysis; Leontief, W.W.

social benefits The total increase in the welfare of society from an economic action. In effect, it is the sum of two benefits: (a) the benefit to the agent performing the action, e.g. the ➤ producer's surplus or ➤ profit made, and (b) the benefit accruing to society as a result of the action, e.g. an increase in tax revenues (➤ externalities). The phrase is sometimes used to describe the second of these on its own. ➤➤ social welfare.

social capital The total stock of a society's productive assets, including those that allow the manufacture of the marketable outputs that create private sector profits, *and* those that create non-marketed outputs, e.g. defence and ➤➤ education. ➤➤ capital.

social cost The total cost to society of an economic activity. It is the sum of the ➤ opportunity costs of the ➤ resources used by the agent carrying out the activity plus any additional costs imposed on society from the activity. For example, when people drive their cars they incur the private cost of petrol and wear and tear on the vehicle, but the social cost of them driving also adds wear and tear on the roads, and the congestion and pollution they cause, which they do not pay for directly. By taxation, social costs can be incorporated into private costs so that market prices properly represent the true costs to the community. ➤➤ externalities; Pigou, A.C.; shadow price.

socialism A social and economic system in which the means of production are owned collectively and equality is given a high priority. There are various forms of socialism, from Marxism to the social democrat systems in Western Europe, but all share a belief in the necessity for collective intervention in economic affairs. ➤➤ planned economy; state planning.

social net product The difference between the ➤ social benefits and the ➤ social cost arising from the use of some ➤ factor of production or from some form of economic activity.

social overhead capital ➤ infrastructure.

social security A system of government-financed income transfers designed to effect a distribution of income considered desirable. The main component of most social security systems is welfare benefits, given to those in ➤➤ poverty. This can be done in two ways: (a) by identifying groups that are likely to be poor, and giving benefits to them (e.g. the unemployed, the elderly and the disabled), irrespective of their actual income; (b) by identifying, through ➤ means tests, people who are poor. Approach (b) is a less expensive method of eradicating poverty but leads to the problem of the ➤ poverty trap. ➤➤ conditional cash-transfer; life-cycle hypothesis; minimum wage laws; National Insurance.

social welfare The total well-being of a community. It is not measurable because it is not possible to add together the benefits or ➤ utilities enjoyed by the individuals comprising the community. It is possible, however, for the community to judge whether it prefers one situation to another. ➤➤ Atkinson index; compensation principle; indifference-curve analysis; Pigou, A.C.; Rawls, J.; social welfare function; welfare economics.

social welfare function An expression of society's taste for different economic states. The analysis of social welfare is analogous to ➤ indifference-curve analysis for individuals. Just as the individual's taste can be defined by his/her ranking of different combinations of commodities, social priorities can be defined by a list of preferences of alternative national combinations of commodities. The comparison between individual and social welfare functions can be taken no further, however, because the individual only has to decide how much of each commodity to consume. Society has to choose how much of each commodity should be produced, *and* how it should be distributed. For this reason, unlike the individual's utility function – which is expressed in terms of commodity quantities – the social welfare function is usually expressed in terms of the utility of the members of society. A social welfare function is used to determine the relationship between overall welfare, and the welfare of different citizens. The function may, for example, be the simple sum of all individual preferences or it might attach a high weighting to the preferences of a particular group of citizens and a low weight to the rest. ➤ Value judgements are necessarily made in determining what is held to constitute social welfare.

The importance of the social welfare function is that it provides a criterion for choosing between different economically efficient (➤ economic efficiency) states. Suppose moving from an efficient allocation, A, to another efficient allocation, B, makes one person better off and another worse off; the social welfare function can be used to determine which of state A or B is to be preferred. This is more flexible than using other criteria for deciding between A and B, notably ➤ Pareto optimality or the ➤ compensation principle criteria.

There are two approaches to the derivation of the social welfare function: (a) to impose it from on high: by using the social welfare function of each individual – representing an own ranking of different allocations of resources – a government, monarch or dictator could produce one for society as a whole; or (b) to devise a constitution or voting system that could turn the rankings of each individual into a single social ranking. To find such a constitution that can guarantee to provide consistent, appealing and decisive results is, however, not possible, as ➤ Arrow shows in the ➤ impossibility theorem. It is this issue that has dominated discussion of social welfare functions in economic literature. ➤ Sen, A.; welfare economics.

soft currency A ➤ currency whose ➤ exchange rate tends to fall because of persistent ➤ balance of payments deficits or because of the building up of speculative selling of the currency in expectation of a change in its exchange rate. Governments are unwilling to hold a soft currency in their foreign exchange reserves. ➤ reserve currency.

soft loan A ➤ loan bearing either no ➤ rate of interest, or an interest rate that is below the true cost of the ➤ capital lent. It is the policy of the ➤ International Bank for Reconstruction and Development working through its affiliate, the ➤ International Development Association, to give 'soft' loans to ➤ developing countries for long-term capital projects.

sole proprietorship, sole trader An unincorporated business owned by one person that may or may not have employees. The majority of small firms are sole traders or ➤ partnerships. ➤➤ company law.

Solow, Robert M. (b. 1924) Having been educated at Harvard University, where he also received his Ph.D. in 1951, Solow remained in Cambridge, Massachusetts, taking a position at the Massachusetts Institute of Technology where, with the exception of those periods spent visiting academic institutions abroad, he has remained. He received the ➤ Nobel Prize for Economics in 1987. His major works include *Linear Programming and Economic Analysis* (with Dorfman and ➤ Samuelson) (1958), *Capital Theory and the Rate of Return* (1963), *The Nature and Sources of Unemployment in the US* (1964) and *Growth Theory: An exposition* (1970). He has also published numerous articles on ➤ depletion theory, including 'The Economics of Resources or the Resources of Economics', *American Economic Review* (1974). Above all, he has played a dominant role in debates on ➤ growth theory, developing a standard growth model based on ➤➤ neo-classical economics that contrasted in its assumptions with that of the then prevalent ➤ Harrod–Domar model. He has also questioned the effectiveness of ➤ market forces in clearing the labour market. ➤➤ capital reswitching.

sources and uses of funds An accounting statement describing the ➤ capital flows of a business. Sources of funds are ➤ profits from trading operations, ➤ depreciation provisions, sales of ➤ assets and borrowing, including capital issues. Uses of funds are purchase of fixed or financial assets (including ➤ cash), and distribution of ➤ income. ➤➤ self-financing.

sovereign risk The hazard that political risk may arise in a country, threatening overseas investments or trading, or an excessive government debt burden may force a country to default (➤ structural budget deficit). ➤ Stability and Growth Pact.

sovereign wealth funds State-owned investment funds mainly in ➤ emerging markets. Many of these countries have large payments surpluses and have accumulated foreign currencies and proceeds from exports and also ➤ privatizations. The funds have been invested heavily in securities and other assets in the ➤ advanced countries. China has two such funds and other important investors include Singapore and Abu Dhabi. It has been estimated that the funds had a total value of about $4 trillion in 2007.

sow's ear effect The inability of a country to raise its ➤ productivity or ➤ Gross Domestic Product per capita relative to other countries of comparable development, in spite of policy adjustments in ➤ macroeconomic variables (e.g. the ➤ exchange rate or ➤ rate of interest) because of deficiencies on the supply side of the economy (➤ supply-side economics); particularly because of an inadequately educated labour force (➤ education). The term refers to the old saying 'You can't make a silk purse out of a sow's ear'. ➤➤ convergence; economic development; institutional economics; Smith, A.

special drawing rights (SDRs) The instruments for financing international trade after the Second World War were predominantly the ➤ reserve currencies (e.g. dollars and sterling) and gold. Dependence on gold, as ➤➤ Keynes pointed out, was an anachronism that had been successfully terminated as far as domestic economies were concerned. The problem of depending on the former was that the supply of these currencies was regulated by their countries' ➤ balance of payments deficits or surpluses. The deficit on the US balance of payments had been an important source of the flow of ➤ liquidity into ➤ central bank reserves. The difficulty was that persistent deficits led to doubts about the maintenance of the currency's ➤ exchange rate and made central banks less willing to hold dollars. This problem came to a head in August 1971, when the US government imposed various measures to correct its balance of payments deficit. In December 1971, the dollar was devalued by about 10 per cent.

Keynes had proposed an international currency, to be called bancor, regulated by a central institution (➤ Keynes Plan). This idea was turned down then for fear that the creation of liquidity would generate ➤ inflation. In 1969, the Group of Ten (➤ International Monetary Fund (IMF)) agreed to establish SDRs, which are similar in principle to Keynes' original idea, and their agreement was ratified by the IMF. The SDR was linked to gold and equivalent to US$1 at the gold rate of exchange of $35 per ounce. Until December 1971 an SDR was equivalent to $1 but, with the effective devaluation of the dollar following the ➤ Smithsonian Agreement, the rate became 1 SDR = $1.08571. With the subsequent breakdown of the fixed parity system, the IMF valued the SDR in terms of a 'basket' of sixteen currencies, so that, as from July 1974, the rate in relation to the dollar 'floated'. In 1981 the SDR was simplified to a ➤ weighted average of four currencies that is revised every five years. In 2005, the weights were set at US dollars (44 per cent), euro (➤ European Economic and Monetary Union) (34 per cent), Japanese yen (11 per cent), and UK sterling (11 per cent). Special drawing rights are a very small proportion of countries' ➤ gold and foreign exchange reserves and their main function is as a unit of account (➤ money).

specialization ➤ division of labour.

specie points The limits to which the ➤ exchange rate between two ➤ currencies on the ➤ gold standard could fluctuate. For instance, before the First World War the same amount of gold could be bought in London for £1 and in New York for $4.87, and therefore the par rate of exchange was £1 for $4.87. If the pound fetched less than $4.87 in London, it would be cheaper for a merchant to ship gold to the USA to settle his debts (rather than settle in dollars), provided the costs of freight and insurance were less than the difference between the par rate and the London rate. Therefore, in practice, the rate never fell by an amount more than the cost of shipment. Similar forces applied in reverse to prevent the rate rising by an amount in excess of the cost of shipment.

specific tax ➤ tax, specific.

speculation Buying and selling with a view to buying and selling at a ➤ profit later when ➤ prices have changed. By buying when prices are low and selling when they are high, speculators can help smooth out price fluctuations. However, speculation can also be a destabilizing force when prices are high and expected to rise further and speculative purchases can help to create a ➤ speculative bubble. The use of ➤ derivatives may augment the unfavourable consequences of speculation, as seems to have happened in the 2007 credit crisis. ➤➤ arbitrage; bear; bull; business cycle; efficient markets hypothesis; stag.

speculative bubble A deviation between the price of an ➤ asset in the market, and the price justified by the inherent ➤ value of the asset, sustained by a belief on the part of buyers that they will be able to sell at an inflated price. The interesting thing about a bubble is that, as long as everyone believes in it, the bubble need not burst. The price can indefinitely deviate from fundamental value. While some have suggested bubbles are a sign of irrationality in the financial markets, creating more variability in the price of assets than is merited by fundamental swings in values, attempts have been made to account for them as rational phenomena.

speculative motive The reason that people or firms hold a stock of ➤ money – in the belief that a capital gain or the avoidance of a loss can be achieved by so doing. It is one of three motives for holding money outlined by ➤ Keynes. When the price of bonds falls, the attraction of holding them increases; this is because people will expect their price to rise again, and anyone owning them will make a capital gain when this happens. People will tend to buy bonds when their prices are low and will thus hold little money. When the price of bonds is high, on the other hand, they will believe their price could fall and hold more money. The amount of money held as a result of this motive thus varies with the price of bonds; as the ➤ rate of interest varies inversely with the bond price, the speculative motive for money varies inversely with interest rates. ➤➤ liquidity preference; liquidity trap; portfolio theory; precautionary motive; transactions motive.

Spence, A. Michael (b. 1943) Economist from Stanford University credited with devising the theory of ➤ signalling, for which he jointly won the ➤ Nobel Prize for Economics in 2001. His work, based on his Ph.D. thesis from the early 1970s, centred on the example of ➤➤ education as an observable signal of various unobservable characteristics that we might want to exhibit. In particular, clever people might struggle to show employers how clever they are, so that going to college could be seen as a signal of cleverness. This might justify going to college, even if the substantive benefit of the teaching was itself minimal. The signal would continue to work as long as clever people found it easier to sit through college than less clever people. The account was published in 'Job Market Signaling', *Quarterly Journal of Economics* (1973) and *Market Signaling* (1974). Spence's theory turned out to be complementary to the work of ➤ Akerlof and ➤ Stiglitz, and between them the economics of information (➤ information, economics of) became one of the most potent topics of study over the following three decades.

spillover effect ➤ externalities.

spot market A ➤ market in which goods or ➤ securities are traded for immediate delivery, as distinct from a ➤ forward market. 'Spot' in this context means 'immediately effective', so that *spot price* is the price for immediate delivery.

spot price ➤ spot market.

spot sterling ➤ forward exchange market.

Sraffa, Piero (1898–1983) Sraffa was a Turin-born socialist who moved to the UK in the 1920s and settled in Cambridge. He had a reclusive nature, but was broad in his intellectual company, mixing with ➤ Keynes and the philosopher Ludwig Wittgenstein. His three main published contributions are 'The Laws of Returns under Competitive Conditions', *Economic Journal* (1926), as editor of the eleven-volume *Works and Correspondence of David Ricardo* (1971), begun in 1930 with most of the substance being published in the 1950s, and *Production of Commodities by Means of Commodities* (1960).

His primary preoccupation in the 1920s was to expose the flaws in ➤ Marshall's theory of the firm (➤ firm, theory of the). He inspired others to develop theories of production that were not embedded in ➤ perfect competition, which he did not think adequately reflected the true state of capitalist society. His *Production of Commodities* contributed to the perennial problem of finding an invariable measure of value (➤ value, theories of). He presented a model in which prices of goods reflected costs of production, a return to a notion of value reminiscent of ➤ classical economics.

These prices would be determined by technology and stated in terms of a standard commodity, a composite of the commodities used in what is assumed to be equal proportions in the production of everything. In this, the Sraffa model can be said to adopt the assumptions and derive the conclusions of the ➤ non-substitution theorem.

Some of his results derive from a particular assumption that the ratio of investment to profits is an ➤ exogenous variable, which has led some to conclude that Sraffa's model is a special case of a more general model of economic activity attributable to von Neumann. ➤➤ Ricardo, D.

stability analysis The study of the behaviour of ➤ variables in ➤ disequilibrium to see whether they have a tendency to converge on an ➤ equilibrium level (➤ dynamics). Most equilibria considered in economics are stable, but models have been developed that are unstable. ➤➤ cobweb model; Harrod–Domar model.

Stability and Growth Pact Following the ➤ Maastricht Treaty, agreement was reached for members of the ➤ European Economic and Monetary Union to comply with strict rules controlling fiscal deficits. The thinking behind the agreement was that if one member irresponsibly inflated its budget deficit, the ➤ European Central Bank would have to raise the rate of interest, which might be quite inappropriate for the economies of other members (➤ free-rider problem). The pact determined that member countries' budgets should be in balance or in surplus in the medium term. In addition, any budget deficit should never exceed 3 per cent of ➤ Gross Domestic Product (GDP). If a country should run such a deficit, it would receive a warning and should put measures in place within four months and get the deficit reduced within a year. Failure could lead to a fine of up to 0.5 per cent of GDP. In practice the rules proved difficult to impose and were abandoned in favour of ad hoc measures to support a member having difficulty in reducing its budget deficit and financing its debt. ➤➤ convergence criteria.

stabilization policy 1 Government action aimed at reducing fluctuations in ➤ national income. Such policy – to expand demand when ➤ unemployment exists and reduce demand when ➤ inflation threatens – became the norm after the Second World War in all Western economies, and the low rates of unemployment prevailing during the 1950s coupled with high rates of economic growth were seen as a testimony to its success. In the 1960s, however, the UK faced difficulties sustaining a stabilization policy, with a ➤ stop–go cycle by which ➤ reflation would occur, the economy would 'overheat' and then a rapid ➤ deflation would be necessary. In the 1970s ➤ stagflation developed, and the traditional-style stabilization policy became obsolete. In the 1980s, it was replaced in the UK by an explicit non-stabilizing policy in the form of the *medium-term financial strategy*.

Stabilization policy fell out of favour for two main reasons:

(1) There are immense practical difficulties in implementing it, primarily because of a lack of sufficient information. All that is known about the economy is how it was behaving several months ago, but actions have to be taken several months in advance. The problem has been likened to attempts at controlling the temperature of water coming out of a shower when any twist of the hot or cold tap takes half a minute to affect the temperature of that coming out of the nozzle.

(2) It is argued that the temptation to attempt to keep unemployment below its market level (➤ unemployment, natural rate of) inevitably causes ever-accelerating inflation. Instead, it is suggested, if the ➤ equilibrium level of unemployment is too high, measures affecting the supply of labour, rather than demand, are necessary (➤ supply-side economics).

Despite the criticisms, stabilization returned to a significant extent in the 1990s in Western economies; this time it was in the hands of central banks; it was ➤ monetary policy that was the tool, and low inflation that was the stated objective. The reason this amounts to stabilization is that any decisions on whether inflation is likely to rise or fall away from its target inevitably involve judgements about whether the economy is overheating or not (➤ output gap). So policy is designed to keep the economy growing at a sustainable rate. In addition, in ➤ fiscal policy, there are automatic stabilizing factors (➤ built-in stabilizers) (e.g. in recession, unemployment benefits paid out rise, causing an increase in government spending) that will never be removed.

2 The action of government or trade associations to stabilize the prices of certain commodities. By holding stocks of the item in question, the authorities can, at least temporarily, affect demand and supply in the market and maintain a constant price. ➤➤ international commodity agreements.

stag A speculator (➤ speculation) who subscribes to new issues in the expectation of selling his allotment of ➤ securities at a profit when dealings in them begin. ➤➤ new-issue market.

stagflation The simultaneous existence of ➤ unemployment and ➤ inflation. In the early postwar era, it was believed that stagflation would never occur. Either there would be an ➤ inflationary gap or a ➤ deflationary gap, with inflation or unemployment, respectively, but never the two together. In the 1970s, however, the problem did emerge, largely because the natural rate of unemployment (➤ unemployment, natural rate of) rose, with strong wage pressure. The idea that there cannot be ➤ Keynesian unemployment at the same time as inflation is still credible.

standard costing ➤ management accountancy.

standard deviation A measure of the spread of a series of values of a ➤ variable around its mean (➤ average). It is defined as the square root of the ➤ variance. The formula for the standard deviation is:

$$\sigma = \sqrt{\frac{1}{n}\sum_{i=1}^{n}(x_i - \bar{x})^2}$$

where x_i is the ith value, $\bar{x}$ is the mean and n is the number of observations (➤ normal distribution).

Standard Industrial Classification (SIC) A categorization of economic activity used in compiling and presenting official statistics. The *Nomenclature des activités établies dans les Communautés Européennes* (NACE) was revised in 1990 and the ➤ European Union issued a regulation for it to be applied in all member countries. The classification is hierarchical with sections, subsections, divisions, groups, classes and subclasses. These classifications follow the same principles as the International Standard Industrial Classification of all Economic Activities of 1989, issued by the United Nations.

standard of living The quantity of goods and ➤ services consumed by an individual or a household. A general measure of standard of living made for comparisons between countries or between different time periods is ➤ gross national income per head of population. ➤ externalities; income, distribution of; poverty; retail prices index.

state planning The regulation of any sector or sphere of an economy by public administrators rather than by the ➤ price system. If state planning is comprehensive, a ➤ planned economy is said to exist. In many countries, however, there is partial planning, that can take one of two broad forms:

(1) Very detailed planning in certain key sectors of an economy. For example, the UK National Health Service is controlled by administrators rather than prices: queues ration the supply of certain operations, and the wages and activity of health workers are determined by the administrators, albeit after consideration of where demand is greatest and what supply of labour is available.

(2) Limited planning covering virtually all sectors of the economy, with production targets, performance monitoring and some state subsidies, and in the form of a national plan. ➤➤ input–output analysis; nationalized industries; transition, economies in.

static equilibrium ➤ Equilibrium in which the relevant ➤ variables do not change over time (in contrast to *dynamic equilibrium* in which the variables do change over time). ➤➤ balanced growth.

statistical inference The method of discovering information about a statistical population by sampling procedures (➤ sample).

steady-state growth A feature of an economy in which all ➤ variables grow (or contract) at a constant rate, e.g. population may rise at 3 per cent a year, national income at 4 per cent and the capital stock at 5 per cent. If these rates are maintained indefinitely, steady-state growth exists. It is distinct from ➤ balanced growth in which all variables grow at the *same* constant rate. Steady-state growth is an ➤ equilibrium concept, and much of ➤ growth theory has been concerned with whether it is likely to be achieved. ➤➤ economic growth; Harrod–Domar model.

Stigler, George Joseph (1911–91) Professor Stigler graduated from the University of Washington in 1931 and, after a year at Northwestern University, obtained his Ph.D. at the University of Chicago. In 1936, he was appointed Assistant Professor in Economics at Iowa State University and in 1938 moved to the University of Minnesota. In 1947, he was appointed to the Chair of Economics at Columbia University, where he stayed until 1959, in which year he returned to the University of Chicago as Professor of American Institutions. Professor Stigler was awarded the ➤ Nobel Prize for Economics in 1982. His publications include *Production and Distribution Theories: The formative period* (1941), *Theory of Price* (1946), *Five Lectures on Economic Problems* (1948), *Capital and Rates of Return in Manufacturing Industries*

(1963), *Essays in the History of Economics* (1965), *The Organization of Industry* (1968), *Domestic Servants in the USA, 1900–1940* (1974), *The Citizen and the State: Essays on regulation* (1975) and *The Economist as Preacher and Other Essays* (1982).

Professor Stigler analysed the cost of obtaining economic information by firms faced with a range of prices offered by competitive suppliers. He contributed to the analysis of ➤ unemployment, pointing up the need for workers to devote time to look for the highest available pay rates for the work and conditions they require. He advocated a more empirical approach to the study of government ➤ regulation and demonstrated that often regulations set for the benefit of consumers will instead turn out in practice to benefit producers. ➤ information, economics of.

Stiglitz, Joseph E. (b. 1943) Economist from Columbia University in New York, former chief economist at the World Bank, and joint winner of the ➤ Nobel Prize with ➤ Akerlof and ➤ Spence in 2001. There is little that Stiglitz has not written about. His Nobel Prize was granted for his contribution to the economics of information (➤ information, economics of) and in particular for his work on the subject of ➤ screening in the context of ➤ asymmetric information. He showed how an insurance company might sift high-risk clients from low-risk ones by offering alternative policies with different levels of policy excess and different premiums (the high-risk clients would choose a small excess amount, knowing themselves to be likely to claim). In this account, Stiglitz and his co-authors also introduced the concept of the *pooled equilibrium* (where all customers are treated identically) and the *separating equilibrium*, where the different types of customer are segmented into different product groups. These concepts have transpired to have widespread application.

Stiglitz was primarily responsible for extending the economics of information to accounts of the market for credit; he found that it may pay banks to ration credit quantitively, rather than to raise interest rates to limit lending, because higher interest rates may simply cause bad credit risks to choose to borrow selectively, in the expectation they may not be paying any interest anyway. He also developed the ➤ efficiency-wage hypothesis, again building on information deficiencies. If an employer is unable routinely to tell how much effort workers are providing, he/she may pay them above the going rate, so that in the event they are seen to be shirking, they will suffer a big loss by losing their jobs.

In addition, Stiglitz has made contributions to public economics and was a vocal critic of the International Monetary Fund during the 1990s. Some of his most notable papers are: 'Equilibrium in Competitive Insurance Markets: An essay on the economics of imperfect information' with Michael Rothschild, *Quarterly Journal of Economics* (1976), 'Credit Rationing in Markets with Imperfect Information' with Andrew Weiss, *American Economic Review* (1981) and 'Equilibrium Unemployment as a Worker Discipline Device' with Carl Shapiro, *American Economic Review* (1984).

stochastic process A process subject to random influences (➤ probability; random sample). For example, a dependent ➤ variable may be determined by an independent variable, x, plus a random element, so that the process generating y is not fully determined by x and predictable by x. The process is stochastic because the value of y depends partially on chance.

stock 1 A particular type of ➤ security, usually quoted in units of £100 value rather than in units of proportion of total ➤ capital, as in ➤ shares. Stock, or stocks and shares, have now become synonymous with securities, and the original distinction between shares and stock has become blurred. The term, however, is now coming to mean exclusively a fixed-interest security, i.e. loan stock in a company or local or central government stock.

2 An accumulation of a ➤ commodity. ➤➤ inventory.

3 A share in the ownership of a company, i.e. equity.

stock appreciation Increase in the value of stock (➤ inventories) resulting from an increase in market prices.

stockbroker A member of the ➤ stock exchange, who buys and sells ➤ shares on his/her own account, or for non-members, in return for a ➤ commission on the ➤ price of the shares. ➤➤ broker; market maker.

stock exchange A ➤ market in which ➤ securities are bought and sold. There are stock exchanges in most capital cities, as well as in the larger provincial cities, in many countries. By far the largest stock exchange by domestic market capitalization is the ➤ New York Stock Exchange (including Euronext), followed by the Tokyo Stock Exchange Group and another US exchange, ➤ NASDAQ OMX (➤ over-the-counter market) and the London Stock Exchange (LSE).

On other measures the rankings differ, for example in terms of capital raised by shares, the top three in 2009 were NYSE-Euronext, followed by London and the Australian Securities Exchange. Not all securities trading is transacted through stock exchanges and a growing volume (perhaps 10 per cent) goes through networks organized by ➤ stockbrokers, ➤ commercial- and ➤ investment banks. These networks, referred to as *dark pools*, allow the conduct of large trades without disrupting the market and without the transaction being revealed (although they will be reported after the event). Continental European exchanges are often referred to as *bourses* (Fr.).

The economic importance of stock exchanges is that they facilitate ➤ saving and ➤ investment: (a) by making it possible for investors to dispose of securities quickly if they wish to do so, and (b) in channelling savings into productive investment. Ready marketability requires (a) that new issues (➤ new-issue market) should be made or backed by reputable borrowers or institutions; (b) that information should be available on existing securities; and (c) that there should be both a legal framework and market rules to prevent fraud and sharp practice. Stock exchanges have their own rules and conventions, but their functioning depends also on the existence of company and other law and ➤ financial intermediaries, e.g. the ➤ issuing houses. In the past two decades, stock exchanges have been deregulated (➤ deregulation) and most trading floors have given way entirely to electronic trading systems (though not on the New York Stock Exchange). Trading in many ➤ securities is now a global market (➤ globalization).

stock–sales ratio ➤ inventories; turnover.

stock split An issue of new ➤ shares to shareholders without increasing total ➤ capital. The object of a stock split is to reduce the average quoted price of shares to promote their marketability.

stock turnover ➤ inventories; turnover.

Stone, Sir J. Richard (1913–91) Sir Richard Stone started his career at Cambridge University as an undergraduate, obtained a D.Sc., and became a Fellow and eventually Emeritus Professor there. His academic life was interrupted by a period in the statistical section of the Office of the War Cabinet between 1940 and 1945, and he held visiting posts at different institutions around the world, including Princeton's Center for Advanced Study. He was awarded the ➤ Nobel Prize for Economics in 1984. He has written widely on the measurement of national accounts data and econometric analysis of consumer demand, including *National Income and Expenditure*, with ➤ Meade (1944), *The Role of Measurement in Economics* (1951) and *The Measurement of Consumers' Expenditure and Behaviour in the United Kingdom 1920–1938*, with D.A. Rowe et al. (1954), and many articles, including 'Linear Expenditure Systems and Demand Analysis', *Economic Journal* (1954).

One of his main contributions was to lay the foundation of ➤ national income accounting. He also bridged the gulf between the theory of consumer demand (➤ demand, theory of) and ➤ empirical testing of the subject with what is known as the 'linear expenditure system'. He saw that, by making various assumptions, a tractable system of equations could be used to estimate consumer demand for different groups of commodities more reliably than by estimating the demand for each group in isolation.

stop–go A phrase used to describe the attempted management of ➤ aggregate demand in the UK during the postwar period and particularly in the 1960s as the period of fixed ➤ exchange rates drew to a close. The exchange rate came under pressure during periods of rising economic activity, but as ➤ fiscal policy and ➤ monetary policy were applied to reduce aggregate demand and improve the ➤ balance of payments it soon became necessary to stimulate the economy again to counteract ➤ recession. The stop–go cycle tended to amplify movements in the ➤ business cycle.

stratified sample A method of sampling (➤ random sample) used when the population to be sampled is not homogeneous and the nature of the population's heterogeneity is pertinent to the characteristic of the population about which information is sought. For example, we may wish to find out the percentage of households (the population) owning dish-washers. Households are not homogeneous; they may be classified into subgroups or strata by, for example, social group or income level and, moreover, these subgroups are likely to differ in their ownership of consumer durables, such as dish-washers. Rather than take a random sample of the whole population of households, the population is first subdivided into the appropriate categories, or strata, and random samples taken from each. If the population is heterogeneous a stratified sample will give more accurate results than a simple random sample of the same size.

structural adjustment programmes ➤ economic development.

structural budget deficit A measure of the level of government borrowing, after the effects of the ➤ business cycle have been taken into account. It is what the level of borrowing would be if the year in question were a year without ➤ recession or boom. It is the government's budget deficit in a year in which the ➤ output gap is zero. As there can be no precise measure of the output gap, there can be no precise measure of the structural budget deficit. ➤ built-in stabilizers; cyclically adjusted budget deficit; public sector borrowing requirement; Stability and Growth Pact.

structural unemployment ➤ Unemployment arising from changes in ➤ demand or ➤ technology that lead to an oversupply of labour with particular skills or in particular locations. Structural unemployment does not result from an overall deficiency of demand and therefore cannot be cured by ➤ reflation, but only by retraining or relocation of the affected workforce, some of whom may find work at low wages in unskilled occupations (➤ classical unemployment). Structural unemployment is distinct from ➤ frictional unemployment, which is essentially a short-term phenomenon.

structure–conduct–performance theory ➤ competition policy.

Student's t-test A statistical method for testing whether the ➤ mean of a small sample taken from a population which has a ➤➤ normal distribution can be accepted against a given hypothesis. The test was constructed by W.S. Gosset (1876–1937) to help his work at the Guinness brewery in Dublin and was published under his pen name 'Student'. The method is based on the 't' distribution which yields a set of curves, each of which is based on a specific sample size. As the sample size increases, the t-distribution approaches that of the normal distribution. The formula is:

$$t = \frac{m - \mu}{s/\sqrt{n}}$$

in which m = sample mean
μ = population mean
s = sample ➤ standard deviation
n = sample size.

There is little difference between the 't' distribution and the normal distribution when the number of degrees of freedom (sample size) is greater than 20. ➤ Chisquare test.

stylized fact A broad generalization, true in essence, though perhaps not in detail. It is perhaps the most important, and least acknowledged, form of ➤ empirical testing in economics. Economic ➤ models are judged by their ability to account for real-world phenomena. While some models attempt to capture the detail of a situation, or apply precise estimates of ➤ parameter values and are tested using ➤ econometrics, many models are designed simply to explain behaviour at its simplest, and can be judged only against the broad truth, rather than the detail. An example of stylized fact is the following: 'the profit rate – the level of profits in the economy, relative to the value of the capital stock – is constant in the long run'. This is a fact that traditional models of growth are held to explain. ➤ growth theory.

Sub-Chapter S ➤ corporation tax.

sub-prime Lending to ➤ mortgage borrowers with impaired credit ratings. Sub-prime refers to the borrower, not the interest rate charged, which will be well above the ➤ prime rate. It is believed that defaults by sub-prime borrowers precipitated the 2007 credit crisis.

subsidiaries Companies legally controlled by other companies. Although a share-holding of less than 50 per cent may be sufficient to control a company effectively, it is not correctly described as a subsidiary unless between 50 and 100 per cent of the ➤ shares are owned by another. Companies may choose to retain subsidiaries rather than to integrate them fully into their own organizations for a variety of reasons, e.g. the desire to allow local participation, a wish to conceal a business connection or to avoid the cost and complication of integrating an acquired company. ➤➤ holding company.

subsidiarity The notion that political authority should vest in the most local jurisdiction possible. Under subsidiarity, problems that affect only a town should be decided by the town; those that extend beyond the town should be decided by the county; those that extend beyond the county should be handled nationally and, in the case, for example, of the ➤ European Union (EU), those that extend beyond the member country by the EU. The twin precepts of subsidiarity are that: (a) everyone affected by an issue should be in the jurisdiction with responsibility for it, and (b) that as few people as possible not affected by an issue should be in the jurisdiction responsible for it. ➤➤ public choice theory.

subsidy Government grants to suppliers of goods and services. A subsidy may be intended to keep prices down (i.e. to raise ➤ real incomes of buyers), to maintain incomes of producers or to maintain a service or employment. An essential characteristic of a subsidy, as distinct from a ➤ transfer payment, is that it has the object of keeping prices below the ➤ factor cost of production. Subsidies, by distorting market ➤ prices and ➤ opportunity costs, may lead to a misallocation of resources, although they may be justified in certain circumstances (e.g. to correct for ➤ externalities) and may be used instead of tariffs to protect new industry (➤ infant-industry argument) where not banned by international agreements. It may be possible to achieve the objectives of subsidies by alternative means that have less distorting effects, e.g. by direct income support through the ➤ taxation system. ➤➤ farm subsidies; cross-subsidy.

subsistence theory of wages ➤ wage-fund theory.

substitute A product that at least partly satisfies the same needs of consumers. Products are defined as substitutes in terms of cross-price effects between them. This account is complicated by the fact that, when the price of an item changes, it affects both the ➤ real income of consumers and the relative prices of different commodities. Strictly, one product is a substitute for another if it enjoys increased demand when the other's price rises *and* the consumer's income is raised just enough to compensate for the drop in living standards caused. One product is a *gross substitute* for another if it enjoys an increase in demand when the price of the other rises and no compensating rise in income is made.

Substitution is not a relationship that only holds between individual commodities – groups of commodities can also be substitutes for each other. Vodka may be a substitute for gin, while spirits in general may be a substitute for wine. Both together may be a weak substitute for restaurant meals. Substitution (but not gross substitution) is a symmetric relationship: if apples are a substitute for bananas, bananas are a substitute for apples. ➤➤ complementary goods; cross-price elasticity of demand.

substitution effect The rate at which consumers switch spending to or from a commodity when its relative price changes but the total ➤ utility of consumers is left constant (➤➤ cross-price elasticity of demand). The substitution effect measures how much consumers would switch their spending away from, or towards, an item, its price having changed, if the resultant change in purchasing power were offset by a compensating transfer of income that would allow them to maintain their total utility (enough to keep them on their ➤ indifference curve). It thus isolates the impact of a change in relative prices from the ➤ income effect. In terms of ➤ indifference-curve analysis, the substitution effect represents a swivel of the budget line around a single indifference curve while the income effect represents a parallel shift of the budget line on to a new indifference curve.

The substitution effect is always negative: consumers always switch spending away from items, the prices of which rise as they attempt to shield their living standards from the impact. If the price of butter rises by 10 per cent, no great loss is incurred by the consumer who can switch to margarine. The substitution effect is not a concept unique to consumer theory. It arises in many areas of economic analysis, including, for example, the demand for ➤ labour and ➤ capital by firms. ➤➤ Giffen good; inferior good; substitute.

sukuk ➤ Islamic finance.

sunk costs ➤ Opportunity costs incurred in the past that are irretrievable and therefore not relevant to current decisions; in ➤ Jevons' famous phrase 'bygones are for ever bygones'. For example, a small bakery might buy an oven at a fixed cost, but it could sell it at some future date should it want to. It also might pay out a large amount in advertising its services. However, this latter cost could not be recovered later on – once paid for, the advertising has gone, whether or not the promotion was successful. Sunk costs represent a ➤ barrier to entry in an industry because they scare potential entrants from entering – should they fail, they would have wasted all the sunk costs. ➤➤ contestability.

'sun-spot' theory ➤ Jevons, W.S.

superneutrality of money The inability of changes in the growth rate of the money stock in an economy to affect any variable except the rate of inflation. Money is neutral (➤ neutrality of money) if the level of the money supply only affects inflation. It is superneutral if the rate at which that level changes only affects the level of prices.

super-normal profit ➤ profit.

supply The quantity of a good (or service) available for sale at any specified ➤ price. Supply is determined by a number of influences: (a) *price*: the higher the price, the more profitable it is, other things being equal, for producers to sell a good and the more they will attempt to sell; (b) *cost of inputs*: the lower the costs, the more profitable it is to sell a good at a given price and more will be offered for sale; and (c) *the price of other goods*: when the price of other goods rises, the supplier of a good may find it advantageous to switch production to the supply of the newly high-priced goods rather than stay in the relatively less profitable industry, where supply will fall. It should be noted that supply is *planned* supply, not necessarily what is actually sold. The latter depends on ➤ equilibrium in the market. The conditions of supply constitute but one aspect of the determination of the quantities sold and the market price; the other being the conditions of ➤ demand. ➤➤ firm, theory of the; Marshall, A.

supply curve A graphical representation of the quantity of a good or service supplied at different price levels. With ➤ price on the vertical axis and quantity supplied on the horizontal axis, supply curves normally slope upwards for two reasons: (a) higher prices allow profits to be made at higher levels of production for firms already in the market, and (b) if profits are made, new entrants are attracted into a market.

Supply curves can be drawn for the short term and the long term. In the short term, new firms do not have time to enter a market and higher output results only from an increase in production by market incumbents. In the long term, however, new entry occurs. The long-term supply curve links demand–supply equilibrium points on these short-run curves, which (as shown in the diagram below) will be steeper than the long-run curve. ➤➤ firm, theory of the.

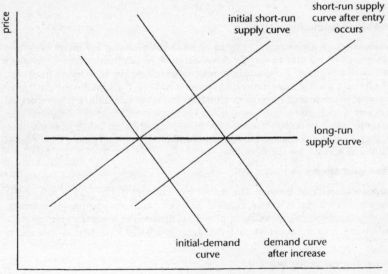

supply-side economics The study of the factors affecting, and the policies appropriate for influencing, the real economy, i.e. the physical behaviour of economic agents, and its response to changes in the structure of relative ➤ prices rather than nominal prices. Supply-side economics is roughly based on a positive and negative thesis. On the *negative* side, supply-side economists tend to deny a role to a ➤ stabilization policy, because, they believe, economic agents are only concerned with their real income and, because markets have a tendency to clear at their ➤ equilibrium levels, an artificial increase in ➤ aggregate demand cannot achieve anything. When demand is boosted, the price of all goods rises and, out of a desire to feed the extra demand, more labour will be sought, requiring an increase in wages. Out of all this, nothing changes in real terms: ➤ real wages are the same as they were, as are relative prices; all economic agents behave in the same way as they did before, even though the absolute price level might have changed, and possibly some temporary aberration from market equilibria occurred.

The *positive* views of such economists relate to the policies that they believe can be effective in influencing the performance of an economy. Anything that attempts to influence the supply of ➤ labour or the supply of goods can be called a supply-side measure. Such policies could include: (a) cutting taxes to improve incentives (affecting people's personal trade-off between going out to work and staying at home); (b) legislating heavily against ➤ monopoly in order to encourage free competition, low prices and incentives to be efficient; (c) diminishing the ability of ➤ trade unions to inhibit the workings of a free labour market; (d) restricting the growth of the ➤ money supply to control ➤ inflation, improve economic stability and encourage investment; (e) increasing the mobility of labour (➤ labour, mobility of); and (f) cutting the benefits available to those out of work to improve their incentive to take on work (➤ unemployment trap).

It would be wrong, however, to believe that supply-side measures are only the concern of free-market economists. State interference in the economy can be classed as on the supply side, and measures of this sort might include: (g) increases in spending on ➤ education to retrain employees; (h) the introduction of ➤ profit-sharing as a means of removing industrial conflict; and (i) the establishment of a state investment bank for subsidizing high-risk, new-technology firms.

In general, supply-side measures can be justified in terms of the findings of ➤ microeconomics, which is concerned with the behaviour of individual workers and firms rather than the behaviour of economic aggregates (➤➤ macroeconomics). Free-market supply-side economics emerged as a body of thought in the early 1980s as a doctrine complementary to ➤ monetarism, which first provided a macroeconomic case against demand-management; it was strengthened by the theoretical revolution that arrived in the form of ➤ rational expectations. ➤➤ Laffer curve; sow's ear effect.

support ratio ➤ dependency ratio.

surplus value ➤ Marx, K.

sustainable development The notion that economic development should proceed at a pace and in a manner that will conserve the environment and depletable natural resources. In its extreme form (steady-state growth) human ➤ population would be stabilized and renewable resources only would be employed. ➤ environmental economics.

swap A transaction in which ➤ securities of a certain value are sold to a buyer in exchange for the purchase from the buyer of securities having the same value, the purpose being to obtain an improvement, in the eyes of either of the parties, in the quality of the security, or to anticipate a change in ➤ yield. ➤ Currency as well as securities are swapped in this way. (➤➤ credit-default swap)

systemic risk A situation in which problems in any one financial institution or market may spread, widely endangering the whole system. This risk is a preoccupation of ➤ central banks and is the subject of prudential regulation (➤ capital adequacy).

Tableau économique The table with which ➤ Quesnay analysed the circulation of ➤ wealth in the economy by setting out the different classes of society. The table showed how the *produit net* produced by the agricultural sector circulated between the owners of the ➤ land, the tenant farmers and other classes, e.g. artisans and merchants. Only agriculture produced any net additions to wealth, all other activities were 'sterile'. The table showed, too, how output is reproduced annually. The sterile classes were essential in that they created the necessary demand for the agricultural sector. ➤➤ Cantillon, R.; Leontief, W.W.; Physiocrats.

take-off in economic development ➤ economic growth, stages of.

takeover The acquisition of one company by another. Takeovers are sometimes financed by paying ➤ cash at an offer ➤ price in excess of the ➤ market price of the ➤ shares, but, more frequently for large acquisitions, by the exchange of shares or loan ➤ stock, possibly with some cash adjustment, issued by the acquiring company for the shares of the acquired company. The term is normally used to imply that the acquisition is made on the initiative of the acquirer and often without the full agreement of the acquired company; as distinct from a ➤ merger. ➤➤ competition policy; reverse takeover.

Takeover Panel A UK committee responsible for supervising compliance with the City Code on Takeovers and Mergers, a non-statutory code issued in 1968 and revised subsequently. The code is intended to protect the interests of shareholders (➤ mergers). One requirement of the code is that any company acquiring 30 per cent or more of the ➤ shares in a quoted company (➤ quotation) must make a full bid at a price not lower than the highest price paid for its shareholding. Similar panels operate in Australia and Ireland. The UK Companies Act 2006 (➤ company law) designated the Panel as the supervisory authority for certain regulatory functions under the European Takeovers Directive (2004/25/EC), but the rules governing takeovers have not been fully harmonized in the member states of the ➤ European Union.

tap issue An issue of ➤ Treasury bills to government departments and others at a fixed ➤ price and without going through the ➤ market; as distinct from a tender issue (➤ tenders).

tariffs, import Taxes imposed on commodity ➤ imports. They may be levied on an *ad valorem* basis (i.e. as a certain percentage of ➤ value) or on a specific basis, i.e. as an amount per unit. Their purpose may be solely for raising revenue, in which case the home-produced product corresponding to the import would bear an equivalent compensatory tax. However, import duties are generally applied for the purpose of carrying out a particular economic policy, and in this context may be used to serve many functions:

1 To reduce the overall level of imports by making them more expensive relative to their home-produced ➤ substitutes, with the aim of eliminating a ➤ balance of payments deficit. ➤➤ devaluation.

2 To counter the practice of ➤ dumping by raising the import price of the dumped commodity to its economic level.

3 To retaliate against restrictive measures imposed by other countries (➤ beggar-my-neighbour policy).

4 To protect a new industry until it is sufficiently well established to compete with the more developed industries of other countries (➤ infant-industry argument).

5 To protect 'key' industries (e.g. agriculture) without which the economy would be vulnerable in time of war.

For example, in respect of members compared with non-members of a ➤ common market, tariffs are preferential. It is an accepted principle under the ➤ most-favoured nation clause of the ➤ General Agreement on Tariffs and Trade (GATT) that tariffs should be non-discriminating and any concessions agreed between two or more countries should automatically be extended to all. It has, however, been accepted that this principle may be waived in the interests of the ➤ developing countries. Significant progress has been made through the GATT in the reduction of tariff levels by means of a series of negotiations, of which the ➤ Uruguay Round of Trade Negotiations was the latest (➤ Doha Round of Trade Negotiations; generalized system of preferences; World Trade Organization).

tatonnement process The *tatonnement* process was suggested by ➤ Walras to illustrate that equilibrium in perfect markets (➤ perfect competition) can be attained at a particular set of prices no matter what the original disequilibrium position of the markets and the route by which prices move before reaching equilibrium. Buyers and sellers make known their prices in the first round. In the second round, buyers and sellers increase their published prices where there is excess demand, and reduce them where there is a shortfall in demand. The process continues until there is a balance of demand and supply in all markets. It is not until this stage that actual transactions take place; no trade is done until equilibrium is reached. ➤➤ price system.

Taussig, Frank William (1859–1940) Apart from a period from 1917 to 1919 when he was chairman of the US Tariffs Commission, Taussig spent his whole career at Harvard University. His works on economics include *The Tariff History of the United States* (1888), *Wages and Capital* (1896), a textbook *Principles of Economics* (1911) and *International Trade* (1927). An economist in the tradition of ➤ Ricardo and ➤ Marshall, he attempted to relate theory to established statistical data.

tax ➤ taxation.

tax, *ad valorem* An indirect tax (➤ taxation) expressed as a proportion of the ➤ price of a ➤ commodity – hence it is 'by value'. ➤ Value added tax is an *ad valorem* tax. ➤➤ sales tax.

tax, 'cascade' ➤ turnover tax.

tax, progressive ➤ progressive tax.

tax, proportional ➤ proportional tax.

tax, regressive ➤ regressive tax.

tax, specific A tax (➤ taxation) of an absolute amount, levied per unit of a ➤ commodity sold or produced. Examples are stamp duty and ➤ excise duties. An indirect tax (➤ direct taxation), not to be confused with a ➤ tax, *ad valorem*. Where tax rates are applied at very high rates on a commodity (e.g. cigarettes, in the UK), specific duties do not unduly penalize higher quality brands of the commodity, which cost a little more before tax, but would be hugely more expensive after tax if an *ad valorem* duty were applied.

tax, turnover ➤ turnover tax.

taxation A compulsory transfer of ➤ money (or occasionally of goods and ➤ services) from private individuals, institutions or groups to the government. It may be levied on ➤ wealth or ➤ income, or in the form of a surcharge on ➤ prices. In the first case, it would be called a ➤ *direct tax*; in the latter, an *indirect tax*. Taxation is one of the principal means by which a government finances its expenditure. While it seems obvious what is tax and what is not, there is an awkward boundary. Would compulsory saving to purchase, for example, a pension, not be equivalent in spirit to taxation? Or, if the government were to apply high prices to the output of ➤ nationalized industries, in order to raise revenue? ➤➤ capital gains; corporation tax; hypothecation; income tax; inheritance tax; local taxation; public goods; sales tax; tax, specific; tax burden; tax expenditures; value-added tax.

taxation, incidence of The ultimate distribution of the burden of a tax. The initial *tax impact*, or formal incidence of an ➤ excise duty on tobacco, for example, may be on the importer or wholesaler who has to pay over the tax to the authorities, but he/she is likely to pass on some or all of the tax in the form of higher prices to the retailer and the consumer. Whether or not a tax is wholly shifted forward will depend on the price ➤ elasticity of demand and supply for tobacco. If the consumer does not reduce purchases following the increase in price, he/she will bear the whole of the tax. If the consumer does reduce purchasing, the wholesaler and the retailer will also be worse off and will be bearing part of the tax.

There are two general rules of incidence: (a) in general, a tax on any company must be paid by its shareholders, its employees or its customers – the company itself does not pay tax, and (b) in the very long term, tax ends up being borne by people in proportion to their ability to transfer the inputs they provide to an economy, or their consumption, from one jurisdiction to another. If capital can move anywhere, governments will find themselves unable to capture revenue from providers of capital. Thus, jurisdictions with high taxes on capital will simply have less capital, and capital will earn high pre-tax returns.

tax avoidance Arranging one's financial affairs within the law so as to minimize taxation ➤ liabilities, as opposed to *tax evasion*, which is failing to meet actual tax liabilities through, for example, not declaring ➤ income or ➤ profit.

tax base The quantity or coverage of what is taxed. The tax base for ➤ income tax is the assessed income of the whole population. The tax base for ➤ value added tax does not include sales of most foods, books and financial services.

tax burden The amount of ➤ money an individual, institution or group must pay in ➤ tax. It should include all costs to the taxpayer that he/she incurs in paying the tax (e.g. the net-of-tax cost of employing an accountant to complete a tax form) as well as the tax itself (➤➤ compliance cost). In most policy discussion, the tax burden is taken as the proportion of ➤ Gross Domestic Product levied by ➤ general government in taxation; according to OECD *Revenue Statistics* 2009, this ratio was 26.9 per cent in the USA, 28.3 in Japan, 30.8 in Australia, and 35.7 per cent in the UK. In every case the ratio had risen significantly since 1975; for the ➤ European Union (15), it rose from 32.1 per cent to 39.7 per cent over the period 1975–2007.

tax equalization account ➤ company reserves.

tax evasion ➤ tax avoidance. ➤➤ informal economy.

tax expenditures The costs of tax allowances and reliefs. It has been argued that tax allowances are similar to ➤ subsidies and may be seen as a form of ➤ public expenditure. However, tax expenditures can never be more than estimates since it cannot be assumed that the ➤ tax base would remain unaltered if the allowances were abolished. There is a wide range of allowances and reliefs, most of which probably lead to the loss of some revenue and all of which complicate the administration of the tax system and raise ➤ compliance costs. Tax allowances and reliefs necessitate higher rates of tax than would otherwise be necessary and lead to distortions in factor markets (➤ factors of production) and probably also to higher ➤ tax avoidance, and there is increasing interest, among economists if not among politicians, in reducing them.

tax impact ➤ taxation, incidence of.

tax tolerance The willingness or ability of a population to support high or increasing levels of taxation. Tax tolerance – and its inverse, tax resistance – has become a fashionable topic among economists interested in ➤ public-choice theory. It is argued that the public have rebelled against the desires of political leaders to raise extra revenue, and the resistance has been shown in the election of governments committed to lower taxation, the growth of the ➤ informal economy, and specific voter initiatives to limit the authority of the state government to levy local property taxes, e.g. Proposition 13 in California in 1978. It has been argued that the growth of government budget deficits (➤ public sector borrowing requirement) has been caused by the inability of governments to curb spending growth, and the unwillingness of populations to pay higher taxes. ➤➤ Buchanan, J.M.; hypothecation.

tax yield The amount of ➤ money that results when the rate of ➤ tax is applied to the money value of the ➤ tax base, minus the costs of collecting the tax.

Taylor, John B. (b.1946) ➤ Taylor rule.

Taylor rule A simple rule for setting interest rates with a view to keeping inflation stable. The rule, proposed by John B. Taylor of Stanford University, says:

Short-term interest rate = 2
+ inflation rate
+ 0.5 (deviation of inflation from target)
+ 0.5 (output gap)

The '2' is derived from the historical average real interest rate. Add this to today's inflation, and you achieve the long-term real average. The next two lines say that rates should be higher than this – the higher inflation is above target the higher the economy is operating above its long-term capacity (➤ output gap). If inflation was on target and the output gap was zero, real interest rates would be 2 per cent.

Taylor wrote about this rule as both an approximate description of what central banks actually do when they set rates and as a possible prescription of what a sensible, responsive monetary policy rule might consist of. In practice, the rule needs calibrating for different countries, and the 'output gap' is not an easily observable variable. Central banks prefer to maintain an air of intelligent discretion over the conduct of their policies than to follow rules, but to some extent they may unwittingly follow a Taylor rule. This makes the rule a useful benchmark against which actual policies can be judged.

technical analysis ➤ chartist.

technical substitution, rate of ➤ rate of technical substitution.

technology The sum of knowledge of the means and methods of producing goods and services. Technology is not merely applied science, because it often runs ahead of science – things are often done without precise knowledge of how or why they are done except that they are effective. Early technology – craft skill – was almost entirely of this sort. Modern technology is increasingly science-based, however, and, rather than relying on acquired skill, is easily communicable by demonstration and printed material to those qualified to receive it. It also includes methods of organization as well as physical technique. Technological change and the diffusion of technology are important in economics because new methods, including those embodied in ➤ investment, play an important part in theories of ➤ economic growth. There is, however, some controversy about the extent to which technological development is an autonomous factor in economic growth. Because it is so difficult to measure, there is also room for doubt about whether or not technological change is, or has recently been, accelerating. ➤ endogenous growth theory. ➤➤ research and development.

tenders Offers to supply at a fixed ➤ price. A ➤ discount house tendering for an issue of ➤ Treasury bills, for example, will offer to take up so many bills at a certain price. ➤➤ contracting out.

term loan A bank advance for a specific period (normally 3–10 years) repaid, with ➤ interest, usually by regular periodical payments. Term loans are common practice in the US commercial banking system for business finance, and for larger borrowings the ➤ loan may be syndicated, i.e. the provision of funds and the interest earned are shared between several banks. Similar facilities are available in the UK, mainly from the ➤ commercial banks or other institutions, but overdrafts are still a common form of ➤ bank loan, and may be a cheaper form of finance. Unlike an overdraft, the interest of a term loan is fixed and the loan cannot be recalled in advance of its maturity date.

terms of trade The ratio of the index of ➤ export prices to the index of ➤ import prices. An improvement in the terms of trade follows if export prices rise more quickly than import prices (or fall more slowly than import prices). ➤➤ United Nations Conference on Trade and Development.

term structure of interest rates The relationship between the interest rate paid on a ➤ bond and the number of years until the bond is repaid. Suppose, for simplicity, bonds are held for either one or two years. People wanting to invest for two years can do so either by buying a two-year bond or by buying a one-year bond now and then buying a new one when that one expires. The term structure compares the annual yield on each type of bond. It is affected by a number of factors. Most important, if interest rates are expected to rise next year, the two-year bond will have to offer a higher annual return than the one-year bond. Otherwise, everyone would sell two-year bonds and hold a one-year bond this year and a higher-yielding one-year bond next year (➤➤ yield curve). ➤ Inflation expectations also determine the term structure (➤ credibility). In general, if ➤ fiscal policy and ➤ monetary policy are 'tight' (i.e. tending to have a deflationary effect) (➤ deflation), then long-term rates will be lower than usual, relative to short-term rates. ➤➤ yield curve.

theories of value ➤ value, theories of.

theory of distribution ➤ distribution, theory of.

theory of games ➤ game theory.

theory of income determination ➤ income determination, theory of.

theory of production ➤ production, theory of.

theory of second best ➤ second best, theory of.

theory of the firm ➤ firm, theory of the.

Thornton, William Thomas (1813–80) ➤ wage-fund theory

Thünen, Johann Heinrich von (1783–1850) A member of the landowning Prussian class of Junkers, after completing his education at agricultural college Thünen attended the University of Göttingen. For the remainder of his life he farmed his estate at Mecklenburg. Volume 1 of *Der isolierte Staat in Beziehung auf Landwirtschaft und Nationalökonomie* (*The Isolated State in Relation to Agriculture and the National Economy*) was published in 1826, and part 1 of volume 2 in 1850. The rest of volume 2 and volume 3 appeared in 1863. Thünen used his farm as a source of facts for his theoretical work in agricultural economics and built a theoretical ➤ model to work out the important factors that determined the most profitable location of various branches of agriculture in relation to their sources of ➤ demand. In so doing, he devised a theory of ➤ rent similar to that of ➤ Ricardo. He set out a theory of ➤ distribution based on marginal productivity, using calculus, which was considerably ahead of his own time, and he could be considered one of the founders of ➤ marginal analysis. ➤➤ location theory.

tied aid The practice by which countries grant aid to ➤ developing countries on condition that they use the aid to buy from the donor country's own suppliers. ➤ foreign aid.

tied loan A ➤ loan made on condition that certain purchases are made from the lender. In the brewing industry, tied loans are made to pubs and clubs for fitting out bars and restaurants on the understanding that beer is supplied by the brewer making the loan. In ➤ foreign aid, loans are made on favourable terms on condition that capital equipment or services are purchased from the lending country.

tie-in sales Sales of a product that have a condition that some other item will be purchased at the same time. An example would be the condition that in order to subscribe to the services of a telephone utility, you have also to rent or buy one of their telephones. It is an example of a ➤ vertical restraint. ➤➤ full-line forcing.

time deposit Money in a bank account for which the bank may require notice of withdrawal, usually of up to three months. ➤➤ deposit account.

time inconsistency A change in preferences that occurs quite predictably after a certain situation has been arrived at. For example, a government that wants to deter the taking of hostages may say that it will never negotiate with hostage-takers, but finds that once a hostage has been taken, it pays to negotiate, whatever its preference beforehand. Or a government that wants to encourage investment and is thus willing to promise tax concessions to firms opening new plants finds that once the new plants are open it would prefer to remove the tax concessions.

Unless they can commit themselves to the original course of action, the existence of time-inconsistent preferences can prevent certain measures of government, or other economic agents, being credible. Whenever agents lay out ➤ sunk costs, it is possible that their options will change and they will exhibit time inconsistency. The problem has been analysed in ➤ game theory. ➤➤ principal–agent problem.

time preference The amount by which consumers value immediate ➤ consumption in preference to deferred or postponed consumption. Suppose an individual has $100; he/she can either spend it now or put it aside and spend it next year. The rate of time preference of that consumer is the amount of money necessary just to persuade him/her to save the $100. If the consumer is expecting to do very well next year and has no need to save, or, out of fear of nuclear war, believes the world will no longer exist next year, there will be a requirement for a large amount of compensation to persuade that consumer not to spend the $100. If, on the other hand, the consumer feels perfectly well off at the moment and conditions are unlikely to change much, he/she may think a rather small amount of compensation makes saving worthwhile.

Several factors affect the time preference of consumers.

1 The level of consumption consumers enjoy in the present. Other things being equal, the more consumption there is now, the lower the compensation needed for ➤ saving. As saving implies a fall in current consumption, the more that is saved, the higher the required level of compensation.

2 A corollary of (1) above is the level of consumption expected to be enjoyed in the future. If great wealth is expected tomorrow, a lot of reward will be needed to induce saving today. Again, as saving today implies higher consumption in the future, the more that is saved, the higher the required level of compensation.

3 The risk the consumer attaches to the arrival of the future: if tomorrow is unlikely to come, huge compensation is needed to cause saving.

4 Consumer taste will influence the time-preference rate – some people may believe that they can only enjoy spending money when they are young, others might believe the reverse.

The market ➤ rate of interest expresses the amount a consumer will actually be compensated for saving, and rational consumers will save enough for their time-preference rate to equal the interest rate. If the interest rate exceeds their time-preference rate, they should save more, raising their time-preference rate until it is equal to the market interest rate. The reverse would be true if their time-preference rate exceeded the interest rate. If the interest rate is lower than their time-preference rate even when they are saving nothing, it is rational for them to borrow money and pay interest on it; this raises current consumption and lowers future consumption and thus lowers their time-preference rate. Optimal consumption through time can be analysed with the help of ➤ indifference curves, depicting the bundles of consumption today and in the future, between which the consumer is indifferent. ➤➤ Fisher, I.; marginal utility of money.

times covered ➤ dividend cover.

time series The values of a particular ➤ variable at consecutive periods of time.

time-series analysis The application of statistical methods to find explanations of movements of ➤ variables over time. ➤➤ cross-section analysis.

Tinbergen, Jan (1903–94) A Dutch economist, from the Netherlands School of Economics in Rotterdam, Tinbergen jointly won, with ➤ Frisch, the first ➤ Nobel Prize for Economics in 1969, 'for having developed and applied dynamic models for the analysis of economic processes'. He spent ten years as director of the Netherlands Central Planning Bureau, where he formulated some important ideas on the conduct of economic policy. Tinbergen is associated with the central principle that there must be as many instruments as there are targets of policy. ➤ gravity model.

tit-for-tat A strategy in a repeated ➤ prisoner's dilemma game (➤ repeated game) by which a player agrees to be cooperative in the first round of the game, and for each subsequent round to do whatever the other player did the round before. The strategy has been shown empirically to be effective when the prisoner's dilemma is repeated a large number of times, or when it continues for an unknown number of rounds. Its importance in ➤ game theory is to have shown that there are circumstances when the cooperative outcome can be sustained in situations that are structurally similar to the prisoner's dilemma. It is not, however, a ➤ dominant strategy.

Tobin, James (1918–2002) Professor Tobin studied at Harvard University, obtaining his Ph.D. in 1947. He moved to Yale in 1950 and was appointed Sterling Professor of Economics. He was awarded the ➤ Nobel Prize for Economics in 1981. Professor Tobin's major published works include 'Liquidity Preference as Behavior towards Risk', *Review of Economic Studies* (1958), *National Economic Policy* (1966), *Financial Markets and Economic Activity* (1967), *Essays in Economics: Macroeconomics* (1971), *The New Economics One Decade Older* (1975), *Essays in Economics: Consumption* *and Econometrics* (1975), *Asset Accumulation and Economic Activity* (1980) and *Essays in Economics: Theory and Policy*, Vol. 3 (1982).

Professor Tobin has made important contributions to the theory of finance through his analysis of the demand for financial assets (➤➤ liquidity preference). He criticized ➤ monetarism for its narrow emphasis on money, arguing that there is a range of financial assets that investors may be willing to hold in their portfolios – not only money but bonds and equities. Precise investor preferences for different assets are determined by their preferences against risk and in favour of higher returns.

He also explored the links between the mix of financial portfolios and the real assets of firms to show how government and central bank policy impinge on real ➤ Gross National Product and employment. In particular, for Tobin, the mechanism by which money may affect the real economy would not so much be the direct relationship of extra money being spent on extra real goods and services (as monetarists are wont to believe), but that extra money would lead to higher prices for shares, thus promoting investment by firms in real expansion (➤ *q* theory; transmission mechanism).

Tobin also contributed to the theory of ➤ econometrics: Tobit, a statistical analytical technique for the estimation of variables subject to ➤ probability, was named after him. ➤➤ Tobin tax.

Tobin tax A tax on ➤ foreign exchange transactions originally proposed by ➤ Tobin. World foreign exchange transactions are very large and it has been estimated that only 2 per cent are connected with trade in goods; most, therefore, are related to ➤ investment or ➤ speculation. Concern has been expressed that the high proportion of such transactions, which are of a short-term nature, can lead to serious instability in ➤ exchange rates because of the speed with which they could switch from one economic region to another in turn (➤ hot money). It has been suggested that a tax would not only help to control these flows but also be a useful source of revenue. Although much discussed, such a tax is probably not a practicable proposition, if only because there would need to be international agreement to introduce it.

Tokyo Stock Exchange The ➤ securities market in Tokyo. It is one of the world's largest and one of the three central Japanese ➤ stock exchanges – Osaka and Nagoya are the other two. The trading floor closed in 1999 and transactions are now all electronic.

total factor productivity ➤ growth accounting; productivity.

total managed expenditure (TME) A measure of total ➤ public expenditure in the UK, comprising departmental expenditure limits and ➤ annually managed expenditure. Total managed expenditure includes some elements of spending by public corporations, which are inside the public sector but outside what is termed 'general government'. Hence, TME tends to be larger than other measures of public spending.

tournament theory The piece of economic thinking that suggests rewards can usefully be based on the *relative* performance of economic agents, rather than on their *absolute* performance. The theory is sometimes used to explain behaviour observed in the ➤ labour market, where patterns of reward are often more subtle than traditional theories (➤ marginal productivity theory of wages) would suggest. In particular, those traditional accounts argue that there should be a close relationship between the value of the output of a worker and the wage the worker receives. But in practice, the ➤ productivity of workers varies, and companies find it hard to observe the individual output of every worker. So, under tournament theory, it is argued, companies can rank workers and pay them on their relative standing. That gives them each an incentive to perform well but does not require as detailed a profile of everybody's performance. Because workers are effectively competing against each other, they are in a tournament. The approach can also be applied to the ➤ regulation of ➤ monopoly utilities, where it becomes a ➤ yardstick competition. It is one of many areas of economic thinking that attempts to justify and explain real-world behaviour on the grounds that the information facing decision-makers is incomplete. ➤➤ efficiency-wage hypothesis; screening; signalling.

toxic assets Financial assets of very low quality for which there is no effective market. During the 2007–2009 credit crisis, some banks and other financial institutions had large portfolios of such assets which threatened their capital position and survival.

trade barrier A general term covering any government limitation on the free international exchange of merchandise. These barriers may take the form of, for example, ➤ tariffs, ➤ quotas, ➤ import deposits, restrictions on the issue of ➤ import licences or stringent regulations relating to health or safety standards. ➤➤ precautionary principle; protection.

trade credit The ➤ credit extended by business firms to other business firms. It may occur explicitly through the issue of a ➤ bill of exchange or may arise from the delay of receipts and payments for services performed. ➤➤ factoring.

trade cycle ➤ business cycle.

trade discount The percentage below the published retail ➤ price at which a manufacturer sells to distributors (wholesale or retail) or at which a wholesaler sells goods to a retailer. In addition, further discounts are sometimes given on a scale related to the quantities of the goods taken. A *'concealed' discount* is one granted by a manufacturer or wholesaler to favoured customers and not made publicly known in order to prevent accusations of unfair trading.

trade diversion and trade creation ➤ customs union.

trade gap The excess of the value of ➤ imports of goods and services over the value of ➤ exports of goods and services. ➤➤ balance of payments.

trade investments ➤ Shares held by one company in another; normally minority holdings in customers or suppliers.

trade promotion authority Authority granted by the US Congress to the President to facilitate US international trade negotiations. Authority was granted by the Trade Act 2002 for a period of five years. Under the Act, while the President had to consult Congress during the course of negotiations, he was assured that any internationally agreed trade agreement put to Congress by the President would not be amended. Such authority was first granted in 1974.

trade unions Trade unions were first established in Britain in the nineteenth century, as a countervailing power against business and as friendly societies giving support in sickness and unemployment to their members. Their history is one of growth and international expansion throughout the nineteenth century and early twentieth century, with the USA reaching a maximum penetration in the workforce in 1945, followed by other countries later, from which point they began to decline.

During this time, however, industrial relations matured from the aggressive tactics of lock-outs, strikes and machinery destruction to reconciliation by debate and collective bargaining. Trade unions became particularly established in many continental European countries so that, for example, the legal right to strike, during which contracts are suspended, is in the French Constitution and in many countries collective agreements have the status of legal contracts. In the UK, on the other hand, legislation was enacted in the 1980s which strictly constrained the methods adopted by unions in their recourse to strike action. From the 1980s union membership throughout the member countries of the ➤ OECD declined. The reasons were the fall in the numbers employed in manual work as economies shifted towards ➤ services, the growth of part-time work and the employment of women, which the unions failed to adjust to.

The basic *raison d'être* of trade unions has been to increase their members' wages and some studies have shown that manual workers could gain a 25 per cent increase on their wage rates through union support in collective bargaining. (This premium, however, was not obtained for skilled workers for whom there was no benefit.) However, these gains could be short-lived because of the consequential increase in their firm's costs and, therefore, lost business through competitive pressure – although, of course, this effect did not apply to employment in the ➤ public sector. Nevertheless, trade unions have succeeded in improving their members' working conditions and have contributed to the realization of the welfare state.

trading currency Currency in which ➤ international trade is invoiced. ➤➤ reserve currency.

transactions costs The costs associated with the process of buying and selling. These are small frictions in the economic sphere that often explain why the price system does not operate perfectly. Transactions costs may affect decisions by an organization to make or buy (➤ contracting out) and the study of transactions costs economics, associated notably with the 2009 Nobel Prize winner Oliver E. Williamson, has implications for a wide range of issues affecting ➤ industrial organization, including ➤ competition policy. ➤➤ Coase, R.; menu costs.

transactions demand for money The holding of cash by people or firms to finance foreseeable expenditures. When people are paid, they usually put their salaries into bank accounts, from which they can withdraw money easily, using cheques or cash taken from machines. If they wanted to, however, instead of putting it in the bank's current account, they could invest it in, say, government bonds, which would pay interest. However, people tend to keep much of their money in easy-access, low-return accounts.

The transactions demand depends on three factors.

(1) The volume and pattern of transactions to be financed. A rich person requires more ready cash than a poor one, because he/she spends more. The pattern of transactions matters too: if spending and income were $20 a day, virtually no

money would be kept for transactions, but if spending were $20 a day and income $140 a week, a positive balance would be kept for the first six days of the week.

(2) The rate of interest, because it represents the sacrifice made from not investing money.

(3) The cost of making transactions in interest-bearing assets, e.g. the brokerage fees, costs of acquiring information.

The foregoing applies equally to the corporate demand for money. It is generally believed that the transactions demand relates to the function of money as a medium of exchange (➤ money) and that, of the various possible definitions of money supply, the most relevant to this demand is a 'narrow' one of very liquid assets (➤➤ money supply). Although it was seen as the only possible reason for holding money by classical economists, it was ➤ Keynes who introduced the idea that the interest rate might be important in determining the demand for money, and outlined other motives for holding cash too. ➤➤ precautionary motive; speculative motive; Tobin, J.

transactions motive The factor causing people or firms to hold a stock of money to finance their foreseeable expenditures. It is one of three motives for holding money outlined by Keynes. ➤➤ precautionary motive; speculative motive; transactions demand for money.

transfer costs The total ➤ opportunity costs of moving goods or materials from one place to another, including loading/unloading costs and administrative costs as well as transport costs.

transfer deed A legal document by which ownership of ➤ securities is transferred from the seller to the buyer. In the UK, it is no longer necessary for both parties to sign such a document when disposing of a share. The seller gives authority to the issuer of the security to remove his/her name from the records while the buyer's ➤ broker simply informs the issuer of the purchaser's name. ➤➤ CREST.

transfer earnings The minimum payment necessary to keep a ➤ factor of production in its existing use and deter movement to other employment. Earnings in excess of transfer earnings are ➤ economic rent.

transfer payments Grants or other payments not made in return for a productive service, e.g. pensions, unemployment benefits and other forms of income support, including charitable donations by companies. Transfer payments are a form of income redistribution, not a return to the ➤ factors of production. ➤ Subsidies that are paid by government to producers are not counted as transfer payments.

transfer pricing Internal (as distinct from ➤ market) prices used in large organizations for transactions between semi-autonomous divisions. A ➤ multinational corporation, for example, will have to set transfer prices for the supply of components from one subsidiary to another. Transfer prices between subsidiaries acting as profit centres may approximate to market prices or may be set above or below them so as to minimize the payment of ➤ tariffs or to shift ➤ profit from a high- ➤ taxation country to a low-taxation one.

transformation curve (production possibility curve) A graphical representation of the maximum amount of one good or service that an economy can produce by reducing production of a second good or service and transferring the resources saved to the production of the first good (see diagram). For example, an economy might be capable of building and equipping fifty hospitals if it does not build any schools, or eighty schools if it builds no hospitals. Either of these combinations would be a point on the transformation curve, which can be plotted on a graph with the number of hospitals built and equipped on one axis, and the number of schools on the other. It traces the number of schools that can be built and equipped using the resources required for any given level of hospital building.

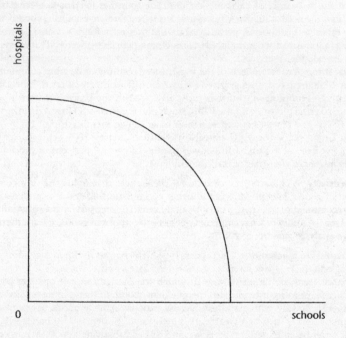

A transformation curve is normally assumed to be concave to (i.e. bulge away from) the origin. This is because the ➤ rate of technical substitution declines the more a commodity is produced: a larger number of schools can be built and equipped for the sacrifice of one hospital if no schools are being built to start with, because the best locations can be used and the people good at building and equipping schools, but poor at hospital-building, can be transferred to building schools productively. However, suppose that only one hospital is being built and the rest of the economy is geared to school-building – transferring resources from hospital-building to school-building will have hardly any effect on the rate of build of schools. Thus, the rate at which hospitals can be transformed into schools declines as school-building rises. ➤➤ economic efficiency.

transition, economies in Countries in transition from a ➤ planned economy to a ➤ free-market economy. The term refers specifically to Russia and the members of the former USSR and other Communist states in Eastern and Central Europe. China, which is moving towards a market economy, is a special case.

The process began in October 1989 with the removal of the Berlin Wall between East and West Germany. The countries in transition, unlike ➤ developing countries, had highly educated populations, substantial, though generally rundown, ➤ infrastructure and large manufacturing sectors. The economies were dominated by heavily indebted state enterprises with low ➤ productivity and generally uncompetitive products and services. Most were characterized by high ➤ inflation and ➤ unemployment and ➤ balance of payments deficits. The countries in transition have had to confront the need to liberalize prices and ➤ interest rates, re-establish property rights and other ➤ institutions, privatize state enterprises, reform ➤ banking systems, invest in infrastructure, introduce ➤ competition policies, reform ➤ taxation systems and develop social services.

Transition to the standards of the ➤ advanced countries is far from complete and from 2008 these countries suffered badly from the world credit crisis, especially in South-East Europe. The countries most advanced in the process of transition are those in central Europe and the Baltic states and especially in Poland, Hungary and the Czech and Slovak Republics, which have gained membership of the ➤ European Union (EU). These EU transition countries had by 2009 achieved levels of GDP per head at ➤ purchasing power parities of over 50 per cent of those in the more advanced countries of the Union.

transitivity A characteristic of rational preferences that holds that if a combination of goods, A, is preferred to another combination, B, and B is preferred to a third combination, C, then A must be preferred to C. Transitivity is also assumed to hold for the indifference relation between combinations of goods. ➤➤ indifference-curve analysis; paradox of voting.

transmission mechanism The process by which changes in the money supply – or changes in the ➤ rate of interest on short-term assets – affect the level of ➤ aggregate demand. There are different ways in which the mechanism can operate: (a) with extra cash (or lower interest rates) people may choose to spend more and save less; (b) more indirectly, with extra cash, people may buy more ➤ bonds or equities, as a means of storing their new wealth. This increase in the demand for bonds will push their prices up and interest rates down and this will stimulate new ➤ investment.

➤ Monetarism concentrates on the more direct process, while ➤ Keynesian economics has tended to play down the power of money, believing that its effects work only through (b). In an ➤ open economy, the transmission mechanism can also operate through the ➤ exchange rate. An increase in ➤ money supply, or a reduction in interest rates, tends to lead to a ➤ depreciation of the exchange rate, and promotes exports.

transnational corporation ➤ multinational corporation.

Treasury bills Treasury bills issued by the US, UK and other governments are short-term debt instruments traded on the ➤ money markets. Also called T-Bills, these securities are issued at a discount to their face value on maturity which might be ninety-one days later. Tenders for these bills are invited weekly. Treasury bills provide governments with a highly flexible and relatively cheap means of borrowing money to meet their fluctuating needs for ➤ cash. ➤ Central banks are able to deal in these securities in pursuit of their ➤ open market operations.

trend growth The level of ➤ economic growth of an economy that is sustainable over the long term, without any tendency for the rate of ➤ inflation to rise or fall. It is sometimes held to be the rate at which the productive capacity of the economy – its potential for production – expands. It could equally be taken as a measure of the growth of the ➤ supply side. It is also interpreted as the long-term growth rate, as it is assumed that, in the long term, the economy must perform according to its potential. The rate is affected by growth in the labour force, and the growth in productivity, itself primarily determined by technology and social institutions. Actual growth in any year may exceed, or under-perform trend growth, usually because fluctuations in ➤ aggregate demand affect actual ➤ Gross Domestic Product more than they affect the long-term capacity of the economy to produce things.

Trend growth is a useful benchmark for whether the economy is growing too quickly (➤ overheating) or too slowly. In the UK's ➤ budget of 2002, Britain's trend growth rate was officially declared to be 2.75 per cent, a quarter point higher than had hitherto been assumed. The government still decided to act on the assumption that it was 2.5 per cent for the sake of caution. Estimates of this magnitude are regarded as reasonable for most highly developed economies, but it is recognized that developing countries may outperform this level for a sustained period of catch-up. Trend growth is a concept more often used by policymakers than theoretical economists. It has largely been ignored by the different theories of growth (➤ growth, theories of), and should not be confused with the natural rate of growth, used in the ➤ Harrod–Domar model; output gap.

trilemma ➤ impossible trinity.

Troubled Asset Relief Program (TARP) Several governments launched programmes to buy up or insure assets that became illiquid (➤ illiquidity) and threatened the financial system during the 2007–2009 credit crisis. TARP was created by the US government for this purpose under the Emergency Economic Stability Act 2008. The sum of $250 billion was authorized immediately under the Act with the possibility of an extension to a total of $700 billion on Presidential authority. Some institutions were able to repay amounts extended to them quite soon and the final overall cost of the programme is expected to be very much less.

The scheme evolved into purchasing equity stakes in banks and even commercial corporations (for example General Motors) and this approach was also taken by other countries, such as the UK, which effectively nationalized some banks. Another approach has been to create *bad banks* to take over from banks' holdings in some illiquid assets, such as the National Asset Management Agency in Ireland.

truck system ➤ fringe benefits.

trust 1 A legal term describing ➤ money or property vested in an individual or group of individuals who will administer it in the interest of others. Trusts of this kind are usually set up to continue interests in accordance with the general instructions of the initiator and to protect them from outside interference or for tax reasons. Thus, people set up trusts or appoint trustees to administer their estates after their death. Certain newspapers are also administered by trusts. Banks act as trustees for a fee.

2 Financial trusts are also established for commercial purposes in which particular protection is required against fraud, e.g. ➤ unit trusts or ➤ investment trusts.

3 A very large amalgamation of firms. ➤➤ anti-trust.

TSE ➤ Tokyo Stock Exchange.

Turgot, Anne-Robert-Jacques, Baron de l'Aulne (1727–81) Educated for the Church, Turgot became an abbé at the Sorbonne in Paris but then took up a career in the civil service, where he remained for the rest of his life. He was the Administrator of the District of Limoges from 1761 to 1774, when he became Secretary of State for the Navy. For a short time he held the post of Controller of Finance.

His economic work appeared in *Réflexions sur la formation et la distribution des richesses* (1766). In this work he gave a clear analysis of the law of ➤ diminishing returns. He demonstrated how more and more applications of a ➤ factor of production (➤ capital) to a constant factor (land) will first increase, then decrease, the return at the margin. He was the first to equate capital accumulation with ➤ saving, a view that became a central feature of ➤ classical economics.

turnover The total sales revenue of a business.

turnover tax A ➤ tax levied as a proportion of the ➤ price of a ➤ commodity on each sale in the production and distribution chain; also called a *cascade tax*. Such a tax encourages ➤ vertical integration. Turnover taxes were widespread in Europe (e.g. in Germany) before the introduction of the ➤ value added tax now standard throughout the ➤ European Union.

turnpike theorem ➤ optimal-growth theory.

two-sided market A market in which a product or service has to attract two distinct groups of consumers, each with their specific needs, and in which each consumer group depends on the presence and size in the market of the other group. Essentially, there is a network (➤ network economics) connection between the consumer groups from which the consumers benefit and which the producer of the product or service exploits. Producers of platforms in these markets have, therefore, to overcome the unique difficulty at their launch of attracting each group without the initial presence of the other. When fixing prices for one group of consumers, producers must be cognizant of the effect on demand of the other group. In some market, products may be priced below cost to one group in order to attract the other group. Superficially, this may appear to be ➤ price discrimination. Examples of two-sided markets are computer operating systems (software users and software designers); credit cards (merchants and cardholders); commercial television (advertisers and viewers); and shopping malls (shoppers and retailers).

unavoidable costs ➤ Opportunity costs that have to be borne even if no output is produced. ➤➤ fixed costs.

uncalled capital ➤ Authorized capital issued to the public, but not called (➤ call) and not ➤ paid-up capital.

uncertainty The state in which the number of possible outcomes exceeds the number of actual outcomes and when no probabilities can be attached to each possible outcome. It differs from ➤ risk, which is defined as having measurable probabilities. Where probabilities are measurable, insurance can be taken out to cover the worst contingencies and the risk of them occurring is spread among many people or taken on by someone who can be reasonably certain to bear them. In the case of uncertainty, however, no insurance company could properly assess the premium to charge to cover bad outcomes – it is simply a possibility that has to be faced. It is the role of the entrepreneur to face each uncertainty that justifies ➤ profit as a reward. ➤➤ Keynes acknowledged the importance of the 'animal spirits' of entrepreneurs in rises and falls of ➤➤ business cycles. In situations in which future outcomes are particularly obscure, such 'animal spirits' may be depressed to the point at which economic activity is brought to a standstill.

uncovered interest parity theory The theory that any difference in the level of the rates of ➤ interest between two countries should tend to equal the expected change in ➤ exchange rates. However, the theory has been repudiated in practice because of particular aspects of the market such as the influence of ➤ risk, and activities such as the ➤ carry trade.

UNCTAD ➤ United Nations Conference on Trade and Development.

undated securities ➤ Securities not bearing a ➤ redemption date or ➤ option, hence ➤ irredeemable securities.

underconsumption ➤ quantity rationing.

underdeveloped country ➤ developing country.

underground economy ➤ informal economy.

undervalued currency A ➤ currency, the ➤ exchange rate of which is below either its ➤ free-market level or the ➤ equilibrium level it is expected to reach in the long term. Conversely, an overvalued currency may develop as a consequence of balance of payments deficits. ➤ carry trade; devaluation; exchange-rate overshooting; revaluation.

underwriting The business of insuring against ➤ risk. An underwriter – in return for a ➤ commission or ➤ premium – agrees to bear a risk or a proportion of a risk. Specifically, an underwriter is a member of Lloyd's, who joins with others to underwrite the risk of damage or loss to a ship or cargo – if the ship sinks and is not recoverable, he/she will pay a proportion of the cost of the loss to be insured – but the term is generally used to describe the basic activity of ➤ insurance. An ➤ issuing house also underwrites directly or indirectly a new issue of ➤ shares – if the public does not take up the whole issue, the balance will be taken up by the underwriters (➤ new-issue market).

unemployment The existence of a section of the ➤ labour force able and willing to work but unable to find gainful employment. Unemployment is measured as the percentage of the total labour force out of work. Four distinct causes of unemployment can be distinguished:

(1) ➤ Frictional unemployment is caused by people taking time out of work – between jobs or looking for a job.

(2) ➤ Classical unemployment is caused by excessively high wages.

(3) ➤ Structural unemployment refers to a mismatch of job vacancies with the supply of labour available, caused by shifts in the structure of the economy.

(4) ➤ Keynesian unemployment results from the existence of a deficiency of ➤ aggregate demand that is simply not great enough to support full employment. A fall in wages – which should cause an increase in the ➤ demand for ➤ labour – merely reduces aggregate demand further because it reduces the spending power of the employed, and thus fails to clear the excess supply of workers. Much economic debate has centred on whether, in the long term, cuts in wages cannot in fact increase demand (➤➤ real balance effect), and thus whether Keynesian unemployment is not just a special case of classical unemployment in which workers are simply pricing themselves out of jobs.

Monetarist and neo-classical economists have tended to argue that all unemployment is either classical or voluntary (➤ unemployment, natural rate of). Either, they assert, the market fails to clear because wages are artificially held too high; or, if the market does clear, the unemployed have chosen not to take a job at the going rate.

However, in practice, it has been shown that at times persistent unemployment can be cured by a boost in aggregate demand. The labour market is widely recognized as being slower to adjust than any other; excess supply in this market persists in a way that it could not elsewhere, despite the high social and human costs of unemployment. In recent years, attention has focused on the particular problem of ➤ long-term unemployment, especially among the unskilled. It is surmised that the market wage of manual workers – especially those in heavy physical occupations – has declined (➤ weightlessness) and that work incentives have correspondingly diminished, too. ➤ unemployment trap. ➤➤ claimant count; education; employment, full; hysteresis; ILO unemployment; labour force; labour-force survey; labour, mobility of; sow's ear effect.

unemployment, natural rate of The level of ➤ unemployment in an economy that is just consistent with a stable rate of ➤ inflation. It is the unemployment that prevails when all markets in the economy are in equilibrium and there is no deficiency of

➤ aggregate demand. It can be thought of as the unemployment rate when output in the economy is just at its potential, no more and no less (➤ output gap). The point about the natural rate is that it is not easily solvable by ➤ fiscal policy or ➤ monetary policy. It is a supply-side feature of the economy (➤ supply-side economics), a reflection of labour-market institutions.

The concept of the natural rate was central to the monetarist critique to the policies motivated by ➤ Keynesian economics (➤ monetarism). It arises out of the failures of policy in the 1950s and 1960s to sustain low levels of unemployment in the 1970s. Somehow, demand had to be stoked up to ever higher levels to maintain the same level of unemployment. The economy appeared to exhibit a natural tendency towards some level, and it was not possible to get that level lower by allowing higher inflation. At best, it appeared possible to get it below the natural rate temporarily, or by ever-accelerating rates of inflation. Indeed, in modern accounts, macroeconomic policy cannot even take unemployment below the natural rate at all (➤ policy ineffectiveness theorem).

Today, the natural rate is accepted by academics of most ➤ economics doctrines, and it certainly motivates the conduct of economic policy day-to-day throughout the Western world. Some think of the natural rate as being the correct definition of 'full employment'. To get the actual level of unemployment below it, it is argued, requires government to consider such factors as: (a) the level of benefits for the out-of-work; (b) the ease with which workers can change jobs; and (c) the stigma attached to being out of work. The natural-rate hypothesis has increased the attention given to ➤ active labour-market policies. The ➤ Organisation for Economic Co-operation and Development has stressed the need for nations to make their labour markets 'flexible'. It estimates that the UK's natural rate has fallen well below that of other European nations as a result of policies of ➤ deregulation of the labour market.

Because unemployment cannot be held below the natural rate without accelerating inflation, it is often called the *non-accelerating inflation rate of unemployment*.

unemployment trap The existence of ➤ social security benefits for the out-of-work that erode any incentive for the unemployed to take a job. The incentive for the unemployed to find a job can depend on: (a) the generosity of state benefits; (b) the level of pay offered; and (c) the tax paid on that pay. ➤➤ poverty trap.

unfunded ➤ pension funds; personal pension.

uniform business rate ➤ local taxation.

Union of South American Nations In 2008, a treaty was signed by the member countries of ➤ Mercosur and the ➤ Andean Pact to establish an economic and political union with a programme envisaging the elimination of tariffs between member countries by 2014. The long-term aim is the development of an economic and monetary union among members. The participating countries are Argentina, Bolivia, Brazil, Chile, Colombia, Ecuador, Guyana, Paraguay, Peru, Suriname, Uruguay and Venezuela.

unit banking ➤ branch banking.

unit cost ➤ average cost.

United Nations Conference on Trade and Development (UNCTAD) A United

Nations conference first convened in 1964 in response to a growing anxiety among ➤ developing countries over the difficulties they were facing in their attempts to bridge the ➤ standard-of-living gap between them and the ➤ advanced countries. Since then, full conferences have been held every three or four years. The twelfth UNCTAD was held in Accra in 2008.

The goal of the conference is to improve prospects for developing countries' trade and to encourage investment. The UNCTAD offers support and advice to assist developing countries in their trade negotiations with the advanced countries, assists them in the promotion of international investment, and offers its expertise through technical assistance projects. The Conference was instrumental in gaining the acceptance of preferential duties on imports from developing countries without having to extend these preferences to all the contracting parties of the ➤ General Agreement on Tariffs and Trade (GATT) (➤ generalized system of preferences). The UNCTAD, which has 193 member states and a budget of about US$75 million, has a permanent secretariat based in Geneva and regularly publishes papers on development problems and an annual report.

United States Emergency Stabilization Act ➤ Troubled Asset Relief Program.

unit of account ➤ money.

unit trust An organization that invests funds subscribed by the public in ➤ securities, and in return issues units that it will repurchase at any time. The units, which represent equal shares in the trust's investment ➤ portfolio, produce ➤ income and fluctuate in value according to the ➤ interest and ➤ dividends paid and the ➤ stock exchange prices of the underlying ➤ investments. The trustees holding the securities are usually banks or ➤ insurance companies, and are distinct from the management company. The subscriber to a unit trust does not, unlike a shareholder in an ➤ investment trust, receive any of the ➤ profits of the organization managing the trust. Management derives its income from a regular service charge as a percentage of the income of the trust's investments and the difference between the (bid) price at which it buys in units and the (offer) price at which it sells them, which may include an initial charge. Unit trusts are ➤ open-ended funds and correspond to *mutual funds* in the USA (➤ mutual company) and first appeared in both countries in the 1930s.

universal bank A bank (➤ banking) that provides a wide range of financial services in one largely unified structure. In some continental European countries, certain large banks have combined the roles of ➤ commercial banks, ➤ investment banks, ➤ insurance and ➤ brokerage. Although in the distant past these functions were performed in the UK by independent organizations, they are now largely offered by partly integrated financial ➤ conglomerates. Alexander Gerschenkron (1904–78), the Russian-born American economic historian, believed that late industrializing countries such as Russia and Germany in the nineteenth century needed state-sponsored universal banks. Such banks were not necessary in the UK or the USA at the time where industrialization was more gradual and could be financed from wealth accumulated through agriculture and trade.

unlisted securities markets 1 Generally, the markets for shares of public companies not included in the Official List for the main market (or first tier) of the ➤ stock exchange. Most of the ➤ advanced countries have organized lower-tier markets or informal 'placing markets' in which unlisted shares are traded. These markets are less stringently regulated and perform an important function in providing a stepping-stone to the main markets (➤➤ over-the-counter market; quotation).

2 Specifically, a market set up in 1980 by the London Stock Exchange to trade in designated unlisted securities and closed in 1996. The Alternative Investment Market (AIM) opened on 19 June 1995 to replace the Unlisted Securities Market (USM) and the Rule 4.2 market (in which members of the stock exchange were allowed to deal in unlisted shares). The AIM's admission requirements are less stringent than those for the former USM and the Official List, and the costs of ➤ flotation are much lower.

unredeemable securities ➤ irredeemable security.

Uruguay Round of Trade Negotiations The eighth round of trade negotiations of the ➤ General Agreement on Tariffs and Trade (GATT) opened at Punta del Este, Uruguay, in 1986. The aim, as with previous rounds, was to reduce trade restrictions and to encourage ➤ free trade on a multilateral basis. The negotiations were concluded and an agreement signed in 1994. Industrial tariffs in advanced countries were to be reduced from an average of 6.3 to 3.9 per cent and the proportion of imports free of tariffs was to be increased from 20 to 43 per cent. All tariffs were to be 'bound', i.e. never raised. For the first time, services were to be, in principle, subject to the same multilateral trading rules as industrial products. However, agreement could not be reached on telecommunications, financial services and shipping.

Under the GATT, agriculture had been excluded from many provisions that applied to other products, e.g. those relating to export subsidies and import quotas. The Uruguay agreement brought agriculture into the multilateral system of trading rules. Non-tariff barriers (➤ protection) were converted into tariffs and these tariffs were to be reduced by 36 per cent over a six-year period. Countries could not impose quotas, minimum import prices, restrictive licences, or variable levies on imports. Constraints were placed on subsidies that distort trade and will become more stringent over time. Agricultural export subsidies were to be reduced (➤ farm subsidies). The ➤ World Trade Organization was set up to replace GATT. ➤ Doha Round of Trade Negotiations.

USM ➤ unlisted securities market.

usury Charging excessive interest on loans. At a much earlier period, religious leaders prohibited the charging of any interest at all on the grounds that it could exploit the poor but restrictions were removed progressively from the seventeenth century onwards with the rise of ➤ capitalism. Today, lenders to private consumers are regulated (➤ Consumer Credit Act) and there continue to be religious restrictions on usury in ➤ Islamic finance.

utilitarianism The philosophy by which the purpose of government was the maximization of the sum of ➤ utility, defined in terms of pleasure and pain, in the community as a whole. It was not hedonistic (➤ hedonism) in so far as pleasure could include, for example, the satisfaction of helping others. The purpose of government was to ensure the 'greatest happiness of the greatest number'. It implied that utility could be measured and interpersonal comparisons made. Its chief advocate was ➤ Bentham. ➤ Human Development Index.

utility The pleasure or satisfaction derived by an individual from being in a particular situation or from consuming goods or services. Utility is defined as the ultimate goal of all economic activity, but it is not a label for any particular set of pursuits, e.g. sensual pleasure or the acquisition and use of material goods. ➤ Bentham described it as that which appears 'to augment or diminish the happiness of the party whose interest is in question', but this barely illuminates the issue, given that the notion of happiness used is a complex one. Some things that appear to make people unhappy, like sad films, can generate utility, while other things appear to make people happy but do not in fact. As no single measure of utility exists (➤ ordinal utility), it is by their choices of combinations of available commodities that consumers reveal what it is that generates utility for them. Economists ignore possible circularities in the concept and rarely argue about what consumers enjoy, taking it as a matter of psychological fact. ➤➤ endogenous preferences; Hicks, J.R.; indifference-curve analysis; marginal utility, diminishing; von Neumann–Morgenstern utility function; Pareto, V.F.D.; Slutsky, E.

utility function ➤ von Neumann–Morgenstern utility function.

V

value The worth of something to its owner. Two concepts of value have been distinguished in economics: (a) value in use: the pleasure a commodity actually generates for its owner, and (b) value in exchange: the quantity of other commodities (or, more usually, ➤ money) a commodity can be swapped for. Water, for example, has high value in use, but low value in exchange. ➤➤ paradox of value; value, theories of.

value, theories of Explanations of what determines the ➤ value of different commodities. The different approaches have tended to distinguish two notions of value: (a) that determined by the ➤ utility it gives a consumer and reflected in the ➤ demand for it (high utility, high value (➤ Galiani, F.)), or (b) the cost of producing the commodity reflected by the ➤ supply of it (high cost, high value).

The ➤ classical economists held that, in the long term, price and hence the exchange value of an item is determined by its costs of production (supply), but that it is the fact that a demand exists for it that determines whether an item has any value at all. ➤ Ricardo developed a ➤ labour theory of value, asserting that value derives from the effort of production, again based on supply. The novelty of his approach was in showing that all costs of production reduce to labour costs, either paid directly or stored in the form of capital. However, there is a need to reward those who store labour, and thus defer consumption, and this undermined his theory. Late nineteenth-century economists like ➤ Marshall subverted theories of value to theories of price, determined by demand and supply, with each determined by ➤ marginal utility or ➤ marginal cost. Since then, the theories of price and value have not been separated except by followers of ➤ Marx. ➤➤ Gossen; Jevons; Walras.

value added, or net output The difference between the total revenue of a firm and the cost of bought-in materials, services and components. It thus measures the ➤ value the firm has 'added' to these bought-in materials and components by its processes of production. Since the total revenue of the firm will be divided among ➤ capital charges (including ➤ depreciation) – ➤ rent, ➤ dividend payments, wages and the costs of materials, services and components – value added can also be calculated by summing the relevant types of cost and subtracting that total from overall revenue. Although 'value added' and 'net output' are often used synonymously, net output in the census of production (UK) is calculated by subtracting the value of materials purchased (allowing for stock changes) from the value of each industry's sales. Payments for *services* rendered by other firms (e.g. ➤ research and development work and hire of machinery) are not deducted, so that in this technical sense, 'net output' is distinguished from 'value added', a term used to describe the contribution of an industry to the ➤ Gross Domestic Product. ➤➤ value added tax.

value added tax (VAT) A general tax (➤ taxation) applied at each point of ➤ exchange of goods or ➤ services from primary production to final consumption. It is levied on the difference between the sale price of the goods or services (outputs) to which the tax is applied, and the cost of goods and services (➤ inputs) bought in for use in its production. The cost of these inputs is taken to include all charges, including all taxes except VAT itself. The method of payment and collection in the ➤ European Union is as follows. Registered traders sells their outputs at a price increased by the appropriate percentage of VAT. They are then liable to the tax authorities for the payment of the tax so obtained from customers, but can claim a refund of any VAT included in the invoices for the inputs purchased from suppliers. Their customers do likewise, and so on down to the final consumer. At each point of exchange the tax is passed on in the form of higher prices. Being at the last point in the chain of exchange, the final consumer bears the whole tax.

Value added tax was first introduced in the then European Economic Community in the late 1960s, largely to replace ➤ turnover taxes. VAT is mandatory for all members and is the basis of the Community budget. VAT was adopted by the UK in 1973 after it became a member of the European Union (EU). Value added tax may be applied to different goods or services or in different industries at different rates, including zero and exempt. The difference between the latter two is that only with the former can refunds be claimed. Some countries have several rates, including a low rate for basic necessities and a higher rate for 'luxury' goods. Supplies by traders in the Union to a customer registered elsewhere in the EU are zero-rated and the customer charges VAT at the country's VAT rate. This is known as the *destination principle*. The intention is ultimately to move to the *origin principle* under which VAT will be charged at the rate prevailing in the country of supply. This will result in some gain or loss of tax revenue in the receiving country, depending on whether its rate is higher or lower than in the country of origin.

Given the political impracticability of completely harmonizing VAT rates in the medium term, the shift from destination to origin principle has proved controversial and probably some sort of clearing mechanism to restore the balance of tax revenues would be necessary. Value added tax is a good revenue raiser and has been adopted by many countries, a notable exception being the USA. Value added tax does impose heavy ➤ compliance costs on ➤ small businesses, much more than a ➤ sales tax, which mainly affects retailers. Japan does not use the European invoice method for VAT but calculates ➤ value added and the tax thereon from company accounts.

value at risk models ➤ efficient markets hypothesis.

value judgement A proposition that cannot be reduced to an arguable statement of fact but that effectively asserts that something is good or that something ought to happen. Economists usually attempt to draw a distinction between facts and value judgements, but the two often merge. For example, the statement 'We can control inflation by cutting the money supply' is clearly arguable but not a value judgement. However, the statement 'Therefore, we ought to cut the money supply' may be a value judgement (based on the belief that inflation is an evil per se) or alternatively could be an economic judgement made on the basis of a belief that the control of inflation stimulates long-term economic growth.

In practice, all statements of economists can be of two types: (a) descriptive statements, e.g. unemployment is falling, or (b) prescriptive, e.g. unemployment should be cut. The former should be devoid of any value judgements. The latter will always be a combination of value and economic judgement. Usually, but not always, the value judgements contained in prescriptive statements are either uncontroversial or explicit enough for the reader to make a clear assessment of them. ➤➤ normative economics; positive economics.

variable A number that may take different values in different situations. For example, the quantity of a good demanded will vary according to its price. ➤ dependent variable.

variable costs Costs that vary directly with the rate of output, e.g. ➤ labour costs, raw material costs, fuel and power. Also known as *operating costs*, *prime costs*, *on costs* or *direct costs*.

variance A measure of the degree of dispersion of a series of numbers around their mean (➤ average). The larger the variance, the greater the spread of the series around its mean. The formula is as follows:

$$\text{variance} = \frac{1}{N} \sum_{i=1}^{N} (x_i - \bar{x})^2$$

where $\bar{x}$ is the mean (➤ average), x_i is the value of the ith item and N is the number of items in the series. For example, consider the two series: (a) 8, 10, 12, and (b) 2, 10, 18. The mean of both (a) and (b) is 10. The variance of (a) is $[(-2)^2 + (2)^2]/3 = 2.67$. The variance of (b) is $[(-8)^2 + (8)^2]/3 = 42.67$. The variance of (b) is greater than (a), reflecting the wider spread of the (b) series. ➤➤ standard deviation.

VAT ➤ value added tax.

Veblen, Thorstein Bunde (1857–1929) ➤ conspicuous consumption; institutional economics.

vector A set of numbers (elements) arranged as a row or a column. For example, [1, 5, 8] is a row vector, and $\begin{bmatrix} 3 \\ 8 \end{bmatrix}$ is a column vector. A vector of n elements is referred to as *n-dimensional*. The above vectors, therefore, are three-dimensional. The *null vector* has all its elements equal to zero. A *unit vector* is a vector with one element equal to unity and the rest all equal to zero. There are, therefore, n unit vectors possible for an *n-dimensional* vector. There is an algebra for vectors, with appropriate rules for addition and multiplication. ➤➤ matrix.

velocity of circulation The speed with which the money in an economy circulates. Each $10 bill that exists is used many times, and each time it is used a transaction of value $10 occurs. It is possible to imagine two economies, one with twice as much money in it as the other, but where on average the money is used half the number of times. The total value of all transactions in each economy would be the same because it equals the value of the stock of money multiplied by the velocity with which it circulates. The income velocity equals the money value of ➤ national income divided by the stock of money in the economy.

The velocity of circulation is related to the demand for money (➤ money, demand for): if people hold cash, it circulates slowly. If, on the other hand, they do not wish to hold cash, they dispose of money holdings and the circulation of money increases. The velocity of money is central to the debate between ➤ monetarism and ➤ Keynesian economics. Monetarists hold that ➤ interest rates do not much affect the demand for money or its velocity. They claim that institutional factors (e.g. the frequency with which people are paid or the number of people who have bank accounts) affect it and these factors are unlikely to change in the short term. Keynesians, on the other hand, believe that the velocity of money varies substantially with the interest rate. Under both doctrines, however, a higher than expected ➤ inflation rate would increase the velocity. This is seen in an extreme form in an economy enduring ➤ hyperinflation, in which anyone holding money is holding a depreciating asset; everybody attempts to rid themselves of cash and acquire goods, the values of which are stable. ➤ deflation; ➤➤ neutrality of money; quantity theory of money.

venture capital ➤ risk capital.

vertical integration The extent to which successive stages in production and distribution are placed under the control of a single ➤ enterprise. Oil companies that own oilfields, tankers, refineries and filling stations exhibit a high degree of vertical integration. Firms move to integrate, either forwards towards retailing or backwards towards sources of raw materials, in order to eliminate the profit margins of intermediaries or to secure sources of supply or markets.

vertical restraints Restrictions or conditions imposed on the seller or buyer of an item. Common restraints are resale price maintenance and ➤ tie-in sales. They are usually either: (a) structured to extend a ➤ natural monopoly in one market to a more competitive market, e.g. when national telephone operators demand that customers obtain their telephone handset from them, or (b) designed to affect the retail conditions in which a product is sold, e.g. when perfume-makers refuse to supply downmarket stores with their produce.

Competition authorities have been concerned to limit the application of these restrictions, although it has been argued more recently that in most cases vertical restraints are as much against the producer's interest as the public interest where they are against the public interest at all. ➤➤ Chicago School; competition policy.

vicious circle of poverty ➤ economic development.

Vickrey, William (1914–96) A Canadian-born economist, who was based at Columbia University in New York, Vickrey was a joint winner of the ➤ Nobel Prize for Economics just days before his death. His most enduring legacy will be the design of an auction named after him (➤ auction). It was just one example of his interest in designing economic mechanisms for overcoming the problems associated with ➤ asymmetric information (in that case, the fact that the seller of an item does not know the true value placed on it by potential buyers). The main design feature of his auction was the fact that it gave potential buyers the incentive to tell the truth about how much they value the item being sold. Other economists have designed similar mechanisms for other contexts. ➤➤ incentive compatibility.

Viner, Jacob (1892–1970) ➤ customs union.

visible balance The ➤ balance of payments in ➤ visible trade (➤ imports and ➤ exports of merchandise).

visible trade ➤ International trade in merchandise, ➤ imports and ➤ exports. ➤➤ invisibles.

von Neumann–Morgenstern utility function A representation of a consumer's preferences that describes the utilities a consumer enjoys from the resulting outcomes of alternative choices. The approach pioneered by John von Neumann and Oskar Morgenstern in 1947 imposed various assumptions to the ➤ utility function, to derive some appealing results. In particular, the von Neumann–Morgenstern approach is applied to consumer choice under uncertainty. For example, it allows us to predict which of two lottery tickets a particular consumer would prefer, without the consumer having to make a specific choice between them. Suppose Lottery 1 offers a prize of $1000 but a potential loss of $1000 (each with a 50 per cent chance) and that Lottery 2 offers a $100 win or $100 loss. (Note that each lottery has the same average outcome – no gain and no loss.) Under the von Neumann–Morgenstern approach, we can answer which lottery is preferred. The first ticket yields expected utility $E(U_1)$,

$$E(U_1) = 50 \text{ per cent} \times U(\$1000) + 50 \text{ per cent} \times U(-\$1000)$$

where $U(x)$ is the utility function that maps $\$x$ to the consumer's overall welfare. Similarly,

$$E(U_2) = 50 \text{ per cent} \times U(\$100) + 50 \text{ per cent} \times U(-\$100)$$

Note that $E(U_1)$ is not equal to $U(50 \text{ per cent} \times \$1000 + 50 \text{ per cent} \times -\$1000)$ (➤ expected utility). Lottery 1 is preferred if $E(U_1)$ is greater than $E(U_2)$. The key advantage of this approach is that it allows us to work out which uncertain outcome is preferred from a utility function that has no uncertainty built into it at all. In practice, of course, it is not particularly realistic at describing human choice under uncertainty (➤ behavioural economics).

voting shares ➤ Equity shares entitling holders to vote in the election of directors of a company. Normally all ➤ ordinary shares are voting shares, but sometimes a company may create a class of non-voting ordinary shares if the holders of the equity wish to raise more equity capital but exclude the possibility of losing control of the business. ➤ Preference shares are rarely, and ➤ debenture shares never, voting shares.

W

wage drift The difference between wage rates set by national agreements and the total earnings received by workers, which includes overtime pay, special bonuses and commissions. If wage negotiations take place between union leaders and management bodies at a national level, whatever the outcome of those negotiations in certain areas of the country, the wage agreed may not be high enough to attract all the workers demanded. In this case, local employers will attempt to entice workers with side payments that do not directly infringe national agreements. If wage drift could lead to cuts in pay as well as increases, it would be a more economically efficient means of introducing pay flexibility. As it happens, though, wage drift has the consequence of making a nationally agreed pay rate the bare minimum anyone receives, with 'top-ups' the norm. ➤➤ bargaining theory of wages.

wage-fund theory The idea that ➤ Smith took over from the ➤ Physiocrats, i.e. that wages are advanced to workers in anticipation of the sale of their output. Wages could not be increased unless the ➤ capital destined to pay them was increased. Capital, in turn, was determined by ➤ savings.

The ➤ Classical School developed its theory of wages around these ideas. In the short run, there was a given number of workers and a given amount of savings to pay their wages. The two together determined the average wage. In the long run, the supply of ➤ labour was related to the minimum of subsistence needed to sustain the ➤ labour force. (This subsistence level was not simply physiological; it was related to a ➤ standard of living accepted by custom.) If the wage rate rose above this, the ➤ population increased; if it fell below it, it contracted. In the long run, the level of the demand for labour was determined by the size of the wage fund, and this, in turn, by the level of savings. This meant that, as ➤ Mill put it, 'the demand for ➤ commodities is not the demand for labour'. If you increased ➤ consumption you reduced savings and therefore the wage fund. ➤ Productivity did not influence ➤ real wages – what mattered was the level of ➤ profits, for savings depended on profits. The argument assumed that savings flowed into fixed capital and variable (wage) capital in equal proportions so that what ➤ Marx called the 'organic composition of capital' remained constant.

➤ Ricardo worried about this point in his analysis of the effect of machinery on employment. Investment bypassed the wage fund and the demand for labour was reduced. Thornton criticized the wage-fund doctrine on the ground that wages were determined by ➤ supply and ➤ demand in the market. Mill accepted some of Thornton's points and admitted that the wage-fund theory might be more appropriate in the context of a discontinuous production process (akin to seed-time to harvest) rather than a continuous flow of output, which was the true state of affairs. There was some popular confusion at the time, because it was thought the economists meant there existed a definite fund available for wages so that there was no hope of workers obtaining higher average earnings.

wage rates ➤ earnings.

Wall Street ➤ New York Stock Exchange.

Walras, Marie-Esprit-Léon (1834–1910) A mining engineer by training, Walras accepted the offer of a newly created Chair of Economics in the Faculty of Law at Lausanne University in 1870. He held this post until he was succeeded by ➤ Pareto on his retirement in 1892. His publications include *Éléments d'économie politique pure* (1874–7), *Études d'économie sociale* (1896) and *Études d'économie politique appliquée* (1898).

One of the three economists to propound a ➤ marginal utility theory in the 1870s, he set out the theory of diminishing marginal utility and showed how ➤ prices at which ➤ commodities are exchanged are determined by the relative marginal utilities of the people taking part in the transaction (➤➤ Gossen, H.H.; Jevons, W.S.; Menger, C.). He also constructed a mathematical ➤ model of ➤ general equilibrium as a system of simultaneous equations in which he tried to show that all prices and quantities are uniquely determined. This is regarded as one of the foremost achievements in mathematical economics, of which Walras is considered the founder. ➤➤ Arrow, K.J.; *tatonnement* process.

warranted rate of growth ➤ growth theory; Harrod–Domar model.

warrants ➤ Securities giving the holder a right to subscribe to a ➤ share or a ➤ bond at a given price and from a certain date. Warrants, which are commonly issued 'free', alongside the shares of new ➤ investment trusts when launched, and carry no income or other rights to ➤ equity, immediately trade separately on the ➤ stock exchange, but at a price lower than the associated share or bond. This provides the investor in warrants with an element of ➤ gearing since, if the associated share or bond price ultimately rises above the subscription price, it will have a value corresponding to the difference between the subscription price at which the warrant rights may be exercised and the market price of the share or bond. Similar to an ➤ option.

wasting assets ➤ Assets with strictly limited, though not necessarily determinate, lives, e.g. a mine, timber lands or a property on lease. Wasting assets have many of the characteristics of ➤ current assets, but they are normally included under fixed assets.

watering, stock The issue of the nominal capital of a company in return for less than its money value, thus overstating the capital of the company and reducing its apparent return on capital (➤ rate of return).

wealth A stock of assets held by any economic unit that yields, or has the potential for yielding, income in some form. Wealth can take a multitude of forms, e.g. cash, bank deposits, loans or shares are all financial assets. Diamonds, factories and houses are examples of physical assets. To these should be added human wealth, which consists of the earnings potential of individuals (➤ human capital). These forms of wealth can be divided into those that constitute a liability to another economic agent (e.g. loans) and those that do not, e.g. physical assets. For the community as a whole, it is only really the latter that constitute net wealth, just as in a family, if a brother owes his sister $100, it comprises part of the sister's wealth, but not that of the family as a whole. ➤➤ Ricardian equivalence.

In perfect markets, assets should be priced at the ➤ present value of the future income they are expected to earn. However, the notion of income is general and would include, for example, the pleasure the owners of a picture would derive from its display (➤ income). The bulk of most individuals' wealth is held in the form of a house or accumulated assets invested in a pension fund. ➤ personal pension.

wealth tax ➤ inheritance tax.

weighted average An ➤ average in which each item in the series being averaged is multiplied by a 'weight' relevant to its importance, the result summed and the total divided by the sum of the weights. For example, suppose the price of meat has risen by 10 per cent and of vegetables by 20 per cent, the average rise is 15 per cent, being the arithmetic mean of 10 and 20. This could be misleading if we were considering the effect of the price increases on a particular household. The above mean assumes that the household regards meat and vegetables as equally important. If, however, the household spends $10 on vegetables for every $25 on meat, a more accurate representation of the average price change would be a weighted average, i.e. [(10 per cent × 25) + (20 per cent × 10)]/(25 + 10) = 450/35 = 12.9 per cent. In the example, the weights are 25 (for meat) and 10 (for vegetables), so that the result is more in keeping with the importance the household attaches to meat in its budget. At the extreme, if no vegetables were bought at all, the 'vegetable' weight would be zero. ➤➤ index number.

weightlessness The term used to describe the decreasing material component in the value of world output. The decline of heavy industry (➤ de-industrialization) and the relative growth of the ➤ services industries in richer countries (➤ economic growth) account for the decline in physical ➤ value added. In particular, it is argued, more value derives from 'knowledge-based' industries. The software for a computer game is the more important component of its value, and the resources for writing the software are those that are most scarce, as opposed to those deployed in the manufacture of the console on which the game is played. One important consequence of weightlessness is the potential for activity and value to flow across national boundaries without incurring a burden of transport costs; another is the tendency for workers whose main attribute in the ➤ labour market is physical strength to suffer a relative decline in attainable income. ➤ globalization.

weights ➤ weighted average.

welfare economics The study of the social desirability of alternative arrangements of economic activities and allocations of ➤ resources. It is, in effect, the analysis of the optimal behaviour of individual consumers at the level of society as a whole. Just as, at the level of the individual, there is a need for a subjective ranking of bundles of goods dependent on the consumer's taste (➤➤ indifference-curve analysis), at the level of a society there is a need for a ranking of economic states, and this will usually rely on subjective or normative criteria – judgements of taste about how society should look. Carrying the methods of indifference analysis from individuals to groups of individuals is not straightforward, however (➤➤ social welfare function) and thus welfare economics is a broader subject than the theory of demand (➤ demand, theory of).

The study of welfare economics consists of the following: (a) the determination of efficient states in which no individual can be made better off without an offsetting loss to another individual (➤ economic efficiency); (b) the choice between the many efficient states that can exist, either through a decision imposed by a dictator, or through democratically determined decisions (➤➤ impossibility theorem; social welfare; social welfare function); and (c) coverage of a number of other smaller topics, e.g. the optimal provision of ➤ public goods, ➤ externalities, and the theory of the second best (➤ second best, theory of). All these topics share the common aim of helping to show when it is desirable to move from one economic state to another. ➤➤ compensation principle; cost–benefit analysis; Pigou, A.C.; Scitovsky, T.; Sen, A.

welfare to work ➤ active labour-market policies.

wholesale banking The making of loans or acceptance of deposits on a large scale between banks and other financial institutions, especially in the ➤ interbank market. As distinct from *retail banking*, a term for the business of the ➤ commercial banks carried out with customers of their branches. ➤➤ overseas banks.

wholesale markets Generally a ➤ market in which goods or services are bought and sold on a large scale among professionals. The *financial wholesale markets* ('the financial markets') include the ➤ money market, the ➤ foreign exchange market and the ➤ stock exchange.

wholesale trade Enterprises in the distributive trades which in principle sell to other businesses. Wholesalers act as middlemen between retailers (➤ retail trade) and manufacturers and other suppliers. Wholesalers perform important economic functions by buying in bulk on advantageous terms and selling on in smaller quantities. They handle imports and exports, may offer credit, and are particularly important sources of supply for small retailers, who can buy many lines from one source and more cheaply than they could buy direct.

Wicksell, Knut (1851–1926) Educated at Uppsala University in Sweden, where he studied mathematics and philosophy, Wicksell was appointed to the Chair of Economics at Lund University in 1904, a post he held until 1916. His major publications include *Über Wert, Kapital und Rente (Value, Capital and Rent)* (1893) and *Geldzins und Güterpreise (Interest and Prices)* (1898). A synthesis of his work was published in 1901 and 1906 with the English title of *Lectures on Political Economy*.

He assimilated the ➤ general equilibrium analysis of ➤ Walras with the work of ➤ Böhm-Bawerk and worked out a theory of ➤ distribution based on the new ➤ marginal analysis of ➤ Jevons, Walras and ➤ Menger.

In addition, he had a significant influence on monetary theory. He pointed out that high ➤ rates of interest often coincided with high prices, which was contrary to what then current theory predicted. He drew attention to the significance of the relative level of interest rates rather than their absolute level. Prices were related to the difference between changes in the real or natural rate of ➤ interest (which was determined by the expected rate of ➤ profits) and the money rate. The ➤ central bank had an important influence over the price level through its operations on the discount rate (➤ bank rate). These theories were incorporated into his theory of the ➤ business cycle. ➤➤ interest, natural rate of; Wicksell effect, price.

Wicksell effect, price A phenomenon noted by ➤ Wicksell in his ideas on the derivation of ➤ factor prices from the value of ➤ marginal products. He pointed out that in equilibrium the rate of interest would be greater than the value of the marginal product of capital. This is because the whole of the existing stock of capital is revalued when rates of interest change (➤ capital reswitching).

Wieser, Friedrich von (1851–1926) Wieser succeeded ➤ Menger in the Chair of Economics at Vienna University in 1903 after a period at Prague University. His most important works include *Über den Ursprung und die Hauptgesetze des Wirtschaftlichen Wertes (The Nature and Essence of Theoretical Economics)* (1884), *Der natürliche Wert (Natural Value)* (1889) and *Theorie der gesellschaftlichen Wirtschaft (Social Economics)* (1914).

He developed a law of costs which became known later as the principle of ➤ opportunity cost – ➤ factors of production would be distributed by competition such that, in ➤ equilibrium, the value of their marginal outputs would be equal. The costs of production of any ➤ commodity reflect the competing claims in other uses for the services of the factors needed to produce it. The law became an important element in the theory of ➤ resource allocation (➤➤ economic efficiency).

Williamson, Oliver E. (b. 1932) ➤ transaction costs.

windfall tax Specifically, a once-and-for-all direct tax (➤ direct taxation) on privatized (➤ privatization) utility companies imposed by the UK government in 1997.

Generally, any tax imposed on persons or organizations deemed to have benefited from external events outside the normal course of their economic activities. The justification is usually made on the grounds that the taxpayers have benefited unfairly from gains that are due to society as a whole. Windfall taxes are controversial. It is usually difficult to design taxes that will extract from the ultimate beneficiaries revenue proportionate to the gains made. This is because of the usual problem of establishing incidence (➤ taxation, incidence of). A theoretical justification for windfall taxes is that they are unlikely to distort behaviour or resource allocation because they are once and for all (➤ life-cycle hypothesis). They may also be argued to promote 'social justice' in a rough and ready way, even though they breach the convention that taxes should not be imposed retrospectively (➤ Smith, A.).

winding up ➤ liquidation.

window dressing Financial adjustments made solely for the purpose of accounting presentation, normally at the time of auditing of company accounts, e.g. the sale of ➤ securities so as to show large holdings of cash at the ➤ balance sheet date, only to repurchase them immediately afterwards.

withholding tax ➤ Taxation deducted from payments to non-residents. Withholding taxes are usually in the form of a standard rate of ➤ income tax applied to ➤ dividends or other payments by companies and are often reclaimable against tax liabilities in the country of residence of the recipient under a double-taxation agreement.

workfare Programmes that make the receipt of unemployment-related benefits conditional on participation in some local work scheme. Workfare, an example of an ➤ active labour-market policy, can reduce ➤ long-term unemployment. This is partly because participation in any kind of work has been shown to improve the labour-market prospects of the unemployed (countering ➤ hysteresis), and also because it encourages benefit claimants who have viable options to work to take them. The relative weight of the 'carrot-and-stick' elements can be tailored scheme by scheme.

working capital That part of current ➤ assets financed from long-term funds. ➤➤ current ratio.

World Bank Group ➤ International Bank for Reconstruction and Development; International Development Association; International Finance Corporation; Multilateral Investment Guarantee Agency.

World Customs Organization The Customs Co-operation Council was established in 1952 for the application of customs procedures and the provision of advice and assistance. The Council developed a classification of commodities for the application of customs ➤ tariffs. In 1994, the Council changed its name to the World Customs Organization (WCO) to better reflect its global status. By 2010, the WCO covered 176 customs authorities and virtually all ➤ international trade. The work of the WCO includes the maintenance of the international Harmonized System for goods nomenclature and the administration of agreements on customs valuations and the rules of origin. Its work also extends to matters relating to customs enforcement, anti-counterfeiting and piracy.

World Trade Organization The World Trade Organization (WTO) was set up in Geneva in 1995 following the conclusion of the ➤➤ Uruguay Round of Trade Negotiations. It replaced the ➤ General Agreement on Tariffs and Trade (GATT). The WTO is charged with further development of, and policing of, the multilateral trading system along the principles followed by the eight rounds of trade negotiations concluded under the GATT and which the WTO continued in the ➤➤ Doha Round of Trade Negotiations. It provides the resources and the legal status for the resolution of trade disputes through independent disputes panels. A member may appeal to the WTO Appeals Tribunal but must accept its ruling. The failure of a member country to accept the WTO ruling would subject it to trade sanctions. The WTO is financed by contributions from its member states based on their shares of international trade. In 2009, the total budget was Swiss Francs 189 million and there were 153 members.

writing-down allowance ➤ capital allowances.

X

X-efficiency The effectiveness of a firm's management in minimizing the cost of producing a given output or maximizing the output produced by a given set of inputs. There is often a discrepancy between the efficient behaviour of firms, as implied by economic theory, and their observed behaviour in practice. This is frequently a result of a lack of the competitive pressures assumed. It was called *X*-efficiency by H. Leibenstein in 'Allocative Efficiency vs "*X*-Efficiency"', *American Economic Review* (1966). ➤ firm, theory of the.

Y

yardstick competition A device used in the ➤ regulation of an industry, dominated by a number of regional ➤ monopoly producers. Although the companies do not compete with each other directly, the regulator can use the performance of all the local monopolies as a benchmark for judging each of them. For example, in deciding what level of costs is a reasonable level to be reflected in the price (➤➤ price regulation), a regulator can take the average cost of the companies. Those who can achieve lower costs would then be able to make larger profits than the others. This gives the companies an incentive to cut costs while allowing the regulator a firm basis for deciding what can reasonably be expected of a producer. ➤➤ tournament theory.

yield The ➤ income from a ➤ security as a proportion of its current market price. Thus, the *dividend yield* is the current ➤ dividend as a percentage of the market price of a security. The *earnings yield* is a theoretical figure, based on the last dividend paid as a percentage of the current market price. The *redemption yield* is normally applied only to fixed-interest securities, and is the interest payment over the remaining life of the security, plus or minus the difference between the purchase price and the redemption value, i.e. it is the earnings yield adjusted to take account of any ➤ capital gain or loss to redemption. With fixed-interest securities, the nominal interest, or ➤ coupon, is unlikely to be the same as the actual yield. An ➤ irredeemable security in the form of a government bond having a flat yield of 3 per cent with a ➤ par value of $100 but a market price of $50 provides an earnings yield of 6 per cent. The earnings yield will fluctuate with the price of the security, rising as security prices fall, and vice versa. ➤➤ gilt-edged securities.

yield curve A graphical representation of the relationship between the annual return on an asset and the number of years the asset has to run before expiring. Longer-term assets usually offer some premium over short-term ones and yield curves thus typically slope upwards. This effect is more pronounced if short-term interest rates are expected to rise. ➤➤ term structure of interest rates.

yield gap The ➤ yield on ➤ ordinary shares minus the yield on ➤ gilt-edged securities, e.g. 2½ per cent irredeemable ➤ consols. If the latter exceeds the former, it is called the *reverse yield gap*.

Z

zero-sum game A game (➤ game theory) in which one player's gain is equal to other players' losses, whatever strategy is chosen. The players can only compete for slices of a fixed cake; there are no opportunities of overall gain through collusion. The sum of gains will always equal the sum of losses, the whole amounting to zero. ➤➤ bilateral monopoly.